A READER IN THEMED AND IMMERSIVE SPACES

A READER IN THEMED AND IMMERSIVE SPACES

Scott A. Lukas (Ed.)

Carnegie Mellon: ETC Press

Pittsburgh, PA

Copyright © by Scott A. Lukas (Ed.), et al. and ETC Press 2016
http://press.etc.cmu.edu/

ISBN: 978-1-365-31814-6 (print)
ISBN: 978-1-365-38774-6 (ebook)
Library of Congress Control Number: 2016950928

TEXT: The text of this work is licensed under a Creative Commons
Attribution-NonCommercial-NonDerivative 2.5 License
(http://creativecommons.org/licenses/by-nc-nd/2.5/)

IMAGES: All images appearing in this work are property of the respective
copyright owners, and are not released into the Creative Commons.
The respective owners reserve all rights.

Contents

Part I.
1. Introduction: The Meanings of Themed and Immersive Spaces — 3

Part II. The Past, History, and Nostalgia
2. The Uses of History in Themed Spaces
   By Filippo Carlà — 19
3. Pastness in Themed Environments
   By Cornelius Holtorf — 31
4. Nostalgia as Litmus Test for Themed Spaces
   By Susan Ingram — 39

Part III. The Constructs of Culture and Nature
5. "Wilderness" as Theme
   Negotiating the Nature-Culture Divide in Zoological Gardens
   By Jan-Erik Steinkrüger — 47
6. Flawed Theming
   Center Parcs as a Commodified, Middle-Class Utopia
   By Steven Miles — 53
7. The Cultures of Tiki
   By Scott A. Lukas — 61

Part IV. The Ways of Design, Architecture, Technology, and Material Form
8. The Effects of a Million Volt Light and Sound Culture
   By Stefan Al — 77
9. Et in Chronotopia Ego
   Main Street Architecture as a Rhetorical Device in Theme Parks and Outlet Villages
   By Per Strömberg — 83
10. Remediation on the High Seas
    A Pirates of the Caribbean Odyssey
    By Bobby Schweizer and Celia Pearce — 95

11. Research Dialogue — 107
    The Ways of Design, Architecture, Technology, and Material Form
    By Filippo Carlà, Florian Freitag, Gordon Grice, Scott A. Lukas

Part V. The Aspects of Immersion, Experience, and Phenomena

12. Questioning "Immersion" in Contemporary Themed and Immersive Spaces — 115
    By Scott A. Lukas
13. Movies, Rides, Immersion — 125
    By Florian Freitag
14. Sensory Design in Immersive Environments — 131
    By Gordon S. Grice

Part VI. The Notions of Identity, Self, and Ideology

15. Autotheming — 141
    Themed and Immersive Spaces in Self-Dialogue
    By Florian Freitag
16. Six Degrees of Navigation — 151
    Titanic Belfast's Identity Issues
    By Stephen Brown
17. Research in Themed and Immersive Spaces — 159
    At the Threshold of Identity
    By Scott A. Lukas

Part VII. The Deployments of Rhetoric, Performance, and Affect

18. Believe It and Not — 173
    The Playful Pull of Popular Culture-Themed Tourism Attractions
    By Derek Foster
19. Spatial Machines of Subjection — 183
    A Materialist Account of Macau's Themed Integrated Casino Resorts
    By Tim Simpson
20. Atmosphere, Immersion, and Authenticity in Colonial Williamsburg — 195
    By Christina Kerz

Part VIII. The Politics of the Space

21. Revisiting The Lost City — 209
    The Legend Lives On
    By Jeanne van Eeden
22. Our Chemical Romance — 219
    Body Worlds and the Memorialization of the Self
    By Kent Drummond and Lei Jia

23. Dark Theming Reconsidered — 225
By Scott A. Lukas

Part IX. The View of the Critic

24. Complicated Agency — 239
By Brian Lonsway

25. North Dakota Wins the Internet — 249
Sincerity and Irony in an Olive Garden Review
By Michael Mario Albrecht

26. Judgments Passed — 257
The Place of the Themed Space in the Contemporary World of Remaking
By Scott A. Lukas

Part X. The Place of the Future

27. Disney's Immersive Futurism — 271
By Davin Heckman

28. Resetting the Clock — 279
Theme Parks, New Urbanism, and Smart Cities
By Markus Reisenleitner

29. Theming and Immersion in the Space of the Future — 289
By Scott A. Lukas

30. Research Dialogue — 301
The Place of the Future
By Filippo Carlà, Florian Freitag, Gordon Grice, Scott A. Lukas

Selected Bibliography — 305
Contributors — 343
About the ETC Press — 349

PART I

1

Introduction: The Meanings of Themed and Immersive Spaces

Since the late 1990s, the themed space has been the subject of widespread analysis and criticism in academic communities as well as a popular source of entertainment for people around the world. Themed spaces have, in their foundation, an overarching narrative, symbolic complex, or story that drives the overall context of their environs. Theming, in some very unique ways, has expanded beyond previous stereotypes and oversimplifications of culture and place to now consider new, uncanny, and often controversial topics, themes, and storylines. At the same time, immersion—or the idea that a space and its multiple architectural, material, performative, and technological approaches may wrap up or envelop a guest within it—has expanded to become an overarching concern of many consumer spaces around the world. Casinos, theme parks, lifestyle stores, and museums and interpretive centers have looked to immersion as a means of both selling products and educating the masses. This collection in themed and immersive spaces brings together researchers, critics, and design professionals from around the world in order to consider the many cultural, political, historical, aesthetic, existential, and design contexts of themed and immersive spaces.

The Symbolic Added Value of Themed and Immersive Spaces

It certainly goes without saying that every space in human existence bears the example of a theme or narrative that provides an overarching conceptual purpose for that space. Any form of the human material environment—whether a gas station, bus stop, fast food restaurant, or bathroom—has multiple contexts of thematic significance. Some of this significance is established by the function or use of a space. For example, by its mere fact of having a toilet, sink, towels, and the like, a bathroom expresses its purpose to any individual who would enter that space and who would have reasonable cultural knowledge to understand these material cues. Beyond this level of functionality, a space may also express purpose through more symbolic and semiotic means. To take the example of the same bathroom, if the owner of a house adds to the functional items of the toilet, sink, and towels a series of photographs, perhaps related to the person's memorable vacations, the bathroom takes on added meaning and extends its narrative beyond the functional fact of being a bathroom. The space is imbued with the meanings of the owner or user who establishes new context in the space through forms of personal markers like the travel photographs.

It may also be said that all forms of space, by their nature, are immersive. It is impossible to enter a space and not be immersed by its various functional, thematic, symbolic, material, and existential purposes. The word immersion suggests, etymologically, a plunging or dipping into something or an "absorption in some interest or situation," and, when applied to space, offers the idea that a person who enters such a space will be transformed.[1] Geographer Yi-Fu Tuan once wrote of the significance of a medieval cathedral as it represented an immersive potential to envelop any individual who entered its environments.[2] Its ability to immerse an individual who walked into its environs was related to its multi-sensorial modes as well as the ideational foundations and narratives that are involved before, during, and after any visit to the space.

What is key in terms of the themed and immersive spaces considered in this text is that when we speak of such spaces we are considering those that inherently involve contexts of a public and consumerist nature. A themed restaurant, as an example, is defined by its function as a restaurant—in terms of having tables on which to eat food, servers to provide food, and so forth—but it is the added value of the theme or narrative that is told through and beyond the functioning of the space as a restaurant that clarifies its status as a themed space. Likewise, while one could be said to be immersed in a bank while he or she is dealing with all of the stories, narratives, and contexts such as accounts, balances, and the like, when that same individual enters a museum space he or she experiences unique, evocative, and extraordinary symbols in that space. It is thus the "added value" in terms of the symbolic properties that is brought to these spaces above and beyond other contexts that so defines these places as themed and immersive. This fact of the symbolic construction of such space is brought to clear light in the sixth section of this reader.

The focus of "The Deployments of Rhetoric, Performance, and Affect" section is on the contexts of themed and immersive spaces as places in which rhetoric, performance, and affect are active, if not foundational, aspects of the venues. Many themed spaces utilize forms of performance that act in tandem with design elements of the space to create captivating forms of immersion for guests. At the same time, these performative (and related rhetorical and affective) approaches display ideological foundations that need to be interpreted and analyzed. The first author, Derek Foster, in "Believe It and Not: The Playful Pull of Popular Culture-Themed Tourism Attractions," looks at the emerging trend of popular culture-themed tourist attractions, specifically those connected to the popular media franchises *Game of Thrones* and *The Hunger Games*. Notable in his focus on these properties is the emphasis on the themed space "as a site of symbolic action, an environment filled with texts to be read and textures to be felt." As Foster says, themed spaces "act as places of cultural performance where popular culture is not simply read or interpreted but re-inscribed. Visiting fans use theming, on a personal level, to remind them of why they care about the text and to re-animate its magical qualities…Through theming, a potentially otherwise mundane environment can be re-animated."

In his chapter, "Spatial Machines of Subjection: A Materialist Account of Macau's Themed Integrated Casino Resorts," Tim Simpson extends these representational and symbolic concerns to the spaces of Macau—notably those of themed casinos. Simpson avoids the typical postmondern analyses of these spaces and instead focuses on Macau and "its gaming environments as a distinct post-socialist spatial formation." He details how Macau's urban and touristic spaces act as neoliberal and biopolitical forces in the lives of everyday citizens. What is prescient in Simpson's analyses of the spaces of Macau is the sense that we get that the impact of such spaces, including in venues outside of Macau, will be realized increasingly through seen, but more importantly, unseen forces on all of us. In her contribution to this section of the reader, Christina Kerz, in "Atmosphere, Immersion, and Authenticity in Colonial Williamsburg," considers the challenging topic of authenticity as it is inscribed in the many performative, affective, and interpretive contexts of the popular Colonial Williamsburg. Kerz writes not only as an observer of the site but as a participant in it and she importantly draws attention to the fact that themed and immersive spaces, at any one point in time, are much more than material, spatial, and architectural entities. They are spaces in which stories are told and meanings are contested. Importantly, she illustrates that "authenticity is a dynamic construct" as well as a "matter of collective identity." Locations like Colonial Williamsburg, in fact, remind us that the contexts of themed and immersive spaces do matter and it is incumbent on researchers to draw out the nuances of such venues.

The Contexts of Themed and Immersive Spaces

As reflected in Table 1.1, theming and immersion have numerous complementary modes through which they operate. Material cultural, including décor, and architectural forms are foundational for their obvious role in creating narrative, fantasy, and otherworldly space. Equally important are the expressions that involve forms of performance. Actors, workers, and performers in these venues use a variety of tools—costume, rhetoric and acting, and behavior—to better immerse guests and more effectively play out the theme or context of the spaces at hand. Narratives that, not unlike those of fictional and filmic worlds, are deployed through textual, audio-visual, or other more indirect means increase the immersive and thematic potentials of spaces as they impact guests. Another expression that is present in all themed spaces, though often missed by those who research them, are forms of phenomenology, psychology, existential state, and identity—"guest role/drive" as a way of expressing these elements—that are connected to the spaces in a number of senses. It should be noted that the modes of theming and immersion that are addressed in Table 1.1 did not emerge independently from other significant cultural, material, and narrative trajectories in the world. World's fairs and world expositions, including the notable World's Columbian Exposition of 1893, have had considerable impact on the architecture, design, technology, and other elements that appear in today's themed and consumer spaces.

Table 1.1 – The Modes of Theming and Immersion

Mode	Example
Architecture	Thematic architectural forms, often related to place, brand, or other context
Material Culture and Design	Décor, interior design, and other sensory forms that offer an evocative potential
Narrative	Text or backstory that expresses the purposes or meanings of the space
Technology	Various technological forms that increase the thematic and immersive potentials of the space
Performance	Forms of acting and aesthetics that enhance the design, architecture, and material elements of a space
Guest Role/drive	The interpretations, desires, and feedback of guests as they respond to a themed or immersive space

Today's themed and immersive spaces, as reflected in Table 1.2, are illustrated in many types or venues around the world. With rare exceptions, such spaces have at their heart consumerist, popular, and social foundations. While not all of these locations are analyzed directly in this reader, the authors who have contributed consider spaces that include theme parks, museums, and branded and lifestyle spaces.

Table 1.2 – The Locations of Theming and Immersion

Location	Example
Theme park	Disneyland (Anaheim, CA)
World exposition	World's Columbian Exposition (Chicago, IL, 1893)
Themed restaurant/bar	Giger Bar (Switzerland)
Lifestyle store	BMW Welt (Munich, Germany)
Brand space	KidZania (numerous worldwide locations)
Cruise ship	Oasis of the Seas Central Park (Royal Caribbean)
Casino	The Venetian (Las Vegas, NV)
Museum/interpretive center	The Mind Museum (The Philippines)
Home	An Egyptian themed bathroom
Immersive performance space	Cirque du Soleil
Virtual space	Second Life
Affective and subcultural themed community	The Tribes of Cologne

With these many impactful modes and contexts of these spaces in mind, it is appropriate to mention the work that is considered in the third section of the collection; these contributions in "The Ways of Design, Architecture, Technology, and Material Form" segment focus on the many issues and contexts of design, architecture, technology, and numerous other material forms. One of the predominant emphases noted in the study of the material forms of themed and immersive spaces is the idea that this materiality is of primary, if not fundamental, significance. While the architectural expressions of themed and immersive worlds are obvious sources for cultural criticism, their primary inclusion in such criticism has led to a de-emphasis of other important issues. The authors in this section thus emphasize underrepresented concerns of themed and immersive spaces that take design, architecture, technology, and materiality as topical starting points for richer analyses and criticisms.

In his contribution, "The Effects of a Million Volt Light and Sound Culture," architect Stefan Al analyzes the case of the historic themed casinos along the Las Vegas Strip, with attention to the design and technological approaches of signage and electricity. As he writes, "Las Vegas in the 1960s was like an open-air laboratory experiment, pushing the limits of technology in architecture, with sign designers as uninhibited amateur scientists building structures of neon and light bulbs." Al reminds us that the exteriors of themed spaces like those of casinos have significance, regardless of how garish or over the top they may seem. Such forms of the material, particularly as they establish evocative, symbolic, and performative effects on guests, further remind us of their power as thematic and immersive entities in our worlds. In a similar light, though outside of Las Vegas, Per Strömberg, in "*Et in Chronotopia Ego*: Main Street Architecture as a Rhetorical Device in Theme Parks and Outlet Villages," looks at the many resonances of main street architecture and design—from the spaces of Coney Island, Disney theme parks, and, most significantly, outlet villages common to the United States and Europe. Strömberg interprets the architectural and design forces behind such themed spaces as rhetorical devices that instill in visitors senses of nostalgia, among other orders.

In a syncretic and multi-spatial perspective, Bobby Schweizer and Celia Pearce, in their chapter titled "Remediation on the High Seas: A Pirates of the Caribbean Odyssey," consider the interesting context of Pirates of the Caribbean—the popular branded Disney form. As they illustrate, the Disney phenomenon, which began as a popular, immersive dark ride, has now spawned video games, virtual reality experiences, and a series of popular motion pictures. In their analyses, Schweizer and Pearce illustrate how the processes of remediation and adaptation that began with the theme park ride do not operate in a logical or linear matter, and we are reminded of examples of auto-poaching and retrofitting that serve to extend the story, often in surprising directions. And, as they offer us, the processes common to the multi-platform, convergent, and transmedia case of Pirates are certainly indicators of the future of theming and immersion in the world. The section on "Design, Architecture, Technology, and Material Form" closes with the first of two research dialogues conducted between authors Filippo Carlà, Florian Freitag, Gordon Grice, and Scott A. Lukas. This particular dialogue grew out of a series of research and interpretive experiments within the contexts of themed and immersive spaces.

The Foundations of Themed Spaces

Previous studies of themed and immersive spaces, including Mark Gottdiener's *The Theming of America*, which clearly brought public and academic attention to the nature of theming in popular culture, have tended to emphasize a series of concerns and contexts that resonate, more generally, with the nature of public, consumer, branded, media, and technological cultures—namely, simulation and authenticity, hegemony, corporatism and brandism, and other culture industry concerns.[3] These issues are, certainly, vital ones that are referenced in the many contexts of themed and immersive spaces. Yet, in order to complement them, we might begin to imagine other areas of analysis, criticism, and research that have been neglected in the focus on these spaces. In 2007, *The Themed Space: Locating Nation, Culture, and Self* was published as a response to the dearth of study in some of these areas.[4] While the text did broaden the literature—particularly as many of the chapters emphasized the specificity, nuance, and phenomenology of themed spaces—a lack of attention on the breadth and wide-scale impacts of theming on the world (and us) was evident. In the years since the publication of these texts, journals and edited collections too numerous to mention have filled in many of these gaps. In one area of theming—the themed restaurant—we have witnessed an exciting growth in the studies of the specifics of themed space.[5] This current collection builds on these previous insights, contributions, and analyses.

It should be noted that four authors from *The Themed Space* have also contributed chapters for this collection, and it goes without saying (as four of us will reflect upon in the research dialogues) that the study of these spaces is made much more profound only given the opportunities for collaboration, dialogue, and debate that are made possible through the establishment of networks of concerned researchers. On at least six occasions, many authors from the current collection have met in various academic and professional meetings in the United States and Germany.[6] It is hoped that this trend will continue in the future, perhaps in additional dialogue that may be developed through the multi-media and social media spaces available to all of us.[7]

In considering both the foundations of themed spaces in symbolic senses and the foundations of criticism, analysis, and research, it is interesting to note that so much attention has been given to the source materials that constitute the many consumer spaces in our world. As Table 1.3 illustrates, any given space may draw on varieties of source materials that may be seen, metaphorically, as being as variable and hybrid as the sources and performance pathways of a DJ or remix artist.

Table 1.3 – The Source Materials of Theming and Immersion

Source	Example
Nature	A famous mountain range (Disney's Cars Land)
Culture	Pop Polynesian culture (tiki bar)
Place	A famous city (Paris Las Vegas)
Time, period, epoch	Ancient Egypt (Luxor Las Vegas)
Person	A celebrity singer (Dollywood)
Brand	A revered automobile brand (BMW Welt)
Lifestyle	The outdoors (Bass Pro Shops Outdoor World)
Cultural form	Music (Hard Rock Hotel)
Media	A popular film franchise (*Star Wars* Land, Disney)
Trope	Time (Coffeemin, Singapore)
Meta	The form itself (The Simpsons Ride, Universal)

What is often lost in the consideration of these source materials is the fact that the reconstitution and remaking of them, to again reference the DJ and remixing metaphor, is quite variable, hybrid, even contradictory. As the simplified Chart 1.1 examines, we might be more leery of research that draws such broad brushstroke comparison of these consumer spaces. Surely, it is ridiculous to consider the Venetian Las Vegas in the same light as the Luxor Las Vegas. Not only are their source materials quite different, the deployments of them are as well. To return to Chart 1.1, we might become more adept at analyzing spaces of the future in terms of how such sources are utilized—whether they are remixed in postmodern, eclectic or more representational, realist senses—and then be more able in focusing more attention on the contexts that are developed, on the ground, as these spaces are used, imagined, reflected on, and remade.

Chart 1.1 Dimensions of Theming

Representational	Abstract
Realist	Metonymic
Conventional	Postmondern

Perhaps one of the most relevant sources of these spaces is the past. Section 1 of the reader, "The Past, History, and Nostalgia," addresses how the past, forms of history, and nostalgia commonly constitute the foundations of these consumer spaces. The past is an evocative foundation for many spaces as it promotes a sensibility of "something that was," often in an unreflexive or unproblematic way. The chapters include emphasis on the ways in which the past is explored in themed and immersive spaces—whether through deployments of history, pastness, affective appeal, time and alternate notions of temporality, heritage, enchantment, nostalgia, memory, and other forms.

Filippo Carlà begins these considerations in "The Uses of History in Themed Spaces," and he writes of the many ways in which history inspires the design of themed spaces. As he illustrates, we could say that the past—however constituted in themed spaces as a ruin, ghost town, or other evocative form—is one of the most common source materials for such venues. Carlà points to the challenging fact that the idea of the past that is promoted in such spaces has a seductive and ideological appeal to guests: "It should not be underestimated how powerful such images of the past, how emotionally loaded, directly experienced, and thus 'naturalized' they are when compared to the argumentative structure of a traditional historical publication." Carlà's curiosity of how the past is deployed in consumer spaces is shared by archaeologist Cornelius Holtorf, who in his chapter, "Pastness in Themed Environments," addresses the concept of pastness. As he writes, "Pastness is different from age and denotes the perceived quality that a given object is of the past. Pastness is not immanent in an object but may derive from the object's physical condition…its immediate context…[and] preconceived understandings of the audience." Holtorf expresses the important fact that theming and immersion does not begin and end with the materiality of the space at hand but extends to the contexts of interpretation, phenomenology, and affect that make up the guest's experiencing of any given space.

Susan Ingram, in "Nostalgia as Litmus Test for Themed Spaces," considers the curious dynamics of time and temporality in the theme park Disney California Adventure. As she notes, "nostalgia used to be simple," and one of the reasons for its complexity is that theme parks like California Adventure have established notable symbolic and thematic structures, including, importantly, retro-futurism, that interpellate the psychic realms of guests. The appeal to specific consumer modes of identification that are common in themed spaces—including, as Ingram notes, ego gratification—illustrates the problematic ways in which spaces like those of Disney theme parks co-opt the experience, identity, and enjoyment of their guests. Ultimately, as we reflect on Disney's complex play with time, we may be cognizant of how spaces like Disney California Adventure may continue to colonize the time-spaces of our lifeworlds.

Culture and nature, as the authors of Section 2, "The Constructs of Culture and Nature," address, is a prominent foundation for many themed, immersive, and consumer spaces. A key consideration shared by the authors is the issue of how and why certain places, peoples, and cultures are re-created in themed and immersive spaces. Connected to these representations of culture are the issues of essentialism, stereotyping, overdetermination, and numerous others that emphasize the idea that the representations common to themed and immersive spaces are problematic—not merely for their senses of inauthenticity, which is, itself, an unproblematized notion that this volume addresses—but for their unwillingness to offer different nuances, other views, or unknown aspects of cultures that might be deemed to be controversial, ideological, or contrary to the purposes of the space, its designers and operators, and the many other actors within the society in which themed and immersive spaces are created. The authors of these chapters are especially concerned with the contrasts and contradictions that are entailed in the conceptual, political, and representational spaces in which theming and immersion and their various antecedents meet.

In his contribution, "'Wilderness' as Theme: Negotiating the Nature-Culture Divide in Zoological Gardens," Jan-Erik Steinkrüger considers the understudied themed and immersive space of the zoological garden. He notes of the particular way in which zoos and their varied thematic constructs represent not only an experiencing of animals in their habitations but an expression of a "quasified 'wilderness.'" Steinkrüger illustrates a fact of the zoological garden that is common to many themed and immersive spaces today—namely, that such space is "located at the intersection of education and entertainment." Maintaining this interesting focus on the construction of nature in themed space is Steven Miles who, in his contribution, "Flawed Theming: Center Parcs as a Commodified, Middle-Class Utopia," focuses on a very curious construction of nature in the popular European Center Parcs holiday villages. In his analysis, the spaces of Center Parcs act as "a redefinition of nature as something to be bought as a means to the broader end of belonging." Center Parcs' reconstitution of nature, as he illustrates, is a specific project aimed at "reproduc[ing] a particular and distinctive version of what it means to be middle class." After reading his piece, we may be less than surprised with his reminder that the Center Parcs model—with emphasis on a certain type of consumer civics, the pleasures of social class, and middle-class lifestyle dynamics—may come to impact more and more of the immersive and consumer spaces to come.

Closing the section is "The Cultures of Tiki," by Scott A. Lukas. In it, he writes of the case of tiki subculture and specifically focuses on the idea of culture as a plural construct—a facet of remaking in which individuals fashion a subcultural lifestyle in creative, idiosyncratic, and, ultimately, self-affirmative respects. Tiki, as he relates, has often been understood—not unlike other domains of theming—as a primarily material construct. Lukas cautions us to focus on the other dimensions

Image 1.1. Market on Street (© Eladora | Dreamstime.com)

of theming that appear not in the form's material cues but in the affective, subjective, behavioristic, and even existential expressions of its adherents.

Spaces Beyond the Fictive and the Real

Excitingly, the study of themed and immersive spaces has benefited from multidisciplinarity that is reflected in terms of the contributing authors in this collection as well as in the wider literature on these spaces. Interestingly, the analysis, research, and criticism related to themed and immersive spaces have often highlighted certain limited and predictable concerns, which are summarized in Table 1.4.

Table 1.4 – The Major Critiques Applied to Themed and Immersive Spaces

Critique	Concern
Mimesis	The spaces—as imitations and remakes of other places, people, or things—suffer from the syndrome of mimesis or bad copying
Authenticity	The spaces lack authenticity and display qualities that make them inherently fake
Semiosis	The spaces rely on forms of semiotic admixture in which disconnected or unrelated symbols, things, and qualities are brought together in what appears to be a unified and meaningful whole
Stereotype	The spaces utilize forms of stereotyping, simplification, essentialism, and uncomplicated design in their re-presentations of other places, people, or things
Sanitization	The spaces focus on re-presentations that are sanitized, such that they lack the complications of the presumed real world
Escapism	The spaces are geared at forms of escapism in which individuals are told that their choices are limited to simplistic aspects of consumption, fantasy, and the like
Branding/Consumerism	The spaces are too heavily focused on branded expressions and associated forms of consumption
Values	The spaces reflect values that are inherently negative, such as consumerism, hedonism, individuality, competition, and others
Hegemony	The spaces are constructed in ways so as to allow the powerful to dominate those who enter and enjoy them
Nature and Associations of Space	The spaces focus our attention on certain contexts, behaviors, and experiences that have negative potentials for individuals and society

With many of these contexts from Table 1.4 in mind, the chapters in the eighth segment, "The View of the Critic," emphasize the topic of criticism as it relates to themed and immersive spaces. One of the foundations for this section is the issue of the critic's gaze as it is applied to these spaces. Often, this gaze is one in which the critic assumes a position of superiority or privilege in terms of the understanding and the interpretive dissemination of these spaces. Designers are sometimes assumed to be complicit as agents of the culture industry as themed and immersive spaces are created and operated in ways that trap guests (and workers) inside processes and forms that are inauthentic, simulated, conformist, and hegemonic. Such simplistic views will be challenged and the authors will address the uneasy dialogues that might be created between critics of spaces, their designers, operators, and guests.

Brian Lonsway's chapter, "Complicated Agency," opens the considerations of this section with a provocation: "Themed environments are authentic. They are in every way genuine, original, real, primary. They are of their own, and fashion themselves after other environments not to imitate them, but rather to reconstruct or re-contextualize them in new (authentic) ways." Lonsway focuses on the case of the branded and lifestyle space KidZania as a means of understanding the complex relationships of guests, brands, and themed and consumer spaces in the world, particularly as these relationships illustrate the complications of agency, as the title of his chapter suggests.

In "North Dakota Wins the Internet: Sincerity and Irony in an Olive Garden Review," Michael Mario Albrecht considers the curious case of Marilyn Hagerty, a food critic for the *Grand Forks Herald*, who had written a review of a newly opened Olive Garden in Grand Forks, North Dakota. Albrecht situates the Olive Garden as "part of a larger phenomenon in which the logic of themed spaces is increasingly prevalent in contemporary consumer culture" and he uses the instance of Hagerty's review of the restaurant as a way of considering the global issues of irony, sincerity, and authenticity, especially as these emerge in the many public considerations of consumer spaces in venues like the website Gawker. Ultimately, he cautions us that the many "modes of engagement in these spaces reflect…multiplicities, complications, and contestations."

In "Judgments Passed: The Place of the Themed Space in the Contemporary World of Remaking," Scott A. Lukas considers the nature of criticism that has been applied to themed, immersive, and consumer spaces. Using the re-created cave art site Caverne du Pont d'Arc as an example, he discusses the curious tendency of criticism to rely on age-old and tired dichotomies of original and copy, real and simulation, among others. He points to the idea that spaces of simulation illustrate the critic's obsession with remaking as an illegitimate if not profane act, which suggests a certain "kitsch" quality of criticism itself. In the end, he argues that criticism be remade, interestingly enough, in such a way that it becomes a more vital force in the worlds of theming and immersion around us.

Immersion and Experience

The authors in the section on "Immersion, Experience, and Phenomena" (the fourth in the reader) address the many contexts in which themed and immersive spaces emphasize, nearly exclusively, the intimate, direct, and personal connections of the guest to those spaces. Since the burgeoning of this form in Disney theme parks—in which the dynamics of all park operations are geared at the enjoyment of the guest—technologies and methods of immersion have grown and adapted to the cultural, economic, and branded forces at play in the world. The authors of these chapters will illustrate the expansions of such technologies and methods and will focus on the complex and sometimes unsettling aspects of experience within themed and immersive spaces.

Image 1.2. Gardaland, Italy (© Martinkaxxx | Dreamstime.com)

Scott A. Lukas' contribution, "Questioning "Immersion" in Contemporary Themed and Immersive Spaces," opens the segment with a focus on the fundamental notion of immersion—something recognized for its ability to dip or plunge the guest into the context, experience, and even existential quality of a given space. Yet, he illustrates how immersion is a much more complex concept (and practice) than is sometimes identified by critics of these spaces and their designers. Immersion—whether understood from the design-side of a space or its research-analytical side—should not be envisioned, he warns, as a formulation of a strict dichotomy of the real-fictive. In fact, we should ask critically why immersion is viewed as a positive entity in a philosophical and conceptual sense.

Florian Freitag's "Movies, Rides, Immersion" considers one of the most significant contexts of immersive and themed space design—that of intermediality. Specifically, Freitag endeavors to analyze the complementary, and sometimes contradictory, relationships between theme parks and movies. These relationships, as he shows, have been particularly fertile, and he illustrates four significant ways in which ride designers have utilized filmic and cinematic techniques—cinematic shorthand, ride pacing, ride adaptations, and movie-based rides. Ultimately, Freitag reminds us of the significance of the "theme park's multifarious and reciprocal relations to other media."

Gordon S. Grice, a creative director at Forrec Creative Studio, writes of the sensory aspects of theming and immersion in his contribution, "Sensory Design in Immersive Environments." Grice's perspective is particularly unique as he bridges the academic, theoretical, and applied sides of theming and immersive design. He points to the many roles that the senses play in the design of contemporary consumer spaces and suggests that the senses represent "a rich and largely untapped design resource that can and should provide the raw material for more immersive and more memorable environments." Yet, he also indicates that due to challenges and complexities of the design process, some spaces will suffer as a result of the marginalization and overlooking of multi-sensory design.

Representations of Spaces in Popular Culture

Themed and immersive spaces are particularly evocative. They beckon us to consider them—whether this entails a mere enjoyment of their environs or a more in-depth analysis—for the fact that they utilize some of the most significant, recognizable, and culturally embedded symbols, architectural forms, design approaches, and other notable elements. In fact, it is interesting to note the representations of themed and immersive spaces—those material and discursive—that have emerged in spaces, contexts, media venues, and textual instances beyond those of academia.[8]

Popular design and eclectic space television shows, such as *Bar Rescue, Extreme Homes, Extreme Makeover: Home Edition, You Live in What?, Monster House*, among many others, provide meta-opportunities to focus on the many representational issues that are connected to theming, immersive spatial design, and other aspects of material and performative consumer space. Although the representational contexts of such shows are often focused on matters of economics or the enjoyment of homeowners or patrons of such spaces, they do allow us to analyze an important understanding of these spaces that has become part of the growing discourse about themed and immersive spaces. What this discourse reflects is an expansion of the considerations of these spaces beyond academic, critical, and research accounts. The growth of popular online and social media discussion and review fora, including Facebook, TripAdvisor, Yelp, and Cruise Critic, emphasizes that much more is at stake in today's consumer and popular culture world, in which themed and immersive spaces play a notable role. At many levels, the research in this collection draws on these many popular insights that have emerged in the last ten or so years.

The chapters in "The Politics of the Space" (the seventh section in the collection) address the political implications of themed and immersive spaces. One of the initial considerations is the extent to which the analyses and critiques of such spaces have reflected limited understandings of the political. The authors in this section focus on new interpretations of themed and immersive spaces in terms of their political realms. The topics of otherness, race, the body, controversy, and ideology emphasize the complex dynamics of themed and immersive spaces and their varied constructions at political, social, cultural, and ideological levels.

Themed and immersive spaces often invite troubling political contexts into their venues—whether intended in the design or resultant as an after effect of the design and theming. In "Revisiting The Lost City: The Legend Lives On," Jeanne van Eeden revisits a space that has occupied her previous academic studies of theming. She considers the many ways in which the Lost City bases its thematic representations on stereotypical and essentialist notions of Africa—whether derived from movies, contexts of archaeology, or other sources. Beyond the theming, the backstory of the site reminds us that such spaces rely on forms of archetype and shorthand in creating their evocative environs. Much of her analysis is focused on the important ways in which the Lost City is symptomatic of larger tendencies of the "experience economy"—this, the important construct of Pine and Gilmore.

Kent Drummond and Lei Jia, in "Our Chemical Romance: Body Worlds and the Memorialization of the Self," consider a much different political context of theming—that of death. Their research focuses on analyses conducted at the popular Body Worlds exhibits, popularized by Dr. Gunther von Hagens. Drummond and Jia take us through the many spaces that one experiences while on site at Body Worlds and they use this ethnographic opportunity as a way of stressing larger themes—death and immortality—that will likely be present in themed and immersive spaces to come. Along similar lines, Scott A. Lukas, in his piece "Dark Theming Reconsidered," continues this emphasis on the darker and political sides of space and he specifically addresses dark theming—an offshoot of dark tourism. In his mind, contemporary spaces have the ability to engage guests and visitors in new and disturbing political senses, especially as they, more and more, have begun to focus on "extreme forms of politics and culture, emphasi[ze]…avant-garde tendencies and aesthetic experimentalism, and consider…taboo and forbidden topics." Lukas analyzes numerous spaces and their forms of dark theming that not only reflect the tendencies of postmondernity but also suggest some new directions in terms of the spaces of museums, theme parks, and other venues.

The focus of the fifth section, "Notions of Identity, Self, and Ideology," is on the various ways in which themed and immersive spaces entail an emphasis on space that is personalized for the enjoyment of the guest. Like the fourth section on Immersion, the authors in this section focus on the ways in which spaces are constructed in evocative senses that aim to connect to the guest's innermost desires. Above and beyond immersion and experience, there is the domain of the self in which the design and operation of a space is geared at getting inside the head of the individual—to populate that person's consciousness with ideas, memes, brands, symbols, concepts, stories, and ideologies that are simultaneously fulfilling to the individual and ideologically problematic. The authors included in this section aim to expand on previous understandings of spaces of consumption by placing greater emphasis on the nuances of self, identity, personality, and ideology that are inherent in contemporary themed and immersive spaces.

Florian Freitag's chapter "Autotheming: Themed and Immersive Spaces in Self-Dialogue," which begins the section, focuses on the significant yet understudied arena of self-referential theming or "autotheming." Freitag considers the many ways in which a theme park engages in self-referential citation of its own attractions, forms, branded properties, or the theme park industry itself and suggests that this practice is not only an emerging trend within theme parks of the present but that it represents the growing "popularity, ubiquity, and impact of themed spaces in contemporary society." Included in Freitag's analysis of this understudied dimension of theming are the spaces of Disney theme parks, Europa-Park, and Universal Studios Hollywood, notably The Simpsons Ride.

Notions of identity are also applicable at the much more macro level of a city. In the case of "Six Degrees of Navigation: Titanic Belfast's Identity Issues," the chapter by Stephen Brown, the author identifies a unique if not peculiar "identity issue" in the case of the popular Titanic Belfast attraction. What Brown discovers is a rather beguiling process in which identity is mapped—historically, mythologically, metaphorically, nationally, culturally, and commercially—to Belfast through its association with the ill-fated cruise ship. Brown illustrates how the dual identities of a city and an attraction (Titanic Belfast) are caught up in the complex politics of theming. In a much different light, Scott A. Lukas, in "Research in Themed and Immersive Spaces: At the Threshold of Identity," looks at identity as a trope that resonates through the research that is conducted in themed and immersive spaces. He argues that new, complex, and hybrid forms of research be developed such that they challenge the notions of inauthenticity, simulation, hegemony, and others that have been privileged in previous forms of research in these spaces. His work suggests the possibility that the future study of themed and immersive spaces be as diverse and multifaceted as the varied uniqueness of the same spaces.

Themed and Immersive Futures

The idea of the future has strong resonance for themed and immersive spaces. On the one hand, many spaces—particularly world's fairs and theme parks—often use the future as a form of reassurance that suggests to guests and society the idea of better things to come. On the other, many themed and immersive spaces, through their futuristic leanings, suggest to us a vision of how space—whether consumer or otherwise—may appear in the time to come. In Section 9, "The Place of the Future," the authors address this concept and analyze spaces that have the potential to transform architecture, design, culture, society, politics, and sociality in ways unimagined. The themed and immersive space is viewed here as an agent of change that could likely impact urbanism, tourism, and other realms in the future.

Davin Heckman, in "Disney's Immersive Futurism," addresses the significant context of the future in terms of the designs of Disney's theme parks. Heckman's analysis includes Tomorrowland, Walt Disney's plan for EPCOT, and the EPCOT Center theme park, and besides their notable impacts on themed spaces as utopian visions, Heckman reminds us that one of their most significant effects—that of transmedia—is with us today. As he writes, "immersive environments thrive insofar as they have a strong, distributed narrative backbone." Similarly, Markus Reisenleitner, in his contribution, "Resetting the Clock: Theme Parks, New Urbanism, and Smart Cities," considers the many ways in which theme park design and urbanism have coincided and even have impinged on one another. As he writes, in this context, "Theming and immersive spaces emerge as the foundation of imaginaries of urban dwelling that profoundly influence the planning and development of twenty-first-century urban spaces." Reisenleitner considers a number of relevant spaces in his analysis—including Los Angeles; the theme parks of Disney; Celebration and Seaside, Florida; among other spaces—and illustrates, importantly, how the New Urbanist movement has coincided with other influences in urbanism, most notably, the smart city and nostalgia trends.

Scott A. Lukas then extends these concerns to an even more general level in his chapter, "Theming and Immersion in the Space of the Future." He begins with the example of Disney's planned community in Celebration, Florida, which he considers in the startling example of the city's inability to move forward in time in line with Disney's rather utopian and futuristic visions of urbanism. He then addresses how the world exposition tradition, specifically the version from World Expo 2015 in Milan, has typically suggested a vision of the future in a variety of senses—spatial, political, cultural, social. In this last sense of the social—particularly the communal—he argues that we will note the greatest influence as themed and immersive spaces of the future will play a significant role in imagining collective futures. The reader concludes with the second of the two research dialogues between authors Filippo Carlà, Florian Freitag, Gordon Grice, and Scott A. Lukas, with this one emphasizing how the nature of themed and immersive spaces may appear in the future as well as what their study may be like.

There is no doubt that themed and immersive spaces will continue to influence our senses of space, our notions of self, and our overall everyday cultural, social, economic, political, and existential sensibilities. It is hoped that the chapters offered in this collection will continue the interesting dialogue that has emerged at the intersections of these spaces and our lives.

Notes

1. Online Etymology Dictionary, <http://www.etymonline.com/>.
2. Yi-Fu Tuan, *Topophilia: A Study of Environmental Perception, Attitudes, and Values* (New York: Columbia University Press, 1990), 11.
3. Mark Gottdiener, *The Theming of America: Dreams, Visions, and Commercial Spaces* (Boulder, CO: Westview, 1996).
4. Scott A. Lukas, ed. *The Themed Space: Locating Culture, Nation, and Self* (Lanham, MD: Lexington, 2007).
5. As examples of the analyses of the themed restaurant, see, Natalie T. Wood and Caroline Munoz, "No Rules, Just Right or Is It?: The Role of Themed Restaurants as Cultural Ambassadors," *Tourism and Hospitality Research* 7, no. 3–4 (2007): 242–255, Stephen Brown and Anthony Patterson, "Knick-Knack, Paddy-Whack, Give a Pub a Theme," *Journal of Marketing Management* 16 (2000): 647–662, and Chen Tsang Tsai, and Lu Pei-Hsun, "Authentic Dining Experiences in Ethnic Theme Restaurants," *International Journal of Hospitality Management* 31, no. 1 (2012): 304–306.
6. Of note is the "Here You Leave Today": Time and Temporality in Theme Parks project that was established by Filippo Carlà and Florian Freitag at the Johannes Gutenberg University of Mainz, Germany.
7. It should be noted that there are a few gaps in the current reader that are a result of key authors being unable to participate in the collection. The editor has attempted to fill in some of these with his own work, but doing so has been very challenging. The editor is grateful for the participation of all of the authors in this collection.
8. One of the most provocative contexts of theming is that which emerges through an aesthetic and design pleasure that is promoted in contemporary, innovative themed office spaces. Google and Epic Systems are two companies that have valued theming as a means of producing collaborative, creative, and enjoyable workspaces. See, Carey Dunn, "8 of Google's Craziest Offices," *Fast Company*, April 10, 2014,

<http://www.fastcodesign.com/3028909/8-of-googles-craziest-offices> and Abby Rogers, "This Awesome Office Was Inspired by Indiana Jones, NYC Subways and The Stock Exchange," *Business Insider*, November 17, 2001, < http://www.businessinsider.com/take-a-tour-of-epic-systems-corporations-amazing-office-2011-11>.

PART II

The Past, History, and Nostalgia

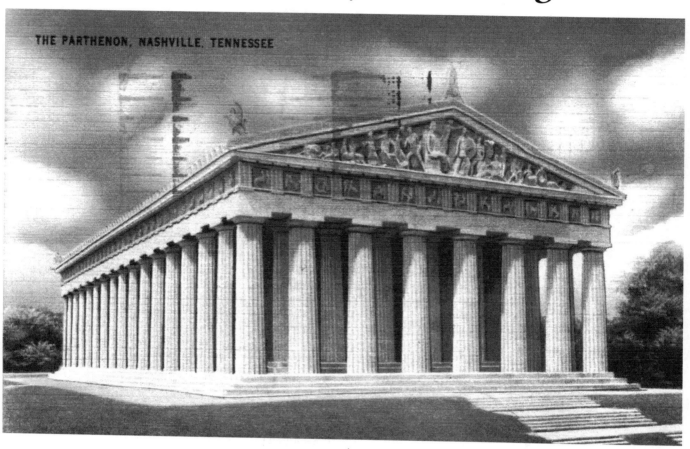

2

The Uses of History in Themed Spaces

By Filippo Carlà

Themed spaces are very often inspired by history, either in their general conception or in single parts or details: they feature recreations of historical civilizations, which are made accessible in the form of traditional architecture, clothes, sounds, as well as through references to their culture, religion, mythology, and other forms. The "history" referred to can encompass a broad variety of times—the nearer past of the twentieth century (as in the area Berlin, in Phantasialand in Brühl, Germany), the Middle Ages of castles and tournaments (for example, in parts of the Puy du Fou, Les Epesses, France), the antiquity of myths and heroes, or the one of decadence and sin (for example, Caesars Palace or the Forum Shops in Las Vegas)—as well as of regions: it can be the history of the region or country where the themed space is built (as in the "mini-countries," see below), or a faraway exotic society (for example, the Mexico area in Phantasialand; or the Holland represented in Japan in the park Huis Ten Bosch).[1]

Both the temporal and the geographical axes must be carefully considered when approaching the study of a themed space: the European Middle Ages represented in the area Medieval Faire in the theme park Canada's Wonderland in Vaughan, Ontario, may be chronologically on a line with the medieval Hungarian village reconstructed at Élménybirtok near Pécs, but while the former refers to a past which is not part of the cultural memory of Ontario, the latter aims to reconstruct the past life of the very region in which it has been built, insisting on the potential geopiety of the visitors from the area. The ancient Greece presented in Terra Mítica, Spain, even if not a direct part of Spain's "national history," is still a part of a Mediterranean and Western European identity—which does not apply when ancient Greece is represented in the theme parks Happy Valley in Beijing, E-Da in Taiwan, or Dunia Fantasi in Indonesia.[2] As formulated by Hochbruck and Schlehe, "what is staged in themed environments is either the creation of a history of a nation, region, or ethnic group, as an offer to the visitor for imaginative identification, or it is the creation of a seemingly timeless exotic Other, juxtaposed to the Self and serving to stabilize and position it in the global world."[3] These two alternatives must be perceived as ideal types at the ends of a spectrum, and many themed spaces can play simultaneously with both forms of recognition and self-ascription.

How can a "historical themed space" be defined? This would seem to overlap with what has been defined a "cultural" themed space: "cultural theme parks are parks which use cultures as their themes. Themes are seen as structured narratives."[4] But the category of cultural themed space seems very elusive, not only because "culture" is a difficult concept to define, and even more difficult to represent, but also because such a definition does not allow taking into consideration two central elements. The first are the different chronological layers and the already mentioned structures of nearness/distance (past vs. modern cultures, local vs. exotic cultures), with all their ideological implications; and the second, the complexity of reception, which very often does not proceed directly from the culture A to its representation in the context B, but travels via many intermediate steps of remediatization—iconographies connected to a particular "culture" derive from art, movies, or comics which are already popular and well known to the visitors. Parc Astérix in Plailly, France, for instance, is a theme park representing the ancient world (and, in one area, modern France, too), but the Egyptians, the Greeks, and the Romans one meets there have been filtered through the popular comics by René Goscinny and Albert Uderzo. To decide if such a park should be considered "cultural" is challenging, since it does not directly represent a "culture," but at the same time it shapes and reinforces the visual ideas of the ancient world shared by many visitors.

Rather than recurring to the concept of culture, therefore, it may be useful to adopt the more neutral one of history to identify themed spaces whose themes are not completely the product of fantasy (they must refer to societies and civilizations which did exist, even if they are remediatized, and not to fantasy worlds as Harry Potter's) and whose themes portray these societies and civilizations in a particular phase which is chronologically placed before the possible extension of memory of a living being in the moment of the construction of the park—therefore a moment which surely escapes biological memory and makes the representation of that society a part of cultural memory.[5] It is thus possible to read such representations of the "past" in their specific cultural, political, and social contexts and to understand, also in consideration of previous steps in the chain of receptions, the specific (ideological) values with which every theme is loaded.

Such historical themed spaces are immersive environments that allow visitors to feel as if they were traveling through time and directly experiencing the historical Other.[6] As argued by Cornelius Holtorf, to the two traditional approaches to history, the "evolutionary" and the "political" one, respectively stressing the historical "facts" and their sequences, and the construction and representation of different pasts in different presents, the last decades have added a third, new one, namely, "time travel," or "an experience and *social practice* in the present that evokes a past (or future) reality."[7] This approach to the past generates a form of knowledge that derives first and foremost from experience, is of a sensorial nature and, as such, cannot be reached with the traditional methods of historiography.

What is provided is a powerful historical image with which "professional historians are unable to compete" because of the sheer amount of visitors.[8] One can think here of the 14 million visitors whom Disneyland welcomes every year and whom the park provides with an image of the American small town at the beginning of the twentieth century in Main Street, U.S.A., or one can even think of the half a million visitors per year for Terra Mítica—a number which, while it does not guarantee the park's survival, is still higher than the sales records of almost all books of popular history.[9] Additionally, it should not be underestimated how powerful such images of the past, how emotionally loaded, directly experienced, and thus "naturalized" they are when compared to the argumentative structure of a traditional historical publication. Since they can be experienced directly, the discourses proposed to the visitors of the themed space appear "objective" and "true"—"such experiences can only be validated, not disputed."[10]

The three approaches must be considered as ideal types, which do not exist in a pure form—historical themed spaces are a form of time traveling because of their immersive and therefore experienced, not argumentative nature; nonetheless they do not cease to be evolutionary and political, too. Since every representation of the past is the product of a present, of its social and political context, and of its ideologies, it is always political:

> Making history is a way of producing identity insofar as it produces a relation between that which supposedly occurred in the past and the present state of affairs. The construction of a history is the construction of a meaningful universe of events and narratives for an individual or collectively defined subject.[11]

A good example of this is the theme park Terra Mítica in Benidorm, Spain, in which the different themed areas, organized in a loop, bring the visitors from ancient Egypt to Classical Greece, the islands of the Mediterranean, the Roman Empire, and finally to medieval and early modern Spain, which is approached progressively both in a chronological and a geographical sense. The underlying message is a teleological construction in which thousands of years of Mediterranean history build up to produce, as their highest point, the Spanish nation—thus fostering an evolutionary approach.[12] While the last example requires visitors to recognize in the represented past a transhistorical (and essentialistic) Same, in other contexts they might be confronted with the Alterity of a complete Otherness, which will in the end once again reinforce their sense of belonging to the Same. This applies to the area Deep in Africa in Phantasialand, a strongly colonial representation of Africa, which insists on the stereotypes representing the continent as "near to nature" and "adventurous," thus reinforcing the feeling of belonging to the European, colonizing, civilization.[13]

The choice of historical themes is thus political, since it is connected to the structures of identity of the context in which the themed space is built, as well as to the selection of the represented elements, which are carefully chosen in accordance with the underlying ideologies—all these choices influence and condition the way in which the public of reference understands and remembers the past, and how it understands the relevance of this past for their own lives and times. The customers of the Caffe Tito in Sarajevo, for example, are offered a vision of their recent past (indeed I would not include it in my definition of "historical") which is very explicit in identifying a "glorious period" of Yugoslavian history to be cherished and nostalgically missed; a planned theme park on the Roman Empire in Rome and another one on Napoleon in France (projected on the site of the battle of Montereau, 1814, in which Napoleon defeated the Austrians) are as explicit in seeking to provide the visitors with a sense of pride for the great past of their "nations."[14] It is not a coincidence that both projects, never realized, were fostered by politicians belonging to right, nationalist parties, namely, the then major of Rome Gianni Alemanno, famous for his post-fascist ideology, and the French MP Yves Jégo, member of the radical party and advocate of a strong souverainism.[15]

Image 2.1. Caffe Tito in Sarajevo (Photo by Filippo Carlà)

If the underlying messages can sometimes shift away from the traditional nationalistic discourses—in a globalized world the commercial enterprises involved in the realization of themed spaces may be interested in reaching a much broader public—popular history in the theme park is definitely not losing "its ideological impetus."[16] Popular history, and especially "time traveling," reproduces political discourses about the past which reinforce themselves continuously through repetition. This is a structural aspect, deriving from the nature of historical reception itself: the public needs to recognize the object—without the element of recognition (be it the Roman legionaries, the medieval knights, or the Native Americans in their teepees), there is no interest in the sensorial and emotional experience offered by the immersive space: "visitors to amusement parks seek to maximise their enjoyment by preferring rides and attractions linked to historic themes that are easy to recognise, simple to grasp, and fun to experience."[17] Historical illustration has always been very conservative and repetitive in its motives and figures.[18]

Power and commercial interests thus support each other, and it is very hard to isolate specific agendas or agency. Some themed spaces, however, may be built after a precise political commission, which facilitates understanding their underlying ideology. The Indonesian park Taman Mini Indonesia Indah, opened in 1975, represents the unity in diversity of Indonesia by portraying its different regions and their local history. The national identity of this country is problematic since it was born from the union of many different islands and areas with different histories, religions, and traditions: the park is the direct expression of the will of then dictator Sukarto (actually, the plan was conceived by his wife in 1971). It is no coincidence that the park has no entrance fee, considering how the political power wished the population to visit it frequently.[19]

This is only one of the themed areas known as "mini countries," which foster national identities through minimized representations of specific nation-states, thus giving material and visual support to the discourses that shape the "imagined communities." Even when their foundation and operation is in private hands, and the State is not involved at all, their political message remains very clear. For example, Mini Israel, which opened in 2002 in the Ayalon Valley, shows 350 replicas of buildings and landmarks from Israel, insisting on the multicultural nature of the country (Christian and Muslim religious buildings are included in the park), while at the same time distributing them so to give to the entire park the shape of David's star.[20] The main aim and ideological background of the park, in a context in which issues of identity and nationhood can only euphemistically be defined problematic, is very evident.

Even if an explicitly political agenda should be missing, therefore, such themed areas in the end do in most cases reinforce, reproduce, and spread stereotypes, structures of identity, and forms of cultural memory that are already the dominant ones. This is not surprising, since dominating discourses are recognizable by the public, therefore fulfill the already mentioned requirement for success, and can activate in the visitors a strong emotional reaction, especially when they appeal to senses of community and national identity: "the historical theme park will content itself with rearranging those things the visitors knew before into forms that appear simultaneously new and familiar."[21]

Postmodernism, Temporality, and History

The recent popularity of "time traveling" needs to be further considered in the context of postmodern culture and aesthetics, since it could at first seem to contrast with the loss of temporality which has been deemed typical of postmodernism. In contrast to space, time has been considered less relevant to postmodernism, which sort of presses time on space in an eternal present: "now a foreign country with a booming tourist trade, the past has undergone the usual consequences of popularity. The more it is appreciated for its own sake, the less real or relevant it becomes. No longer revered or feared, the past is swallowed up by the ever-expanding present; we enlarge our sense of the contemporary at the expense of realizing its connection with the past."[22] Such a broader present is the precondition for "time travel."[23] The death of the future has been sung contextually by many scholars since it seems that this age does not have any idea of the future as a realm of completely different social, political, and economic structures—figurations of the future can only be imagined as a hyper technological present, or as final catastrophe.[24] While I cannot discuss the reasons for this evolution in detail here, I will simply mention as possible causes the political events of the late 1980s, a reaction to the deconstructionist wave of the 1960s and 1970s (Lowenthal), the digital revolution (Gumbrecht), the struggle for natural resources, which would have caused a negative attitude towards the future and social and political change (Torpey, Assmann).[25]

What is important is that this does not at all indicate a loss of interest in the past or the dismissal of any form of knowledge of ancient worlds—futurism is not postmodern, it is on the contrary one of the highest points of modernism. What is at stake is the end of a particular conception of time and temporality that was born at the end of the eighteenth century and characterized Western modernity.[26] In this "time regime," time was conceived as linear, physical time was objectified as a natural dimension in which to situate human action, the present represented a point between the past and the future, while these three temporal spheres were kept radically and strictly separate.[27] This meant a loss of significance of the past in shaping activities and values of the present—the death of the concept of *historia magistra vitae*, while history was born as an academic subject with a pretense of objectivity which postulates the separation of the different time levels—and a re-orientation of human activity away from an inspiration by the past, seen as "golden" and better, and towards the future.[28] This conception of time—since "time regimes" are a culturally conditioned aspect of mentality—had replaced the earlier, teleologically oriented history of the Christian Middle Ages, and seemed for centuries, also because of its base in physics and natural sciences, to be "objective" and "true," before entering into a deep crisis and losing its dominance with the 1980s, when a "temporal revolution" created a new, postmodern, time regime, in which the past reconquered a big space in human conscience and daily life.[29] This "need for history" generates a typical nostalgia and retro-taste, while cultural values and personal identities are again oriented by the past and based on historical origins, on cultural memory, and on "historical consciousness."[30] Consequently, not only history as an academic discipline is challenged by the right of each individual and community to be interested in history (also as a form of entertainment), but also by an always broader range of "history providers," which include themed spaces.[31]

Such a new interest in the past is indeed characterized by a new approach to history and its knowledge—what Vanessa Agnew has identified as an "affective turn," characterized by a "collapsing of temporalities" and a "privileging of experience over event or structure."[32] The "new past" must be approached "directly," through a form of presentification which

Image 2.2. Fishermans Wharf, Macau (© Simon Gurney | Dreamstime.com)

makes it the object of a direct personal and possibly pansensorial experience and which allows each individual to directly identify with persons from different epochs, their daily life, their needs, and their challenges. What is expected is again the destruction of the linear timeline, and an experience of the past that is not purely educational, but also entertaining, personalized, and strongly connected to structures of memory and identity.[33] While history was, in the modern chronotopos, the place where emotions were neutralized, it becomes now a field of strong affectivity and self-finding.[34]

As a consequence of this new approach, a new concept of "authenticity" has developed, according to which what is "real" is not what really comes from the past, but what generates "real feelings" of identification with it; at stake is not what is ancient, but what "feels authentically ancient," an "existential authenticity," different and distinguished from a "museological authenticity."[35] The past "disappears" and is replaced by "pastness," the quality possessed by an object which is perceived as "old," as belonging to a historical period or society, independently from when it was actually produced.[36] Historical themed spaces, which inspire an idea of "traveling back in time" with their "new" structures and buildings, are a perfect example of this quality.[37] The "historical themed space" thus has to be interpreted together with such other immersive and direct sensorial experiences as video games and particularly Second Life virtual worlds, but also with particular forms of "presentification," such as historical sewing and historical modeling, "historical reality shows," and the increasing success of reenactments, which respond to the same interests and needs and pursue the same agenda as themed spaces.[38]

All this has been widely recognized in the educational sector, too, as evidenced by the revolutions this caused in the fields of museology, of didactics, of experimental archaeology, and so forth.[39] Indeed, many themed spaces with a historical theme have been developed with a primarily educational aim, as a support, or actually as the "real way" to teach (and learn) history. This is the case of what Kirsti Mathiesen Hjemdahl calls "historical theme parks" (but they are not theme parks in strict sense), where school children are allowed to spend one or more days recreating the life conditions of the past, and thus apparently learn "history" in a much more effective way through a direct experience with which the "detached" and "aseptic" atmosphere of the traditional museum cannot compete.[40] The visitors of a living history museum experience a form of "transformation of the self," of a theatrical nature, which gives way to the affective identification with the members of the past society represented.[41] Living history museums have thus become increasingly popular, while traditional museums offer activities and "theming," too, and experimental archaeology centers provide a growing number of opportunities to directly experience life in other epochs, dressing in "historical clothes," baking pottery "as they did," among other examples.[42] A case in point is the "living history program" which has been developed over the years at Colonial Williamsburg.[43] Alternate reality games are meanwhile entering the daily life of schools and classes as a useful tool for teachers to develop immersive, participatory teaching.[44]

These educational themed spaces, which are supposed to challenge existing stereotypes, are nonetheless an exception. Most historical themed spaces have a commercial aim, or, as shown, even an explicitly political one. Here, the representation of history revolves mostly around the appeal to the visitors' existing pre-knowledge—without a reference to something recognizable there would be no possibility of reception, and therefore no "interest." This implies that the themed space has almost no possibility to stay clear of existing and rooted stereotypes. But this is not the only reason why such historical themed spaces are innately conservative—in addition to the necessity of adhering to and reproducing the dominating discourses, there is an implicit assumption underlying the affective turn, namely, the assumption that many aspects of human life are "natural" and not "cultural," are constant through time and space. Indeed, only through postulating the existence of meaningful "constants" in human life—not only from a biological perspective—can one assume that the past or another culture can be experienced on one's own skin and be meaningfully reenacted.

Image 2.3. Europa-Park, Rust, Germany (Photo by Scott A. Lukas)

According to Jörn Rüsen, there are four kinds of historical consciousness: a traditional one, which "furnishes us with traditions, it reminds us of origins and the repetition of obligations," an exemplary type, which through examples transmits rules and values, a critical one, which shows the existence of a rupture between a past perceived as Other and us, and a genetic type, which accepts the change but not the rupture, and sees the present as the product of successive transformations of the past.[45] While the critical type is hard—but not impossible—to find in the themed space (the completely exotic past), the other three forms of historical consciousness are all relevant for the affective and immersive past. Particular structures, rites, and relationships are projected back in time and thus naturalized and universalized, and the same happens with values. Main Street, U.S.A. (in Disneyland) provides the model of the good, true America of the small town; the different countries in Europa-Park in Rust, Germany, are presented with their traditional clothes, buildings, and food; shows in Terra Mítica present values such as masculinity, military bravery, and respect of the gods as universal by placing them in the sphere of myth and prehistory, while at the same time—as already noted—proposing a teleological and therefore "genetic" vision of history.[46]

The Contested Past

The new interest in the past and its location outside academia, in connection with the loss of credibility of the idea of an "objective" history, which can exist only in the modern frame of a clear-cut separation of past, present, and future, has generated controversial discussions about the possibilities, legitimacy, and dangers of the "affective turn," the alternative forms of contact with history provided by popular history, living history, and the themed spaces, and the possible cooperation between academic history and these new forms of historical consciousness.[47] The consequence was—and still is—a wide identity crisis among professional historians concerning the aims, methods, and duties of research, a crisis deepened by the extreme increase in the number of professional historians after the Second World War and the consequent progressive lack of public funding for the Humanities since the 1980s—the very moment in which the "time regime" changed.

The reaction of academic historians has been, especially when the phenomena described first emerged, a huge skepticism about the possibilities of "public history," which was denigrated as "amateur history," a focus on the responsibilities of "making history," and on the possible dangers ensuing from the diffusion of historical themed spaces. The high point of this critique was represented by the debate surrounding the project of Disney's America, a theme park planned in Haymarket, Virginia, at the beginning of the 1990s. The concept became known in 1993 and the opening was planned for 1998—the park, which would be built in an area thick with historical memories, in a town destroyed during the Civil War in 1862, would have consisted of 9 themed areas: Crossroads USA (a Civil War village), Native America (a native American village), Civil War Fort, We the People (Ellis Island), State Fair (inspired by Coney Island), Family Farm (a "traditional" American farm), President's Square (featuring a copy of the Magic Kingdom's Hall of Presidents), Enterprise (a nineteenth-century industrial town, celebrating the Industrial Revolution), and Victory Field (celebrating the US participation in the two world wars).[48]

The project attracted—unexpectedly for Disney—a very strong resistance, "by comparatively small organizations, advocacy groups and thousands of concerned citizens."[49] While part of the protest was rooted in concerns about the impact of the project on the region and in the possible worsening of life quality, worries were raised also regarding Disney's particular approach to and representation of history. More specifically, there were two main points: on the one hand, the white-washed and highly ideologized way in which American history would be presented in a celebratory fashion as the triumphal march of middle classes towards the construction of the best of all possible worlds, "sanitizing" conflict (even if the company insisted that conflict would be represented), repression of minorities, slavery, among other issues, and, on the other hand, the negative impact on the "real" historical sites of the region—both because of the subsequent urbanization (which also moved environmentalist groups) and of the potential loss of visitors such sites would have suffered.[50] Disney decided in a first moment to leave Haymarket and consider relocation, responding to the "local" and the environmental issues, but the importance of the other points became clear when such relocation did not take place. Even the project of re-theming Knott's Berry Farm in Buena Park, California, which was being sold at the moment, along these lines, caused the Knott family to decide to not sell the park (officially out of fear that the original park would have been too radically re-built). The project was then abandoned and some of the already planned attractions were incorporated in Disney's California Adventure (Anaheim, California), albeit rethemed.

While most scholars simply frowned at the idea that Disney could be a legitimate "history teacher" and only saw the dangers inherent in the project, some of them demonstrated some openness for the park, but asked for a thorough rethinking of it: "the company must decide whether it wants to use its resources to educate and engage visitors, as does a historic site like Colonial Williamsburg, or to entertain them with nostalgia and fantasy-like playlands."[51] Both positions developed from a huge misunderstanding: the scholarly community, with very few exceptions, had not realized the change in historical interests and perceptions of history and the extent of the affective turn; it thought that historical theming could be legitimate only in presence of an educational purpose, and claimed in the end an absolute and exclusive right to "do," "show," and "teach" history "in the right way," not acknowledging the necessities of time traveling and the aesthetic developments running through society.[52]

In more recent years, a broader agreement has been reached about the impossibility of maintaining the ideal of a value-free and independent historical research. It is now clear to all that academic history is just one of the sources of cultural memory, and that academic historians have the duty to confront alternative forms of history if they do not want to remain trapped in the ivory tower but instead want to continue playing an important role in society.[53] At the same time, the sharp differentiation between a "professional" and a "public" history is questioned by the postmodern destruction of the distinction between "high" and "low" culture. Surely, the dangers of affective history, particularly in themed spaces, should be clear to everybody—the non-argumentative, instinctive approach and the deriving impression of "objectivity," the basically conservative character, the strong stereotypization. None of the above constitutes, however, a good reason to ignore or to violently attack popular history, and to turn our backs to it with the presumption of being the detainers of a "responsible" history.[54] The same dangers are inherent to academic history when it is not aware of its influences and conditionings, as they have been progressively "revealed," starting with Hayden White's *Metahistory*.[55]

The central question of who "possesses" history and the authority to speak about it must be framed differently. We must recognize on the one hand that no one can presume to have a privilege or a right to historical interpretation, and that history is a "public good," and on the other hand continue to show—and this can be done only in a continuing dialogue—that "professional historians" acquire, during their education, skills which differentiate them from other people, and which make sense only if they are made available to the entire public. A complete appraisal of what heritage, cultural memory, and uses of the past mean "is only possible if historians understand something of how museums, theme parks, and so on function, the discussions in which those who work in them engage, and the frameworks that are being developed under the umbrellas of museum studies and material cultural studies," as well as cultural studies, theme park studies, and aesthetics.[56]

Notes

1. For more on the antiquity of myths and heroes and decadence and sin, see Margaret Malamud, *Ancient Rome and Modern America* (Malden, England: Oxford, 2009), 229–252, and for more on Huis Ten Bosch, see M. Treib, "Theme Park, Themed Living: The Case of Huis Ten Bosch (Japan)," in *Theme Park Landscapes: Antecedents and Variations*, eds. Terence Young and Robert Riley (Washington, D.C.: Dumbarton Oaks Research Library and Collection, 2002), 213–234, and Judith Schlehe and Michiko Uike-Bormann, "Staging the Past in Cultural Theme Parks: Representations of Self and Other in Asia and Europe," in *Staging the Past: Themed Environments in Transcultural Perspectives*, eds. Judith Schlehe, Michiko Uike-Bormann, Carolyn Oesterle, and Wolfgang Hochbruck (Bielefeld, Germany: Transcript, 2010),

2. On the reception of ancient Greece as a part of a "monolithic" and "exotic" Western world in Japanese popular culture, see Maria G. Castello and Carla Scilabra, "Theoi Becoming Kami: Classical Mythology in the Anime World," in *Ancient Magic and the Supernatural in the Modern Visual and Performing Arts*, eds. Filippo Carlà and Irene Berti (London: Bloomsbury 2015: 177–196).

3. Wolfgang Hochbruck and Judith Schlehe, "Introduction: Staging the Past," in *Staging the Past: Themed Environments in Transcultural Perspectives*, eds. Judith Schlehe, Michiko Uike-Bormann, Carolyn Oesterle, and Wolfgang Hochbruck (Bielefeld, Germany: Transcript, 2010), 8.

4. Schlehe and Uike-Bormann, "Staging the Past in Cultural Theme Parks," 57.

5. Jan Assmann, *Das kulturelle Gedächtnis: Schrift, Erinnerung und politische Identität in frühen Hochkulturen* (Munich, Germany: Verlag C.H. Beck, 1992).

6. The historical dimension, as defined above and subtracted from biographical memory, is by definition "Other": "Being human means being in history which means being mortal; popular historical texts have this at their heart. Popular history, or the manifestation of the past in the cultural text, reconciles us to at the same time as repelling us from death. We recognise the otherness of the past and its complete difference from now—that otherness allows us to control our reactions to it." Jerome De Groot, "Afterword: Past, Present, Future," in *Popular History Now and Then: International Perspectives*, eds. Barbara Korte and Sylvia Paletschek (Bielefeld, Germany: Transcript, 2012), 285–286.

7. Cornelius J. Holtorf, "On the Possibility of Time Travel," *Lund Archaeological Review* 15 (2009): 33; see also, Cornelius J. Holtorf, "Time Travel: A New Perspective on the Distant Past," in *On the Road: Studies in Honour of Lars Larsson*, eds. Birgitta Hardh, Kristina Jennbert, and Deborah Olausson (Stockholm: Almquiest and Wiksell, 2007), 127–132.

8. Michael Wallace, "Serious Fun," *The Public Historian* 17, no. 4 (Autumn, 1995): 33.

9. Nonetheless, the first and principal means by which people enter into contact with history is nowadays television, which also is immersive and immediate. On the other hand, the commercial success of history on TV is a product of the increasing interest in history, especially since TV's immediacy highlights how historical representations relate to current and actual issues, selecting, as they do, popular topics and reinforcing stereotypes. On all this, see Gary Edgerton, "Introduction: Television as Historian: A Different Kind of History Altogether," in *Television Histories: Shaping Collective Memory in the Media Age*, eds. Gary Edgerton and Peter Rollins (Lexington: University Press of Kentucky, 2001), 1–16.

10. Vanessa Agnew, "Introduction: What Is Reenactment?" *Criticism* 46, no. 3 (Summer 2004): 331.

11. Jonathan Friedman, "The Past in the Future: History and the Politics of Identity," *American Anthropologist* 94, no. 4 (December 1992): 837; see also Jonathan Friedman, "Myth, History, and Political Identity," *Cultural Anthropology* 7, no. 2 (May 1992): 194–210.

12. Filippo Carlà and Florian Freitag, "Ancient Greek Culture and Myth in the Terra Mítica Theme Park," *Classical Receptions Journal* 7 (2015): 242–259. On the disputed Spanish national identity, see Pedro Ruiz Torres, "Political Uses of History in Spain," in *Political Uses of the Past: The Recent Mediterranean Experience*, eds. Jacques Revel and Giovanni Levi (London: Routledge, 2002), 95–116.

13. Jan-Erik Steinkrüger, *Thematisierte Welten: Über Darstellungspraxen in Zoologischen Gärten und Vergnügungsparks* (Bonn, Germany: Transcript, 2013), 272–276.

14. See <http://www.caffetito.ba/>.

15. See Anon. "Plans Revealed for Theme Park to Recreate Glories of Ancient Rome," *DailyMail.com*, <http://www.dailymail.co.uk/travel/article-2136083/Romaland-Plans-revealed-theme-park-recreate-glories-Ancient-Rome.html>.

16. De Groot, "Afterword," 292–294, 283.

17. Holtorf, "Time Travel," 129.

18. Raphael Samuel, *Theatres of Memory: Past and Present in Contemporary Culture* (London: Verso, 2012), 32.

19. For more on this park, see Noel B. Salazar, "Imagineering Tailor-Made Pasts for Nation-Building and Tourism: A Comparative Perspective," in *Staging the Past: Themed Environments in Transcultural Perspectives*, eds. Judith Schlehe, Michiko Uike-Bormann, Carolyn Oesterle, and Wolfgang Hochbruck (Bielefeld, Germany: Transcript, 2010), 95–97, and Schlehe and Uike-Bormann, "Staging the Past in Cultural Theme Parks," 73–85.

20. Michael Feige, "A Dorian Gray Reflection: Mini Israel and the Subversive Present," in *Time and Temporality in Theme Parks*, eds. Filippo Carlà, Florian Freitag, Sabrina Mittermeier, and Ariane Schwarz (Hanover: Wehrhahn, 2016).

21. Hochbruck and Schlehe, "Introduction," 11.

22. David Lowenthal, *The Past is a Foreign Country* (Cambridge: Cambridge University Press, 1985), xvii.

23. François Hartog and Jacques Revel, "Historians and the Present Conjuncture," in *Political Uses of the Past: The Recent Mediterranean Experience*, eds. Jacques Revel and Giovanni Levi (London: Routledge, 2002), 7–8.

24. Lowenthal, *The Past is a Foreign Country*, 3–4; John Torpey, "The Pursuit of the Past: A Polemical Perspective," in *Theorizing Historical Consciousness*, ed. Peter Seixas (Toronto: University of Toronto Press, 2004); Aleida Assmann, *Ist die Zeit aus den Fugen? Aufstieg und Fall des Zeitregimes der Moderne* (Munich, Germany: Carl Hanser Verlag, 2013), 67–69.

25. Lowenthal, *The Past is a Foreign Country*; Hans Ulrich Gumbrecht, *Unsere breite Gegenwart* (Berlin: Suhrkamp, 2010); Torpey, "The Pursuit of the Past," 240–255. Assmann, *Ist die Zeit aus den Fugen?*

26. Reinhart Koselleck, *Vergangene Zukunft. Zur Semantik geschichtlicher Zeiten* (Frankfurt, Germany: Suhrkamp, 1979), in particular 130–143.

27. Koselleck 1979:38–66; Assmann, *Ist die Zeit aus den Fugen*, 179–191.

28. Koselleck 1979:38–66; Assmann, *Ist die Zeit aus den Fugen*, 179–191.

29. Assmann, *Ist die Zeit aus den Fugen*, 9–22.

30. For more on postmodern nostalgia and retro-taste, see Simon Reynolds, *Retromania: Pop Culture's Addiction to Its Own Past* (London: Faber and Faber, 2011); on cultural memory, see Assmann, *Ist die Zeit aus den Fugen*, 239–244; and on historical consciousness see Jörn Rüsen, "Historical Consciousness: Narrative Structure, Moral Function, and Ontogenetic Development," in *Theorizing Historical Consciousness*, ed. Peter Seixas (Toronto: University of Toronto Press, 2004), 66–68.

31. Effi Gazi, "Claiming History: Debating the Past in the Present," Historein 4 (2003): 5–16; Assmann, *Ist die Zeit aus den Fugen*, 276–280.

32. Vanessa Agnew, "History's Affective Turn: Historical Reenactment and Its Work in the Present," *Rethinking History* 11, no. 3 (September 2007): 301.

33. Assmann, *Ist die Zeit aus den Fugen?*, 291–293.

34. Assmann, *Ist die Zeit aus den Fugen?*, 296–297.

35. Cornelius J. Holtorf, *From Stonehenge to Las Vegas: Archaeology as Popular Culture* (Walnut Creek, CA: Altamira, 2005), 135–136. Friedman, "The Past in the Future," 845–846.

36. Cornelius J. Holtorf, "The Presence of Pastness: Themed Environments and Beyond," in *Staging the Past: Themed Environments in Transcultural Perspectives*, eds. Judith Schlehe, Michiko Uike-Bormann, Carolyn Oesterle, and Wolfgang Hochbruck (Bielefeld, Germany: Transcript, 2010).

37. Hochbruck and Schlehe, "Introduction," 8–9.

38. On the topic of video games, see, Brian Rejack, "Toward a Virtual Reenactment of History: Video Games and the Recreation of the Past," *Rethinking History* 11, (2007): 411–425, and Jerome De Groot, *Consuming History: Historians and Heritage in Contemporary Popular Culture* (London: Routledge, 2009), 133–145. I thank Danielle Fiore, a former student and historical model, for attracting my attention to sewing and historical modeling; her homepage is indeed a perfect example of this particular cultural phenomenon, <http://www.daniellefiore.blogspot.co.uk/>. For historical sewing, see <http://historicalsewing.com/>. An online shop for ancient clothes (eighteenth century), which organizes events such as picnics, rents clothes, and offers clients the chance of an experience of the past can be found at <http://www.anticoatelier.com/>. On historical reality shows, see Alexander Cook, "The Use and Abuse of Historical Reenactment: Thoughts on Recent Trends in Public History," *Criticism* 46, no. 3 (2004): 487–496, and De Groot, *Consuming History*, 165–172. A good example of reenactments is the organization of the Fiestas de Carthagineses y Romanos" which take place every year in Cartagena, Spain—a town founded by the Carthaginians but which shares, at the same time, the Spanish idea of a Roman "descent" and identity. The population of the city takes part in the events, they are organized in "groups" of Carthaginians and of Romans (there are 50 active associations, 25 Carthaginian and 25 Roman, collected in a "Roman Senate" and a "Carthaginian Council"), see, <http://www.cartaginesesyromanos.es/>. Similarly, Mutina Boica in Modena, Italy, re-enacts every year, with a program of other events and lectures, the battle which took place there in 43 BCE, see <http://www.mutinaboica.it/home/>. On reenactments, see, among others, Agnew, "Introduction."

39. De Groot, *Consuming History*, 116–119.

40. Kirsti Mathiesen Hjemdahl, "History as a Cultural Playground," *Ethnologia Europaea* 32, no. 2 (2002): 105–124.

41. Carolyn Oesterle, "Themed Environments–Performative Spaces: Performing Visitors in North American Living History Museums," in *Staging the Past: Themed Environments in Transcultural Perspectives*, eds. Judith Schlehe, Michiko Uike-Bormann, Carolyn Oesterle, and Wolfgang Hochbruck (Bielefeld, Germany: Transcript, 2010). See, also, Christina Kerz, "Atmosphere, Immersion, and the Production of Authenticity in Colonial Williamsburg," in this volume.

42. One example is the center Archea in Benevagienna, Italy, which offers four different themed spaces: one for Prehistory, two for the Roman period, and one for the Middle Ages. Here the school classes are introduced—again in a direct and "affective" way—first to archaeological practice, then to "daily life" in the ancient communities, with activities such as realizing Paleolithic parietal paintings or Roman mosaics, minting Roman coins, grinding wheat with reconstructed ancient millstones, or writing on parchment with a goose feather in the "scriptorium" of a medieval monastery. See, <http://www.archea.info/index.html>.

43. Eric Gable and Richard Handler, "Deep Dirt: Messing Up the Past at Colonial Williamsburg," in *Marketing Heritage: Archaeology and the Consumption of the Past*, eds. Yorke Rowan and Uzi Baram (Walnut Creek, CA: AltaMira, 2004), 170–171.

44. <http://blogs.kqed.org/mindshift/2014/10/how-students-can-channel-the-odyssey-into-an-alternate-reality-epic/> is an example of an ARG developed to teach the Odyssey.

45. Rüsen, "Historical Consciousness," 70–78.

46. Michael Wallace, "Mickey Mouse History: Portraying the Past at Disney World," *Radical History Review* 32 (1985): 34–37; Filippo Carlà and Florian Freitag, "Strategien der Geschichtstransformationen in Themenparks," in *Geschichtstransformationen: Medien, Verfahren und Funktionalisierungen historischer Rezeption*, eds. Sonja Georgi, Julia Ilgner, Isabell Lammel, Cathleen Sarti, and Christine Waldschmidt (Bielefeld, Germany: Transcript, 2015), 131–149.

47. See Hartog and Revel, "Historians and the Present Conjuncture," 1–2. Ann-Louise Shapiro, "Whose (Which) History is It Anyway?" *History and Theory* 36, no. 4 (1997): 1–3.

48. On the Hall of Presidents, see Wallace, "Mickey Mouse History," 37–39. On the Manassas controversy, see, Joan M. Zenzen, *Battling for Manassas: The Fifty-Year Preservation Struggle at Manassas National Battlefield Park* (University Park, PA: Penn State University Press, 1997).

49. Marcia G. Synnott, "Disney's America: Whose Patrimony, Whose Profits, Whose Past?," *The Public Historian* 17, no. 4 (1995): 44–45.

50. Synnott, "Disney's America," 52–54, 45–48.

51. On the "history teacher" issue, see, Wallace, "Mickey Mouse History"; Patricia Mooney-Melvin, "Beyond the Book: Historians and the Interpretive Challenge," *The Public Historian* 17, no. 4 (1995): 75–76. Synnott, "Disney's America," 57. It is interesting to underline how Colonial Williamsburg is a "clean" reconstruction, too, in which "dirt, ruin, and decay" have been introduced "in the restoration" to counter accusations of kitsch and inauthenticity, and whose historicity relies in the end mostly on the topographic collocation. See, Gable and Handler, "Deep Dirt."

52. See, Horton's statements in Synnott, "Disney's America," 57. Cary Carson acknowledged that the entire debate was not so much about Disney and this park as about the "ownership" of history. Carson opposed the construction of the park but considered the ensuing, more general debates about popular history to be necessary for the discipline. Cary Carson, "Mirror, Mirror, on the Wall, Whose History Is the Fairest of Them All?," *The Public Historian* 17, no. 4 (1995): 62–63.

53. Among many others, see Gazi, "Claiming History," and Cook, "The Use and Abuse of Historical Reenactment," 490–492.

54. See Wallace, "Mickey Mouse History," 48–49, with notions such as "bad history" and "historicidal enterprise."

55. Hayden White, *Metahistory: The Historical Imagination in Nineteenth-Century Europe* (Baltimore: Johns Hopkins University Press, 1973).

56. Ludmilla Jordanova, "Public History," *History Today* 50, no. 5 (2000): 20–21. See, Carson, "Mirror, Mirror, on the Wall, Whose History Is the Fairest of Them All?," 65–67, and Richard Francaviglia, History after Disney: The Significance of "Imaginereed" Historical Places," *The Public Historian* 17, no. 4 (1995): 69.

3

Pastness in Themed Environments

By Cornelius Holtorf

Theme parks and other themed environments commonly evoke stories about the past in order to provide their customers and audiences with enjoyable experiences, often giving the impression that they are immersed in the past. Usually, such depictions of the past are only very loosely related either to historical accounts based on academic research or to surviving remains of the past. Drawing on previous research, I discuss with examples in this paper how the past is designed in theme parks and other themed environments by an evocation of *pastness*. Pastness is different from age and denotes the perceived quality that a given object is of the past. Pastness is not immanent in an object but may derive from the object's physical condition (for example, visible decay), its immediate context (for example, suggestive association in a museum or historic town center), or preconceived understandings of the audience (for example, expectations about historic appearance). I conclude by discussing the significance of fictitious heritage in themed environments and indeed in society at large.

The Presence of Pastness

Theme parks and other themed environments commonly evoke stories about the past in order to provide their customers and audiences with enjoyable experiences, often giving the impression that they are to some extent immersed in the past. Usually, such depictions of the past are only very loosely related either to historical accounts based on academic research or to surviving remains of the past.

To give one specific example, the theme and amusement park High Chaparral near Värnamo in southern Sweden engages guests in a built environment and activities associated with the American Wild West. The impressions given are to a large extent neither based on historical research nor on surviving remains of that period in North America. Instead they are largely derived from TV series (*The High Chaparral*), movie scenes, movie making (a stunt show), and other forms of popular culture such as the comic hero Lucky Luke (see image 3.1).

In past research, I discussed how the past is designed in theme parks and themed environments such as High Chaparral.[1] I have been arguing that an important precondition for success in this respect is an evocation of pastness. Pastness is different from age. It denotes the perceived quality that a given object is of the past. After all, it is the assumption of antiquity that matters for the experience, not its veracity.

Pastness is not age-specific but generalizing: although the quality of pastness may be present to larger or lesser degree, there is no linear, quantifiable scale as there is with age expressed in years. Unlike age, pastness is not inherent in an object and therefore, for an archaeologist or other relevant experts, not deductible from a scientific analysis of its physical properties either. Instead, pastness is a perception in a given context and for a specific audience. Pastness may derive from an impression given by the object's physical condition, its immediate context, or from its correspondence with the audience's expectations of historical appearance. Consequently, contemporary buildings, artifacts, and sites can be subjected to various processes that enhance their pastness. These processes include:

Adding-on material decay and other forms of patina (as in the case of artificial ruins).

Displaying in a major cultural institution (like a museum) or creating another form of seamless link to a familiar historical narrative (for example, as part of a historic town center).

Image 3.1. Western Show at the American Wild West theme park High Chaparral near Värnamo, Sweden (Photo by Cornelius Holtorf)

Improving the match with expectations of historic appearance (as in sets of historical movies).

Contemporary objects enhanced like that can fulfill many of the societal functions of cultural heritage in the present and, arguably, therefore they become cultural heritage.[2]

These insights about pastness are confirmed by inverting the argument. An object will not possess pastness when its physical condition looks new, its immediate context is not suggestive of the past, or when it does not match the audience's expectations of historical appearance. For example, when the Sistine Chapel in Rome reopened in the 1990s after a decade of diligent restoration to its original appearance, the familiar scenes lacked cracks and patina so that the painting, for some, looked too new although it resembled its actual historic appearance much more. For example, the Irish artist William Crozier stated in an interview that "What they have taken away is the age of the paint."[3] Similarly, material evidence said to be associated with extraterrestrial creatures that visited Earth in distant prehistory, to many visitors lacks pastness because it is not presented by the main cultural and educational institutions and thus not suggestively associated with the historical narrative familiar to many. By the same token, although the temples of Classical Greece were originally painted in bright colors, contemporary depictions or models in which they appear like this, make them look new to many because they are not expecting them to look like this. Pastness is thus firmly situated in a given social and cultural context of the present and is inherently audience specific.[4] However, it is unclear at this point to what extent the concept of pastness is applicable globally or only in the global West from where the short case studies that follow are derived.

Case Studies

Pastness and Decay

Since the 1970s the American artist Charles Simonds (born 1945) has been creating hundreds of ruined dwellings of a population of imaginary Little People, first in New York City but also elsewhere.[5] Simonds' work is part of a larger movement in art known by the title of a major German exhibition as *Spurensicherung*— the forensic securing of traces as evidence.[6] Simonds constructed tiny structures made of small, unfired clay bricks and originally built into the gaps of the modern city: gutters, window ledges, crevices in walls of dilapidating buildings, and so forth. In later years, Simonds produced similar miniature constructions and landscapes, even in galleries and public spaces, often inspired by global folk myths and the native heritage of the American Southwest.

As Simonds explained in a short text, his ruins were by one of three imaginary peoples who all related to past and future in different ways.[7] Whereas one people, in building the future, reconstructed their past buildings mathematically exact, a second people operated in a circular way letting buildings go through phases of abandonment, excavation, and rebuilding. The third people simply left their buildings behind as they moved on and built a new civilization, letting the earth gradually reclaim the architecture of the past (see image 3.2).

Image 3.2. Charles Simonds, *Dwellings of the Little People in New York, PS1*, 1975, clay, sand, and wood (*Reproduced with permission of the artist*)

All these fragile little structures tell stories about the past lives of their imaginary builders that are no longer there. Because of the visible decay, they are full of pastness even though they do not represent any historical reality. These structures constitute miniature themed environments, affecting our present by inspiring passing audiences to reflect upon their own culture: how come we never noticed the Little People while their civilization was still flourishing? How will our own culture end one day and what will remain of us, both physically and in other people's memories?

Pastness and Context

In recent years, in the Swedish town of Ystad (right at the Baltic Sea), a heritage has emerged that possesses pastness because it is presented as part of the historical narrative of the town. Ystad is the hometown of Inspector Kurt Wallander, a character invented in 1991 by the bestselling Swedish author Henning Mankell (1948–2015). As in other cases of a growing trend of literary tourism, many tourists seek to find the reality behind the fiction and visit Ystad in the footsteps of Kurt Wallander.[8]

As they walk through the town center, the visitors recognize many of the places and buildings they know and associate with Wallander and the 1990s. They are effectively transforming a pre-existing townscape into a themed environment through an act of suggestive association facilitated by recalling the books and films about Wallander.

For example, in Ystad's Santa Maria church visitors may now recall that Inspector Wallander is said to have married his ex-wife Mona here in 1970. For tourists visiting Ystad in the footsteps of Wallander, places such as the Santa Maria church are authentic because the stories and movies about Inspector Wallander explicitly refer to them in their account of

34 A Reader in Themed and Immersive Spaces

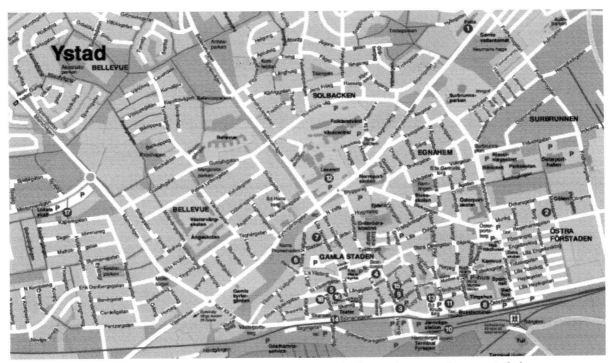

Image 3.3. Map of sites associated with Inspector Wallander in Ystad, Sweden (© Ystad Tourist Information Office)

Ystad's recent past. They possess pastness through suggestive association: it seems utterly possible that among all the town buildings and among all the inhabitants of the town, there just might have been an Inspector Wallander, as portrayed in Mankell's stories, temporarily inhabiting some of them during the second half of the twentieth century.

Pastness and Expectations

My final case is Jakriborg, a housing estate in Hjärup, located between Lund and Malmö in the very southeast of Sweden. Constructed from the late 1990s onwards by the real estate firm Jakri AB, this suburb is built in an architectural style inspired by pre-industrial town architecture (see image 3.4). The estate has many features of medieval towns that might otherwise be found for example in Northern European towns associated with the Medieval Hanseatic League or Hanse, a confederation of merchant guilds and market towns during the late Middle Ages and early modern period.

Jakriborg is a themed environment manifesting an international trend championing traditional architecture and historicizing building styles.[9] About 500 families rent apartments in Jakriborg, evidently appreciating the atmosphere created by a town wall, pointed gables, and maze-like passageways.

The pastness of Jakriborg relies on the familiar historical scenery provided by the houses, the streets, and the squares. Much like in a film set, the scenery matches the onlookers' pre-existing understandings and expectations about historic appearance and thus "sets" the entire scene in a familiar past. Although until the 1990s the area was used for agriculture, this is now a picture-book historic town from the Middle Ages and for many an attractive place to live.

Pastness in Context

Pastness is a significant concept because it disassociates cultural heritage from age and links the historicity of cultural heritage with a particular experience in the present, thus making it easier to discuss the forms and functions of cultural heritage that operate in contemporary society. The notion of "fictitious heritage" is not a contradiction in terms or a designation of falseness and fake. As my examples of artwork, a town center, and a housing estate demonstrate, themed environments in the real world may successfully employ fictitious elements that saturate them with pastness and provide very historical experiences indeed.

Image 3.4. Medieval architecture in Jakriborg, Hjärup, Sweden (Photo by Cornelius Holtorf)

The places I discussed in this chapter are places of the imagination that bridge the gap between fiction and reality by focusing on what is *imagined* to have taken place at existing sites. According to the Dutch media scientist and cultural analyst Stijn Reijnders, places of the imagination are material reference points "which for certain groups within society serve as material-symbolic references to a common imaginary world," that is, to something that "is not actually present."[10] Intriguingly, after only a few years, many people can forget that seemingly old buildings, despite their pastness, had until recently not actually existed in their present locations.[11] The boundary between fictitious and non-fictitious heritage is thus very fluid and all places may also be places of the imagination.

This corresponds to recent trends in heritage thought, according to which the core values of heritage are deemed to reside in the cultural meanings and values humans invest in heritage, not in the properties of their physical fabric.[12] Accordingly, it is the values embodied by the heritage, and their functions and benefits in society, that need to be maintained and enhanced, not the fabric of the heritage. The notion of pastness is arguably a cornerstone in this emerging new philosophy of conservation.

By way of concluding, there are three important implications of my argument for the way we understand the temporality of themed environments and indeed of cultural heritage:

1. Temporal experiences are not dependent on assessments of actual age but on the perception of pastness among specific human audiences.

2. Experiences of the past are necessarily anachronistic and need to be evaluated not in terms of their historical veracity but in terms of the functions, benefits, and values they provide for contemporary societies.

3. Everybody is competent to determine whether or not a particular item is successful in evoking the past in a meaningful way in the present.[13]

The so-called Faro Convention expresses some of this new thinking concerning cultural heritage at the level of policy.[14] It acknowledges in its preamble very clearly not only "the need to put people and human values at the centre of an enlarged and cross-disciplinary concept of cultural heritage" but also "the need to involve everyone in society in the ongoing process of defining and managing cultural heritage." What is more, the preamble also states that as an implication of individual human rights "every person has a right to engage with the cultural heritage of their choice." Cultural heritage must increasingly serve society and accommodate people's needs and preferences. Arguably, themed environments have for some time been pointing the way.

Notes

1. Cornelius Holtorf, "The Presence of Pastness: Themed Environments and Beyond," in *Staging the Past: Themed Environments in Transcultural Perspective*, eds. Judith Schlehe, Michiko Uike-Bormann, Carolyn Oesterle, and Wolfgang Hochbruck (Bielefeld, Germany: Transcript, 2010), 23–40; Cornelius Holtorf, "On Pastness: A Reconsideration of Materiality in Archaeological Object Authenticity," *Anthropological Quarterly* 86 (2013): 427–444; Cornelius Holtorf, "Changing Concepts of Temporality: From Age to Pastness in Heritage and Theme Parks," in *"Here You Leave Today": Time and Temporality in Theme Parks*, edited by Filippo Carlà, Florian Freitag, Sabrina Mittermeier, and Ariane Schwarz (Hanover, Germany: Wehrhahn, 2016).

2. Tolina Loulanski, "Revising the Concept for Cultural Heritage: The Argument for a Functional Approach," *International Journal of Cultural Property* 13 (2006): 207–233; Cornelius Holtorf and Graham Fairclough, "The New Heritage and Re-shapings of the Past," in *Reclaiming Archaeology: Beyond the Tropes of Modernity*, ed. Alfredo González-Ruibal (London: Routledge, 2013), 197–210.

3. Brian Fallon, "William Crozier," *Irish Arts Review Yearbook* 9 (1993): 183.

4. See also Raphael Samuel, *Theatres of Memory: Past and Present in Contemporary Culture* (London: Verso, 1994); Edward Bruner, "Abraham Lincoln as Authentic Reproduction: A Critique of Postmodernism," *American Anthropologist* 96 (1994): 397–415; Mike Crang, "Magic Kingdom or a Quixotic Quest for Authenticity?" *Annals of Tourism Research* 23, no. 2 (1996): 415–431.

5. Museum of Contemporary Art, Charles Simonds (Chicago: Museum of Contemporary Art, 1981).

6. Günter Metken, Spurensicherung. *Kunst als Anthropologie und Selbsterforschung: Fiktive Wissenschaft in der heutigen Kunst* (Cologne, Germany: DuMont, 1977), 77–80.

7. Charles Simonds, *Three Peoples* (New York: Samanedizioni, 1975).

8. Stijn Reijnders, *Places of the Imagination: Media, Tourism, Fan Culture* (Farnham, England: Ashgate, 2011); Anne Marit Waade, *Wallanderland: Medieturisme og skandinavisk TV-krimi* (Aalborg, Denamrk: Aalborg Universitetsforlag, 2013).

9. Vva von Engelberg-Dočkal, "Rekonstruktion als Architektur der Gegenwart? Historisierendes Bauen im Kontext der Denkmalpflege," kunsttexte.de 2007/3, <http://edoc.hu-berlin.de/kunsttexte/2007-3/engelberg-dockal-eva-von-8/PDF/engelberg-dockal.pdf>.

10. Reijnders, *Places of the Imagination*, 14.

11. Uwe Altrock, Grischa Bertram, Henriette Horni, and Olaf Asendorf, *Positionen zum Wiederaufbau verlorener Bauten und Räume*. Forschungen 143, Bundesministerium für Verkehr, Bau und Stadtentwicklung (Bonn, Germany: Bundesamt für Bauwesen und Raumforschug, 2010), 102–103.

12. Loulanski, "Revising the Concept of Cultural Heritage"; Noel Fojut, "The Philosophical, Political and Pragmatic Roots of the Convention," in *Heritage and Beyond*, ed. Council of Europe (Strassbourg, France: Council of Europe, 2009), <http://www.coe.int/t/dg4/cultureheritage/heritage/identities/PatrimoineBD_en.pdf>.

13. See also Holtorf, "Changing Concepts of Temporality in Cultural Heritage and Themed Environments."

14. Council of Europe, Framework Convention on the Value of Cultural Heritage for Society ("The Faro Convention"), European Treaty Series 199 (Strasbourg, France: 2005), <http://conventions.coe.int/Treaty/EN/Treaties/Html/199.htm>.

4

Nostalgia as Litmus Test for Themed Spaces

By Susan Ingram

Nostalgia used to be simple. As its etymology tells us, one left behind one's home, the place of one's birth, and then longed to return to it (in Greek *nostos* means to return home and *algia* means longing). For the Swiss physician Johannes Hofer, who coined the term in 1688 as a synonym for *mal du pays* to diagnose the malaise that mercenaries fighting abroad suffered from, that return was spatial. However, as modernity proceeded, nostalgia came increasingly to be understood as having a temporal dimension. For the Romantics it was the longing for the premodern past that rampant industrialization was rapidly obliterating, a longing that the rise of individualism quickly transferred onto one's personal past: "As one critic has succinctly put this change: 'Odysseus longs for home; Proust is in search of lost time.'"[1] By the time Fredric Jameson was diagnosing the postmodern condition in the 1980s, nostalgia was firmly established as one of its primary temporal characteristics despite the "waning of the great high modernist thematics of time and temporality," supporting Hutcheon's argument about irony being one of the key markers of the postmodern.[2]

What does this mean for themed spaces? Nostalgia has long been recognized as an integral component of the Disney practice of theming. Susan Willis has suggested that "Disney World might be thought of as an immense nostalgia machine whose staging and specific attractions are generationally coded to strike a chord with the various age categories of its guests," while Scott Bukatman sees in "the 'retro-futures' of Disneyland's theme parks" exemplars of what he calls a "meganostalgia."[3] We have entered, Bukatman claimed in the early 2000s, "a 'seemingly inexhaustible period of meganostalgia' with an 'obsessive recycling of the past,' in response to the sense that the future is no longer distant and unattainable but has already arrived."[4] Disney parks have played a key role in de-ironizing nostalgia in the contemporary period, keeping it in the sphere that Svetlana Boym has termed restorative, as opposed to reflective, in that it pretends "to rebuild the mythical place called home" and "ends up reconstructing emblems and rituals of home and homeland in an attempt to conquer and spatialize time."[5]

By no means all themed environments or even all immersive themed environments are as beholden to nostalgia as the wonderful world that is Disney. Nor have all of Disney's themed environments been equally successful. By examining one of Disney's most spectacular failures, California Adventure, which was such a bust after it opened on February 8, 2001 that a mere six years later Disney undertook a major $1.1 billion redesign and expansion of a significant portion of the park, this contribution mobilizes nostalgia as a critical concept in order to detail the psychodynamics by which Disney's immersive environments have succeeded in maintaining a hegemonic hold over the corporate glorification of childhood, a form of what Kant understood as *Unmündigkeit* that supports fantasy-generated commodity consumption.[6] After first tracing California Adventure's backstory, I then analyze the temporality of park visitors' psychic structures and locate Disney's success in their ability to interpellate visitors primarily as families through a form of restorative retro-futurism.

The original plan for the California Adventure site, which was built next door to Disneyland in Orange County, California, on what had for forty years served as one of Disneyland's parking lots, was to build a west-coast version of Epcot Center at Walt Disney World in Florida. That park, which opened on October 1, 1982, celebrated human achievement, technological innovation, and international culture, and its west-coast equivalent, to be called WestCOT, was to have hosted a Future World, with attractions that carried utopian names, such as Horizons, Journey Into Imagination, The Living Seas, Wonders of Life, and The Land, and a World Showcase that resembled the one in Florida except with the countries grouped by regions rather than pavilions for individual nations as in Florida. However, "[t]he high price tag of the proposed park as well as the company's financial and public relations problems with the newly opened Euro Disneyland (now Disneyland Paris)," not to mention the cancellation in 1994 of Disney's America—a theme park planned for Haymarket, Virginia, which was to be dedicated to the history of the United States and which met with so much citizen opposition that the plans had to be shelved, led Disney CEO Michael Eisner to rethink his company's expansion strategy.[7] Unable to push through his pet project in Virginia, he settled instead for a park in Anaheim that themed the history and culture of the state of California so that it would knowingly appeal to adults in the same way that Disneyland next door to it unknowingly appealed to children, and in the process made use of some of the attractions he had planned for Disney's America. More to the point, California Adventure was conceptualized to knowingly appeal in the same way the hit films and TV shows did that Eisner had overseen during his tenure as President and CEO of Paramount, the position he held before coming to Disney in 1984.[8] Films such as *Saturday Night Fever*, *Grease*, the *Star Trek* film franchise, *Raiders of the Lost Ark*, and *Beverly Hills Cop*, and hit TV shows such as *Happy Days*, *Laverne & Shirley*, *Cheers*, and *Family Ties* were all successful in evoking recognizable aesthetics that appealed to youth while at the same time containing utopian potential—those same youth as future adults would look back at them the way that contemporary adults also enjoyed them, namely, with Boym's reflective nostalgia, distinguished from restorative nostalgia in that it puts emphasis on the *algia*, on dwelling "in longing and loss, the imperfect process of remembrance" rather than the *nostos*, which "proposes to rebuild the lost home and patch up the memory gaps."[9] Eisner's plans to build on his Paramount success by turning the 1990s into a "Disney Decade" by re-styling the Disney theme parks in the manner of his screen successes did not work out as planned. After the Disney America fiasco, Euro Disney's shaky start, and California Adventure's persistently low attendance figures, there was something of a palace coup led by Walt's nephew Roy Disney. Eisner stepped down as Disney CEO in 2005, a year before his contract was up.

How should Eisner have known that a knowingly playful, stylish restaging of history and culture in a theme park setting would not appeal the way it did in film? How should he have known, in other words, that retro in the form of postmodern restorative nostalgia would not work in a Disney theme park such as California Adventure? Eisner may not have partaken in any of the scholarly debates on postmodernism involving Jameson, Baudrillard, Eco, and others, but by 1995 he knew enough to understand that a utopian Futureworld such as the one celebrated at Walt Disney World in Florida had lost its appeal for a post-Cold War world.[10] Moreover, given the success of cyberpunk and darkly dystopian, ultra-violent video games such as *Doom*, he could not but be aware of the fact that postmodern dystopia was the flavor du jour. When the "science fiction horror-themed first-person shooter (FPS) video game" *Doom* was released in 1993 by id Software, it was heralded as "one of the most significant and influential titles in the video game industry" for the breakthrough it represented in 3-D graphics and for popularizing the first-person shooter genre, while at the same time coming in for sharp criticism for its graphic violence and satanic imagery.[11] Such environments might have had great appeal for kids, who enthusiastically immersed themselves in the rapidly expanding market for games such as *Doom*; however, there was no way Eisner could sell family visits to such material environments to their parents. He therefore attempted to go not back to the future but back to the past—in the first instance, to the past of the United States, but when that was shot down, to the past of the state which had been home to Disney's original success. However, miscalibrating that past proved, literally, to be his doom.

Not only do Disney theme parks generally try to avoid history in Jameson's understanding of it, namely, as what hurts, but they are also "systematically elaborated to eliminate carnival."[12] As the Project on Disney noted, "the drunkenly reeling and lewdly gesturing crowd in the French Quarter [in New Orleans] was as antithetical to the folks at Disney World as aliens to Earthlings."[13] We can understand these sanitizing tendencies by drawing on William F. Van Wert's observation that the adults who visit Disney parks, even or especially the academic ones, tend to be primarily parents first, who understand their mission in similar terms to nineteenth-century museums: namely, as a palatable mix of edification and entertainment suitable for those considered to be less developed creatures, such as the working classes and children. The history that is presented in the Disney context can therefore be seen to be what Wert terms "posthistories repressing the shame, vitality, and all traces of race-class-gender-sexuality of a more accurate history."[14] Wert's study shows:

> how Disney World was built as metaphor (the atemporal grid, the repression of shame and lack, the various namings, from Space Mountain to Spaceship Earth). And perhaps in its ideal state (that is, with no people there,

before the gates have opened or after they're closed), this metaphoric operation succeeds, for machinery feels no endlessness of desire. But, as soon as people are admitted to the park, they bring metonymy along with them. They bring their mortal bodies and their lived time, their spatial contiguity, their knowledge gained by passing through, their side-by-side contrasts, their sexual and cultural differences.[15]

In drawing on his own discomfort with the way the park tried to interpellate him and work against his experiencing the excess of metaphor metonymically, Wert was able to identify the type of analysis that Disney theme parks are usually designed to minimize, and that usually works, unless academics switch off their finely tuned critical radar together with their cellphones.

In departing from Disney's well-tested techniques and introducing spaces for reflection, California Adventure trapped itself and its visitors in a postmodern bind of occupying multiple spots on the rapidly compressing time-space continuum. The park was only able to recover by being "re-imagineered" in proper Disney style, which is, as Miles Orvell notes, "a nostalgic and idealized representation of small-town America" that is "the essence of the inauthentic [and actually] represents nothing but itself, its own factitious universe."[16] Each part of California Adventure was reimagined to transform the park from a veritable postmodern spoof of California culture to "a romanticized, idealized version of the state."[17] In other words, the "California" in California Adventure was recalibrated from reflective to restorative in Boym's sense so that it better reflected what Orvell identifies as the key components of Disney's spirit: namely, "the general liveliness and good humor [that] conjures up a dream of the McKinley era at the turn of the century, when William McKinley could declare, with the economic depression and labor unrest of the 1890s over, 'Now every avenue of production is crowded with activity, labor is well employed, and American products find good markets at home and abroad.'"[18] The main entrance and Sunshine Plaza were turned from a reflective "giant postcard" of California into the restorative Buena Vista Street, a representation of Los Angeles as it appeared when Walt Disney moved there in the 1920s, and a new statue of a young Walt and Mickey was added to Buena Vista Street to encourage visitors to make this connection. Similarly, Paradise Pier was turned from a reflective comical contemporary representation of California boardwalks into a restorative representation of turn-of-the-century Victorian seaside amusement parks, reusing designs for a themed area about Atlantic City in the roaring 1920s that had originally been created for Disney's America. In the same vein, Maliboomers and Mulholland Madness were among the off-the-shelf rides designed to appeal to adult knowingness that were done away with, replaced by restorative, less popular cultural savvy attractions, such as Goofy's Sky School and Silly Symphony Swings. The restorative re-theming placed a greater focus on Disney characters, most obviously in the case of Mickey's Fun Wheel. The success of California Adventure's restoratively nostalgic new direction was immediate with attendance to the park increasing twenty-three percent in 2012, the year the renovations were completed.

In looking to account for the new direction's success, one can turn to Cars Land, an area that simulates Radiator Springs from Disney-Pixar's *Cars* film franchise, which was added to the southeast portion of the park and includes the very popular Radiator Springs Racers, during which the vehicles reach a top speed of 40 mph.[19] Cars Land points us in the direction of what Dean MacCannell has identified as "the secret of Disney's success"—namely, ego gratification.[20] MacCannell has observed that:

> Disneyland (Anaheim, Tokyo, and Paris) and Walt Disney World are fictional habitats for tourists that were built on the principle of ego mimesis and on the positive superegoic command to enjoy. The X factor in the tourist economy is no longer an unknown. It is the ego-mirroring component of the attraction. Mimesis means to imitate, mimic, or copy. The tourist experience, the tourist destination, increasingly the entire environment built by advanced capitalism, are mimetically modeled on the structure of the ego.[21]

He goes on to identify the importance that commodity consumption plays in this tourist experience:

> The ego also goes shopping for itself. And the ego actually believes that it is enhanced by all the wonderful things it surrounds itself with. The ego pauses over every item of attire, cosmetic, and accessory that builds up surface appearances while effectively obscuring anything that might be happening within. It will snap up anything that has an aura of power and aggressivity. It especially identifies with the automobile with its steel

skin and soft interior, with its ideal synthesis of power, control, and silence, perhaps the most ego mimetic of all commodities.[22]

With Cars Land, Disney resorted to tried-and-proven appeal. One of the early attractions at Tomorrowland was Autopia, "where youngsters could drive actual, though miniature, automobiles."[23] As Scott Bukatman relates, Walt Disney's intent was "that young citizens-to-be would thereby learn traffic safety at an early age and hence be prepared to enter the LA freeway system," but "the children took 'demented delight' in crashing the cars, and the ride had to be put on tracks."[24] In having a race akin to the very popular *Fast and Furious* franchise, which is also at home in Los Angeles and which recently became an attraction at Universal Studios, Cars Land shows the way that Disney learns from its own experience at the same time that it taps into proven parts of popular culture, whether or not it is aware of the psychoanalytic implications of that material.

An awareness of the temporality of the ego, whose gratification MacCannell has identified as the secret of Disney's success, is necessary, however, to understand California Adventure's recalibration and the different appeals of restorative vs. reflective nostalgia. For that we can turn to Jane Gallop and her reading of Lacan's "Mirror Stage" essay. Gallop draws our attention to the fact that "the temporality of 'The Mirror Stage' is in some way alien to the logic of chronology."[25] She shows how "[t]he mirror stage is a decisive moment…This moment is the source not only for what follows but also for what precedes. It produces the future through anticipation and the past through retroaction…Both future and past are thus rooted in an illusion…In other words, the self is constituted through anticipating what it will become, and then this anticipatory model is used for gauging what was before." The mirror stage itself is "a turning point. After it the subject's relation to himself is always mediated through a totalizing image which has come from outside. For example, the mirror image becomes a totalizing ideal which organizes and orients the self. But since the 'self' is necessarily a totalized, unified concept—a division between an inside and an outside—there is no 'self' before the mirror stage," a structure that Gallop shows holds for Lacan's essay as well.[26] "In an introduction to the section of *Ecrits* which contains 'The Mirror Stage,' he writes: 'It happens that our students delude themselves in our writings into finding "already there" that to which our teaching has since brought us.'"[27] Gallop elucidates that:

> Lacan's students are reading earlier writings in view of later Lacan teachings. This implies reading what comes 'after,' 'before,' and what comes 'before,' 'after.' Such a violation of chronological order is encouraged by *Ecrits* which presents the 1956 "Seminar on 'The Purloined Letter'" before the earlier texts. But even more to the point, here, is an analogy between the students' illusion and the infant's "mirage" in the mirror stage. According to Lacan, in the mirror stage, "the subject anticipates in a mirage the maturation of his power." The student anticipates in the early texts the maturation of Lacan's teachings. Thus, somehow, the effect of Lacan's text on his students is analogous to the effect of the mirror on the infant. Lacan's text functions as an illusory mirror image.[28]

When Disney's theme parks are successful, they also function in this way, as illusory mirror images, ones that provide the type of ego gratification MacCannell identified. California Adventure failed in that it initially disrupted this process, reflecting back to visitors a distorted, postmodern funhouse version of California that did not create a gratifying mirage of the maturation of the state's power or project a possible mirage into the future in the way a utopian Futureworld would have. On the contrary, the original California Adventure was relatively honest, not to mention ironical, about the state's shortcomings. A knowing, adult orientation may have worked for the *Who Framed Roger Rabbit?* franchise in the cinema, where audiences could fantasize in the dark. However, in the bright light of a California day, it did nothing to further the ego projects of identificatory-hungry parents eager to buy into the myth of sun-drenched orange groves that had originally attracted settlers to Southern California from the Midwest.

Why, then, style the successfully refurbished California Adventure in a retro-futurist aesthetic? In the final section of *Retro*, Elizabeth Guffey describes retrofuturism as a hankering "for a world of flying cars and plastic houses" and situates its Disney connection historically: "By the time Monsanto Chemical Company opened 'The House of the Future' (1957), many visitors anticipated a future resonant with Disney's slogan, 'if you can dream it, you can do it.'"[29] However, the "shiny futurism of previous decades" began to tarnish, as evidenced by such works as Alvin Toffler's *Future Shock* (1970), and as it did, retrofuturism began to seep into popular and academic discourse, only to first dissolve into postmodernism proper and then re-emerge as postmodernism waned and became the stuff of museum exhibitions such as the one at London's Victoria and Albert Museum in 2011.[30] Disney's was by no means the first, or only, resuscitation of retrofuturist aesthetics. As Sharon Sharp makes clear in her analysis of the last *Star Trek* TV series, *Enterprise* (2001-2005), retrofuturism was a sign of the millennial times, which she substantiates with a number of examples: Henry Jenkins' work on critical comics by Dean Motter; George W. Bush's appeal in January 2004 "to the space-age, utopian ideas of the 1960s New Frontier era to direct attention away from his faltering international war on terrorism"; conservatively nostalgic films such as *Sky Captain and the World of Tomorrow*; her own analysis of the *Enterprise* series and Scott Bukatman's discussion of the retro-futures of Disneyland's theme parks as exemplars of meganostalgia, "a return to a [seemingly inexhaustible] period of (imaginary) mastery; and an attempt to answer the question 'How did I get here?' when cause and effect have vanished within the random intricacies of quantum reality…[and] futures past are exhumed and aired, their quaint fantasies simultaneously mocked and yearned for."[31] The retro-futures of the 1920s through the 1950s, whose return Bukatman identifies as speaking "to a perceived loss of subjective comprehension of, or control over, the invisible cyberhistories and cyberspaces" of his millennial present, clearly inflects the retro-restyling of California Adventure and similarly serves to "locate and center the subject. The popularity of these theme parks bespeaks the massive need for reassurance and resituation that many continue to feel in the face of the invisible and hence unknowable spaces of terminal culture."[32] Not only does this retrofuturism function "as comfort for assuaging the technological anxieties of the present," Sharp notes that its pervasiveness can be attributed to the perception of the acceleration of historical time.[33]

To conclude on a more reflective than restorative note with a few questions: what does the fact that space-time continues its accelerated compression and we are bouncing more and more quickly along various intersecting virtual timelines mean for our sense of the future? Will the future of Disney theme parks continue to colonize the present of our lifeworlds? The massive recalibration and overhaul that was successfully given to California Adventure would seem to suggest so. However, if "retrofuturism points to 'a crisis in modern futurity,' in which futures seem to be coming and going at an accelerated pace," it also points to the malleability of futures.[34] It further "reminds us how decisively our imagination of futures can change in response to changing times [and] leads us to ask what sorts of cultural work are necessary to make new futures cohere."[35] Since the end of the Cold War, it has been difficult to go "forward without forgetting" with much of a sense of optimism. Yet that is where we continue to go, and as long as we maintain the ability to translate the types of memories the lyrics of Brecht's 1931 "Solidaritätslied" embodied in its day, and to be critical of the demand that our yesterdays have tomorrows, perhaps our presents will continue to have them.

Notes

1. Linda Hutcheon, "Irony, Nostalgia, and the Postmodern," *Studies in Comparative Literature* 30 (2000): 189–207.

2. Fredric Jameson, *Postmodernism or the Cultural Logic of Late Capitalism* (Durham, NC: Duke University Press, 1991), 64. Hutcheon, "Irony, Nostalgia, and the Postmodern."

3. The Project on Disney, *Inside the Mouse: Work and Play at Disney World* (Durham, NC: Duke University Press, 1995), 10. Cited in Sharon Sharp, "Nostalgia for the Future: Retrofuturism in Enterprise," *Science Fiction Film and Television* 4, no. 1 (Spring 2011): 26.

4. Scott Bukatman, *Matters of Gravity: Special Effects and Supermen in the 20th Century* (Durham, NC: Duke University Press, 2003), 14.

5. Svetlana Boym, *The Future of Nostalgia* (New York: Basic Books, 2001), 49, 50.

6. Immanuel Kant, "Answer the Question: What is Enlightenment?" <https://archive.org/details/AnswerTheQuestionWhatIsEnlightenment>.

7. "Disney California Adventure," Wikipedia, <http://en.wikipedia.org/wiki/Disney_California_Adventure>.

8. "Michael Eisner," Wikipedia, <http://en.wikipedia.org/wiki/Michael_Eisner>.

9. Boym, *The Future of Nostalgia*, 41. Jameson tried to gesture towards this dynamic in identifying them as "nostalgia films" or "la mode retro." However, with the benefit of hindsight and the substantial literature on nostalgia that has emerged since Boym's pivotal work, we are better placed now to understand what was going on.

10. See Jameson, *Postmodernism or the Cultural Logic of Late Capitalism*; Jean Baudrillard, *Amérique* (Grasset, Paris 1984); Umberto Eco, ""Casablanca": Cult Movies and Intertextual Collage," *SubStance* 14, no. 2 (1985): 3–12.

11. "Doom (1993 Video Game)," Wikipedia, <http://en.wikipedia.org/wiki/Doom_(1993_video_game)>.

12. The Project on Disney, *Inside the Mouse*, 4.

13. The Project on Disney, *Inside the Mouse*, 4.

14. William F. van Wert, "Disney World and Posthistory," *Cultural Critique* 32 (Winter, 1995–1996): 213.

15. Wert, "Disney World and Posthistory," 211.

16. Miles Orvell, *The Death and Life of Main Street: Small Towns in American Memory, Space, and Community* (Chapel Hill: University of North Carolina Press, 2012), 39.

17. "Disney California Adventure," Wikipedia, <http://en.wikipedia.org/wiki/Disney_California_Adventure>.

18. Orvell, *The Death and Life of Main Street*, 41.

19. "Disney California Adventure," Wikipedia, <http://en.wikipedia.org/wiki/Disney_California_Adventure>.

20. Dean MacCannell, "The Ego Factor in Tourism." *Journal of Consumer Research* 29, no. 1 (June 2002): 149.

21. MacCannell, "The Ego Factor in Tourism," 149.

22. MacCannell, "The Ego Factor in Tourism," 149.

23. Bukatman, *Matters of Gravity*, 13.

24. Bukatman, *Matters of Gravity*, 13.

25. Jane Gallop, "Lacan's 'Mirror Stage': Where to Begin," *SubStance* 11.4–12.1, Issue 37–38 (1982/1983): 119.

26. Gallop, "Lacan's 'Mirror Stage,'" 120–121.

27. Gallop, "Lacan's 'Mirror Stage,'" 120.

28. Gallop, "Lacan's 'Mirror Stage,'" 120.

29. Elizabeth Guffy, *Retro: The Culture of Revival* (London: Reaktion, 2006), 152, 153.

30. Guffy, *Retro: The Culture of Revival*, 152.

31. Sharp, "Nostalgia for the Future: Retrofuturism in *Enterprise*," 25, 26.

32. Cited in Sharp, "Nostalgia for the Future: Retrofuturism in *Enterprise*," 26.

33. Sharp, "Nostalgia for the Future: Retrofuturism in *Enterprise*," 27.

34. Sharp, "Nostalgia for the Future: Retrofuturism in *Enterprise*," 27.

35. Daniel Rosenberg and Sandra Harding, "Introduction: Histories of the Future," *Histories of the Future* (Durham, NC: Duke University Press, 2005), 8.

PART III

The Constructs of Culture and Nature

5

"Wilderness" as Theme
Negotiating the Nature-Culture Divide in Zoological Gardens

By Jan-Erik Steinkrüger

Zoological Gardens are an aporetic institution. They present animal individuals, who at least today are most commonly raised in human custody, in an artificial setting to represent the beastly nature of their conspecific "out there in the wilderness."[1] Zoos commoditize the wild within our urban society in a highly human controlled and engineered setting to simultaneously appeal to our anxieties about the erosion of the natural world through urbanization, industrialization, and commoditization.[2] Zoological gardens (and similarly aquariums) are a fascinating form of themed and immersive spaces as they are located at the intersection of education and entertainment—of the "zoological gaze" and the "tourist gaze".[3] Alan Beardsworth and Alan Bryman have already pointed out, that the zoo today can be considered not only a themed, but a Disneyized institution, as it follows principles ideally perceivable at Disney's theme parks, namely theming, dedifferentiation of consumption, merchandising, and emotional labor.[4] Today's zoos have become multifunctional entertainment enterprises, which not only offer an opportunity to watch wild animals, but "a trip around the world" in a day with restaurants, shops, playgrounds, and sometimes even offering rides and lodging to prolong the wildlife experience.[5] Seeing Disney's own zoo, Disney's Animal Kingdom, as a model for future zoo designs, Beardsworth and Bryman conclude:

> [It] could be that we are also witnessing a basic shift in the object of the tourist gaze. There exists the probability that the exhibition of animals will become subordinate to the staging of elaborate quasifications of the "wild." Rather than the animals being the primary attraction, the settings themselves will become the main objects of the location in which urban humans can experience a quasified form of the "wild" with maximum comfort, convenience and safety. These developments are very much in tune with the theme park and its emergence as a tourist destination.[6]

As I will argue, the same can be said not only of today's zoos. The zoo has always been more than an exhibition of animals, but also a place for the experience of a quasified "wilderness" within urban society. It has been and still is a place for the representation of our understanding of "the wild" and the negotiation of the difference between "culture" and "nature" with two crosscutting themes: "the theme of the gaze and the theme of power."[7] What has changed, however, is the understanding of "culture," "nature," and "wilderness," and the mode of representation from its beginnings in aristocratic menageries of the seventeenth and eighteenth century and the early public zoos of the nineteenth century to today's zoos.

Menageries and Early Zoological Gardens

Until the end of the eighteenth century and beginning of the nineteenth century, the ownership and display of "exotic" animals were predominantly a province of the noble and wealthy.[8] Especially since the Middle Ages, animals were held for the "gratification of curiosity and the underlining of the magnificence and the power of their owners."[9] They were given and traded within aristocracy as bribe, tribute, or ceremonial gift and shown in menageries as a symbol of power not only over the royal's subjects, but over nature itself. This authority over nature was archetypically represented in Louis XIV's menagerie at Versailles founded in 1665, which became paradigmatic for the design of Baroque menageries. The

Image 5.1. Wilderness on Display (© Daveallenphoto | Dreamstime.com)

dominant feature of this style was a central two-story pavilion surrounded by a courtyard passing the animal enclosures. The enclosures were all directed towards the central pavilion, from whose balcony one could overlook the courtyard and enclosures. In *Discipline and Punish* Michel Foucault not only interprets the menagerie of Versailles as a representation of (one) man's power over nature, but also as a model for Jeremy Bentham's Panopticon prison design of omnipresent observation and surveillance:

> [O]ne finds in the programme of the Panopticon a similar concern with individualizing observation, with characterization and classification, with the analytical arrangement of space. The Panopticon is a royal menagerie; the animal is replaced by man, individual distribution by species grouping, and the king by the machinery of a furtive power. With this exception, the Panopticon also does the work of the naturalist.[10]

Although the animals were also used for scientific research in comparative biology, the enclosures of Louis XIV's menagerie were not scientifically arranged to teach an order of species, but can be seen as "a mirror, albeit distorted, of the cultural and aesthetic ideals of the aristocracy."[11] The animals were shown as graceful, tame, peaceful, and peaceable beasts under the king's order.

The foundation of the first public zoological garden, the Jardin des Plantes in Paris, partly owed its existence to the menagerie of Versailles and a makeshift during the French Revolution. When the uprising of the people led to the release and slaughter of parts of the collection in Versailles, the remaining animals were transferred to the Jardin du Roi in 1793 soon to become part of the newly founded Muséum National d'Histoire Naturelle. Following the example of Paris, the Zoological Society of London opened its zoo in Regent's Park in 1828, with many others to follow during the nineteenth century. The common ground of these early zoos was that the animals were shown in taxonomical order in often small cages within an English garden park:

> Dangerous and wide-roaming animals were confined in small cages and placed along well-marked paths, in manicured parks that seemed natural only in contrast to the surrounding urban landscapes. The horticultural

displays that routinely adorned the borders, often composed of plants from all over the world, emphasized the artificiality of the setting, as did the constructed lakes, a feature of every zoo that was spacious and prosperous enough to build them.[12]

Carl Hagenbeck's Revolution

The main attraction of many early zoological gardens was the presentation of large carnivores like bears, tigers, and lions. The control of their "beastliness" was a powerful expression of the human dominance over nature. The appeal of their display was based, following Ritvo, "on the contrast between their natural ferocity and their artificial powerlessness."[13] It was this repression of the beastly nature, though, which later turned into pity and compassion for the captive animals. Lacking the capacity to build "natural" compounds for larger animals and carnivores, many European zoos designed their animal houses in a so-called "exotic" style to look like the "cultural environment" of the animal. They were to resemble castles, mosques, Indian palaces, or Arabic houses: "the designs were used as exotic settings for exotic animals housed in a European environment."[14] The architectural style, however, only changed the façade, not the husbandry conditions. It was Carl Hagenbeck, an animal dealer, circus proprietor, and impresario of human zoos from Hamburg, though, who not only changed the design of animal compounds, but the visitor's perception of nature in zoological gardens.[15]

When he got his "natural-scientific panorama" (*Naturwissenschaftliches Panorama*) patented in 1896, Hagenbeck built on his experiences in animal trade, the circus, and a small zoo in Hamburg to create compounds with moats instead of bars and fences. He determined in example the width and depth of moats by observing the distance which animals were able to jump in a circus arena. Although many of his principles were not entirely new, the innovations lay in the outline of a series of such barless and fenceless enclosures as scenery. The compounds were set behind each other with the ones in the background slightly higher than the ones in the foreground, separated by concealed moats, while the animal houses were screened by artificial rocks and hedges.[16] This stage setting made it possible to not only show mixed animal groups, but even carnivores next to prey from the same geographical region. As Eric Ames emphasizes, the term "panorama" may seem rather misleading for Hagenbeck's innovation, as it was not a circular display viewed from a central platform normally associated with the term. "At the same time, however, [Hagenbeck] no doubt sought to benefit from some of the cultural connotations such as 'reality' and 'immersion' that were already attached to its name."[17] The panorama was more than just a painted background; it made it possible to not only watch animals, but immerse oneself in an animated landscape picture.

In 1907 Hagenbeck opened Hagenbeck's Tierpark (animal park) in Stellingen, a suburb of Hamburg, based on the principles of his panorama. It featured several panoramas within a themed environment and seemed to foreclose ideas normally associated with the development of the modern theme park:

> Hagenbeck's park distinguished itself from nineteenth-century zoological gardens not simply by its interest in geographical space, but also by its coordinated effort to create an imaginary universe that visitors could inhabit (albeit momentarily) in the presence of wild animals. Open enclosures and natural settings invited the free play of the spectator's imagination…To offer such divergent spaces, to permit such experience of adventure, and to do so by combining live animals with the latest display technologies, [the park] was to create an exciting alternative to the zoological garden, while at the same time expanding the zoological imagination and immersing the spectator's mind and body in a mythical world of exotic adventure.[18]

Zoos Today

When Hagenbeck's Tierpark opened, Hagenbeck's animal dealership was the world's largest and oldest. But, as he became a direct competition to the established zoological gardens, the German zoo directors boycotted his animal trade and denounced his Tierpark as a mere sensation for the masses.[19] With few exceptions Hagenbeck was also not able to sell his patent to the established zoological gardens. In the long term, however, his patent changed the idea of zoo design. Since the 1970s, "habitat immersion" or "landscape immersion" are becoming popular as new forms of display, in which it seems as if animal and spectator are standing in one landscape:

> Instead of standing in a familiar city park (known as a zoological garden) and viewing zebra in African setting,

both the zoo visitors and the zebra are in a landscape carefully designed to "feel" like the African savanna. Barriers separating the people from the animals are invisible and, no matter where the viewer turns, the entire perceptual context appears consistently and specifically African.[20]

To be convincible, however, these exhibits have to, following Nigel Rothfels, "outdo nature."[21] Compressed into the small space of a zoo, the experience becomes so intensified that the "real" nature may seem dreary in comparison, as there is not an animal around each corner. Whereas some zoos like the Koninklijke Burgers' Zoo in Arnhem immerse the humans into a "natural" landscape representing an ecosystem, other zoos like Disney's Animal Kingdom stage the cultural and natural environment of the animal's "native" region. Stephan Spotte, however, emphasizes that that even an immersive space can neither deceive neither the spectator nor the animal:

> As a denotative entity, an "immersion" exhibit depicting a tropical rainforest has more in common with another zoo exhibit—even one displaying polar bears—than it has with a rainforest. The world can't be copied. In art, an attempt to represent reality involves only people duping other people who know they are being duped. Builders of "immersion" exhibits promote the notion that the animals inside are being duped along with the rest of us. People who believe this are only duping themselves.[22]

After all, how should an animal individual, raised in human custody and living in an artificial setting resembling the supposedly "natural" or "cultural and natural environment" of its conspecifics know the wilderness "out there?"

Image 5.2. Berlin Zoo (Photo by KLMircea, Attribution-ShareAlike 2.0 Generic)

Zoos: Nature and Culture

Zoos are and have been representations of "nature" within (urban) society. What has changed, though, is the understanding of "nature." Whereas "nature" has been a curiosity and a symbol of aristocratic power in the royal menageries, it became an object of scientific research and taxonomic education in early zoological gardens. Additionally it became a symbol of human power over nature. With Hagenbeck's panorama, "nature" turned into an aesthetic experience and an adventure, which it still is today. Whereas menageries and early zoo were characterized by a strict border between the gazing cultural subject and the gazed natural object, the zoo after Hagenbeck's revolution immerses the visitor in a themed environment. This immersion, however, should not deceive us that the border between spectator and spectated have blurred. It is still an environment built for the tourist's gaze in a hierarchical asymmetry between human and nature. An interesting phenomenon which I was only able to scratch superficially in this chapter is the representation of "culture" in zoological gardens, as it connects the representation of "nature" as the Other of "culture" to the representation of the "exotic," that is, the cultural Other. Whereas "African," "Asian," and "Native American" culture are still presented in zoological gardens, it would be considered irritating to find an immersive exhibit representing bears next to the Kremlin or boars in Berlin.

Notes

1. Stephen H. Spotte, Zoos in *Postmodernism: Signs and Simulation* (Madison, NJ: Fairleigh Dickinson University Press, 2006).
2. Alan Beardsworth and Alan Bryman, "The Wild Animal in Late Modernity: The Case of the Disneyization of Zoos," *Tourist Studies* 1, no. 1(2001): 83–104.
3. Adrian Franklin, *Animals and Modern Cultures: A Sociology of Human-Animal Relations in Modernity* (London: Sage, 1999). John Urry and Jonas Larsen, *The Tourist Gaze 3.0* (London: Sage, 2011).
4. Beardsworth and Bryman, "The Wild Animal in Late Modernity."
5. See, <http://www.zoom-erlebniswelt.de/english/START/index.asp>.
6. Beardsworth and Bryman, "The Wild Animal in Late Modernity," 100.
7. Beardsworth and Bryman, "The Wild Animal in Late Modernity," 88.
8. R. J. Hoage, Anne Roskell, and Jane Mansour, "Menageries and Zoos to 1900," in *New Worlds, New Animals: From Menagerie to Zoological Park in the Nineteenth Century*, eds. R. J. Hoage and William A. Deiss (Baltimore: Johns Hopkins University Press, 1996), 15.
9. Lord S. Zuckermann, *Great Zoos of the World* (Boulder, CO: Westview Press, 1980), 8.
10. Michel Foucault, *Discipline and Punish: The Birth of the Prison* (New York: Pantheon Books, 1977), 203.
11. Peter Sahlins, "The Royal Menageries of Louis XIV and the Civilizing Process Revisited," *French Historical Studies* 35, no. 2 (2012): 267.
12. Harriet Ritvo, "The Order of Nature: Constructing the Collections of Victorian Zoos," in *New Worlds, New Animals: From Menagerie to Zoological Park in the Nineteenth Century*, eds. R. J. Hoage and William A. Deiss (Baltimore: Johns Hopkins University Press, 1996), 47.
13. Ritvo, "The Order of Nature," 48.
14. Harro Strehlow, "Zoological Gardens of Western Europe," in *Zoo and Aquarium History: Ancient Animal Collections to Zoological Gardens*, ed. Vernon N. Kisling (Boca Raton, FL: CRC Press, 2001), 100.
15. Hilke Thode-Arora, "Hagenbeck's European Tours: The Development of the Human Zoo," in *Human Zoos: Science and Spectacle in the Age of Colonial Empires*, eds. Pascal Blanchard, Nicolas Bancel, Gilles Boëtsch, Éric Deroo, Sandrine Lemaire, and Charles Forsdick (Liverpool, England: Liverpool University Press, 2008).
16. Herman Reichenbach, "A Tale of Two Zoos: The Hamburg Zoological Garden and Carl Hagenbeck's Tierpark," in *New Worlds, New Animals: From Menagerie to Zoological Park in the Nineteenth Century*, eds. R. J. Hoage and William A. Deiss (Baltimore, MD: Johns Hopkins University Press, 1996), 59.
17. Eric Ames, *Carl Hagenbeck's Empire of Entertainments* (Seattle: University of Washington Press), 147.
18. Ames, *Carl Hagenbeck's Empire of Entertainments*, 178–179.
19. Ludwig Heck, "Volkbildungsanstalt und Schaugeschäft," *Berliner Tageblatt*, January 28, 1909.
20. Jon C. Coe, "Design and Perception: Making the Zoo Experience Real," Zoo Biology 4 (1985): 206.
21. Nigel Rothfels, *Savages and Beasts: The Birth of the Modern Zoo* (Baltimore, MD: Johns Hopkins University Press, 2002), 201.
22. Spotte, *Zoos in Postmodernism*, 62.

6

Flawed Theming

Center Parcs as a Commodified, Middle-Class Utopia

By Steven Miles

On the surface Center Parcs appears to be nothing more than a fairly rudimentary family holiday destination. It provides a carefully organized, at least partly regimented, rural retreat in which families can enjoy the benefits of a forest setting away from the tribulations of everyday life. And yet at one and the same time Center Parcs promotes an almost utopian feeling of escape, of choice, and of family-driven identities. In this chapter I want to suggest that if we begin to dig beneath the surface to examine the values that Center Parcs represents and how it is consumers are obliged to engage with those values, we can begin to chart how it is that experiential forms of consumption have come to play an increasingly fundamental, and indeed, ideological, role in propping up the world in which we live. Furthermore, the case study that Center Parcs provides will enable us to begin to re-evaluate the role that themed spaces play in how an individual begins to make sense of his or her place in a consumerist society.

Progress

My analysis of Center Parcs can only be understood in the context of a broader notion of social and historical change and specifically in an understanding of how the individual fits into this process. Modernity was founded upon the notion of progress and the belief that human beings could take the world and shape it in their own guise. Human beings thus went about manipulating the world, but in doing so they simultaneously promoted notions of privacy and self-exploration. Ironically, the social change that emanated from a desire for sustainability produced an increasingly unstable world that was preoccupied with the preservation of human personality or with what Tuan calls "a progressive awareness of self" to the extent that the individual sought to express him or herself through the opportunities he or she had to escape from the "real" world.[1] Our existence came to be about achieving a balance between communal belonging and self-identity. For this reason, and not least since the second half of the twentieth century, consumption and spaces for consumption have come to play an ever-important role in how the individual relates to society.[2] Themed space is one example, an increasingly significant example, of how such space has undergone a process of constant re-invention in order that the individual can at least indulge in the sense that he or she can explore ever-new ways of asserting a sense of self while simultaneously maintaining a sense of belonging in a rapidly changing consumerist world.

Nature

Nature and human beings' relationship with it, as is indicated elsewhere in this volume, has long been an evocative means of embellishing the relationship between the individual and society. Historically, Modernity came to define Nature as something that was in need of being subdued and controlled, a sense that the maximization of economic growth was more desirable than environmental sustainability.[3] But for many authors the power of Modernity is such that nowadays very little remains that is genuinely "natural," unexplored, or untainted by human touch.[4] Nature is in fact a social construction. The form of nature we "consume" depends on the lens through which it is culturally construed and class plays a particularly significant role in underpinning what is thus a cultural process. In this light, one of the key notions I wish to explore through the remainder of this chapter is the suggestion that our relationship with Nature, notably within the context of tourism, is in fact largely a middle-class construction, given that the middle classes have effectively appropriated it for their own ends. This reflects a state of affairs in which the form citizenship takes has itself been transformed: "Contemporary western societies have begun to shift the basis of citizenship from political rights to consumer rights, and within the bundle of the latter, environmental rights, especially linked to conceptions of nature as spectacle and recreation are increasingly significant."[5]

What nature is or what we see it to be, is highly dependent upon historically and geographically specific social practices, not least that of tourism and recreation. But the point here is that a society in which the seduction of the marketplace is so central and in which the "feeling and emotions generated by seeing, holding, hearing, testing, smelling and moving" is so fundamental, has created a world in which Nature is defined, above all, by recreational pleasure-seeking. This process is reconstituted in the form of a class struggle in which class groups intent on distinguishing themselves from one another do so through education, occupation, residence, and consumption.[6] From this point of view, tourism isn't necessarily about the mere act of escape, leisure, or recreation, but embodies other higher order social and cultural proclivities. Tourism provides one of the key arenas within which the new petit bourgeoisie or alternatively the new service class, compensate for their lack of economic capital by expressing their difference through taste.[7] From this point of view tourism, particularly as regards its propensity towards "worthwhile experiences," is fundamentally an act of classification.[8]

Center Parcs as an Act of Classification

It's in the above context that I turn to Center Parcs. Center Parcs is a network of holiday villages located around Europe and specifically, the Netherlands, Belgium, France, Germany, and the United Kingdom and Ireland. Each of the parks takes on a familiar pattern. They constitute what could be described as mini "rural communities," offering visitors a central village hub that includes a Subtropical Swimming Paradise, chain restaurants, bars, and a supermarket, while spiraling outwards from this hub are a series of log cabins (plus a hotel), primarily designed for family occupation for periods of either a week or perhaps over a long weekend. These cabins provide a home away from home; a rural idyll with trails and cycle-friendly paths providing the consumer with a somewhat sanitized rural experience. Visitors are embraced by the greenery that surrounds them. They are able, obliged even, to partake in a range of rural activities from archery to cycling, from quad biking to the Segway experience, to boating and the Aqua Sana Spa. Such activities are highly individualized, and yet at one the same time the consumer is made to feel that he or she belongs to a bigger communal picture in which everyone is committed to the same vision of a land respected and utilized to the full.

Interestingly, with the exception of swimming, all activities taking place in the grounds of Center Parcs incur an additional cost. Such an arrangement is itself a further indication of a particular way of understanding the world that underpins the Center Parcs experience. As García Canclini argues in his discussion of consumer citizenship, our weekend engagement with the natural environment outside the city provides us with a focal point upon which we can attach our fantasies.[9] A consumer ethic underpins these fantasies: consumption has effectively become both the arena and the subject matter for their "fulfillment." Center Parcs provides a graphic demonstration of this insofar as it constitutes a manifestation of the freedoms and choices that a consumer-driven lifestyle can offer. The Center Parcs experience is all about the commodification of the rural landscape through activities that imply a pro-active engagement, but which actually encourage a passive process of commodification. In effect, the individual defines his or relationship to nature according to his or her ability to consume it like he or she would any other product made available on the market.

From this point of view a visit to Center Parcs is a self-affirming, class-based experience in which:

> The new petit bourgeoisie are best conceived as *ego*-tourists, who search for a style of travel which is both reflective of an "alternative" lifestyle and which is capable of maintaining and enhancing their cultural capital…Furthermore, it is a class fraction that attempts to compensate for insufficient economic capital, with an obsessional quest for the authentication of experience.[10]

Such experiences are not enough for their own sake, they say something profound about a group's class position and, specifically, as a reaction against the perceived crassness of tourism and a determination to establish particular forms of social distinction.

The Center Parcs experience is one based upon the familiarity and comfort-bearing qualities of rationalization.[11] The whole process is highly predictable and formalized from the ritual of the arrival where families pick up the keys to their lodge, drop off their luggage, and then return their car to the car park. At this point the family is ready to indulge: to indulge in the freedom to relax, perhaps retiring to the reassuring comfort of the Subtropical Swimming Paradise with its water slides and its programmed artificial waves. Center Parcs constitutes what is effectively a packaging of Nature. Such packaging is reflected elsewhere on the site, so, for example, the Longleat Forest site in the UK offers a workshop, habitat, and Rangers Lodge providing interactive nature-themed activities for children.[12] It is not Nature itself that is being sold to tourists here, but rather the feeling that they are "at one" with Nature—a commodified idealization in which middle-class notions of Nature-based leisure are carefully packaged. What's important here is that this version of Nature appears on the surface to be communal and family-driven, but is actually highly individualized, and individualized in such a way that the consumer is paramount. In this sense Center Parcs is ideological. It provides a terrain within which the consumer's status, and the aspirational lifestyle that this entails, is utterly beyond question.

Critiquing Center Parcs

The most comprehensive single treatment of the Center Parcs experience is to be found in the work of O'Callaghan who argues that Center Parcs provides a consistent standardized product, a brand that exists independently of a single location or geography and which meets the needs of a captive consumer-driven audience.[13] Center Parcs comes out of the British tradition of the holiday camp that reached its peak in the form of Butlins and Pontins in post-war Britain. Center Parcs succeeded in offering something different, something that exceeded perfunctory working class needs and which went above and beyond the even more highly regimentalized nature of the holiday camp. This is, or at least purports to be a peculiarly middle-class experience, to the extent that O'Callaghan argues that "there is little difference between the experience of Center Parcs and life in a typical suburb," providing a way of life in which personal development and self-awareness have become an increasingly significant agent of social change.[14] Arguably then, Center Parcs could be said to have very little at all to do with nature:

> Despite the fact that just eighteen per cent of the land is actually built on, Center Parcs maintains a suburban density; it is by no means nature. It is nature coerced for the individual enjoyment of the "guests." Artificially cultivated and enhanced to give the impression of abundance and fertility. The quality of wilderness and untouched nature is thereby sacrificed for the pleasures of a garden.[15]

For O'Callaghan this is a benign and tame nature that symbolizes human beings' assertion of their supremacy: "Nature has been tamed, packaged and commodified for the convenience of holidaymakers. It is the inevitable consequence of bringing nature to a mass audience; nature must be cultivated, protected and enhanced just to maintain an appearance of 'naturalness.'"[16]

This relationship between the need to find an escape and to do so in a way that meets middle-class aspirations of distinction creates its own set of tensions and arguably a challenge to the sense of a themed space as a straightforward place of entertainment. In other words, I want to argue in the remainder of this chapter that themed spaces are more than simply economic or cultural transactions, but rather they are the product of an ideological process through which key dimensions of social change are articulated. Miodrag Mitrasinovic talks about "systematic totality" and the fact that totalizing narratives are built into the core of the modern movement and into modernity itself.[17] From this point of view themed spaces are complex artifacts that reproduce a normative notion of harmony. But this isn't about the issue of entertainment as the dominant form of cultural reproduction and public discourse. Yes, such processes naturalize the commodity form.[18] But they do so in a way that not only do they define the contemporary citizen through what it is they consume—they create a set of conditions where the consumer actively seeks the kinds of distinctions that such forms of consumption can provide. In many respects Center Parcs can be said to have the characteristics of an immersive world.[19] Center Parcs provides the consumer with a particular sense of escape and yet, simultaneously, of belonging. It has an evocative quality. It provides a multi-sensory experience in which the consumer finds him or herself at the center of a rural narrative. It does so by providing what feels like a hands-on experience of nature, providing an edge that gives that experience a sense of authenticity when such authenticity is actually socially and culturally constructed.[20]

Beyond Nature

But the idealized world that Center Parcs has created is under threat from the very class-based aspirations that made it what it is in the first place. My point is that the immersive space that Center Parcs creates is not simply one based on a redefinition of nature as defined by the middle classes. It actually constitutes a means to an end: the end being the need to reproduce a particular and distinctive version of what it means to be middle class more generally. In effect then, I am seeking to extend O'Callaghan's argument.[21] While acknowledging the way Center Parcs has provided a successful model of tourism through the presentation of a morally superior package of natured-based physical family activity and good health, by creating such a monster, Center Parcs has arguably sown the seeds of its own thematic downfall.

As I established above, the Center Parcs experience is a highly commodified one. What we know about commodified experiences is that they succeed on an aspirational level. In other words, the social groups that buy into the values implied by such a process are not just the groups to whom such values come naturally. The middle-class theme that lies at the heart of Center Parcs is one that appeals to working-class consumers who want to see themselves through the lens that Center Parcs provides. Social scientists have long investigated the ways in which social groups use forms of consumption to demonstrate belonging.[22] The aspirational working-class consumer buys into the world that Center Parcs represents. For example, although Center Parcs itself is notionally car free at least after the point of arrival—the car is actually at the heart of the experience. It plays a key part of the ritual of arrival and departure and its absence actually reasserts its significance to what it means to be a middle-class consumer. Meanwhile, as far from offering a car free future, Center Parcs' relationship with the car is based upon "a hypocritical present in which the absence of the car is affected as a curiosity, a pleasure that can only be enjoyed on a temporary basis and in an artificially created scenario."[23] The car effectively signifies the escape that is entailed in a Center Parcs break. It is also a physical expression of the power of the family unit that sits at the heart of the Center Parcs experience.

The version of family life that Center Parcs presents is one that asserts the freedoms implied by a weekend or week away. The middle-class family resident at Center Parcs is together and yet apart at one and the same time. Although the family comes to Center Parcs as a unit, once there they will often partake in their own individual or perhaps child/parent only activities so that it is the notion of the family unit, rather than any commitment to dedicated family time, that is reproduced here. Of course, at key points of the day, notably meal times, the family is likely to come together, but such occasions further emphasize the individualistic nature of the broader experience and in particular the way it is broken up into commodified activity-based elements.

My suggestion then is that the theme propagated by Center Parcs, albeit arguably sub-consciously, is not nature, nor even middle-classness, but is in fact, *aspirational* middle-classness. In effect, Center Parcs is a gated weekend community. Once you arrive at the park you are positively discouraged from exiting prior to the end of your stay. Far from being an escape, the Center Parcs experience is actually a form of cultural captivity. Visitors to Center Parcs are effectively obliged to adhere to a Center Parcs code of middle-class conduct. They are entering what appears to be a utopic rural state but in fact such a state is a thinly veiled reproduction of a consumerist world of aspiration and belonging. The point here is that any definition of belonging to, or taking ownership for the values associated with this way of being is not resource dependent. Center Parcs doesn't demonstrate belonging to a particular class grouping, but rather the aspiration for such belonging.

Another way of explaining what I mean here is through a brief consideration of Bauman's notion of the "flawed consumer" which I will now extend to consider the notion of "flawed theming." Consumers are flawed in the sense that not everyone has the resources to fully partake in the world of consumption set before them. Bauman's argument is that in fact in order to be available to be secured by the market its customers must be ready and willing to be seduced by that market. In a consumer society being "normal" is defined by the ability to consume. Furthermore the experience of poverty brings with it a particular relationship to the opportunities that consumerism provides. Bauman argues that the work ethic has thus gradually been demoted from its position as a supreme regulatory principle. Meanwhile, "poverty" means being excluded from whatever passes as "normal" life and not having the ability or the opportunity to partake in a "happy life":

> This results in resentment and aggravation, which spill out in the form of violent acts, self-depreciation or

both…in a society of consumers, it is above all the inadequacy of the person as a consumer that leads to social degradation and "internal exile." It is this inadequacy, this inability to acquit oneself of the consumer's duties, that turns into bitterness at being left behind, disinherited or degraded, shut off from the social feast to which others gained entry.[24]

The poor members of a consumer society are therefore defined first and foremost in terms of their ability or otherwise to consume, and they seek any means possible to assert their belonging through the symbolic value of consumption. They are "flawed consumers" in that their resources will only allow their consumerist imaginations to go so far.

Flawed Theming

The theme of Center Parcs is itself, flawed in the sense that what it delivers is a space in which middle class values can be enacted, but those given those values are essentially aspirational—they are not actually built upon very secure foundations. This reflects a process in which Center Parcs, "the producer," has consciously or otherwise, gone about reproducing a stage set upon which consumers can feel they are living out a particular set of values. This is of course an inevitable result of the management of Center Parcs identifying a successful model and running with it. But there is also a kind of "trickle-down" process going on here that effectively dilutes the middle-classness of the theme. Given the world of consumption is ever changing, so too are the spaces within which consumption-based classed membership is enacted. In other words, the cultural capital that underpins the Center Parcs experience does not have the same status it may have had twenty years ago. Having visited Center Parcs at both points in time, I would argue that not only has the Center Parcs infrastructure been subject to a degree of wear and tear, not only is Center Parcs no longer arguably "of the moment" (not least as a result of the growth of cheaper international tourism via budget airlines in the 2000s), but the park is also, anecdotally at least, attracting more and more working-class consumers who actively aspire to the lifestyle Center Parcs promotes. The danger here then is that the Center Parcs brand is undermined by its apparent accessibility in a similar way to how the fashion brand, Burberry was damaged by its associations with the aspirational consumption of the so-called "chav" in the UK.[25] It may well be that the theme that underpins Center Parcs is eventually undermined or indeed usurped by those consumers who partake in it.

As far as the actual experience of Center Parcs is concerned, the genuineness of the Center Parcs experience as an engagement becomes less and less significant as Center Parcs comes to represent the broader and commercialized nature of tourists' holiday aspirations. O'Callaghan suggests that the evolution of Center Parcs reflects the wider gentrification of post-war British society and of course, at least to an extent, this is a perfectly plausible interpretation.[26] But the point here is that gentrification in this form effectively has the reverse effect to that which O'Callaghan describes. It actually undermines the themed space by de-gentrifying it to the extent that the spaces that it provides are available to a broader non-elite social group. Center Parcs promotes a passive, controlled, and predictable form of middle class tourism but in doing so it undermines the brand that sits at its core. Or to put this a different way, the social force of commodification is so axiomatic and so dependent upon changing markets and patterns of consumption that the theme of middle-class nature consumption that underpins Center Parcs is simply unable, any longer, to hold "sub-tropical" water. The middle-class values that lie at the heart of the Center Parcs experience can no longer be maintained in a world in which there is so much more to be consumed than the limited world that Center Parcs represents.

Nature, Redefined

In their discussion of the evolution of the park, Jones and Wills suggest that nature seems increasingly peripheral in modern parkscapes, given that such spaces are increasingly driven by the image and the artificial rather than the geographical reality. A focus on Center Parcs suggests something slightly different: a state of affairs in which the boundaries between image and reality are increasingly blurred. This reflects a broader state of affairs in which public space and private space are increasingly hard to decipher and in which, in effect, public space is ever more marginalized. From this point of view, nature, as Center Parcs perhaps demonstrates, has been rendered less of a fundamental element of people's everyday lives and more of a "weekend escape"…and a weekend escape to be paid for, "Nature has become a museum object, a cultural artefact and a place only for visiting."[27] The process being described here is one of reinvention. The park was traditionally a paradigm for a reaction against society's problems, as Jones and Wills put it, it provided a tonic to civic alienation. Center

Parcs demonstrates how it is that this relationship has been redefined along the lines of consumption to the extent that such problems are barely even remembered. To consume is to forget.

Far from being a tonic to any notion of civic alienation, the nature that Center Parcs represents is a redefinition of nature as something to be bought as a means to the broader end of belonging. The nature it represents is a space that actively reproduces and reasserts the status quo, not one that is designed to provide a challenge or escape from it. But the market value of the consumer experience is only sustainable if it is adaptable and able to respond to the changing needs of its market. The potential danger with Center Parcs is that the experience it offers is fundamentally the same as it was twenty years ago and that on this case the consumer has changed more quickly than what it is he or she is consuming. Themed spaces might well operate as "scholastic program[s] for the naturalization of the commodity form" but they also serve as a microscope on the unforgiving nature of social change.[28]

By visiting Center Parcs, consumers breathe life into consumer capitalism.[29] However, what Center Parcs ultimately represents is the inherent limitations of a model of themed space that is more interested in the past than it is the future. The narrative that Center Parcs presents is in danger of not keeping up with those narratives that consumers use to construct themselves. In discussing Skultan's work, Meethan suggests that, "In order to be intelligible, narratives, like other forms of experience, must be rendered into forms that are both culturally specific and common, and this ordering and accounting for experiences is an active, rather than a passive process in which people interpret, negotiate and create their own particular meaning."[30] For Meethan the successful tourist experience provides a means by which tourists can "work at" creating their own personal space narratives.

Perhaps the danger here is that the theme that Center Parcs presents is simply too prescriptive. It is so indebted to a notion of aspirational middle-classness that the room it provides for individual notes of transformation is actually peculiarly limited. The notion of freeing up the individual and the family to the opportunities that nature offers only goes so far. Center Parcs "performs" nature in such a way that while it offers self-discovery on the one hand, on the other it takes it away, by so closely defining the routes through which self-discovery can be achieved. It may be that the time for totalizing narratives has gone; that the demands of social change are such that themed space is itself vulnerable to the constraints imposed by its own rationale. The principle of themed spaces may be experience-driven, but the reality tends to be somewhat different. The consumerist ideology that underpins such spaces is inevitably more powerful than any practical commitment to provide the individual or his or her family to create their own experience. Themed spaces allegedly work insofar as they provide the space within which consumers can narrate their own biographies. Perhaps the next generation of themed spaces will enable such aspirations more than they currently constrain them.

Notes

1. Yi-Fu Tuan, *Segmented Worlds and Self: Group Life and Individual Consciousness* (Minneapolis: University of Minnesota Press, 1982).
2. Steven Miles, *Spaces for Consumption: Pleasure and Placelessness in the Post-Industrial Society* (London: Sage, 2010)
3. Scott Lash and John Urry, *Economies of Signs and Space* (London: Sage, 2001).
4. John Urry, *Consuming Places* (London: Routledge, 1995).
5. Phil Macnaghten and John Urry (2005) "Towards a Sociology of Nature," in *Nature: Critical Concepts in the Social Sciences*, eds. David Inglis, John Bone, and Rhoda Wilkie (London: Routledge, 2005), 147.
6. Lash and Urry, *Economies of Signs and Space*, 296.
7. On the new petit bourgeoisie, see, Pierre Bourdieu, *Distinction: A Social Critique of the Judgement of Taste* (London: Routledge, Kegan and Paul, 1979); and on the new service class, John Urry, *The Tourist Gaze: Leisure and Travel in Contemporary Societies* (London: Sage, 1990).
8. Shaw and Williams, *Tourism and Tourism Spaces*.

9. Néstor García Canclini, *Consumers and Citizens: Globalization and Multicultural Conflicts* (Minneapolis: University of Minnesota Press, 2001).

10. Ian Munt, "The 'Other' Postmodern Tourism: Culture, Travel and the Middle Classes," *Theory, Culture and Society*, 11, no. 3 (1994): 108.

11. George Ritzer, *The McDonaldization of Society: An Investigation into the Changing Character of Contemporary Social Life* (London: Pine Forge, 1992).

12. Tim O'Callagahan, "Center Parcs," *The Journal of Architecture* 13, no. 6 (2008): 675–700.

13. O'Callaghan, "Center Parcs."

14. O'Callaghan, "Center Parcs," 682.

15. O'Callaghan, "Center Parcs," 690.

16. O'Callaghan, "Center Parcs," 691.

17. Miodrag Mitrasinovic, *Total Landscape, Theme Parks, Public Space* (Burlington, VT: Ashgate, 2006).

18. See, Neil Postman, *Amusing Ourselves to Death* (London: Methuen, 1987).

19. Scott A. Lukas, *The Immersive Worlds Handbook: Designing Theme Parks and Consumer Spaces* (New York: Focal Press, 2013).

20. Christian Mikunda, *Brand Lands, Hot Spots and Cool Spaces: Welcome to the Third Place and the Total Marketing Experience* (London: Kogan Page, 2004).

21. O'Callagahan, "Center Parcs."

22. Thorsten Veblen, *The Theory of the Leisure Class* (London: Constable, 1899).

23. O'Callagahan, "Center Parcs," 696.

24. Zygmunt Bauman, *Work, Consumerism and the New Poor* (Buckingham, England: Open University Press, 1998), 38.

25. The "chav" refers to the "stereotypical white working-class delinquent looking for trouble," *The Economist*, "Burberry and Globalisation: A Checkered Story," January 20, 2011, <www.economist.com/node/17963363>.

26. O'Callaghan, "Center Parcs."

27. Karen Jones and John Wills, *The Invention of the Park: From the Garden of Eden to Disney's Magic Kingdom* (Cambridge: Polity, 2005), 172–173.

28. Stephen Fjellman, *Vinyl Leaves: Walt Disney and America* (Boulder, CO: Westview Press, 1992), 402.

29. See, John Fiske, *Reading the Popular* (London: Unwin Hyman, 1989).

30. Vieda Skultans, *The Testimony of Lives: Narrative and Memory in Post-Soviet Latvia* (London: Routledge, 1998). Kevin Meethan, "Introduction: Narrative of Place and Self, in *Tourism, Consumption and Representation*, eds. Kevin Meethan, Alison Anderson, and Steven Miles (Wallingford, England: CAB International, 2001), 8.

7

The Cultures of Tiki

By Scott A. Lukas

We are what we pretend to be, so we must be careful about what we pretend to be. — Kurt Vonnegut, *Mother Night*

In 2015, while conducting research at the Aria in Las Vegas, I stumbled upon a surprising theme among the many other themes inside a relatively unthemed casino. Nestled among the slot machines that featured an array of exotic representations of the past, culture, and branded entities—the Lord of the Rings, Amazonian princesses, cuddly pandas, among others—was the conspicuous game Tiki Beach (IGT). Like the other slots, Tiki Beach was designed to attract the potential player with its mesmerizing lights, cute cartoon characters, and promises of lucrative bonus games, but these features were not the facets of the slot machine that drew me to its surface. This was the first sighting that I had of a tiki-themed slot machine—a fortuitous event as I was, at that time, trying to grasp the elusive nature of this cultural form. As I glanced more closely at the representations on the slot, it occurred to me that the surface symbols of the game reaffirmed my sensibilities of tiki—a kitschy, less-than-serious, and now dated pop culture entity—yet as I reflected more deeply at conceptual and meta levels, my senses of tiki began to change. My mind began to focus on one of the iconic humanoid tiki statues represented on the slot and I started to obsess on one of the tikis that was adorned with sunglasses. At first, it seemed to me that the sunglasses fit the representation in that tiki has come to stand for a beach lifestyle, having eroded any of the semiotic and cultural foundations of Polynesian cultures, and now having landed in popular culture as a lifestyle, not unlike that of Jimmy Buffett, Parrotheads, and Margaritaville.[1] Yet, on second glance, it occurred to me that the sunglasses were blasphemous, as odd as this sounds, in that they have taken the essences of tiki and have transformed and remade them too excessive, and extravagantly such that the resonances of tiki are now too diluted—the overall thematic complex of which is left, ironically, with near-empty signifiers. The sunglass-wearing tiki at once demonstrated to me the ascendancy of tiki as a lifestyle form and, now, its nadir. Reflecting today on my encounter with Tiki Beach, I struggle to answer a series of questions that not only informs this study of tiki but also speaks to paramount issues in the nature of themed spaces and themed living. Do material representations of tiki like the iconic American backyard tiki bar identify a new direction in the nature of themed and immersive spaces? Can any forms of tiki be considered "authentic" given the fact of tiki's illicit material and cultural borrowing? Are those associated with tiki and its complex lifestyle politics guilty of forms of cultural essentialism and appropriation, of celebrating primitivism, and of an overall ethnocentric lack of appreciation of material, religious, and cultural forms which have given rise to such lifestyle? Is it possible to imagine tiki as anything other than a joke, wink, or form of kitsch?

This writing builds on ethnographic study of the cultures of tiki that includes archival research, interviews with individuals enmeshed within tiki culture, and research visits to a number of famous tiki venues, including the revived Don the Beachcomber in Huntington Beach, California; the Tonga Room and Hurricane Bar in San Francisco, California; and Trader Vic's in Emeryville, California. The work begins with a focus on the material, cultural, and lifestyle essences of tiki with an emphasis on the idea of postmodern culture. It then addresses tiki through the lens of "culture sampling" or the ways in which tiki represents the sampling and remixing of various cultures, lifestyles, and affective realms. It then focuses on the resonances of tiki with an emphasis on the various material, performative, and lifestyle instances of tiki and is followed by a discussion of authenticity and kitsch. The writing concludes with a consideration of the dynamics of cultural appropriation and the ethics of tiki lifestyle, especially in the context of numerous other examples of contemporary cultural appropriation in popular culture and the media and the various related lifeworlds of lived theming such as Civil War reenactment and other thematic forms of lifestyle. A general concern of this research is to analyze tiki as a conceptual midpoint between the forms of theming and immersion common to contemporary themed spaces like theme parks and examples of lifestyle immersion or lived theming found in reenactment and other avocational circles.

The Original Image and Its Reflection

Among the cultures of the Maoris and of the islands of Polynesia, a Tiki—the first being and creator—is fashioned as an image, a tiki, which is a re-presentation of the Tiki in wooden sculptural form. In Maori culture, the tiki is often worn as a pendent, fashioned out of greenstone.[2] Both of these indigenous meanings of Tiki highlight the practice of the re-presentation of cultural and cosmological orders in material and immaterial forms—a practice that is common to most cultures in the world, those indigenous and those popular. Re-presentation and forms of remaking are always caught up in the very tricky politics of (presumed) origins and their dissemination. Tiki, in both its indigenous and popular forms, is no different. It is an entity that expresses the illicit nature of any form of remaking. Yet, it is the popular form of tiki that has most dramatically illustrated the stakes of representation and remaking and which may, I will argue, provide fertile grounds on which to more fully consider the nature of theming in both architectural and lifestyle dimensions.

Image 7.1. Tikis (photo by Infrogmation of New Orleans, Creative Commons Attribution 2.0 Generic)

According to tiki expert and Taschen author Sven Kirsten, whose numerous lavish and creative books on tiki have had a notable impact on the popular construction of what some have also called "Polynesian Pop," tiki took root in the 1940s as sailors returned from calls of duty in the Pacific. The work of popular author James Michener (particularly his *Tales of the South Pacific* and its later adaptation as the musical *South Pacific*), Thor Heyerdahl's Kon-Tiki expedition (as well as his texts *The Kon-Tiki Expedition: By Raft Across the South Seas* and *Aku-Aku: The Secret of Easter Island*), popular chain restaurants Don the Beachcomber and Trader Vic's, Hawaiian statehood and associated tourism, television shows like *Gilligan's Island,* music of Martin Denny (and others connected to the exotica genre), the Enchanted Tiki Room ride (Disneyland), tiki-themed apartments and hotels (and certain architectural style influences, such as A-frame design), and the ubiquitous backyard tiki bar are all, according to Kirsten, notable foundations in the evolution of tiki.[3] As suggested with Kirsten's list, a number of the influential moments in the evolution of tiki include architectural, material culture, and décor elements—all of which situate tiki within the traditions of other themed and immersive spaces. Particularly famous spaces like those of themed restaurants (Don the Beachcomber and Trader Vic's), themed hotels (Caliente Tropics in Palm Springs, California), tiki apartments (Tiki Apartments in Redondo Beach), themed casinos and tiki bars (Harvey's in South Lake Tahoe, California), and theme parks (Disneyland's Enchanted Tiki Room and the associated primitivism of Adventureland, the never fully realized tiki theme park of Danny Balsz known as the Tikis) assisted in forging a new form of Polynesian Pop design in the United States. Bamboo, rattan, and thatched structures and features; artwork depicting tropical paradise and various fauna (turtles, parrots, sea life); muted versions of the colors orange, brown, tan, red, and green; and numerous tiki statues were some of the many noticeable and distinctive styles of the tiki lexicon. Somewhat unique to tiki's evolution is the growth in popularity of the backyard tiki bar. In this example tiki may be said to be one of the most popular choices of homeowners in the United States in terms of using an evocative theme by which to theme their home (or at least a part of it). Yet, tiki, as a cultural form, is much more than any of these material details would suggest. For many people, tiki begins and ends with a few tiki torches, a couple of statues, and a tropical drink, but as I discovered visiting the International Tiki Market Place at Don the Beachcomber in 2015, there are significant lifestyle components to tiki as well.

My trip to the International Tiki Market Place was necessitated by a desire to connect with the many individuals who are part of a number of loosely knit communities—the "cultures" of tiki, as I call them. Cultures, in the plural, is used to connote two facets of this study. First, is the tendency within cultural anthropology to regard the construct of culture as a multiplicity opposed to its once monolithic and all-encompassing definition and, second, is the idea that tiki represents the convergence of cultural forms—material, lifestyle, and ideational—that is characteristic of postmodern subcultures and avocational tendencies outside of the world of tiki. My goal to study ethnographically the cultures of tiki stems from an interest to move beyond tiki's materiality and surface expressions—a somewhat ironic goal, as I have discovered—and to better understand the avocational, lifestyle, and even existential expressions of its adherents.

Samples of Culture

One of the most interesting narrative currents that runs throughout the many Sven Kirsten tiki texts is the idea that tiki is best studied from the perspective of an explorer or, more properly, an urban/pop archaeologist or anthropologist who is willing to research strange and seemingly arcane rituals of those involved in tiki culture.[4] Kirsten's reliance on this narrative likely relates to his efforts to make his important texts funny and more readable for his audience, but considered in a more conceptual light, the narrative of the ethnographer seeking out a strange and "primitive" culture has important implications for an overall understanding of tiki's constructions. Otto von Stroheim offers a similar metaphor in an interview about tiki: "You have to take tiki at face value and run with it."[5] For a cultural anthropologist, taking something at "face value" is an interesting proposition. Anthropologists have traditionally focused on the most in-depth, holistic, and even subterranean views of a given culture and its various phenomena. As Clifford Geertz once remarked in terms of "thick description," it is incumbent on the anthropologist to push beyond the surface meanings of cultural phenomena. As he famously wrote about in terms of the difference between a wink and a blink, there is much to be learned by delving deep into a culture, its people, and meaning systems.[6] The problem arises when we attempt to apply Geertz's interpretive framework to the case of tiki. Were an anthropologist to do so, he or she would likely discover either what appears to be a lack of deep meaning (as tiki seems to deliberately reside on the surfaces of culture—winking at us all the while) or a sense of meaning that is imbued with all of the things that he or she, as an anthropologist, is patently against—cultural stereotyping, essentialism, primitivism, and the like. The adherents of tiki would likely admonish an anthropologist for first desiring to study tiki and then second for any conclusions that might be critical of tiki's core. The whole point of tiki, as I heard time and time again in many field observations, is to eschew the serious and the conventional and to delight in the campy and the controversial.[7]

During my time at the International Tiki Market Place (Huntington Beach, California, 2015), I had the opportunity to speak to a number of the attendees of this quasi-conference. One of the initial questions that I posed to tikiphiles was, "Why did you get involved with tiki?" As one might expect, there was considerable variance in the responses that I received.

Image 7.2. International Tiki Market Place (Photo by Scott A. Lukas)

Some saw tiki as an expression of individuality (especially common among the sculptors and artisans), others viewed it as an escape from everyday life, and some, quite interestingly, saw tiki as a sort of spiritual calling. Such was the case with Vontiki, a tiki sculptor from Ventura, California.[8] In his mind, "If life gives you a bunch of palm trees, you carve tikis." Vontiki spoke of his aesthetic work as a devoted religious person might speak of his belief system. He told me that he used only traditional tools, but occasionally supplemented them with power ones. What I found interesting in his discussion of carving was the hybrid sense of authenticity that he expressed about his practices. As Ryan Moore has written of punk subcultural practices, the notions of authenticity that are often part of a subculture's ethos can seem, to the outsider, to be contradictory in nature.[9] I believe that Vontiki's sensibilities about his carvings suggest an awareness to maintain what he determines to be "traditional" techniques but also an ability to adapt, modify, and rework those techniques so as to create a new hybrid aesthetic. As well, due to tiki's inherently constructed and overdetermined nature, carvers like Vontiki ruminate on the discourse of authenticity as a means of balancing out the nature of tiki. Like many forms of contemporary, postmodern culture, tiki, as a hybrid entity, represents a balancing act in terms of its playing with the politics of authenticity and culture.[10]

It is this playing with culture and winking at us, at least a bit, that gives tiki its charm as well as its outrage in the views of social critics. During my conversations with Vontiki, I became more and more aware of the playfulness inherent in the form. He explained that styles and movements that have little or nothing to do with tiki of the past—like surf culture and car culture—are now becoming a part of tiki culture. In his mind, this was acceptable, but other variations of tiki's remaking, such as a "Chinese restaurant using tiki to sell food [was a] bastardization [of the form.]" What seemed evident in Vontiki's constructions of tiki, was that the choices of cultural mixing and remixing that are a part of tiki's world are highly personalized and adaptable to the individual and context at hand. In my time spent with tiki adherents, I have felt a great sense of openness and non-judgment, and this may also explain this artist's openness to new and expanded versions of tiki.[11] As well, I would suggest that an acceptance of tiki's adaptability and its constant redeployment as a cultural form illustrates tiki's reliance on on re-presentations of culture. Tiki is, by its nature, a remade form. In fact, some critics have charged that it is too much a product of remaking and thus lacks authenticity or cultural sensitivity. I will address these critiques shortly, but let me argue that, on the contrary, tiki represents a manifestation of what I have called "culture sampling" or "the tendency to draw on (or sample) a culture for the purpose of recreating and remixing that culture, or numerous variations of it, in another place."[12] Like the forms of theming common to consumer themed spaces, the material and architectural expressions of tiki rely on certain essences that connote the associations intended by tikiphiles.[13] The classic backyard tiki bar, as I will consider later, is an example of a themed spatial form that is highly dependent on iconic, over-the-top, and even stereotypical colors, material, aesthetics, and narrative. Part of tiki's pleasure relies on such material expressions for their inherent emotional import and effects—both internally and externally within straight or mainstream society—and in some ways it shares affinities with Egyptomania.[14] In addition to such forms of sampling in the material senses, we see that tiki's other expressions—including its iconic exotica music, its social gatherings, and the origin myths detailed by its members—also follow a pattern of cultural sampling.

Authenticity and the Fake

One of the most enduring associations with that of tiki is the notion of the fake and inauthenticity. The casual observer of the form would likely view tiki as one would velvet Elvis paintings, garden gnomes, pink flamingo lawn art, colorful depictions of mystical unicorns, and any number of other items which have been labeled as kitsch. Tiki, with its garish colors, over-the-top caricatured sculptures, cheap bamboo bars and furniture, Martin Denny exotica music, conformist Hawaiian shirts and island sarongs, among other features, represents, to such an antagonist, the most base and lurid of popular culture forms. An aficionado of tiki, whether a person who enjoys her backyard tiki bar on the weekend or a more involved individual who follows tiki bulletin boards on the Internet and who attends tiki conferences, is a person who suffers from inauthenticity in terms of her connection with culture; or, in the words of Gillo Dorfles, "whose attitude towards works of art is definitely and hopelessly wrong."[15]

As I have suggested throughout this work, many of the tiki aficionados with whom I spoke had little, if any, difficulty in terms of these claims of the form's inauthenticity. My time at the International Tiki Market Place reminded me of other cultural traditions, including those at Comic-Con and other fan conventions, in which humor, reappropriation, and strongly believing in oneself go hand in hand. At the tiki event, I noted one individual who was wearing a very garish and over-the-top tiki mask that would have been welcomed at a fan convention like Comic-Con (see image 7.2). The humor and constant winking at straight (or non-tiki) society is part of what gives the form its social draw. In one of the most interesting descriptions of the nature of tiki, Otto von Stroheim, a contemporary of Sven Kirsten and publisher of *Tiki News*, suggested that tiki is a cultural form that is, in fact, "fake." As he said, "Tiki is a culture in and of itself—not Polynesian, not island style or, say, Jimmy Buffett. It is anchored by tiki bars, which are fake representations of Polynesian islands here on the mainland."[16] Other tiki aficionados also share von Stroheim's sense of tiki's "fake" nature. As one offered, he didn't want any authentic Polynesian artifacts in his tiki-themed spaces of home, "Those belong in the British Museum…I only want the fake stuff—the fake-real stuff."[17]

Tiki's members are extremely comfortable with tiki's lack of fidelity and, again, there are parallels to be drawn between this spirit and that of punk. The difference is, of course, that punk has had an edgier, nihilistic, and counter-cultural spirit in terms of its reactions to those who disapprove of its core symbols, values, performances, and personal expressions. In my observations of similar tiki groups, I have only heard laughter and good wishes in the responses to any outsiders who might deem tiki to be inauthentic, fake, or even kitsch. The topic of kitsch is a particularly complex one that is covered in more depth in numerous excellent studies of popular culture.[18] For purposes of this study, it is important to note a series of concerns that might be raised in terms of the assertions of critics who would likely challenge the authenticity of kitsch popular culture generally and tiki culture more specifically. First, as sociologist Herbert Gans has written of taste publics and taste cultures, the distinctions between so-called high and low culture (and their constituent determinants of taste) have been exaggerated.[19] In fact, new research on contemporary popular culture suggests that, more and more, presumed high and low cultures are involved in forms of cross-fertilization and convergence[20] As well, as Gans further argues, high and low culture distinctions are born of particular social class dynamics which are often forgotten in discussions of kitsch and inauthenticity in popular culture. As I will consider later in comparisons of tiki culture to American and German reenactment subcultures, the reactions against those who favor tiki are, discursively and politically, representative of the rhetoric of class warfare and loathing disguised as the politics of taste.[21] A third concern relates to the vacuous grounds of distinction on which kitsch rests. Present in the discourse of kitsch are universalist claims of cultural superiority in which

Image 7.3. Tiki-Ti Los Angeles (photo by Sam Howzit, Creative Commons Attribution 2.0 Generic)

those who differentiate kitsch from high culture claim to be able to make such distinctions in the first place—claims which violate relativistic theories of popular culture that suggest that "all taste cultures are of equal worth."[22]

As we noted earlier, we may look at how such self-identified, even celebrated forms of the "fake" may, in fact, promote stronger senses of group identity, community, or communitas among members of the tiki community. Anthropologist Daniel Miller, in a study of home cultures that predates his important *The Comfort of Things*, writes of an ethnographic study in which he interpreted the material object "kitsch" collections of one of his informants as not a matter of taste but a means by which the individual could come to terms with tragedy, coming of age, loss, and feelings of existential insignificance.[23] In my own ethnographic observations of tiki communities, I noted a similar sense of comfort that was provided by tiki material culture, performance, and lifestyle among individuals who, like the woman in Miller's study, were disinterested in external perceptions about tiki's inauthenticity, phoniness, or kitsch quality. As my informant Vontiki expressed in a discussion of his approach to tiki carvings, "When the tiki bug bites you, then you get hooked." In his mind, participation in tiki events was natural and, certainly, authentic in terms of the meanings of community, individualism, and aesthetic craft that are a part of his notions of tiki. But this begs the question, to what extent does tiki's internal ethos impinge on those outside of its community?

Cultural Appropriation and the Ethics of Tiki

In 2015, the story of Rachel Dolezal dominated the news. Dolezal was the chair of the Spokane, Washington chapter of the NAACP and a part-time instructor at Eastern Washington University and it was discovered that she had fabricated numerous details of her life history in order to claim African-American ancestry. Dolezal was interviewed on numerous major media programs and even when confronted with clear evidence of her European-American ancestry, she maintained her identity as being African American. A number of Dolezal's critics suggested that by making her claims that she had culturally, politically, even existentially appropriated aspects of the African-American experience. The Dolezal case is certainly not the first, and will not be the last, example of the complex politics of cultural appropriation. Within the world of popular music, the rapper and former model Iggy Azalea has raised similar concerns about the ethics of appropriating other aesthetic and cultural styles. Azalea's signature is her uncanny re-creation of Southern African-American voice in her rapping performances. Many have called this signature style, as well as music videos that depict Azalea in potentially culturally insensitive contexts—such as the Bollywood-styled India (*Bounce*)—inappropriate cultural appropriation, even blackface.

Image 7.4. Don the Beachcomber, Huntington Beach, CA (Photo by Scott A. Lukas)

Tiki, as a cultural form, is no stranger to the world of cultural appropriation. Tiki, particularly in reference to its primitivistic roots and its sampling of Polynesian cultures, has been interpreted as a form that is inherently problematic for its reliance on cultural appropriation. Especially troubling for those who have studied tiki, Polynesian pop, and other related forms, is the common reliance on the "savage slot"—the figure of the primitive indigenous person and her culture appropriated for western cultural and aesthetic forms.[24] All forms of theming, including tiki, entail such forms of appropriation. Like earlier examples of cultural appropriation common to the art of Gauguin, Picasso, and van Gogh, tiki's drawing on Polynesian and Pacific cultures suggests problematic constructs and foundations related to colonialism, racism, sexism, among other issues. As George Lewis has suggested, cultural appropriation is much more about the reframing of "dreams and desires" of the appropriating culture than it is a form of homage to that culture.[25] One of the most curious facets of tiki is the fact that so many of its proponents are willing to address this aspect of the cultural form. In one interview about tiki parties, *Tiki News* magazine publisher Otto von Stroheim calls tiki forms "fake representations of Polynesian islands here on the mainland."[26] In a similar vein, heralded exotica composer and musician Martin Denny described his music—which has become highly associated with tiki—as a construct: "My music is fictional, but it's based on different ethnic sounds and instruments. It was sort of all [a] make believe type of thing…fiction. It's what people think the islands might be like in your own mind."[27] Of course these admissions do not necessarily justify the representations that are characteristic of forms of Polynesian pop culture. What they do suggest, like the Dolezal and Azalea cases, is a certain postmodern hybridity that has come to characterize much of contemporary popular and public culture. Especially in a world of signification's endless deferral, as Jacques Derrida offered, it becomes incredibly challenging to make sense of originals, copies, sources, and citation. Tiki's problem and, simultaneously its draw, is its loose and carefree approach to cultural appropriation. Its adherents admit fully to tiki's lack of "authenticity" (using the term of the mainstream and its critics), accept its playful recombination of cultural forms, and feel delight in an apolitical response to those who critique tiki's problematic connections to cultural appropriation. One analysis of tiki conducted in 2014 suggested that the form's easy and carefree drawing on culture was no more a given: "A growing sensitivity to the poor treatment of indigenous people made many uncomfortable with the idea of drinking from a glass shaped like a native girl."[28] The stereotypical women depicted in tiki culture suggest a related issue of the ethics of cultural appropriation.

In addition to tiki's problematic connections to primitivism and racial essentialism, there is the issue of its constructions of gender and sexuality. Donn Beach (born Ernest Raymond Beaumont Gantt) is best known for his successful Don the Beachcomber restaurants and bars, but many see him, along with Vic Bergeron (Trader Vic's), as the primogeniture of the tiki movement. Many other males appear in the pages of Sven Kirsten's numerous tiki books, along with numerous scantily clad or nude women, some of whom are women of color. It could be said that much of the aesthetic of tiki is a male-centered one with emphasis placed on a male, relaxed on a beach and sipping a tropical drink while beautiful women walk by. As Amy Ku'leialoha Stillman writes, "Tiki culture identifies with the figure of the white male beachcomber living in paradise, whose object of desire is an exotic brown-skinned island girl."[29] Interestingly, many of tikis founders suggested that tiki emerged, in the 1950s, as a response to sexual puritanism in the United States. As Kirsten relates, "[with tiki], the generation of our parents, for the first time, were ridding themselves of the Christian heritage of Puritanism."[30] Of course, in cases like these, a subculture's attempt to escape sexual puritanism or the other mores of society does not necessarily result in equality among its members. In this sense, subcultures like those of tiki exist between the unease of social criticism and the suggestions of social change fueled by its members and their values. Tiki has not been characterized as a new social movement, and certainly not an alternative or redemptive social movement that seeks to either change behaviors of people or society itself. Its existence as a subculture that specifically has a checkered history in terms of its drawing on cultural appropriation and heteronormativity has resulted, in the minds of some critics, as a force counterproductive to other social movements that may have intentions of social change. Lisa Kahaleole Hall describes such a situation in reference to tiki and other forms of pop Hawai'ian-ness. The tourist representations common in Hawaii, for example, have "significant political implications, because by making Hawai'ian-ness seem ridiculous, kitsch functions to undermine sovereignty struggles in a very fundamental way…Bombarded with such kitsch, along with images of leisure and paradise, non-Hawai'ians fail to take Hawai'ian sovereignty seriously and Hawai'ian activism remains invisible to the mainstream."[31]

Postmodern Subcultures and Backyard Tiki Bars

For many individuals, including those who enjoy tiki but who do not share as much passion for it as someone like Vontiki, the idea that tiki could be connected to the politics of cultural appropriation, colonialism, and heteronormativity would likely never enter the person's consciousness. Instead, he or she would likely be too caught up in the milieu of fruity island drinks, rattan furniture, and kitschy tikis that make up his or her backyard tiki bar. Of all of the connotations that people have of tiki, it is the tiki bar—whether the backyard or the public establishment variety—that holds the strongest meanings. The Internet is flooded with how-to guides that describe the themes, techniques, and materials needed to create a tiki bar. The DIY cosmology of tiki, which I have noted in my conversations with adherents in numerous spaces, certainly offers a proletarian spirit that is part of its appeal. As Moore notes of punk subcultures, the DIY spirit holds a special legacy for many subcultures.³² What is curious in the case of Polynesian pop is that the very openness and non-serious spirit that may attract a newcomer to the subculture is also the ethos that may suggest to the same person that tiki is not exclusive in that anyone can be a part of it. As Dick Hebdige and others have written of other subcultures, the contradictory spirit of tiki is part and parcel of its notable cultural manifestations.³³ And perhaps this open appeal to be a popular form—as Sven Kirsten said, tiki "emerged from the common subconscious"—has led to its untimely transformation.³⁴

Image 7.5. Keith's Tiki Hut, Edinburgh, Scotland (photo by Amanda, Creative Commons Attribution 2.0 Generic)

Numerous contemporary tiki businesses, such as those on the Internet, suggest a gradual movement of the form beyond its Polynesian Pop roots. In this case and other examples, one notes pirate and Parrothead (Jimmy Buffett) merchandise being sold on the website.³⁵ Again, as illustrated in Vontiki's narratives of the form, tiki aficionados would not necessarily chastise an individual for drawing on Jimmy Buffett iconography in his or her own construction of tiki. Doing so, it would seem, would go against the openness and tolerance that seem to characterize the ethos of the cultural form. At the same time, within tiki's diehard community, there is some admonishment given to the individual who wishes to create his or her backyard themed space while taking too many liberties with it. In the mind of Sven Kirsten: "Don't use parrots or monkeys or pirate stuff. Nautical, yes. Asian, some. Mexican, never! Remember first and foremost, the culture is about the Polynesian triangle, the South Seas or South Pacific."[36]

Interestingly and quite telling for this study is the fact that Kirsten's admonishment comes not from the pages of one of his tiki tomes but from the piece "How to Go Tiki," written by the paint company Dunn-Edwards.[37] The author Kastle Waserman produced a very intriguing series of features on tiki subculture including emphases on major tiki gatherings (Tiki Caliente in Palm Springs, California), famous artists (Shag), and the many connections of tiki to material culture. Quite obviously, the focus of Dunn-Edwards is on paint colors, décor, and design. The company has a series of paints that they recommend were a typical person to create his or her own backyard tiki bar—these include Tiki Torch (DE5453) and Bamboo Screen (DE6193).[38] Waserman's articles, which are incredibly interesting in their own right in terms of how they detail the connection of the paint industry to themed spaces, reflect some of tiki's core principles, notably the emphasis on humor and campiness. At other levels, however, the writing parallels other industry-consumer guides to tiki that seem to "high culture" tiki up a bit. An article written on the subject in *Essence* suggests a variety of Polynesian-style items that would be appropriate for a backyard tiki party, while *Martha Stewart Living* offers an upscale, chic look at tiki by suggesting that first-timers focus on sophisticated material culture and culinary cues like leaf-covered candleholders, tropical fruit centerpieces, Hawaiian flower cushions, banana party cones, pineapple decoupage votives, grilled tuna skewers, and many other items.[39] The same tone of sophistication has been applied to the ubiquitous tiki drink—the zombie, scorpion, Mai Tai—with claims that "the faux-Polynesian aesthetic [of tiki] came off as phony" and there is a need to remake the signature tiki cocktail into something more refined.[40] Not all of the calls to remake tiki are based on high-culture arguments or a desire to focus on tiki's materiality. To return to cultural appropriation, we see that numerous critics have called for stylistic changes in tiki's core foundations in order to make room for more authenticity in tourism in Hawaii and Polynesian cultures.[41] The curious thing will be to assess to what degree tiki can maintain the spirit that drives its most die-hard followers to attend conventions like those described in this writing and also link its relevance to the larger culture. Of course, this last idea may belie its intentions of maintaining a postmodern locus as a subculture.

The Play of Culture: Themed Space, Themed Living, and Identity

Throughout my research I have discovered that tiki, in line with other forms of theming, is very commonly only understood through its material manifestations—the fruity drinks, the thatched bars, and the eponymous statues. In other work, I have suggested that theming is much more than an architectural or material approach to the world, it is a catalyst for social interaction and communitas, a performative practice, even an existential state.[42] During my years as a trainer in the themed spaces of Six Flags AstroWorld, I became more and more attached to forms that I called "lived theming"—or the ways in which material expressions of theming are internalized by individuals in numerous ways.[43] In the case of tiki, it is very unfortunate that few people ever stop and ask, "What does tiki mean to the aficionado," or "How does tiki provide meaning to an individual in an otherwise chaotic world?" Instead, the emphasis on the form is a reductionist one with little attention to these phenomenological and existential concerns. To the outsider, it may sound silly to speak of existential issues in the same context of tiki, but this is exactly what is needed. Earlier I wrote of the disturbance that resulted from my viewing of a tiki wearing sunglasses at a Las Vegas casino. My feeling came on the heels of extensive research in tiki's communities, and upon the occasion of seeing this image in Las Vegas, I could only imagine that all of the subcultural, existential, and counter-cultural spirits that are present in tiki will only be consumed by the popular forces that surround it—a fate not disconnected from the churning of cool-hunting in the world.[44]

As is the case with the material elements considered in tiki cultures, the ideational foundations—the existential, political, and ideological cues that form the ethos of tiki—also bespeak of tiki's postmodern form. The "play" of tiki in terms of culture suggests the meanings of process (as tiki is always "on the move") and of frolic, humor, and jubilation (as in tiki is a form that exists on the margins of serious culture). Not unlike the famous "tiki" bar Sip n' Dip in Great Falls, Montana—which combines tiki décor with live, performing mermaids—the ethos of tiki is deliberately contradictory. Some of its followers speak of its message of sexual freedom, fun, and a carefree lifestyle as a counter cultural statement. Sven Kirsten once said that tiki represented "a symbol of rebellion for the man in the gray flannel suit and the escape from his rigid lifestyle."[45] Others have suggested something quite the opposite with tiki framed as a "just...want to have fun" movement, nothing more.[46] Contemporary theorists of culture and subculture would say that such contradictions are not surprising given the nature of hybridity and flow in the modern world. As Michel Maffesoli has written, elective affinity groups are characteristic of contemporary society.[47] They are groups not unlike tribes—those entities of classic anthropology—yet they are organized "as a plural series of affinities."[48]

Tiki followers, not unlike those of themed reenactment and themed lifestyle communities, use tiki's iconic material and ideational forms to orient themselves in a world that often appears to be contradictory to the feelings that tie them to their movement. In common with Indianists, or individuals who thematically represent Native American cultures, is tiki's claiming of a certain authenticity in the face of outsiders' belittling discourse of inauthenticity, fakes, and kitsch.[49] Tiki also shares with other groups, such as those described in Anja Dreschke's ethnographic documentary *Die Stämme von Köln* (*The Tribes of Cologne*), in which the use of themed material culture, costume, architecture, performance, and games to create a lifestyle orientation suggests a playing with culture, or "playing ethnology," as Dreschke says.[50] The use of certain indigenous cultural foundations in forms of remaking suggests, on the one hand, a playful, creative, and expressive identity on the part of the user, and, quite problematically on the other, an identity that is formed without enough attention given to the consequences of the remaking.[51] Specific to reenactment communities is the growing suggestion that certain forms of reenactment and remade identity construction not take place, thus confirming, as Stephen Gapps writes, the fact that the act of reenactment exists on the knife-edge of the ethics of the appropriate and the politics of the inappropriate in terms of competing communities.[52]

Tiki's attractiveness is related to its inherently postmodern form. For its followers, it is apolitical (lacking the controversies inherent in Civil War reenactment circles); it is lifestyle focused (being a culture of entertainment, enjoyment, and nonchalance), and it is deliberately irreverent (sharing in common with Goth, renaissance fair enthusiasts, and other subcultures the Rabelaisian pleasures of "not caring all that much," as one person expressed to me). Tiki's failure lies not in its soft misogyny, cultural appropriation and essentialism, or its willingness to align itself with the all-too-popular, kitschy, or campy forms of culture, but in its inability to act on the nascent counter-insurgency that is evident within its cultures. Concerns with Victorian sexuality and unrealistic expectations of masculinity could be addressed with new expressions of gender and sexuality, perhaps paralleling the metrosexuality and pansexuality trends outside of tiki cultures, as well as with more critical reflections on gender, sexuality, race, and other intersectional and postcolonial issues. The desire to play with cultures in the plural, hybrid, and recombinant sense could be expressed with deeper reflections on the politics of appropriation which might result in the opening up of forms of cultural dialogue and intercultural communication. The attractiveness of overtly popular and even kitschy forms of culture could be met with a more critical and postmodern spirit that could challenge politically the forms of elitism and high culture that make up much of United States public and popular cultures—a parallel with groups like the Tribes of Cologne, Goth, and punk subcultures that illustrates, at least on one level, the desirability of challenging the status quo, of adopting and reformulating the mass hegemonic popular cultures of elites and corporations, and of celebrating politically the material markers, expressions, and lifestyles of "bad taste." Of course, a tiki aficionado would say that none of these expressions of response to the failures that I have identified are true reflections of tiki. But, then again, what *is* tiki?

Notes

1. See, John Mihelich and John Papineau, "Parrotheads in Margaritaville: Fan Practice, Oppositional Culture, and Embedded Cultural Resistance in Buffett Fandom," *Journal of Popular Music Studies* 17, no. 2 (August 2005): 175–202. Note: a video of this chapter is available at <https://youtu.be/z7SQTbcIz14>.

2. *Oxford English Dictionary*, <http://www.oed.com>.

3. The range of Sven Kirsten's books includes *Tiki Pop: America Imagines Its Own Polynesian Paradise* (Köln, Germany: Taschen, 2014), *Tiki Modern* (Köln, Germany: Taschen, 2007), and *The Book of Tiki* (Köln, Germany: Taschen, 2003).

4. See Kirsten, *Tiki Modern*, 14. Also worth noting is the mention of anthropology on the website of Trader Vic's—"Trader Vic's Worldwide has a full-time team of Anthropology experts who scour the globe to collect these hand-crafted pieces." Unfortunately, Trader Vic's corporate did

not return my requests for more information on this use of anthropology at their restaurants. See, <http://tradervics.com/brands/trader-vics-restaurant-brand/>.

5. Richard von Busack, "Tiki It to the Limit," *Metro: Silicon Valley's Weekly Newspaper*, January 4–10, 1996, <http://www.metroactive.com/papers/metro/01.04.96/tiki-9601.html>.

6. Clifford Geertz, "Thick Description: Toward an Interpretive Theory of Culture," in The Interpretation of Cultures: Selected Essays (New York: Basic Books, 1973), 3–30.

7. In fact, "There were no studies about that stuff," von Stroheim says of the first wave of tiki. Von Busack, "Tiki It to the Limit."

8. Vontiki is mentioned in Lisa McKinnon, "All Things Tiki Finds a Home on Main Street in Ventura," *Ventura County Star*, August 31, 2013.

9. Ryan Moore, "Postmodernism and Punk Subculture: Cultures of Authenticity and Deconstruction," *The Communication Review* 7 (2004): 305–327.

10. See Peter Burke, *Cultural Hybridity* (Cambridge, UK: Polity, 2009).

11. The same can be said of acceptance among Goth members. See the documentary Goth Cruise, directed by Jeanie Finlay (2008).

12. Scott A. Lukas, "Culture Sampling." Unpublished paper. <https://www.academia.edu/2249945/Culture_Sampling>.

13. Etymologically, essence is tied to the verb "to be" and, from the 1600s, has suggested "that ingredient which gives something its particular character." Online Etymology Dictionary, <http://www.etymonline.com/index.php?term=essence>.

14. See Bob Brier, *Egyptomania: Our Three Thousand Year Obsession with the Land of the Pharaohs* (New York: St. Martin's Press, 2013).

15. Gillo Dorfles, "Kitsch," in *Kitsch: The World of Bad Taste*, ed. Gillo Dorfles (New York: Bell, 1969), 15.

16. Barbarella Fokos, "Tiki Time," *San Diego Reader*, August 13, 2008.

17. David Thompson, "The Tiki Tribe," *Honolulu Magazine*, January 12, 2012 <http://www.honolulumagazine.com/Honolulu-Magazine/January-2012/The-Tiki-Tribe/>.

18. Other significant texts in the study of kitsch include Monica Kjellman-Chapin, ed. *Kitsch: History, Theory, Practice* (Newcastle upon Tyne, UK: Cambridge Scholars Publishing, 2013), Ruth Holliday and Tracey Potts, *Kitsch!: Cultural Politics and Taste* (Manchester: Manchester University Press, 2012), Celeste Olalquiaga, *The Artificial Kingdom: On the Kitsch Experience* (Minneapolis: University of Minnesota Press, 2002), Matei Calinescu, *Five Faces of Modernity: Modernism, Avant-garde, Decadence, Kitsch, Postmodernism* (Durham, NC: Duke University Press, second edition, 1987), and the journal *Home Cultures* (Volume 3, no. 3, 2006).

19. Herbert Gans, *Popular Culture and High Culture: An Analysis and Evaluation of Taste* (New York: Basic Books, second edition, 1999).

20. Peter Swirski, *From Lowbrow to Nobrow* (Quebec: Mcgill-Queen's University Press, 2005); Henry Jenkins, *Convergence Culture: Where Old and New Media Collide* (New York: New York University Press, 2008).

21. A similar example can be found in the rhetoric of many on the Left in the United States who disguise a class loathing of lower socioeconomic class shoppers and workers at Wal-Mart as a form of cultural critique.

22. Gans, *Popular Culture and High Culture*, x–xi.

23. Daniel Miller, *The Comfort of Things* (Cambridge Polity, 2008). Daniel Miller, "Things that Bright Up the Place," *Home Cultures* 3, no. 3 (November 2006): 235–249; see, in particular, 245–246.

24. Michel-Rolph Trouillot, "Anthropology and the Savage Slot: The Poetics and Politics of Otherness," in *Recapturing Anthropology: Working in the Present*, ed. Richard G. Fox (Santa Fe, NM: SAR Press, 1991). See also Sally Price, *Primitive Art in Civilized Places* (Chicago: University of Chicago Press, 1989) and Marianna Torgovnick, *Gone Primitive: Savage Intellects, Modern Lives* (Chicago: University of Chicago Press, 1990).

25. George Lewis, "Beyond the Reef: Cultural Constructions of Hawaii in Mainland America, Australia and Japan," *The Journal of Popular Culture* 30, no. 2 (Fall 1996): 123–135.

26. Fokos, "Tiki Time."

27. *The Air-Conditioned Eden*, BBC, documentary film (1996).

28. Joseph Flaherty, "The Bizarre Rise and Fall of the Tiki Bar," *Wired*, July 16, 2014.

29. Amy Ku'leialoha Stillman, "Pacific-ing Asian Pacific American History," *Journal of Asian American Studies* 7, no. 3 (October 2004): 263

30. Von Busack, "Tiki It to the Limit."

31. Lisa Kahaleole Hall, "'Hawaiian at Heart' and Other Fictions," *The Contemporary Pacific* 17, no. 2 (Fall 2005): 409.

32. Moore, "Postmodernism and Punk Subculture," 308.

33. Dick Hebdige, *Subculture: The Meaning of Style* (New York: Routledge, 1979).

34. Kirsten, *Tiki Pop*, 180.

35. One example is Tiki Kev, <http://tikikev.com/>.

36. Kastle Waserman, "How to Go Tiki," *Dunn-Edwards Specs+Spaces*, January 8, 2012 <http://www.specsspaces.com/Blogger/KastleWaserman/Article/HowtoGoTiki.aspx>.

37. Kastle Waserman, "How to Go Tiki."

38. See <https://www.dunnedwards.com>.

39. Jorge Arando and Jonell Nash, "Tiki to Go-go: Throw a Polynesian-style Beach Bash!" *Essence*, June 2001, 143–146. *Martha Stewart Living*, "Tiki Party Ideas," <http://www.marthastewart.com/901705/tiki-party-ideas/@center/905082/party-themes-and-ideas>. Again, a worthy study in parallel with the study of theming and paints would be a focus on themed party concepts like those of *Martha Stewart Living*.

40. Caroline Pardilla, "The New Tiki," *Los Angeles Magazine*, May 1, 2015.

41. Audrey McAvoy, "Nix the Tiki Bar and Coconut Bras: Hawaii Tourism Getting Authentic in Latest Offerings," The Associated Press, September 7, 2012.

42. Scott A. Lukas, "How the Theme Park Gets Its Power: Lived Theming, Social Control, and the Themed Worker Self," in *The Themed Space: Locating Culture, Nation, and Self*, ed. Scott A. Lukas (Lanham, MD: Lexington, 2007), 183–206.

43. Scott A. Lukas, "How the Theme Park Gets Its Power," 187. See, also, Derek Foster, "'Wii're Here for a Good Time': The Sneaky Rhetoric of Wii-Themed Parties," *The Journal of American Culture* 33, no. 1 (2010): 30–39.

44. See the documentary, *The Merchants of Cool* <http://www.pbs.org/wgbh/pages/frontline/shows/cool/etc/hunting.html>.

45. Becky Ebenkamp, "Tiki's Transcendency," *Brandweek* 38, no. 9 (1997): 42.

46. Kastle Waserman, "Shag: Cocktails with a Splash of Tiki," *Dunn-Edwards Specs+Spaces*, December 5, 2011 <https://stilettocity.files.wordpress.com/2013/03/kastle_waserman_shag.pdfv>.

47. Michel Maffesoli, *The Time of Tribes* (London: Sage, 1995).

48. Kevin Hannam and Chris Halewood, "European Viking Themed Festivals: An Expression of Identity," *Journal of Heritage Tourism* 1, no. 1 (2006): 24.

49. Petra Tjitsk Kalshoven, "Things in the Making: Playing with Imitation," *Etnofoor* 22, no. 1 (2010): 59–74.

50. Anja Dreschke, "Playing Ethnology," in *Staging the Past: Themed Environments in Transcultural Perspectives*, eds. Judith Schlehe, Michiko Uike-Bormann, Carolyn Oesterle, and Wolfgang Hochbruck (Bielefeld, Germany: Transcript, 2010), 253–267.

51. See Rory Turner, "Bloodless Battles: The Civil War Reenacted," The Drama Review 34, no. 4 (Winter, 1990): 123–136.

52. Stephen Gapps, "Mobile Monuments: A View of Historical Reenactment and Authenticity from Inside the Costume Cupboard of History," *Rethinking History* 13, no. 3 (September 2009): 395–409. See, also, Hannam and Halewood, "European Viking Themed Festivals."

PART IV

The Ways of Design, Architecture, Technology, and Material Form

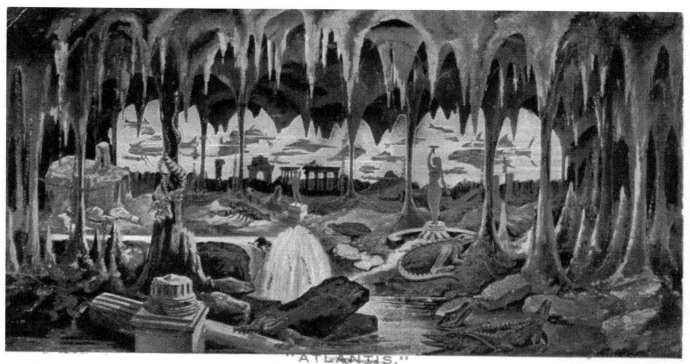
"ATLANTIS," THE SUNKEN CITY

8

The Effects of a Million Volt Light and Sound Culture

By Stefan Al

In 1963, Lee Klay, corporate art director of the Federal Sign Company, was charged to design a new sign for the Dunes casino in Las Vegas. At 181 feet tall, it was the largest freestanding electric sign in the world, as tall as the Leaning Tower of Pisa. Klay had designed not a simple shaft but a figure made of two white pylons that rose up to form a bulbous shape evoking an onion dome—it held two-story tall Dunes letters and a shimmering diamond, the size of a car (see image 8.1). A total of 624,683 watts or 3 miles of neon tubing and 7,200 electric lamps made it a significant upgrade from the Dunes' old sign, a 30-feet fiberglass Sultan with a single headlight—to the pleasure of General Electric, who awarded it the Sign of the Year.

The Dunes' sign shone so strong in firehouse red, patrons in the adjacent hotel tower complained of trouble sleeping, forcing hotel management to drape windows with blackout curtains. Yet, the Dunes' new pillar made it clear to everyone that the tall freestanding pylon sign was excellent at attracting attention from a distance. More and even bigger electric signs followed. The Dunes sign ignited what one sign designer called the "Golden Age" of signage in Las Vegas.[1] Electric signs were even bolted on entire casino façades. In 1965, sign company Ad-Art covered the Thunderbird casino with a 560-feet long sign, as wide as the entire front. Massive teal blue and green metal panels formed a sheer wall of light bulbs, 37,000 points of light in total (about the same amount as a low definition television), which flickered non-stop (see image 8.2). Architecture critic Reyner Banham wrote, "So the humble globe is to Las Vegas what the humble brick is to more conventional townscapes—the basic unit for building monuments and fantasies along the Street and Strip."[2]

Las Vegas in the 1960s was like an open-air laboratory experiment, pushing the limits of technology in architecture, with sign designers as uninhibited amateur scientists building structures of neon and light bulbs. It made other less technologically endowed places—New York or Los Angeles, for instance—look like Luddites. Why did other cities not build electronic architecture like in Las Vegas?

Architects were too repressed by "the traditions of architectonic culture, training, and taste," architect Reyner Banham claimed. Las Vegas' architecture of signage was so far out the norm, that it represented a paradigm shift: "a change from forms assembled in light to light assembled in forms."[3] Instead of being the stuff of bricks, Las Vegas' walls were made of energy. This architecture of "pure environmental power, manifested as colored light" was more "convincing" than conventional architecture: "...the effectiveness with which space is defined is overwhelming, the creation of virtual volumes without apparent structure is endemic, the variety and ingenuity of the lighting techniques is encyclopaedic."[4] This is why architects should get educated by studying the Strip: "a visit to Las Vegas would be as mandatory as a visit to the Baths of Caracalla or La Sainte-Chapelle."[5] Banham titled his first article about Las Vegas as a manifesto of technology: "Towards a Million Volt Light and Sound Culture."[6]

The Strip showed the potential of "electrics-as-place," the British avant-garde architecture group Archigram argued. "Las Vegas suggests that a really powerful environment can be created simply by passing an electric current—in daytime the hardware is nothing."[7] Electricity had turned the desert into an exciting place: "Lights combined with cinema projection can make the whole place a city where there is no city."[8] To prove their point, they used the city as inspiration for their speculative project the "Instant City," a touring assemblage of instantly mounted screens and sound systems that would wake up sleepy provincial towns with audio-visual bombardments. They only placed one critical side note regarding the

Image 8.1. The 181-feet tall Dunes sign (Nevada State Museum Archives, Las Vegas, 1963)

lack of interactivity of Las Vegas' signs: "It is suggested that the visitor himself could play with large areas of this lighting so that he makes it happen rather than gawk at it."[9]

But Hunter S. Thompson was less thrilled with such a possibility, describing a new invention he saw at Circus Circus casino:

> Stand in front of this fantastic machine, my friend, and for just 99$ your likeness will appear, two hundred feet tall, on a screen above downtown Las Vegas. Ninety-nine cents more for a voice message. "Say whatever you want, fella. They'll hear you, don't worry about that. Remember you'll be two hundred feet tall." Jesus Christ. I could see myself lying in bed in the Mint Hotel, half-asleep and staring idly out the window, when suddenly a vicious Nazi drunkard appears two hundred feet tall in the midnight sky, screaming gibberish at the world: "Woodstock Uber Alles!"[10]

Tom Wolfe had also cautioned about the oppressive effects of technology on human beings. He describes a gambler called Raymond, "a good example of the marvelous impact Las Vegas has on the senses."[11] A 34-year old engineer from Phoenix, he was showing symptoms of "toxic schizophrenia" and kept droning: "hernia hernia hernia hernia hernia hernia."

Like all visitors to the Strip, Raymond had been bombarded with a barrage of visual and audio components, starting with his drive into the city. "He had been rolling up and down the incredible electric-sign gauntlet of Las Vegas' Strip, U.S. Route 91, where the neon and the par lamps—bubbling, spiraling, rocketing, and exploding in sunbursts ten stories high…"[12] Downtown, where casino signs stood closer to another making one continuous façade of neon, was even more extreme. The juxtaposition of these various competing lighting sequences made downtown's Fremont Street appear like a television, tuned to all channels at once. Raymond had also been exposed to constant audio stimulation, from the ubiquitous Muzak to the rumbling of the slot machines.

> Muzak pervades Las Vegas from the time you walk into the airport upon landing to the last time you leave the casinos. It is piped out to the swimming pool. It is in the drugstores. It is as if there were a communal fear that someone, somewhere in Las Vegas, was going to be left with a totally vacant minute on his hands."[13]

Add to that to the sound of slot machines, "churning up over and over again in eccentric series all over the place, like one of those random-sound radio symphonies by John Cage."[14] This is why Wolfe titled his essay "Las Vegas (What?) Las Vegas (Can't Hear You! Too Noisy) Las Vegas!!!!"[15]

Las Vegas, claimed Wolfe, "has succeeded in wiring an entire city with this electronic stimulation, day and night, out in the middle of the desert."[16] And while some stimuli were more low-tech, such as the humming of the card dealers, and, "a stimulus that is both visual and sexual—the Las Vegas buttocks décolletage," (a sexually provocative dress for waitresses exposing the back) in the juxtaposition of these stimuli, "the casualties start piling up," including poor Raymond—who gets escorted out of the casino.[17] And whether Las Vegas' electrifying potential was desirable or not from a psychological standpoint, one crucial element explains why it could not be repeated elsewhere: cheap and plentiful energy, which made it all possible. In the early 1960s, Las Vegas per capita electrical consumption exceeded the national average by almost 300%, for only half the cost per kilowatt-hour.[18] One energy blackout or price hike and all of Las Vegas' audio-visual architecture would vanish into the silent night.

The Las Vegas walls of light were only possible because of that 660-feet thick wall wreaking havoc on the Colorado River—Hoover Dam—with its unstoppable supply of cheap hydro-electricity. Tom Young, founder of the YESCO sign company, had already anticipated its significance back when the dam was constructed in the 1930s. "Oh Mama! Think of all that electricity that's going to be available for our signs there in Las Vegas!"[19] All this cheap electricity explains why energy wastage did not bother casinos. On the contrary, they bragged about it. The light bulb galore of the Thunderbird screen, for instance, was publicized to use as much power to light 300 homes.

Image 8.2. The 560-feet long Thunderbird sign (University of Las Vegas, Nevada, Special Collections, 1965)

Light bulbs were particularly energy inefficient because of their use of a metal filament, heated to thousands of degrees

Fahrenheit, to generate light. Converting this electricity to heat meant a lot of energy waste, and a dramatic heating up of the environment. Downtown offered the most intense experience because the concentration of lights was so strong. Normal Mailer observed, "The Fremont was one electric blaze, the Golden Nugget another, the sky was dark, the streets were light, lighter than Broadway on New Years' Eve, the heat was a phenomenon. Was it ninety degrees at nine minutes to five, five in the morning now?"[20] Walking down Fremont Street felt like a piece of toast being browned on both sides, stuck in a toaster two stories tall.

Energy was also blown at cooling the desert. Without air conditioning, gamblers would not bear the desert landscape. As early as the 1950s, Las Vegas led the nation in per capita air-conditioning sales.[21] In casinos, the coolers were especially blasted high. "As everywhere else in Las Vegas," Wolfe wrote, "someone has turned on the air conditioning to the point where it will be remembered."[22]

But where in other deserts thick walls would have kept the cool air inside, Las Vegas' casinos removed their entire ground façades, so gamblers could more easily wander into the casino. A cool blast of air conditioning, an "air curtain," would seal off the desert heat, and in the process, waste more energy. Once again, developers did not waste time fretting about all this energy loss. In 1959, the Lucky Strike Bingo Hall had the first air curtain in Las Vegas, which it deliberately advertised on its sign: "Walk Thru the *Air Curtain.*" A quintessential modern experience, it offered gamblers a shower of cool in the midst of desert and filament heat.

Las Vegas' sign, sound, and air-conditioning systems drew so much heavy voltage that it exhausted the city's supply from Hoover Dam. City leaders had to leave the Nevada source to tap into the New Mexico gas fields in 1960. To add to the supply, they built coal-burning plants in Southern Nevada, which became the primary energy resource, the first of which burned 1,050 tons of coal a day.[23] All this energy came at a large environmental cost. Bulldozers carved out natural environments in search for coal. Pumps sucked up water to supply the plants, which drastically dropped and polluted the water table. Chimneys filled the air with nitrogen oxides, chromium, and arsenic emissions. While hidden to gamblers on the Strip, it was crystal clear to the Moapa Band of Paiutes adjacent to one of the plants, their families suffering from unusual high rates of asthma, lung disease, and cancer.

Blinded by their technological enthusiasm, Banham and Archigram had overlooked some essential implications. While Las Vegas pointed to exciting architectural possibilities in its integration of technology, if it had been mimicked in other cities, aside more casualties like Raymond, their hinterlands required a makeover. Bulldozers, river barricades, and scorching ovens devastating local ecologies embossed the other side of the electric coin, invisible from the escapism in Las Vegas. Meanwhile, on the front end of the electric supply chain, a one-of-a-kind profession emerged to maintain the spectacle of Vegas: neon sign patrollers, who drove around at night to spot broken lamps, like cable guys fixing a dead channel of a television set.

Notes

1. Charles F. Barnard, *The Magic Sign: The Electric Art–Architecture of Las Vegas* (Cincinnati, OH: ST Publications, 1993), 104.
2. Reyner Banham, "Las Vegas," *Los Angeles Times*, November 8, 1970.
3. Reyner Banham, *The Architecture of the Well-Tempered Environment* (London: The Architectural Press, 1969), 270.
4. Banham, *The Architecture of the Well-Tempered Environment*, 269.
5. Banham, *The Architecture of the Well-Tempered Environment*, 269.
6. Reyner Banham, "Towards a Million-Volt Light and Sound Culture," *Architectural Review* 141 (May 1967): 331–335.

7. Peter Cook, Ron Herron, and Dennis Crompton, "Instant City," *Architectural Design* (May 1969): 280.

8. Cook, Herron, and Crompton, "Instant City," 280.

9. Cook, Herron, and Crompton, "Instant City," 280.

10. Hunter S. Thompson, *Fear and Loathing in Las Vegas: A Savage Journey to the Heart of the American Dream* (New York: Vintage, 2010), 47.

11. Tom Wolfe, *The Kandy-Kolored Tangerine-Flake Streamline Baby* (New York: Macmillan, 2009), 5.

12. Wolfe, *The Kandy-Kolored Tangerine-Flake Streamline Baby*, 5.

13. Wolfe, *The Kandy-Kolored Tangerine-Flake Streamline Baby*, 6.

14. Wolfe, *The Kandy-Kolored Tangerine-Flake Streamline Baby*, 6.

15. Tom Wolfe, "Las Vegas (What?) Las Vegas (Can't Hear You! Too Noisy) Las Vegas!!!!" *Esquire*, February 1964.

16. Wolfe, *The Kandy-Kolored Tangerine-Flake Streamline Baby*, 6.

17. Wolfe, *The Kandy-Kolored Tangerine-Flake Streamline Baby*, 21.

18. Jay Brigham, "Lighting Las Vegas: Electricity and the City of Glitz," in *The Grit Beneath the Glitter: Tales from the Real Las Vegas*, eds. Hal Rothman and Mike Davis (Berkeley: University of California Press, 2002), 105.

19. John Hollenhorst, "Neon Museum in Las Vegas a Tribute to Utah Company," *KSL.com*, August 19, 2013.

20. Norman Mailer, *An American Dream* (New York: Dell, 1965), 250.

21. "Air Conditioning Is Important Here," *Las Vegas Review-Journal*, March 1, 1955.

22. Wolfe, *The Kandy-Kolored Tangerine-Flake Streamline Baby*, 16.

23. Jay Brigham, "Lighting Las Vegas: Electricity and the City of Glitz," in *The Grit Beneath the Glitter: Tales from the Real Las Vegas*, eds. Hal Rothman and Mike Davis (Berkeley: University of California Press, 2002), 105.

9

Et in Chronotopia Ego

Main Street Architecture as a Rhetorical Device in Theme Parks and Outlet Villages

By Per Strömberg

There is a connection between commerce and theater that can be traced back in time. The Parisian passages of the early 1800s are often referred to as a precursor of staged commercial venues. In Walter Benjamin's view, the commercial arcades of the nineteenth century appear as typical arenas for luxury consumption of the bourgeoisie and the life excesses of the modern city.[1] In similar ways, contemporary commercial spaces offer a seductive and dreamlike architecture that touches the internal lifeworld of humans.

This chapter investigates the nostalgic Main Street architecture, that is, the small-town idyll of the early 1900s as a rhetorical device for consumption in theme parks and outlet villages during the last three decades, and how this fictionalized setting interacts with corporate interests. In the analyses, I consider the small-town idyll as a mental and architectural archetype in two interchangeable contexts. First, how theme parks—such as Disneyland, and Liseberg and Astrid Lindgren's World in Sweden—have expanded and focused their establishments for food and souvenir-retailing to pedestrian streets of a small-town character. Second, how this Disneyesque Main Street, U.S.A. architecture and entertainment plays a more and more important role in retailing. A lucid example of this latter development is the creation of outdoor shopping malls in the shape of small towns, so-called outlet villages, exemplified by La Vallée village outside Paris and Baberino near Florence. The use of the small town as an architectural archetype is also a rhetorical way of turning these outlet villages into veritable tourist destinations.

The Miniaturization of Everyday Life

The combination of industrial expositions and fairgrounds is one of the legacies from the major world expositions of the nineteenth century. In Paris 1867, the organizers launched the idea of a separate fairground that gathered restaurants and rides at one site. The idea was well received and from that moment carnival culture became a regular, if not mandatory, ingredient at world expositions. Soon, historical and fictive settings of idyllic small-towns became a popular feature in various forms.

Garden architecture, such as Tivoli (1850s) in Copenhagen, and Paris' nineteenth-century passages and fairgrounds of world expositions with their machine-driven attractions, were the first themed environments in a modern sense, according to the urban sociologist Mark Gottdiener.[2] These theming techniques and attraction technologies were soon adopted by independent amusement parks such as Dreamland, Steeplechase Park, and Luna Park (1900s) at Coney Island on the outskirts of New York City. The architect Rem Koolhaas has described Coney Island as a test site for architectonic and social experiments. One of the attractions was Midget City, a miniature version of old Nuremberg with three hundred residents short in stature. Midget City—also called Lilliputia—was built in half scale with houses, squares, a fire station, and its own parliament. *The New York Times* noticed that: "grown people who visit it can see into third-story windows of the houses without standing on tiptoe." (3) The villagers, short in stature, were supposed to live an everyday life in front of the visitors but in completely different conditions. Promiscuity, homosexuality, and nymphomania were encouraged and promoted in order to attract and lure more visitors. If Dreamland was a laboratory for Manhattan, Midget City was a laboratory for Dreamland, Koolhaas argues.[3] During the Gilded Age at the turn of the century, Coney Island appeared as a haven of refuge for immigrants and the working class away from the urban life, social hierarchies, and self-discipline. The commercial interests were omnipresent. Steeplechase Park, Luna Park, and Dreamland appear as prototypes for the twentieth-century theme park in the way they integrate scenography, entertainment, technology, and commerce.[4] Devoid of the pedagogy of innocence, employed later by Walt Disney, Midget City was a strained if not perverted version of what would become a frequent ingredient at expositions and amusement parks around the world.

Image 9.1. The entrance to Midget City at Coney Island, Brooklyn (New York Public Library, date unknown)

In connection to Gothenburg's industrial exhibition in 1923, a similar miniature town called Lillköping (literally "small market town" in English) was built in the new amusement park area, Liseberg. Similar to Midget City at Dreamland, around twenty-five midgets were supposed to act as villagers in this miniature small-town setting. The idea was to let inhabitants short in stature perform a fictitious everyday life, celebrating weddings, and having parties. Lillköping was planned for the purpose of children's activities on a suitable scale. However, soon after the closure of the exhibition, the children's activities were given a completely different focus and the village was replaced by a dance floor.[5]

This phenomenon of miniaturization of an imagined world was not only inspired by Jonathan Swift's Lilliputian world, but it was also about the pleasure and power of visually embracing a fictional world of wondrous nature. Cynically, the midget towns paradoxically defined normality, that is, an innocent, everyday small-town fiction with the help of the "abnormal," that is, the actors short in stature.

The Chicago World's Fair in 1933 was the last big exposition with midget cities. However, main street architecture as a concept was already institutionalized and later adapted to modern theme parks, notably Main Street, U.S.A. at Disneyland (1954). At the street level, the architecture of Main Street, U.S.A. was full-scale, but it diminished gradually on the second and third floors through a series of false perspectives in two-thirds scale. The reduced scale displacement is an imaginative transposition of the architecture to an emotional level. The miniaturization represents a poetic metaphor for sentimentality, comparable to the blurred edges of an old sepia photograph. This illusionistic device was later put to work at other theme parks. In mid-1980s, the amusement park of Liseberg created its own main street setting called Storgatan (literally "main street" in English) with the same architectural device as used by Disney's Imagineers. It was a part of Liseberg's strategy to sentimentalize the theme park with references to old Gothenburg.[6]

The Idyllic Main Street as a Nostalgic Time Space

Main Street, U.S.A. at Disneyland occupies a central position within the theme park—both geographically and mentally.

Image 9.2. Lillköping at the theme park of Liseberg, Sweden (Museum of Gothenburg/Göteborgs stadsmuseum, 1923)

A railway station serves as the entrance to Disneyland. From this point, the visitors could reach the central hub in the middle of the theme park by strolling along a fin-de-siècle American main street. The whole area was structured like a Cartesian coordinate system with two axes representing reality-fantasy and history-future, in which Main Street, U.S.A. signifies "reality."[7] However, rather than referring to an existing reality, Main Street, U.S.A. is a national sign related to a metonymic place image of America and an overall expression of nostalgia, as well as Walt Disney's own biography and attempt to revive old memories from his childhood in Marceline, Illinois. He wished that the stores would sell the shoes he once used to buy, not because they were sought after, but because Disney recalled his childhood main street as such.[8]

Main Street, U.S.A. is nostalgia in materialized and visualized form. It is the original home of the petty-bourgeois lifeworld. The difficulties in talking about nostalgia in an unbiased manner are that nostalgia is often regarded as an ethical and aesthetic failure. The concept of nostalgia was introduced in the late seventeenth century and was described as a state of homesickness. Since then, the concept has been given a different meaning. Nowadays, nostalgia is a longing for a home that no longer exists or never existed, a sense of loss and displacement, which is a contemplative romantic fantasy, and also, the other side of the coin of modernity in times of change in society.

The historian Karin Johannisson divides the concept of nostalgia into two entities: first, the sentimental memory as an emotional state of mind, and second, the past as a "hidden and covered memory of something real and authentic."[9] The latter entity is the retroactive perception or feeling of how it was before the transformation, the change. By its selective nature, nostalgia filters and may create deceptive feelings of belonging, especially when businesses transform nostalgia into a commodity, Johannisson argues. The criticism of nostalgia has partly been addressed in its commercialization, its sentimentality and the lack of authenticity, and finally, its reactionary trace.[10]

Main Street, U.S.A. is perhaps the best example of the idyll placed in an idealized small-town bourgeois setting. The

Image 9.3. Main Street, U.S.A., Walt Disney World in Orlando, Florida (Photo by Per Strömberg)

origins of the concept of the idyll is found in the ancient poetry and pastoral landscape painting with its stylized rural and prosperous landscapes, often named Arcadia. However, the urbane reader's dream of an uncomplicated life was already represented in garden architecture, especially in pastoral English gardens and Queen Marie-Antoinette's private farm Le Hameau (1783–1785) next to Versailles. In the late 1700s, the German poet J. H. Voss made the idyll more domestic and homelike for the petty-bourgeois audiences with everyday family tableaus of realism and idealism. Since then, the idyllic dreamscape has become established in small-town environments clearly shielded from society's concerns and demands. The idyll is a picture of a congenial everyday life in silent euphoria. It is often clearly linked to an idealized small-town bourgeoisie that is clearly community-based—*Gemeinschaft*—in the sociologist Ferdinand Tönnies' words.

Time and space are the main entities of these fictional environments. The Russian literary historian M. M. Bakhtin introduced the concept of chronotope (literally, "time space") in order to describe the intrinsic relationship between time and space artistically expressed in literature.[11] A chronotope is both a cognitive concept and a narrative feature of language, but it can also be used as a concept to analyze themed environments of different temporality and geography. Although the chronotope only exists on a cognitive level, it can also be understood as real in a social context whenever it constitutes the setting for people's nostalgic play at Main Street, U.S.A. or as Storgatan at Liseberg.

The Theme Park as a Shopping Center

The idyllic small-town setting of Main Street, U.S.A. indisputably forms an extraordinary context for merchandising and consumption, as noted by Umberto Eco during his travels in the Disneyesque "hyperreality" in the mid-1970s. To him, the picturesque stores at Main Street, U.S.A. seem to be the first stage in a fantasy world that simultaneously attracts visitors to enter. Still, "their interior is always a disguised supermarket, where you buy obsessively, believing that you are still playing."[12] Although Eco's perspective is somehow reductionist and Eurocentric, there some truth in his statement. In fact, Main Street, U.S.A. at Disneyland conceals four big supermarkets from the 1950s covered with turn-of-the century façade.[13] They are "decorated sheds," as Venturi and Scott would have put it, which work as funnels through which the visitors must pass in order to reach other attractions with the risk of being stuck in a store.[14]

Similarly, as mentioned earlier, the goal of restructuring Liseberg in the 1980s aimed to emphasize the sentimentality of old Gothenburg. Of utmost importance, however, was to replace the previous modernist kiosks with a more logistically efficient and more attractive setting for eating and shopping. Another Swedish example in this genre is Astrid Lindgren's World in Sweden whose main street attraction Bråkmakargatan (literally "Troublemaker Street" in English) gathers all the stores and restaurants along one themed street based on one of Lindgren's books for children and once built as a setting for filmmaking.[15]

Image 9.4. Storgatan at the theme park of Liseberg, Sweden (Photo by Per Strömberg)

Hence, this business-driven "main street grammar" became a device frequently applied in theme parks around the world in the 1980s with Main Street, U.S.A. as a role model. Alan Bryman argues that merchandising and hybrid consumption (various forms of spin-off consumption) in themed environments are two of the most important business principles applied by Disney Company. Bryman takes a step further claiming that other sectors of society, the economy, and areas of cultural life are increasingly being infiltrated by a process he calls *disneyization*, that is, "the process by which the principles of the Disney theme parks are coming to dominate more and more sectors of American society as well as the rest of the world."[16] One might criticize Bryman for attaching too much importance to the Disney Company as a mediator of these ideas and strategies. However, his claims sound reasonable in view of how spaces of consumption have evolved in recent decades, how frequently Disneyland is referred to, and how main street architecture has been applied in settings other than theme parks.

The Shopping Center as a Theme Park

As mentioned earlier, the core of the mythical-poetic small-town setting in theme parks is the fusion between business and experiences, between shopping and entertainment. This connection has an extended history, but in the last few decades, commercial festival culture has evolved into various forms of which main street architecture has become an important element. The concept of shopping malls located in the urban sprawl developed after World War II. One of the most influential architects in this development, Victor Gruen, considered motoring to be a threat to the city center. He stressed that the solution would be to lead the traffic to the suburbs and to create greater self-sufficient complexes with adequate parking. In his view, the main attraction was an abundance of shops, giant store windows, entertainment, fountains, spinning sculptures, and rose beds. Moreover, this modernist consumer paradise would simultaneously also serve as a social meeting place. In the end, Gruen realized with resignation that his idealistic visions of modern social venues had paved the way for pure profit motives while the city centers had been emptied of stores.[17] This is still an urgent global problem, and cities have approached this dilemma in different ways in order to reclaim the historical townscape of commerce, or at least the image or feeling of it. One solution practiced in San Francisco (in 1964) was the reuse of historic buildings for commercial purposes. At Ghirardelli Square, an old chocolate factory was converted into a shopping district with a series of restaurants and small shops with boardwalks under the open sky.

As a defensive strategy by the commercial city centers, this concept of so-called festival marketplaces was invented and further developed by the Rouse Company at Faneuil Hall Marketplace in Boston, 1976. The marketplace, also known as Quincy Market, consists of older buildings of historical value near the harbor area that have been converted into a commercial center. The successful example of Faneuil Hall had many followers in the United States such as Harbour Place (Baltimore, 1981), the South Street Seaport (New York, 1983), the Riverwalk (New Orleans, 1986), and the Aloha Tower Marketplace (Honolulu, 1994).[18] Earlier, the Rouse Company has been described as a "commercial developer that regenerates down-market neighborhoods into Thumbelina-clean commercial strips Walt would have loved."[19] During his working life, James Rouse was a prominent urban planner in the United States and participated in the construction of several hotels and shopping malls. Not surprisingly, he has described Disneyland as "the greatest piece of urban design in the United States today."[20] In the anthology *Variations on a Theme Park*, the urbanist M. Christine Boyer adopts a more critical approach to festival marketplaces by characterizing them as city tableaus with no consideration of the life forms that are supposed to take place there.[21]

The reclaim of the old townscape also took other expressions at themed regional malls like West Edmonton Mall or the Mall of America in which whole city streets were covered with a giant transparent roof similar to the enormous Italian urban arcades built in the late 1800s. However, the clearest expression for the reinvention of the convivial small-town marketplace is the advent of outlet villages or outlet centers, which sprung from the traditional factory outlet; that is, a store attached to a factory or warehouse. The definition of an outlet village is a themed open-air center with branded outlet stores often offering discounted prices.

Main Street Architecture as a Rhetorical Device

The concept of outlet villages originates from the United States, but it has been spread around the world. In 1970, one of the first opened in Reading, Pennsylvania. Since the 1990s, the number of outlet villages has increased significantly in the United States. European cities have gradually adopted the American concept in the 1990s, notably in the United Kingdom, France, Germany, and Italy. One of the biggest players in the European market, Value Retail, was initiated by the American Scott Malkin in the mid-1990s. His plan was to create a consortium of outlet villages with sales of exclusive brands. As a result, Bicester Village in Oxfordshire opened in 1995. Today, several companies own and manage outlet villages in Europe of which Value Retail, McArthurGlen, Freeport, and Realm are the largest.

Outlet villages offer an alternative atmosphere to the modernist big-box mall. It is an exclusive and informal open-air setting for consumption located on the outskirts of bigger cities, as accessible as the standard malls. Since 1995, Value Retail has expanded to several European cities such as Wertheim, Barcelona, Oxford, Madrid, Paris, and Munich. The trend is to build small-town environments based on a vernacular main street architecture, sometimes with historical references, cast in a postmodern mold and adapted to today's consumer culture: "form follows fiction"—to quote the urbanist Nan Ellin's paraphrase of Sullivan's "form follows function."[22]

One prominent example is La Vallée Village outside Paris, managed by McArthurGlen. Here, the developer alludes to "the charming towns and villages of the Ile-de-France region," according to their webpage. McArthurGlen Group is the other large player on the market, and manages around twenty designer outlet villages in Europe. In Italy, several large outlet villages have been constructed in the last fifteen years designed by the architectural firm Hydea in Florence. Castel Romano, outside Rome, is a themed Roman forum, while at Barberino, close to Florence, the architects have picked up the design from the Renaissance and neighboring Tuscan villages: "it is an architecture of citation," according to their head architect.[23]

Image 9.5. South Street Seaport, New York City (Photo by Per Strömberg)

Convivial small-town idylls like the outlet villages recall the pre-industrial marketplace with allusions to a shared dream of authentic trade relations and spontaneous social interactions between people, what Jon Goss calls "agorafili," ultimately the myth of the genuine public space.[24] Thus, to recall the city's imaginary lifeforms has become an important ingredient in developing new attractive spaces of consumption of which the outlet village is a clear example. Architecture's main function in commercial settings is to encourage consumers to spend more money, in other words, an architectural setting that seduces.

According to Mark Gottdiener, the ability to "realize" capital (when the investments pay for themselves) is also linked to these spaces of consumption. There has been a shift from a producer-oriented to a consumer-oriented economy that is born out of global production competition where goods and services can be produced and delivered cheaply in low-wage countries. Thus, the difficulty of capitalism today is not the production system in itself (unless you consider the negative externalities of industrial production—for example, environmental destruction) but to create demand for products and sell them. Media, marketing, and advertising are crucial in creating this demand, although these are not enough. Therefore, it is in the interest of investors and entrepreneurs to look for new kinds of spaces of consumption that are more attractive and more able to give profitable returns.[25] Furthermore, the adoption of main street architecture in two different contexts demonstrates the interchangeability of different industries and their modes of consumption.

An increasingly common solution is to create narrative and themed spaces of consumption and turn them into tourist attractions in themselves in addition to being shopping centers—to make people stay and offer them a spatial experience as well. Gottdiener claims that the realization of capital is a driver towards more associative shopping settings. The symbolic values of goods and services—the very base of conspicuous consumption—are not only of importance when purchasing the product. The spatial context in which the purchase is made is of utmost importance as well.[26] If the purchase of goods and services fits with the setting, the consumer event becomes even more accurate. In this discussion, Sharon Zukin's analogy

Image 9.6. La Vallée Village, Marne-la-Vallée, Paris (Photo by Per Strömberg)

to Fredric Jameson's notion that "architecture is the symbol of capitalism" is very apt. She argues similarly that "architecture is the capital of symbolism" in consumer society.[27] In short, the idyllic backdrop of main street architecture functions as a rhetorical device for both theme parks and outlet centers to lure consumers into their stores. The small-town original home is supporting the business while it offers a sentimental, convivial, and somehow informal setting for the shopping experience in a framed time space, which is sometimes sought after by the consumers.

Et in Chronotopia Ego

The last heading alludes to a frequently depicted subject matter in arts and literature: *Et in Arcadia Ego* ("Even in Arcadia, there I [Death] am"). The essence of this proverb is that even in Arcadia, in fact a fictitious place—a pastoral idyll far away from fear and human degeneration—there are death and decay. Like a *momento mori* ("Remember [that you have] to die"), it reminds us about our own perishable existence. Likewise, chronotopia—a spatiotemporal fictive experiencescape beyond the dull everyday life—also has its undoing. The complications of the everyday idyll are implied in the reduction, of what is excluded. Idyllic serenity raises suspicion that things are not what we think they are.

Consequently, the Imagineers have to deal with this ambiguity and they have to design the idyllic setting so that it does not crack. Joseph Pine and James Gilmore, authors of the influential book *The Experience Economy*, recommend the managers of experiences to not only enhance the positive impressions but also "eliminate anything that distracts from the theme."[28] The authors stress the importance of pursuing the theme so that it appears as a veritable law. Or, to quote one of Disney Imagineering's own design rules—"out of sight, out of mind." In other words, what is sought after is a kind of visual and experiential homogeneity. Hence, it is in the interest of the suppliers of these commercial spaces to avoid distractions of the tourists' gazes, both visually and socially. First, technical installation and logistics are visually hidden behind and within the decorated sheds. Second, the main street architecture offers the appearance of a public space. However, theme parks and

Image 9.7. Temples of consumption at Castel Romano in the suburbs of Rom (Photo by Per Strömberg)

outlet villages are just semi-public spaces that are privately owned and not places for "social pollution," nor manifestations of civil rights.[29]

Different control strategies, such as guards and security cameras, are parts of the company's own defensive strategies against violence, harassments, and theft. According to Alan Bryman, control is the precondition for the four dimensions of Disneyization (theming; hybrid consumption; merchandising; and performing staff) to function optimally. This is done primarily through strategies of monitoring and control of criminal elements and deviant behaviors, personnel management, logistics, and design in order to enhance the experience, and ultimately increase the business profits.[30] Reassurance is crucial for Disney and a part of their pedagogy of innocence towards children. It is manifested in precautionary measures as well as in architectural design—the "architecture of reassurance," in Karal Ann Marling's words.[31] Or, to put it differently by using another of Nan Ellins' analogies, "form follows fiction *and* fear."[32]

Sharon Zukin goes further in the criticism of the Disney Company in her book *Landscapes of Power: From Detroit to Disney World* by claiming that Disney not only promotes its own commercial purposes, but also configures classes and ethnic groups through the exercise of spatial control. Almost on the edge of reductionism, she stresses that the main street architecture of reassurance is projected into a coherent landscape of corporate power. Walt Disney World represents a macro level of social control, while at Main Street, U.S.A. control is adapted to a micro level in the form of individualized, domesticated consumption.[33]

The decorated shed, hidden logistics, and technical installations as well as surveillance and social control in these themed environments remind of what Leo Marx describes as the "Machine in the Garden"—places that encourage visitors to think of the good life. At the same time, the idyll is overrun by "the machine," that is, modernity—logistics, rationalization, surveillance, and unrestrained capitalism—which is omnipresent.[34] Imagined havens say much about the present, and

Image 9.8. Barberino Designer Outlet outside Florence (Photo by Per Strömberg)

so does the criticism. Some people would argue that the idyllic existence is pure imagination, and if it does exist, it would probably mask negative implications. As the architectural historian Claes Caldenby notes, the idyll has always been problematic for the modernist movement. Modernism wants change, but formulates, paradoxically, utopias, albeit of a different nature. The idyll and the idea of "the good life" have always existed as an undercurrent to the dominant modernist movement. Caldenby believes that architecture, unlike other art forms, should not portray evil. At the same time, architects and city planners have to vouch for poetic power with a firm connection with political reality when designing idyllic settings.[35] How this balance may be achieved is still an unanswered question.

Notes

1. Walter Benjamin, *The Arcades Project* (Cambridge: Belknap Press, 2002).

2. Mark Gottdiener, *The Theming of America: American Dreams, Media Fantasies, and Themed Environments* (Boulder, CO: Westview Press, 2001), 45–50.

3. Rem Koolhaas, *Delirious New York: A Retroactive Manifesto For Manhattan* (New York: Monacelli Press, 1994), 49.

4. Scott A. Lukas, *Theme Park* (London: Reaktion, 2008), 21–64.

5. Per Strömberg, *Upplevelseindustrins turistmiljöer: Visuella berättarstrategier i svenska turistanläggningar 1985–2005*, Dissertation, Uppsala Universitet (Uppsala, Sweden: Fronton Förlag), 203.

6. Strömberg, *Upplevelseindustrins turistmiljöer*, 209.

7. Louis Marin, *Utopics* (London: Macmillan, 1984), s. 252

8. Karal Ann Marling, *Designing Disney's Theme Parks: The Architecture of Reassurance* (Paris: Flammarion, 1997), 82.

9. Karin Johannisson, *Nostalgia: en känslans historia* (Stockholm: Bonnier, 2001).

10. Johannisson, *Nostalgia*, 145–152.

11. Michail Michajlovic Bakhtin, *The Dialogic Imagination* (Austin: University of Texas Press, 1981), 84–85.

12. Umberto Eco, *Travels In Hyperreality* (San Diego: Harcourt Brace Jovanivich, 1986), 43.

13. Marling, *Designing Disney's Theme Parks*, 29.

14. Robert Venturi, Denise Scott Brown, and Steven Izenour, *Learning from Las Vegas* (Cambridge: MIT Press, 1972).

15. Strömberg, *Upplevelseindustrins turistmiljöer*, 200.

16. Alan Bryman, *The Disneyization of Society* (London: Sage, 2004), 1–2.

17. Jeffrey M. Hardwick, *Mall Maker: Victor Gruen, Architect of an American Dream* (Philadelphia: University of Pennsylvania Press, 2004), 212–224.

18. Kent A. Robertson, "Downtown Retail Revitalization: A Review of American Development Strategies," *Planning Perspectives* 4, no. 12 (1997): 390.

19. Bryman, *Disneyization*, 35.

20. Marling, *Designing Disney's Theme Parks*, 170.

21. M. Christine Boyer, "Cities for Sale: Merchandising History at South Street Seaport," in *Variations on a Theme Park: The New American City and the End of Public Space*, ed. Michael Sorkin (New York: Hill and Wang, 1992), 187.

22. Nan Ellin, *Postmodern Urbanism* (Cambridge: Blackwell, 1996), 135.

23. Strömberg, *Upplevelseindustrins turistmiljöer*, 229, 238.

24. Jon Goss, "Disquiet on the Waterfront: Reflections on Nostalgia and Utopia in the Urban Archetypes of Festival Marketplaces," *Urban Geography* 3, no. 17 (1996): 232.

25. Gottdiener, *The Theming of America*, 44.

26. Gottdiener, *The Theming of America*, 44.

27. Sharon Zukin, *Landscapes of Power: From Detroit to Disney World* (Berkeley: University of California Press, 1991), 260.

28. James H. Gilmore and Joseph B. Pine, *The Experience Economy: Work is Theatre and Every Business a Stage* (Boston: Harvard Business School, 1999), 51.

29. John Urry, *Consuming Places* (London: Routledge, 1995), 187–188.

30. Bryman, *Disneyization*, 131–135.

31. Marling, *Designing Disney's Theme Parks*, 81–86.

32. Ellin, *Postmodern Urbanism*, 145.

33. Sharon Zukin, *Landscapes of Power*, 232–233.

34. Leo Marx, *The Machine in the Garden: Technology and the Pastoral Ideal in America* (New York: Oxford University Press, 1967), 3–11.

35. Claes Caldenby, "Är inte idyllen nästan all right," *Artes* 2 (2002), 57–58, 64.

10

Remediation on the High Seas
A Pirates of the Caribbean Odyssey

By Bobby Schweizer and Celia Pearce

Pirates of the Caribbean presents the ideal case study on the complexities of remediation, adaptation, and immersion, because of the ways the fragmentary storyworld established in the theme park ride became codified in a transmedia narrative nearly thirty years after its inception. Unlike many other transmedia and cross-media franchises, Pirates of the Caribbean initially constructed its storyworld as a pastiche of intertextual references from different sources in the unique form of the theme park attraction. This attraction eventually came together as a film series and, in turn, was retrofitted to match the movies. Works in the franchise engaged in a form of—building on the work of Henry Jenkins and Michel De Certeau—"auto-textual poaching," where it plundered from itself, then adapted to accommodate its new form.[1]

This auto-poaching process can be traced back to the original 1967 Disneyland ride, which was itself a collage of elements poached from prior Disney animated and live-action films, as well as quasi-historical references. The subsequent remediations of this ride s and its offshoots draw heavily on indexical references between theme park and virtual reality attractions, films, consumer video gamesvideo games, and other licensed products. For over a half a century, Pirates of the Caribbean has been a textbook case of Bolter and Grusen's "remediation," complete with the hypermediacy for which Disney is so famous.[2]

In "Sequelizing Spectatorship and Building Up the Kingdom: The Case of Pirates of the Caribbean, Or, How a Theme Park Attraction Spawned a Multibillion-Dollar Film Franchise," film studies scholar Carolyn Jess-Cooke details the narrative sequelization of the Pirates storyworld, by framing the first movie *Curse of the Black Pearl* as itself a sequel to the ride.[3] Jess-Cooke's work provides a compelling account of the creation of a commercial media franchise around the "retextualization" of the Pirates storyworld through the mythology of Captain Jack Sparrow.[4] Significantly, this retextualization is seen by Anne Petersen as Disney attempting to "close" the open-ended text of the ride to limit the interpretive possibilities.[5] Petersen asserts that the depiction of Sparrow by Johnny Depp actually helps leave gaps in the story through Sparrow's whimsical disregard of expectations., However, by limiting the discussion to the movies, she neglects to consider the role of the spectator as participant in other franchise media. Both Jess-Cooke and Petersen's works are limited to the moment of the third film's release in 2007 and lack an account of the many Pirates spin-offs, including video gamesvideo games, that remediate and expand the Jack Sparrow and Pirates universes. Jess-Cooke sees the move to film as the "transposition of a spatial source to a textual 'world' and commercial franchise" and while certainly the commercial impact of the movies cannot be argued, the original rides were themselves a franchise distributed across the globe in Anaheim, Orlando, Tokyo, and Paris, both before and after the film series.[6] The Pirates of the Caribbean ride itself was a major marketing draw during the early years of Disneyland, helping increase annual park attendance by three million visitors between 1966 and 1969.[7] Furthermore, Jess-Cook neglects to account for the origins of the ride itself, drawn from films, which were in turn drawn from literature, as well as the pre-Jack Sparrow spin-offs, such as the DisneyQuest virtual reality ride.

The Curse of the Black Pearl is almost an anomaly for Disney—a successful translation in a period where other ride-to-film adaptations included the commercial failures *Mission to Mars* (2000), *Country Bear Jamboree* (2002), and *The Haunted*

Mansion (2003). Retrospectively, the success of *Black Pearl* seems guaranteed. However internal criticisms at the time within the Disney company that Johnny Depp's swaggering portrayal was "ruining the movie" reveal that the Jack Sparrowization of Pirates of the Caribbean was not the original intention.[8] The full integration of the Pirates world was something of an afterthought, with a pivotal turning point occurring not at the release of *Curse of the Black Pearl*, but at the release of the second film *Dead Man's Chest*. With this movie, a somewhat ragtag collection of adaptations comes together into a more unified whole. Disregarding historical anachronisms, the storyworld of Pirates of the Caribbean is most significant for depicting a specific place at a specific time. The spatial qualities of the Disneyland attraction, as far as the media empire is concerned, set the heading for a course in which the mythology of piracy in the Americas during the seventeenth and eighteenth century could be plundered for stories, characters, and visually evocative environments.

Media scholars Neil Randall and Kathleen Murphy criticize the first movie within the context of fidelity in adaptation studies, writing that:

> the film [*Curse of the Black Pearl*] borrows the title, certainly, and also the overarching subject matter of not-very-serious pirates and some of the visual images. Other than that, the film differs enormously from the ride, to the degree that calling it an adaptation strains the definition of "adaptation" to the breaking point.[9]

Perhaps a better framework for understanding how the ride became a movie emerges from looking back at how the ride created a narrative space by piecing together pirate mythology with imagery from swashbuckling tales, including Disney's own early films *Treasure Island* and *Peter Pan*. A simple approach to designing a ride about pirates could have been to recreate scenes from *Treasure Island* in their original narrative sequence, but Disney instead plucked elements from the historical imagination in much the same way that media scholar Henry Jenkins describes film and television fans as "textual poachers" who use pieces of existing stories to tell their own.[10] *Curse of the Black Pearl*, then, is better seen as Disney poaching the text of its own ride rather than adapting the source material.

While Jess-Cook's analysis focuses on the films from a cinema studies perspective and Petersen's work considers the role of the audience in negotiating the narrative, in the context of this collection of essays on theming and immersion, we wish to complement their work with an exploration of the various immersive and interactive experiences that have emerged from the Pirates franchise, as well as explore the auto-textual poaching, remediation, and indexicality that occurs throughout all the various elements of this paradigmatic transmedia storyworld. The complexity of the analysis presented here is punctuated by the diagram below (Chart 10.1), created by the authors, which attempts to map the relationships and influences between the various instantiations of the Pirates world.

Storyworld and Story Space

In *A Theory of Adaptation*, Linda Hutcheon argues that the pleasure of adaptation is in the repeated re-telling of a familiar story.[11] However, the enduring multigenerational appeal of the Pirates franchise is more a matter of a love affair between fans and the familiar tropes of not so much a story as a story*world*, to borrow from Marie-Laure Ryan.[12] According to Ryan, as a general rule, storyworlds are "not a collection of fragments," but can be "felt as a totality or a whole." But what is interesting about the most successful storyworlds is that they are not conceived all at once.[13] They are pieced together over time. The underlying logics that govern the *Pirates* storyworld across media are, to use the words of Captain Barbossa, "more what you'd call 'guidelines' than actual rules."

While it's true that J.R.R. Tolkien's self-proclaimed act of "subcreation" entailed conceiving an entire world prior to embarking on the "storification" of Middle Earth, many more contemporary fictional worlds, such as *Star Trek* and *Star Wars*, and certainly the worlds portrayed in superhero comic books, are designed to be open-ended and extensible.[14] In many respects, the Pirates world that encompasses all the different properties explored in this chapter is in fact very much the "collection of fragments" Ryan claims cannot build storyworlds. Pirates is composed of the fragments from two early classic Disney films and the literature from which they were derived, fragments of a ride woven into the newer films, fragments of the films woven into the games and back into the ride, …and so forth. It is more of a collage than a totality

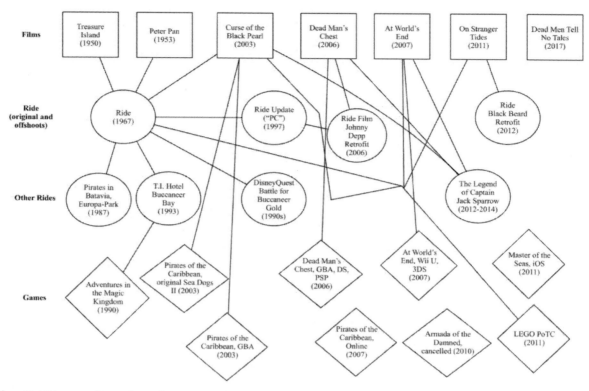

Chart 10.1 Diagram of Interrelationships Between the Various "Pirates" Remediations

or a whole and the looseness of its fragments afford the creative interpretation that immerses park-goers, movie watchers, and game players in different ways.

The relevance of storyworld—particularly the "world" aspect—can also be seen in conversations about space and place. In some senses, the Pirates world is more of a place to be explored through narrative than a narrative per se, although the two are intimately intertwined. Psychogeographer Yi-Fu Tuan argues that the distinction between space and place lies in three elements: experience, meaning, and story.[15] The Pirates of the Caribbean ride constructs just such a meaningful place, interweaving its hypermediated remediation of history, myth and fiction with the ride's intergenerational appeal that has been woven into the lore of family histories.[16] Hence, the indexing of story elements back and forth between the ride, films, and games adds pleasure to those who have experienced all three.[17]

Turning the Tides on the Original Ride

The original Disneyland ride Pirates of the Caribbean was a landmark in the emergence of the theme park. What set the Disney theme park apart from other earlier amusement parks such as Tivoli Gardens and those of Coney Island was the tighter integration of narrative with attraction. Although Walt Disney's vision for Disneyland was initially unconnected to his company's animation and film properties, colleagues (including his brother, Roy Disney, who ran the business side of the operation), encouraged a more integrated approach by including the company's other assets in the rides.[18] This made the Disney Company perhaps the first true producer of "transmedia," adapting and repurposing works from other sources, as well as from its own work across a variety of different media.

The original Disneyland ride, completed in 1967 shortly after Walt's death, did not have a one-to-one relationship with any existing film or character. Many of the park's other attractions were derived directly from its intellectual property, such as Tom Sawyer's Island (1955) and the Swiss Family Robinson Treehouse (1962), both of which were based on popular (notably derivative) Disney films. Pirates, instead, was a pastiche of film references, which included primarily the studio's first live-action film *Treasure Island* (1950), the pirate sequences in the animated feature *Peter Pan* (1953), oblique references to the *Swiss Family Robinson* film (1960), and also historical and fictional pirate worlds. Thus the Pirates storyworld, as instantiated in the original ride, was already cobbled together from several different sources across multiple media.

Hypermediated in the extreme, the ride has a number of distinctive features. As with all theme park experiences, it is highly social, with guests traveling in shared boats. While the ride is essentially a passive "on rails" theme park experience, it is perhaps the most immersive of the Pirates world instantiations. This is in part due to the physical embodiment required by the ride participation, as well as the "practical" (physical) effects that surround riders. The preponderance of water means you can actually get wet, and also creates a strong olfactory sensation that is entirely unique to the physical theme park attraction medium: you can actually smell the world, with its dank, moldy, dusky aroma; it is at once evocative of a pirate world, but also smells distinctly like a theme park ride. Additional practical effects, such as pyrotechnics, also add smells and even temperature changes. The portion where you sail into the middle of a cannon battle is a particularly compelling example: You hear the cannons exploding, the cannonballs flying overhead and splashing in the water next to your boat. Pirates also exemplifies an early use of Audio-Animatronics—the life-sized, pre-programmed robotic characters pioneered by Disney.

Although it is on rails, the ride uses spatiality in an interesting way because the 360-degree view means you cannot look at everything at the same time. Primarily sound, and secondarily light and practical animation effects, draw your attention to various parts of the panoramic scene. Because of this, although short, the original Pirates of the Caribbean ride makes for a highly repeatable experience in which the audience cannot see everything on one pass-through. As Walt Disney said to animator and ride scriptwriter Xavier Atencio: "Think of it this way… it's like a cocktail party: you hear bits and pieces of conversation, and you get the idea of what's going on. Our boat ride is even better; if you want to hear the rest of the conversation, come back for another ride!"[19] Walt Disney also saw merchandising, in which visitors are fed directly into the gift shop after the ride, as an integral part of the immersive experience that would allow guests to take home a piece of the world with them.[20] Judging by the popularity of *Pirates*-themed action figures, toys (such as swords and goblets), and Halloween costumes, the merchandising strategy has successfully supplemented the property's numerous other remediations.

A typically short experience, the original ride runs at around fifteen minutes in length and subsequent versions in other parks were shortened to around ten minutes. The format does not lend itself well to the long-term narrative or character development that is better captured in novels, films, or even long-play games. Instead, it relies largely on two narrative modes. The first is spatial storytelling, in which a static scene conveys a narrative arc. One example is the pirate's cave with its lushly appointed bedroom filled with mounds of gold. Without actually showing us the conquest which led to this bounty, our imaginations can fill in the blanks. The second narrative mode is the Audio-Animatronic character vignettes that play throughout and collect to make up the world—the "cocktail party" chatter that Walt described. Rather than a fully developed narrative arc, these vignettes are used to create tension, conflict, drama, and humor. The battle mentioned earlier, with cannonballs whirring overhead and splashing in the water, with commensurate yelling by combatants on each side, is a prime example of the use of immersive vignettes in the ride. Perhaps the most infamous of the vignettes is the notorious wench-chasing scene. Here, a bristly pirate drunkenly pursues a buxom woman, just out of reach, in endless circles. In the service of political correctness, in 1997, this vignette was updated to depict the woman carrying a pie, downplaying the ribald nature of the original scene. The fact that this scene is both literally and figuratively circular also explains the underlying limitations of the format. As guests sail through in their boats, they may pick up a scene at any point, so scenes must repeat in such a way that they can be seen by all visitors.

Because the films were based directly on the ride, there are a number of cross-referential indexical moments in the films. For instance, the subtitle of one of the films, *Dead Man's Chest,* is a direct line taken from a song that recurs throughout the ride. *Dead Men Tell No Tales*, the title of the film in production at this writing, is the inscription that greets players at the entrance to the ride. *Curse of the Black Pearl* opens with a young Elizabeth Swann singing "Yo Ho (A Pirate's Life For Me)" and, the film's introduction of Tortuga subtly portrays the extras in the scene as if they were in a loop like the ride's animatronic characters. The ride's portrayal of skeleton sailors also introduces notion of the supernatural ghost world that appears throughout the films. As Scott A. Lukas points out, multiple generations have integrated their memory of this ride into family lore.[21] Older adults watching the movies will get the references to the original ride, while younger people seeing the ride for the first time, having seen the movie, will perceive the reciprocal connections between the two.

The vignette technique also created a perfect opportunity during the ride's 2006 retrofitting to make indexical references to the movies and, in particular, the character of Jack Sparrow. This update was a turning point in the "Pirates" worldbuilding enterprise. Prior to this, the world continued to function as a kind of remix, bringing together disparate elements from the ride, the films, and the early games which were retrofitted by Disney from generic pirate-themed games to connect to the film properties. From this point forward, a more deliberate integration seems to occur, in which a conscious effort is being made to construct a cohesive storyworld from a vast collection of components across multiple media. The integration of Jack Sparrow into the physical ride marks a paradigm shift in the overall approach to the transmedia blockbuster the franchise has become.

Before Jack Sparrow: Pre-Film Instantiations

Prior to the advent of the *Jack Sparrow* films, several attempts were made at reenvisioning the Pirates world in other immersive media that are critical for understanding how this world has evolved through the pastiche approach mentioned previously. These various instantiations also demonstrate the strengths and weaknesses of different media at creating a sense of immersion, as well as helping us to better understand the complex relationships between the remediations that have taken place in various media.

Derivative Attractions and Media

Adventures in the Magic Kingdom (Nintendo Entertainment System)

A sole example of a game that adapted the ride before the influence of the film series can be found in the 1990 Nintendo Entertainment System game *Adventures in the Magic Kingdom*. Developed by Capcom, a notable Japanese video game company, the game revolves around a boy who arrives at the Disney theme park only to be informed by Mickey Mouse that the keys to unlock Cinderella Castle have been misplaced by Goofy in various places around the park. The game adapts a number of well-known rides, including Pirates of the Caribbean, into short games that each reward the player with one of the lost keys for completion. This first adaptation of the Buccaneering ride into a game followed the scenes and narrative of the boat trip relatively closely, though the game level is designed after the "platforming" genre that involves controlling a character that can walk across a scrolling screen as they jump on platforms, climb ladders, dodge enemies, and collect items. The player arrives on the island on a boat and must rescue six captured villagers while encountering different areas representing parts of the ride that include the port, the rowdy streets of Tortuga, depictions of the burning village, and a skeleton-filled treasure trove reminiscent of the last scene in the ride.

This first attempt atnd adapting the ride to a game has perhaps the most fidelity of any of its digital offspring. This is because it takes place within the ride itself, allowing players to go "off the rails" and become participants. Without a movie franchise narrative to adhere to, the spirit of the ride's aesthetic is maintained through the linear narrative progression of the stage and the familiar scenes from the original ride.

Treasure Island Hotel, Las Vegas

The Treasure Island hotel, while not a Disney property, is perhaps the most direct homage to the original theme park ride of all the property's pre-film series manifestations. Built in 1993 and designed by the Jerde Partnership, including a number of theme park professionals who had worked on Disney theme park projects, the hotel draws many of the same visual portrayals and narrative techniques from the ride. "Buccaneer Bay," the original live show at the front of the hotel, ran hourly and included water, fire, and a physical ship battle in which a pirate vessel actually sailed from behind a mock pirate village into a giant pool of water at the front of the attraction. At the time it opened, pirate theming could also be seen throughout the Treasure Island Hotel. The hotel had a makeover in 2003, rebranding itself as "TI." The pirate theming was abandoned and "Buccaneer Bay" was replaced with another more adult-themed pirate show, "The Sirens of TI," which closed in 2013.

DisneyQuest: Battle for Buccaneer Gold

The DisneyQuest Pirates of the Caribbean: Battle for Buccaneer Gold virtual reality experience emerged at the peak of the high-end virtual reality craze of the late 1990s. It was part of a large indoor attraction that included a variety of immersive experiences based on various Disney properties. It should be noted that DisneyQuest was created by a team within the theme park division, the so-called "Imagineers," coming out of its virtual reality lab, and predates both the film and consumer game series by about a decade. The attraction also uses many of the techniques used in theme parks.[22] Opening in 1998, it was a high-end virtual reality attraction that attempted to bring more interactivity to the Pirates storyworld by focusing on sea battles. Four players stepped into a simulated pirate ship, complete with motion base platform, a physical steering wheel and physical cannons, surrounded by a 360-degree screen. By combining physical and virtual elements, the experience created a high degree of both agency and immersion, but in a very focused and specific way. It did not include, for example, land or sword battles, or a treasure-hunt mechanic. It also did not include practical effects as were seen in the original ride or in the derivative Treasure Island Hotelhotel. Whereas the original ride had character vignettes (as opposed to full-blown narratives), the first-person nature of the game put players themselves in the roles of pirates on the high seas.

The designers of Battle for Buccaneer Gold describe a delicate balance between providing agency and creating a consistently satisfying experience for players. The steering of the ship, a level of agency not afforded by the dark ride, introduced the problem that players could run adrift and go to the wrong place. The designers employed the technique of the "weenie," a term invented by Walt Disney himself to indicate a visible landmark that draws visitors to a certain geographic area. In Disneyland, the weenies are the high points that establish the various zones throughout the park: The Matterhorn for Adventureland, Sleeping Beauty's Castle for Fantasyland, Space Mountain for the World of Tomorrow. Additionally, since the players were chasing simulated pirate ships, the designers could have those ships move in a direction they wanted the developers to follow, leading them to the desired destination.[23]

The Jack Sparrow Universe

The release of *Pirates of the Caribbean: Curse of the Black Pearl* in 2003, directed by Gore Verbinski, represents a significant shift in what had previously been only a fragmentary storyworld. Before the film, as previously detailed, the Pirates mythos is constructed not of a unifying narrative but rather a series of adaptations and translations. The film's release signaled the universe of the Pirates ride transitioning from this series of fragments and tableaus into a cohesive narrative universe centered around the charismatic ne're-do-well Captain Jack Sparrow played by Johnny Depp. At this point, as Jess-Cooke describes, "the Pirates [film] franchise becomes an 'original' or source, insofar as Sparrow's relation to the franchise becomes defined as a secondary textualization of an originating work."[24]

Jess-Cooke describes the movies as being "reexperienced" by a spectator, relying on knowledge of the original source ride to constitute their relationship to these new texts by way of sequelization.[25] But, it can be argued that very little knowledge of the ride is required to understand *Curse of the Black Pearl*. Instead, translations of ride elements to the big screen function more as winks and nods to the members of the audience who recognize that the prisoners in Port Royal that are attempting to coax the key-carrying dog over to their jail cells are making reference to a scene from the ride. The savvy audience member would also have picked up on Jack Sparrow's fourth-wall breaking warning to the prisoners that, "you can keep doing that forever, that dog is never going to move." The film does illustrate, however, that the dog *must* move when the formal structure of narrative cinema extends a moment trapped in cyclical time beyond the ride spectator's' passing glances. Thus, the spatial storytelling of the immersive ride environment gives way to visual and temporal qualities of film, as well as a stronger investment in the characters it portrays.

Yet, the transition to the Gore Verbinski films as the new "original" was neither immediate nor elegant. In fact, while *Curse of the Black Pearl* is often seen as the turning point, it was merely just a change in the prevailing winds. It was not until the release of *Dead Man's Chest* that the impact of the first movie was seen in updates to the theme park attractions and companion video games whose stories aligned with the films. The years between the two movies are decidedly less cohesive than one might expect from a major media corporation's attempt at transmedia synergy. The many Pirates of the Caribbean video games, in particular, reveal that the Walt Disney Company's attempts to bring in the narrative universe established in *Curse of the Black Pearl* was not as simple as creating quick spin-offs and movie tie-in products. The process of adaptation involves as much retrofitting as it does translation between media sources. Thus, despite their release alongside the films of the same name, the Pirates of the Caribbean movie tie-in games change the narrative universe in small ways. Video games based on Pirates of the Caribbean demonstrate the challenge of adapting linear narrative media into digital game form and the complexity of aligning media franchise storyworlds as they are being developed on a massive scale.

When the ride opened in 1967 in Disneyland, video games had not yet emerged into popular culture. But, by the premiere of the first movie in 2003, games had become a cultural force and the world of Pirates had new waters to sail in. Over a dozen games have remediated different aspects of the rides and films, illustrating the ever-changing world of the Pirates fiction, video game technology, and corporate influence on the products of a successful media franchise. Rather than being in perfect lock-step with the stories told in the films, most of the video games set in the Jack Sparrow universe stray from the course to varying degrees as they reconstitute and remediate the player's immersion as participant and spectator in the Pirates storyworld.

The success of the film *Pirates of the Caribbean: The Curse of the Black Pearl* was not guaranteed. However, propelled by the weight of the Mouse Machine, the force of Producer Jerry Bruckheimer, and a bankable cast of movie stars, the summer blockbuster stood a better chance than most spin-offs. And yet, the synergy that companies strive for in their transmedia properties was not evident in the tie-in game released in time for the first movie's premier. Bethesda Softworks, the publishing company for a Russian development studio called Akella, had been brought on by Disney to take a pirate-themed game already in development and retrofit it to relate to the movie. Because it was too late in the development process to integrate the film's story into the game, Akella retrofitted their role-playing game *Sea Dogs II* to include brief narration from Keira Knightley as Elizabeth Swann and to make occasional reference to the Black Pearl ship. Despite Disney's intervention, much of the original game persisted in the PC and Xbox release simply titled *Pirates of the Caribbean*. Much as the film was a blank canvas to capture the spirit of high-seas adventuring, the game was a classic tale of a young pirate captain named Nathaniel Hawk embroiled in a larger political conflict between nations in a large, open 3-D world. Free from the constraints of the Disney narrative, Akella's game could flourish on its own in an adventurous pirating world. In fact, this game became its own jumping-off point for a series of fan-based textual poaching—modifications that retrofitted the game with updated graphics, technical fixes, and new ship and character models.[26]

The consumer demographic of the PC and Xbox were not necessarily the younger audience of video game players that Disney typically targeted with its movie and cartoon game adaptations. Instead, Disney also published a game for the extremely popular Nintendo Game Boy Advance handheld system with the full title *Pirates of the Caribbean: Curse of the Black Pearl*. Similar to its Akella produced counterpart, this game by Pocket Studios bears no similarity to the movie with which it shares its name. The player takes on the role of a sailor named Jack (but not Jack Sparrow) who has been kicked off the Black Pearl by Barbossa for insolence. Like the Akella game, the gameplay is a mix of exploring and fighting on land with a naval combat component in which the player is left to assume that the game somehow extends the universe of the film. Yet, because both games diverge so wildly from the *Curse of the Black Pearl* movie, they're perhaps both most appropriately thought of as additional fragments in the broader pirate mythology that originally fascinated Walt Disney. The Sparrow-ization of the Pirates empire would really not take hold for another three years.

Dead Man's Chest and the Sea Change

Dead Man's Chest represented a major shift in the constitution of the Pirates experience, wherein the previously fragmentary world of themed spaces became bound to the pervasive narrative re-centered on Jack Sparrow. The movie retroactively figured *Curse of the Black Pearl* as the first in a trilogy, despite its closed ending. During this period, Disney's many media releases relied more heavily on the plot of the films than they did broader pirate mythology. The experience of imagining what it might be like to go adventuring on the open waters of the Caribbean Sea in the ride, Xbox and Game Boy games, and even in the first movie, was replaced by the spectatorial position of watching the familiar faces of Captain Sparrow, Elizabeth Swann, Will Turner, and the rest of the cast embark on a story arc that spanned two movies.

As Petersen writes, using "a static message and a concrete text (film), Disney could effectively commodify and capitalize upon its narrative, its character, and its sequels."[27] This commodification attempted to shift the role of the park-goer, movie watcher, and video game player into consumer rather than participant. However, surveying the media that succeeded the movie illustrates that this role shift was not cut and dry.

Thematically, *Dead Man's Chest* is a much darker film than *Curse of the Black Pearl*. With Davy Jones' crew of grotesque sea-creatures, a story of a scorned lover, new forces of outside authority, and its themes of purgatory and death, *Dead Man's Chest* strayed from the relatively lighter—even comical—tale of swashbuckling skeleton pirates that originated with the ride. Though *Curse of the Black Pearl* concludes with Captain Jack Sparrow setting upon the high seas in search for more adventure, its story does not demand a sequel because there are no loose threads. Rather, it invited the possibility of the continuing adventures of Jack Sparrow and the Black Pearl crew. *Dead Man's Chest* does the double-duty of both serving as a sequel while establishing a line of continuation that could sustain the all-popular trilogy format of film franchises.

Re-Remediation: The Ride Retrofit

As mentioned previously, the theme park attractions in Anaheim and Orlando were refurbished and retrofitted in 2006 to incorporate the inimitable Captain Jack Sparrow in an attempt to weave a larger storyline into the experience. The changes were highly indexical, with the implicit assumption that most riders had seen at least one of the films and would thus recognize Johnny Depp popping up out of a barrel or yelling at his adversaries from the helm of a ship. Not only does Johnny Depp's likeness appear in a number of places, parts of the script were altered to create a more linear narrative in the ride. Unlike the tableaux of Caribbean life in the ride's original instantiation that pieced together pirate mythology into a loose chronology, the retrofitted ride adapts the movie's premise that Sparrow is entangled in all pirating affairs. This is largely accomplished through depictions of Jack Sparrow hiding in plain sight while pirate ruffians warn that he is about and seeking the treasure. This character is used as a narrative through-line, albeit roughly, that the audience can immediately identify with and, at the ride's conclusion, Sparrow is seen sitting atop a pile of treasure singing "Yo Ho (A Pirate's Life For Me)," like at the end of *Curse of the Black Pearl*. Additionally, the initial waterfall was updated to include a curtain of mist on which is displayed a projection of Davy Jones welcoming boats into the dangerous waters, and the battle in the harbor was modified to become helmed by a cantankerous Captain Barbossa.

Not only was the ride retrofitted for the movie but other changes were made in the parks as well. In the Adventureland area outside of the Pirates of the Caribbean ride in the Magic Kingdom, "Captain Jack Sparrow's Pirate Tutorial" treated audience members to a simple stage show of swashbuckling and swaggering that incorporated audience participation. And in Disneyland the original Tom Sawyer's Island was updated in 2007 to become Pirate's Lair on Tom Sawyer Island, completely overhauled and re-themed to focus on elements from the movies. Each addition demonstrates how the initially contained experience of being immersed in the space of the ride was expanded outside the bounds of the attraction walls.

Playing Pirates: The Game Franchises

Unlike *Curse of the Black Pearl*, which debuted with two movie tie-in games that had clearly been rushed through production, *Dead Man's Chest* and *At World's End* (both films having been shot at the same time) demonstrated a more coordinated effort to extend the movies into video game worlds. In a press release on April 18, 2005, Buena Vista Games—the interactive entertainment division of The Walt Disney Company—announced the release of a slate of games that would be offered alongside the film sequels.[28]

What is most remarkable about the *Dead Man's Chest* games is that their timing and platforms required separate development studios to produce three distinct pieces of software. Typically, mass-market releases like movie tie-in games would be developed for one target platform and then the software would be translated and adapted to run on a different platform's hardware. This process is difficult even when all of the hardware produces similar looking games, but the *Dead Man's Chest* games were planned for three distinct platforms. While the Nintendo DS and Sony PlayStation Portable (PSP) could both render 3-D graphics, the older Nintendo Game Boy Advance could only render 2-D. The DS hardware featured two screens, the bottom of which was a touchscreen display. And the PSP, though only a single screen, had better

3-D graphical capability than the DS. Three distinct platforms produced three distinct games, though their common thread was that they featured characters and actor-likenesses from the movie and loosely followed the film's plot.

Perhaps even more unusual than the three different versions of the *Dead Man's Chest* game on handhelds was the timing of the release of *Pirates of the Caribbean: The Legend of Jack Sparrow*, an entirely separate game for the PlayStation 2 and PC. *The Legend of Jack Sparrow* revisited scenes from *The Curse of the Black Pearl* while also detailing all-new adventures of the eponymous captain. Released in 2006, the game uses a flashback narrative conceit in the form of Jack Sparrow recounting embellished (or perhaps completely fictional) stories to Will Turner while they await being sentenced to the gallows. The odd timing of the game's development period between the first and second movies and its lack of reference to the *Dead Man's Chest* story make it a curious media artifact that doesn't fit with the typical assumptions of movie-to-game synergy. In some ways, *The Legend of Jack Sparrow* acts as a meta-commentary on the process of adaptation, declaring that when it comes to the history of pirates, it's impossible to separate fact from fiction.

The synergistic efforts culminated in a swath of *At World's End* games for the newly released PlayStation 3 and Xbox 360, the still popular PlayStation 2, Windows PC, Sonys PlayStation Portable, and both the Nintendo DS and Wii. Once again, Disney adapted, remediated, and poached from itself when the game begins—not just with the events of its movie namesake, but rather—bizarrely—with a retelling of the preceding film (and thus a retelling of the games). In other words, the *At World's End* game is also simultaneously a *Dead Man's Chest* game as well.

Though the console video games composed the most active part of the Pirates transmedia strategy, the example of *Pirates of the Caribbean Online* is an interesting edge case that borrows from the ride, the film franchise, and the DisneyQuest VR attraction. Launched in 2007, right around the release of the third film, the online massively multiplayer game (MMOG) was created within Disney by members of the Imagineering team, some of whom had worked on the DisneyQuest virtual reality attraction nearly a decade before. The online game borrowed some of the same techniques as the virtual reality game, such as the use of attention-drawing weenies, which had in turn been borrowed from the parks, to guide players to quest locations. When a player is given a quest, a beam of sunlight in the distance points to a visible landmark that the player must go to complete the quest. Additionally, the movement of non-player- character- controlled boats also leads players to sail to desired destinations, avoiding the "lost at sea" problem that had been an issue with the DisneyQuest attraction. Also featured throughout the online game are vignettes not dissimilar from those in the original ride.

Knowing that the online game was created by Imagineers and creators of the DisneyQuest attraction sheds some light on some of its "auto-textual poaching." The MMOG introduced player agency to the experience at a much larger scale than was afforded by the limitations of the four-person DisneyQuest attraction. The game too used an extensive multiplayer sea battle mechanic in which players could board various ships and engage in large-scale cannon battles with teams of other players on the open seas. The game also adds sword fighting to the mix. Players can sink a ship, but they can also instead choose to disable and board it, a more dangerous enterprise, but possibly more lucrative as there may be loot on -board. The game also takes place in a vast, open world that players can explore at whim, with new zones opened for access as a reward for quest completion or, in some cases, real money payments. By inhabiting a customized avatar in the MMOG's persistent virtual world, players could develop a history with the place while feeling a powerful sense of immersion.[29]

A New Course: Post-Trilogy Films and Games

On Stranger Tides, the fourth movie in the Pirates franchise, was released in theaters in May of 2011. Whereas *Curse of the Black Pearl* harkened back to the pirate mythology that informed the ride's design, and its sequels *Dead Man's Chest* and *At World's End* capitalized on the Sparrow-verse established in the first film, *On Stranger Tides* had the unique task of dropping existing characters into a previously conceived pirate story that was over two decades old. Most filmgoers were likely unaware that *On Stranger Tides* was actually an adaptation of a 1987 pirate-themed novel unaffiliated with Disney. Unlike the Gore Verbinski trilogy, whose narrative universe was without connection to the real Atlantic and Caribbean pirates, author Tim Powers' original novel dealt with the line between historical fact and historical fiction.[30] Because the supernatural was a central concern of the Pirates trilogy, it's not surprising that Powers' *On Stranger Tides,* which also included a supernatural component, was an appropriate source to adapt to the big screen. But the movie's release did not have as significant an impact on the storyworld as previous films. The only ride retrofits for this film were the 2011 update that replaced the Davy Jones introduction with Blackbeard from *On Stranger Tides*, and the 2012 addition of a few brief images of the mermaids that featured prominently in the film.

On Stranger Tides saw two different approaches to including games in the armada of the Pirates franchise. The first was a "social" game for Apple iOS devices in which players created and upgraded a ship, went on expeditions to find treasure and take over islands, and worked to assemble a crew by connecting to other players in game. Though in the Pirates universe, the game did not specifically refer to any of the three original movies nor the movie that had released earlier that same year. *Pirates of the Caribbean: Armada of the Damned*, another game that was intended to be separated from the Sparrow-centric movie trilogy, was cancelled in 2010.

LEGO game developer Traveler's Tales had established a reputation for taking popular franchises such as Star Wars and Harry Potter and adapting them into games composed of LEGO figures and environments. Coinciding with the 2011 release of *On Stranger Tides* in theaters, the LEGO Pirates game not only adapted the fourth movie, but the original trilogy as well. Not only does the game remediate the movies but it also was able to create a familiar visual world by reaching back to the pirate-themed sets and minifigs that were a part of LEGO's toy history. *LEGO Pirates of the Caribbean* was able to engage with players on multiple levels including their fondness for the movies, enjoyment of the TT Game's previous LEGO games, nostalgia for the original pirate themed sets, contemporary Pirates of the Caribbean branded LEGO sets, and, surprisingly enough, the ride itself. Like the other LEGO games developed by TT, LEGO Pirates relies on abstraction as it remediates live-actors on a screen into toy worlds and the LEGO brand and Pirates franchise are inherited in this playable world.[31]

Following the typical LEGO game formula, LEGO Pirates is composed of a hub world of a Port that the player is free to explore before entering the Story Mode in which the events of all four movies are played in order. Each movie story is segmented into chapters and the level of abstraction presented by the LEGO visual style supports the condensed narratives. LEGO games of the time were known for forgoing real voice acting and dialogue in favor of cartoonish exclamations like barks, grunts, sighs, whistles, and other filler sounds. Without dialogue, the animation of the characters and the objects in the world needed to tell the story—a technique that lies somewhere in between the temporal narratives of the film stories and the vignettes used to tell the spatial story of the ride.

Collection is a significant component of the gameplay of the LEGO games and *Pirates of the Caribbean* provides a unique reward for completing the daunting task of collecting all 85 eighty-five Gold Bricks in the game. This unlocks a secret area called "The Ride," which begins by dropping the player into the level aboard a small boat that descends a waterfall. As the LEGO version of Jack Sparrow, the player can exit the boat and climb onto the scenery to fight enemies and collect gold in three sequences of attraction-like vignettes. During this short bonus level, the original ride soundtrack plays and the booming bass of Thurl Ravenscroft singing "yo ho, yo ho, a pirate's life for me!" punctuates the third and final sequence. While not an exact recreation of the ride, this Easter egg stage pays homage to the theme park attraction that started it all.

The nearly twenty Pirates of the Caribbean franchise games show the complexities of remediation and adaptation.[32] Not only do they all attend to the ride and the movies to varying degrees, but they are also engaged with pirate history, mythology, and fiction in the popular imagination. Players of these games have taken on a range of character roles from sailor and scallywag to noble navigator. Each game is an opportunity to re-orient the player's relationship to the franchise through characters, story, and environment. And, with the fifth movie *Dead Men Tell No Tales* on the horizon for 2017, there will undoubtedly be new adventures that continue to evolve the Pirates of the Caribbean universe.

Coming Ashore

In December of 2012, Disney opened a new attraction in Walt Disney World's Hollywood Studios to replace the Journey into Narnia shows that had occupied the space between 2005 and 2011. The Legend of Captain Jack Sparrow was a single-room, immersive performance experienced in the theatrical format of "the round" in a stage composed of physical sets and digital projection. Welcomed by a digital projection of the same skull and crossbones figure that once warned riders of the original Disneyland attraction that "dead men tell no tales," audience members were invited to test their merits in order to join Jack Sparrow's crew. The show was short-lived, however, and closed two years later for reasons unannounced. This thirteen-month run, and the relative lack of impact of *On Stranger Tides* on the transmedia landscape of the franchise, raises questions about the direction the Pirates storyworld is heading as the fifth movie looms on the horizon. Looking back at the storyworld's fragmented history, however, it's possible to conclude that the franchise has always used a compass that doesn't point north because it's never looked for north. Instead, it's precisely the lack of direction that has always benefited the storyworld and that cohesion and finitude are at odds with the immersive potential of the original source.

Notes

1. Henry Jenkins, *Textual Poaching: Television Fans and Participatory Culture* (New York: Routledge, 1992). Michel De Certeau, *The Practice of Everyday Life* (Berkeley: University of California Press, 1984).

2. Jay David Bolter and Richard Grusin, *Remediation: Understanding New Media* (Cambridge, MA: The MIT Press, 1999).

3. Carolyn Jess-Cooke, "Sequelizing Spectatorship and Building Up the Kingdom: The Case of Pirates of The Caribbean, or, How a Theme Park Attraction Spawned a Multibillion-Dollar Film Franchise," in *Second Takes: Critical Approaches to the Film Sequel*, eds. Carolyn Jess-Cooke and Constantine Verevis (Albany, NY: State University of New York Press, 2010).

4. Jess-Cooke, "Sequelizing Spectatorship," 209.

5. Anne Petersen, "You Believe in Pirates, Of Course...Disney's Commodification and 'Closure' vs. Johnny Depp's Aesthetic Piracy of 'Pirates of the Caribbean,'" *Studies in Popular Culture* 29, no. 2 (April 2007): 64.

6. Jess-Cooke, "Sequelizing Spectatorship," 209.

7. Marty Sklar, *Dream It! Do It!: My Half-Century Creating Disney's Magic Kingdoms* (New York: Disney Editions, 2013), 118–119.

8. Patti Smith, "Johnny Depp Talks to Patti Smith About Working with Angelina Jolie, Jack Sparrow, and His Own Musical Aspirations," *Vanity Fair*, November 30, 2010.

9. Neil Randall and Kathleen Murphy, "The Lord of the Rings Online: Issues in the Adaptation of MMORPGs," in *Dungeons, Dragons, and Digital Denizens: The Digital Role-Playing Game*, eds. Gerald A. Voorhees, Joshua Call, and Katie Whitlock (New York: Continuum Books, 2012), 115.

10. Jenkins, *Textual Poachers*.

11. Linda Hutcheon, *A Theory of Adaptation* (New York: Routledge, 2006).

12. Marie-Laure Ryan, *Narrative as Virtual Reality* (Baltimore, MD: Johns Hopkins University Press, 2001).

13. Ryan, *Narrative as Virtual Reality*; Michael Heim, *Virtual Realism* (New York: Oxford University Press, 1998).

14. J.R.R. Tolkien, *The Tolkien Reader* (New York: Ballantine, 1966).

15. Yi-Fu Tuan, *Space and Place: The Perspective of Experience* (Minneapolis: University of Minnesota Press, 1977).

16. Bolter and Grusen, *Remediation*. Scott A. Lukas. *Theme Park* (London: Reaktion, 2008), 182.

17. Jess-Cooke, "Sequelizing Spectatorship."

18. Karal Ann Marling, ed. *Designing Disney's Theme Parks: The Architecture of Reassurance* (Quebec: Flammarion, 1997).

19. Marty Sklar, *Dream It! Do It!*, 36–37.

20. Marling, *Designing Disney's Theme Parks*; John Hench, *Designing Disney: Imagineering and the Art of the Show* (New York: Disney Editions, 2008).

21. Lukas, *Theme Park*, 182.

22. Jesse Schell and Joe Shocket, "Designing Interactive Theme Park Rides," *IEEE Computer Graphics and Applications* 21, no. 4 (July 2001): 11–13.

23. Schell and Shocket, "Designing Interactive Theme Park Rides."

24. Jess-Cooke, "Sequelizing Spectatorship," 215.

25. Jess-Cooke, "Sequelizing Spectatorship," 208.

26. See <http://www.moddb.com/mods/potc-build-mod> for more on this mod.

27. Petersen, "You Believe in Pirates, Of Course," 65

28. *Business Wire*, "Buena Vista Games to Build Treasured Video Game Franchise for 'Pirates of the Caribbean'—BVG Announces Development of 'Pirates of the Caribbean: Dead Man's Chest', Next-Gen Handheld Games and Sets Course for Next Generation Console Titles," *Business Wire*, April 18, 2005.

29. Celia Pearce, *Communities of Play: Emergent Cultures in Multiplayer Games and Virtual Worlds* (Cambridge, MA: The MIT Press, 2009).

30. Tim Powers, *On Stranger Tides* (New York: Harper, 2011).

31. Jessica Aldred, "(Un)Blocking the Transmedial Character: Digital Abstraction as Franchise Strategy in Traveller's Tales' LEGO Games," in *LEGO Studies: Examining the Building Blocks of a Transmedial Phenomenon*, ed. Mark J.P. Wolf (New York: Routledge, 2014), 105–117.

32. The Pirates universe has not exclusively been limited to movie-tie in games. Much like the ride is a single part of the broader theme park, Pirates has often functioned as a segment of a larger game, including the PlayStation 2 game Kingdom Hearts II (2005), the Disney's "toys-to-life" game Disney Infinity (2013), and Disney Magical World (2014) for the Nintendo 3DS.

11

Research Dialogue

The Ways of Design, Architecture, Technology, and Material Form

By Filippo Carlà, Florian Freitag, Gordon Grice, Scott A. Lukas

This chapter is the first of two research dialogues that focus on the insights that may be gained from research collaborations within the worlds of themed and immersive spaces. The dialogue focuses on the idea of creating cross-pollination between the academic and design arenas of themed and immersive spaces. The research group that forms this conversation has initiated a series of field, design, and academic-critical experiments that focuses on fuller understandings of these spaces. This first dialogue focuses on the contexts of Design, Architecture, Technology, and Material Form.

Lukas: I have suggested this dialogue as a way of influencing collaboration between the academic and design arenas of themed and immersive spaces. I believe that this dialogue has been many years in the making. In 2013, Filippo Carlà and Florian Freitag, invited me to participate in a guest professorship at Johannes Gutenberg University in Mainz, Germany. Florian and Filippo were significantly transforming the ways in which we approach the study of themed and immersive spaces and my time in Germany was especially significant as I was able to engage in extensive conversations about theme parks in some very fresh and innovative senses. To give readers some context about your work, perhaps you could each briefly state what led you to develop extensive studies of theme parks and themed spaces.

Carlà: First of all, I think I have to qualify myself. I am an ancient historian and my studies were all in the fields of Classics. Through this path I came to be interested in the various form of reception of the ancient world in modern culture, and especially in popular culture, and I worked on movies and comics with an ancient "topic" or "set." It is in this way that I started investigating the creation of immersive environments inspired by Classical antiquity—with a particular eye for re-enactments and for theme parks. Since I am interested in immersion as an educational tool, too, and thus in the birth and development of living history and experimental archaeology, my interest in theme parks developed around two main axes: the role of Classical antiquity in modern popular culture and entertainment (why do we like it? Why do we want to spend time and money in reconstructed "classical" environments?), and the role of immersion in postmodern approaches to history (pastness, the affective turn, and so on). From there it was a short step to start investigating, in broader terms, representations of the past, even if Greece and Rome remain my main "case studies" and areas of interest. The rest came when I met Florian and we started our cooperation.

Freitag: I had never seriously considered studying theme parks until shortly before I finished my Ph.D. in American studies. I had been interested in theme parks; as an undergraduate, I even spent a year working at Disneyland Paris—in order to improve my French, I had told my professors—and used much of my time off exploring the park and talking to the designers and architects at Imagineering. At my home university in Germany, however, American studies at the time mostly meant American *literary* studies; everything else—movies, pictures, virtual media—was left to the media studies department. For our oral examinations, however, we were supposed to come up with a thesis in a subject other than that in which we wrote our dissertation. I saw my chance and wrote something about intermedial connections between theme parks and movies. After finishing my Ph.D., I reworked this piece and sent it to *The Journal of Popular Culture*. And then I met Filippo.

Lukas: Why was the focus on time and temporality significant?

Carlà: For me it is significant to identify how immersive environments, and theme parks among them, create a space which is outside our temporality, and they make "time traveling" possible.[1] Not only can you immerse yourself in an ancient Roman world, but you can easily cross a few minutes afterwards in the future, and then back in the medieval ages. I think this is an aspect which has been quite neglected in theme park studies until now, and it is the one on which I focused my attention. So, how do you choose the temporal layers to represent? How do you select the elements of that period that you want to reproduce? How do you create the immersion into another period? And, from a broader cultural perspective, why do you do that at all? What role do other time layers—all the possible pasts and futures—play in creating our identities, confirming our sense of belonging, reinforcing our beliefs and values? Can we see a new approach to history and, more generally, to temporality in the decades starting with the 1980s, as claimed by Hans Ulrich Gumbrecht and Aleida Assmann?[2] And how does this interplay with the representation of such time layers in a commercial, and theoretically entertaining, reality such as a theme park? These are the questions that prompted me to start the research.

Freitag: Yes, we definitely felt that aspects of time and temporality had not been given due attention in theme park studies. And the topic is even more complex than Filippo has suggested. Again, the time I spent working at Disneyland Paris proved significant here. Like theme park visitors, theme park employees are confronted with a complex temporality—various temporal layers that influence the way they perceive and navigate the themed environment. Some of these layers overlap, others are completely different. "The parade starts in an hour" has a different implication for employees than for visitors. For the latter, it means they should start hunting for a good spot to see the show. For the former, it means that they should leave for lunch now, because with the parade crowds, it will take you twice as long to get to the cafeteria, and you only have one hour of lunch break.

Lukas: One of the things that has struck me is how different and innovative the study of themed and immersive spaces in the European context is. I have expressed some disappointment in the lack of fertile approaches to the study of themed and immersive spaces in the United States. Many of these studies have either been dismissive of these spaces or have relied on now stale concepts—theme parks are spaces of simulation and hegemony, and so forth. Am I correct in this assessment of the European study of these spaces? Is there something to the nature of the research or criticism at play? Is there something about how theming and immersion is approached in Europe that contrasts with American cases?

Carlà: I think there are two important elements here. One is the bigger "homogeneity" of the United States compared to European States and cultures. In the case of my interests, you can clearly see how different European countries, bigger or smaller, have a completely different approach to different historical periods, related to the role they play in their identity construction. Ancient Rome in Italy is not ancient Rome in Britain, for instance. The other point is that theme parks are strongly perceived as an "American" product, so it is important to consider the way in which they are "incorporated" into the European context and market (for example, Parc Astérix as an anti-Disneyland) or even resisted.

Freitag: I think the latter point is extremely important. Some of the most influential early studies of theme parks, almost all of which are highly critical of their subject, were written by European scholars—Jean Baudrillard, Umberto Eco, Louis Marin.[3] Compare these texts and their quite explicit critique of Disneyland in particular and the United States in general to the early, almost celebratory writings of a Margaret J. King and you'll see what I mean.[4] This scholarly legacy notwithstanding, I think that today there are oceans between the different disciplines, as well as between academia and designers, that are even bigger than the Atlantic. Historians, tourism scholars, geographers, cultural studies people, anthropologists, and designers all talk about theme parks, but they rarely talk to each other about theme parks. This is why this research dialogue is so important. Theme park studies, or themed environment studies, need to start conceiving of itself as an interdisciplinary venture.

Grice: Each of us has a deep professional interest in theme parks, but our backgrounds couldn't be more dissimilar. Florian Freitag is a lecturer of North American Studies in Germany; Filippo Carlá is a lecturer in classics and ancient history in England; Scott Lukas is an author, anthropologist, and professor of theme park studies in the United States; and I'm a Canadian architect. As it happens, this quirky mix is perfectly suited to Creative Research, which we have chosen to define as: the examination of a subject, approached simultaneously from a variety of directions, with the intent of stimulating new insights—in a manner of speaking, serious research conducted as a creative act. Creative Research, as the name suggests, combines two disparate elements into a single exercise that is spontaneous and deliberate, carefree and rigorous, cerebral and visceral, mindful and mindless—all at the same time. The tension that exists between the two parts—the disorder of creativity and the methodical orderliness of research—is what provides the motive force, as well as the unpredictable results. So, to further test the effectiveness of our methodology, we decided that, before our presentation at the 2014 meetings of the American Studies Association, we would both expand and focus our minds by strolling through some local theme parks (Disneyland, Disney's California Adventure, and Universal Studios Hollywood)—a decision that introduced a whole new adjective to our exercise, creating what we might call Ambulatory Creative Research.

Lukas: Something that I have enjoyed immensely about the current state of my studies of themed and immersive spaces is the ability to engage in dialogues such as these. In 2013, as part of T*he Immersive Worlds Handbook*, I was introduced to the work of Gordon Grice.[5] Gordon ended up providing one of the key interviews in the text. Since this time, Gordon took part in the Time and Temporality conference at the Johannes Gutenberg University in Mainz, Germany (in 2014). As well, he was part of the panel that the four of us took part in at the American Studies Association Conference in 2014. Gordon's collaborations with the three of us have been particularly significant, as in addition to his numerous publications Gordon is a creative director for Forrec Ltd. Gordon, I wonder if you could comment on your work and how you began to develop collaboration between the study and practice of themed spaces?

Grice: First of all, thanks for those very kind and encouraging words. The study-and-practice approach predated my interest in theme parks. Way back when I started working with Forrec, about 35 years ago, I was an architect and freelance architectural illustrator.[6] I had always been interested in understanding the design decisions that my clients made, and I think the quality of my work depended on it. I've always believed that you can't draw something unless you understand what it's meant to represent. The thing that I really enjoyed about Forrec projects was that they gave me the opportunity to explore ideas about form, space, and human activity, beyond the constraints of "traditional" architectural conventions. I also liked working with them. When my career turned to writing and editing, Forrec became my major client and now, I got to open the curtain and really find out what was behind the design of themed environments. Whenever I wrote something—a storyline, a marketing piece, a magazine article, or a proposal—I learned something new about the underlying discipline and philosophy. What a learning curve that was! Now I started doing research in the many areas of thought that intersect with theme park design. Not coincidentally, this also led to the discovery of your (Lukas') books, which stood out from the theme park books and treatises because they treated themed environments as a legitimate and important field of study—not something to be scorned and dismissed. Since then, having met Filippo, Florian, and many others involved in the serious study of themed environments, I have focused a lot more of my attention in this direction. And as a creative director, I get the chance to apply this theorizing to the work that we do—not by applying specific discoveries to specific projects, but by changing the way I think about certain design directions.

Lukas: Perhaps you could say a bit about what this collaboration has meant for you? Is it possible to say that this sort of collaboration has influenced your approaches to the study and design of themed and immersive spaces? If so, how?

Grice: I think that the collaboration with you, Filippo, and Florian represents a logical development in my career, and the beginning of an exciting new chapter. I am presented with different ways of seeing things although, surprisingly, our observations are often quite similar and, as I keep discovering, your observations and comments often have more relevance to the field of architecture and design than those of my fellow practitioners. As editor of an architectural journal, I'm still involved with architectural thinking, but now I get to test that thinking against the practical aspects of immersive design. It's less about form and more about space. What kind of activity are we trying to encourage, and how do our forms and spaces support that activity? Are people having fun?

Lukas: During the time that the four of us visited Los Angeles for the American Studies Association meetings, we took part in a series of site visits that included Disneyland, Disney's California Adventure, and Universal Studios Hollywood. I wondered if each of you could describe what these visits represented and how they impacted your understanding of the study, design, and criticism of theme parks?

Grice: Regrettably, I missed the Universal Studios tour, so I only got to share the Disney experience with the three of you. I think the main advantage of these visits was that they demonstrated the value of Ambulatory Creative Research. It may seem slightly unorthodox, but it isn't really: four researchers from four disciplines, examine the same phenomena with an open mind and no vested interest, comparing ideas and modifying them, on the fly. In real terms, this is probably a good way to stir up ideas for more conventional research—observations and assumptions leading to hypotheses to be tested. But subjective human experience is notoriously resistant to quantitative analysis. So how better to analyze it than to *experience* it and make informed observations? The most memorable realization (almost an epiphany) that I gained from the visits had to do with the subject of nostalgia. I had been doing some reading on the subject for my part of the American Studies Association presentation, so I was sensitized to it. I began to realize what a powerful element nostalgia is, and was a little surprised at how frequently we had been using it in our design narratives. But I was unprepared for the nostalgic tidal wave that the two Disney parks presented. Even now, I'm not sure I have fully recovered. Another important factor—and key to the success of the venture—is that the four of us appear to share certain characteristics (curious, analytical, iconoclastic, and possessing a wry sense of humor). I've noticed that other people working in the theme park business display some of these same characteristics. It is also important that we are all from different disciplines—and especially from different *collections* of disciplines—since this prevented us from going off on pragmatic tangents, or wandering off the subject completely, since there was someone always able to offer an insight from a viewpoint unfamiliar to the rest of us that would push the conversation along productive lines.

Carlà: The three parks we visited together are not directly relevant to my project, since none of them contains at the moment representations of Classical Antiquity (even if I had an interest in studying the Revenge of the Mummy ride at Universal Studios because of its archaeological "background.") What was important for me was first of all to see in Disneyland the park from which "everything started"—and whatever the topic is that you approach in theme park studies, you cannot escape of course Disney, since most parks do show elements of imitation, reference, reaction to what is done in Disney parks. California Adventure was probably the most interesting for me, because it has a very strong historical theme, with the definition of a clear identity to be referred to, and because it incorporates parts of the plans for the never realized Disney's America park, which would have been a purely historical theme park.

Freitag: I agree with Gordon in that our visits were, above all, highly conducive to stimulating new research questions. Two aspects especially contributed to this: first, none of us was an expert on these particular parks, no one felt like he had to give the others an insider's tour of the place, which would have channeled the discussion. As it was, we simply reacted to what we noticed—and we noticed the same things, although we called them by different names. Indeed, we realized that although we speak different "technical" languages, we talk about the same things. This is an experience I had again when I visited Gordon at Forrec to introduce our research project on time and temporality in theme parks. After my short lecture, I talked to a landscape designer about a field trip to a theme park she had recently been on to, and although I would have put it quite differently, I knew exactly what she was talking about.

Lukas: I agree that these collaborative experiences have been quite instructive. The experiences took me back to my days working at Six Flags AstroWorld. Then, along with other AstroWorld employees, I took a number of field trips to other Six Flags parks. While on site, we "compared notes," so to speak, in terms of the quality of the theme parks that we visited in relationship to AstroWorld. Like this experience from my past, I found that the dialogues that occurred in situ were valuable for the fact that we were also able to compare notes on the various attractions that we experienced together. Especially exciting were conversations with Filippo and Florian related to the Mummy and Simpsons rides at Universal Studios Hollywood—for discussions related to theming the past and autotheming—and the dialogue that we exchanged as a group, along with Gordon, at Disney California Adventure. And a key point that I took away from these experiences was the need to (sometimes) suspend the academic-critical conversations that we often have about these spaces.

Carlà/Freitag: Indeed, Florian's Forrec experience as well as the Los Angeles field trips made us realize that studies of theme parks need to look beyond academia and take into account insights from people who are professionally involved in theme parks in a non-scholarly way: designers, managers, and employees. We are not talking about studying employee behavior in theme parks here—this has been done by some scholars and it constitutes, or should constitute, a fundamental part of studying theme parks, along with studying guest behavior and other aspects that transcend the theme park proper, such as the relationship between the theme park and its immediate local surroundings or theme park metatexts (books, movies, and other media about theme parks). Indeed, conceiving of the theme park not as a mere place, but as a performance, a daily interaction between places (designed by artists and managers) and people (operational employees and guests), may be one of the new directions in which studies of theme parks need to evolve in the future. Rather, we believe that not least due to their frequent—in some cases, daily—encounters with theme parks, which starkly contrast with scholars' necessarily infrequent field trips, designers and employees perceive the theme park in radically different ways that are otherwise inaccessible to the researcher.

Lukas: During Gordon's presentation at the American Studies Association meetings, I was particularly intrigued with his focus on the background and foundations on which many of his designs are envisioned and built. Perhaps the two of you could comment on this aspect of the design of themed and immersive spaces and what it implies for study and criticism.

Carlà: Surely it was extremely fascinating to have a clear insight in the creative moment, which helped me to realize that there is much more in theming than what we "see" as visitors and users—there might be extremely complicated narratives underlying the design which are not visible, but which influenced the design. I think that the most important thing I learned is exactly that the basis for the design is indeed always a narrative, and not only a "set" or a "period," and this must be considered thoroughly when analyzing a single ride, or a section of a theme park, or the entire park. I think it would be necessary to study how much of the theming is "understood" by the visitors, and if they care at all about that—it seems clear that the visitors do privilege strong themes and strong immersion.

Freitag: As someone who was trained in literary studies in the late 1990s and early 2000s, I grew up with Barthes's dictum of the death of the author, and this has also influenced the way I study themed spaces: I try, first and foremost, to find out how the space works as a space, not how well it reflects the designer's original intentions. I rather think of design narratives as a separate area of study, just like visitors' reactions to a themed space, especially when, as in the case of Disney parks, certain aspects of the genesis of the place are used for promotional purposes. Disney keeps telling us, for instance, that Main Street, U.S.A. is based on Walt Disney's hometown of Marceline, Missouri. The question is not whether this is really the case but rather: why do they do that?

Lukas: Florian's last point is very interesting. I have to say that one of the things that I have learned in my movement from the academic study of themed and immersive spaces to the more practical considerations of the design and narrative aspects of these spaces is that there is a great deal of attention that is placed on elements of backstory and the like that establish the significance of a themed space like Main Street, U.S.A. Years ago, while consulting for Disney Imagineering, I became acutely aware of the fact that backstory (or what Filippo refers to in the "extremely complicated narratives underlying the design which are not visible") is a foundational part of the theme park design process. This, of course, presents a challenge in terms of unpacking and analyzing the "text" of any themed or immersive space, as Florian might suggest. To go back to some of Gordon's work, the reverse of this consideration is the circumstance of the designer being influenced by those who study and often critique themed and immersive spaces. Gordon, I am wondering if you could discuss how such study and criticism could impact the conceptualization of these spaces?

Grice: I think the criticisms that have most motivated me are the ones with which I disagree most strongly. After having read the well-considered comments of such critics as Michael Sorkin and Ada Louise Huxtable about the general evils of themed environments, I have been motivated to think about my own response to these criticisms.[7] Some of the most helpful support has come from the members of the Time and Temporality conference in Mainz, especially on the subject of authenticity—something that you have written about on a few occasions as well. The presentations by Cornelius Holtorf and Per Strömberg (both authors in this collection) were especially eye opening, and have affected my thinking on architectural heritage and preservation, as well as my ideas about theme park design.

Notes

1. Cornelius J. Holtorf, "On the Possibility of Time Travel," *Lund Archaeological Review* 15 (2009): 31–41.
2. Aleida Assmann, *Ist die Zeit aus den Fugen?: Aufstieg und Fall des Zeitregimes der Moderne* (Munich, Germany: Hanser, 2013). Hans Ulrich Gumbrecht, *Unsere breite Gegenwart* (Frankfurt am Main, Germany: Suhrkamp, 2010).
3. Michael Immerso, *Coney Island: The People's Playground* (Piscataway, NJ: Rutgers University Press, 2002), 69.
4. Margaret J. King, "The New American Muse: Notes on the Amusement/Theme Park," *Journal of Popular Culture* 15 (1981): 56–62. Margaret J. King, "Disneyland and Walt Disney World: Traditional Values in Futuristic Form," *Journal of Popular Culture* 15 (1981): 116–140.
5. See "Space and the Senses, Interview, Gordon Grice," in Scott A. Lukas, *The Immersive Worlds Handbook: Designing Theme Parks and Consumer Spaces* (New York: Focal, 2013), 200–203.
6. See <http://forrec.com>.
7. Michael Sorkin, "See You in Disneyland," in *Variations on a Theme Park*, ed. Michael Sorkin (New York: Noonday, 1992), 205–232. Ada Louise Huxtable, *The Unreal America: Architecture and Illusion* (New York: New Press, 1999).

PART V

The Aspects of Immersion, Experience, and Phenomena

12

Questioning "Immersion" in Contemporary Themed and Immersive Spaces

By Scott A. Lukas

In the contemporary consumer world, more and more, we are told of the value of becoming immersed in the worlds and spaces around us. Cultural anthropologists, since the days of pioneering fieldworker Bronislaw Malinowski, have understood the deep desirability of appreciating an "emic" or insider's view of the world that is possible after completing rigorous and often challenging forms of cultural immersion in the fieldsite of study. This describes the method of participant observation whose anthropologist fieldworker attempted "to grasp the native's point of view, his relation to life, to realize *his* vision of his world."[1] Interestingly, the posthumous and controversial publication of Malinowski's diary resulted in the anthropological community confirming what any fieldworker has likely known all the while in the field—namely, that cultural immersion and its many methodological and representational dynamics is an arena of notable contradictions.[2] Malinowski's "immersion" in his fieldsites, as reflected in his classic ethnography *Argonauts of the Western Pacific*, was later contradicted by the expressions in his diary. Disturbing sensibilities, anxieties, and expressions of culture shock in the diary suggest the anthropologist's discomfort with his immersion. Since the days of Malinowski's fieldwork, cultural anthropologists have agreed with his suggestion of "getting off the verandah"—avoiding the observation of culture from afar—in order to get deeply wrapped up in the culture being studied.

The world of consumer spaces has also been influenced profoundly by such notions of immersion. The word immersion, etymologically, suggests a plunging or dipping into something or an "absorption in some interest or situation."[3] In the contemporary world—particularly in popular culture, media, and consumer spaces—immersion has taken on new and important meanings. As Frank Rose suggests, today's media and consumer world is influenced by new forms of narrative that are participatory and immersive.[4] In themed spaces of the present, immersion involves taking a patron or guest and placing that person directly within the given (and typically symbolically marked) context of those spaces. Very commonly, narratives or forms of storytelling are used to immerse guests within spaces—as are forms of technology, social media, and many other manners of material, media, and performative culture. Such spaces exemplify the nature of the "experience economy" and the "dream society" as defined by Pine and Gilmore and Rolf Jensen respectively.[5] Guests who enter any number of spaces today—whether a cruise ship, restaurant, or even, a library—are seen not simply as automata who mindlessly move in and use the space, but they are viewed as active participants who often complete the story, experience, or context at hand within the space. Narratives like "Be a part of it all," "Feel like it really feels," "Have an authentic experience," "Go out there and do it," among others, suggest the value of becoming deeply engaged in a space and experiencing all that it offers. These narratives of immersion, whose embodiments often result in forms of pleasure experienced by guests, have been viewed typically by researchers and social critics of the popular as being representative of the many problematic issues of popular culture and associated consumer spaces—hegemony, commodification, hedonism, and related areas. The greater involvement of guests in these spaces, such as at the Cerritos Millennium Library (which was created as the first library to be designed using principles of Pine and Gilmore's experience economy), could be argued to be resultant in various negative effects. This begs the question for this study: Is immersion a desirable state in the world?

Cults of Immersion

Beyond the anthropological and consumer cultural contexts, we may review others in which immersion is considered of fundamental importance to the space at hand. Of course, it is worth noting, that each and every space—no matter a

Image 12.1. Cerritos Millennium Library (Photo by Scott A. Lukas)

theme park, museum, or office cubicle—may be denoted as an "immersive space," with the idea that any space "wraps us up within it" by the nature of the activity or context specific to that space. We may, however, choose to engage or disengage in the space, its people, ideas, and activities as we desire and thus, we are not necessarily fully engaged in every space of which we are a part. Because some of our engagement with or immersion in certain spaces may be considered unpleasurable—such as standing in line at the DMV to receive our driver's license—we create other spaces, like theme parks, to provide an opportunity to immerse ourselves in a more pleasurable space and, likely, to allow us to forget about the other less pleasurable spaces of our lives. Curiously enough, as I will discuss later, some of the most intriguing immersive spaces in existence (and some, perhaps, to come) are those that indeed engage us, but often in disturbing, unsettling, avant-garde, and uncanny senses. Most contemporary themed and consumer spaces, however, do not engage the guest at the level of these negative feelings or associations and instead strive for a pleasurable form of immersion. In my years working in the theme park industry, I found that while we spoke of engaging the guest in our many themed spaces, we very often did not reflect on the nuances of that immersion. In our training department, we instructed employees on the many techniques necessary to engage guests in our spaces and, typically (at least during my years at the theme park), we emphasized the idea of movie making as a metaphor for how successful guest immersion might occur.[6] In assessing our employees, we observed and asked questions as to whether their service work, performance, and guest interaction behaviors led to the engagement of the guest in our theme park, but we never asked questions such as: Should guests be immersed in our themed spaces for the entirety of their visit? What about when they are going to the bathroom? Are there some spaces and contexts that, akin to the employee backstage, are even "out of bounds" for the guest—perhaps meta-spaces and meta-contexts that supersede or negate the immersive world at hand?

Our guest relations department did interview guests upon leaving the theme park on a given day and thus did obtain feedback about guest satisfaction which could include reflections on guests' feelings in regards to how successful the immersive efforts of our employees were. However useful for park operations these forms of feedback were, they did not provide context—at least in terms of this study—as to the nuances of guest immersion. In my research related to this concept, including my work on *The Immersive Worlds Handbook*, I have come to understand that the concept has been accepted, by multiple communities, for its simplicity.[7] Social critics and many researchers, when detailing the "typical" exploits of guests in themed and consumer spaces, offer superficial interpretations of guest behaviors in those spaces—they shop, enjoy, consume, laugh, and so forth.[8] Similarly, for some designers, trainers, and assessors in the theming industries, there is a reliance on oversimplified notions of guest immersion—the guest should feel escape, fantasy, delight, and the like.[9] In both cases, the simplification of how a guest experiences (or might experience) a themed space is remarkable. Cultural anthropologists remind us that the behaviors, attitudes, and existential reflections of individuals in any space are incredibly complex—perhaps too complex to re-present in any form, ethnographic or otherwise.[10]

In a much different but useful example, in the case of a "cult" (more properly, a high demand religious movement), we typically interpret the context of the immersion or engagement of the individual as a negative one. Individuals who leave such groups and are "deprogrammed," speak of the inherent toxicity of being part of a group whose social and other spaces are incredibly determinant in the lives of group members. We call these groups "high demand" because they require that individuals give up a good deal, if not all, of their previous social lives in order to engage in the social spaces of the new group. We may look at the similar context of the "total institution"—Erving Goffman's concept of a space, such as a prison, in which the effects of the space on the individual are total.[11] Each and every aspect of the individual's life are prescribed and enforced by the institution. Again, we might say that in this context the desirability of the individual to be immersed in such a space is low, but a key point is that the effect of the immersion on that person is often high. High demand groups and prisons are, certainly, unique and arguably extreme spaces of immersion, but the dramatic nature of their effects on individuals within them reminds us of some significant foundations of immersion. Immersion is always related to the deployment and exercise of symbols. In the case of a prison, the symbolic deindividuation of the prisoner is a key aspect of bringing him or her in line, potentially even resulting in resocialization of the individual. In the example of a theme park, it is the highly evocative forms of thematic symbols—represented in architecture, material cues, types of performance, and other forms—that similarly impact how well the individual becomes immersed in the space. In its various modes of effect on individuals, we also note that immersion is socially manifested. Proponents of language immersion programs, for example, emphasize that language is easier to learn if the student surrounds him- or herself with the people from the culture who speak the given language.

Immersion, then, is context dependent. It is related to the specifics of the space at hand—its uses, activities, and themes; it is also connected to the desires of the individual undergoing immersion, especially as her or his level of connection with the space may vary, for a number of reasons. It is also highly dependent on the myriad social relationships that constitute the space—contemporary alternative spaces like Burning Man in the Black Rock Desert remind us that likemindedness (similar to Victor Turner's notions of communitas) may result in more positive feelings of mutual engagement in a space.[12] As cultural anthropologists have suggested as a result of their fieldwork, immersion is a mixed bag—in some cases, there is a lack of welcome afforded to the anthropologist attempting to become immersed in a given ethnographic setting; in other cases, the ethnographer might have to disengage from a field setting (sometimes quite abruptly) in order to preserve the political stability of the setting. What cultural anthropology has educated us in terms of immersion is that it is a multi-faceted, nuanced, and, indeed, highly subjective entity. Of course, anthropologists have a certain luxury in that they may spend a much longer time in a setting and thus have opportunities for deeper sorts of engagement in it as compared to individuals in other settings that reflect a much shorter temporal duration of immersion; as well, anthropologists communicate the dynamics of their fieldwork in ethnographic forms that allow for expressive, detailed, and nuanced considerations of all facets of the fieldsite, including the immersion experienced by the ethnographer.

In contrast with these two contexts of ethnographic immersion—the field and the textual—we discover that many spaces of the contemporary consumer world do not allow for similar levels of corporeal or existential engagement. In some cases, such as in a ride like Pirates of the Caribbean at Disney theme parks, the entire length of the ride is a mere fifteen minutes. While this does not include the immersion of the guest that may occur in spaces related to the ride, such as the queue house, even including these, the time in which guest immersion may occur is relatively brief—thus, we see the high stakes of guest engagement when it comes to the world of themed spaces. Added to this challenge is the fact that a given guest, as in this Disney example, upon leaving Pirates of the Caribbean, moves to a new space, perhaps after leaving other interspaces that connect rides and attractions or entire themelands to one another. It may be a strange and uncanny experience for such a guest to shift, existentially, from all of the feelings, moods, and story effects of Pirates of the Caribbean as he or she then boards It's a Small World. In contrast with other immersive media, like video games and novels, the guest is taken on a series of thematic, conceptual, and contextual turns in which he or she may be unable to make sense of the whole of the experience—either the themeland in question or the entire theme park. Save some postmodern forms of fiction, the reader of a novel is typically able to become wrapped up in the story because of the consistency of the elements (setting, characterization, narrative, and so forth) that has been provided by the author. As we reflect on the fact that immersion is nuanced, subjective, and context dependent, the question that framed this section—namely, is immersion a desirable state in the world?—becomes even more curious. Many advocates of cultural and language immersion programs suggest that a key value—pedagogical and, in some cases, moral and ethical—of such programs is that they alter radically the perspective of the learner; as some have put it, immersion creates "perspective shift" in the individual with the idea being that the preponderance of cultural contexts, experiences, sensations, and activities results in a total effect on that person.[13] Yet, we might ask, what is entirely entailed in such a shift of perspective and, what are its impacts on that individual, intended and unintended?

Questioning Immersion

Many years ago, I was asked to draw on my experiences as a cultural anthropologist *and* a researcher of theme parks at an extensive collaborative event held by a major media corporation—what I will call "The Workshop." Due to my non-disclosure agreement, I am unable to detail the nature of this event, but I mention it here so as to emphasize the interesting worlds that I have engaged as an anthropologist and themed industry consultant. Notably, my involvement in these worlds—that of theoretical and methodological professional anthropology, professional theme park training, and themed and immersive design consultation—suggests a curious and often contradictory engagement with the concept of immersion. While participating in the Workshop, I found myself continually posing queries in the form of internal dialogues: How, exactly, could I help develop better strategies for the forms of immersion suggested by the company that organized the event? Is it possible to use critical awareness of the issues and problems associated with immersion (those of Plato's cave, which I will address shortly) in order to fashion new spaces, modalities, and understandings of immersion that are more critical, conceptual, even political?

In the midst of this work, I was contacted by a large publisher of practical guidebooks and was asked to write a text that would detail approaches to creating themed and immersive spaces. This work became *The Immersive Worlds Handbook*—a text that attempted to establish considerations of design practices that could be used to create immersive environments in theme parks, museums or interpretive centers, and many other spaces. The initial impetus of the text was based on some of the concepts that I had developed for the Workshop. One of the daunting tasks of working on the book was to consider a shift from my role as an ethnographer-analyst to a practitioner who was advising others on how to create immersive spaces for the guest. I welcomed this challenge, especially as my consulting work with some of the major players in the themed amusement industry had allowed me to consider my relationship to themed spaces in new senses; in fact, I eventually formed my own consulting operation that emphasized practical approaches to many of the research, analysis, and design sides of the themed entertainment industry.[14] At the same time, I felt some degree of trepidation as I began to reflect on the notable contradictions between the critical views of immersion and those focused more decidedly on pleasures and experiences of guests in immersive spaces.

In the film *The Matrix* (1999), the viewer is presented with the interesting heuristic of the red and the blue pill. As suggested in the film and its rumination on a faux and hegemonic world that is lurking behind the "real," were an individual to take the blue pill, she or he would be allowed to remain in the world of illusion or simulation and experience bliss; were an individual to take the red pill, he or she would be confronted with the opposite—the stripping away of illusion and fantasy and, in its place, the realization of the harshness of reality. The "red and the blue pill," as an allegory, reminds of Plato's famous tale of the "cave" in *The Republic*.[15] In that telling, we see a similar emphasis on the delusional and illusory quality of a "themed" and "immersive" space as the dwellers of the cave know only the reality of what its masters have projected on the walls. Aside from being an important allegory for understanding the contemporary world, both the "red and the blue pill" and the "cave" offer an opportunity for an interesting reorientation of the guest (and the critic) in the world of themed and immersive space. In my own research and practical efforts in terms of the Workshop and the *Immersive Worlds*

Handbook, I have noted some curious parallels between the fictional suggestions about immersion in the *Matrix* and Plato's cave and the concerns that have been offered in the literature on immersive spaces.

One concern that has been expressed is the idea that one is never immersed in any space—whether a consumerist one or a presumably "authentic" one, such as an ancient church—because one can never fully (existentially) become one with that space. There will always be a divide between an individual and any space in the world. Of course, this may only suggest that there are levels of engagement—nuance—that should be understood in any context in which we consider immersion. A second expression of critique is that one is never able to become immersed in a consumer space because, unlike other spaces (again, the ancient church), the consumer space is emblematic of simulated and therefore inauthentic experiences.[16] This critique relies on antiquated notions of immersion and of the passive, non-acting guest within the immersive space. A third concern is that one is, indeed, able to be immersed in a consumer space but he or she is participating in a ruse—a fantasy world created by the culture industry with various economic, political, and other hegemonic intentions. As stated here, the critique would suggest that while immersion is occurring, the outcome of it is inherently negative to the actor. Yet, as relevant as these critiques are, we might imagine a fourth possibility—one that highlights these concerns but also complicates them. Slavoj Žižek, in an interview focused on the *Matrix*, suggested the need for a "third pill" in terms of the *Matrix's* choice of a red and a blue pill. In his mind, this "pill…would enable [one] to perceive not the reality behind the illusion, but reality in illusion itself."[17] Referencing Zizek's notion of a third pill, we might imagine the fourth possibility of immersion. In this one, the guest is immersed in a space and thus feels all of the sorts of connections to it as one might but that individual realizes that his or her experience is partial and contingent—all the time understanding that all spaces, whether themed, consumerist, or otherwise, are constructions that imply fluctuations between active-passive, agent (subject)-object, creator-consumer. The guest also realizes that this circumstance is not entirely the doing of the maker or the operator of the space (as social criticism so often implies) but that she or he is complicit in these mixed and ambivalent connections with the space. In this sense, he or she is operating, metaphorically, at the level of the "middle voice"—not an agent acting upon or a subject being acted upon but an individual who is, along with all others, in the midst of things.[18]

In the title of this chapter, I have placed in scare quotes, quite deliberately, the word "immersion" so as to suggest the hopelessness of relying on eroded notions of the real-fictive, authentic-inauthentic, original-copy. By questioning immersion and all of its contexts, we may become better able to appreciate the complex nature of contemporary themed and consumer space as well as the experiences that occur within it. We should thus challenge both the guest of any themed space who wishes to have an uncomplicated, seamless immersive experience in which he or she suspends fully his or her own disbelief and enters the reality of the immersive space and the social critic who assumes that he or she understands fully the experiences entailed in any form of immersion—whether in a "faux" space or a "real" one. As well, we might begin to question the very boundaries that seem to define the immersive from the non-immersive.[19] It would be quite easy for any of us, whether our role be guest, designer, or anthropologist-critic, to simply assume our position in relationship to immersion that has been defined for us. Greater dialogue among these actors—who represent the sort of collaborative-conflicting roles that I suggested in the Workshop and *The Immersive Worlds Handbook*—may result in greater understanding of both the nuances of themed and immersive spaces and their varied psychological, existential, and social uses by their many actors.

The parables of the *Matrix* and Plato's cave necessarily simplify the vicissitudes of the real and the fictive. There is neither one real world nor one fictive one. As well, it is difficult, if not impossible to determine the boundaries between such worlds. As participants in the Jejune Institute, discovered—a curious experiment in San Francisco in which participants were not clear on when an extensive, real-world game began or ended—certain reflections of the real-fictive, in today's world, suggest the stuff of the existential complexity that we discover in great works of conceptual art, open-ended art film, and other aesthetic forms that eschew clarity, closure, and "world definition" in favor of complexity, openness, and fabula.[20] Thus, in our questioning of all forms of immersion—whether those of contemporary themed spaces or other spaces and everyday life forms—we should avoid the simplicity that is suggested in an assertion that there is a clear, definable real and an equally identifiable, doppelgänger of it in the fictive.

Avant-Garde Futures of Immersion

In the American television series *Fantasy Island* (1977–1984), well-to-do visitors found themselves in the remarkable position of having any of their fantasies granted—a starlet who wished to just be anonymous and unknown, an aspiring detective who wanted to solve the case of Jack the Ripper, a bumbling individual who wished to time travel back to World War I to battle the Red Baron. Viewers of the show were never clear as to how the fantasies were granted to the island's guests by its mysterious Mr. Roarke, and this is exactly what made *Fantasy Island* an engaging show—the idea that one could be *fully* immersed in any fantasy space, whether of the past, present, or future. What's more is that on many occasions, the immersive experiences of guests were all too realistic, particularly when their fantasies became so "real" that they were nearly killed as a result of their participation in them. Mr. Roarke, who likely had supernatural powers, often warned guests of the dangers posed by their fantasies and reminded them that once the fantasies had begun, they could not be stopped. On numerous occasions, Roarke did intervene and save some of the guests from certain peril—an act which was often followed by the guest's realization of some sort of lesson that Roarke had intended. Conceptually, we may view this point of Roarke's intervention in the fantasy world to save the guest as an imposition of the "real" as it relates to all fantasy and, ultimately, to all immersive spaces. Other fantasy spaces that, like those of *Fantasy Island*, are too immersive in their dangerous potentials include the holodeck in the numerous *Star Trek* series and films—in which an individual could enter an immersive, virtual space that could replicate any desired place, time, or context—and the fantasy theme park of the film *Westworld* (1973) in which gunslinger robots go out of control and attempt to kill the park's guests. As in the case of *Fantasy Island*, the desires of guests to be immersed in fantasy spaces—that often become as real as the "real"—are posed to viewers as being highly problematic. In fact, in some versions of *Star Trek*'s holodeck, a safety feature was introduced such that certain virtual re-creations, such as dangerous weapons, would either not be created by the computer's simulation systems or would be negated in a circumstance in which the holodeck user might be harmed. This feature suggests, not unlike the many metaphors implied by Plato's cave and *The Matrix*, that the desire to be immersed in fantasy spaces is not without consequence.

Today's academic and cultural critics of the immersive space fulfill Plato's role of the philosopher who, in the case of the immersive cave of the *Republic*, is able, presumably, to see the contradictions between the world of the cave and the outside world—the fictive and the real. As powerful as Plato's parable is today, as well as the many works that have struggled with the implications of the often contradictory worlds of the simulated and the "real," we might discover a subtle form of elitism inherent in the idea of the philosopher being able to sort out the complications of these worlds. Like Plato's philosopher, the critic who claims to be able to clearly demarcate the boundaries of fictions and realities—of simulated immersive space versus everyday, mundane space—is operating from a position of supremacy. As Slavoj Žižek, Peter Sloterdijk, and others have expressed, the position of the critic is often, at best, ideologically unproblematized, or, at worst, a form of enlightened false consciousness (or cynicism).[21] At the same time, returning to the allegories of shows like *Fantasy Island*, we should acknowledge the many problematic ways in which all of us, whether researchers of themed and immersive spaces or not, are caught up in the complex semiotic, political, and identity webs that are part and parcel of our everyday worlds. Using fictional worlds of immersion as exemplars, I argue that we should not be any less critical of our spaces of the future but more aware of our own conceptual, political, and personal limitations as these critiques continue to emerge.

As I have argued throughout this chapter, it is incumbent on all of us—researchers, cultural critics, designers, operators, consultants, and guests—to appreciate and express the nuance, complexity, and ambiguity inherent in the idea of immersion. We must jettison the simplistic view of the concept as, metaphorically, some sort of on-off switch as well as leave behind the related dualisms and simplifications, such as authenticity, as they only prevent us from acting on the warp and woof—the true nuances—of immersion. We should reflect this complexity in our research papers and our personal enthusiast blogs, in our design schema and our training curricula, and we should all generally approach immersive spaces with open, honest, and reflexive sensibilities. There are no fail-safe switches of the sorts found on the fictional holodeck and thus it is impossible for any of these parties to immunize itself from whatever negative effects might be the outcome of immersion and its various modalities and conceptual implications.

As well, in terms of the design side of themed and consumer spaces, we should consider new approaches to the immersion of guests in space. I do not intend this as an argument about new and innovative spaces, but rather a push to combine these

Image 12.2. Tio's Tacos, Riverside, CA (Photo by Scott A. Lukas)

more complex understandings of immersion with a deeper appreciation of the conceptual and existential opportunities of using new and cutting-edge design to alter the phenomenology of immersion. Contemporary venues like those of the pavilions at World Expo 2015 (Milan) remind us that the emerging technologies of virtual and augmented reality, conceptual and postmodern design and architecture, and new approaches to presenting history, self-other concepts, and cultural meaning need not be used as simple, awe-inspiring moments, nor, ironically enough, as means of "better immersing" the guest in space. Rather, taking cues from the most innovative and tricky of contemporary spaces—notably Dennis Sever's House in London; the Museum of Jurassic Technology in Culver City, California; Juan Pollo's corporate headquarters and McDonald's tribute museum in San Bernardino, California; Tio's Tacos in Riverside, California; Robber's Roost Ranch Antiques and Collectibles in Inyokern, California; and the DDR Museum in Berlin, Germany—we may use new design approaches to inspire doubt, existential anxiety, feelings of complicity, middle-voiced experiences, and even meta-immersive potentialities in the spaces of the future.[22] Immersion need not imply simply telling a story or creating a fictive world for the guest to experience; it might, instead, suggest some powerful unraveling of the everyday world around us—this, the avant-garde potential of *Fantasy Island* and its not-quite-realized critique of the relationship of the real and the simulated.[23]

We must also reorient the experiences, roles, and sensibilities of guests within themed and immersive space. The notions of guests being passive, robotic, and non-agentic in consumer space are, fortunately, beginning to pass and in their place are new and expressive understandings of the complex, active, and creative roles that guests play in the consumer world. Media theorist Henry Jenkins has spoken of media convergence in which users of media become more active creator-agents of media. As well, the research in themed living communities (such as those of Civil War reenactment), themed avocational groups (such as the Tribes of Cologne), LARPs or live-action role playing (such as Darkon), and experimental life-fiction games and experiences (like the Jejune Institute and Dismaland) all provide ample ground on which to build greater involvement, participation, and indirect and direct dialogue of guests in the spaces to come. The spaces of the future will, no doubt, be highly immersive, yet the nature and stakes of that immersion is in ALL of our hands. Let us, then, suspend our disbelief, at least for this moment and a few more to come.

Notes

1. Bronislaw Malinowski, *Argonauts of the Western Pacific* (London: Routledge and Kegan Paul, 1922), 25. 4. Note: a video of this chapter is available at <https://youtu.be/wO_u0VzFm4A>.

2. Bronislaw Malinowski, *A Diary in the Strict Sense of the Term* (Stanford: Stanford University Press, 1989).

3. Online Etymology Dictionary, <http://www.etymonline.com/>.

4. Frank Rose, *The Art of Immersion: How the Digital Generation Is Remaking Hollywood, Madison Avenue, and the Way We Tell Stories* (New York: W.W. Norton, 2011).

5. Joseph B. Pine II and James H. Gilmore, *The Experience Economy: Work Is Theatre and Every Business a Stage* (Boston: Harvard Business School Press, 1999); Rolf Jensen, *The Dream Society: How the Coming Shift from Information to Imagination Will Transform Your Business* (New York: McGraw-Hill, 2001). See, also, Anna Klingmann, *Brandscapes: Architecture in the Experience Economy* (Cambridge, MA: MIT Press, 2007) and Brian Lonsway, *Making Leisure Work: Architecture and the Experience Economy* (New York: Routledge, 2009).

6. See Florian Freitag, "Movies, Rides, Immersion," in this collection, for more on the significance of film-ride relationships and Scott A. Lukas, "The Cinematic Theme Park," <https://www.academia.edu/17321873/The_Cinematic_Theme_Park>.

7. Scott A. Lukas, *The Immersive Worlds Handbook: Designing Theme Parks and Consumer Spaces* (New York: Focal, 2012).

8. Numerous studies of theme parks and themed and branded spaces have argued that guests or consumers in such spaces display forms of inauthenticity, hedonism, among other behaviors. Such assertions have in common a denial of the emic or insider's perspective of the guest in such spaces as well as an assumption of the homogeneity of the guest.

9. Indeed, in some cases companies develop lists of adjectives that describe the effective ways to immerse guests in themed spaces.

10. This concern parallels the "crisis of representation" in anthropology. See, James Clifford and George E. Marcus, eds., *Writing Culture: The Poetics and Politics of Ethnography* (Berkeley: University of California Press, 1986).

11. Erving Goffman, "On the Characteristics of Total Institutions," in *Asylums: Essays on the Social Situation of Mental Patients and Other Inmates* (Garden City, New York: Anchor Books, 1961), 1–124. Interestingly, at least one article suggests some curious parallels between the total institution of Goffman's prison and other "total institutions" like those of cruise ships. See, George Ritzer and Allan Liska, "'McDisneyization' and 'Post-tourism:' Complementary Perspectives on Contemporary Tourism," in *Touring Cultures: Transformations of Travel and Theory*, eds. Chris Rojek and John Urry (London: Routledge, 1997), 106.

12. Victor Turner, "Liminality and Communitas," in *The Ritual Process: Structure and Anti-Structure* (Chicago: Aldine, 1969), 94–113.

13. See, Karen Rodriguez, Cultural Immersion: Achieving The Elusive Perspective Shift," <http://www.transitionsabroad.com/publications/magazine/0005/cultural_immersion.shtml>.

14. The firm is known as "Culturespace," see, <http://www.culturespaceconsulting.com>.

15. See, Plato, *The Republic*, Book VII, 514a–521d.

16. One of the clear concerns about contemporary immersive techniques is their inherent connection to forms of the culture, branding, and marketing industries. As one such example, see, "Engage Shoppers with an Immersive Retail Experience," <https://lusens.com/immersive-retail/immersive-retail/>. Of note is the following suggestion from the website, "Installing a well designed immersive experience in your store will increase sales, improve brand recognition and increase chances [that] shoppers will come back to your store as they will feel an experience that is less overwhelming and intrusive than the 'pitch' of a sales associate."

17. Slavoj Žižek, "A Third Pill," video, <https://www.youtube.com/watch?v=k-0VMnFmnL0>.

18. For more on the middle voice, see, Stephen A. Tyler, "The Middle Voice: The Influence of Post-Modernism on Empirical Research in Anthropology," in *Post-Modernism and Anthropology*, eds. Karin Geuijen, Diederick Raven, and Jan de Wolf (Assen, Netherlands: Van Gorcum, 1995).

19. There is no doubt that such conceptual work on the matter of immersion is needed. Very likely, it may need take place at the curious intersection of cultural anthropology and existentialist philosophy.

20. See the documentary, *The Institute* (2013), directed by Spencer McCall.

21. See Slavoj Žižek, *Living in the End Times* (London: Verso, 2011) and Peter Sloterdijk, *Critique of Cynical Reason* (Minneapolis: University of Minnesota Press, 1988). See, also, Scott A. Lukas, "Judgments Passed: The Place of the Themed Space in the Contemporary World of Remaking" in this collection and Rita Felski, *The Limits of Critique* (Chicago: University of Chicago Press, 2015).

22. There are many other spaces that illustrate immersive innovations. I list these as a few examples of such spaces.

23. In an ever-more branded, multi-meme, and saturated consumer world, it would be easy to simply cast aside the value of immersion as something of the past. For more on the impacts of such a world, see, Kenneth Gergen, *The Saturated Self: Dilemmas of Identity in Contemporary Life* (New York: Basic Books, 2000). Immersion, one might argue, is too complicated in a world that in its postmodern and intertextual sensibilities seems to promote conceptual modalities not of the whole and the organic but of the part, rhizome, and the inorganic. But, I would say that the point is not to jettison immersion as a concept but to reorient it within this world of globalization, flux, and postmodernism. One possibility of such

reorientation is to situate immersion in the methodological worlds suggested by actor-network theory. See Bruno Latour, *Reassembling the Social – An Introduction to Actor-Network-Theory* (Oxford: Oxford University Press, 2005).

13

Movies, Rides, Immersion

By Florian Freitag

Theme parks in general and theme park rides in particular can be described as multimedia installations that seek to immerse visitors into multisensory environments by combining kinetics with a variety of different art forms or media, including architecture, landscaping, painting, sculpture, music, theater, and film. Time and again, however, the theme park has also been categorized as a medium in itself.[1] As a medium in its own right that combines and fuses various other media that have historically and conventionally been viewed as distinct, the theme park—similar to the movie, the theater, or the opera—can be classified as a "hybrid" medium, a "composite" medium, or a "meta-medium" that entertains numerous intermedial relations.[2]

Among these intermedial relations, it is undoubtedly the connections between theme parks and movies that have received the most critical consideration. The reason for the particular attention scholars have paid to theme park-movie relations can be attributed to the fact that historically, both theme parks and one of their historic predecessors, namely, amusement parks, have been closely linked to the cinema from their very beginnings. In *Electric Dreamland* (2012), Lauren Rabinovitz has pointed out that movies and amusement parks appeared almost simultaneously in the mid-1890s, were frequently joined (with nickelodeons often being located adjacent to or even inside early amusement parks and early movies, in turn, frequently counting amusement parks among their subjects), offered visitors similar, mechanically induced thrills or "shocks" to the senses, and thus both substituted "spectacle for natural beauty and sensation for aesthetic contemplation."[3] With respect to theme parks, it is important to note that Disneyland, arguably the first theme park, was designed by filmmakers, a fact that has been stressed in promotional material for the park from the very beginning: a 1957 Disneyland brochure, for instance, notes that "an experienced movie maker himself, one of Walt's [Disney] major considerations in the design and construction of Disneyland was arrangement for visual—and camera—effect."[4]

However, many of the critical discussions concerning the intermedial relationship between theme parks and movies have taken the form of insightful but scattered remarks in texts that focus on some other topic and have only rarely constituted the main interest of scholarly work.[5] Moreover, many of the various theme park elements and design strategies that critics have identified as having been "borrowed" from the movies are, in fact, not exclusive to either theme parks or movies, and thus constitute transmedial rather than intermedial phenomena.[6] For example, many critics have commented on how the sight-restricting, spinning ride vehicles in the various versions of Disney's Haunted Mansion dark ride frame visitors' views like a movie camera. Thus Andrew Lainsbury has noted that the Haunted Mansion ride vehicles:

> were designed to function like movie cameras by twisting, turning, and directing the gaze of passengers from scene to scene. Their high backs and sight-restricting sides, not to mention the metal lap bars that held guests firmly in their seats, guided the experience further by erasing from view anything that might spoil the illusion.[7]

However, the strategy of visual framing is not exclusive to either the cinema or the theme park, but is also employed in other visual media such as photography and painting and therefore constitutes a transmedial phenomenon.

Elsewhere, I have attempted to classify genuinely intermedial relations between movies and Disney theme parks in general according to Wolf's and Rajewsky's typology of intermediality.[8] In this essay, I would like to focus on theme park rides and explore the role of movies in them by identifying four different ways in which ride designers draw on individual movies and cinematic techniques: cinematic shorthand; ride pacing; ride adaptations; and movie-based rides. These four different ways can be heuristically separated, but are frequently combined in actual rides; and while some of them reach back to early fusions of motion pictures and mechanized movement in turn-of-the-century amusement parks and elsewhere, others have emerged from contemporary "convergence culture" in general and multimedia corporations' strategies of cross-media promotion and synergy in particular.[9]

Cinematic Shorthand

As commercial spaces that seek to address a maximum amount of people, theme parks generally select themes that are well-known to the public and represent them in a way to make them as easily and quickly recognizable as possible. To ensure a high level of recognizability, some theme park rides borrow specific elements such as the mise-en-scène (the production design) from particular movies without necessarily being related to that movie in other ways. The movie reference functions like a cinematic shorthand here, then, an easy and quick way to establish a certain mood or atmosphere. Cinematic shorthand is often used when movies represent the most well-known visualization of a theme (as in my first example) and/or when other channels of communication with the visitor are closed (as in my second example).

Terra Mítica's El laberinto del Minotauro ride employs references to multiple film genres. Themed to Greek mythology and housed in a stylized replica of the Palace of Cnossos, this interactive dark ride takes visitors through the labyrinth of the Minotaur, which has generally been identified with the Palace.[10] Before riders actually meet the Minotaur in the ride's climactic final scene, however, they encounter the protagonists of various other Greek myths that are in no way related to that of the Minotaur; among them Pan, Arachne, Adromeda, or Cerberus. As Filippo Carlà and I have shown elsewhere, to make sure that all visitors, even those who are not overly familiar with Greek mythology such as children, get the tone and mood of the ride, the designers drew on the visuals of various movie genres and particular movies, most notably the horror movie, the adventure movie, and *Clash of the Titans* (1981), one of the most influential peplum movies.[11] Cinematic shorthand results in some glaring anachronisms and other incongruities here (neither tropical plants nor gravestones seem to fit into the Minoic setting of the attraction), but successfully conveys an atmosphere of adventure and horror.

Parc Disneyland's Phantom Manor dark ride, too, uses cinematic shorthand to convey a specific atmosphere and to communicate the ride's theme to its visitors. Unlike its counterparts in Anaheim, Orlando, and Tokyo, the Paris version of the Haunted Mansion ride is housed not in a seemingly well-maintained, otherwise inconspicuous building, but in a dilapidated mansion that strongly resembles the Bates mansion from Alfred Hitchcock's *Psycho* (1960). Except for the shared horror theme, of course, the ride itself has no connections whatsoever with the movie, but the designers apparently felt that the name change from Haunted Mansion to Phantom Manor (with "phantom"/"fantôme"/"Phantom" meaning "ghost" in English, French, and German) was not enough to communicate the ride's potentially frightening nature to a multilingual European audience—hence the visual reference to *Psycho* and its iconic setting.[12]

Ride Pacing

Theme park rides not only borrow from the mise-en-scène of movies, but also from their mise-en-chaîne (that is, their editing). Indeed, as Scott A. Lukas has pointed out:

> like pacing in film, the newest dark rides use the unexpected—a quick turn of the ride and a sudden jolt of a monster, scene or other sight—to heighten the sensory experience of the ride. Similar to jump cuts in film, ride pacing creates constant visual and kinetic situations.[13]

Rather than specific movies or movie genres, then, ride pacing references a general cinematic technique, which is, however, unlike cinematic mise-en-cadre or visual framing (see above), unique to the medium.

In contrast to what Lukas suggests, however, ride pacing cannot only be found in the "newest" dark rides, but also in such classics of the genre as Disneyland's Mr. Toad's Wild Ride, Pinocchio's Daring Journey, or Alice in Wonderland. In all of these rides, extremely sharp turns in the ride track and hydraulic doors in-between show scenes prevent riders from seeing the next scene until the very last moment, thus introducing visual barriers that imitate filmic cuts. While the ride vehicles travel at the same speed throughout the entire ride, the sharp turns, in combination with, for example, a switch to a faster soundtrack, also enhance the illusion that the vehicles travel faster in some scenes than in others, thus also imitating filmic cuts.

More technologically advanced rides imitate cuts through the use of so-called Enhanced Motion Vehicles (EMVs) or trackless ride vehicles. EMVs can be described as motion simulators on wheels and have been used in a variety of Disney theme park rides since 1995, amongst others in Disneyland's Indiana Jones Adventure, Disney's Animal Kingdom's Dinosaur, or Tokyo DisneySea's Journey to the Center of the Earth. The ride vehicles can tilt forward, backward, and sideways to give the illusion of driving over rough terrain and even moving backwards; most importantly, however, they can slow down and accelerate at strategic points of the ride. In Journey to the Center of the Earth, for instance, the vehicle speeds up dramatically after the pivotal encounter with the "lava monster," thus "cutting" from a close-up of the monster to a frantic phantom shot. Trackless dark rides have been featured in theme parks at least since the year 2000, when Pooh's Hunny Hunt and El laberinto del Minotauro opened at Tokyo Disneyland and Terra Mítica, respectively. Since then, they have been used in such rides as Aquatopia at Tokyo DisneySea and Ratatouille at Walt Disney Studios Park in Paris. Being able to actually move backwards and spin around themselves, trackless ride vehicles offer an even greater range of motion than EMVs, although their maximum speed appears to be lower than that of the latters. Nevertheless, when they pick up speed after a complete stop—for example, in front of a show scene—the ride imitates a cut from a close-up to a phantom shot.

Ride Adaptations

In addition to drawing on and imitating filmic mise-en-scène and mise-en-chaîne, numerous dark rides allow visitors to re-experience specific movies. Such ride adaptations work with (partial) reproductions of the movie's key elements (including its main plot, main characters, famous lines, production design, and music), which is possible due to the medially hybrid nature of both movies and theme park rides (for instance, both fuse images, language, and music). Examples of ride adaptations include Disney's Fantasyland dark rides, which are all based on the company's animated movies. Of course, these movies themselves often constitute adaptations, for example, from literature and theater: thus Disneyland's Peter Pan's Flight ride, opened in 1955, is an adaptation of the movie *Peter Pan*, released two years before and itself an adaptation of James M. Barrie's play *Peter Pan; Or, the Boy Who Wouldn't Grow Up* (1904). This sometimes plays a role in the design of the ride adaptation, too: at Parc Disneyland, for instance, Fantasyland dark rides were arranged according to the national origins of the authors and playwrights who created the original stories.[14] Due to the limited length of dark rides, however, generally only the most memorable elements or scenes of a movie are reproduced in the rides, with storylines, for example, being considerably simplified. Some rides even focus on but one particular scene of a movie, such as Disneyland's Mad Tea Party, which refers to the "Unbirthday Celebration" scene of *Alice in Wonderland* (1951).

Box office success appears to be the central criterion that determines whether a movie is adapted to a theme park ride or not—the Wizarding World of Harry Potter at Universal Orlando Resort and Pandora–the World of Avatar at Disney's Animal Kingdom are cases in point. There are interesting exceptions, however: for instance, unlike *Avatar*, director James Cameron's second-highest-grossing movie to date, *Titanic* (1997), has never been adapted for a theme park, quite probably because its being based on a real-life tragedy makes it unsuitable for a family-oriented space.[15] By contrast, Disneyland's Splash Mountain, opened in 1989, constitutes an adaptation of the animated segments from the movie *Song of the South* (1949), itself a remediation of Joel Chandler Harris's "Uncle Remus" stories (first published in 1880). That Disney would choose to base a ride on a movie that has been surrounded by controversy over its depiction of the South and that is not available on home video or DVD is interesting insofar as it potentially inspires debates about a "dark" topic—namely, slavery—that is usually excluded from theme parks (see the case of *Titanic* above) and as it cannot drive video and DVD sales.[16] Merchandise based on the movie's animated segments is available at the park, however, and points to the role of ride adaptations in multimedia corporation's synergy strategies: although compared to, for example, video games or other merchandise, theme park rides usually lag behind when it comes to the cross-media promotion of movies, they help to keep the brand alive.[17]

Movie-based Rides

Descendants of turn-of-the-century Hale's Tours and similar, less well-known installations, movie-based rides use actual film technology—that is, the projection of moving images on a screen—and combine them with in-theater effects to induce the sensation of movement and to create a multisensory experience.[18] Movies featured in movie-based rides are so-called phantom rides and usually consist, as did the earlier Hale's Tours movies, of travelogues (see, for instance, Soarin' over California at Disney California Adventure), but may also include, as did later Hale's Tours, narrative elements (for example, the former Le Visionarium attraction at Parc Disneyland, which featured original characters and a plot).[19] Movie-based rides may simultaneously constitute ride adaptations, thus allowing visitors to re-experience a particular movie (as virtually every ride at Universal Studios Hollywood), with rides using already existing footage from the movie, new footage, or a combination of the two.

Frequently, movie-based rides feature special projection techniques to further enhance the immersion, with wide screens, Circlevision, 3-D technology, and IMAX being among the most popular. Thus Impressions de France at Epcot's France pavilion is projected on five adjacent screens, giving a 220-degree coverage. The circle is completed in such movie-based rides as Le Visionarium (see above) or O Canada at Epcot's Canada pavilion, where visitors are surrounded by screens. With its transformation from Star Tours to Star Tours–The Adventures Continue in 2011, Disney's first simulator ride, originally opened in 1987, was upgraded to 3-D technology. And in Soarin' over California (see above), visitors enjoy a movie projected on an IMAX-dome. A particularly interesting case is Disneyland's Finding Nemo Submarine Voyage, which includes underwater screens. In-theater effects, in turn, serve to "extend" the diegetic world of the movie into the "cinema" by appealing to visitors' senses of sight, sound, touch, balance, and smell. Light effects within the theater room and surround-sound systems, moving seats (as in Terra Mítica's Templo de Kinetos) and entire moving theaters (as in such simulator attractions as Star Tours), but also scents and air blasts (as in Soarin' over California), all synchronized with the images projected on the screen, contribute to enhance the immersion of visitors.

The latest generation of movie-based rides combines elements from "classic" dark rides (moving ride vehicles and three-dimensional props) with projections. In such rides as Universal Studios Hollywood's Transformers–the Ride 3-D or Walt Disney Studio Park's Ratatouille: The Adventure, trackless ride vehicles travel from one screen to the next, with the movement of the ride vehicle often imitating the movement of the camera (for example, both the camera and the vehicle moving backwards) to ensure smooth segues in-between different screens. Props in the show building take up elements from the movie and thus also "extend" the diegetic world of the movie into the theater space and occasionally even beyond: in Ratatouille, for example, the last movie scene is set at a restaurant and the screen on which it is projected is surrounded by giant tables, matching those shown on the screen. The ride vehicles then travel to the unloading station of the ride, from where visitors can already see the Ratatouille-themed restaurant, which is located right next to the ride and features similar tables.

Future theme park rides promise to link movies, specifically phantom shots, and actual movement even more closely. In September 2015, Europa-Park (Germany) tested so-called "VR coaster" technology at one of its existing coasters. During the ride, visitors wear VR headsets and watch a computer-generated phantom shot of a roller coaster whose turns and drops are synchronized with those of the actual coaster visitors are riding. The virtual film is created on the spot by hardware mounted on the coaster cars. The designers state that "for the very first time, [riders] can experience real airtime, real drops, intense g-forces and moments of zero gravity in a simulated world" and invite theme parks to upgrade their coasters.[20] Re-theming a ride or coaster (or even theming it in the first place) in real life no longer seems necessary, as rides can be virtually themed. Considering the various ways in which existing theme park rides have always drawn on movies and cinematic techniques, this new development makes perfect sense: as Lauren Rabinovitz has stated with respect to simulator ride adaptations of movies, "it is much easier to simulate reality when the reality being depicted is already a movie. It's not difficult to make a movie that looks like another movie."[21]

The Intermediality of Theme Parks

Due to limited space, this brief overview or typology of the intermedial relations between theme park rides and movies has covered neither the various ways movies "borrow" from theme park rides (see, for instance, the movies based on such rides as Pirates of the Caribbean or Haunted Mansion) nor the ways in which theme parks in general use and imitate cinematic themes and techniques, nor the ways in which theme parks and theme park rides interact with other media such as theater, architecture, music, and so forth.[22] As "hybrid," "composite," or "meta-media," however, theme parks entertain intermedial relations with all of these other media, and while a careful distinction between intermedial and transmedial relations seems absolutely necessary, more detailed, systematic, and critical discussions of the theme park's multifarious and reciprocal relations to other media are sorely needed. Such discussions would help us not only to better understand how theme parks work, but also to get a deeper insight into intermedial networks in general.

Notes

1. See, amongst many others, Margaret J. King, "The New American Muse: Notes on the Amusement/Theme Park," *The Journal of Popular Culture* 15 (1981): 59.

2. On the "hybrid," see, Irina O. Rajwesky, *Intermedialität* (Tübingen, Germany: Francke, 2002), 203. On the notion of the "composite," see, Werner Wolf, "Intermediality," in *Routledge Encyclopedia of Narrative Theory*, eds. David Herman, Manfred Jahn, and Marie-Laure Ryan (London: Routledge, 2005), 253. On the "meta," see, Alexander C.T. Geppert, *Fleeting Cities: Imperial Expositions in Fin-de-Siècle Europe* (New York: Palgrave Macmillan, 2010), 3.

3. Lauren Rabinovitz, *Electric Dreamland: Amusement Parks, Movies, and American Modernity* (New York: Columbia University Press, 2012), 2, 7, 19, 36, 107.

4. Quoted in Eric Avila, *Popular Culture in the Age of the White Flight: Fear and Fantasy in Suburban Los Angeles* (Berkeley: University of California Press, 2004), 126.

5. See, for instance, Scott Bukatman, "There's Always Tomorrowland: Disney and the Hypercinematic Experience," *October* 57 (1991): 107–129; J. P. Telotte, "Theme Parks and Films," in *Disneyland and Culture*, eds. Kathy M. Jackson and Mark I. West (Jefferson, NC: McFarland, 2011), 171–182; and, on the "cinematizing" of world's fairs and Disney, J. P. Telotte, "Disney and 'This World's Fair Thing,'" in *Meet Me at the Fair: A World's Fair Reader*, eds. Laura Hollengreen, Celia Pearce, Rebecca Rouse, and Bobby Schweizer (Pittsburgh: ETC Press, 2013), 409–422.

6. Transmediality refers to formal strategies and thematic complexes that are non-specific to individual media and whose possible origin in one specific medium is either uninteresting or unknown. See Rajewsky, *Intermedialität*, 13.

7. Andrew Lainsbury, *Once upon an American Dream: The Story of Euro Disneyland* (Lawrence: University Press of Kansas, 2000), 61.

8. Florian Freitag, "'Like Walking into a Movie': Intermedial Relations Between Disney Theme Parks and Movies," *The Journal of Popular Culture* (2016) [in print]. For a brief introduction to this model, see Wolf, "Intermediality."

9. Jenkins uses the term convergence culture to identify the increasing circulation of media content across different media platforms and the ensuing blurring of the strict dividing line between media consumers and media producers. See Henry Jenkins, *Convergence Culture: Where Old and New Media Collide* (New York: New York University Press, 2006).

10. For a much more detailed analysis of Terra Mítica and El laberinto, see Filippo Carlà and Florian Freitag, "Ancient Greek Culture and Myth in the Terra Mítica Theme Park," *Classical Receptions Journal* 7, no. 2 (2015): 242–259.

11. See Carlà and Freitag, "Ancient Greek Culture," 255.

12. See Lainsbury, *Once upon an American Dream*, 61.

13. Scott A. Lukas, *Theme Park* (London: Reaktion, 2008), 126.

14. Didier Ghez, *Disneyland Paris: From Sketch to Reality* (Paris: Nouveau millénaire, 2002), 181.

15. Scott A. Lukas, however, discusses a "Taitanic" bar in Tokyo, which "uses shipwrecks, life vests, and video images of the Titanic to produce a space that references the Titanic and other ship disasters of the past. See Scott A. Lukas, "A Politics of Reverence and Irreverence: Social Discourse on Theming Controversies," in *The Themed Space: Locating Culture, Nation, and Self*, ed. Scott A. Lukas (Lanham: Lexington, 2007), 278. Located in a former ticketing office of the White Star Line, the Titanic Bar & Grill in Cobh, Ireland, is themed to the ship, using enlarged photographs and period-appropriate furniture, but entirely excludes the disaster that made the vessel famous; see <http://www.titanicbarandgrill.ie/>. See, as well, Stephen Brown, "Six Degrees of Navigation: Titanic Belfast's Identity Issues," in this collection.

16. See Jason Sperb, *Disney's Most Notorious Film: Race, Convergence, and the Hidden Histories of* Song of the South (Austin: University of Texas Press, 2012).

17. See Celia Pearce and Bobby Schweizer, "Remediation on the High Seas: A Pirates of the Caribbean Odyssey," in this collection.

18. First appearing in 1904 and remaining popular for about a decade, Hale's Tours combined phantom shots with kinetics and in-theater effects to simulate railroad or auto travel; see Rabinovitz, *Electric Dreamland*, 67–94. Another important example of such a ride is the famous Trip to the Moon, which premiered at the Pan-American Exposition in Buffalo, New York (1901) and which made later appearances at Coney Island's Luna Park.

19. See Rabinovitz, *Electric Dreamland*, 88.

20. See <http://www.vrcoaster.com/faq.php>.

21. See Rabinovitz, *Electric Dreamland*, 167.

22. For some suggestions on this point, see Freitag, "'Like Walking into a Movie.'"

14

Sensory Design in Immersive Environments

By Gordon S. Grice

The Supremacy Of The Visual

Try this: next time you enter an unfamiliar space—a building or an environment—close your eyes and take a deep breath. The way a place smells can have a profound effect on the way that you think about it and remember it, so your early olfactory impressions, unencumbered by other senses, are very important. If you want to add to your sensory inventory, keep your eyes closed and just listen. Every environment has characteristic sounds, dependent on a number of things, including reverberation times, reflection, absorption, and background noise. Now, feel the texture of the ground or floor under your feet and, if you can, reach out and touch a surface. Without having looked at the space, you have now compiled a complex—and perhaps memorable—impression of it.

The recorded history of architecture is a pictorial history. Most of the knowledge we have about famous buildings, past and present, comes from visual images of those buildings. Never having had the chance to visit the Guggenheim Museum in Bilbao, the Parthenon, or the Hanging Gardens of Babylon, most of us are comfortably familiar with the buildings because we have seen countless drawings, photographs, and YouTube videos. Even when we actually visit great monuments, we are content to snap a cellphone photo and move on.[1]

For those of us who create buildings and spaces, the process is far more rigorous and intense: no detail can be overlooked. And yet "detail" refers almost exclusively to visual detail, the other sensory perceptions being left largely to chance. When Frank Lloyd Wright spoke of the importance of nature in architectural design, he meant "visible" nature. For the great French architect Le Corbusier, architecture represented simply a "magnificent play of masses brought together in light."[2]

The preeminence of the visual sense was given a huge boost by the introduction of the rules of linear perspective in the fifteenth century, then in the nineteenth century with the introduction of photography. In the twentieth century, the advent of digital modeling virtually (literally) replaced perspective drawing as the standard for architectural creation and communication. The problem is that, for those of us who claim expertise in the design of immersive environments, all modes of sensory perception need to be considered, otherwise, what does "immersive" mean? If our job is to expand human experience, we are compelled to explore more facets of that experience than the visual. In the world of architecture and environmental design, sensory design needs to be paid a little more attention.

Touch

We should begin the discussion with the sense of touch, if for no other reason than that all our senses are adaptations of that one sense. There can be no sight without photons striking the retina, no hearing without sound waves knocking on the eardrum, no taste or smell without molecules—ingested or inhaled—tickling our gustatory and olfactory receptors.

There are many examples of architecturally designed forms and spaces being enhanced, even characterized, by an attention to the tactile qualities of their surfaces. The Brutalist architecture of the mid-twentieth century relied on it heavily. Frequently, however, we are content to admire the rich textures visually, from afar, only imagining how they feel. It seems somehow wrong to physically touch them.

Steen Eiler Rasmussen describes the textural effects of paving stones, but even here, he can't help resorting to their visual qualities.

> Cobblestones, which for aeons have rubbed against each other, are ideally smooth....Granite flagstones which have been worn smooth by the feet of generations of walkers have the same character. By being polished, stone can be made to shine even more.[3]

If you want to experience for yourself what difference a truly tactile environment can make, you have only to visit a traditional Japanese garden, where vegetation, water, rocks, and raked sand all contribute to a rich textural experience. Consider Rasmussen's recollection of a Japanese garden, with "tiles and stepping stones designed to be walked on with wooden clogs."[4] In this description, there is even the added aural component of the clopping of wooden shoes. A Japanese temple provides an almost complete sensory experience, beginning with the changing textures underfoot, as we step from an ancient stone doorsill onto equally ancient floorboards, continuing with the striking aroma of aged cedar and burning incense that also adds a faint smoky cloud to the murky interior and, finally, the striking of a brass bell to engage the aural sense. This might be likened to the environment of a European cathedral—rough granite, sweet incense, soft light from above, and reverberant organ music, but here in the west, this tradition tends to feel quaint and nostalgic, not a living, contemporary experience, as in Japan.

In themed environments, tactile qualities are often downplayed for reasons of durability or economy. Concrete can be painted to resemble wood or brick, and plastics can substitute for stucco, plant material, and anything else imaginable. Visually, these substitutions can be made to appear convincing. But making them *feel* convincing is another matter.

Smell

Amazingly, the aroma of coffee consists of 18 separate and distinct smells. These include such exotic descriptions as "cereal/malty/toast-like… rancid/rotten… rubber-like."[5] If you think about it, smells such as coffee can strongly affect the way we feel and may even alter our impressions and expectations about our surroundings. A good example of aroma-persuasion is the custom of popping an apple pie into the oven before prospective buyers turn up to look at a house we're hoping to sell. A pot of fresh coffee probably doesn't hurt either.

When we hear the word "smell," our noses tend to wrinkle up a little. In current Western vernacular, "aroma" indicates something pleasant; "smell" is the opposite, defined in one dictionary as: "to give out an offensive odor; stink."[6] And yet our sense of smell normally delivers to us some of the most lasting memories that we have—both pleasant and unpleasant.

In fact, it was the smell of madeleine cakes that appears to have launched Proust's *In Search of Lost Time*—in translation, the longest work of fiction in the English language. How is it that one rarely considered sense can hold such surprising power over us? According to Walter Benjamin, our visual sense may even influence the olfactory sense as well.

> No one who is aware of the peculiar toughness with which memories are preserved...will be able to dismiss Proust's sensitivity to smells as in any way random. Certainly, most of the memories we look for come to us as visual images. And even the things that float up freely from the *mémoire involuntaire* are largely isolated visual images—somewhat mysteriously present."[7]

What would Proust or Benjamin think of the current vogue of piping pleasant smells into public and commercial spaces, in order to entice people into stopping and making a purchase?

Novelist Orhan Pamuk describes his disappointment in learning that the relatively tasteless cinnamon rolls he purchased from a New York bakeshop had no connection with the aroma in the shop. As his friends patiently explained to him "the heavenly cinnamon smell that made you long for the sweet rolls the moment you walked into the bakery was actually an artificial fragrance they pumped into the store....in fact there wasn't even an oven in the back."[8] Thinking of Proust's "Lost Time," Pamuk suggests that his experience might best be called "lost illusion."

But duping unsuspecting patrons is not the same as intensifying an experience by introducing pleasant aromas. Professional scent designers, or "olfactive branding" specialists such as Tracy Pepe represent "a handful of North American scent designers who [work] with architects and interior designers to ensure that the smell of a space is as pleasing as the décor."[9] Even homeowners can get professional advice to perk up and individualize the aroma of their environment. For example, "the Delos, a high-end Manhattan condo, perfumes the apartments of its residents…with custom fragrances."[10]

In the world of theme park design, olfactory design is beginning to gain adherents. Here is a partial description of Ferrari World in Abu Dhabi, which promises to:

> offer guests the time of their lives with a host of attractions that indulge the senses in ways never experienced before…with…eye-catching surroundings, authentic aromas and distinctive sounds of Italy.[11]

In Timbertown, Australia, meanwhile an effort is made to lend sensual authenticity, to a re-creation of a pioneer village:

> where the Horse and Carriage still runs, timber is still sawn and the bullock team still hauls its heavy load. You'll smell the distinctive aroma from the steam engines, the smell of sawn timber and the smell of home-style cooked meals.[12]

Before leaving the subject of the horse-and-carriage, a particularly memorable historic recreation takes place in the stables at Warwick Castle in the United Kingdom. Lighting and animatronics lend an immediacy to the reenacted twelfth-century events, but the experience is driven home by the strong, artificial, but seemingly authentic stable aromas. In these examples and many others, the introduced artificial aromas aren't intended to create an aura that doesn't exist, but to augment an experience with contextual aromas that expand and intensify it.

Taste

In discussions about the built environment, the word "taste" often crops up, but it invariably refers to the metaphorical sense of the word: style or preference. It is hard to imagine architectural ingestion and gustation of the built environment. Yet, examples have been cited.

Our local architectural journal published a story about a concrete contractor who was able to establish the readiness of a concrete batch by touch (palpation of a mix to evaluate its texture), sound (the "splat" of a handful slung against a wall), and taste (touching the wet glove with the tongue—although one suspects that the aroma of the mixture was equally relevant). It all seemed entirely believable, even when the author confessed he had made it up.

Then there's this confession by sensory architecture specialist Juhani Pallasmaa:

> [C]ertain qualities of stone…certain metals, detailing of wood can be so subtle that you feel it in your mouth, and I'm myself, in my own work, conscious of that possibility….Maybe 20 years ago in California [I] was just about to enter a grey, rough stone building by the Green Brothers and when I opened the door, I saw the shining white marble threshold and that whiteness of marble juxtaposed with the rough stone almost made me automatically kneel and taste the surface with my tongue.[13]

Did Professor Pallasmaa taste the floor? The word "almost" suggests otherwise. But before we write this off as an extreme exercise in architectural appreciation, remember that infants and toddlers routinely experience the material world in this way. *De gustibus non disputandum.*

There are so few examples of our taste buds being involved in the appreciation of our environment, and so many examples of our environment affecting the way things actually taste, that it might be useful to look at the taste-environment relationship the other way round. Think, for example, of a really nice restaurant that you have visited recently, and how much the ambience contributed to your appreciation of the food.

From my own experience, I very well remember a multi-course meal in a Canadian winery. The wine was very good, but it was more than the flavor of the wine that enhanced the meal. It was also the *idea* of the wine—present in every detail of every room—that enhanced the taste of the food. The main course took place in a candle-lit room, with aged French oak barrels lining the walls, where the acoustic characteristics created by the barrels, as well as the low light level, the aroma of the wine—and perhaps the quantities being consumed—all had the effect of heightening the gustatory delight.

Applying this lesson to the creation of immersive spaces, designers only need to place themselves in the shoes of the consumer. If the goal is to provide a memorable experience and the heart of that experience consists of the pleasurable consumption of food and drink, then an environment that supports this can be considered a successful one.

Perhaps this is a good time to introduce a new area of sensory design. Biomedical engineer Irwin Adam Eydelnant is "part of a new group of *flavour architects* who blend science, design, and technology to intensify taste"[14] The word "architect" doesn't just lend a sense of class to the enterprise. It also hints at the fact that architecture may be one of the factors that influence the way we taste things. Emilie Baltz, another flavor architect, and founder of the Food Design Studio at Pratt Institute in New York,

> is looking at ways to redesign the dining experience by playing with the slate of sensations—smells, sights, sounds—that ultimately influence how things taste. Her work ranges from the fully immersive and wildly experimental—hosting a dinner party 25-metres underground in a dark, decommissioned nuclear reactor—to smaller, more specific tweaks."[15]

The example of flavor architecture points up that in an ideal environment, the specific sensory focus of enjoyment is immaterial. All the senses contribute to a single pleasurable experience.

Hearing

you close your eyes as you stand inside a building, your ears will receive the sounds of the building, but what you hear depends a great deal on how you listen.[16]

As mentioned above, every space possesses a distinct auditory signature. Some are purposely designed with this in mind. In performance spaces, for example, acoustic properties are critically important, although other considerations mustn't be overlooked. If you're going to sit for several hours to listen to a symphony orchestra, you need to be comfortable. In ages past, before electronic amplification, music and architecture were frequently designed to complement each other.

In *Experiencing Architecture*, Steen Eiler Rasmussen describes how the history of architecture is intertwined with the history of acoustics and music.[17] St. Peter's Basilica (precursor of the present St. Peter's) consisted of many hard surfaces and big volumes, resulting in long reverberation times, so a rhythmic kind of recitation evolved, with special attention to the "sympathetic note" that was perfect for the open vowels of Latin speech. The text became song, which led to the Gregorian chants, especially composed for the space.[18] Organist and composer Giovanni Gabrieli, created music to be played in domed music galleries and heard simultaneously by the congregation. Much of Johann Sebastian Bach's music was composed especially for St. Thomas Church in Liepzig, where the installation of numerous, reverberant, baroque wooden boxes made it possible for much more complex forms of music to evolve.[19] Rasmussen traces this coevolution through the rococo and classical revival eras, to the era of radio transmission. Of the modern era Rasmussen writes, "There is no longer any interest in producing rooms with differentiated acoustical effects—they all sound alike."[20]

Rasmussen's book was first published in 1959, but more than a half-century later, there is still some truth to this observation. With the exception of performance spaces, developments in digital sound creation and reproduction have greatly diminished the importance of acoustic design.

Just as commercial scent design, or "aromascapes" seek to create an impression that wouldn't exist otherwise, soundscapes of the post-WWII era attempted to "perfume" or sometimes even obliterate their context.[21] The terms "elevator music" and "mall music" refer to such soothing, out-of-context background soundtracks.[22] But in an anonymous environment such as that found in many shopping malls, transportation hubs, and public spaces, this aural blanket can't create an environment all by itself. Even today, in their most artful applications these soundscapes, sometimes called "environmental music," need the support of an overall theme, established visually, and perhaps texturally and aromatically as well.

For designers of non-performance entertainment spaces music provides a useful resource in enhancing the theme or narrative of the space. Many theme and amusement parks employ an overall soundtrack to generate a desirable mood among visitors. A particularly good example is Disney California Adventure, where a soundtrack follows visitors wherever they go, spilling softly from invisible speakers in the landscape. Like the environment itself, the music is adapted from a loosely defined bygone era—one that is familiar to very few of us personally, but to most of us culturally. Not only does the music relieve anxiety, like mall music does, it also creates a subtle mental time-scape that alters our perceptions and transports us back to a fictional trouble-free past, reinforcing the park's overall theme.

But theme parks are meant to be fun, and lulling visitors into a nostalgic dream doesn't entirely accomplish that. A much more effective fun-oriented noise source is not musical at all. If you think about your recent visits to a theme or amusement park, you might recall that, rising above the tootle of the calliope or the din of rock music, there was one unforgettable sound: the screams of terror-and-delight that come from the thrill rides. It seems that the sound of other people enjoying themselves can be very effective in raising the spirits of anyone within earshot.

> You go to a place like [a boardwalk or an arcade], and it is the sound of people having fun, and that is pretty contagious. When you hear other people having fun, you can have fun vicariously without even realizing it. It is a group experience.[23]

The sounds of people screaming in delight, the overlapping theme music, even the hoarse sounds of visitors attempting to carry on a conversation above the din, are not haphazard. They are an integral part of an amusement park tradition that goes back more than 100 years.[24]

A Second Sense of Touch: Kinesthesia

A special branch of the sense of touch, kinesthesia or proprioception is an internal mechanism that keeps track of our physical orientation and location. This sense comes last in our discussion because it is possibly the most overpowering, and because it is unique to entertainment environments.

In addition to the excited aural stimulus, such as the screams of terror-and-delight described above, thrill rides can also create a vicarious physical stimulation. In his essay "Roller Coasters for the Non-Enthusiast," ride designer Jeff Havlik points out that the physical sensation of a monster coaster involves more people than those with the courage to ride it.[25] "The ride should engage the guest on the surrounding walkways where the speed, force, and exhilaration can be experienced by everyone."[26]

This kinesthetic sense is of special interest to designers of immersive experiences because, where most designers are required to ensure that the environments they create will allow end-users maintain a constant peaceful equilibrium—nothing that might cause discomfort—designers of immersive environments have the delightful opportunity to design experiences that are intentionally stimulating. This includes those that are disorienting and physically unsettling—roller coasters, drop towers, and various other thrill rides. The fictional character Dr. Nick Laslowicz explains the appeal of such rides: "Gravity is a mistake," he says. "We fight the forces that hold us down. And our whole life is an effort to escape from [this] reality."[27] When you add the stimulation of the traditional five senses, the result can be more than exhilarating; it can be memorable.

You might wonder how this relates to the design of immersive environments themselves. With a roller coaster or a wave swinger, it's mostly the lack of an environment (being suspended in space, for example) that provides the thrill. But consider the importance of rides and attractions. In their most extreme form, there is the sensation of complete disorientation that comes from a sudden drop or a high-speed curve. In these instances, the designed environment accedes to the requirements of ride engineering. But the ride is only part of the thrill. Before the ride, there is the build-up of anticipation and excitement of the preshow, then the cooling-down and memory imprinting period of the exit—not forgetting the exit retail. And, of course, those timid individuals standing comfortably on firm ground, watching.

I recently had the opportunity to do some un-thrilling research on thrill rides. A Japanese filmmaker, asked me to review some of the world's wildest thrill rides for a Fuji TV feature. In no special order, the rides were:

1. Tower of Terror II (Dreamworld, Gold Coast, Australia)
2. Formula Rossa (Ferrari World, Abu Dhabi)
3. Insano (Beach Park, Fortaleza, Brazil)
4. Gravity Max (Lihpao Land, Taichung, Taiwan)
5. Giant Canyon Swing (Glenwood Caverns Adventure Park, Glenwood Springs, Colorado, United States)
6. X Scream at the Stratosphere (Las Vegas, Nevada, United States)
7. Insanity at the Stratosphere (Las Vegas, Nevada, United States)
8. Takabisha (Fuji-Q Highland Theme Park, Fujiyoshida, Japan)
9. Kilimanjaro water slide (Aldea da Águas Park Resort, Rio de Janeiro, Brazil)

I was asked to rate the top three, giving reasons for my choice—in other words, offer a cerebral response to a visceral experience. The task was made possible, but a lot tamer, by the fact that I wasn't actually going to go on the rides (I have never been on any of them). My impressions were to be based on videos that I viewed on my laptop. This is my description of my favorite:

> Takabisha, Fuji-Q Highland Theme Park, Fujiyoshida, Japan: The vertical assent is worrying enough. Then the drop propels the coaches downward at an angle greater than 90 degrees, so that riders are lifted from their seats as they fall. The application of positive gravitational force is sudden and extreme, but the thrill isn't over. Riders are subjected to a great deal of further disorientation, before their trajectory is finished. To me, this ride represents the most extreme experience combined with the longest period of disorientation—the biggest value for the money.

I recall that merely watching the rides on my computer screen provided a mild adrenaline rush. Even rereading these words causes my heart to race a little bit.

More recently, along with the Forrec Creative Studio, I made a research visit to Canada's Wonderland, home of the Behemoth and the Leviathan (which replaced it in 2012 as Canada's tallest and fastest coaster). The nature of our research required that we record our experiences on these rides, as well as the park's other coasters. The sheer exhilaration of the two major coasters (we went on each of them twice, being sure to sit in the front seat and then the back seat) cannot be duplicated by any other passive experience. And as for the spatial experience, this is perhaps an example of sensory stimulation regardless of environment. The steel supports whizzing past at more than 100 miles per hour provide all the structural context required.

"Architecture of inconvenience" (also called "design for discomfort") is a useful phrase. It describes situations in which designers abandon their mission to create ease and convenience, in order to intentionally force or encourage people do things and go places that they might otherwise avoid. One goal of this apparent subversion may be to cause them to spend more money (the milk and eggs are always at the back of the supermarket), but in theme parks, creating inconvenient and unexpected routes and diversions is a good way of enriching the visitor experience. Discomfort and inconvenience is epitomized in thrill rides, our tactile sense is stimulated to its very limits to create an intense and unforgettable experience.

Afterword

For most of us, the overwhelming dependence on our visual sense is unlikely to abate any time soon. It has been with us far too long and has been responsible for too many important human developments: astronomy, microscopy, linear perspective, and so forth. It has even been proposed as one of the main reasons that we walk upright, since bipedalism affords a better view of our surroundings. Many of today's most exciting technological innovations deal with the visual realm. Ultra-high-definition and 3-D television, virtual spaces with real-time simulated visual experiences, holography,

3-D printing, and all of the amazing applications available for our smartphones—these things entrench our dedication to the realm of the visual, and make it even more difficult to convince clients and investors of the importance of sensory design. Seeing is believing, they might say. "Pics or it didn't happen."[28]

In the Forrec office, we are currently working on a winery resort project, both a working winery and a resort/recreation environment—in this case, an immersive one. As described in the Taste section above, a winery presents the unique opportunity to explore the entire sensory spectrum, including taste. In our concept statement for this project, we describe our design approach:

> The intricate art, background music, tactile fabrics and finishes of interior spaces harmonize with the full menu of senses, differentiating the feel of each environment and transporting the guest to a magical, far-away place. There, while dining, tasting, sleeping, and relaxing the guest can absorb and appreciate the experience using all five senses.

The environment promises to be a fully immersive sensory experience. But, in the design world, the bulk of conceptualizing, developing, presenting, documenting, and even constructing the physical environment are all dependent on powerful digital—that is, visual—modeling programs. So the possibility of non-visual design ideas surviving to the finished project is never assured.

As designers of immersive environments, we invariably involve as many ways of looking at the environment as possible throughout the design process. This includes a consideration of the entire sensory range. However, as important—and as exciting—as sensory stimuli are, clients and developers are often reluctant to embrace things they can't see and, as a result, multi-sensory design runs the risk of being overlooked, marginalized, or budgeted out of the final project.

Research on the behavioral effects of sensory input has increased in recent years. This is due in part to new areas of exploration in neuroscience, the emergence of commercial phenomena such as olfactive branding, and sensory research projects such as "smellwalks."[29] The increasing sophistication of simulation attractions involving motion, aromas, sound, and movement has also contributed to the expectation of more sensually engaging environments. But in general, the study of sensory experience is still heavily reliant on trial and error and educated guesswork. For architects and designers, there is no better reference source than personal experience and the observation of the experiences of others, during daily life, as well as under the special circumstances presented by immersive environments. The realm of the senses is a rich and largely untapped design resource that can and should provide the raw material for more immersive and more memorable environments.

Notes

1. John Urry, *The Tourist Gaze, Leisure and Travel in Contemporary Societies* (London: Sage, 1990), 11. Urry discusses the "tourist gaze" phenomenon, whereby, initial impressions may be "preconditioned through the experience of mass produced images of heritage sites for marketing purposes." In some cases cited, "individuals often express the sentiment that they prefer the experience of consuming the image to experiencing the original monument or site."

2. Le Corbusier, *Towards a New Architecture* (London: The Architectural Press, 1927), 31.

3. Steen Eiler Rasmussen, *Experiencing Architecture* (Cambridge, MA: MIT Press, 1989), 174–175.

4. Rasmussen, *Experiencing Architecture*, 174–175.

5. International Coffee Organization, "The Aromas and Flavors of Coffee: What You Smell, Taste and Feel," <http://www.thenibble.com/reviews/main/beverages/coffees/aromas.asp>.

6. *Random House Unabridged Dictionary* (New York: Random House, 1983).

7. Walter Benjamin, "Picturing Proust," in *The Work of Art in the Age of Mechanical Reproduction* (London: Penguin, 2008), 110.

8. Orhan Pamuk, *Other Colours: Essays and a Story* (Toronto: Vintage Canada, 2007).

9. Matthew Hague, "Bottled Influence," *The Globe and Mail*, September 11, 2014.

10. Matthew Hague, "A Sense of Occasion: How Luxury Hotels and Condos Seduce You with Signature Scents," *The Globe and Mail*, September 10, 2014.

11. Ferrari World Abu Dhabi, "World's First Ferrari Theme Park Opens in 100 Days," <www.ferrariworldabudhabi.com/en-gb/media-centre/press-releases/worlds-first-ferrari-theme-park-opens-in-100-days.aspx>.

12. Greater Port Macquarie, "Timbertown Heritage Theme Park," <www.portmacquarieinfo.com.au/explore/location.aspx?id=378>.

13. Alan Saunders, host, quoting Juhani Pallasmaa, "Beyond Appearances: Architecture and the Senses" in *The Comfort Zone* (radio program presented by Australian Broadcasting Corporation, November 6, 2004).

14. Matthew Hague, "Technology Is Changing the Way We Eat—But Gizmos Will only Get Us so Far," *The Globe and Mail*, February 10, 2015. Italics are mine.

15. Hague, "Technology Is Changing the Way We Eat."

16. Bill Gastmeier, *OAA Perspectives*, Fall 2010, 18

17. Rasmussen, *Experiencing Architecture*, "Chapter X: Hearing Architecture."

18. Rasmussen, *Experiencing Architecture*, 226–230.

19. Rasmussen, *Experiencing Architecture*, 231–232.

20. Rasmussen, *Experiencing Architecture*, 235.

21. Ethan Trex, "Muzak History: The Background Story on Background Music," <http://mentalfloss.com/article/28274/muzak-history-background-story-background-music>. According to Trex, Muzak gained its foothold in North America in the 1940s, as a means of stimulating office workers.

22. SensualMusic4You, "Best of Blevator Music and Mall Music," <https://www.youtube.com/watch?v=HZiSPYWgd5E>. The site promises "2 hours of remix playlist video. This elevator and mall music collection is compiled for your enjoyment."

23. Alexander Verdoni, "The Sound of Fun: A Brief Survey on the Soundscape of Amusement Places," (dissertation UC Santa Cruz, 2011) transcription of an interview with Jem Gruber, The Pacific Pinball Museum, <https://www.academia.edu/1558561/The_Sound_of_Fun_A_Brief_Survey_on_the_Soundscape_of_Amusement_Places>.

24. Verdoni, "The Sound of Fun."

25. Jeff Havlik, "Roller Coasters for the Non-Enthusiast," Bemusement Blooloop Blog, February 5, 2015, <www.blooloop.com/blog/2015/02/roller-coasters-for-the-non-enthusiast/>.

26. Havlik, "Roller Coasters for the Non-Enthusiast."

27. Till Nowak, KurzFilmAgentur Hamburg, "The Centrifuge Brain Project," <www.youtube.com/watch?v=RVeHxUVkW4w>. Dr. Nick Laslowicz is played by actor Leslie Barany.

28. Jacob Silverman, "'Pics or It Didn't Happen'—The Mantra of The Instagram Era: How Sharing Our Every Moment on Social Media Became the New Living," *The Guardian*, February 26, 2015 <www.theguardian.com/news/2015/feb/26/pics-or-it-didnt-happen-mantra-instagram-era-facebook-twitter>.

29. Nathan Collins, "Eau de Cité: Mapping the Smells of a City May Help Governments Plan Better, Richer Cities, Researchers Argue," *Pacific Standard*, June 2, 2015, <http://www.psmag.com/books-and-culture/mapping-the-smells-of-a-city>.

PART VI

The Notions of Identity, Self, and Ideology

15

Autotheming

Themed and Immersive Spaces in Self-Dialogue

By Florian Freitag

"At Disneyworld in Florida," Jean Baudrillard notes in *Cool Memories II*, "they are building a giant mock-up of Hollywood, with the boulevards, studios, etc. One more spiral in the simulacrum. One day they will rebuild Disneyland at Disneyworld."[1] And why would they not? In the land where "[e]verything is destined to reappear as simulation," as Baudrillard characterizes the US elsewhere, even Disneyland, this "perfect model of all the entangled orders of simulacra," would surely be rebuilt or simulated at some point, too.[2] Baudrillard may have intended his comment to be deliberately exaggerated or ironic. Instead, it turned out to be prophetic: for at least two decades, theme parks have increasingly relied on theme parks and their historic antecedents (trolley parks, amusement piers, and county fairs) as themes for rides, shops, restaurants, and entire themed areas. Indeed, Clavé's list of recurring themes in contemporary theme parks—he mentions comics, the future and science, history, children's tales, the world of toys, travel, nature, the cinema, local mythological culture, and music—should also include theme parks themselves: Paradise Pier at Disney California Adventure, Toyville Trolley Park at Tokyo DisneySea, and the Boardwalk section at Knott's Berry Farm, but also Parc Disneyland's Walt's restaurant and the Disney & Co. shop, Universal Studios Hollywood's The Simpsons Ride, and Europa-Park's Historama experience, all offer theme park visitors an opportunity to encounter simulated versions of either theme parks themselves or their historic predecessors.[3]

As I will argue in the following, such cases of self-referential theming or "autotheming," as I will call it, reflect a number of concerns and issues in current theme park design and in today's theme park industry.[4] While all of the above examples illustrate theming's inherent goal to represent a place, time, or atmosphere that is as remote from visitors' daily lives as possible, the Historama and Walt's restaurant mirror the growing relevance of branding in the theme park industry. The comparatively "light" theming of, for instance, the Boardwalk or the original Paradise Pier points, in turn, to the budget concerns of theme park operators. Autotheming may not only help to cut costs and to establish the theme park as a brand, however, but also to depoliticize theming and to avoid the kind of controversies that have arisen over more or less explicitly political, cultural, or historical themes, as in the case of the ultimately abandoned Disney's America project. Conversely, with their explicitly ironic or dark approach to theme parks, The Simpsons Ride and Dismaland, Banksy's Bemusement Park in Weston-super-Mare (UK), seem to deliberately invite controversy and instigate discussions about theming in general and its inherent politics of inclusion/exclusion in particular.

Autotheming Strategies

In the general context of themed and immersive spaces, the term "autotheming" refers to places whose theming reflects their function, such as a shop themed to a shop, a restaurant themed to a restaurant, a hotel themed to a hotel, and so forth. Prominent examples (all taken from the Disneyland Resort Paris resort hotels) include the General Store, a souvenir shop themed to the general store of a small town in the US West; Parkside Diner, a restaurant themed to a New York diner; and the Hotel Sequoia Lodge, a hotel themed to an American National Park hotel. Autothematic references may be even more specific: with its name, its menu, and the green-and-white color scheme of its interior, the Café du Monde in downtown Tokyo, one of twenty franchised Cafés du Monde all over Japan, refers to the world-famous coffee shop opened in 1862 in the New Orleans French Market.[5] Even before the officially licensed autotheming of Tokyo's Café du Monde, the façade of Café Orléans, located in the New Orleans section of Tokyo Disneyland's Adventureland, evoked the original Café du Monde with its characteristic green-and-white awnings (although the Café Orléans serves crepes rather than Café du Monde's signature beignets).

In the more restricted context of theme parks, two forms of autotheming can be distinguished: firstly, theme park spaces (rides, restaurants, shops, entire themelands) that are themed to the parks themselves and/or their history (one might call this "autobiotheming"); and secondly, theme park spaces that are themed to predecessors of the theme park genre, such as amusement parks. In both forms, just like in other, non-theme park cases of autotheming, but unlike elsewhere in the theme park, theming and function are inextricably linked. Steinkrüger points out that in theme parks, the symbols used to establish a specific theme usually do not have the same function and symbolic meaning as in their original context. An Egyptian pyramid in a theme park, for instance, neither serves as the tomb of a pharaoh nor represents the god-like status of the deceased, but may house a shop, a restaurant, or a ride and simply denotes "(ancient) Egypt."[6] The Ferris wheel in Disney California Adventure's Paradise Pier, by contrast, not only helps to establish the section's theme—an early-twentieth century West coast amusement pier—but also really functions as a Ferris wheel, offering riders a thrill experience and great views of the surrounding area.

To be sure, there are counterexamples, especially in cases where theme parks apply autotheming not to entire areas or "lands," but to individual shops, restaurants, or rides. The theming of Disney & Co., for instance, a souvenir shop on Parc Disneyland's Main Street, U.S.A., evokes a turn-of-the-century county fair. At the entrance, banners in the American national colors welcome customers to the Pike County Fair, point out the "Games of Skill!" featured there, and invite visitors to "Try [Their] Luck!"[7] Throughout the shop one can find funhouse mirrors and humorous posters that announce the fair's attractions, from the "animal trainer extraordinaire" "Mr. Mickey Mouse" to the "gentleman juggler and equilibrist" "The Great Donaldo." The Pike County Fair even features a carousel: the shop's central room is round, the shelves on the walls feature panels with painted landscape scenes at their top, and there is a calliope behind the cash register, whose music provides the soundtrack of the shop. This stylized "carousel" does not function as a carousel, of course. Instead, it simply helps to establish the county fair theme and provides display space for the merchandise.

With the exception of the relationship between theming and function, however, autotheming is remarkably similar to other themes employed in theme parks. In fact, autotheming can be argued to expose the very rationale or essence of theming. In *The Disneyization of Society*, Alan Bryman defines "theming" as follows:

> Theming consists of the application of a narrative to institutions or locations. Typically, the source of the theme is external to the institution or object to which it is applied. This externality is usually revealed as being external in terms of space, time, sphere or any combination of these sources.[8]

Yet for Steinkrüger the "externality" of the theme is not only typical for a themed space. As he argues in *Thematisierte Welten*, it is a necessary condition for a place to be perceived as a themed space: "The fact that they constitute representations does not sufficiently differentiate themed from other spaces. The difference lies in what is represented there; namely, something that is different from what one may expect at this place in ordinary or daily life."[9] And what could be more different from ordinary or daily life than a theme park? Hence, by simulating theme parks and their predecessors, autotheming offers theme park visitors a maximum of externality.

Moreover, like theming in general, autotheming, too, is governed by specific strategies of cultural and medial translation that guide or dictate the transfer from the theme's "sources" to its representation in the theme park. Richard Schickel has used the somewhat disparaging term "Disneyfication" to describe these strategies, Scott A. Lukas has generally spoken of theming's "politics of inclusion/exclusion," and Filippo Carlà and I have identified selection, abstraction, immersion, and transmediality as the most important of these strategies.[10] However one may describe the processes of translation that theme park designers use to establish a theme, they also apply to autotheming. Autothemed spaces represent theme park versions of theme and amusement parks, that is, heavily edited versions of the theme that highlight specific aspects of theme parks and their antecedents while de-emphasizing others. This becomes particularly obvious when theme parks choose to represent themselves (rather than their historic predecessors), as, for instance, in the case of Europa-Park's Historama attraction. Simultaneously, the Historama illustrates one of the reasons why autothemed elements, and especially autobiothemed elements, have become increasingly popular in theme parks: namely, the way in which they can help to establish the theme park as a brand.

Celebrating the Brand

As one of the highlights of its thirty-fifth anniversary celebrations in 2010, Europa-Park (Germany) opened the Historama attraction in the huge cone-shaped building next to the Dutch section of the park. Previously, the building had housed the Lila Chocoland, a brand space dedicated to a well-known Swiss chocolate brand. The building housed attractions, restaurants, and shops, all themed around the chocolate brand and its products: a café that served hot chocolate and other chocolate-related items, a store that offered the company's entire product range, an interactive experience where children could learn about chocolate manufacturing, a monorail ride painted in the company colors, and, most importantly, Das Lila Geheimnis (The Purple Secret), a revolving theater show about the history of chocolate. When the Lila Chocoland was rethemed to the Europa-Park Historama in 2010, the shop, the interactive experience, and all references to chocolate and purple cows (the brand's mascot) were removed, the monorail was repainted, and the revolving theater no longer told the history of chocolate, but instead that of Europa-Park itself.

Prior to 2010, the history of Europa-Park had been the subject of a somewhat hidden and comparatively simple exhibition in the park's Italian section. That exhibition, called Mack-Rides Ausstellung (Mack-Rides Exhibition), featured several glass cases with old newspaper clippings, artifacts from the park's beginnings, and pictures of celebrity visitors, as well as, as its centerpiece, a huge scale model of the park that was continuously updated with each new addition to the park. In 2010, parts of the model and some of the artifacts and newspaper clippings were transferred to the waiting area of the new Historama, and the park added numerous videos, signs, and timelines providing background information. Much like the original Mack-Rides Ausstellung, then, the waiting area presents the park and its history in a museal, non-immersive manner. The Historama's main show, by contrast, offers visitors a theme park version of Europa-Park and its story.

For instance, the four-act show employs animatronics, projections, light and other in-theater effects, as well as music and sound effects to give an overview of the park's history (Act 1), to tell the history of the park's parent company and offer glimpses behind the stage (Act 2), and to present the park's main rides (Act 3) and shows (Act 4). The last two acts are particularly impressive: in Act 3, point-of-view shots of various Europa-Park coasters, reminiscent of the so-called movie rides of the early cinema of attractions, are projected on a wide screen and combined with special effects such as spraying water on viewers when water coasters are shown.[11] In Act 4, still shots of the park's various shows are combined with lasers, fountains, mist screen projections, and epic music. Hence, the Historama uses various media to immerse visitors into rides and shows that are located right outside and, in some cases, just a three-minute walk away from the Historama itself.

But Historama's versions constitute "enhanced" versions of these theme park rides and shows, in the sense that theming's "politics of inclusion/exclusion" or its strategies of selection and abstraction are used to full extent here. The film collage in Act 3, for instance, only shows the highlights of the various coasters (for example, the "big splash" in the case of water coasters) and cuts from one coaster to the next without any segue. The film shows neither visitors waiting in line for the coaster nor people getting on and off the vehicles, nor people walking from one coaster to the next, let alone breakdowns or accidents. Instead, visitors of the Historama get the coaster experience pure and simple, without any of the negative side effects that actually riding the coaster may have. This also applies to the representation of the park in general: as we do not get to see visitors traveling to Europa-Park, standing in line and paying for the park tickets, eating, taking breaks, going to the bathroom, getting lost in the park, or arguing over what to do next, the show implies that the Europa-Park experience simply consists of enjoying the park's rides and shows.

The representation of the park's and its parent company's history are perhaps even more selective: similar to Disney's Carousel of Progress, on which it was modeled with respect to both ride technique and underlying ideology, the Historama show tells the history of Europa-Park and Mack-Rides as a teleological narrative of progress. From their humble beginnings as a wagon manufacturer in 1780 and a small regional park in 1975, respectively, the company and the park are depicted as steadily progressing to develop into an innovative and successful ride designer and into Germany's largest theme park.

In this success story, there is no room for setbacks, failures, or false modesty: the first act presents the current CEOs of the company, brothers Jürgen and Roland Mack, as talking marble busts in a Greek temple, reminiscent of the bronze bust of Walt Disney at Disneyland Paris (see below).

Much like the illustrated books and the videos about Europa-Park that are sold as souvenirs in the park's shops, then, the Historama offers visitors a highly selective, idealized version of Europa-Park and its history, though it does so not through the medium of print or film, but through the medium of the theme park. Even after its transformation from the Lila Chocoland into the Historama, then, the cone-shaped building can still be considered a brand space, but instead of the chocolate brand, it celebrates Europa-Park as a brand. Indeed, as various scholars have pointed out, the issue of branding has become more and more important in the theme park business. In *Theme Park*, for instance, Scott A. Lukas writes that in the contemporary world, "the most significant transformation of the theme park" involves the brand, and in *The Immersive Worlds Handbook*, he dedicates an entire chapter to "The Brand and the Senses."[12] Autotheming offers theme parks an immersive, engaging way to establish and celebrate themselves as a brand, and Europa-Park has continued to use autotheming for these purposes: for its fortieth anniversary in 2015, the park has developed a 4-D animated movie in which the park's mascots travel through time and encounter none other than the parent company's founder.

As the example of Europa-Park has shown, autothemed branding in theme parks is often tied to self-referential temporalities—namely, park anniversaries—although this is not always or necessarily the case. At Parc Disneyland in Paris, Walt's–An American Restaurant has welcomed visitors since the park's opening in 1992. As its name and its entrance suggest, the restaurant appears to be themed to the park's founder and his life: the entrance hall features a bronze bust of Disney, the walls are decorated with his pictures, and his initials can be found everywhere from windowpanes to lampshades. The main dining rooms, however, evoke four of the five themed sections of the park: through its Art Déco furnishings, carpets, wallpaper, and lighting fixtures, and particularly through the framed pieces of concept art hanging on its walls, for instance, one of the rooms refers to the park's Discoveryland section, which, in turn, uses design elements of steampunk and Art Déco as well as motifs and storylines from Jules Verne's novels to evoke a late-nineteenth century retrofuture. Hence, this dining room does not merely share a theme with Discoveryland, it is *themed to* Discoveryland. Similarly, the other dining rooms do not simply refer to the Western, North African, and medieval fairy tale themes of the park's Frontierland, Adventureland, and Fantasyland sections, respectively, but—again particularly through concept drawings by the park's designers—to the sections themselves.

A visit to Walt's restaurant thus allows patrons to immerse themselves into the park's themed lands without actually visiting them (it is no coincidence that Walt's restaurant is located in Main Street, U.S.A., towards the entrance of the park). Moreover, the sheer materiality of the themed space of the restaurant not only naturalizes the park's apparently random selection of themes and presents them as an organic ensemble, but also inextricably links the park to the person and life story of Walt Disney. Although Disney had been dead for more than 25 years by the time Parc Disneyland opened, Walt's restaurant brands the space as Walt's park. Given the controversies about the park even prior to its opening, with French intellectuals calling the park a "cultural Chernobyl" and French demonstrators throwing eggs and ketchup at Disney executives, it seemed to make sense to connect the park with a man whose popular image was that of a kindly smiling, elderly uncle, rather than with an aggressively expanding multinational entertainment corporation.[13] Of course, this has also and routinely been done in the various books, videos, and shows about Parc Disneyland that the Disney company has released and produced—the *EuroDisney Führer*, for instance, tells us much more about Walt Disney than about Michael Eisner, the Walt Disney Company's CEO who supervised the project—but in the case of Walt's restaurant, it is done through the medium of theming.[14] Again, autotheming is used to help establish the theme park as a brand.

Budget-conscious Theming

Autotheming, both autobiotheming as well as autotheming that refers to the historic predecessors of the theme park genre, has also often been employed in theme parks to keep budgets under control. Tomorrowland at Disneyland in California and The Boardwalk at Knott's Berry Farm are cases in point, although Paradise Pier at Disney California Adventure illustrates that this particular use of autotheming does not work in every park and/or can be carried too far. With respect to Disneyland's Tomorrowland, the designers introduced autobiotheming as a solution to the daunting challenge of constantly keeping the themed section ahead of its time. As John Hench, one of the designers involved with Tomorrowland, complained: "Obviously, it's impossible to design the future…this minute it's now and tomorrow it will be yesterday."[15] Opened in 1955 along with the rest of the park, Tomorrowland had already been completely rebuilt in 1967 to keep up with (and overtake) the fast-paced technological and architectural changes of the mid-twentieth century. By the mid-1980s, however, the "heavy-handed concrete buildings and uninterrupted façades" of the 1967 redesign had again come to look "commonplace," too much like "the thousands of anonymous office buildings and warehouses that line[d] America's cities and suburbs," and yet another redesign seemed in order for the section to continue to live up its claims of depicting the future rather than the present or even the past.[16]

For the Tomorrowland section of Parc Disneyland, which was being planned at the time for its 1992 opening, Disney's designers therefore chose to take a different approach to the topic and focus on past—more precisely, late-nineteenth century—rather than contemporary visions of the future (see above). Similarly, in 1995 the Tomorrowland of the Magic Kingdom in Florida, whose original design was based on Disneyland's 1967 version of Tomorrowland, switched to past visions of the future, although the clock was not turned back as far as in the case of Discoveryland: descriptions of the Magic Kingdom's new Tomorrowland list cultural productions from the 1930s as the main sources of inspiration for its architecture, amongst others the 1939 New York World's Fair, Dick Calkins's *Buck Rogers* comics, Alex Raymond's *Flash Gordon* comics, and the popular science magazine *Mechanix Illustrated*.[17] Finally, retrofuturistic ideas also played a role in the 1998 redesign of Disneyland's Tomorrowland. Yet here, the designers did not draw on "external" sources such as Jules Verne's novels (as in Paris) or *Buck Rogers* (as in Orlando), but on Disney's own depictions of the future in its various Tomorrowlands.

Indeed, when Disneyland opened its new Tomorrowland, it featured references to both Discoveryland's retrofuture—notably the brown-and-gold color scheme and a copy of the Orbitron spinner ride, which functions as Discoveryland's kinetic centerpiece—as well as Disneyland's original Tomorrowland: a scaled-down copy of the TWA Moonliner, which had dominated the Tomorrowland landscape from 1955 to 1962, a prominently placed model of the Monsanto House of the Future, an iconic walk-through attraction in Tomorrowland from 1957 to 1967, and a mural featuring other long-gone Tomorrowland rides.[18] In 2005, even more references to Disneyland's original Tomorrowland were introduced, among them a revised color scheme that harkens back to that of the 1960s, a modernist topper for the Tomorrowland Terrace stage that strongly resembles the one that Rolly Crump designed for the 1967 Tomorrowland, and a new soundtrack featuring rearranged versions of the theme songs of old Tomorrowland attractions. The new Tomorrowland, then, immersed visitors neither into today's nor into past futures, but into the old Tomorrowland. Autobiotheming is used here to evoke nostalgia for the 1950s and 1960s as well as for Disneyland, of course, but like the retrofuturistic approaches at the Magic Kingdom and at Parc Disneyland, it also helped designers to break through the cycle of having to completely redesign and rebuild Tomorrowland every 20 years.

Similarly, the autotheming of the Boardwalk section at Knott's Berry Farm allowed designers to gather a maximum of thrill and family rides in a relatively small area without having to worry too much about how they would fit together. Originally opened in 1996 to replace the park's Roaring 20's section, the Boardwalk is themed to a seaside amusement pier and currently features thrill rides, a number of family rides, and some classic boardwalk games. Interestingly, however, some of the other attractions that one would conventionally associate with an amusement pier, such as a Ferris wheel or a merry-go-round, are located elsewhere in the park. Moreover, there is very little that holds the area together from a thematic point of view. To be sure, upon its opening the Boardwalk had its own mascot, and in 2013 the park added some rides with a light ocean theme (Surfside Gliders and Pacific Scrambler) as well as a subsection called Boardwalk Pier, whose artificial lake, palm trees, and wooden boardwalk add considerably to the section's seaside atmosphere. In addition, some of the restaurants, as well as the area's soundtrack, refer to the 1950s. Yet apart from that, the various buildings and rides, their individual shapes, themes, and color schemes, seem to compete for the visitor's attention rather than form one coherent, immersive whole.

Indeed, one could argue that it is the Boardwalk's very visual and thematic eclecticism that differentiates it from the park's other, more homogenous sections (the Western-themed Ghost Town, the character-themed Camp Snoopy, and the Mexican-themed Fiesta Village) and thus marks its thematic identity. In that, the Boardwalk is remarkably similar to "real" amusement piers as, for instance, the Santa Monica Pier, located a mere 50-minute drive from Knott's Berry Farm. Hence, in this case autotheming provided designers with a comparatively easy and cost-efficient frame to bring together a number of otherwise unrelated rides and elements. The park could even add non- or extremely lightly themed off-the-shelf rides without necessarily "breaking" the boardwalk theme (if anything, this would rather enhance the theme). In fact, one of the latest additions to the Boardwalk (in 2013) has been Coast Rider, a generic wild mouse coaster whose only boardwalk-themed element or, indeed, whose only *themed* element, is its name.

Opened five years after Knott's Boardwalk, Disney California Adventure's Paradise Pier originally seemed to use a similar theme to pursue a similar strategy. To be sure, with its recurring sun icon logo (on lampposts, trashcans, and rides), its calliope soundtrack, and its vague maritime/surfer theme for such attractions as King Triton's Carousel or California Screamin' and such restaurants as Avalon Cove or Pizza Oom Mow Mow, the amusement pier-themed area offered visitors a slightly more distinct and thematically coherent experience than the Boardwalk. Yet here, too, visitors could find stereotypical amusement park rides with their own individual theme as, for instance, the Sun Wheel (a Ferris wheel), the Orange Stinger (a swing ride), or the Games of the Boardwalk. In the case of Paradise Pier, however, fans in online forums and blogs regularly criticized the pier theme as a cheap excuse for putting generic carnival rides into a theme park, and the park's acronym (DCA) was re-interpreted as Disney's Carny Adventure.[19] In 2007, Disney eventually acknowledged these and other criticisms (as well as the low attendance figures engendered by, amongst other factors, bad word-of-mouth) and announced a USD 1.2 billion "extreme makeover" for the park. While in the course of this extensive redesign, some of the park's areas (most notably the entrance) were completely rethemed, however, the autotheme of Paradise Pier was generally left intact.

Of course, one visually prominent carnival ride—namely, the Maliboomer "space shot" attraction—was simply removed and others, such as the Ferris wheel, the swing ride, or the wild mouse coaster, received new themes based on classic Disney characters. Yet the most fundamental changes that Paradise Pier underwent in the context of the makeover consisted of various strategies of "distancing." For instance, views of various buildings outside the park such as the Anaheim Convention Center were blocked and explicit references to what some may consider the more seedy offerings at amusement piers (for example, tattoo parlors) were entirely dropped. Most importantly, the temporal setting of the area was shifted from the present to the past, more precisely, the late 1920s: box-like stucco structures were replaced with ornate wooden buildings; employees received new, period-appropriate costumes; the new soundtrack features 1920s jazz music; and the designers added a newsstand with copies of old magazines and the November 18, 1928, issue of the fictional *Daily Boardwalk Breeze* on display.[20] Even the Disney characters in Paradise Pier look the way they did in the 1920s (see, for instance, the giant Mickey face on the Ferris wheel).[21] In contrast to its original version (as well as in contrast to Knott's Boardwalk), the rethemed Paradise Pier offered visitors a more immersive, but also, and especially from a temporal perspective, a more "external" experience (in Bryman's and Steinkrüger's sense; see above).

Paradise Pier's revamped autotheming suggests at least two things: firstly, *quod licet* Knott's, *non licet* Disney. The Boardwalk at Knott's Berry Farm and the original Paradise Pier at Disney California Adventure were remarkably similar in the sense that both used autotheming and, more specifically, the theme of a contemporary seaside amusement park, to cut back on the expenses of theming individual rides, restaurants, and other attractions, to an overarching area theme. What has apparently been considered acceptable in the case of Knott's, a lower-priced park with a more limited catchment area, however, proved offensive to fans and visitors of Disney California Adventure, located right across from the prototype of all theme parks, Disneyland. This does not mean that autotheming in general and amusement park themes in particular are unsuitable for "quality" theme parks such as Disney's. The crucial difference lies, I suggest, in the different degrees of externality that such autothemed areas can provide. Indeed, as is also evidenced by Toyville Trolley Park, a theme park version of a turn-of-the-century electric amusement park located in the American Waterfront section of Tokyo DisneySea, Disney customers accept autotheming, but they seem to expect a maximum degree of externality.

Secondly, the example of Paradise Pier illustrates that autotheming, too, may cause controversy. In "A Politics of Reverence and Irreverence: Social Discourse on Theming Controversies," Scott A. Lukas suggests that designers may increasingly "emphasize apolitical and non-cultural themes" in order to avoid "political controversies" such as the ones about the about Disney's America, Dracula Park, or the Holy Land Experience that Lukas discusses in his writing.[22] Compared to other historical and cultural themes, autotheming may appear as a "safe" option to thus depoliticize theming, but as the debates about Paradise Pier have shown, it isn't. In fact, as my last two examples will demonstrate, autotheming has even been used to deliberately create controversy and to instigate discussions about the politics of theming and themed spaces.

Theming the Theming Debate

Like many other attractions at Universal Studios Hollywood, The Simpsons Ride simultaneously constitutes a ride adaptation of a movie or TV series—in this case, the popular animated TV series *The Simpsons*—and a movie-based attraction that features projections as well as simulator and various in-theater effects.[23] Opened in 2008, the ride is themed around Krustyland, a fictional theme park owned by and themed to Krusty, the series' tragicomic TV clown. Visitors enter the ride through a giant Krusty head (which represents the entrance to Krustyland), see a map and attraction posters of Krustyland in the ride's waiting area, and eventually accompany the Simpsons family on a turbulent visit to the park, flying from one attraction to the next in a runaway ride vehicle. While similar to the other autothemed areas discussed here, then, The Simpsons Ride employs the strategies of theming to immerse visitors into a theme park, the tone of the attraction, in keeping with the tone of the TV series, is notably different.

Indeed, like some of the other fictional theme parks featured in *The Simpsons* (for example, Duff Gardens and Itchy & Scratchy Land), Krustyland contains many satirical references to Disneyland, from the Krustyland Main Street and Sleeping Itchy's Castle to the Krustyland Hotel and Captain Dinosaur's Pirate Rip-off (Krustyland's version of Disneyland's Pirates of the Caribbean). Krustyland not only features some of Disneyland's most characteristic elements, however, it has also adopted some of the operational practices that Disneyland has regularly been criticized for: the park appears to be run by overworked, underpaid, and unhappy teenagers; seeks every opportunity to rip off customers (Krustyland Main Street offers "The America of 1895 at Today's Prices"); does not care too much about visitors' safety; and features long lines (one of Krustyland's attractions is called It's a Long, Long Line!) as well as unthemed carnival rides (for example, the Unoriginal Log Ride). Most importantly, some of Krustyland's attractions focus on aspects of a particular theme or raise general social and political issues that Disneyland, following theming's "politics of inclusion/exclusion," attempts to downplay or silence: for instance, Krusty's L.A. Traffic Jam does not focus on the joy of cruising the freeways (as does Disneyland's Autopia), but rather on the unpleasant aspects of using the city's traffic system. Krusty's Dustbowl Jalopy Rush is themed to one of the most devastating natural disasters in twentieth-century America. And Krusty's Haunted Condo invites visitors to meet Krustyland's "999 Unhappy Teen Employees," thus pointing to labor issues at theme parks.

Hence, in some ways the theming of Krustyland—and thus the autotheming of The Simpsons Ride—functions as a mirror to the theming of Disneyland, in the sense that it includes, and even foregrounds, what Disneyland excludes. Yet whereas Krustyland still pretends to operate like a regular theme park, yet another autothemed space—namely, the Dismaland Bemusement Park—carries the idea of "mirroring" Disneyland to its ultimate conclusion. Opened on August 22, 2015, in a former lido in Weston-super-Mare (UK), and closed on September 27, 2015, Dismaland was created by the British graffiti artist, political activist, and film director Banksy and features contributions from a total of 61 artists from all over the world.[24] In promotional material, Dismaland identifies itself as "A festival of art, amusements and entry-level anarchism" and as "The UK's most disappointing new visitor attraction!," but perhaps the space can be more accurately described as a combination of autotheming and dark theming that seeks to instigate a discussion about the politics of theming—expressed through the medium of the theme park.[25]

With respect to autotheming, Dismaland's references to Disneyland are even more obvious and direct than Krustyland's: the Dismaland logo uses the characteristic Disneyland font and castle silhouette, the façade of the central building closely resembles that of Disneyland's iconic Sleeping Beauty Castle (albeit in a dilapidated state), and various Disney characters, from Cinderella to the Little Mermaid, make their appearance (although, again, in somewhat disheveled conditions). In keeping with the overall atmosphere of decay, disillusion, and forlornness that pervades the site, however, the themes of Dismaland's individual "rides" and attractions are almost directly antithetical to those of Disneyland's offerings. For instance, the exhibition inside the castle shows Cinderella surrounded by paparazzi after a fatal accident in her carriage, Jimmy Cauty's Model Village depicts a town after a riot, and in the "Amusements" section, visitors can hook oiled rubber ducks and steer remote-controlled boats full of refugees.

Dismaland constitutes, of course, by no means the first or only space to be themed around death, destruction, or disaster. As Scott A. Lukas has pointed out, citing such examples as prison-themed restaurants in Japan and the planned Crash Café in Baltimore, "dark theming" has become a growing trend in both museums and other themed spaces.[26] Neither does it constitute, as I have tried to show, the first or only autothemed space. Yet whereas other dark and autothemed spaces "merely" apply the strategies of theming to what some may consider "unusual" themes (namely, theme parks and death, destruction, and so forth), Dismaland, by combining dark theming with autotheming, employs the medium of theming to start a discussion about the politics of themed spaces in general and theme parks in particular. Dismaland is not so much a dystopian theme park or an anti-Disneyland, as some have suggested, but rather a contribution to the debate about the social functions of themed spaces and theming.[27]

Indeed, whereas themed spaces have often been dismissed as "mere places of entertainment and folly," Lukas has wondered to what extent they may also "provide suggestions for social change and opportunities for cultural critique."[28] Using the language of theming, Dismaland asks precisely this question. In fact, in an interview with *The Guardian*, Banksy, asked what Dismaland is, at first responded by quoting from the official tagline of the site ("In essence it's a festival of art, amusements and entry-level anarchism"), but eventually offered the following: "I guess you'd say it's a theme park whose big theme is—theme parks should have bigger themes."[29] Elaborating on Banksy's statement, I suggest that Dismaland acknowledges the popularity, ubiquity, and impact of themed spaces in contemporary society and argues that precisely because of their social relevance they should also tackle topics that up to now have been considered unsuitable for them.

The Relevance of Autotheming

Among a list of "[t]hemes that will appear in the future development of theme parks in the USA," park operators gave, in 2001, the highest degree of accord to "interactive adventure," "fantasy and mystery," and "movies and TV shows."[30] Autotheming—or anything that resembles autotheming—apparently did not even figure among the 16 pre-given answers respondents could choose from, and even if it did, it probably would not have been among the top answers. Nevertheless, I maintain that in the future autotheming is likely to remain and perhaps even become more popular with park designers due its potential to celebrate the theme park brand, to cut on budget costs, and to instantly and easily provide a general atmosphere of leisure and fun. However, autotheming could also become more relevant for theme park designers, theme park scholars, and the general public thanks to the possibilities it offers to comment on the politics and limitations of theming and the social relevance of themed spaces. Indeed, autotheming might change both the way we look at themed spaces as well as themed spaces themselves.

Notes

1. Jean Baudrillard, *Cool Memories II: 1987–1990* (Durham: Duke University Press, 1996), 42.

2. Jean Baudrillard, *America* (London: Verso, 1989), 32. Jean Baudrillard, *Simulacra and Simulation* (Ann Arbor: University of Michigan Press, 1994), 12.

3. Mark Gottdiener, Alan Beardsworth, and Alan Bryman have discussed a somewhat similar phenomenon in the context of themed restaurants. Gottdiener writes that because "the names of franchises like Kentucky Fried Chicken or McDonald's are so famous, promotional advertising develops the name itself as a corporate theme that functions along with the efficiently designed fast-food interior scheme as a total environment." See Mark Gottdiener, *The Theming of America: American Dreams, Media Fantasies, and Themed Environments* (Boulder, CO: Westview, 2001), 80. Beardsworth and Bryman refer to this as "reflexive theming" since "the theming principle is internally generated, and then endlessly reproduced." See Alan Beardsworth and Alan Bryman, "Late Modernity and the Dynamics of Quasification: The Case of the Themed Restaurant," *The Sociological Review* 47 (1999): 254, 243. See, as well, Alan Bryman, "McDonald's as a Disneyized Institution," *American Behavioral Scientist* 47, no. 2 (2003): 156–158. However, although it is also "internally generated," autotheming is different from reflexive theming in that it uses much more than just the brand name as its theming principle.

4. Salvador Anton Clavé, *The Global Theme Park Industry* (Wallingford: CABI, 2007), 35.

5. See <http://www.cafedumonde.jp/>.

6. Jan-Erik Steinkrüger, *Thematisierte Welten: Über Darstellungspraxen in Zoologischen Gärten und Vergnügungsparks* (Bielefeld, Germany: Transcript, 2013), 65–66. However, Steinkrüger also mentions the various churches at Europa-Park, which really do function as places of worship; see Steinkrüger, *Thematisierte Welten*, 66n188.

7. A reference to Disney's 1948 feature film *So Dear to My Heart*, in which the eponymous fair plays a central role. "Disney & Co." is

autothemed in a double sense, then: by evoking a county fair, it refers to the history of the theme park medium, by specifically evoking one of Disney's movies, it refers to the company's own history.

8. Alan Bryman, *The Disneyization of Society* (London: Sage, 2004), 15.

9. Steinkrüger, *Thematisierte Welten*, 55 (my translation).

10. Richard Schickel, *The Disney Version: The Life, Times, Art, and Commerce of Walt Disney* (London: Pavilion, 1986), 225. Scott A. Lukas, "A Politics of Reverence and Irreverence: Social Discourse on Theming Controversies," in *The Themed Space: Locating Culture, Nation, and Self*, ed. Scott A. Lukas (Lanham, MD: Lexington, 2007), 277. Filippo Carlà and Florian Freitag, "Ancient Greek Culture and Myth in the Terra Mítica Theme Park," *Classical Receptions Journal* 7, no. 2 (2015): 244–246.

11. Tom Gunning, "The Cinema of Attractions," *Wide Angle* 8, no. 3/4 (1986): 63–70.

12. Scott A. Lukas, *Theme Park* (London: Reaktion, 2008), 172. Scott A. Lukas, *The Immersive Worlds Handbook: Designing Theme Parks and Consumer Spaces* (New York: Focal, 2013), 177–204.

13. Gottfried Korff, "Euro Disney und Disney-Diskurse: Bemerkungen zum Problem transkultureller Kontakt- und Kontrasterfahrungen," *Schweizerisches Archiv für Volkskunde* 90, no. 2 (1994): 208. James B. Stewart, *DisneyWar* (New York: Simon and Schuster, 2005), 127.

14. Régine Ferrandis, *EuroDisney Führer* (n.p.: Walt Disney Company, 1992).

15. Quoted in Beth Dunlop, *Building a Dream: The Art of Disney Architecture* (New York: Harry N. Abrams, 1996), 134.

16. Dunlop, *Building a Dream*, 140.

17. See, for instance, Dunlop, *Building a Dream*, 143.

18. See <http://www.yesterland.com/1998mural.html>.

19. See, for instance, <http://www.mouseplanet.com/7505/Mailbag>.

20. The date refers to the date of release of Disney's animated short film *Steamboat Willie*, which is considered the debut of the Mickey Mouse character.

21. Paradise Pier thus contains autobiothemed elements, too.

22. Lukas, "A Politics of Reverence and Irreverence," 285.

23. See my other contribution to this volume, entitled "Movies, Rides, Immersion."

24. A complete list of the artists involved, as well as other material, could be found on the official website of Dismaland, <http://www.dismaland.co.uk/>.

25. See <http://www.dismaland.co.uk/>.

26. Lukas, "A Politics of Reverence and Irreverence," 277–278.

27. See, for instance, <http://www.thisiscolossal.com/2015/08/dismaland/>.

28. Lukas, "A Politics of Reverence and Irreverence," 287.

29. See, Banksy, "I Think a Museum Is a Bad Place to Look at Art," *The Guardian*, August 21, 2015, <http://www.theguardian.com/artanddesign/2015/aug/21/banksy-dismaland-art-amusements-and-anarchism?CMP=twt_gu>.

30. Ady Milman, "The Future of the Theme Park and Attraction Industry: A Management Perspective," *Journal of Travel Research* 40, no. 2 (2001): 143.

16

Six Degrees of Navigation

Titanic Belfast's Identity Issues

By Stephen Brown

Let's set sail with a simple question. What is the connection between George Clooney and the *Titanic*? Yes, there is one. And no, it's not that George was considered for the lead role in James Cameron's blockbuster movie of the terrible maritime tragedy. Matthew McConaughey is the man you're thinking of. He was the actor who almost pipped Leonardo DiCaprio to the post of Jack Dawson, the part that transported Leo to superstardom and beyond.[1] Nor, for that matter has Gorgeous George appeared in—much less produced/directed—any of the many other movies, mini-series, docudramas, and reality television shows that retell the oft-told tale of the "night to remember" when the largest steamship in the world hit an iceberg on its maiden voyage from Southampton to New York and sank with awful loss of life. Granted, George made a guest appearance in the fifth series of *Downton Abbey*, the first of which commenced with the sinking of the immemorial vessel and the death of Downton's presumptive heir, James Grantham. But the connection between the star of *Ocean's Eleven* and the dark star of the Atlantic Ocean has nothing to do with movie making. It's more indirect than that.

It's a connection, though, that was loudly trumpeted when a massive, money-no-object, *Titanic*-themed visitor attraction opened in Belfast, Northern Ireland, on March 31, 2012. For several weeks prior to Titanic Belfast's official launch, timed to coincide with the centenary of the sinking it "commemorates," an energetic public relations company had been feeding the world's media with increasingly extravagant stories about "the most famous ship since Noah's Ark." These were stories that centered on the *Titanic*'s associations with the infamous city of Belfast. Ripley's Believe It or Not was as nothing compared to the often bizarre, occasionally preposterous, links between popular culture—Clooney included—and the city that built the stupendous steamship. Most of the world's media, admittedly, were baffled by Belfast's attempt to build its place brand around one of the most epic fails of all time. But the bottom line, believe it or not, is that this counter-intuitive promotional tactic worked brilliantly.

Three years after its PR-pimped opening, Titanic Belfast is one of the biggest tourist attractions in Ireland, within spitting distance of its nearest direct rival, the Guinness Storehouse in Dublin. The architecturally striking building has won several prestigious awards—plus a brickbat or two—and, with ever more cruise ships choosing to include the once taboo city of Belfast in their itineraries, the multiplier effect on the region's restaurants, bars, hotels, and the hospitality industry more generally has been immense.[2] Far from being a liability, the *Titanic* connection has turned out to be the city's USP (Unique Sinking Proposition)—a distinctive brand identity that helps it stand out on the crowded shelves of the themed attraction supermarket. It's an identity, nevertheless, that's congenitally conflicted, confused, contorted, and controversial. It's an identity that has issues, shall we say, six of which impinge on Titanic Town's eponymous tourist trap.[3] Let's call them the six degrees of navigation.

Historical Identity

Back in the day, that day being Sunday, April 14, 1912, RMS *Titanic* was the largest moving object on the face of the earth. Built by Harland & Wolff in Belfast, Ireland, *Titanic* was the absolute pinnacle of cutting-edge engineering at the absolute zenith of the great British Empire which not only ruled the waves but waived the rules when it felt so inclined.

Image 16.1. Titanic Belfast (Creative Commons Attribution-Share Alike 4.0 International; NITB, Northern Ireland Tourist Board)

The pride of Liverpool's White Star Line, *Titanic* was approximately 900 feet long, weighed 50,000 tons, carried 3,500 passengers and crew, and had a top speed of 24 knots. It was the last word in luxury, what's more. A floating grand hotel, copiously equipped with the latest technological gizmos and sybaritic customer services, including electric light, elevators, telephones, Turkish baths, swimming pools, squash courts, and Marconi's innovative wireless telegraph, RMS *Titanic* far eclipsed its competitors on the lucrative transatlantic routes. True, it was ever so slightly slower than its nearest rivals (the sleek greyhounds *Mauretania* and *Lusitania* operated by Cunard), and another prominent shipping line, Hamburg-Amerika, was about to bring an even bigger vessel into service. But on that fateful Sunday, four days into its inaugural voyage from Southampton to New York—with brief stops to pick up extra passengers in Cherbourg, France, and Queenstown, Ireland—*Titanic* was the undisputed master of all it surveyed (mistress, rather).[4]

One of the things the ship's lookouts surveyed was ice, lots and lots of ice, much more than usual at that time of year. Tragically, Captain Smith chose to ignore the warnings he had received from passing vessels and, at twenty minutes to midnight, *Titanic* collided with an iceberg. Less than three hours later—less time than it takes to sit through Cameron's mega-successful movie—the majestic steamer sank with the loss of 1,500 lives. Luckily, more than 700 passengers and crew managed to escape on the lifeboats, the total carrying capacity of which was insufficient to accommodate all those on board. Many of the lifeboats were launched less than full, thereby compounding the catastrophe, as did the shambolic combination of wireless messages, distress flares, and emergency evacuation procedures that prevailed as the brand new steamship, still smelling of fresh paint, slipped beneath the flat calm, freezing cold waters of the North Atlantic. If it weren't for the heroic actions of Captain Rostron, the commander of the nearby *Carpathia*, which sped through the ice field to the last reported position of the *Titanic* despite considerable risk to itself, the death toll would have been even more appalling.

Appalling, however, doesn't begin to describe the post-sinking behavior of the White Star Line. Apart from inexcusable delays in informing the families of the victims (the belated bulletins about the casualties were riddled with typographic errors, which exacerbated the agony); apart from the disrespect shown to the bodies of the dead (first-class cadavers were embalmed and transported to shore in coffins, third-class corpses were buried at sea); apart from the maltreatment of surviving crew members, some of whose wages were docked pro rata (for failing to complete the voyage they had signed on for), White Star officials dissembled repeatedly during the official inquiries into the accident, albeit it was J. Bruce Ismay (the company president who leapt into the last lifeboat) who bore the brunt of the opprobrium.

Mythological Identity

Part of the hatred heaped on J. "Brute" Ismay, as the American gutter press described him, pertains to the accusation that he dressed up as a woman in order to effect his escape from the stricken steamship.[5] Utterly unfounded, the Ismay "myth" is just one among many that attached themselves to *Titanic*. The leaky leviathan had hardly settled on the floor of the Atlantic Ocean—in two separate parts, surrounded by a vast debris field of coal and cargo—before innumerable myths, legends, fables, yarns, tall tales, and shaggy dog stories sought accommodation on board. It is said, for example, that the ship's cat and its kittens sneaked off the *Titanic* in Southampton and survived thanks to her feline intuition. It is said that 55 passengers cancelled their bookings beforehand, due to premonitions of disaster. It is said that an ancient Egyptian mummy being transported in the hold cursed the ship and all who sailed in her. It is said that several passengers managed to scramble on to the iceberg, where they froze to death after failing to attract the attention of passing rescue vessels. It is said that a "mystery ship" passed very close to the foundering giant but refused to pause to pick up survivors. It is said that the sinking was an elaborate White Star insurance scam that went disastrously wrong. It is said that Sir Cosmo Duff Gordon bribed the crewmen on near-empty Lifeboat One to stand off and stay safe rather than return to assist those screaming for help. It is said that Jack Johnson, the world heavyweight boxing champion, was denied passage by a racist booking agent who added "We ain't haulin' no coal." It is said that the catastrophe was a Dan Brown-style conspiracy concocted by Jesuit extremists like Father Browne of *Titanic* photographs fame (who disembarked at Queenstown). It is said that Captain Smith urged his fellow officers to "Be British!" before standing to attention, snapping a salute and adjusting his upper lip to the requisite level of stiffness before going down with his ship (as all true blue Brits do). It is said that the *Titanic* was trying to break the transatlantic speed record on its maiden voyage (not true, impossible too). It is said that the shipbuilders claimed *Titanic* was unsinkable (not true, though they came close). It is said that the band played "Nearer, My God, to Thee" as the leviathan slowly slipped beneath the swell (doubtful, despite considerable wishful thinking). It is said that the greatest poem of the twentieth century, T.S. Eliot's *The Wasteland*, was inspired in part by the sinking (possible, but unproven). It is said that a science fiction novelist wrote a speculative book back in 1898 which told the unthinkable tale of an unsinkable ship called *Titan*—yes, *Titan*—that hit an iceberg on its maiden transatlantic voyage and sank with huge loss of life caused by a shortage of lifeboats (not only true, but the dimensions of the fictional craft almost exactly matched those of White Star's finest).[6]

In addition to myths with a small "m," RMS *Titanic* soon sailed at top speed into the realm of capitalized Myth. The very name of the ship is mythic—the titans too came to an unfortunate, unanticipated end—and it has since become an enduring symbol of human folly, an emblematic instance of vaunting pride and overweening ambition brought low. As Wade brilliantly observes:

> When the dream ended in a nightmare, the material world lost its credibility and, for a moment in passing time, myth became reality. The *Titanic*'s mystique is therefore a poetic realm, in which her maiden voyage expresses the blind justice of Greek Tragedy and the allegorical warning of the medieval morality play. Here, the *Titanic* is an eternal symbol: She was, is, and will be. She was the Titans' struggle against Jove, the Babylonians' ziggurat to heaven. She was Lucifer's fall from grace, the Night-Sea crossing of the medieval alchemists, and the moment of truth realized too late by the tragic hero whose aspirations led him fatally beyond his limitations. She is not mere history, but a parable to the effect that the mighty of each age must fall. In a word, she is Hubris.[7]

Metaphorical Identity

Above and beyond its embodiment of hubris, *Titanic* has become a figure of speech, part of the vernacular. Cameron contends that Titanic is one of the three most frequently used words in the English language after Jesus Christ and Coca-Cola.[8] This may or may not be an exaggeration—Facebook, Google, and Kim Kardashian would surely contest his claim—but there's no doubt that the T-word packs a prodigious metaphorical punch. Even before the traumatized survivors arrived in New York City, the disaster was being used as a metaphor for American party politics. *Titanic* was employed as a figurative stand-in for the sin of pride in manifold post-sinking sermons preached throughout Britain and America during 1912, and by contemporary commentators as a symbol of vainglorious Victorian society, soon to be humbled in the killing fields of the Great War. The steamship's tropic power has not dimmed in the century since the calamity, what's more. On the contrary, it has become an "all-purpose metaphor for any doomed enterprise."[9] Whether it be rearranging deckchairs, iceberg ahead warnings, manning the lifeboats, women and children first, going down with the ship, playing music in the face of catastrophe, or indeed on-board social stratification—patricians up top, plebeians down below—each component of the fateful incident is a simile in itself.

It is little wonder, then, that *Titanic* is the go-to trope for columnists, cartoonists, comedians, sub-editors, speechwriters, and after-dinner speakers. It is the name of a satirical magazine in Germany (and several hotels forbye). It is the subject of a classic headline in *The Onion* ("World's Largest Metaphor Hits Ice-Berg"). It features regularly in critiques of western capitalism, network television, the music industry, Britain's creaking health service, and the financial travails of the Eurozone. It has been adapted to executive development programs, where able-bodied managers ruminate on lifeboat leadership lessons, iceberg avoidance strategies, and sink or swim scenarios going forward. It made an appearance on 9/11, moreover, when the following unspeakable exchange occurred:

> Survivors even reported a reference to the *Titanic* in the midst of the chaotic attempts to evacuate the south tower of the World Trade Center. On the seventy-eighth floor, soon to be directly hit by the second plane, a man supposedly blocked two women who were trying to squeeze past him into an elevator and said, "This isn't the *Titanic*, ladies. It's not women and children first."[10]

National Identity

Although the *Titanic* looms large in western culture, it looms especially large in Ireland, where the sinking long-symbolized deep political, social, ethnic, and national divisions between north and south. The great ship was conceived, designed, and built in Belfast, an industrial enclave in the northeast of a predominantly agricultural island, by thousands of Irish workmen, most of whom were devout Protestants and Unionists. That is to say, they were British in outlook and affiliation. If not quite a Protestant ship for a Protestant people, *Titanic* was British to the last bolt and rivet. The leviathan was built, what's more, at the height of Ireland's "home rule" campaign, which agitated for a modicum of independence from British dominion. This prospect filled northern Protestants with dread, since they would be a tiny minority huddled in one corner of an entirely Catholic island.

Thus the success of Belfast's shipyard—the biggest and best in the world back then—denoted continuing Protestant ascendancy, as did its pride and joy, the largest and most luxurious liner ever built. However, the catastrophic failure of the region's single greatest achievement was a devastating blow to Protestant pride, a devastating blow reinforced by Irish partition in 1922, when the six northern counties clung on to British citizenship, like beggars at a feast. The south's territorial claim on the north, meanwhile, led many to make admittedly glib comparisons between the foundering of the ship and the founding of Northern Ireland. The fates of the two were somehow intertwined, as the symbolic ship of state cruised dangerous waters dotted with "the chillingly impersonal iceberg dynamics of Irish nationalism."[11]

What this all boils down to is that, for the best part of eighty years, *Titanic* was an accursed word in Ireland, north and south. In the north, it was not only an unmentionable badge of shame, but Harland & Wolff used its influence to stifle any discussions and/or debates about the disaster. In the south, *Titanic* embodied the unbearable arrogance of northern Protestants and the sinking was regarded as God's punishment on shipyard workers, many of whom profaned the pope during the construction of the blasphemous vessel. No memorial was erected to (southern) Irish victims of the tragedy until 1998, even though a large proportion of steerage passengers were (Catholic) Irish emigrants to the new world, seeking a better life in the United States of America.

Cultural Identity

Titanic may have been taboo in Ireland throughout the twentieth century, but it wasn't everywhere else. As Biel and Howells' cultural histories of the disaster reveal, *Titanic* is nothing less than a global phenomenon, a shipshape celebrity of sorts.[12] True, her allure has ebbed and flowed through time. However, an ever-rising trajectory of human interest is evident too. Largely forgotten in the aftermath of the First and Second World Wars, whose horrors vastly exceeded those of April 1912, the ill-fated steamship resurfaced in the 1950s, thanks to a bestselling book by Walter Lord. An advertising copywriter for J. Walter Thompson, Lord's breathless retelling of the terrible tale—a real-time account that anticipated the non-fiction novels of Truman Capote and Norman Mailer—was made into an enormously successful British movie, *A Night to Remember*.[13] The ship picked up further steam when Robert Ballard discovered the wreck in September 1985 and whose dramatic undersea photographs triggered a spate of touching remembrance, tasteless scavenging, and lucrative touring exhibitions by the salvors-in-possession.[14] The momentum increased a decade later when James Cameron's staggeringly expensive movie of the tragedy—widely expected to sink without trace on release—not only triumphed at the box office, with worldwide receipts of $1.8 billion, but bagged a record haul of eleven Oscars, including Best Picture, which put it on a par with Golden Age Hollywood classics like *Gone With the Wind* and *Ben Hur*.[15]

Top speed, however, was attained in 2012, when the centenary of the sinking was commemorated. In addition to the 3-D rerelease of Cameron's classic, which did gangbusters business in China, manifold works of popular culture poured out of the rusting wreck: musicals, murals, mini-series, magazine articles, ocean cruises, video games, requiem masses, light shows, pop songs, poetry recitals, photographic exhibitions, pornographic movies, and books beyond number, including a biography of the iceberg! A veritable tsunami of tie-in merchandise, from teddy bears and tote bags to baseball caps and candy bars, swamped supermarkets, department stores and smart phones worldwide. The cities most associated with the tragedy pushed the boat out big time. Southampton built a brand new Sea City Museum; Cherbourg extended and upgraded its seafaring attraction, *La Cité de la Mer*; Cobh (formerly Queenstown) laid out a Tourist Trail, then added a Heritage Centre; and Liverpool, the luxury liner's port of registration, retold the terrible tale in its Merseyside Maritime Museum.

Commercial Identity

In such circumstances, the city of Belfast faced a dilemma: should the deep-seated trauma in its collective civic psyche stop citizens cashing in on a cornucopian commercial opportunity? Of course not! Money talks at the best of times and yells especially loudly in post-industrial cities such as Belfast which suffered a Detroit-style decline during the 1970s—a decline that was deepened by a prolonged, low-level civil war between the ethnic groups mentioned above. For the best part of three decades, Belfast became a byword for brutal, bare-knuckle bigotry, a dystopian symbol of urban destitution, desolation, dereliction, and death.[16]

Set against this, it still had *Titanic*. Although Harland & Wolff no longer built new ships to order, the old slipways, graving docks, pump rooms, drawing offices, and more lay rusting and unloved. In the aftermath of Cameron's *Titanic*, which recast the once sectarian ship in a Celtic Catholic-Irish light, the ship shed its Anglo-Saxon Protestant connotations and became, bizarrely, a symbol of cross-community cooperation. A series of small-scale *Titanic*-themed events in Belfast City Hall proved successful and, more importantly, uncontroversial. This led to the announcement of a massive mixed-use property development on the riverside site of the former shipyard, which was opportunistically renamed "Titanic Quarter." Much of this metropolitan wasteland was allocated to the familiar tropes of inner urban redevelopment, *à la* Baltimore and Bilbao: expensive apartments, bijou hotels, fancy restaurants, riverside walkways, rinky-dink marinas, upscale retail stores, glossy office blocks, and assorted entertainment attractions. The mooted centerpiece, moreover, was a massive *Titanic*-themed tourist trap—sorry, commemorative facility—that its boosters boasted would be bigger, better, and more beautiful by far than all the second-rate *Titanic* attractions from Liverpool to Las Vegas. The greatest ship ever built deserved nothing less from the city where she spent more time than anywhere else. Southampton? A week at most. Cherbourg and Cobh? A couple of hours, tops. Liverpool? Never went near the place. Pigeon Ford, Tennessee? You cannot be serious. The Luxor Hotel, Las Vegas? WTF![17]

She spent three years in Belfast. Titanic Belfast. It's a branding no-brainer, isn't it? Not exactly. Many of Belfast's citizens were somewhat skeptical, to put it mildly, about the grand plan. Some regarded the monster property development as an egregious ruse to raise the price of land in a rundown part of town, where only the backers would benefit. Some were scandalized by the very idea that a terrible tragedy, one of the worst blots on the city's amply blotted history, should be packaged, promoted, and profited from in such a disgusting, disgraceful, disrespectful, and downright Disneyfied manner. It's a graveyard not a goldmine, they said. Some, perhaps the majority, thought that the whole idea was perverse at best and demented at worst. If you're going to sell Belfast as a comeback city, aligning it with the worst maritime catastrophe of all time isn't exactly the best way to go about it.

As if that wasn't enough, there were interminable debates about the physical form of the proposed visitor attraction. By far the most popular option, among the general public at any rate, was an exact replica of the original. The blueprints were still available, Harland & Wolff needed the business, and the dry dock Titanic once occupied lay empty, ready to be filled by a replicant. Health and safety concerns soon ruled out a replicant however and, when push came to shove, a striking six-story, star-shaped, stainless steel-clad showcase for all things *Titanic* was built at enormous expense. Its dimensions echo those of the original, its sharp edges evoke the prows of vast, ocean-going vessels and, although many locals reckon it looks more like a North Atlantic iceberg than a White Star steamship, the $150 million building is undeniably arresting (see image 16.1). With the aid of state-of-the-art audio-visual equipment and dark ride technology, its nine grand galleries tell the story of the celebrity ship's conception, construction and catastrophic maiden voyage, as well as the awful aftermath. The final gallery features live footage from the rusticle-covered wreck, which is disintegrating by the day and forecast to disappear within the next couple of decades.[18] Whether it disappears from popular culture remains to be seen.

Propelled by the polished promotional campaign previously mentioned—George Clooney's great-great aunt, incidentally, worked in a factory that supplied the carpets—Titanic Belfast's light show-illuminated launch went without a hitch or hiccup. Except for one, a calamity that if not quite a commercial iceberg, unsettled more than a few early visitors who found that history was repeating itself in farcical form.[19] Titanic Belfast includes a duplicate of the Grand Staircase, which figured prominently in Cameron's blockbuster movie. Access to the staircase is strictly limited, however, because it is situated in the attraction's banqueting suite and reserved for corporate functions, wedding parties, and similar showcase occasions. For fat cats and the affluent only, in other words. Ordinary punters and passing tourists don't get to see it and are thereby denied the opportunity to pose for Jack and Rose selfies on the steps of *Titanic*'s iconic staircase. The first class/third class divide still obtains. The former guzzle canapés and chocolates on the top floor of Titanic Belfast, while the latter line up for tea and biscuits in steerage. No doubt the in-house string quartet plays "Nearer My Godiva to Thee" as the urban elite relive the good old days like Sunday, April 14, 1912. Monday the 15th awaits.

As the concerned citizens' comments about Disneyfication suggest, themed attractions are often dismissed as trite and tawdry tourist traps managed by malevolent, mendacious, mercenary marketing types who kick puppies, drown kittens, and rip the ears off bunny rabbits in their spare time. Some do, no doubt. But, as the issues appertaining to Titanic Belfast attest, assembling an appealing attraction is a difficult task. Juggling multiple identities, balancing conflicting demands, satisfying influential stakeholders, managing investor expectations, creating unforgettable experiences, crafting compelling narratives, ensuring customer satisfaction, and making sufficient money to cover the operating costs—while remaining one step ahead of the competition—is challenging at the best of times and almost impossible when the chosen theme is something as stupendous as *Titanic*. So vast is the story, so intimate the human interest, so powerful the emotional impact, so opinionated are the pressure groups, so indefinite are the "hard" facts, so sensitive is the subject matter, and so brutal is the struggle for consumers' disposable incomes that the visionaries behind Titanic Belfast can only be commended for keeping their facility afloat despite the slings, arrows, icebergs, and identity issues that assail them.[20]

Notes

1. Nor, in case you're wondering, was Gorgeous George considered for the female lead, Rose DeWitt Bukater, the role that made Kate Winslet's reputation. Gwyneth Paltrow was slated for that one, then scratched because Cameron wanted to cast comparative unknowns. His studio bosses weren't best pleased, needless to say. But the rest is history.

2. The backers of Titanic Belfast boast that it's the city's equivalent of Paris's Eiffel Tower, Sydney's Opera House, and Rio's Christ the Redeemer. Maybe so, but the building has also been nominated for the annual Carbuncle Cup, a competition organized by *Building Design* magazine, which aims to identify the most unsightly new building in Britain.

3. The term "Titanic Town" was coined by a Northern Irish novelist, Mary Costello, whose semi-autobiographical book of the same name was later made into a movie starring Julie Walters. Her nickname has stuck.

4. The gendering of *Titanic*—and ships generally—is a fascinating subject. The historical background is discussed by Jonathan Eyers, *Don't Shoot the Albatross: Nautical Myths and Superstitions* (London: Adlard Coles, 2011). The seminal source, however, is Ann E. Larabee's brilliant article "The American Hero and His Mechanical Bride: Gender Myths of the Titanic Disaster," *American Studies* 3 (1990), 5–23.

5. Aptly described by A.N. Wilson as "the world's whipping boy" ("Sunken Aspirations," *Financial Times*, April 15, 2012, 13), Ismay has often been portrayed as the villain of the piece. The reality, as you might expect, is rather different. The part he played in Titanic's traumatic tale has been retold many times. See for example Richard Davenport-Hines, *Titanic Lives: Migrants and Millionaires, Conmen and Crew* (London: Harper, 2012).

6. Just as there are numerous histories of the sinking, so too the manifold "myths" are well covered. Greg Ward's *Rough Guide to the Titanic* (London: Rough Guides, 2012) offers a balanced overview. To get some idea of how obsessive things can get, see Senan Molony, *Titanic and the Mystery Ship* (London: History Press, 2006).

7. Wyn Craig Wade's book about the American inquiry, *The Titanic: End of a Dream* (New York: Penguin, 1986), is both an outstanding account of the events as they unfolded and deeply moving to boot, not least when describing the committee's reaction to Captain Rostron's testimony.

8. Stephen Cameron, *Titanic: Belfast's Own* (Newtownards, Ireland: Colourpoint, 2011).

9. Senan Molony, *The Irish Aboard Titanic* (Cork: Mercier Press, 2012).

10. Steven Biel, *Down With the Old Canoe: A Cultural History of the Titanic Disaster* (New York: Norton, 2012).

11. John Wilson Foster, *The Titanic Complex: A Cultural Manifest* (Vancouver: Belcouver Press, 1997).

12. Biel, *Down With the Old Canoe*. Richard Howells, *The Myth of the Titanic* (Basingstoke, England: Palgrave, 2012).

13. Walter Lord, *A Night to Remember* (New York: Holt, Rinehart and Winston, 1955).

14. Robert Ballard, *The Discovery of the Titanic: Exploring the Greatest of all Lost Ships* (London: Orion, 1995).

15. Kevin S. Sandler and Gaylyn Studlar, *Titanic: Anatomy of a Blockbuster* (New Brunswick, NJ: Rutgers University Press, 1999).

16. William J.V. Neill, "Belfast. Rebranding the Renaissance City: From the Troubles to Titanic Quarter," in *Urban Design and the British Urban Renaissance*, ed. John Punter (London: Routledge, 2010), 305–321.

17. Yes, indeed, there's a *Titanic*-themed attraction in Pigeon Ford, Tennessee—Titanic Pigeon Forge. It comprises a part-replica of the ship. You enter via the iceberg. See, <http://www.titanicpigeonforge.com>. There's no shortage of competition for "share of sinking." Plans have recently been announced for a $200 million *Titanic* theme park in Sichuan Province, China, which not only includes a full-scale replica but all sorts of special effects including "iceberg-strike" and "capsize" experiences. Can't wait!

18. The fate of the wreck is discussed in great detail by Charles Pellegrino, *Farewell, Titanic: Her Final Legacy* (New York: John Wiley, 2012).

19. Perhaps the most farcical element of Titanic Belfast is the dark ride. If you were designing a *Titanic*-themed dark ride, what element of the story would you focus on? In Belfast, believe it or not, it's the construction of the ship's rudder. I kid you not. If awards were given out for the most dire dark ride on the planet—Rotten Rides, *à la* movies' Rotten Tomatoes—Titanic Belfast would be on the shortlist, no question.

20. As with most themed attractions, one of the biggest challenges is generating return visits. Once you've seen it, there's no great urge to see it again. Refreshing the offer is a key consideration and Titanic Belfast's managers have been assiduous in that regard (mainly with the aid of loaned artifacts, remodeled displays, and the like). They've also broadened the building's appeal by hosting non-Titanic themed events like rock concerts, boxing matches, "Victorian Christmas" extravaganzas, and temporary exhibitions devoted to the HBO series *Game of Thrones*, which is made in Northern Ireland. The dark ride issue needs to be addressed, however.

17

Research in Themed and Immersive Spaces

At the Threshold of Identity

By Scott A. Lukas

In 2013, while conducting research at a famous themed outdoor mall, I was confronted by three security guards. During a conversation, I discovered that the three had approached me because, in their words, "I looked strange," particularly as I was seen talking into my video camera and filming aspects of the quasi-public space. I explained that I was a researcher of themed and immersive spaces and that I shoot such video for my YouTube page, which features some of the results of my research. I was told that I had to cease my shooting of video but that I could remain in the space. I ended up leaving right after the altercation occurred. Later, in my perusal of some of the video that I had shot at the mall, I discovered that one of the guards had his hands on his mace during the entire encounter—presumably meaning that he was willing and able to use the pepper spray if needed. Two years later, while taking similar video at a famous Southern California mall—one that had been on my list of inspiring themed and immersive spaces to visit—I had a similar though much more pleasant encounter with a guard who informed me that I was forbidden from shooting video. Again, I explained my research and even provided him a flyer for my book on themed and immersive spaces—an item that I began to keep on my person after the incident in 2013. Once again, I left the space without having fully completed my filming. In the same year, I had a third such incident of this sort while taking some still photographs of a small but elaborately themed casino in Nevada. In this case, I was accosted by an irate server who became upset with my photography and shouted, at the top of her lungs, "You may not take any photography in here!" Her voice was so dramatic that I decided to immediately make my way to the exit. "So much for the theming," I thought, as I exited into the parking lot.

These three incidents are presented as an introduction to the type of research that I have been engaged in for the last twenty or more years.[1] I am a cultural anthropologist who studies themed and immersive spaces—theme parks, casinos, themed restaurants, museums, heritage sites, and various other consumer lifestyle spaces. I also used to be an employee trainer at Six Flags AstroWorld in Houston, Texas, and in the many years since I worked there, I have gained new appreciation for the understanding and analysis of the variety of themed and immersive spaces that I study. In this writing, I wish to use the context of my research to offer new insights about theming and immersion. The title of my chapter addresses two senses of these terms. Theming, or a "theme," refers to a foundational topic or issue that is the focus of one's speech—a proposition, deposit, or "something set down"—while immersion indicates a situation in which one is plunged or dipped into something or is absorbed in some situation or interest.[2] When I speak of research in themed and immersive spaces I intend to focus on the meanings of theming and immersion both in the sites of concern (their deployments in the consumer spaces that I study) and in the context of contemporary, postmodern ethnographic research—particularly as contemporary ethnography has focused on specific thematics of research and writing and as classic Malinowskian participant observation has privileged the notion of immersion as a site-based research strategy. I will endeavor to connect these two domains of the terms with specific emphasis on the issue of identity, whose meaning of "sameness, oneness" suggests an opportunity—even need—to create more dialogue between the two worlds entailed in my writing.

To return to my opening field anecdotes, let me suggest some concerns that govern this research. First, while nothing in my encounters is necessarily unique to participant-observation field settings—after all, any ethnographer is likely to encounter research hurdles that make the work more challenging, and sometimes impossible, to complete—there is a rather curious dynamic to research that is conducted in consumer spaces. I would argue that this dynamic involves the desire of the anthropologist to become more immersed in the space and the will of the many social control agents to sometimes prevent that immersion. So, I wish to draw attention to some of the unique circumstances of this research in themed and immersive spaces and indicate some possible trajectories that future study might follow. Along with this concern is a second that relates to the position of such sites and their accompanying research in the context of contemporary ethnography. Quite surprisingly, for all of the everydayness and public popularity of these spaces, they remain understudied—especially by American anthropologists.[3] Many years ago, I had the opportunity to meet an anthropologist who had written such a book that related to the analysis of consumer spaces. When I expressed my excitement about that study, the author replied, "Yes, that was just a fun study that I didn't put much effort into." At the time, I was shocked to hear this, but later, I realized that this is the attitude that governs the spaces that I study—they are not worthy of serious research and, certainly, not by an anthropologist. This reminds of a third overarching issue or the fact that so many "analyses" of themed and immersive spaces are represented by overly generalized writing—for example, hypothetically, "I walked down Disney's Main Street, U.S.A. and found the entirety of the space to be so hegemonic and consumerist in nature"—that expresses the lack of first-person, on-the-ground research that addresses either (or both) of the domains of the consumption practices of guests and workers and the design practices of those who create public consumer spaces. In fact, these analyses are characterized not so much by on-the-ground, phenomenological research but by research essays or editorials that make vast and sweeping generalizations about people in the spaces (that is, when people actually appear in such writing). I will argue for the expansion of research in themed and immersive spaces such that we begin to see the nuances of the spaces—their guests, workers, and designers—more so than we see the opinions of the authors. Finally, I will suggest that there are wide-scale, game-changing shifts in media, popular culture, public space, and existential reality that necessarily impact—and often at dramatic levels—the study of consumer space, especially as guests and designers of them are engaged in their own forms of "research."

An Entropic State of Research

Entropy—which suggests a turning inward, transformation, or a general decline or disorder of a system—has a dynamic relationship to the research conducted in themed and immersive spaces.[4] As a worker and anthropologist at Six Flags AstroWorld, I became very familiar with this concept as each and nearly every day of work in the park related to some pending disorder that employees needed to prevent. The sense of a disaster on the horizon is related to the public nature of these spaces, their overwhelming scale of concern (particularly for theme parks that have thousands of employees, tens of thousands of guests in a given day, and many potential mishaps that can occur to park rides, shows, and attractions), and very tenuous brands to protect in a marketing sense.[5] Since the years that I worked at AstroWorld, my research has evolved in such ways that the entropy I experience no longer relates to that disorder that I noted and often tried to prevent as a worker in a consumer space but to the context of the research itself as a site of disorder. My opening examples involving three consumer spaces could be seen, metaphorically, as apt expressions of the nature of the research that I am describing. As I suggested earlier, there is resistance within academia to the immersive studies of consumer spaces that I am describing in this work. As well, there is considerable challenge that ethnographers experience when they are on site and attempt to capture the essence of a space that is presumably open and public in nature. Of course, it doesn't take long for the researcher to realize that such space is not truly public and that certain uses of that same space—whether for research, an artistic project, or a political action—will be forbidden. Initially, when I reflected on the first encounter with security guards in 2013, I felt quite inept, thinking that I should have made an effort to arrange a press meeting—something that I had done in many other research visits to theme parks and other spaces. Later, as I reflected more on the incident, it occurred to me that the outcome was, ironically, a desirable one, especially as it pointed to a trope of my research—this, the loss of control.

For many ethnographers, a loss of control experienced in the course of field research may be an undesirable state, but I want to suggest that in the context of the study of popular culture, particularly its consumer spaces, the entropic state that I have experienced in my own research is particularly important. During the course of my work in the worlds of themed and immersive spaces, I have moved from the position of a pure ethnographer of these spaces to a consultant working in them. This has not been a particularly easy transition, but, again, this speaks to a desired state of process in terms of my ethnographic work. On one occasion, I was asked to provide anthropological guidance on a project related to themed and immersive spatial design. I cannot directly comment on the event since I am bound by a non-disclosure agreement, but let

Image 17.1: The author conducting research (Photo by Scott A. Lukas)

me suggest that the event was particularly instructive for me as I began to again experience a situation in which my own agency as a professional anthropologist was challenged. Initially, I expected to enter the consulting events with a sense of power due to my presumed expertise as an anthropologist. The projects involved focus on my knowledge as it related to cultural systems that were being analyzed, produced, and remade by the participants. As time went on, I discovered that I was less and less able to express my expertise about cultural systems (and themed spaces) because the designers involved were operating from different paradigms than those often employed by anthropologists.[6] My frustration turned to delight as I began to witness the unfolding of the seminars—this included fascination with being able to see how a themed space is created, in a generative sense, and also a curiosity with the fact that the participants in the seminars were, essentially, engaging in their own research protocols, in some ways paralleling the approaches of professional researchers. As Douglas Holmes and George Marcus have argued, more and more, contemporary ethnographic research is determined by an uneasy collaboration between ethnographers and informants—"a more complex scene of multiple levels, sites, and kinds of association" in terms of the field.[7] This changing scene of the ethnographic, which I have identified through this theme of entropy, may suggest to traditional researchers a sense of loss; in fact, I believe that such loss represents an emerging ethos for research. More specifically, George Marcus has written of the crisis of representation that has impacted contemporary ethnography, and he has suggested the need to revise outdated models of ethnographic research such that fieldwork will begin to parallel the complexities, uncertainties, and fluctuations that are representative of the (postmondern) world at large.[8] Combined with other emergent epistemological and methodological innovations, such as Actor-Network Theory (ANT), new ethnographic approaches illustrate the potentiality of research in spaces of consumer and popular culture, particularly as such research represents a struggle to cope with loss, entropy, and other social and cultural forces that are on the horizon. ANT, in particular, represents an exciting opportunity for the study of these spaces, in no small part for the fact that it both recognizes the complexity of the social world in terms of any particular thing, entity, or context and suggests a relational model that situates such complexity in processes of interpretation, translation, and convergence.[9] Applied to the venues of theme parks and other themed and immersive spaces, we leave behind the model of the lone researcher who visits any such space as a solitary, detached, and omniscient individual and instead welcome an approach that addresses the complexity, ambiguity, relationality, convergence, and complicity that are implied in the space, its researcher, and its many, many actors—human and non-human.

It should be noted that such reformulation of the research conducted in consumer spaces need not be interpreted as a "loss of objectivity" or an admission of guilt as some have suggested in terms of the crisis of representation within contemporary cultural anthropology. In fact, the reformulation of research in the wake of entropic cultural forces suggests a coming to terms with the changing world and a desire to engage new researchers in this complex, though methodologically and epistemologically inhabitable, arena. It is also important to note that one of the results of both the crisis of representation in the social sciences and the adoption of more complex models of the world, such as ANT, is a notable effect on the status, and identity, of the researcher involved in the field of study.

Material Expressions of the Surface and Experiments Beyond

The consulting seminars that I have described began with considerations of the material cues realized through images, associations, mood boards and the like that are often a part of a charrette or other planning session that establishes the basis of a consumer space. I did not participate in future seminars with these designers, so it is unlikely that the conversations continued to focus *only* on the materiality of the design process, but it is curious to me that the seminars that I did experience focused so exclusively on the material expressions of theming. In striking parallel with social critics of themed spaces, the participants in the seminar seemed to have suggested that theming was best understood or designed through its obvious, material expressions.[10] The study of any form of theming—whether a lived or experienced version like that of Civil War reenactment or a more material or atmospheric version like that of a Venetian themed casino—necessitates deep questions about what exactly constitutes the theming. For an ethnographer of Civil War reenactment communities, the initial perceptions of the theming being a material phenomenon—with the varied symbols of guns, tents, costumes, and historical and period accoutrements—may shift into insights of theming as a lived, phenomenological, emotional, and affective entity.[11]

Ethnographic studies of theming, in dramatic contrast with analyses of social critics, emphasize the total, holistic nature of theming. In Civil War reenactment, the combination of material cues, performative practices, phenomenological happenings, and existential conditions all matter in terms of understanding the foundations of this form of theming. A significant proportion of the literature on themed spaces, however, has eschewed this focus on the holistic and ethnographic nature of theming and has instead emphasized domains of concern that include authenticity, hegemony, consumerism, and corporatism. While these are significant issues that do have direct bearing on the understanding of theming, these concerns, as part of a discursive worldview, have certainly impacted the perceptions that academics and laypersons have of specific themed spaces, themed communities and lifestyles, as well as theming as an overall construct in consumer society. General perceptions of theming noted on social media sites and through Internet searches, for example, include sensibilities that themed spaces and themed communities like those of Civil War reenactment are characteristic of shallowness, campiness, inauthenticity, overt consumerism, and tourism run amuck. With this general discursive construct of theming in mind, the study of theming is particularly challenging as guests, workers, and designers alike may sometimes privilege discourse that is focused on the material expressions of theming, as opposed to those expressions of phenomenological, ideological, political, and existential contexts that are often considered in the study of reenactment communities.

Given the fact that theming relies on certain material, architectural, and performative cues—some of which could be considered "stereotypical" in nature—it is not surprising that so much of the discourse related to it is focused on these non-ideational facets. The challenge, however, exists in the ethnographic desire to consider (seriously) the phenomenological, affective, and existential states beyond the material expressions of the theming.[12] Take, as an example, the account of a family enjoying a gondolier ride at the Venetian Las Vegas. A critic, whether having observed the account or not, may likely focus on the material cues present in the situation—the gondolier, the architecture, the gondola—and connect these presumably "surface" details to the idea of the family being duped in the situation at hand. An ethnographic observation of the same situation would necessitate that the analysis of the material cues be balanced by a focus on the lived and

Image 17.2. Civil War reenactment (Photo © Jack Schiffer | Dreamstime.com)

existential characteristics of the people within the event. Workers in such service industry spaces would argue that the gondolier's status as a performer within that space is much more complex than accounts within the literature on theming would suggest. The same could be said for analyses of the family within this space—their behaviors, sensibilities, and motivations could fall between engagement and apathy, enjoyment and dread. Unfortunately and somewhat ironically, the focus on the surface elements of theming's materiality within the discursive world of theming criticism has resulted in similar superficiality in the understanding of the actors involved in the spaces of theming. The focus on the materiality of the event—the surface, metaphorically—reminds of the classic, though now heavily critiqued, notion of the inside-outside ("emic"-"etic") distinction in anthropology. While I cannot delve into this debate in detail, let me say that a very simple requirement for the research of themed and immersive spaces is to consider aspects of the spaces beyond the material. This sounds somewhat simplistic and obvious, but this fact alone speaks to the incredible dearth of phenomenological research in these themed and immersive worlds. In this case, we might agree that the trope of immersion, surprisingly enough, should be considered as an appropriate means of engaging these spaces.

Not surprisingly, for the critic or researcher who feels that he or she is above the object of study—in these recent examples, the stereotypical themed Las Vegas casino—it is difficult, if not impossible, for that researcher to engage the space in question by becoming immersed in it. This is, however, exactly what needs to take place. In my own ethnographic observations of Las Vegas theming, I have begun a series of videographic experiments that, in many ways mimic the approaches of the "typical" Las Vegas tourist. Internet searches of "Las Vegas Strip" or "themed casinos" will result in some interesting popular examples—many of which are YouTube videos (see image 17.3). After analyzing these many videos, I decided to create my own videos that though based in a research protocol—typically, one focused on the theming of a given casino—were primarily voiced through a tourist or "guest" lens.[13] The experiments, though often focused on the materiality of the themed spaces, imagine a space of the mind and attempt to posit what experiences for typical guests are like in these spaces. The videos have the appearance of a tourist review film that is quite common on Youtube, yet they feign a sense of research in that the focus of each film is on an anthropological or design dynamic that would not be typically found in a tourist video. I see this hybridity of the form as an example of blurring the lines of immersion—those of the themed space and those of traditional anthropology—and also as a focus on the further blurring of the lines between popular (Internet and social media) "research" and traditional academic research.

Image 17.3. The author's YouTube page (Photo by Scott A. Lukas)

A second example of pushing the precarious dynamics of the material and ideational expressions of theming relates to a research group that began in 2012. The group includes two academics (Filippo Carlà and Florian Freitag) of themed spaces (the second of whom is also a former Paris Disneyland employee), myself, and a fourth colleague (Gordon Grice) who is a professional designer of themed spaces. The activities of the research group have included the traditional considerations of theming at academic conferences, but most intriguing have been a series of on-site research visits to a number of theme parks and subsequent e-mail conversations. As in the other cases that I have described, the initial considerations of the themed spaces began with the obvious material cues of theming, but what followed was a dynamic discussion of the ideational aspects of the spaces. As an example, while conducting a field visit at Universal Studios Hollywood, Carlà, Freitag, and I had opportunities to engage in in-depth discussions about the representations of the past in various park attractions (notably the Revenge of the Mummy–The Ride) as well as consider the issue of autotheming or the ways in which a theme park expresses, reflexively, sensibilities about itself, its industry, or its meta-representation.[14] Additionally, on another visit to both Disneyland and Disney California Adventure, we were joined by Grice. His expertise in the design of themed and immersive spaces was particularly valuable as we were able to pose questions to him about the interplay of the various dynamics of theming—including design, execution and implementation, guest responses in the park, and other matters. What was most insightful for me was our implicit focus on the differences between and the paralleling of academic-critical, design-praxis-focused, and popular-entertainment-based discourses about themed spaces.[15] These research protocols, and many others, suggest opportunities for future research experiments in themed and immersive spaces.

A Made-Up Theme Park

Image 17.4. Robber's Roost Ranch Antiques and Collectibles, Inyokern, CA (Photo by Scott A. Lukas)

In 2015, I made a brief research trip to Robber's Roost Ranch Antiques and Collectibles—a small and otherwise unassuming store on CA-14 in Inyokern, California. Robber's Roost had long been on my theming radar as I had read that the store had created a rather unique and imaginative ghost town. This themed site is a challenge to describe in writing, but, very generally, it is a small space spread over a few acres that includes a number of enclosed, themed structures.[16] I discovered that the current owners of the site—who, it should be noted, also own a modern, unthemed convenience store next to the themed town—purchased the Mojave Desert Inn and Station and then began the slow process of transforming the old motel rooms and accompanying buildings into a themed ghost town. It is actually a bit of a misstatement to describe the site as a ghost town. While it does have elements that one finds in such a themed space, the way that it develops the space—notably through techniques of inventive bricolage and beguiling narratives in the form of signage and other text—suggests that it is far from a typical ghost town. The various spaces within the site include the ubiquitous jailhouse complete with an interesting combination of a door-sized Christian cross and a "Buy Something, Buy Anything" sign that greets the visitor; Hans Bellmer-like stuffed dummies and texts like "My old lady can go to hail"; a labeled "Big Rock Garden" that consists of four unremarkable rocks; a sign to a museum that leads to no museum; an old water tower rethemed with discarded and repurposed telephones (complete with misspellings of common words); and a space, labeled "House" on the door, that is themed somewhat like a typical house but whose arrangements have been adapted for a more aesthetic purpose—a pile of paintings on a chair displayed in odd juxtaposition with other objects in the room and, most curious, a discarded door and lock tumbler laid out next to a "Support Our Troops" sticker.

Image 17.5. Robber's Roost Ranch Antiques and Collectibles, Inyokern, CA (Photo by Scott A. Lukas)

In fact, I believe that Robber's Roost represents an avant-garde vision of theming that invites us to ruminate on a metadiscourse about theming and immersion. In some respects, the space shares innovative design approaches with Tio's Tacos in Riverside, California.[17] Both of these spaces illustrate what has been called outsider or folk art. As artist Jean Dubuffet said of such work, it is "created from solitude and from pure and authentic creative impulses—where the worries of competition, acclaim and social promotion do not interfere."[18] Folk art, bricolage, and indigenous repurposing, as Allen F. Roberts describes, suggests a critical awareness of space, culture, and design and indicates a sensibility of irony with its various "meta" underpinnings.[19] In the cases of Robber's Roost and Tio's Tacos, we have a much different project of theming and immersion. While each space does suggest an awareness of the common elements of theming and immersion and likely invites guests to the spaces to enjoy them as they would more traditional venues, each also portends a simultaneously marvelous and disruptive discourse about theming and immersion. As researchers, after visiting spaces like these, we cannot help but focus on how these spaces are the future of theming (they are reflexive and, in some ways, too critical and ironic in how they remake the discourses of theming), and we cannot avoid considering the "mistakes" that we might discover in failed theme parks like Hard Rock Park, the design directions that could never be materialized in a typical, corporate themed space, and the "winks," ironic ploys, and unanswered questions that are more commonly found in a conceptual museum like the Museum of Jurassic Technology, in such ways that we are left asking new questions about these other spaces beyond their environs that they reference.

In another important respect, these conceptual themed spaces suggest a reworking of the dynamics that are typically involved in the study of consumer spaces. Grant McCracken, in his work *Culturematics*, speaks of a new era of consumer society in which everyday individuals are remaking the popular world around us by deploying their own forms of cultural "research."[20] Robber's Roost and Tio's Tacos are expressions of such culturematics as they represent a reworking of both the material and the discursive statements of theming and immersion of the past. As McCracken writes, a culturematic is a "little machine for making culture...designed to do three things: test the world, discover meaning, and unleash value."[21] Beyond these material constructions, we may imagine additional examples of culturematics that similarly move forward the discourses of theming and immersion as well as the research that is focused on its analysis. As I referenced earlier in an experiment involving YouTube, contemporary discourse about theming and immersion is, very much, constituted in the various media, social media, and other crowd-based spaces on the Internet and on mobile media. Social critics have largely ignored these reflections of theming and have thus limited our understandings of its nature and have prevented us from discovering these new "research" insights from the popular, crowd-sourced world.[22] While there are hints of a new, constitutive approach to the study of themed and immersive spaces—Edward Bruner's work on the multiple forms of authenticity present in tourist spaces is one example—there is a need for the development of truly collaborative, interfaced, and constitutive approaches to such research.[23] As well, as I argued earlier, high time it is to jettison traditional models and interpretations of popular and consumer culture and the themed and immersive spaces that such culture entails. New theoretical and methodological approaches, such as that of Actor-Network Theory, suggest that any given space—including these insurgent or avant-garde versions that I have examined—be understood as a complex product of multiple actors (human and non-human) and actions, contexts (seen and unseen), interpretations (explicit and implicit), images and memes (extant and extinct), and numerous other multiplicities of the world.

Future Directions of Research in Themed and Immersive Spaces

Describing the tendencies of research that may take place in themed and immersive spaces, years from now, is akin to predicting the nature of how these same spaces will appear in the future.[24] Both are challenging matters due to the changes, fluctuations, and uncertainties in the worlds of technology, economics, and popular culture that, no doubt, befuddle the researcher and designer of themed and immersive spaces alike. Let me suggest five specific trajectories of research to come in themed and immersive spaces. First, as I have alluded to earlier, subsequent research in these consumer spaces need take into account the reconceptualizations of the social and research worlds as suggested by Actor-Network Theory. Using ANT's complex models that were first tested in the social worlds of science and technology, we may begin to apply them to popular and consumer culture in order to stimulate new interpretations, conversations, and collaborations related to the spaces that we study. Imagine, just for a moment, if we resist the previous configurations of our research as consisting of a solitary, disconnected, and heroic figure of the critic-researcher of themed and immersive spaces (such as in the work of Ada Louise Huxtable, Paul Goldberger, and others) and instead imagine that same researcher as one node among many nodes and multiplicities within the field known as "themed and immersive space."

Second, and quite related to the first, is the tendency in which we witness the changing status and identity of the researcher. I began this chapter with a focus on failures, or at least difficulties, in the research process, not to suggest the impossibility of the project but to allow more effective rumination on how such challenges inform the research and offer some pathways forward. In the case of ethnographic research and other fieldwork forms that follow in the wake of the crisis of representation, the avant-gardes, postmodern epistemology, and cutting-edge research protocols like those of ANT, we realize that all share in common the tendency to cast doubt on, or otherwise ask new and probing questions of, the researcher in the middle of it all. Thus, I argue that reflexive research and the complex interactions that it creates between subject and object, space and criticism, theory and practice, event and re-presentation, results in the researcher developing a more tenuous and unstable relationship with the field.[25] In the case of the study of themed spaces, the notion of ethnographic complicity is a prominent voice. As George Marcus writes, the spaces of contemporary research suggest "...access to a construction of an imaginary for fieldwork that can only be shaped by complicitous alliance with makers of visionary or anticipatory knowledge who are already in the scene or within the bounds of the field. The imaginaries of knowledge makers are what the dreams of contemporary ethnography are made of."[26] Thus, future research in these venues may be more balanced in terms of the deployment of forms of cultural critique—perhaps critical in some cases, and empathetic in others—and may be better able at illustrating the complicity of the researcher in terms of the specific spaces and the more general cultural, consumerist processes that form them.[27]

Next, I would suggest that given the crises of representation and methodology that I have mentioned, as well as the changed status of the researcher, we need focus on forms of research that privilege postmondern, experimental, and avant-garde tendencies. Experiments in the nature of fieldwork (as I emphasized with the collaborations with Carlà, Freitag, and

Grice earlier), transformations of the written text that result from such fieldwork (as an example, in the "mystory" genre of Gregory Ulmer), and relocations of the "site" of research from an academic, scholarly location in staid, underpopulated, 8 a.m. Sunday conference rooms to a popular, collaborative, and ultimately public location (such as that which emerges in the contexts of public charrettes employed by architectural and community development firms) are all opportunities that owe some of their legacies to postmondern, experimental, and avant-garde tendencies in the world at large.[28]

Fourth, and related to this last desire to make the study of themed and immersive spaces open to the public is to imagine ways to give voice to the spaces that we study, their designers, and their users (in terms of guests). As Grant McCracken's work indicates, there is incredible value in addressing the cultural analytical and researcher models (as "quasi" as they may be) that are created by other actors outside of the research sphere of the ethnographer.[29] New research collaborations, including those between the various and often competing players of consumer spaces (researchers, designers, workers, and guests) could be imagined. We should also consider ways to address the innovations that are being experienced in popular, media, and public cultures, particularly as they are changing the ways in which themed spaces are designed (and studied). The work on contemporary branding, such as Kevin Roberts' *Lovemarks*, and on convergence cultures (Henry Jenkins), represents two significant arenas of future exploration.[30] Fifth, I suggest that there needs to be greater seriousness and attention given to the study of the nuances of themed and immersive spaces.[31] These spaces have been relegated to the junk pile of social research in that they either are not studied at all or they are addressed through simplistic, reductionistic, and essentialist analyses. Sober study of these spaces will entail complex analyses of the design processes that give rise to the spaces as well as consideration of the ethnographic dynamics of their use by guests. These and many other research protocols suggest the interesting possibility that the innovative, unexpected, and surprising facets of themed and immersive spaces of the future will be paralleled by even more surprising and innovative forms of their research, analysis, and criticism.

Notes

1. Portions of this work draw on my paper, "Research in Consumer Spaces: Emergent Issues," <https://www.academia.edu/3746281/Research_in_Consumer_Spaces>. Note: a video of this chapter is available at <https://youtu.be/1a4XWEh7SqI>.

2. Online Etymology Dictionary, <http://www.etymonline.com/>.

3. Surprisingly, in the one major ethnographic study of Disney theme parks, *Vinyl Leaves*, the anthropologist admits to never having spoken to any people while inside Walt Disney World. Stephen M. Fjellman, *Vinyl Leaves: Walt Disney World and America* (Boulder, CO: Westview Press, 1992), 18.

4. Online Etymology Dictionary, <http://www.etymonline.com/>.

5. For more on entropy and the theme park, see Scott A. Lukas, "An American Theme Park: Working and Riding Out Fear in the Late Twentieth Century," in *Late Editions 6, Paranoia Within Reason: A Casebook on Conspiracy as Explanation*, ed. George E. Marcus (Chicago: University of Chicago Press, 1999), 405–428.

6. In many ways, the situation paralleled Edward Bruner's description of events when he encountered individuals within the tourism industry "chasing anthropology's discarded discourse, presenting cultures as functionally integrated homogeneous entities outside of time, space, and history." Edward M. Bruner, *Culture on Tour: Ethnographies of Travel* (Chicago: University of Chicago Press, 2004), 4.

7. Douglas R. Holmes and George E. Marcus, "Refunctioning Ethnography: The Challenge of an Anthropology of the Contemporary," in *Handbook of Qualitative Research*, third edition, eds. Norman Denzin and Yvonna Lincoln (London: Sage, 2005), 1102.

8. George E. Marcus, *Ethnography Through Thick and Thin* (Princeton: Princeton University Press, 1998).

9. See Bruno Latour, *Reassembling the Social – An Introduction to Actor-Network-Theory* (Oxford: Oxford University Press, 2005).

10. While the context of much of my chapter has related to the field of academic research in themed and immersive spaces, it is important to apply the critiques and recommendations in this writing to all contexts of research. As an example, many contemporary design firms in the themed and immersive industries regularly engage in forms of research that are formative aspects of their approach to the design of such spaces. Yet, in some cases, I have noted that such research may operate at a level of superficiality that parallels some of the problems associated with academic research.

11. See Rory Turner, "Bloodless Battles: The Civil War Reenacted," *The Drama Review* 34, no. 4 (Winter, 1990): 123–136, Gordon Jones, "Performing Authenticity," in *The Immersive Worlds Handbook: Designing Theme Parks and Consumer Spaces* (New York: Focal, 2013), 107–110, and Scott A. Lukas, "The Cultures of Tiki," in this collection.

12. Many accounts that emphasize the problems associated with theming focus almost entirely on the materiality of the theming. In the case of Medieval themed restaurants, the costumes and swords of knights, the décor of the tables and wall coverings, the ubiquitous turkey legs, and so forth, are the primary entities in the social critic's reconstruction and analysis of the events or spaces. When behavioral or quasi-existential states are

implied in such studies, they tend to privilege a heavily etic- or critic's-based account and assume inauthenticity, being duped, and false consciousness on the part of the individual in that space or event. See, Mark Schatzker, "Historical Fiction: How Do Medieval-Themed Restaurants Get It Wrong?" *Slate*, October 6, 2004.

13. The results of my Las Vegas videos may be viewed at the playlist <https://www.youtube.com/watch?v=JX-HQG3umCM&list=PLTetG9GSbApDwyrVXPmQl83MCTn_e2R9i>.

14. See Florian Freitag, "Autotheming: Themed and Immersive Spaces in Self-Dialogue," in this collection

15. The conversations that developed are included in two research dialogues in this collection.

16. For a visual description, see https://www.youtube.com/watch?v=whhB6GGSDp8>.

17. See the video, <https://www.youtube.com/watch?v=qs9JWIQw1Xc

18. Jean Dubuffet, "Place à l'incivisme (Make way for Incivism)," *Art and Text* 27 (December 1987–February 1988).

19. Allen F. Roberts, "Chance Encounters, Ironic Collage," *African Arts* 25, no. 2 (April 1992): 54-98 and "The Ironies of System D," in *Recycled Re-Seen: Folk Art from the Global Scrap Heap*, eds. Charlene Cerny and Suzanne Seriff (New York: Henry N. Abrams, 1996), 82–101.

20. Grant McCracken, *Culturematic: How Reality TV, John Cheever, a Pie Lab, Julia Child, Fantasy Football . . . Will Help You Create and Execute Breakthrough Ideas* (Boston: Harvard Business Review Press, 2012).

21. McCracken, *Culturematic*, 3.

22. In the future, we may discover that there will be less of a need to place "research" in quotes. At that time, we may come to the realization that there is a complementarity between traditional academic research and more popular forms conducted by non-academics.

23. Bruner, *Culture on Tour*, 149.

24. See Scott A. Lukas, "Theming and Immersion in the Space of the Future," in this collection, for more on the contexts of themed and immersive spaces and their possible future states.

25. See, Mats Alvesson and Kaj Sköldberg, *Reflexive Methodology: New Vistas for Qualitative Research*, second edition (London: SAGE, 2013).

26. George E. Marcus, "Affinities: Fieldwork in Anthropology Today and the Ethnographic in Artwork," in *Between Art and Anthropology: Contemporary Ethnographic Practice*, eds. Arnd Schneider and Christopher Wright (Oxford: Berg, 2010), 91.

27. See, Scott A. Lukas, "Judgments Passed: The Place of the Themed Space in the Contemporary World of Remaking," in this collection for more on these new contexts of criticism.

28. Gregory Ulmer, *Teletheory* (New York: Atropos, 2004), particularly "Derrida at the Little Bighorn," and *Applied Grammatology: Post(e)-Pedagogy from Jacques Derrida to Joseph Beuys* (Baltimore, MD: Johns Hopkins University Press, 1984). Along with Ulmer's work, we might consider many other new openings of research that in general have a "meso," hybrid, or middle-voiced tendency to them. We may imagine new forms of research and textuality of representation that attempt to bridge the gaps between professional researcher and layperson, researcher and designer, among other dichotomies, and begin the process of creating new forms of collaborative, emergent, and dialogic fieldwork approaches and texts. One recent example of a "bridging device" in terms of such research is IDEO's "Method Cards;" see, <https://www.ideo.com/work/method-cards>.

29. McCracken, *Culturematic*.

30. Kevin Roberts, *Lovemarks: The Future Beyond Brands* (New York: powerHouse Books, 2004). Henry Jenkins, *Convergence Culture: Where Old and New Media Collide* (New York: New York University Press, 2008).

31. As examples of some excellent directions in the study of space, see, Jan Gehl and Birgitte Svarre, *How to Study Public Life* (Washington, D.C.: Island Press, 2013) and Linda N. Groat and David Wang, *Architectural Research Methods* (Hoboken, NJ: Wiley, 2013).

PART VII

The Deployments of Rhetoric, Performance, and Affect

18

Believe It and Not

The Playful Pull of Popular Culture-Themed Tourism Attractions

By Derek Foster

Television shows and movies obviously provide the narrative foundation for much of popular culture. But these popular media increasingly are the source for "non-mediated" experiences such as TV- and popular culture-themed tourist attractions. For instance, while places such as Northern Ireland and Iceland are locations for filming episodes of *Game of Thrones*, these places also use the television series to encourage new forms of tourism and consumption behavior. Similarly, U.S. locations in North Carolina and Georgia offer tours of *Hunger Games* filming sites, attracting enthralled fans of that franchise with the chance to peek behind the curtain of movie magic. The field of tourism studies, with its healthy tradition of investigating film tourism and literary tourism before that, frequently confronts questions about the blurring of the boundary between the real and the fake. Indeed, the figure of the "post-tourist" is one whose travels are concerned with the search for blatantly unreal and contrived experiences.[1] How these tourist sites are themed (and how these themes are encountered by visitors) becomes an important question, then, for those who seek to understand the pull of the patently inauthentic.

I will examine two particular constellations of such popular culture themed entertainments: Those based on *The Hunger Games* (indebted to films based on books) and *Game of Thrones* (a TV series, based on books). Beyond simply acknowledging the truism that, "Today's themed environments constitute, in fact, a part of our popular culture," I seek to analyze examples of popular culture that congeal into themed environments.[2] The source material for these themed attractions transports readers and viewers alike into fantastic, unreal narratives and places derived from fantasy and science-fiction genres. This is important because, unlike some other popular culture themed tourism sites, neither of these exist in the real world. One can never directly visit Panem, District 12, or the world of Westeros. One can, however, visit real-world places where these unreal places were staged. Fans of *Game of Thrones* can be led on themed excursions in Ireland, Iceland, or Croatia (to name only a few of the major destinations where the TV series was filmed). Meanwhile, *Hunger Games*-based tours offer to familiarize visitors with North Carolina or Georgia (where its movies were filmed). Both the *Game of Thrones* and *Hunger Games* franchises are particularly relevant for an examination of theming because of the pervasiveness and plasticity of their themes. For instance, some of these tours offer visitors a chance simply to visit the places that serve as the source code for their favorite filmic fictions. Other tours insert fans into the fantasy world more directly, not by re-enacting particular scenes but by giving visitors the chance to playfully perform along with the theme and engage the imagination in a more multi-sensorial, lived experience. Here, fans, through their reenactment practices, "can challenge and change the limits of present-ness through the creation of an affiliation to a particular era or place which is not dependent on the materially real or authentic."[3] Also, both of these franchises have created traveling exhibitions designed to give fans the opportunity to further interact with the narrative underpinning the fictional worlds. At these themed sites, one can see the real elements used to construct the filmic fantasies (movie props, costumes) and even engage in virtual reality immersion into the fictional world.

Quasification and the Blurring of Reel and Real Spaces

It goes too far to suggest that the power of these themed spaces overwhelms visitors' cognitive faculties. For sure, some literature on theming points out how consumers can, in some settings, have difficulty distinguishing between fact and fiction.[4] But the purely fictive foundation of the theming in question here means that visitors are ever aware that they are partaking of real simulations, not simulations of the real that threaten to undermine reality but rather real representations of fictional worlds. These are examples of "a burgeoning global tourist trade for places that do not exist except in popular culture and imagination."[5] As such, the fan-tourist does not get lost in a hyper-reality of veneers but makes "concrete comparisons between imagination and reality…driven by an emotional longing for these two worlds to converge."[6] Instead of unreality trumping reality through the application of a (fantastic) narrative to institutions or locations, theming becomes the means by which people find themselves "in the 'real' world, an empirically measurable reality, defined by time and place [and]…a world of imagination, an interconnected complex of fantasies, daydreams, and stories."[7] Far from confusing imagination and reality or believing that imaginary stories or settings could be made real, popular-culture themed tourism allows visitors to enter into or engage with a world of make believe without actually believing in it. I'm interested in investigating instances where fans of themed entertainments deploy their cultural capital in order to "'believe it and not'—rather than 'believe it or not.'"[8] These themed sites present us with examples of quasification wherein an environment "can be experienced as if it were something other than what it essentially is."[9] So, one can visit a landscape in Iceland and gaze upon a vista as if one was wandering beyond the Wall and encountering White Walkers. Or, one can engage in archery as if one were a character in either *The Hunger Games* or *Game of Thrones*. Quasification means pretending that one's experience is real even when one knows that it can never be. This kind of theming is not a device meant to seduce cultural dupes who are all-too-willing to believe in the illusion of the theme. "In fact, quasification works so well precisely because consumers know that they are being presented with fabricated and fantasized images and settings which are underpinned by a business ethic."[10]

While the quasifying imagination is "an imagination which need not be limited too literally to the mundane world of phenomena," it behooves scholars of theming and popular culture to question how that imagination manifests itself as consumers encounter these themes.[11] So let us now investigate how the fictional worlds of *The Hunger Games* and *Game of Thrones* are brought to life in traveling exhibitions and tours of their filming sites. By investigating the marketing of each of these, I can first establish how such spaces are positioned for consumption by fans and then, by investigating comments of visitors to these tours and exhibits on the popular website TripAdvisor, I can assess the reception of these themed environments. One of the goals of this study, therefore, is to take up the challenge of those who "argue for a contextualization of the role of film tourism within cultural and media studies."[12] In essence, I'm examining multiple instances of "mediatized tourism" wherein people use online social media to circulate their responses to tourist sites.[13] Through their behavior online, people act as both consumers (detailing their actions and opinions of tourist attractions) and producers (circulating this media content and potentially affecting subsequent experiences by other visitors). For the analyst, these posts demonstrate how people are affected by their experience at these sites and how such posts help constitute the conditions for potential affective experiences by others.

Insights from Being On-Set: Learning and Laboring at Film Locations

If movie "locations provide a site where fictional places become actualized and tangible," theming provides the connective tissue between the actual and the imaginary geography encountered by visitors at these places.[14] So, how are such tourist experiences themed in order to encourage affective encounters and ignite the imaginations of visitors? The marketing of these tours gives us an initial hint. Pictures provided on the TripAdvisor site for *Hunger Games Unofficial Fan Tours* show a bus emblazoned with the slogan "Walk in the footsteps of your favorite characters" while visitors pose at various locations and participate in archery tag. Seeing the sights where one's favorite fictions were filmed obviously is important, but one's visit to the actual site invariably is not sweetened by CGI and post-production techniques that overlaid an unreality onto these locations and made them so attractive when one saw them for the first time on screen. Thus, in some instances, the opportunity to partake in activity similar to that undertaken by one's favorite characters is designed to make the experience that much more memorable and mimic that which was depicted on screen. Reviews of *Hunger Games* Unofficial Fan Tours demonstrate their affective, experiential appeal. TripAdvisor user djstories summarized the Atlanta Day Tour iteration on January 11, 2015 as such: "*Hunger Games* Unofficial Fan Tours make you feel like you are standing in the middle of the *Hunger Games!*" Meanwhile, on November 22, 2014, Toni G reviewed the North Carolina iteration in detail: "We even got to do camouflage in clay! Probably my favorite time was eating a *Hunger Games* style lunch on the flat rocks on Triple Falls trail. Our lunch consisted of things that Katniss would have eaten during the games such as goat cheese, berries and 'nightshade!'"

Here we see the sensual nature of the themed experience tying the real to the fictional. The food consumed by Toni G calls to mind the quasified nature of the experience, seamlessly recalling a Katniss-esque repast. Visitors could eat food as if they were Katniss even though they were never in her dangerous circumstances. Also, reality never disappears altogether although it is filtered through the lens of fictional characters. The real-world location (Triple Falls Trail) gets mentioned in this review, as it is an important feature of DuPont State Forest and a major filming location for the first movie. Yet it was a picturesque but nameless feature momentarily captured on film and not mentioned in the books given that the location was a stand in for the fictional Arena. So why was Katniss invoked instead of Jennifer Lawrence, the actor who portrayed the character and was filmed eating at that same location? The way in which this experience was recalled demonstrates how seamlessly the real and the imaginary can interweave. The ease with which people connect with fictional characters and imagine communing with them in unreal places reinforces how, "Through popular culture and media, places…are collectively reimagined, with certain elements and features exaggerated and others ignored."[15]

In a similar vein, the official visitor website for Northern Ireland trumpeted its own fictionalized heritage. It recommended a number of *Game of Thrones* pursuits, highlighting not just the appeal of certain sites as backdrops for sightseeing, but also marketing them based on the experiential nature of visiting the sites. Visitors were encouraged to step into the shoes of fictional characters and recreate scenes from the TV series: "Now you can experience the world of 'Westeros' for yourself on a *Game of Thrones* inspired activity!" The first option announced, "Become a Stark of Winterfell for a day…[and] immerse yourself in the land of Westeros. Why not dress up in character, take to the archery range, tour the movie set or hire a glamping pod?"[16] No visitors remarked on the absurdity of their favorite characters engaging in glamorous camping. But reviews of this *Game of Thrones* Winterfell Set Tour typically noted the fun involved in practicing archery. For many the highlight was seeing actual filming locations, meeting the quasified direwolves (Northern Inuit dogs), and gaining insider knowledge from tour guides who had previously appeared as extras in the series. Comments that praised the opportunity to wear authentic Stark family costumes and act as if one was a character from the show tended to be subsumed within a larger narrative of the pleasures of partaking in a behind-the-scenes privilege. Of course, not every location offers the cosplay-potential of becoming one's favorite characters. For other locations, seeing was the key to believing.

While visiting Belfast, for instance, one can embark upon the Stones and Thrones tour. Here, one is entreated to "explore the scenic splendor of the seven kingdoms and see where so many of the pivotal *Game of Thrones* scenes were shot." One is offered the chance to "Travel to Ballycastle—home to the world famous Lammas fair and the birthplace of *Game of Thrones* Star Conleth Hill (Varys)—to see where Varys was born as a slave in the Free Cities."[17] Clearly, one has to be a fan of the franchise to distinguish the fake from the real among the tour details. The Lammas fair sounds like it could be featured in *Game of Thrones* but is, instead, a real-world, three-hundred-year-old celebration that marks the end of summer and the beginning of the harvest season. Meanwhile, one is told that a star from the series was born in this locale while it is also highlighted as the setting for her character's birth. This tour offers the popular-culture-minded pilgrim the chance to situate the fictive landscape alongside the factual one. Representative reviews of the tour lauded beautiful coastline scenery and destinations that weren't used in *Game of Thrones* alongside those that were instantly recognizable from watching the series. It was not uncommon to encounter reviewers commenting that one did not have to be a fan of the show to enjoy the tour but it meant one would get more from the experience.

In like-minded fashion, reviews of Icelandic tours trumpet the stunning landscapes and picturesque locales that formed the backdrop for *Game of Thrones* scenes. Comments tend to focus on the natural beauty of the land as a frame for further appreciating the series (rather than having the series prime visitors' appreciation for the landscape). While locality is an ephemeral concept, it is also a structure of feeling that helps partially constitute the theme, infusing the particular place with both the spirit of the show and an affective response of wonder.[18] The recursive nature of the themed reality is demonstrated in the following comment posted on October 31, 2013 by TripAdvisor user SouthWestSmoggy about The Traveling Viking's tour in Akureyri in Northeast Iceland: "If you go beyond The Wall expect the cold. The weather alone, which was at its wintry best was superb in helping to capture a GoT atmosphere." Of course, the *Game of Thrones*-like atmosphere was itself a product of Iceland's weather, but the experience of the themed excursion meant that the weather now could be felt as if it were an adjunct of the series. Locality is meaningfully invoked in a different fashion in Croatia where reviewers of *Game of Thrones* walking tours consistently noted their newfound appreciation of local history. Reviewing the *Game of Thrones* – Day Tour in Split, Croatia, Marija A on June 15, 2015 noted, "The guide was very interesting in comparing the film spots and the historical events of the region. On the Klis Fortress we could feel the spirit of slaves and masters." Travis T. on September 1, 2015 titled his review, "Incredible experience for GoT fans and history buffs alike!" At least in this setting the themed attractions seemed to cultivate a newfound knowledge and enjoyment of local history, likely indebted to but also clearly distinct from the fictional narratives that enticed tourists there originally. Elsewhere, Annette T reviewed the Atlanta History Center on 10 June 2014 with the following title: "Obsessed. Go for the Hunger Games Capitol Tour." Here, opportunities to see historical dwellings such as the Swan House (President Snow's residence on film) were valued more for the frisson that comes from coming into contact with a fictional world rather than their historical significance. The important thing to take away from these reviews is not that real history or fake histories are valued above the other but to understand that all such themed experiences are forms of affective history or, "historical representation that both takes affect as its object and attempts to elicit affect."[19] Visitors to these themed sites filtered their experiences through their affective investment in popular culture and had the opportunity to not just learn history but also feel it, sometimes in creative, unexpected ways.

Clearly, these various examples of themed tourism demonstrate more than just the obvious fact that fans are affected by visiting filming sites. Beyond the observation that theming, in general, depends upon and also sustains those who exhibit the "affective sensibility" of popular culture fans, we might understand these themed attractions as opportunities for affective labor.[20] This type of work or investment is "labour that produces or manipulates affects such as feelings of ease, well-being, satisfaction, excitement, or passion."[21] Clearly, this is a consideration of "Imagineers" responsible for envisioning themed experiences as well as the responsibility of those leading visitors through them. A staple of all such tours comes when operators highlight the correspondence points between a visitor's view and scenes that were filmed at the same spot. Another opportunity for such labor sometimes comes in the form of guiding visitors through costumed revelry. However, visitors are not just the recipients of such labor; they can produce it too. In their enumeration of affective intensities like anger, gratitude, joy, disappointment, and surprise (and by communicating memories of themed experiences) visitors also have the capacity to produce an affective state in other people. But, more importantly, affective labor entails "a self-transformation…[wherein] the bodily activities of the commemorating individual themselves become the mnemonic substrate."[22] In this capacity, people's TripAdvisor reviews demonstrate not merely that individuals are emotionally affected by the narrative of the theme but that theming's affects extend to an appreciation of local extra-narrative features such as landscape and history. Through first performing as theme-saturated sightseers, and then laboring online to report upon their experiences, visitors help make the tours meaningful, both for themselves and others.

Ex situ Affect: Theming and the Traveling Exhibition

The very public nature of TripAdvisor's reviews underscores how affect, as a rhetorical phenomenon, is distinguished "from a felt state on the part of an individual subject. In a sense, affect is a condition of possibility for such feeling states, in its status as a circulating affinity, rather than a space of interior emotional content."[23] This begs the question, then, how do certain kinds of themed experiences seem to matter more for visitors and how are these affective states activated differently by the application of the same narrative but in different circumstances? To begin such an investigation, we can examine traveling exhibits dedicated to *Game of Thrones* and *Hunger Games*. While these lack the "authentic" theming of place that in-situ film location tours can offer, these exhibits are designed to also cultivate the affective response of wonder as one is given the chance to come face-to-face with the "real" objects used to construct the fantasy and gain additional insight into its construction while interacting with favorite characters and stories in a new way.

The *Game of Thrones* traveling exhibition is relatively small (compared to the *Hunger Games* exhibit which trumpets ten times the number of props and costumes) but both offer interactive experiences designed to cultivate an emotional authenticity and appeal to a fan-driven affect-fueled economy. For instance, The 2015 *Game of Thrones* Exhibit, Experience the Realm, featured an interactive performance in which visitors took a wooden sword embedded with wireless technology and swung at targets projected onto a screen in front of them which would explode and cast series-related artwork onto the screen in the form of blades, dragon claws, raven feathers, and direwolf fur. In the end, each visitor received a personalized *Game of Thrones* themed self-portrait.[24] The feature of the exhibit that seemed to attract the most attention, however, was the Ascend the Wall virtual reality experience. Here, one stepped into a physical recreation of the Castle Black winch elevator from the series and, donning an Oculus Rift headset, "ascended" to the top of the series' iconic 700-foot-tall wall, immersed in a virtual *Game of Thrones*-esque world as if one were a character in the series. Speaking to the blend of the virtual and the real, visitor Madtv261 noted in a review on May 18, 2014 that upon ascending the wall in Toronto, you "almost think you are going to run off, get shot at by arrows, and fall to your death." Similarly, Myles J reviewed the exhibit in Belfast on June 14, 2014: "You also get to do a virtual reality type activity that takes you to the top of the ice wall in the show. This was amazing and maybe abit [sic] scary." Clearly, this exhibit did more than help fans suspend disbelief and revel in the fakery of visiting with and living in a fantasy world. Far from playing at "make believe" in which one's performances maintain the distinction of what is real and what is pretend, the virtual reality experience at least seems to cultivate performances that "potentially generated belief in make-believe."[25]

The *Hunger Games* exhibition seems, at first glance, to affect visitors slightly differently. Fans of both series surely "want to marvel at the fabrications and the relics that are presented for their delectation."[26] Yet different subject matter is likely to attract different fans. Jordan Hoffman reviewed the exhibit for the *Guardian* on July 1, 2015 when it debuted and predicted that with "a well-curated mix of props, sets, costumes, holograms and interactive displays…many obsessed teens may just want to shiver in front of Katniss Everdeen's quiver." However, this says more about assumptions regarding the affective sensibility of this particular fandom than it does about the associational power of the exhibit. Indeed, one's self-identification as a fan did not guarantee an awesome or even an enjoyable experience. For instance, Nathan K's TripAdvisor review on July 5, 2015 reported, "Me and my wife are *hunger game* [sic] fans and when we saw that they had an exhibit for it we had to see what it was. Its [sic] basically just their outfits on mannequins." Ari L had the exact same complaint in her review on July 10, 2015: "Me and [my] wife and our two kids are fans of the *Hunger Games* and we never missed a single movie. Naturally, we rushed to visit the exhibit 3 days after it opened at the Discovery Center. It was a loss of time and money…to see outfits on mannequins!" Interestingly, these comments reveal the disappointment that can come from visiting a themed exhibit as a "specific film tourist." This type of visitor seeks to actively participate in the theme and is motivated by an affective sensibility that seeks some form of self-actualization or larger fulfillment from the film franchise. On the other hand, the "general film tourist" also participates in film tourist activities (such as traveling exhibits based on films). However, such individuals tend to not be specifically motivated to visit because of the films and may be motivated by factors such as novelty or education value.[27] Such motivation may be exhibited in the following TripAdvisor comment posted on August 5, 2015 by Mireya H: "Even though I am not a *Hunger Games* fan I have to admit that the exhibit was beautiful (actual props and costumes from the movies) and very informative (background info on where every one [sic] involved got their inspiration)."

Precisely because different types of visitors record varying degrees of affinity for exhibits such as these, organizers often go beyond the simple presentation of sets and props from the movie. In this case, they tied the *Hunger Games* franchise into contemporary, real-world moral issues and provided visitors the opportunity to interact with the narrative of the unreal world as it was brought alive on film. This is consistent with what Pine and Gilmore suggest are the key points for experiential design: Theme the experience, harmonize impressions with positive cues, eliminate negative cues, mix in memorabilia, and engage all five senses.[28] Of course, not everyone will be positively affected by the particular ratio of these factors. Davec023's TripAdvisor review on July 6, 2015 exclaimed, "To step into the world of Panem was incredible, the costumes and sets were beautiful!" Contrarily, FabianVidela remarked on September 13, 2015, "*The Hunger Games* [exhibition] is basically like going to a museum of memorabilia with very little interaction." While one can never account for variance in visitors' expectations, it seems universally true that "if the show is unconvincing, if the theme simply does not resonate for them, they will feel let down and disappointed."[29] (29) And, yes, a larger proportion of visitors' comments seemed to express a degree of disillusionment with the *Hunger Games* exhibit than with the *Game of Thrones* exhibit. But there may be straightforward reasons for the varying responses. Clearly, one factor that affected visitors was the cost of admission. The *Game of Thrones* exhibit was free, whereas the *Hunger Games* exhibit typically required thirty dollars to enter with an additional cost for a media guide meant to unlock special features during one's visit. Also, even though one can usually expect some memorabilia to be mixed in with any commodified themed experience, an exhibit that contains too much memorabilia and not enough opportunities to exercise the imagination can be accused of leveraging the theme in order to cash in on merchandising opportunities. Of course, each of the *Game of Thrones* and *Hunger Games* traveling exhibits served as mobile marketing devices for their respective media franchises. The Exhibition Store for the latter offered 149 items for sale from a $2.99 pen to a $7,500.00 gold pendant. Both exhibitions are paratexts that only exist alongside upcoming TV seasons and film debuts, reminding visitors of what whet their appetites before, giving them opportunities to delve deeper into these imaginary realms, and feeding a demand for future consumption. Also, another factor that seemed to negatively impact impressions of the *Hunger Games* exhibit was its location. While it moved on to San Francisco in 2016, its initial stop was for six months in New York City's Discovery Times Square, a giant exhibition space billed as "more than a museum" in perhaps the busiest tourist zone in the country. Here, many "serendipitous" film tourists experienced it.[30] With less motivation to encounter the exhibit on purpose, such consumption-by-happenstance generated reviews of the exhibit frequently indicated that attendance was due less to fascination with the film and related more to a free stop on a pre-purchased NY Pass. Contrarily, in both 2014 and 2015 the *Game of Thrones* exhibit temporarily set up in eight different cities around the world for a period of roughly a week at each location; this created a greater sense of exclusivity and attracted specific *Game of Thrones* tourists.

Thematic Common Ground: Making Belief in Make Believe

It may seem as though the themed traveling exhibits attracted a group of visitors less likely to exercise a quasified imagination compared to those who visited real-world filming sites. However, it is reasonable to suggest that visitors to both real world and traveling exhibition sites continually weave between the world of the imagination and reality, finding points of contact and overlap. Admittedly, when participating in a themed tour, one is literally at a movie set and therefore can imagine as if they are in a fantastic world whereas visitors to a themed exhibit get to experience the fantastic world as if they were on a movie set. In situ tours offer the chance to use the fictive space of one's choice in order to supply "representational files that are dragged onto the actual landscape…where fictive space not only orients the tourist in actual space but also confers new value onto the landscape."[31] This was evident in numerous reviews on TripAdvisor.com. Yet it isn't as simple as dismissing the themed exhibit as less meaningful, but simply full of different meanings. In each themed environment, affective registers are cued as visitors ensconce themselves in "a discursive system of representations where fact becomes as incredible as fiction, and fiction as compelling as reality."[32] When the *Hunger Games* exhibit touts its educational value and is used to teach students about natural resources or propaganda and *Game of Thrones* visitors claim to have learned about local geography and history, visitors' engagement with the theme in each case ties the real world into the fictional world, connecting the actual and the speculative, the already-happened and the provisional future.

These popular-culture inspired tourists searching for themed experiences must not be classified as cultural dupes, confusing unreality with reality. Far from losing themselves in simulacra, real events and places get merged with the hyperreal in people's narratives, describing the real world as if it were filtered through an imaginary one. The theme, then, has the power not to merely distract from reality and transport people to a world of make-believe. Instead, the variety of themed tours and exhibits I've addressed above are all predicated on showing people the real world behind that of the "make-believe" world. And, the act of granting privileged access to apprehend how the thicket of the unreal is constructed helps fans constitute their particular worlds of "make belief." Without suffering from the pretense that the world of the Westeros or the Capitol could be real, people are afforded the temporary luxury of pretending as if they could be nonetheless. Fans know full well that on screen and on the written page, these fictional worlds are inauthentic realities presented for escapist entertainment. However, experiencing these worlds in the context of multi-sensorial, interactive themed spaces creates the conditions for "existential authenticity."[33] Viewed this way, one's touristic activities can offer a liminal space where the requirements and inauthenticity of everyday life are put on hold and one can be fulfilled, seeking not the veneer of authenticity constructed in artificial settings or fake objects but the feeling of being true to oneself, activated by one's participation in an alternative reality. The perceived authenticity of themed experiences is directly related to the extent to which visitors feel connected to these alternate realities, whether they are the world of *The Hunger Games* or *Game of Thrones*. However, it is worth underscoring that the strength of that connection matters more than the degree of artificiality or naturalness of the themed experience. After all, for many, "the 'real' is not even necessarily the point of reference regarding where human experience takes place. What she has seen on TV and in books is just as valid a reference point."[34] This point is underscored by the realization that "heightened reality, not reality may be the true focus of theming."[35] The exhibits I've examined obviously do not gain their significance from strict adherence to historical facts. Far from symbolizing scenes from specific past or even current events, they achieve their popular culture capital by leveraging visitors' affective intensities to imaginary places. These are exemplars, therefore, of cultural artifacts and cultural experiences instructing us that, "while it is unhelpful to draw a strict distinction between the real and the reel in today's media-based society, it is worth thinking about this distinction in relational terms."[36]

Clearly, not all theming has the power to transport people to imaginary places like *Game of Thrones* and *Hunger Games* themed spaces. Nonetheless, all theming, by its very nature, injects some fantasy and fiction into real places. As such, even more than the ability to invoke the imagination, one might argue that the affective power of theming opens up the horizon of the imaginal: "In contrast to the imaginary, which is often associated with the unreal and fictitious...[and] whereas the imaginative is the result of the work of imagination, the imaginal is the medium where such work takes place."[37] Thus, theming helps us acknowledge the intertwined nature of the imaginary and the real and provides people with the means to do more than merely escape from reality. Similarly, while these spaces may blur the line between real and reel places, they do not seem to encourage people to lose the ability to distinguish fiction from reality. Instead, when one feels as if one is on-set or makes a connection with real places that act as filming locations for unreal ones, theming may encourage people to experience reality in a heightened fashion.

Coda: Popular Culture and the Re-animation of the Real

It has been suggested that are three notable inter-related developments within scholarship on film-induced tourism: "The first is the growing realization that individual case studies have been overdone...A second conceptual shift has been from film tourism to media tourism...The third change is a dramatic swing from a supply to a demand focus."[38] This study has taken up the challenge of investigating all three developments. By branching out from site-specific instances of theming, I've attempted to ascertain how the same theme evokes different impressions and leads to different experiences in different settings. I've also explicitly acknowledged the power of popular culture based theming across media. Of course, both *Game of Thrones* and *The Hunger Games* are poly-mediated phenomena, drawing in fans through books and screened representations. But these same fans report on their tourist activities online. Consequently, visitors to these themed spaces do not simply consume themed entertainments; they also produce media about them too. Finally, the ability to analyze these postings allows the researcher to address how these themed spaces affect visitors without relying upon speculation or an isolated, subjective experience of a single group or visit. This research coincides with work that seeks to de-emphasize the role of organizations using themes to promote specific destinations and instead places renewed focus upon tourists and the impact of the themed experience upon them. One of the fundamental points that this research has hopefully demonstrated is the importance of theming in both an attention economy and an affect economy. Theming—especially that based upon popular culture—provides the seemingly disposable fluff that becomes the stuff of import, to both fans visiting and to economies supported by both industrial and affective investments.

While each themed space is unique, each also serves as a site of symbolic action, an environment filled with texts to be read and textures to be felt. They act as places of cultural performance where popular culture is not simply read or interpreted but re-inscribed. Visiting fans use theming, on a personal level, to remind them of why they care about the text and to re-animate its magical qualities. And on a social level, theming demonstrates how popular culture is an important medium of public communication and public memory. Through theming, a potentially otherwise mundane environment can be re-animated. Through the injection of artifice, a place or thing can be made emotionally and existentially more significant to visitors. By visiting and recording their impressions of these visits, people can animate these spaces anew, exploiting the ambiguity of what they are and what they could be. Private recollections become public recommendations and these representations act as rhetorical interventions, adding onto and altering our judgments of what are real and what really matters. As such, even though, "in this world, reality wears the mask of a meaning, the completeness and fullness of which we can only imagine, never experience," through performing and partaking of themed spaces, people can experience what would otherwise only remain imaginary.[39]

Notes

1. John Urry, *The Tourist Gaze: Leisure and Travel in Contemporary Societies* (London: Sage, 1990).

2. Mark Gottdiener, *The Theming of America: Dreams, Visions and Commercial Spaces* (Boulder, CO: Westview, 1997), 3.

3. Elizabeth Carnegie and Scott McCabe, "Re-enactment Events and Tourism: Meaning, Authenticity and Identity," *Current Issues in Tourism* 11, no. 4 (2008): 359.

4. Caroline L. Munoz, Natalie T. Wood, and Michael R. Solomon, "Real or Blarney? A Cross-Cultural Investigation of the Perceived Authenticity of Irish Pubs," *Journal of Consumer Behavior* 5, no. 6 (2006): 222–234.

5. Christina Lee, "'Have Magic, Will Travel': Tourism and Harry Potter's United (Magical) Kingdom," *Tourist Studies* 12, no. 1 (2012): 53.

6. Stijn Reijnders, "Stalking the Count: Dracula, Fandom and Tourism," *Annals of Tourism Research* 38, no. 1 (2011): 233.

7. Alan Bryman, *The Disneyization of Society* (London: Sage, 2004), 15. Stijn Reijnders, *Places of the Imagination: Media, Tourism, Culture* (London: Routledge, 2011), 15.

8. Peter Farrugia, "Convenient Truths: History, Memory, and Identity in Brantford, Ontario," *Journal of Canadian Studies* 46, no. 2 (2012): 122–146

9. Alan Beardsworth and Alan Bryman, "Late Modernity and the Dynamics of Quasification," *Sociological Review* 47, no. 2 (1999): 248.

10. Beardsworth and Bryman, "Late Modernity and the Dynamics of Quasification," 250.

11. Beardsworth and Bryman, "Late Modernity and the Dynamics of Quasification," 253.

12. Rodanthi Tzanelli and Majid Yar, "Breaking Bad, Making Good: Notes on a Televisual Tourist Industry," *Mobilities* 11, no. 2 (2016): 189.

13. Maria Månsson, "Mediatized Tourism," *Annals of Tourism Research* 38, no. 4 (2011): 1634–1652.

14. Lee, "Have Magic, Will Travel," 54.

15. Warwick Frost and Jenifer Laing, *Imagining the American West Through Film and Tourism* (London: Routledge, 2015), 8

16. "*Game of Thrones* Inspired Activities in Northern Ireland," <http://interact.discovernorthernireland.com/blog/5-game-of-thrones-inspired-activities-in-northern-ireland/>.

17. "Stones and Thrones Game of Thrones Location Tour," <http://www.discovernorthernireland.com/Stones-and-Thrones-Game-of-Thrones-Location-Tour-Belfast-P42575>.

18. Arjun Appadurai, *Modernity at Large: Cultural Dimensions of Globalization* (Minneapolis: University of Minnesota Press, 1996), 180–181.

19. Vanessa Agnew, "History's Affective Turn: Historical Reenactment and Its Work in the Present," *Rethinking History* 11, no. 3 (2007): 301.

20. Lawrence Grossberg, "Is There a Fan in the House?: The Affective Sensibility of Fandom," in *The Adoring Audience*, ed. Lisa Lewis. (New York: Routledge, 1992), 50–65.

21. Michael Hardt and Antonio Negri, *Multitude: War and Democracy in the Age of Empire* (New York: Penguin, 2004), 108.

22. Matthew J. Allen and Steven D. Brown, "Embodiment and Living Memorials: The Affective Labour of Remembering the 2005 London Bombings," *Memory Studies* 4, no. 3 (2011): 316.

23. Carole Blair, Greg Dickinson, and Brian L. Ott, "Introduction: Rhetoric/Memory/Place," in *Places of Public Memory: The Rhetoric of Museums and Memorials*, eds. Greg Dickinson, Carole Blair, and Brian L. Ott (Tuscaloosa: University of Alabama Press, 2010), 46.

24. To see this part of the exhibit unfold, see the July 2015 posting "Game of Thrones / Sword Experience" by user Red Paper Heart, <https://vimeo.com/133376161>.

25. Ann Folino White, "Performing the Promise of Plenty in the USDA's 1933–34 World's Fair Exhibits," *Text and Performance Quarterly* 29, no. 1 (2009): 23–24.

26. Beardsworth and Bryman, "Late Modernity and the Dynamics of Quasification," 250.

27. Niki Macionis, "Understanding the Film-Induced Tourist," in *Proceedings of the International Tourism and Media Conference*, eds. Warwick Frost, W. Glen Croy, and Sue Beeton (Melbourne, Australia: Tourism Research Unit, Monash University, 2004), 89.

28. B. Joseph Pine and James H. Gilmore, "Welcome to the Experience Economy," *Harvard Business Review* (July–August 1998): 97–105.

29. Beardsworth and Bryman, "Late Modernity and the Dynamics of Quasification," 251.

30. Macionis, "Understanding the Film-Induced Tourist," 89.

31. Leshu Torchin, "Location, Location, Location: The Destination of the Manhattan TV Tour," *Tourist Studies* 2, no. 3 (2002): 252.

32. Lee, "Have Magic, Will Travel," 64.

33. Ning Wang, "Rethinking Authenticity in Tourism Experience," *Annals of Tourism Research* 26, no. 2 (1999): 349–370.

34. A. Fuat Firat and Ebru Ulusoy, "Living a Theme," *Consumption Markets & Culture* 14, no. 2 (2011): 200.

35. Scott A. Lukas, "From Themed Space to Lifespace," in *Staging the Past: Themed Environments in Transcultural Perspectives*, eds. Judith Schlehe, Michiko Uike-Bormann, Carolyn Oesterle, and Wolfgang Hochbruck (Bielefeld, Germany: Transcript, 2010), 137.

36. Derek H. Alderman, Stefanie K. Benjamin, and Paige P. Schneider, "Transforming Mount Airy into Mayberry: Film-Induced Tourism as Place-Making," *Southeastern Geographer* 52, no. 2 (2012): 217.

37. Chiara Bottici, *Imaginal Politics: Images Beyond Imagination and the Imaginary* (New York: Columbia University Press, 2014), 7.

38. Frost and Laing, *Imagining the American West*, 8–9.

39. Hayden White, "The Value of Narrativity in the Representation of Reality," *Critical Inquiry* 7, no. 1 (1980): 20.

19

Spatial Machines of Subjection
A Materialist Account of Macau's Themed Integrated Casino Resorts

By Tim Simpson

In 1999, after nearly 500 years of colonial administration, Portugal returned the tiny, "sleepy," and largely overlooked territory of Macau to the People's Republic of China (PRC). Like its more prominent neighbor Hong Kong, Macau was subsequently designated a Special Administrative Region (SAR) of the PRC under the "one country, two systems" regime. During the following decade, however, Macau experienced an unlikely transformation into a prominent tourism hub, and became the world's most lucrative site of casino gaming revenue. This brief period also saw a remarkable transformation of the Macau cityscape, with fantastical iconic glass buildings and themed integrated casino resorts emerging alongside the colonial-era Portuguese architecture that had formerly characterized the city's built environment. For example, Macau's new themed Venetian and Sands-Cotai casino resorts, constructed by Las Vegas entrepreneur Sheldon Adelson, are two of the world's largest buildings; the scale of these developments is remarkable given that, with a population of 636,000 in a land mass of only 30 square kilometers, Macau is not only one of the world's smallest sovereign territories, but also the most-densely populated autonomous locale on the planet.

This chapter analyzes the functional role of Macau SAR, and the city's new integrated casino resorts, in the post-socialist economic transition of the PRC. Chinese premier Deng Xiaoping initiated economic reforms in the late 1970s, establishing Special Economic Zones (SEZ) on China's southern coast where foreign entrepreneurs could operate capitalist ventures and Chinese officials could study capitalist enterprise. Today Macau SAR plays an operative role in the Chinese central government's current shift in macro-economic policy, from an initial reliance on an export-driven production regime that used the SEZs to exploit China's vast pool of cheap labor in order to initiate market reforms, to a current emphasis on domestic urban consumption that might contribute to more sustainable growth. The replacement of a production economy with a consumption economy in the PRC depends on the urbanization of China's vast population of rural peasants, 150 million of whom will be relocated to cities over the next decade. Chinese leaders hope that the residential and lifestyle purchasing habits of those newly urbane citizens will enhance economic growth, and that this urban work force will contribute to a knowledge and service economy that will gradually replace China's industrial base.

Prioritizing Chinese cities (and the urbanization process itself) as a strategy of development is a stark reversal of the anti-urban, rural bias characteristic of Maoism. Chinese cities under the socialist regime lacked the dynamic quality of "urbanism" which defined the modern occidental metropolis, and was so important to the development of capitalism in the West.[1] Today, however, China hopes to urbanize the countryside. I contend that as spectacular tourist destinations, Macau's new themed resorts play an unlikely pedagogical role in promoting a Chinese urban lifestyle, what Louis Wirth famously called "urbanism as a way of life."[2] This urbanism constitutes an accumulation strategy that is driving China's economic transition and contributes to the production of a post-socialist, neoliberal Chinese consumer subject.[3]

Neoliberalism and Enterprising Chinese Subjects

The various governmental strategies involved in China's shift to urban consumption may be generally understood within the rubric of Aihwa Ong's conception of "neoliberalism as exception."[4] Ong theorizes neoliberalism in Asia, not as a totalizing ideological or economic system, but as a mobile and migratory set of governmental interventions. These practices are selectively applied by "post-developmental" Asian states to specific territories and populations, based on a market logic, in order to enhance accumulation. Such states carve up national territories into SEZs, SARs, and other locales of juridical exceptionalism, with favorable tax regimes or relaxed labor regulations aimed to attract international investment, and use "graduated" strategies to disarticulate components of sovereignty and citizenship in order that they may be bundled and rearticulated to the trajectories of global capitalism.

Observing that "neoliberalism's metaphor is knowledge," Ong envisions neoliberalism as a governmental technique to manage populations with the aim of "production of educated subjects" who possess entrepreneurial and enterprising characteristics that will enable them to compete in a global marketplace.[5] We will see that tourism consumption is instrumental to China's economic reforms, and the central government uses tourism practices to fashion such enterprising Chinese subjects. Macau's resorts are unlikely but instrumental factors in this process.

Macau as a Post-Socialist Space

As a distinct anterior city-state, with a Portuguese colonial history and the only legal casino gaming industry in the PRC, Macau is an important destination for Chinese tourists. Investment by transnational gaming companies that entered Macau after the post-colonial liberalization of the local gaming industry, has produced a peculiar Macau cityscape anchored by themed integrated casino resorts which are clustered predominantly in two recent land reclamation sites, NAPE and COTAI. These resorts are Macau's primary attraction for tourists, 31 million of whom visited the city in 2014. Those tourists generate huge profits; in 2013 alone Macau's gambling revenues totaled $45 billion, an amount more than seven times greater than the revenues produced by the casinos on the Las Vegas Strip that same year.

Given the obvious superficial similarities among these two gaming cities, it is not surprising that journalists and scholars alike tend to view Macau primarily as an Asian incarnation of Las Vegas, the most recent example of the general globalization of urban spectacle and casino capitalism.[6] Indeed, Las Vegas-based operators like Adelson, Steve Wynn, and MGM have developed casino resorts in Macau. Scholars typically conceive of Las Vegas as the epitome of postmodern architecture and urban design, with simulated, de-differentiated, and hyperreal environments which provide a leisure respite for tourists, an "elsewhere for escape" from the travails of work.[7] However, rather than addressing Macau's integrated resorts in terms of their post-modern signification or compensatory leisure function, I consider the city and its gaming environments as a distinct post-socialist spatial formation which is a crucial component of the urbanization of the PRC. From this vantage point, Chinese tourism to Macau is no simple escape from work life. Macau is a highly differentiated site where Chinese tourists visit themed and integrated resorts to engage in the labor of leisure.

Biopolitical Population Governance in the PRC

My study of Macau's integrated resorts and their function for Chinese tourists should also be understood within the broader context of recent scholarship, influenced by the work of Michel Foucault, which investigates the politics of population governmentality in the PRC. For Foucault, liberal governmental rule is not coercive, but involves "a power that enacts a positive influence on life, that endeavors to administer, optimize, and multiply it, subjecting it to precise controls and comprehensive regulations."[8] Foucault refers to this modern state-enabled vitality as "biopower."

Scholars interested in population governance in the PRC have explored the manner in which Chinese authorities seek to enhance biopower in order to achieve specific administrative or economic outcomes. This governance is focused on optimizing such disparate areas as sexuality, reproduction, education, and labor.[9] Following from this research, my study investigates the production of the post-socialist consumer, a nascent Chinese subject that is the product of specific biopolitical calculations that aim to achieve China's macro-economic goals.

In a manner that parallels the role of the built environment under socialism, Macau's integrated resorts play an operative role in the subjection of a post-socialist Chinese consumer. The socialist Chinese worker (*gongren*) under Maoism was forged in work units (*danwei*); these work units were autonomous, self-contained residential and work communities, financed and operated by Chinese State-Owned Enterprises (SOE), which produced a collectivist proletarian subject and ensured reproduction of labor power. The socialist *danwei* provided all of the necessary components of everyday life and social welfare: accommodation, food, health care, childcare, education facilities, and entertainment. The *danwei* provided workers with a cradle-to-grave social contract that was crucial to the socialist regime. For David Bray, the *danwei* functioned as "spatial machines" for the "production of subjectivity" appropriate to utopian political aims.[10] Similarly, I contend that the post-socialist Chinese consumer subject is forged, at least in part, in Macau's new integrated resorts, which may be understood as "spatial machines" which ensure reproduction of leisure power necessary for China's economic reforms.

As self-contained pseudo-urban enclosures, Macau's resorts offer all the "social benefits" once provided by the *danwei*. However, the socialist Chinese state has retreated in the organization of collective consumption and the provision of the Maoist "iron rice bowl" of social services, and responsibility for these benefits is left to the tourists to pursue in a commodity logic. Those tourists participate in the "work" of leisure necessary for the development of the consumer economy of the PRC.[11] Traveling to Macau and gambling in an integrated resort constitutes a corporeal form of neoliberal governmentality, a pedagogical process whereby carefully calibrated freedoms of mobility and consumption are strategically extended as a mode of vital population governance that aims to create a "quality" (*suzhi*) Chinese consumer.[12]

My interest here is how specific forms of Chinese population mobility are articulated with Macau's built environment in population governance strategies; Macau's integrated casino resorts, which are specifically designed to promote consumption, help to produce an increasingly enterprising neoliberal Chinese subject.

Tourism as Biopolitical Governance

Under China's communist regime, population mobility was discouraged or even prohibited. Workers in cities were attached by both work and residence to their respective *danwei*, and all Chinese citizens were tied to their home city or province through household registration (*hukou*), which required them to remain in that locale in order to qualify for social services. Consumption in general, and tourism in particular, were denigrated as wasteful and bourgeois activities. However, this attitude began to change in the reform era.

The 1997 Asian Financial Crisis demonstrated the weakness of the PRC's production for export regime, by exposing the economy's reliance on neighboring Asian states to purchase Chinese goods. Therefore, the Chinese central government sought to enhance domestic consumption as a strategy of economic development and made tourism a key growth area of the economy. Alongside its economic benefits, the government sees tourism as "an inexpensive substitute for education," says Pál Nyíri, a pedagogical or civilizing practice that helps create "quality" citizens.[13] "Tourism is an arena in which the production of cultural discourse penetrates everyday consumption, one in which Chinese subjects self-consciously consume complex representations of culture and respond to them in quotidian activities," contends Nyíri.[14] "As such, it is a key sphere in which the reinvention of the Chinese subject takes place."[15]

One specific PRC governmental strategy is the Individual Visit Scheme (IVS), which allows residents of select Chinese cities and provinces to travel to Hong Kong and Macau on individual visas, without joining a government-sanctioned group tour. The IVS can be understood as a neoliberal technology of governance, an example of what Ong calls "graduated sovereignty," involving "differential state treatment of segments of the population in relation to market calculations."[16] In this case, the central government uses selectively applied exit visas to allow residents from relatively more affluent locales advantaged access to Macau.

Transnational Transformation of Macau's Casino Properties

Macau's spatial, cultural, and juridical distinction from both Hong Kong and mainland China makes it an important destination for those new Chinese tourists. Gambling has been legal in Macau since 1847, and the industry traditionally operated as a monopoly concession granted by the Portuguese government to a private entrepreneur in exchange for a share of the revenue. By the late-1990s, this monopoly arrangement—combined with Portugal's weak, laissez-faire administration of the territory—made Macau the site of increasingly violent fighting between rival Chinese organized crime groups who sought to claim their shares of vice-related proceeds.

Following Portugal's return of the territory to the PRC in 1999, the Chinese government hoped to restore order in the city, and the local Macau administration liberalized the gaming monopoly and invited the participation of foreign operators in the industry; officials hoped that this competition would help maintain law and order and strengthen the legitimacy of Macau's postcolonial administration.[17] Ultimately six operators were granted casino concessions in the city, including companies that also held gaming licenses in Las Vegas, Atlantic City, and Australia. Since casino operators in those jurisdictions must abide by their applicable regulatory statutes, even when operating properties abroad, the Macau government leveraged these foreign regulatory regimes to indirectly police Macau's gaming operators.

This public-private governmental arrangement is an example of what Ong refers to as a "state-transnational network whereby some aspects of state power and authority are taken up by foreign corporations located in special economic zones" or outside the territory.[18] For their part, the new foreign concessionaires brought a professional service and management regime and constructed spacious, ornamented mega-resorts that imitate the "Las Vegas style." The resorts and accompanying service regime contrasted dramatically with the small, austere, and unadorned casinos typical of the monopoly era.

Understanding Integrated Resorts as Post-Socialist Space

The iconic structure of Macau's casino industry liberalization is Sheldon Adelson's Venetian Macau integrated resort. The Venetian Macau, built at a cost of $2.4 billion, and opened in 2007, was modeled after its namesake in Las Vegas. However, the Venetian Macau is significantly larger than its Las Vegas counterpart and, in terms of total floor space, is in fact the sixth-largest structure in the world. The resort's motifs simulate the Italian city of Venice, with meticulous reconstructions of St. Mark's Square, Campanile Tower, and the façade of Doge's Palace, creating a massive interiorized pseudo-urban space.[19] The resort includes the world's largest casino; 3000 hotel rooms; 350 retail shops; three indoor canals; a 15,000-seat auditorium; 1.2 million square feet of conference facilities; a large clinic; and an off-campus facility of the University of Macau. With residences, shopping, dining, entertainment, waterways, and medical and educational facilities, the Venetian constitutes a city unto itself.

The Venetian is more than simply a massive consumer space; like the socialist *danwei*, it is an urban enclosure that offers all the basic characteristics of urban life, but under a market regime. While it is tempting at first glance to view such resorts as indicative of postmodern architecture—characterized by implosion, simulation, and hyperreality—I suggest that in the context of Macau it is more productive to understand them as distinct post-socialist spaces.

Macau as a Highly Differentiated Site

The integrated resort is a technology of tourist leisure accumulation, which provides all of the diverse components of leisure experience in one self-contained structure. This feature of the integrated resort is often described as exemplary of postmodern implosion. "The term implosion refers to the erosion of boundaries between two, or more, formerly relatively distinct spheres," write Ritzer and Stillman.[20] They contend that "a symptom of postmodernity is 'dedifferentiation' in which the borders between consumption and other aspects of the social world are imploded."[21]

It is certainly true that the Venetian, like other integrated resorts in Macau, comprises a dedifferentiated consumer space. However, this focus on dedifferentiation within a single property overlooks the way Macau's resorts serve collectively as a highly differentiated post-socialist spatial formation. As an SAR with legal gambling, Macau's juridical exceptionalism makes the city distinct from the rest of the PRC. Each integrated resort, in turn, is a discrete, enclosed, and interiorized space, funded by transnational capital, and marked off from the surrounding city by walls that create a differentiated spatial logic.

Integrated Resorts as a Material Spatial Fix for Capital

The Venetian Resort might also seem to be the epitome of postmodern hyperreality. As a copy of the eponymous Venetian property in Las Vegas, itself a romanticized copy of the city of Venice—a site which, in turn, endlessly recycles sentimentalized images of its own past—the Venetian seems a perfect example of a simulation that confounds the meaning of "original." A long line of postmodern cultural critics analyze such themed reconstructions in terms of a simulated and self-referential hyperreal that confounds modernist distinctions between surface and depth, original and copy, real and imaginary.[22] However, while this critical approach certainly identifies representational characteristics of the themed architectural form, it tells us little about the pragmatic functions of the built environment. In the case of Macau it is useful to attend to the function that the integrated resort plays for Chinese tourists. Similar to the socialist *danwei*, the integrated resort in Macau may be understood as a spatial machine, an "apparatus" or *dispositif* of subjection that produces a post-socialist Chinese consumer subject.[23] The integrated resort is a "diagram" of a power relation that does not represent or simulate reality, but rather "produces a new kind of reality, a new model of truth," for those tourists who move through it.[24]

Therefore, to understand the function of Macau's resorts for Chinese tourists, we must look beyond the simulated and hyperreal characteristics of the resorts—their ornamental façades and free-floating historical or geographical motifs—and to the materiality of the environments and the articulation of their design with the spaces of the socialist Chinese city. To focus on the material use-value of Macau's tourist environments is to suggest that there is actually something quite meaningful about Chinese tourism to these sites (see image 19.1). This challenges the hegemony of a visualist paradigm that examines material culture in terms of semiotic veracity, and that trivializes the specific functions of empirical environments.

Image 19.1. Mainland Chinese tour group inside the Venetian Macau resort (Photo by Tim Simpson)

From a materialist perspective, the integrated resort may be understood as a manifestation of what David Harvey calls a "spatial fix" for capital. According to Harvey, capitalism periodically encounters crises of overaccumulations of labor and capital which may sit side by side, but without a way of bringing them together in an economically productive manner.[25] Capitalists usually resolve this crisis "by geographical expansion and geographical restructuring" by which capital is "fixed" in new productive activities.[26] This process is revealing of China's market reforms which deploy the SEZs and SARs to articulate the excess labor indicative of state socialism with over-accumulated transnational capital.

Harvey emphasizes capital's "geographically expansionary" characteristic, pointing out that as transnational capital is deterritorialized and fixed spatially in a new location, like Macau, it is also deferred temporally as "surplus capital gets displaced into long-term projects that take many years to return their value to circulation through the productive activity they support."27 But in the meantime, this "spatio-temporal fix" might also include investments in tertiary circuits of capital like the training or reproduction of the labor force. Over time, regional economies like China's Pearl River Delta emerge "that achieve a certain degree of structured coherence to production, exchange, and consumption, at least for a time."28 This "structured coherence" is not simply evident in economic exchange, but "typically encompasses attitudes, cultural values, beliefs, and even religious and political affiliations among both capitalists and those whom they employ."29 The constellation of beliefs, values, and behaviors which must be naturalized among Chinese tourists in Macau include the kinaesthetic relationships among consumerism, neoliberal economics, and an appreciation of "urbanism as a way of life," which together help produce entrepreneurial subjects, calculating citizens prepared to forego socialism's iron rice bowl in order to embody and embrace the risks (and potential rewards) endemic to capitalist enterprise.

In Macau, transnational capital is fixed in the integrated resorts, as well as devoted to tertiary education of the indigenous work force in local university gaming management and tourism and hospitality programs, construction of transportation networks and relevant infrastructure, and the like. But aside from such investment in tourism infrastructure and education, Chinese tourism itself has an educational dimension, instructing tourists in a project of consumer pedagogy—the process of comporting Chinese consumer bodies and producing an urban imaginary appropriate to China's macroeconomic urbanization strategy. The IVS delivers tourists directly into the vast space of the integrated resorts; like *danwei*, each resort constitutes an enclosed and discrete spatial realm, and therefore functions as a metropolitan factory of biopolitical subjection.30

Macau as a Biopolitical Factory

From this perspective, what is important about the design of the resort is not its simulated hyperreality, but specifically the urban quality of the environment, regardless of what particular city might be thematically referenced. According to Wirth, "urbanism" is characterized by a particular set of qualities, including heterogeneity, density, anonymity, segmented roles, heightened mobility, and a distinct mode of interpersonal contact which is superficial, impersonal, and transitory.31 These are the qualities which tourists experience in the integrated resort, and these characteristics enhance the urban quality of these spaces (see images 19.2 and 19.3). It should be noted that each of these qualities is absent from the *danwei* lifestyle, where the work unit space is designed to discourage or prohibit mobility, to encourage communal sharing of facilities, and to promote deep and long-term engagement with a limited number of homogenous others.

Just as *danwei* design ensures reproduction of labor power by providing daily needs for workers, the integrated resort ensures reproduction of leisure power, but it does so by naturalizing a neoliberal commodity logic. The pedagogical "lesson" materialized in the resort design and attendant activities is that the post-socialist "state-transnational network" ensures availability of housing, education, child care, health care, food, and entertainment—much like was provided in the *danwei*—but it is the responsibility of the individual tourist to compete for and purchase these provisions for a market-determined price (see images 19.4 and 19.5). That is, the capitalist market has subsumed the socialist rice bowl (see image 19.6).

Producing Chinese Consumers

The paradox of the integrated resort regime is that while workers in the *danwei* generally produced some specific industrial product or service, nothing tangible is actually produced in the resort, except perhaps immaterial tourist affect. The object of "work" in the post-Fordist "factory" of consumption becomes the Chinese subject itself—the production of refined, quality, urbane consumers. To that end, the retail and service offerings in the resorts are focused on the body: cosmetics, jewelry, and fashion; spas, health clubs, foot massage, haircare, and cosmetic surgery; and various other means of toning, refining, and perfecting individual bodies and appearances. The resort activities literally comport consumer bodies and fashion quality subjects. In addition, the abstract logic of capitalism—revolving around investment, calculated risk, return, and affective stimulation—is embodied in the gaming attractions of the resort's casinos. From this perspective, the enclosed

Image 19.2. Cafe lifestyle as an experiential quality of an interiorized "urbanism" in the Venetian Resort. (Photo by Tim Simpson)

urban environment of the integrated resort may be understood to function as a biopolitical laboratory of subjection. It is therefore one component of the biopolitical population governance of the PRC.

This analysis of Macau's resorts demonstrates how latent aspects of the socialist built environment, as well as post-socialist "zoning technologies" and biopolitical governmental decisions, inform the integrated resort in Macau.[32] If the *danwei* was a machine for the production of *gongren*, then the integrated resort may be understood as a spatial machine of subjection that functions in a contemporary Chinese market economy. Macau's integrated resorts produce "quality" post-socialist consumers who learn to practice urbanism as a way of life, and who are therefore poised to contribute to the realization of the PRC's urbanization-oriented economic reforms. In addition, this localized and materialist understanding of Macau's integrated resorts and their pragmatic function is in overt contrast to the typical scholarly tendency to understand themed environments from a universalist and visualist paradigm that treats such environments as exemplary of both postmodern architecture and semiotic artifice.

Image 19.3. Chinese tourists experience characteristic qualities of "urbanism" at an indoor park in the Sands-Cotai Resort. (Photo by Tim Simpson)

Notes

1. Fulong Wu, "Neo-urbanism in the Making Under China's Market Transition," *City* 13, no. 4 (2009): 418–431.
2. Louis Wirth, "Urbanism as a Way of Life," *The American Journal of Sociology* 44, no. 1 (1938): 1–24.
3. Wu, "Neo-urbanism in the Making Under China's Market Transition."
4. Aihwa Ong, *Neoliberalism as Exception: Mutations in Citizenship and Sovereignty* (Durham, NC: Duke University Press, 2006)
5. Aihwa Ong, "Neoliberalism as a Mobile Technology," *Transactions of the Institute of British Geographers* 32 (2007): 3–8.
6. Carlos J. L. Balsas, "Gaming Anyone? A Comparative Study of Recent Urban Development Trends in Las Vegas and Macau," *Cities* 31 (2012): 298-307; Kim-Ieng Loi and Woo Gon Kim, "Macao's Casino Industry: Reinventing Las Vegas in Asia," *Cornell Hospitality Quarterly* 55, no. 2 (2010): 268–283. Timothy W. Luke 2010, "Gaming Space: Casinopolitan Globalism from Las Vegas to Macau," *Globalizations* 7, no. 3 (2010): 395–405.
7. Shelton Waldrep, "Postmodern Casinos," in *Productive Postmodernism: Consuming Histories and Cultural Studies*, ed. John Duvall (Albany: State University of New York Press, 2002). Rob Shields, "The Tourist Affect: Escape and Syncresis on the Las Vegas Strip," in *Ecologies of Affect: Placing Nostalgia, Desire, and Hope*, eds. Tonya K. Davidson, Ondine Park, Rob Shields (Waterloo, Canada: Wilfrid Laurier University Press, 2011).
8. Michel Foucault, *The History of Sexuality, Volume 1: An Introduction* (New York: Vintage, 1990), 137.
9. Lisa Rofel, *Desiring China: Experiments in Neoliberalism, Sexuality, and Public Culture* (Durham, NC: Duke University Press, 2007), Susan Greenhalgh and Edwin A. Winckler, *Governing China's Population: From Leninist to Neoliberal Biopolitics* (Stanford: Stanford University Press, 2005), Andrew B. Kipnis, *Governing Educational Desire: Culture, Politics, and Schooling in China* (Chicago: University of Chicago Press, 2011), and Lisa M. Hoffman, *Patriotic Professionalism in Urban China: Fostering Talent* (Philadelphia: Temple University Press, 2010).
10. David Bray, *Social Space and Governance in Urban China: The Danwei System from Origins to Reform* (Stanford: Stanford University Press, 2005).
11. Brian Lonsway, *Making Leisure Work: Architecture and the Experience Economy* (London: Routledge, 2009).
12. Tamara Jacka, "Cultivating Citizens: Suzhi (Quality) Discourse in the PRC," *Positions* 17, no. 3 (2009): 523–535.
13. Pál Nyíri, *Scenic Spots: Chinese Tourism, the State, and Cultural Authority* (Seattle: University of Washington Press, 2009), 154.
14. Nyíri, *Scenic Spots*.

Image 19.4. Childcare facilities for purchase in the Venetian Resort. (Photo by Tim Simpson)

15. Nyíri, *Scenic Spots*, 97.

16. Aiwha Ong, "Graduated Sovereignty in South-east Asia," *Theory, Culture and Society* 17, no. 4 (2000): 55–75.

17. Shin-hing Lo, "Casino Politics, Organized Crime and the Post-Colonial State in Macau," *Journal of Contemporary China* 14, no. 43 (2005): 207–224.

18. Ong, "Graduated Sovereignty in South-east Asia," 57.

19. Tim Simpson, "Macau Metropolis and Mental Life: Interior Urbanism and the Chinese Imaginary," *International Journal of Urban and Regional Research* 38, no. 3 (2014): 823–842.

20. George Ritzer and Todd Stillman, "The Modern Las Vegas Casino-hotel: The Paradigmatic New Means of Consumption," *M@n@gement* 4, no. 3 (2001): 83–99.

21. Ritzer and Stillman, "The Modern Las Vegas Casino-hotel," 92.

22. Umberto Eco, *Travels in Hyperreality* (San Diego: Harcourt Brace Jovanovich, 1986). Jean Baudrillard, *Simulacra and Simulation* (Ann Arbor: University of Michigan Press, 1994).

23. An apparatus involves "a thoroughly heterogeneous ensemble consisting of discourses, institutions, architectural forms, regulatory decisions, laws, administrative measures, scientific statements, philosophical, moral and philanthropic propositions—in short, the said as much as the unsaid…the apparatus itself is the system of relations that can be established among these elements." Michel Foucault, "The Confession of the Flesh," in *Power/Knowledge: Selected Interviews and Other Writings, 1972–1977* (New York: Vintage, 1977), 195.

24. Gilles Deleuze, *Foucault* (Minneapolis: University of Minnesota Press, 1986), 35.

25. David Harvey, *The New Imperialism* (Oxford: Oxford University Press, 2005).

26. David Harvey, *Rebel Cities: From the Right to the City to the Urban Revolution* (London: Verso, 2012).

27. Harvey, *The New Imperialism*; David Harvey, "Globalization and the 'Spatial Fix,'" *Geographische Revue* 2 (2001): 25, 88.

28. Harvey, *The New Imperialism*, 102.

29. Harvey, *The New Imperialism*, 102.

30. Michael Hardt and Antonio Negri, *Commonwealth* (Cambridge: Harvard University Press, 2009).

31. Wirth, "Urbanism as a Way of Life."

32. Ong, *Neoliberalism as Exception*.

192 A Reader in Themed and Immersive Spaces

Image 19.5. Pain relief medications and infant milk formula for sale at a pharmacy in the Venetian Resort. In contrast to the danwei provision of health care as part of socialism's "iron rice bowl," health care products must be purchased at the resort. (Photo by Tim Simpson)

Image 19.6. "Shop your way to a hotel stay" promotion in the Venetian Resort. Tourists who spend sufficient money purchasing consumer items in the resort may be provided with complimentary accommodation; that is, housing is available only under a commodity logic. (Photo by Tim Simpson)

Atmosphere, Immersion, and Authenticity in Colonial Williamsburg

By Christina Kerz

Our images of past and future are present images, continuously re-created. The heart of our sense of time is the sense of "now." Kevin Lynch[1]

In the 1920s, John D. Rockefeller, Jr. and Reverend W. A. R. Goodwin laid the foundation for what is considered to be the world's largest living history museum: Colonial Williamsburg in Virginia. Today, visitors are given the opportunity to immerse themselves in the restored eighteenth-century capital of Great Britain's largest colony: They may begin their morning (set in 1775) by discussing the recent developments of the endeavors for attaining American independence from Great Britain with Thomas Jefferson or Edith Cumbo. They can continue by visiting the Governor's Palace, defending themselves in a trial at the courthouse, and visit the local blacksmith or the printer to learn about the crafts of the era. In the evening (set in 1781), after having seen the General encourage the troops of the Allied American Army to march on to Yorktown ("and Victory!," as the program title foreshadows) and when the fifes and drums have played their last tunes, the visitors can dine in one of the taverns on Duke of Gloucester Street (the main street of the Revolutionary City), or sing and dance along with enslaved people to African-American music.

Image 20.1. Scene from the program "The General Reviews the Troops" (Photo by Christina Kerz)

Ever since the restoration of the colonial capital in the 1920s and 1930s, powerful narratives of American history and identity have been shaped in and through Colonial Williamsburg. Amongst different temporal, tangible and intangible layers of interaction and performance, an atmosphere arises that influences the visitors and their surroundings and colors the situations in a special feeling. While time and technology have enhanced and varied the strategies of research, reconstruction, and interpretation, the mission to be "a center for history and citizenship" and to ensure "that the future may learn from the past" has remained the same.[2] The product of this effort to portray national cultural heritage and to "preserve and re-create the symbols and memorials of a creative and colorful period of American history" has often been questioned with regard to accuracy and authenticity.[3] Critics declare Colonial Williamsburg to have followed "the new world order of Walt Disney Enterprises" by showing history "the way it never was."[4] Others, however, argue that there is often little value from academics "shadow-boxing with Disney, Colonial Williamsburg, and other popularizers of the past."[5] After all, the idea presented in the opening quote—that all we can ever sense is the present—may also apply to the critics themselves.

This chapter begins right here: in the "primitive present" (*primitive Gegenwart*) that arises by *being here now*.[6] By taking the designated Revolutionary City, also known as the Historic Area of Williamsburg, as a case study, I aim to explore how experiencing the overarching atmosphere of this themed environment influences the notion of authenticity of the historic site: How does the atmosphere affect the visitors, and vice versa? What do guests perceive? And what role do those feelings and perceptions play in the construction of authenticity?[7]

Atmospheres and Situations

The academic interest in the concept of atmosphere has grown vastly across disciplines over the past ten years.[8] This chapter will focus on the mediating and constructive qualities of the atmosphere that can be experienced by visitors in Colonial Williamsburg. On a theoretical level, this implies interweaving a phenomenological perspective (How do we experience the world around us?) with a constructivist perspective (How is this environment that we experience shaped and how do we shape our environment after having experienced it?).

An ambiance is a "quality…that registers in and through sensing bodies while also remaining diffuse."[9] It is composed as a "totality" (*Totalität*) and can be described as a "half-thing" (*Halbding*); it is a holistic phenomenon that, similar to a wind gust, only exists in the present without going someplace else when we stop experiencing it.[10] The initial moment of the encounter with this phenomenon is established through affects that link the sensing subject with the environment. Consequently, atmospheres affect the movement and the rhythm of the entity and the authority of the lived body (*Leib*), which is "everything a sensing subject can feel in proximity (not necessarily within the borders, however) of one's corporal or material body."[11] Ecstasies (*Ekstasen*) lead to either a widening (*Weitung*) or a narrowing (*Engung*) of this "felt space in the region of one's body."[12]

This relational quality of an atmosphere gives rise to a "field of pre-personal intensity" which can lead to being registered in the individual's sensing body as the affect has evoked a feeling that eventually transforms into an emotion and hence into a "socio-cultural expression of that felt intensity."[13] We are thus not sensing the atmosphere itself, but perceiving a situation according to the atmosphere that our lived body is immersed in.[14] These emotions can be understood as the enduring outcome of an individual's involvement with an ambiance, which consequently leads to a new state of being that influences our behavior, our thinking, and our actions.

The three keywords addressed so far—the spatial aspect of *here*, the temporal aspect of *now*, the mediating aspect of the *affect*—are important to this experience of and the immersion into the potential of atmospheres. Echoing Eugène Minkowski's triad of *moi, ici, maintenant*—me, here, now—the philosopher Hermann Schmitz explains that all atmospheric immersion revolves around the *primitive present* and affects the lived body.[15] Situations are the key to understanding such encounters between affects and the lived body and thus between the individual and an ambiance. They are "the element in which we live" and they demand our attention, even if we are not aware of it. Situations are both "origin and partner" of all behavior and action. Every situation is a "chaotic and manifold whole" that is characterized by being cohesive and meaningful.[16] Of particular interest for this study are two categories of situations that Schmitz introduced with regard to their chronological sequence. The first is the situation of a current moment (*aktuelle Situation*)—for example meeting someone, walking down a road, or smelling the flowers. These situations are subject to momentary change, whereas the second type, the permanent situations of state (*zuständliche Situation*), are more enduring states such as, for example, friendships or languages.[17] Situations of a current moment are further characterized by some sort of specific interaction between the environment and the sensing subject. The lived movement enhanced by those interactions can generate permanent situations of a state when sensing subjects engage in the situational experience that involves them in the atmosphere.[18]

The Situation of a current moment can be seen as the smallest organizational unit of the lifeworld (*Lebenswelt*).[19] It is characterized not only by an individual's biographical background, but also by a given arrangement of the setting, time, and place.[20] The setting of a situation can be presented in a goal-oriented manner; external actors not present in the current moment can thus influence and shape the atmosphere that arises from the situational encounter. While the atmosphere itself cannot be fully constructed and controlled, the conditions which allow for an atmosphere to appear can be set.[21] Hence, while an atmosphere is experienced by an individual, the "stage set" leading to this atmospheric immersion is programmatically designed.[22] If this program is created by stakeholders in power in a certain circumstance, for example professionals in charge of a living history museum, an overall atmosphere exists at this place that all sensing subjects exploring this place can potentially experience. It is this kind of overarching atmosphere that will be focused on in the case study.[23] But first, let us address a concept that is questioned whenever theming or preservation efforts are at play.

Authenticity, Feeling, and Place

Authenticity is an empty term. Generally speaking, it is a "label for a valuable, deep level of reality" (35) that is omnipresent in everyday life and yet apparitional—especially because one would need to agree upon a universal definition for what's *really real* first.[24] The concept of authenticity has also been widely debated throughout academia.[25] The different notions can be grouped into two approaches: an object-related approach and an activity-related approach.[26] The object-related approach is rooted in realism and cognitivism.[27] It relies on an essentialist perspective that draws on objects and truths.

According to the activity-based approach, which I'm following in this paper, a museum or theme park visit cannot be degraded as a "pseudo-event" because the situational setting cannot be considered a "front stage" that has been designed in contrast to a "back stage."[28] The outcome of any kind of setting is not a "staged authenticity" as opposed to a natural authenticity.[29] Rather, authenticity is viewed more in an experiential manner as dynamic, path-dependent, and relational. Authenticity is "a potential existential state of Being" that can be "activated by tourist activities."[30] This phenomenological understanding of authenticity also includes traces of contingent constructivist thought which echoes concepts such as the "invention of tradition" or "imagined communities" and the suggestion to take fictional qualities of authenticity seriously because they have a real effect on our lives.[31] Consequently, "origins and new beginnings" both shape what we perceive as authentic.[32]

The notion of authenticity is thus not linked to any external object, truth or fact, but instead to the sensing subject in the *primitive present*. It only gains its power through an individual's affective and, consequently, emotional engagement in a specific situation. Thus, all relations a person establishes towards a place, an object, or any given fact—regardless of whether there are fictional elements or copies involved in the staging of specific stories—can potentially be perceived as authentic. Authenticity can hence be defined as a "relational quality attributed to something out of an encounter."[33] It is a "feeling you can experience in relation to place."[34]

If we consider authenticity a feeling that is rooted in place-based experiences by a sensing subject, there are two conclusions we can draw that establish a bridge to the concept of atmospheres: First, authenticity is produced in the present by *being here now* and by immersing and engaging oneself in the atmosphere that arises from situations of a current moment. By emerging as a powerful emotion, the feeling of authenticity can then become a permanent situation of state that is significant for future actions. Authenticity is thus neither based on nor relevant to some*thing* in the past. Instead, it is the perception of "pastness" which adds to the emergence of the feeling of authenticity.[35] Second, by influencing the situational setting of the atmosphere, the probability to evoke authenticity can be increased. In order to responsibly attend to this endeavor, it is important to balance three fields of interest when arranging the elements of the setting: the interests and desires of the audience, the interests and desires of the authors or actors in charge, and the factual background of the subject matter such as historic events. Let us now look at how these elements are expressed in the context of Colonial Williamsburg.

Framing Colonial Williamsburg and the Revolutionary City

Colonial Williamsburg is located within the so-called Historic Triangle on the Virginia Peninsula. The town of Williamsburg was the capital of the Colony of Virginia from 1699 to 1776 and, following the Declaration of Independence, remained the capital of the "new" Commonwealth of Virginia from 1776 to 1780. The town was a hub for political debate and decision-making. It was a strategic meeting place for leading voices of the American Revolution and hence became a place for historically significant events.[36]

In the 1920s, the small town of Williamsburg was transformed by the vision of Reverend W.A.R. Goodwin and the money of John D. Rockefeller, Jr.; Colonial Williamsburg was thereby (re)born and the Revolutionary City came to life. The national narrative has since been reconstructed in tangible and intangible dimensions through this effort of preserving the past: Over 500 structures (which include homes, kitchens, dairies, wells, and trade shops, as well as sites like the Capitol or the Royal Governor's Palace) were rebuilt in the Colonial style. Several hundred buildings were torn down or relocated to make space for the new old part of town. Some of the restored and reconstructed houses today serve as exhibit or performance venues while others are private residences. The urban space that resulted from this initiative stretches across 301 acres and is referred to as the Historic Area, Colonial Williamsburg, or the Revolutionary City.

Today, the visitors find themselves walking public city streets of twenty-first century Williamsburg while at the same time being bodily engaged in the themed museum environment, in situations where place-based history is staged by interpreting and reenacting eighteenth-century streetscapes and everyday routines. The atmosphere is framed by different material, immaterial, and transmaterial elements that are shaped by the Colonial Williamsburg Foundation (CWF), a private, not-for-profit educational institution that is in charge of the living history museum.[37] Visitors can encounter various current situations on the fringe of past and present. The strategies applied involve first- and third-person interpretation, house tours, the staging of scripted scenes, as well as unscripted interactions with tradesmen and actors portraying eighteenth-century citizens of Williamsburg.

Today, Colonial Williamsburg is more than a participatory, living history museum. It is also a historic district and a functioning part of town. Colonial Williamsburg is not walled off. It is therefore a themed area that continuously blends with the twenty-first century environment: the students of the adjacent College of William and Mary jogging past horse-drawn carriages on the museum's main street and trains interrupting Thomas Jefferson's public audience demonstrate this contrasting amalgamation. When guests are told that they are "leaving the twenty-first century" via the "Bridge to the Past," they are actually entering a very sanitized and secured past. They are visiting a cultural heritage site that celebrates the revolutionary era through stories that have been shaped by the Colonial Revival period of the early twentieth century and that gained further public interest through the phenomenon of the "founders chic."[38]

Colonial Williamsburg is also a Foucauldian heterotopia that narrates and hence (re)produces the ideas of the American nation 365 days a year by including stories of achievement and bravery while excluding those of failure and misery.[39] This approach is not openly addressed in front of the visitor, but it is a main directive expressed by the senior management: "We want everybody to go away happy."[40] Visitors should feel "safe and comfortable" throughout their stay. While the museum is "committed to telling the true story of the enslaved," they also try to make history "more palatable to people, more interesting, more fun." This attempt to do justice to historical accuracy and at the same time "meet [the guests] where they are" and give them the eighteenth-century experience that they want (and "they want it candy-coated," as an employee explained) is a difficult endeavor. What is the societal cost for candy-coating adversities like slavery, war, and poverty? This is a question those involved in heritage interpretation have to bear in mind when creating the narratives of public history. However, in order to gain economical *and* educational benefits from this entertainment and to have the visitor indeed leave

Image 20.2. The shoemaker of the Revolutionary City (Photo by Christina Kerz)

with "a little bit more of the truth"—the minimum the museum aims to achieve—it requires active participation from the guests.

As you can see from this brief insight, the City of Williamsburg and the Historic Area form a peculiar mixture of exclusion and inclusion, of past, present, and future, of museum and town. The boundaries of then and now, of old and new, exhibition and daily routine, are blurred. The themed environment of Colonial Williamsburg is a setting that invites visitors to engage in an atmosphere of performed pastness and secretly sanitized history. It is a place where visitors are continuously being convinced through the stories, interactions, and publications revolving around the Historic Area that they are experiencing historical accuracy. It is a playground for those who want to learn about history and those who want to be entertained by it.

In trying to accomplish its mission to educate Americans about citizenship, the Foundation is dependent upon donations and operational revenue for its survival. The CWF therefore feels obliged to attend to the visitors' and donors' needs and to succumb to the laws of the experience industry of a capitalist consumer society. And so visitors will not only encounter Peyton Randolph or Patrick Henry in the streets, but also the Coca-Cola Company, Mars' American Heritage Chocolate, and various benches, trees, and well-manicured flower gardens—all of which wouldn't have been part of the eighteenth-century landscape.

However, it is important to note that strategic decisions and didactical reductions are key elements that are essential for allowing such large-scale educational projects to make historical research publicly accessible and to capture people's attention in the first place.

Image 20.3. Recruitment of "townspeople," visitors for the local militia (Photo by Christina Kerz)

The Five Stages of Atmospheric Immersion

The process of atmospheric immersion takes place on five levels. It is possible to skip a level, to pause or to exit the immersive process; there is no fixed time frame in which the stages have to be completed and the stages aren't. closed entities, but rather fluid sectors that intertwine.[41] It is not possible to tie specific situations visitors might encounter to one stage; instead, one situation can unfold the atmospheric potential of one stage while at the same time allowing another person to reach the same or another stage. The more people let go of any preconceived notions or other distractions from the *primitive present* and the longer they expose themselves to the themed environment, the deeper they experience the immersion into the potential feelings and insights each stage can bring. While the visitor is involved in the situations that the atmosphere is taking shape in, the impact of the atmosphere's character changes from purely pre-reflexive to mediating and finally to constructive: the lived body is involved in all of the stages, but the feeling of authenticity that is constructed in the process is also impacted by the individual's capacities for reflection and imagination which are triggered predominantly in the last two stages of the process.

Gripping

In the first stage of atmospheric involvement, the atmosphere affects the visitors by gripping them. One interviewee describes the encounter that sparks an initial interest for a specific micro-setting as "resistance is futile."[42] The guests are captured by sensing an ecstasy that links them to the environment. There are several fields that provide such a space for atmospheric involvement. One is the realm of personal preferences of visitors that they find echoed in the Historic Area: one visitor might visit the bindery because he is a librarian, another one might be impressed by the reconstructed buildings because they remind him of the years he spent in England. One interviewee was attracted by the "infectious smile" of an actor-interpreter while another one was attracted because of the singing. The personal connection that was established in that moment was the spark that pulled them into the atmosphere: "I came over there because he seemed friendly." Another

Image 20.4. Custis Tenement Garden opposite to Bruton Parish Church (Photo by Christina Kerz)

field that engages people in the atmosphere is the place in the context of its location: Sitting in the pew at Bruton Parish Church that is designated to be the one where George Washington sat or looking at the Capitol where "the Founding Fathers of our nation tried to impact change and make the world better" gives visitors a "tingly feeling." The sense of place that is experienced in this stage is also connected to imaginations of the past that the visitors bring to the Historic Area. Believing to know that the things they encounter in the Historic Area are fact-based reproductions of eighteenth-century life might draw them into the experience: "The small animal pastures with one or two animals in them fit the period, with families having a small menagerie." Besides such images that resonate with the visitor's imagined eighteenth century, it is also *the other* that demands their attention—and that can be anything from cobblestone, lambs, the "impressive architecture" of the Governor's Palace, the "live fire" from the cannons, or the observation that the tradesmen are "actually making things" that are then sold or used in the museum. Last, but not least, the olfactory sense is another field that connects visitors to the atmosphere: "As soon as I can smell the place I have that feeling. It's just the whole place: it smells old, I guess."

Immersing

Even though the whole process of atmospheric involvement can be considered an immersive experience, the second stage of this process is best described as becoming holistically immersed in the atmosphere. After first contact situations, many visitors have started to overcome their insecurity of being in the new environment filled with people, objects, and structures of the past. Many dare to get involved in situations where they are passively interacting with townspeople of Colonial Williamsburg. This stage is characterized by the vital drive gaining momentum and becoming more dynamic—the visitors are opening up towards the situational and the momentary; they feel safe to "take a deep breath and go back in time." Often, this widening is connected to a "lackadaisical feeling" and to impressions of tranquility and freedom that can be caused, for example, by ecstasies rooted in the sounds of the Fifes and Drums, the width of Duke of Gloucester Street, or the lack of any "loud advertisement" or "glaring colors." Many people also appreciate the opportunity of being able to finally attend to "so much history, as much history as the U.S. has history" and to experience their imagined *colonial* Williamsburg at their own pace. Visitors will find several familiar structures along the way that facilitate this immersion; benches in an eighteenth-century courthouse and an eighteenth-century style iced beer are examples of such conveniences. Visitors rarely consider such elements of the setting "modern intrusions," as critics often refer to, but rather as orientation devices. In that function, they actually support the process of atmospheric involvement because they meet the guests' basic needs. This makes it easier for them to engage in the dynamic they become engrossed with at this stage: "[The interpreters] were talking day-to-day stuff, not the war, not General Washington or Governor Henry. Just day-to-day stuff! It was not on any schedule." Those interactions with the townspeople of Colonial Williamsburg are not perceived as staged scenes, but as daily routine encounters where visitors can step in and join in timeless debates about family, love, and town politics. Many visitors describe this emerging feeling of immersion as "pretty natural" and "very normal, almost weirdly so."

Unfolding

In the unfolding stage, visitors become an active participant in shaping the narrative of Colonial Williamsburg. They experience the Historic Area as "the center of [their] universe" and are fully (caught) in the moment. The feelings that have been triggered through the experiences of the two preceding stages become stronger: "It's almost like a spiritual high." This provides them with the self-confidence to explore more details and to gain insights into perspectives and curiosities that they wouldn't have approached at an earlier stage: "Yesterday I asked David, he was Mr. Prentis, and I asked him if he had salt to sell. Because back in that time they claimed that he was hoarding salt. And he was a loyalist, he was very much against the war." Visitors engage in the performances of eighteenth-century Williamsburg more actively and lose track of time: the boundaries of time and temporality become blurred. Sometimes they are also overwritten; the object behind an ecstasy is assigned an eighteenth-century cover. For example, when a train runs by or a maintenance truck approaches, the immersed individual will filter this noise as something more fitting to the eighteenth century. This way, twenty-first century sounds turn into, for example, colonial carriages. This deep immersion also makes visitors experience a sense of community when walking the Duke of Gloucester Street which, especially in this stage, bears resemblance to the mythical image of Disney's timeless Main Street, U.S.A.: "When you walk the Duke of Gloucester Street, it is every street in America, it is your street."

There are different types of communities visitors can feel attached to in this moment: the eighteenth-century colonial Williamsburg, the twenty-first century community of Colonial Williamsburg, or the patriotically infused community of the American nation. The intense feelings revolving around questions of identity and belonging that are atmospherically mediated in this stage make the museum visit become ever more relevant to the visitor's personal lifeworld.

Connecting

In this stage, the atmosphere's character changes from mediating to constructive. Visitors begin to connect their past and present experiences in the Historic Area to existing archives of emotions and knowledge. They learn by bridging the experiences to their own lives and their own realities: "They had to work harder for what they got. And when they say they were fighting for their freedoms, they were really fighting for their freedom! They weren't going to a ballot box, they weren't creating a Facebook page." In the course of this process, new regimes of orientation are formed. The feelings become more permanent; they turn into emotions. Visitors also become more critical about the institution and the staging. However, since they have already achieved a deep immersion into the potential of the atmosphere of the place, they will not simply cut the ties, but rather reflect upon the constructive character of history. Many visitors in this stage understand the difficulty to portray public history. They are "OK with things being fuzzy" and make jokes about, for

Image 20.5. Interpreters and visitors walking the Duke of Gloucester Street (Photo by Christina Kerz)

example, money-making intrusions they encounter: "I expect the squirrels to have little tricorn hats on." In that stage, many visitors have spoken to actors *out of period*, which increased their trust in the Foundation's work. By interacting more with the interpreters, they also learned about issues one could not figure out without engaging in the atmosphere in the Historic Area. Such discoveries include finding out that fifty-two percent of the 1770s population in Williamsburg was made up of free or enslaved blacks, that it is the middle and the upper classes instead of the broad majority of lower class Virginians that are represented in Colonial Williamsburg, or that there were between 10 and 12 shoemakers in Williamsburg back than compared to the single shop one can visit today. Many visitors, in fact, come to appreciate the foundation's "cheating strategy" because they understand the motivation behind it: "To get people of today to come and be interested in Williamsburg and the eighteenth century, you've got to fudge it a little bit. You've got to add the apples and pineapples."[43]

Fulfilling

This stage marks the peak of atmospheric involvement. The new frameworks of emotions and knowledge become embedded into the visitor's everyday life. Colonial Williamsburg has become "like an addictive drug in a good sense." The atmospheric experience becomes an integral part of the visitor's reality. The feeling of authenticity is thus neither rooted in the subject matter of the historical events or the buildings, nor is it embedded in the place itself. Rather, it is an emotion rooted in the atmospheric involvement. It is a permanent situation of state that has become part of the visitor's identity and that has become detached from any place-based situations of a current moment: "It just feels like home. And it has nothing to do with coming here and "Oh, look at all the history." With me it goes beyond that: it's an actual love for the place, just because it is what it is. And getting outside the colonial area into town, I carry that feeling with me. You go a block over and you're out of THIS, but you still feel like you're part of it." The sense of trust and community has become even stronger. Very often, visitors also implement a fragment of their Williamsburg experience in their homes to be reminded (and, as ambassadors, remind others) of that special connection: "All the colors in my house are Williamsburg colors. If you go in the apothecary shop: I built the shelves that hold all the medicines and stuff, I did a replica of that in our dining room." The routines, actions, and images that result from this engagement are powerful foundations for future actions.

Many visitors experiencing this stage plan to learn more about the artifacts, the historical characters, and the complexities of American history. They also make plans to come back and maybe even move to Williamsburg to be closer to their "happy place" and to become involved as donors or volunteers.

Experiencing the Feeling of Authenticity in Colonial Williamsburg

In Colonial Williamsburg, visitors experience authenticity as an emotional state that emerges through the involvement in the atmosphere of the Historic Area. The immersion into this place-based atmosphere does not simply exist when first encountering the surroundings of a specific environment. Instead, it rather gradually develops by engaging with the situational settings. It is especially the widening of the lived body which visitors experience when participating in the various situational settings engineered by museum designers which further draws the visitors into the experience and hence into what the potential atmospheric immersion can hold. Authenticity is thus nothing that is itself staged, faked, or imagined. It is a feeling that is experienced as the outcome of a dialogue between a situational setting, the self, and the subject matter. It therefore varies in its connotation and it is not—and cannot be—the same for every sensing subject.

It is important to remember that the designers of the setting and the stories play an important and powerful role in that process. Especially when aiming for the responsible interpretation of history, museum professionals need to make sure that they balance all fields of interest involved and that they offer the guests orientation to navigate through each stage of atmospheric involvement. While this research has shown that simplifying and candy-coating historical contexts can in fact help guests to become more immersed in the experience, it is necessary to also offer opportunities where they can sever those safety nets and experience different, likely unsettling, stories of history as well. In order to succeed with a responsible interpretation of history, the connection between the authors, the audience, and the subject matter has to remain intimate and personal throughout. This also means that the designers must be honest about their own strategies for framing the atmosphere.[44] The authenticity resulting from the effort to educate the public could otherwise fall victim to the value of the sanitized image that visitors encounter in the first stages of the atmospheric involvement.

Authenticity is not only a result, but also a starting point from which new actions and insights, and thus new places and stories, are produced. By understanding authenticity as atmospherically produced, the power of authenticity to generate senses of identity and community is revealed. The sense of authenticity is evoked by an individual's experience. It is, however, also rooted in the atmosphere that every individual who is familiar with the cultural context in which the settings have been staged can potentially access. Authenticity thereby also becomes a matter of collective identity.

If we want to understand the meaning and the power of authenticity, we must look at the atmosphere that it emerges from. Similar to the concept of identity or sense of place, authenticity cannot simply be found in an artifact, date, or event. Rather, it is established in through negotiation between different agents of various shapes. As an emotional state, it is a permanent situation that is strong and sturdy because it has evolved from an experience over time. With these links to time, place, and self, authenticity is a dynamic construct that can change depending on the stories through which we shape our cultural landscapes. We relate to these stories and thus to our realities through atmospheres. Before denouncing such narratives as unreal, fake or dangerous, we should first immerse ourselves in the stories we encounter and then be attentive to both the power relations that they reveal and the new relations that they establish: "Stories help to open up the world, not to cloak it."[45] And that is worth exploring.

Notes

1. Kevin Lynch, *What Time Is This Place?* (Cambridge: MIT Press, 2001), 65. All photos in this article were taken by Christina Kerz and are used with permission of The Colonial Williamsburg Foundation.
2. The Colonial Williamsburg Foundation. "Our Mission," <http://www.history.org/foundation/mission.cfm>.
3. William Archer Rutherford Goodwin, "The Restoration of Colonial Williamsburg," *National Geographic Magazine* 71, no. 4 (1937): 402.
4. Ada Louise Huxtable, *The Unreal America. Architecture and Illusion* (New York: New Press, 1997), 12.
5. Cary Carson, "Mirror, Mirror, on the Wall, Whose History Is the Fairest of Them All?" *The Public Historian* 17, no. 4 (1995): 63.

6. Hermann Schmitz, Rudolf Owen Müllan, and Jan Slaby, "Emotions Outside the Box. The New Phenomenology of Feeling and Corporeality," *Phenomenology and the Cognitive Sciences* 10, no. 2 (2011): 246.

7. With the revision of the programming in 2006, when the number of actors and staged street interactions were increased, the Colonial Williamsburg Foundation began to narrow its focus to the theme of the Revolution, especially in the time span of 1775 to 1781. The expression *Historic Area* is slowly being substituted by the term *Revolutionary City*. By replacing the presumed dusty connotation of the *Historic Area* by a cooler and more appealing expression, the museum is trying to attract more families and to establish a more distinct image that moves away from the negative reverberation of the *colonial*. The research presented in this chapter is part of a larger Ph.D. project. The results are based on data collected during field research trips to Williamsburg in 2012, 2013, and 2014. The qualitative research methods applied include interviews, participant observation as a visitor, and as an interpreter in period costume in the streets and in two trade shops, and photo documentation. Parts of the empirical fieldwork has kindly been supported by funds from the Institute of Geography at the University of Mainz, The Colonial Williamsburg Foundation (John D. Rockefeller, Jr., Library fellowship), and the German Academic Exchange Service (DAAD-Doktorandenstipendium).

8. There is no consensus in the scientific community of whether the terms atmosphere and ambiance carry different notions. See, Jean-Paul Thibaud, "The Backstage of Urban Ambiances: When Atmospheres Pervade Everyday Experience," *Emotion, Space and Society* 15 (2015): 2. I am using the terms interchangeably here, even though some authors differentiate between the two concepts, placing the notion of atmosphere more in alignment with the approach of scholars of affect theories or non-representational theories and viewing the notion of ambiance as stressing more the subjective or situational perception of and through atmospheres. See, Peter Adey et al., "'Pour votre tranquillité': Ambiance, Atmosphere, and Surveillance," *Geoforum* 49 (2013): 302. An extensive list of academic studies on atmospheres has been compiled by the Italian philosopher Tonino Griffero at <https://atmosphericspaces.wordpress.com/literature>.

9. Derek P. McCormack, "Engineering Affective Atmospheres on the Moving Geographies of the 1897 Andree Expedition," *Cultural Geographies* 15, no. 4 (2008): 413.

10. Gernot Böhme, *Bewusstseinsformen* (Munich, Germany: Fink, 2014), 158. Even though Schmitz's notion of the *Halbding* has been translated by Schmitz, Müllan, and Slaby as "half entity," I am following Riedel's literal translation as *half-thing* because they are, as Schmitz points out throughout his work, "(full) entities just as things, differing from these only in their materiality and hence temporality." See, Friedlind Riedel, "Music as Atmosphere. Lines of Becoming in Congregational Worship," *Lebenswelt* 6 (2015): 89.

11. Translation by Christina Kerz. Hermann Schmitz, "Gefühle als Atmosphären," in *Atmosphären im Alltag. Über ihre Erzeugung und Wirkung*, eds. Stephan Debus and Roland Possner (Bonn, Germany: Psychiatrie-Verlag, 2007), 264.

12. Ecstasies are "states and forms of presence" that describe how things appear to a sensing subject (translation: C. Kerz; Gernot Böhme, "Die Ekstasen des Dinges," in *Rehabilitierung des Subjektiven. Festschrift für Hermann Schmitz*, ed. Michael Großheim (Bonn, Germany: Bouvier, 1993), 63). While the property of a thing (*Eigenschaft*) is more attached to the thing, the ecstasy of a thing is more attached to the subject. Widening and narrowing are the two key terms for Schmitz's concept of the vital drive (*vitaler Antrieb*). Those two modes of experiencing the lived body (*leibliches Befinden*) are not merely physiological impulses, but feelings that are experienced holistically. See, Hermann Schmitz, *Bewusstsein* (Bonn, Germany: Bouvier, 2010): 48. Schmitz, Müllan and Sleby, "Emotions Outside the Box," 245.

13. McCormack, "Engineering Affective Atmospheres," 414.

14. Jean-Paul Thibaud, "Die sinnliche Umwelt von Städten. Zum Verständnis urbaner Atmosphären," in *Die Kunst der Wahrnehmung. Beiträge zu einer Philosophie der sinnlichen Erkenntnis*, ed. Michael Hauskeller (Zug, Switzerland: Die Graue Edition, 2003), 293.

15. Schmitz, Müllan, and Sleby, "Emotions Outside the Box," 246.

16. "The element in which we live," Hermann Schmitz, "Heimisch sein," in *Die Stadt als Wohnraum*, ed. Jürgen Hasse (Munich, Germany: Verlag Karl Alber 2008), 36. "Origin and partner," translation by Christina Kerz. Hermann Schmitz, *Was ist Neue Phänomenologie* (Rostock, Germany: Ingo Koch Verlag, 2003), 91. "Chaotic and manifold whole," translation by Christina Kerz. Hermann Schmitz, *Die Person* (Bonn, Germany: Bouvier, 1980), 17. Schmitz's philosophy, the *New Phenomenology*, is a complex system of philosophical thought that offers little to no links for a methodological analysis and empirical research. His holistic view on situations and atmospheres is based on the principle of "diffuse meaningfulness," implying that the cohesion and integrity of the concepts suspend any efforts to single out certain parts or elements of the whole of the atmosphere, the situation, or the experience. Schmitz's terms and theorems are therefore in this study seen more as navigational notions that enable us to move beyond the Cartesian predominance in empirical social and cultural research. All separations between source and effect, action and consequence, acting subject and perceiving subject are thus only possible on an analytical level and cannot be distinguished in the "lifeworld" (*Lebenswelt*). See, Alfred Schütz and Thomas Luckmann, *Strukturen der Lebenswelt* (Konstanz, Germany: UTB, 2003).

17. Translation by Christina Kerz. Schmitz, *Was ist Neue Phänomenologie*, 92.

18. Hermann Schmitz, *Atmosphären* (Freiburg, Germany: Karl Alber Verlag, 2014), 63.

19. Schütz and Luckmann, *Strukturen der Lebenswelt*.

20. A person's biographical background determines the way an individual experiences a situation: the cultural and political environment a person grew up in, the momentary mood, the intellectual abilities, any existing imaginations or knowledge, as well as a person's ability to dream and fantasize affect the depth of immersion into the atmospheric potential.

21. Gernot Böhme, "The Art of the Stage Set as a Paradigm for an Aesthetics of Atmospheres," *Ambiances* (2013), <http://ambiances.revues.org/315>.

22. Böhme, "The Art of the Stage Set as a Paradigm for an Aesthetics of Atmospheres."

23. Every sensing subject is affected by an atmosphere, but it takes a certain intrinsic motivation, dependent on one's biographical background and current mood, to engage in the atmosphere and to get involved in the immersive experience an atmosphere has to offer. Of the

four types of visitors I found coming to Colonial Williamsburg (transitory tourists, curious return visitors, well-informed return visitors, and homeschoolers), visitors of the second and the third group engage with the atmosphere in the Historic Area more actively than members of the other groups. All interviews have therefore been conducted with members of those groups.

24. Søren Buhl Hornskov, "On the Management of Authenticity: Culture in the Place Branding of Øresund," in *Re-Investing Authenticity. Tourism, Place and Emotions*, eds. Britta Timm Knudsen and Anne Marit Waade (Bristol, England: Channel View Publications, 2010), 81.

25. For a detailed overview of current approaches, see, Ning Wang, "Rethinking Authenticity in Tourism Experiences," *Annals of Tourism Research* 26, no. 2 (1999): 349–370; Yvette Reisinger and Carol J. Steiner, "Reconceptualizing Object Authenticity," *Annals of Tourism Research* 33, no. 1 (2006): 65–86.

26. Reisinger and Steiner, "Reconceptualizing Object Authenticity."

27. Ada Louise Huxtable was heavily drawing on this object-related approach when she wrote about the "unreal America" and the "stunningly doctored reality" that both Williamsburg and Disneyland are "inventing" (Huxtable, *The Unreal America*, 41). In her analysis of the commodification of history she neglected and underestimated the importance of the sensing subject.

28. Daniel J. Boorstin, *The Image. A Guide to Pseudo-Events in America* (New York: Atheneum, 1973). MacCannell uses the terms "front stage" and "backstage" in reference to Erving Goffman. See: Dean MacCannell, "Staged Authenticity: Arrangements of Social Space in Tourist Settings," *American Journal of Sociology* 79, no. 3 (1973): 589–603.

29. MacCannell, "Staged Authenticity."

30. Wang, "Rethinking Authenticity," 352.

31. Eric J. Hobsbawm and Terence Ranger, eds., *The Invention of Tradition* (Cambridge: Cambridge University Press, 2013). Benedict Anderson, *Imagined Communities* (London: Verso, 2006). Sharon Zukin, *Naked City* (Oxford: Oxford University Press, 2010), xiii.

32. Zukin, *Naked City*, 26

33. Britta Timm Knudsen and Anne Marit Waade, "Performative Authenticity in Tourism and Spatial Experience: Rethinking the Relations Between Travel, Place, and Emotion," in *Re-Investing Authenticity. Tourism, Place and Emotions*, eds. Britta Timm Knudsen and Anne Marit Waade (Bristol: Channel View Publications, 2010), 13.

34. Knudsen and Waade, "Performative Authenticity in Tourism and Spatial Experience," 5.

35. Holtorf describes the concept of *pastness* as the "quality of being of the past" and as "the result of a particular perception or experience, and thus not immanent in any material object." See, Cornelius Holtorf, "Authenticity and Pastness in Cultural Heritage Management," in *Encyclopedia of Global Archaeology,* ed. Claire Smith (New York: Springer, 2014), 712.

36. When the Revolution unfolded, it was in Williamsburg where the first document proclaiming inherent rights of men, the Virginia Declaration of Rights, was adopted in June 1776. A few days later Virginia became the first colony to ratify a constitution and to create its own commonwealth. Those two documents heavily influenced subsequent political documents, amongst others, the Declaration of Independence.

37. The museum first opened in 1932 and is run by the Colonial Williamsburg Foundation, a non-profit corporation with an additional for-profit division that manages the museum's restaurants, hotels, and shops. There are currently 2,500 employees and 900 volunteers working for the Foundation.

38. Heike Paul, *The Myths that Made America. An Introduction to American Studies* (Bielefeld, Germany: Transcript, 2014), 232.

39. For more details on what has been made in/visible in the course of the Restoration process, see Eduard Führ, "Becoming Americans. Colonial Williamsburg als Gründungsmythos," in *Building America: Die Erschaffung einer neuen Welt*, eds. Anke Köth et al. (Dresden, Germany: Thelem, 2005), 177–206; Anders Greenspan, *Creating Colonial Williamsburg* (Washington D.C.: Smithsonian Institution Press, 2002); Sabine Schindler, *Authentizität und Inszenierung. Die Vermittlung von Geschichte in amerikanischen historic sites* (Heidelberg, Germany: Universitätsverlag Winter, 2003).

40. Between August 2012 and April 2014, I conducted interviews with 57 employees of different divisions, departments, and positions of the Colonial Williamsburg Foundation. The quotes in this chapter are excerpts from those interviews.

41. Six groups of perceived barriers that might, but not necessarily have to, distract from the experience of atmospheric involvement could be identified: weather conditions, economic barriers, lack of guidance and orientation, barriers of movement, form of interpretation, and presumed inaccuracies of artifacts and narratives.

42. The quotes in this chapter are excerpts from 44 qualitative interviews conducted in Colonial Williamsburg in September 2013 and between February and April 2014.

43. The interviewee is referring to the Christmas decorations that are put on the doors in the Historic Area. The fruit-decked wreaths that have become a symbol of Colonial Williamsburg are rooted in the invented traditions of the Colonial Revival era of the early twentieth century. Like many other irregularities that have become inscribed in the Historic Area over time, the Colonial Williamsburg Foundation is addressing this issue on its website: "They didn't originate in Williamsburg…nor did they begin during colonial times," <http://www.history.org/almanack/life/christmas/dec_doors.cfm>. While the gentle visitor will uncover those inscribed modifications to historical accuracy, they might remain historical accuracies for visitors that are not engaging in the atmosphere on site or in the online lecture.

44. With regard to Colonial Williamsburg, Handler and Gable have stressed that the institution has to become "more open and honest with itself" already nineteen years ago in their much-quoted analysis of the "new history in an old museum." See, Richard Handler and Eric Gable, *The New History in an Old Museum. Creating the Past at Colonial Williamsburg* (Durham, NC: Duke University Press, 1997).

45. Tim Ingold, "The Temporality of the Landscape," *World Archeology* 25, no. 2 (1993): 171.

PART VIII

The Politics of the Space

21

Revisiting The Lost City

The Legend Lives On

By Jeanne van Eeden

The popular South African destination resort Sun City was the creation of the innovative local leisure entrepreneur Sol Kerzner of Sun International. When it opened on December 7, 1979, it consisted of a hotel, casino, and entertainment complex unique in South Africa, although it was not technically "in" South Africa since it was located in the neighboring "homeland" of Bophuthatswana. According to government legislation at that time, many forms of social life were censored, and gambling and public entertainment involving nudity were prohibited in South Africa. Kerzner used the apartheid government's segregation policy of supposedly independent homelands to construct an entertainment resort in Bophuthatswana because it was conveniently situated for visitors from the metropolitan areas of Johannesburg, Pretoria, and Vereeniging. Sun City was immediately welcomed by South Africans seeking entertainment that evoked the glamour of Las Vegas—primarily gambling and spectacular live shows in the Sun City Extravaganza Theatre. Sun City was structured around what Marietta Kesting and Alosja Weskott call the "sun trope," consisting of a "stereotypical constellation of sun-leisure-tourists-exotic places."[1]

Although initially the majority of visitors to Sun City were South Africans, by the 1990s the changing political landscape in South Africa opened it up to the international market eager to experience "Africa." Kerzner therefore decided that Sun City should expand its association with wildlife and include a new type of entertainment landscape, inspired by Disney theme parks. He accordingly conceptualized, in conjunction with the American destination designers Wimberley Allison Tong and Goo (WATG), the Lost City theme park and The Palace Hotel on the Sun City site, in 1992. The Lost City was inspired by popular culture, myths, and perceptions about Africa, and used a unifying "Legend" to create a backstory and give thematic unity to a new kind of immersive and experiential entertainment that extended the existing sun trope.

By the late 1990s, the 150km circumference of the site made Sun City one of the biggest resorts in the world, encompassing four hotels, numerous restaurants, and a variety of entertainment options, outdoor recreational spaces, and sports activities (see images 21.1, 21.2).[2] The resort currently includes two golf courses, the Motseng cultural village and *shebeen* or informal tavern, an animal farm, aviary, butterfly sanctuary, Kwena Gardens crocodile sanctuary, Waterworld, Unreal ZIP 2000 extreme adventure slide, Segway Personal Transporter tours, horse riding stables, game drives and game walks, a health spa, and the Valley of the Waves waterpark structured around the Legend of the Lost City.

In this chapter, I consider some of the strategies that Sun City, and in particular the Lost City, has used to maintain its market sector. The purpose is not to critique the Lost City and Sun City as fantasyscapes that profited from apartheid policies or to comment extensively on how they maintain colonialist attitudes towards Africa.[3] The implicit point of departure is that Sun City is rooted in and informed by contested and controversial histories and that it originated in South Africa at a very specific time in its socio-political history.[4] The fact that the Lost City is based on the stereotypical and essentialist formation of "Africa" is referred to as necessary, but the aim of this chapter is rather to explore why the Legend of the Lost City continues to survive in a jaded postmodern world of knowing consumers who are familiar with sophisticated technology. In particular, I shall suggest that a greater emphasis on immersive experiences helps consolidate the idea that the Lost City is indeed metonymic of "Africa," a beguiling simulacrum that stands in for and replaces the "real"

Image 21.1. NuMaps Bird's Eye View of Sun City (Cape Town, NuMaps, 1992)

Africa. I thus agree with Martin Hall and Pia Bombardella that the Lost City is "intended as an improvement on Africa, an experience without the distracting unpleasantness of the organic…[it is a] true simulacrum—a copy for which there is no original."[5]

I start this chapter by looking at some of the strategies that Sun City has used recently to re-position itself in the national and international leisure and entertainment market. Thereafter, I focus specifically on how the Lost City has moved across a number of other entertainment platforms to create pleasurable immersive experiences that absorb or engage visitors anew.[6]

Re-positioning Sun City

Gambling, now known by the more benign term "gaming," benefited from its de-regulation in South Africa in 1996, leading to the erection of many theme-driven casinos and resorts in metropolitan areas.[7] This loss of Sun City's virtual monopoly on gambling had important consequences. As previously mentioned, by the 1990s, Sun City was starting to re-position itself as a leading destination resort for foreign tourists, and expanded its timeshare offerings.[8] Ashton remarks that the growth of national competition clearly had an influence on how Sun City was trying to change its image: "Sun City has mellowed. It's no longer the temptress in the wilderness."[9] The promotional material generated by Sun City since the late 1990s echoes this sentiment: it is no longer "the sinful gambling mecca…[it] has segued into its new position as an imperative African *experience* destination for international travellers. Locally, it has become the preferred destination for incentive groups and conventions, and the loyal local leisure market is highly valued."[10]

In spite of increased competition and the loss of its gambling monopoly, Sun City remains unique in terms of its scale, scope, and continued popularity as an up-market resort. The growing number of worldwide tourists to South Africa increased from 1.09 million in 1990 to 4.48 million in 1995.[11] Although Sun City has traditionally relied on attracting local day visitors, it has been established that foreign visitors spend more time and money at the resort, and the challenge

Image 21.2. The Lost City and the Palace Hotel (The Lost City at Sun City, Johannesburg, Art Publishers, 2000)

is therefore to accommodate the needs of both demographic groups.[12] Christel Botha, John Crompton, and Seong-Seop Kim comment that it is not easy for a resort to totally re-imagine itself in the minds of visitors and it is therefore preferable to reinforce "key features of the position the resort already possessed" and to expand on unique differentiating attributes.[13] Accordingly, to attract and retain visitors, it became vital to identify the perceived benefits of visiting Sun City and to establish positive differentiation between it and other places in terms of meeting people's personal motivations for traveling.[14] As a result of the growing sophistication of tourists and their expectations, it is essential for resorts to meet their changing needs, including internal social-psychological ones, and to allay concerns about any constraints that may inhibit them.[15] So, for example, in the face of great competition from other resorts, Sun City has to convince potential visitors that the journey there will be worthwhile and that they will be rewarded by a distinctive experience.

In a survey on the re-positioning of Sun City/the Lost City, the following were the most positive things that people reported about their experiences: they could escape from crowds; they felt safe; there were ample opportunities to view wildlife; they enjoyed the variety of entertainment and indoor recreational activities; gaming was available if wanted;

golf and other sports were a drawcard; and being able to see and do many things in close proximity in a short space of time.[16] The first and last points are particularly significant. The seclusion that could easily have worked against Sun City's accessibility has been used positively to differentiate it from resorts in busy metropolitan areas. In addition, Sun City's broad spectrum of "African" attractions and activities almost invalidates the need for foreign visitors to visit other parts of South Africa, with the possible exception of Cape Town. As noted above, Sun City has regularly worked to update its image in response to changing market needs, but what has remained consistent at "Africa's kingdom of pleasure" is the promotional rhetoric that invokes notions of royalty, majesty, magic, pleasure, romance, adventure, luxury, exclusivity, and exotic indulgence, all of which speak to people's emotional needs and the desire for diverse experiences. Consequently, the persuasive discourse is unabashedly directed at self-indulgent and self-absorbed experiences: "Journeys that allow you to *find yourself and lose yourself* at the same time. *Escape* into the thrill of your journey" and "Sun City's emphasis [is] on the *African experience*, including access to the Big Five in the nearby game-rich, malaria-free Pilanesberg National Park."[17] We see here how the notion of the journey becomes an end in itself, part of the experience, rather than a tedious obstacle, and at the same time, fears about tangible realities such as malaria are dispelled.

The Legend Made Real

The Legend of The Lost City, originally formulated by Gerald Allison from WATG, provided the backstory and framework for the visual identity, iconographic program and thematic content of The Lost City. Extracts from this Legend are found throughout the Lost City site and remind visitors about its ostensible origins:

> Centuries before tall ships were ever dreamed about, long before the dawn of a western civilisation, a nomadic tribe from northern Africa set out to seek a new world, a land of peace and plenty. The tribe wandered form many years in search of such a magical place, and at last their quest was rewarded. The land they discovered to the south became the legendary valley of the sun, known today as the Valley of Waves. Not only did they bring with them a rich culture, but also architectural skills which were exceptional even by today's standards. Something special was created: from the jungle rose an amazing city with a magnificent Palace, a world richer and more splendid than any they had ever known. Then a violent earthquake struck this idyllic valley, the survivors fled, never to return and left it to be found and restored by archaeologists centuries later.[18]

This Legend was the backstory used to thematize the environment and render the space into a meaningful, self-referential and intertextual narrative structure that tells a compelling story. As Margaret King argues, theming involves "shorthand stylizations of person, place and thing, an archive of collective memory and belief, symbol and archetype…the 'bank' of popular culture."[19] Martin Hall contextualizes the Legend of The Lost City and relates it to three common components of mythic discourse that are related to this bank of popular culture: an idyllic Lost Age that is brought to an end by a Dark Disaster, leaving only an Enchanted Ruin as evidence of former greatness.[20] The Legend merges popular ideas of colonial travel to and exploration of Africa, as well as the romance of archaeological excavations. These ideas resonate with key, overarching themes commonly found at themed environments—adventure, the exotic, luxury, and the search.[21] This "Indiana Jones" type of story suggested by the Legend seizes the imagination of visitors as it is built on a complex network of inscriptions in film and literature about Africa.[22] The colonial romance is reinforced by the hermetic isolation and safety of Sun City where visitors are immersed in a nostalgic, timeless world that maintains the entitled myth of leisure and pleasure. Renato Rosaldo explains that imperialist nostalgia is an ideological construct that sanctions the longing "for more stable worlds, whether these reside in our own past, in other cultures, or in the conflation of the two."[23] The Legend relies on this random conflation and people's imprecise ideas concerning the past. It is taken for granted that a theme park past does not have to be specific to be believable; rather, its credibility can be measured by its plausibility, its "persuasive ambience," and its ability to create memorable and pleasurable experiences.[24]

Living the Legend: Immersive Experiences

The contemporary emphasis on immersive experiences is not new—already in 1997, a former Vice-President of WATG reasoned that themed architecture allows architects to "create [their] own legends—in the same way that a screenplay writer invents a storyline—and these 'scripts' form the backbone for our architecture…Guests are invited to *immerse* themselves in our creative vision and, thereby, enrich their *experiences*."[25] The recent rise of the multisensory experience economy is based on "the commodification of visual and sensory distraction."[26] Joseph Pine and James Gilmore note that the experience economy is part of the shift from an industrial to a service economy whereby consumers pay for experiences that have been staged for them rather than for commodities.[27] The creation of total environments, such as the Lost City, is typical of the experience economy, and the backstory, as noted above, creates the believable fiction in which visitors participate. For example, in keeping with the royal theme of the Legend, visitors to the Palace Hotel can expect distinctive and indulgent experiences in an "atmosphere of luxurious tranquillity which [reflects] the hospitality extended by kings."[28] Visual and textual signifiers of royalty are used throughout the Lost City to invoke and sustain the romantic majesty of the lost civilization, which relates back to the Queen of Sheba theme that is implicit in the Legend, according to Hall.[29]

Themed experiences are inherently personal and rely to some extent on customer participation (which can be passive or active) and absorption or immersion "in the sights, sounds, and smells" that make up the experience.[30] At a location such as a theme park, it is likely that the experiences will be mainly aesthetic or escapist, and will rely on quite a high degree of immersion.[31] The most compelling themed experiences are based on a unified storyline that creates a captivating experience for the consumer.[32] In terms of Scott A. Lukas' taxonomy of customer immersion, the Lost City would probably constitute a 'middle of the road' experience. In other words, although it would almost certainly not be life changing or awe-inspiring, the associative power of the Legend could awake people's desire for adventure and inspire a better appreciation for "the past."[33]

The Lost City creates an illusion of a lost culture and in order to be successful as a themed environment, it should invoke many senses and be multi-experiential; in other words, the story should be compelling so that people are drawn into it, the created world should not feel artificial, and there should be a connection to the "real" world.[34] The sensory environment, consisting of the rides, attractions, sounds, textures, smells and light can to a large extent determine the credibility of the themed environment. There are a number of instances of successful immersion in the artifice at the Lost City. Firstly, the appearance of the fake stones used to construct the "excavated" columns, the Royal Staircase, the Royal Observatory, the Royal Baths, the platinum mine, the Royal Arena, the Valley of Waves, the Valley of the Ancients, the Monkey Spring Plaza, the Kong Gates, and the Bridge of Time is very convincing. Broken "stone" columns, boulders, mouldings and ornamentation were replicated out of other materials, and the passing of three millennia is artfully suggested by fake chips, fade marks, fissures, and cracked, uneven flagstones. (see image 21.3) The fact that people have to walk over these flagstones reinforces the immersive experience as the "past" is literally felt underfoot. A huge amount of work went into the construction of the fake rocks and stone. All the columns and rockscapes were made from glass fiber reinforced concrete, moulded from real rocks; the large slabs of rock were moulded from cement, and then plastered and carved by hand. To create a tactile and convincing illusion of age, care was "taken to ensure that everything which looks like stone and is within *touching* distance, does indeed *feel cold* to the fingers."[35]

Secondly, the experience economy demands that as many senses as possible should be engaged by means of sensory stimulants.[36] This is best illustrated at the Lost City on the Bridge of Time that forms the physical transition from the Entertainment Centre building to the Lost City. This kind of "lead area" signals that another world is being entered and it ought to create a specific kind of atmosphere.[37] The Bridge of Time, a 66-meter-long pedestrian bridge, stands eight meters above ground on an air float, and functions as a threshold to the themed space. The bridge was equipped with special effects by Hollywood experts that mimic the effects of the volcanic eruption and earthquake that supposedly destroyed the Lost City three millennia ago.[38] At each hourly re-enactment of the volcanic eruption, the bridge shakes and moves about two millimeters and smoke and steam issue from cracks on the bridge. Lava hisses and bubbles and ominous rumblings are heard. The bridge is one of the most popular sites at the Lost City, and it is here where the experience of being in a catastrophic, awe-inspiring event is felt firsthand by visitors. The fact that volcanic eruptions are unknown is this region of Africa, is irrelevant in this context.

A third example is the converse of the action embodied in the previous example. In order for people to be absorbed or immersed in certain kinds of landscapes, it is important for them to experience tranquility and to be able to reflect in quiet areas.[39] An example of this is the extensive themed Garden located around the Palace Hotel. The Lost City Garden is a constructed 25-hectare tropical fantasy forest planted from scratch in the normally dry bushveld terrain. It comprises

Image 21.3. The fake columns at the Royal Arena at The Lost City (Photo by Jeanne van Eeden)

artificial lakes, pools, fountains, waterfalls, overgrown mock ruins, and meandering paths. Extracts from the Legend are found at strategic places in the Garden and they remind visitors about the backstory: "Forbidden to use the stairway to the Palace villagers had to trek this winding path. Today it is a walk through time. You *lose yourself* in the wonder and mystery of the great civilization that thrived here" and "Even a cursory *exploration* into the Lost City's jungle will *enfold* you in exoticism and mystique."[40] The Garden calls to mind European picturesque gardens of the eighteenth century and also evokes John Urry's account of the romantic tourist gaze in nature: "solitude, privacy and a personal, semi-spiritual relationship with the object of the gaze."[41] Similarly, immersion in the "healing powers" of the Royal Bath might be seen as an invitation to an embodied experience located in a setting evocative of the luxury of the past.

In the experience economy, is it is important that consistent cues be delivered to consumers, and merchandising, for example, should also continue the theme and the experience.[42] Accordingly, an up-market outlet in the Palace Hotel sells glossy guidebooks, books, jigsaw puzzles, exclusive logo-bearing items, postcards, and a video about the Lost City. Various retail outlets in the Entertainment Centre sell less exclusive items that may remind visitors of their experience. In addition to these experiential elements at the Lost City, it has moved across a number of other immersive, multimedia entertainment platforms, such as *The Lost City* iOS game by Fire Maple Games available on iPhone and iPad. This game picks up the theme of archaeology embodied in the Legend, but constructs another narrative that is gendered as female and highlights ecological and cultural restitution rather than colonial exploitation:

> Your grandmother loved telling you bedtime stories from her times as a famous archaeologist…by far your favourite story was that of the Lost City, a mystical place that always seemed more like a fairy tale to you…too old to travel now herself, she hands you her journal and a chiselled heart-shaped stone…the only artefact taken from their expedition. She has come to believe that taking the stone has somehow disturbed the natural harmony of the land and needs to be returned. Using her map as a guide, you set off on an adventure to see this magical place with your own eyes, and to unveil the secrets of the Lost City."[43]

Computer games are known to require a high level of consumer immersion and have been the driving power behind creating personal immersive experiences and environments.[44] The player of the Lost City game is accordingly invited on a quest that she sees with *her own eyes* and the experience thus becomes personal and unique. The game has all the formulaic elements beloved of colonial adventure stories and heroic quests, including a journal, map, ciphers, threats to life and safety, and puzzles that have to be solved.

Image 21.4. *Pamphlet by Sun International for the Maze at The Lost City*

The last example of immersive experience at the Lost City concerns the latest addition to the site, the Maze of the Lost City that opened in September 2012 (image 21.4). The Maze is reached from the Entertainment Centre by crossing a 90-meter bamboo themed suspension bridge, which moves perceptibly as one crosses it, again signaling a personal and embodied experience similar to the Bridge of Time (image 21.5). Thereafter, a winding path, constructed in the same manner as the stone paths in the Lost City, takes one to the Maze. Upon successful completion of the Maze, the real destination is reached—a refreshment area called the Brewers Roof and the maze lookout area that affords a panoramic view over the Lost City. A separate entrance fee is charged for the Maze, and the refreshment area hosts functions, conferences, and teambuilding events; the latter builds on the idea that adventure and testing oneself can be a bonding experience.

Image 21.5. The suspension bridge leading to the Maze at The Lost City (Photo by Jeanne van Eeden)

The Maze was conceived by Tim Dawson, CEO of Unreal The Company (Unique Recreational Experiences and Leisure), which specializes in adventure activity design, construction and consultancy. The Maze is 2200 square meters and is apparently one of the largest permanent mazes in the southern hemisphere; its constructed mythology resonates with the genealogy of mazes that encompasses Egyptian labyrinths and the Cretan labyrinth of King Minos. Dawson started with a backstory that extends and complements the existing archaeological theme of The Lost City:

> The Ancients that once inhabited the valley where the Sun City resort now stands constructed many wondrous and beautiful buildings, structures and monuments to honour their kings and their gods. It was thought that all of the structures and ruins had been discovered. But after listening to local folklore telling of other structures into which some would enter and never return, I started searching. For the past three years I have been searching for parts of the Lost City that were still lost. And finally I found it, "The maze of the lost City."[45]

The Maze is reminiscent of a semi-ruined Mayan stone maze; this stylistic inconsistency is typical of the eclecticism of The Lost City, which combines Greco-Roman with North Africa architecture, Versailles, and the Taj Mahal with gothic gargoyles, all overlaid with decorative motifs derived from African flora and fauna. Just like the Lost City, the Maze is constructed out of artificial rock, stone and wood, "creating the illusion of an ancient archaeological discovery, reflecting the time of the legendary Lost City…When night falls, flaming torches [in the] seated area, bathe it in peaceful ambience."[46] Where possible, existing trees were incorporated into the ruin, which suggests that nature is still repossessing the land. Based on my recent personal experience of the Maze, it seems that people really engage with the notion of exploration and adventure it embodies and camaraderie is created between visitors trying to solve the puzzle. The archetypal significance of the Maze is suggested on Sun International's website, where visitors are alerted to the anticipated sensory experience: "Symbolically, mazes are said to represent human beings' *experience of intuition and the senses.*"[47]

The Allure of the Lost City

Whether as its earlier incarnation as "sin city" or as the more recent family resort, Sun City is an indelible part of South African popular culture and part of its imaginary psychogeography, despite its dubious political origins. In this chapter, I looked at the current position of the Lost City theme park in terms of growing competition from other resorts. In spite of this, however, it is clear that Sun City is doing well, specifically with international tourists. The reason seems to be that it has built on its strengths of being close to nature and wildlife and offering respite from urban chaos, and has continued to upgrade and extend its facilities. In comparison with international theme parks, the Lost City has been quite modest in its use of new technology and expanding its rides and attractions. The challenge for entertainment landscapes is to avoid stagnation and to provide new experiences for their customers. As Innocent Pikrayi comments, the past sells, and the allure of places such as the Lost City is that they use the past, "regardless of the fact it is usually presented in a manner that negates historical accuracy" to cater for a privileged set of people.[48] The Lost City is an elaborate illusion, the ultimate fake: its history and legendary past are not real; stone, ivory, crystal, the jungle, lakes and sea are simulated; the Palace is not a palace; the city is not a city; and everything that appears old is actually new. Despite this, and however cynically one looks at it, it offers a beguiling experience that kindles the imagination by means of its scale and ability to create a believable and fantastical "pseudo-world."

Notes

1. Marietta Kesting and Alosja Weskott, "Dream Machine–Introduction," in *Sun Tropes: Sun City and (Post-) Apartheid Culture in South Africa*, eds. Marietta Kesting and Alosja Weskott (Berlin: August Verlag, 2009), 17. At the time of writing, two extravaganzas were showing at Sun City—Heavenly Bodies and B'dazzled, both of which seem to perpetuate the tradition of showgirl entertainment.

2. Christel Botha, John Crompton, and Seong-Seop Kim, "Developing a Revised Competitive Position for Sun/Lost City, South Africa," *Journal of Travel Research* 37, no. 4 (May 1999): 341.

3. For the critical discourse about Sun City and The Lost City, see for example Martin Hall, "The Legend of the Lost City; or, the Man with Golden Balls," *Journal of Southern African Studies* 21, no 2 (1995): 179–199; Kesting and Weskott, eds. Sun Tropes (Berlin: August Verlag, 2009); Jeanne van Eeden, "The Colonial Gaze: Imperialism, Myths and South African Popular Culture," *Design Issues* 20, no. 2 (2004): 18–33; Jeanne van Eeden, "Theming Mythical Africa at The Lost City, in *The Themed Space: Locating Culture, Nation, and Self*, ed. Scott A. Lukas. (Lanham, MD: Lexington Books, 2007), 113–135; Jeanne van Eeden, "Mapping Fun in the Sun," in *Sun Tropes. Sun City and (Post-)Apartheid Culture in South Africa*, eds. Marietta Kesting and Alosja Weskott (Berlin: August Verlag, 2009), 187–224.

4. Kesting and Weskott, "Dream Machine," 9–38.

5. Martin Hall and Pia Bombardella, "Las Vegas in Africa," *Journal of Social Archaeology* 5, no. 1 (February 2005): 9.

6. See Scott A. Lukas, *The Immersive Worlds Handbook: Designing Theme Parks and Consumer Spaces* (New York: Focal, 2013), 4, 6.

7. These include Emperors Palace and Montecasino in Johannesburg, Grandwest in Cape Town, and the forthcoming gaming and entertainment complex on Time Square at Menlyn Maine in the affluent eastern suburbs of Pretoria.

8. S. Bridge, "Jacko to Become new Sun King," *Sunday Times Business Times*, March 25, 1999, 1.

9. Leigh Ashton, "The Temptress in the Wilderness Goes Legit," *Saturday Argus Out and About*, September 20–21, 1997, 3.

10. Sun International, "Foreign Markets Targeted for Future Growth," *Pretoria News Business Report*, June 28, 1999, 9; my emphasis.

11. Botha, Crompton and Kim, "Developing a Revised Competitive Position," 341.

12. Botha, Crompton and Kim, "Developing a Revised Competitive Position," 341.

13. Botha, Crompton and Kim, "Developing a Revised Competitive Position," 341.

14. Botha, Crompton and Kim, "Developing a Revised Competitive Position," 343–344; Seong-Seop Kim, John L. Crompton and Christel Botha, "Responding to Competition: A Strategy for Sun/Lost City, South Africa," *Tourism Management* 21, no. 1 (February 2000): 40.

15. Botha, Crompton and Kim, "Developing a Revised Competitive Position," 342.

16. Botha, Crompton and Kim, "Developing a Revised Competitive Position," 345–350.

17. Sun International, "The Palace of The Lost City at Sun City," undated brochure, 1, 12; my emphasis; Sun International, "Sun City–Fact Sheet," (2014), 1; my emphasis.

18. Sun International, "Fact Sheet: The Palace," Press release, May, 1997, 1

19. Margaret J. King, "'Disneyfication'? Some Pros and Cons of Theme Parks, 'Never Land' or Tomorrowland?," *Museum* 43, no. 1 (1991): 6.

20. Hall, "The Legend," 180–181.

21. Lukas, *The Immersive Worlds Handbook*, 30–31.

22. The most obvious filmic examples, apart from the Indiana Jones trilogy (*Raiders of the Lost Ark* (1981), *Indiana Jones and the Temple of Doom* (1984), and *Indiana Jones and the Last Crusade* (1989)), are *Romancing the Stone* (1984), *The Jewel of the Nile* (1985), the television series *The Relic Hunter* (1999–2002), *The African Queen* (1951), *The Lion King* (1994), *Out of Africa* (1985), *The Gods Must be Crazy* (1981), and *Heat of the Sun* (1998). Literary examples include Sir Henry Rider Haggard's colonial adventure stories *King Solomon's Mines* (1885), *She* (1887), *Allan Quatermain* (1887), and *Ayesha, or the Return of She* (1905), *The Lost World* (1912) by Sir Arthur Conan Doyle, and Edgar Rice Burroughs' *Tarzan* stories (1912–1944), many of which were filmed from the 1920s onwards. There is a further level of intertextuality—Sun City has become a ready-made film set for fashion shoots and television commercials. The Lost City, as a metonym for "Africa," was used as a mise-en-scène for an American television series *Tarzan: The Epic Adventures* (1996–1997) and large sections of the American film *Blended* (2014, directed by Frank Coraci), were filmed at Sun City.

23. Renato Rosaldo, "Imperialist Nostalgia," *Representations*, 26 (Spring 1989): 108.

24. Hall and Bombardella, "Las Vegas in Africa," 9.

25. M.R. Paneri, "Is Themed Architecture Legitimate?" <http://www.watg.com/>; my emphasis.

26. Albert S. Fu and Martin J. Murray, "Glorified Fantasies and Masterpieces of Deception on Importing Las Vegas into the 'New South Africa,'" *International Journal of Urban and Regional Research* 38, no. 3 (2014): 848.

27. B. Joseph Pine and James H. Gilmore, "Welcome to the Experience Economy," *Harvard Business Review* July–August (1998): 97–98.

28. "Works of Wonder," *Habitat* 114 (1993): 47.

29. Hall, "The Legend," 29.

30. Pine and Gilmore, "Welcome to the Experience Economy," 98–99, 101–102.

31. Pine and Gilmore, "Welcome to the Experience Economy," 102.

32. Pine and Gilmore, "Welcome to the Experience Economy," 102–103.

33. Lukas, *The Immersive Worlds Handbook*, 137, 139.

34. Lukas, *The Immersive Worlds Handbook*, 107.

35. Sun International, "Sculpting an Architectural Tribute at The Lost City," Press release, December 1993, 4; my emphasis.

36. Pine and Gilmore, "Welcome to the Experience Economy," 104.

37. Lukas, *The Immersive Worlds Handbook*, 145–146.

38. They include people who collaborated on films such as *Alien*, *Death on the Nile*, *King Kong Lives*, *Terminator II*, and *Licence to Kill* (Sun International, "Sculpting an Architectural Tribute," 2).

39. Lukas, *The Immersive Worlds Handbook*, 147.

40. "Explore the Jungle of the Lost City," <http://www.suninternational.com/stories/travel/destinations/pages/articles.aspx?>; my emphasis.

41. John Urry, *The Tourist Gaze. Leisure and Travel in Contemporary Societies* (London: Sage, 1990): 45, 86.

42. Pine and Gilmore, "Welcome to the Experience Economy," 104.

43. iPhone game *The Lost City*. Games©. 2012, <https://www.youtube.com/watch?v=xPvJjMP5mlA>.

44. Pine and Gilmore, "Welcome to the Experience Economy," 99.

45. "The Maze of The Lost City," accessed December 31, 2014, <http://www.lostcitymaze.co.za/index.php>.

46. J. Warburton, "Mazes Provide Adventure and Mystery," <http://www.suninternational.com/Stories/lifestyle/outdoor-adventure/Pages/mazes.aspx>.

47. J. Warburton, "Mazes Provide Adventure and Mystery," <http://www.suninternational.com/Stories/lifestyle/outdoor-adventure/Pages/mazes.aspx>.

48. Innocent Pikirayi, "The Kingdom, the Power and Forevermore: Zimbabwe Culture in Contemporary Art and Architecture," *Journal of Southern African Studies* 32, no. 4 (2006): 767.

22

Our Chemical Romance

Body Worlds and the Memorialization of the Self

By Kent Drummond and Lei Jia

The Dead Are Always with Us

The museum blockbuster Body Worlds has been touring the globe for over 20 years. Billed as the exhibit that features "real human bodies," Body Worlds has become the most successful touring show in the history of the world, having appeared in more than 90 cities and attracted more than 40 million visitors worldwide. Simply put, Body Worlds is the most globally significant immersion experience for the memorialization of dead bodies. To understand how Body Worlds attracts and sustains consumers is to understand much about dark tourism in general and memorial theming in particular. Accordingly, our research question addresses this very issue: How does Body Worlds accomplish its memorial theming, and how has it become a popular stop on any dark tourist's itinerary?

In order to answer this question, we offer an interpretive, impression-based analysis of Body Worlds. Having visited six Body Worlds shows in four cities over the course of five years, we have observed the behavior of hundreds of visitors to Body Worlds. We interviewed curators, security guards, and museumgoers. We also purchased artifacts from museum gift shops, and collected notes, quotes, and information on the persona of the inventor of Body Worlds, Dr. Gunther von Hagens. Heeding the call issued by leading consumer researchers Alladi Venkatesh and Fuat Firat over 20 years ago, we focus as much on what producers display as what consumers apprehend.[1] As von Hagens told an interviewer over a decade ago, "I am making the dead lifeful again. This exhibition is a place where the dead and the living mix."[2]

What does it look, feel, and sound like to visit a Body Worlds exhibit? In the following sections, we take the reader on a descriptive tour of a typical Body Worlds exhibit, even as we realize that each show is unique.[3] Yet we submit that all shows excel in memorializing the dead in idealized, life-like ways that make dark tourism not only palatable, but pleasurable.

Paint It Black

Immediately upon entering a Body Worlds exhibit, the visitor is greeted by waves upon waves of black velvet drapes. Like dark tsunamis, they stretch from the floor to the ceiling, blocking out all sound and light. Voices are hushed accordingly. A somber mood pervades, in stark contrast to the buoyant anticipation of the box office and lobby. Here, there's a feeling of liminality: we've left one space, but we haven't quite entered another.

Then, as we enter the first gallery, three giant light boxes confront us. They project human faces that morph swiftly and silently from young to old, male to female, black to white. No sound effects here. We witness the passing of time in these strangers' faces. We want to help them—to stop the aging process!—yet we are powerless to do anything about it. There's something sad and elegiac about this tableau, an undeniable memorialization. The message on a nearby placard does little to lighten the mood: "The exhibit focuses on the nature of our physical being, not on providing personal information on private tragedies." The tone here, possibly translated from the German, is oddly foreboding. What private tragedies? Whose personal information? By stating what it won't be focusing on, the exhibit calls our attention to that very thing. Are the cadavers, soon to be encountered, somehow linked to the faces on the light boxes?[4]

After another short, dark passage (more velvet drapes), the path opens into a room focused on conception, called, It Starts With a Single Cell. Lines of text greet the visitor, explaining how cells combine to form a unique human who has never existed and who will never be recreated. An endless-loop video narrates the story of conception, backed by piano and flute accompaniment. Six fetuses in different stages of development line the walls. Having undergone the process of plastination invented by Dr. Gunther von Hagens, they look like plastic dolls a very young child might play with. Yet these "dolls" were once dead babies. Their lives were over before they really began. This memorialization of nascent life only amplifies the dark, sad ambiance of the initial part of the exhibit.

As we continue through the exhibit, shafts of light pierce the dark and land on various piles of bones. In this segment featuring the skeletal system, casements are filled with arrangements of bones. Some bones bear the markings of arthritis, and many visitors grimace as they view them. Short personal narratives emanate from some visitors, accompanied by small gestures. One spectator moves close to the shoulder joint, explaining to friends that his shoulder pops a lot and wants to see what's going on. Another straightens his spine as he encounters a casement containing a healthy spine. Another says, "I have a herniated disk in my back. I haven't talked to my doctor about it since I was nine; my cousin caused it." Still another worries to a companion that the exhibit will leave him with the impression that youth is fleeting, and that by the end, he'll be saying, "No, youth! Come back!" This is certainly the impression given by the light boxes at the exhibit's beginning, and by the first several segments of the exhibit itself. A memorial quality is palpable from the start. The sense that time is passing, and there's nothing anyone can do about it, pervades the first portion of the exhibit.

Walk Towards the Light

In fact, the theme of *tempus fugit*—and the personal choices we make as time flies—is developed early and repeated often. Yet as the exhibit continues, the mood transitions from sad resignation to tentative elation. Posters and placards with various titles—some ominous, others reassuring—persuade us that "Good health is a highly fragile condition." Skin ages, we are shown, but what ages the skin is largely determined by the choices we make. Although time passes uncontrollably, what we do within the time we have is entirely within our control. For example, exposure to ultraviolet rays, smoking, stress levels, and amount of sleep are all within our control, one poster reminds us. Another poster contains a less didactic, more poetic message. Featuring an Asian boy caught in a contemplative moment, the quote is from Lebanese poet Khalil Gibran:

> Your body is the harp of your soul. And it is yours to bring forth sweet music from it or confused sounds.

Other quotes follow from philosopher-kings such as Abraham Lincoln, Gandhi, the Dali Lama, and Albert Einstein. In contrast to the purely informational posters, these messages serve to soften the grit of the exhibits and take the spectator to a higher plane. Great thinkers and great humanitarians elevate the discourse, in sharp contrast to the finely detailed anatomical displays. For the first time, the focus moves slightly from memorialization to idealization. As visitors move through the galleries, bodily systems become more elaborate. Sinew, muscle, ligaments, and tendon are added to the skeletal system. It is at this moment that we encounter our first whole-body plastinate, the Baseball Player.

Plastinate Power

As the Baseball Player illustrates, full-body plastinates are oddly captivating. And it's understandable: after many casements filled with fractionated body parts, it's a relief to see a body fully assembled, however unusual that assemblage might be. Visitors crowd around the figure isolated in a large acrylic casement. Bat swung far to his left, torso dynamically twisted, the Baseball Player has just hit what looks like a home run. Plastinates, we soon learn, are invariably winners. With muscles of bright red and connective tissue of pale cream, he strides like a fat-free god, daring us to ignore him. But we can't. After all, his mouth is agape as his glass eyes follow the stupendous arc of an imaginary ball. Body bent back and feet improbably balanced, he is frozen, like most plastinates, in a heroic act of great physical exertion. It looks like he could topple over at any moment. Yet unbeknownst to most visitors, he is held together by dozens of wires, clamps, and blocks threaded throughout his body. What the spectator sees is a subcutaneous idealization, a paragon of Man.

And what a man! Hanging between the Baseball Player's legs is a generous endowment of genitalia, drawing fleeting, embarrassed glances from the spectators pressed against the glass casement in which he resides. It turns out that whatever their status in real life, plastinates in the afterlife (with the exception

of the effete Flamenco Dancer) are awarded perfectly-formed breasts, taut buttocks, large penises, and fulsome vaginas that draw giggles from some, admiring glances from others. And as onlookers press up against the casements, a curious thing happens. Since all glass casements are highly reflective in the track lighting set against the black drapery, spectators see their reflections overlaid onto the plastinates. They can literally see themselves in von Hagens's creations.

Better Living Through Chemistry

This subtle but profound act of what Burke would call identification takes on an ask-not-for-whom-the-bell-tolls quality.[5] The cadaver was once a man or woman, and she or he was probably a lot like you. But now, something's happened to them and not you. And yet you could become—*will* become, if you wish—this transformed being, a kind of cyborg. And would that be such a bad thing, given how fierce, fresh, and fearless these plastinates are?

It is here that the exhibit moves quietly from memorialization to unrestrained celebration, by way of idealization, and chemistry. What was sad and somewhat repulsive has been transformed into something strangely sanguine and seductive. The proof is in the behavior of the visitors: they're not pulling back from the casements; they're drawing closer. And so the show continues, from one gallery to another, one plastinate to another. Although the length and focus of Body Worlds exhibits vary, visitors must always follow a pre-determined path through the exhibit, and backtracking is discouraged. Nor are visitors likely to tarry long, as the temperature is relatively cool. As one security guard notes, the plastinates cannot get overheated, or they might disintegrate. Besides, backtracking would ruin the optimistic effect the plastinates have on spectators. To experience the show in reverse would be to disassemble the plastinates and arrive at a conclusion of only body parts.

After the Baseball Player comes the Runner. He is posed mid-stride, with all of his muscles peeled back to reveal key junctures of the skeleton beneath. Next is Nerve Leonardo, a plastinate referencing da Vinci's famous drawing, Vitruvian Man. Other prominent plastinates include Body of Open Doors (revealing how all internal organs are packed tightly into the body by displaying them outside it), the Hockey Players (wielding hockey sticks, two plastinates contend for a puck), and the Winged Man. Wearing a hat, this plastinate is accompanied by a quote from von Hagens': "I put the hat on this plastinate to make it look more lively and humorous. Beauty and humor motivate learning, while horror hinders it." Therein lies one secret to dark tourism: use beauty and humor to lighten the mood.

Dr. Feelgood

In fact, Dr. von Hagens is never far from the exhibit; his presence is felt from start to finish. Beginning with banners announcing the exhibit's title (officially, Gunther von Hagens' Body Worlds), and ending with a benedictory photograph of the inventor backlit by the sun, spectators cannot escape knowing that a single man is responsible for this singular display. Von Hagens' flamboyant persona is enacted boldly, both within the show and beyond it.

Variously described as concentration camp survivor, prison escapee, precocious medical student, savvy entrepreneur, and diabolical provocateur, von Hagens embraces whatever descriptors are leveled at him, for it gives him the chance to further fan the flames of controversy. He bears more than a passing resemblance to Dr. Victor Frankenstein, decked in an omnipresent hat and, occasionally, a white smock. More vitriolic critics have likened him to Joseph Mengele, Angel of Death at Auschwitz. Von Hagens wears a fedora, he explains, because all the great anatomists do. Quite deliberately, he seems the living embodiment of one of the figures in his favorite painting, Rembrandt's *The Anatomy Lesson of Dr. Nicolaes Tulp*. After all, operating rooms were originally surgical theaters, and von Hagens is nothing if not theatrical.

Yet none of von Hagens' adventures or opinions would matter if he weren't, first and foremost, a brilliant anatomist. Here is how one museum curator, a biochemist by training, describes him:

> I've been to his workplace in Germany, and I can tell you, he's brilliant. His knowledge of biochemistry is remarkable. That's how he was able to develop plastination. Rather than infusing the body with a preservative

substance, which is what embalming does, he discovered a way to draw the fluid in. No one had ever done that before.

Once von Hagens' perfected this process, he decided to take his show on the road. The impetus, according to the same curator, was political rather than financial:

> Most people don't realize this, but von Hagens refers to himself as a medical socialist. He wants to put the information in the hands of the people and let them decide. That's why so many of the preserved parts show pathologies. You see this, and you make the choice. Is this how you want to end up?

Many religious leaders, outraged by what von Hagens has done with human bodies, have protested the presence of *Body Worlds* within their communities. Their inclination is to bury the plastinates out of respect for the dead. And this concern raises the question of von Hagens' own perspective on religion and spirituality. The final placard in the exhibit, written by von Hagens, is typically and strategically ambiguous:

> The presentation of the purely physical reminds visitors to Body Worlds of the intangible and unfathomable. The plastinated post-mortal body illuminates the soul by its very absence. Plastination transforms the body, an object of individual mourning, into an object of reverence, learning, enlightenment, and appreciation. I hope for *Body Worlds* to be a place of enlightenment and contemplation, even of philosophical and religious self-recognition, and open to interpretation regardless of the background and philosophy of life of the viewer.

This message, only recently added to Body Worlds shows, represents a sea change in von Hagens' worldview. In earlier exhibits, he would not have considered any reference to a "soul" or "religious self-recognition." Now, he encourages a peaceful interchange of these ideas.

Parting Is Such Sweet Sorrow

As Body Worlds continues to circle the globe, we offer three observations that help explain the tremendous popularity of this exhibit. First, Body Worlds walks a fine line between promoting the living and memorializing the dead. Body Worlds is a highly visual exhibition that highlights the inner workings of the body and organs. The exhibited bodies are open, eye-catching, colorful, and odorless. They desperately seek interaction with consumers, which is why, once the plastinates appear, the exhibit truly connects with spectators. Eye contact alone accomplishes much of this. A creative as well as alluring exhibition that displays educational and artistic ambitions, Body Worlds transforms the way we experience dead bodies by portraying them as anything but dead.

Part of what makes Body Worlds so compelling is that the plastinates have been posed to perform various actions and activities from everyday life, suggesting vitality even in death. Yes, the plastination process reveals how bodies function in a mundane world, but they also suggest a world in which the dead are in fact very much alive, performing activities that few of us mere mortals would even attempt to undertake. The subtle suggestion is that what awaits visitors after their own death is a very active afterlife—one which may be more enticing than the lives they lead now. "Don't Fear the Reaper" would make a suitable theme song for this dark but idealized themed space.

Second, Body Worlds strips away individual characteristics to present a generalized notion of the self. Whether through clothing, hair, skin color, or makeup, human bodies signal social identities such as ethnicity and status. Body Worlds, however, exfoliates these signifiers. It literally strips away the outer layers of our identity. In so doing, it deconstructs human beings into universal entities with similar deep structures, despite superficial differences that enable us to judge, envy, and subjugate one another. The implication is that "Underneath, we're not all that different." Body Worlds thus offers a new, depoliticized portrait of the self, stripped of its individual characteristics and replaced with a generalized, global notion of self. It's the United Colors of Benetton taken to the extreme. Perhaps this is why the show plays so well around the world: It is impossible to tell where the bodies are from, what their station in life was, or how old they were when they died. Under this dark cloak of chemically induced anonymity, consumers find a kind of universality. Devoid of distinguishing characteristics, the plastinates in Body Worlds redirect our attention to the inner characteristics that make us all alike. "Consider," they seem to suggest, "the fine qualities we all possess, the vulnerability of our bodies, the fact that we are all cut from the same cloth." From this perspective, is it still meaningful if we keep being judgmental, envious, and condescending? By promoting a generalized, affirming sense of self, Body Worlds creates a mindset of community among its guests, encouraging them to gaze inside rather that care too much about the uniqueness that separates them from one other.

Finally, Body Worlds satisfies an innermost consumer desire—To Live Forever. From the dark velvet drapes to the hushed tones of awestruck visitors, Body Worlds immerses its visitors in darkness, literally rendering dark tourists of us all.[6] Yet what emerges by the exhibit's end, at least symbolically, is a sense of light and hope for the world that awaits. Body Worlds deals in dead bodies, yet it idealizes them to the point where we no longer see them as such. Once repulsive cadavers, they have been transposed, through a brilliant act of biochemistry, into strangely attractive gods. And we observe these gods playing soccer, dancing, speaking in public, even having sex. In accomplishing these feats so convincingly, Body Worlds contradicts the experience many of us have had visiting nursing homes. As we age, our bodies will not necessarily fail us. In fact, they may supersede us.

Body Worlds educates its visitors, as von Hagen intended it to do. Following cutting-edge museum pedagogy, the show provides consumers with "buddies" to accompany them on a journey through the wonders of the human body. That is the superficial effect. Underneath the surface, Body Worlds presents consumers with the breathtaking possibility that their egos, as well as their bodies, may live on, fully intact, after that excellent adventure called death has been experienced. In this exhibit, consumers meet themselves coming and going. They visit Elysium and depart with the seductive suggestion that someday they'll get to live there. It's the ultimate Hollywood ending. That's the true genius of Gunther von Hagens, and why Body Worlds is the blockbuster it is.

In an ironic twist, Dr. von Hagens has recently been diagnosed with Parkinson's disease. Despite his rapidly deteriorating health, he completed a Crucifixion plastinate consisting of a body made out of thousands of scarlet arteries. The body is hanging on a cross. He would like to give it to Pope Francis. And in the ultimate act of memorialization, he has entrusted his own body to his wife (from whom he is separated) for plastination.

Notes

1. Fuat Firat and Alladi Vankatesh, "Liberatory Postmodernism and the Reenchantment of Consumption," *Journal of Consumer Research* 22, no. 3 (December 1995): 254.

2. For a feature article on von Hagens, his work, and his philosophical stance on plastination, see <http://www.theguardian.com/education/2002/mar/19/arts.highereducation.html>.

3. A similar version of this "tour" can be found in Kent Drummond and Eric Krszjzaniek, "Theatre of the Abject," in *Death in a Consumer Culture*, ed. Susan Dobscha (London: Routledge, 2016), 242–254.

4. For more on Body Worlds, consult its website, <http://www.bodyworlds.com/en.html>.

5. Kenneth Burke, *A Rhetoric of Motives* (Berkeley: University of California Press, 1950).

6. For more on the foundations of dark theming, see Scott A. Lukas, "Dark Theming Reconsidered," in this collection.

23

Dark Theming Reconsidered

By Scott A. Lukas

It is not you who will speak; let the disaster speak in you, even if it be by your forgetfulness or silence. — Maurice Blanchot.[1]

In 2013, the Emoya Luxury Hotel in Bloemfontein, South Africa received a rather dubious distinction in the press. CNN, Gizmodo, *Time*, and the Colbert Report criticized the Emoya for what many called its appeal to slumming, poorism, and poverty tourism—"A Fake Slum for Luxury Tourists Who Don't Want to See Real Poverty," as one of these news sources titled its story.[2] The source of the outrage was the Emoya's unique approach to hotel theming. The hotel is designed to resemble a shantytown—the informal settlement common to South Africa and typically inhabited by the poor. The Emoya's version includes corrugated iron sheet dwellings, outdoor fire pits, and interior rooms complemented by long-drop effect toilets, paraffin lamps, battery-operated radios fashioned in a manner reminiscent of indigenous forms of bricolage art, as well as the conveniences of contemporary hotels like Wi-Fi and heated floors.[3] For any admirer of themed and immersive spaces, the Emoya would likely be described as one of the most interesting and creative of themed hotels, but given the other context that is brought into harsh juxtaposition with the theming—the issue of poverty and social oppression—the space would likely be seen in a much different light. The Emoya Luxury Hotel highlights what is at stake in the contemporary world of postmodern leisure and tourism. In one respect, the hotel represents an inauthentic, offensive, colonialist project, while in another, it suggests signs of the future of tourism and theming—complex, politically problematic, and entirely avant-garde in orientation. I will return to the case of the Emoya later in this writing, but for this moment let me use this example as a way of reviewing and refining the existing work on dark tourism and of suggesting a reevaluation of dark theming.[4]

There is a rich and important literature on the topic of dark tourism. Philip Stone has defined dark tourism as the "act of travel to tourist sites associated with death, suffering and the seemingly macabre."[5] Typically, dark tourism has been associated with sites that include museums, places at which natural disasters or human tragedies have taken place, and other venues that generally focus on aspects of death or the macabre. Previous considerations of dark tourism have focused quite exclusively on the meanings of "dark" that connote "gloomy, sad, cheerless, and sinister."[6] In this research I wish to suggest the conceptual movement away from these meanings of the word and towards the more distant Proto-Germanic etymology of "hidden, concealed." In this way I hope to argue that tourism that is dark is much more than death-focused—thanatourism as some have called it—and is instead characterized by a range of activities, symbols and narrative constructions, actions and interpretations that include reflection on extreme forms of politics and culture, emphasis on avant-garde tendencies and aesthetic experimentalism, and consideration of taboo and forbidden topics.[7]

There are three general concerns with the previous constructions of dark tourism that inform this study. First, the literature focuses quite exclusively on what P.E. Tarlow indicates as places of tragedy or death, and what Chris Rojek suggests are "black spots," such as places to which tourists flock because of a great tragedy (for example, a celebrity death) having occurred there.[8] While such sites are significant, they are not the only ones that complete the oeuvre of such tourism. Again, I suggest the need to expand considerations of both dark tourism and dark theming to include meanings beyond death and the macabre. Second, much of the literature, while focused on site-specific examples of darkness, is unable to analyze the spatial, thematic, and narrative underpinnings of such sites.[9] Venues, whether museums or theme park attractions, are seen as staid and non-evolving spaces that consist of monolithic narratives in terms of their topics of death, tragedy, and genocide. As Paul William's suggests in his important *Memorial Museums*, spaces of darkness exhibit a "sense of spatial orchestration" that is part and parcel of the meanings of such spaces.[10] I thus aim to focus more attention on the spatial significance of darkness in this expanded analysis of dark tourism and theming. Third, many of the writings on dark tourism focus on interpretations of the form that suggest negativity in terms of the ways in which the spaces are perceived and understood by guests. Similarly, many of these analyses focus on binaries—pedagogy/entertainment, authentic/inauthentic, location-based/non-location-based, and others—with the suggestion being that certain dark venues (particularly theme park rides, "campy" dungeon attractions, and casinos) are inappropriate in terms of their use of such themes in their spaces. In this writing I will emphasize that the deconstruction of these binaries and simplistic assumptions about the themed representations of darkness is necessary.

With these three concerns in mind, let me suggest the concept of dark theming as a subset of dark tourism which describes the ways in which disturbing, controversial, political, or other hidden topics and concerns are narrativized and performed in spaces that include museums, theme parks, casinos, restaurants, and other venues. Throughout this chapter, I will express how dark theming is much more than a novel or entertaining way in which to orient the guest in a themed or immersive space. It is an approach to space that is simultaneously creative and controversial, innovative and off-putting, avant-garde and offensive. I will suggest a series of characteristics of dark theming that simultaneously illustrate its nature and express emerging tendencies of contemporary tourism, leisure, and popular amusement. Throughout this writing I will argue for the necessity of dark theming (and related forms of dark tourism) as a meaningful way of expressing existential, nihilistic, and postmodern interpretations, experiences, and ideas in the contemporary world.

Dark Theming's Doppelgänger

During my years as an employee trainer at Six Flags AstroWorld, I became intimately familiar with what might be called the doppelgänger image of the theme park. What often consumed my work as a trainer—especially my time conducting undercover, plain-clothes audits of park locations—involved my seeking out and erasing any traces of AstroWorld's dark side. If AstroWorld represented safe, clean, wholesome, family entertainment, it was my job to assess and act on situations in which the opposite—the doppelgänger—was present. An employee not properly dressed, excessive garbage outside of a restaurant, and many other examples, expressed the theme park's doppelgänger.[11] Even when a theme park is functioning in a near-perfect manner, signs of the theme park double are omnipresent. In such cases, the narratives of particular spaces or rides point to dark or absent meanings. One example of such a case is the fact that the foundational narratives of many rides and attractions deliberately eschew political, dark, disturbing, or existential meanings. Stephen Fjellman, in his text *Vinyl Leaves*, points to such exclusion of meaning in the Walt Disney World ride The Hall of Presidents. The Vietnam War, what would be considered a dark period of American history, is only referenced in an oblique manner on the ride.[12] Indeed, for many theme parks and themed spaces, particularly those that are part of larger brand or media conglomerates, the focus on avoiding negative associations with rides, attractions, or other entities is paramount.[13] Consider the recent controversies that have been attributed to SeaWorld theme parks in the wake of the documentary film *Blackfish* (2013). The film suggests that SeaWorld's use of killer whales in captivity is problematic for its impact on the whales and for deaths and injuries of human trainers that have occurred. In this case, we see that the doppelgänger is an absence that if made present could negatively impact the theme park and its ability to sell its products.

In 2005, the controversial artist Paul McCarthy opened a new installation in a London warehouse called Caribbean Pirates. The piece is notable for its riffing off of the famous Disney ride and now transmedia form Pirates of the Caribbean. The work occupied a series of rooms in the warehouse—each featuring video screens that depicted horrific and macabre pirates engaged in various acts of violence and debauchery. According to the artist, "We started working on that piece and made all these vignettes from the ride at Disney. It's a way of doing things: flip it around on itself so it's a new world."[14] Not unlike McCarthy's re-presentation of Disney's iconic ride, much of the fictional literature on theme parks, including Mitch Albom's sentimental *The Five People You Meet in Heaven*; Robert Stuart Nathan's *Amusement Park*; Lincoln Child's *Utopia*; Julian Barnes' satirical *England, England;* and many films, including *Rollercoaster* (1977); *Westworld* (1973); and *Futureworld* (1976), all tend to focus their concerns on the dark and Oedipal aspects of theme parks—mechanical park disasters, terrorism and violence, and bringing to the surface disturbing, tawdry, unwholesome, or inappropriate elements that are typically excluded from real-world places of amusement.[15] The most recent of such examples, the cult film *Escape from Tomorrow*

(2013), follows a similar path and brings in absent theme park signifiers like creeping corporatism and brandism and overcharged and anti-familial masculinity. These examples all point to the desire to give voice to the absent and dark double that is implied, and sometimes made manifest, in all theme parks. Theming's doppelgänger is, however, more than a mere Oedipal reflection of popular amusements; it represents the growing institutionalization of dark theming within the industry. I argue that the emergence of dark theming coincides with a new period of leisure and popular amusements in which the figure of the doppelgänger is especially privileged. As other areas of this writing will explore, the desire to give voice to the dark and absent sides of popular amusements is a trend that will likely result in more examples of darkness that is not implied or brought to the surface after the fact but is actually a foundation of the space from its inception.

Dark Theming: A Reflection of Postmondernity

In 2009, the London company Dutch By Design created a controversial duvet cover and sheet set that received notable attention in the popular press.[16] The company's design included a photographic representation of a cardboard box on the duvet cover and a similar photographic reproduction of what appears to be the concrete of a typical street. The design was meant to mimic the bedding arrangements of a homeless person—a fact that upset many critics in the press. The representations, they suggested, were created without taste and without concerns for the politics of homelessness. What made the controversy even more curious was the fact that Dutch By Design donated thirty percent of its profits from the bedding items to the UK charity Centrepoint. The company's representatives argued that "the Home Duvet lets you sleep under a cardboard box so a homeless person doesn't have to!"[17] Even with this caveat, many critics were of the opinion that such a re-presentation of reality was unwarranted. I suggest a counter-reading of Dutch By Design's bedding and use it to offer my next premise about dark theming, namely that it reflects the cultural, aesthetic, and economic orientations of postmodernity.

In *Dark Tourism*, John Lennon and Malcolm Foley argue that dark tourism represents "an intimation of post-modernity," particularly as it highlights the convergence of a series of facets of postmodernity—the interplay of media and communication technologies and resultant global-local blurring and time-space compressing, the intertwining of educational and commercial-consumer facets of the world, and, most significantly, the expression of "an anxiety and doubt about the project of modernity."[18] Dark themed venues like the DDR Museum in Berlin highlight these many facets of postmodernity and dark tourism that are identified by Lennon and Foley. The museum is one of many new European venues that focuses on the darkness of the past. In the case of the DDR Museum, the difficult era of East Germany and the Stasi is considered in highly technological, immersive, and interactive exhibits. At one point during the guest's visit to the space, he or she has the opportunity to take part in a faux Stasi interrogation.[19] Critics have charged that the museum is guilty of "Ostalgia"—a shallow re-presentation of Berlin's Communist past with little attention to education or critical analysis.[20] What is curious about such criticisms is that they appear to take issue with the manner in which context is developed in the space—the displays are too technological or interactive, there is less direct commentary about the displays given to the guest, there is too much of a consumer drive in the museum as it has a restaurant and a gift shop, are among the criticisms that have been suggested. To return to Lennon and Foley's work, I would argue that the museum reflects two of the facets they offer in terms of dark tourism's relationship with postmodernity—namely the concern with technology and media and the merging of educational and consumer tendencies—and that the responses to the DDR Museum's approach to content reflect anxiety with the new directions that are emerging in themed spaces. As well, the museum's blurred approach to presenting information to the visitor suggests opportunities to reformulate tired notions about the Truth and its sober representation in museum spaces.[21] In line with the Museum of Jurassic Technology, which I will consider later, the DDR Museum's approach to troubling and disturbing periods of history is accomplished by its postmondern use of technology, design, immersion, and narrative. Dark theming's interfacing with other facets of postmondernity—particularly those found in the worlds of new media, aesthetics, information design, and consumer culture—suggests that more museums will follow the DDR Museum's trends in the future.

Earlier, I wrote of the many controversies that surround the Emoya Luxury Hotel in Bloemfontein, South Africa. As I discussed, the main concerns about the Emoya centered on the idea that the re-presentation of a South African shantytown was in bad taste, offensive, and reflective of new forms of consumer society that are politically and morally unsavory. Indeed, these and many other issues should be considered in the context of this and other themed spaces that focus on dark issues. As Malte Steinbrink writes of slum tourism, one of the consequences of new interest in slums is a certain "ethnicization" of slumming that occurs when guests to such spaces of tourism develop ethnocentric stereotypes about those people who live in slums or socio-economically depressed places.[22] Certainly ethnocentrism is one possible result of the guest's immersion in a space like the Emoya, however, it may not be the only outcome. As a cultural anthropologist who studies themed and immersive spaces and a former theme park trainer, I would claim that there exists no one monolithic guest in the world and thus it is a misassumption to presume that every guest would leave a slum-themed space as a bigot or even a racist. In fact, in the world of postmondern tourism there is a new tendency in which guests seek out new, experimental, even dangerous, forms of tourism.[23] Certain guests who might visit or stay at the Emoya might indeed use their experience in the space as a form of experimental tourism. Likewise, other guests could leave the space entirely transformed and politically motivated to deal with pressing issues like those of post-Apartheid South Africa—including poverty and racism. At the moment in which the guest is forced to confront his or her complicity in *both* the systems of oppression that includes Apartheid South Africa and its correlates (violence, racism, and poverty) and in the consumerist re-presentation in which he or she is involved while staying at the hotel, this is the point at which one may argue that the Emoya offers an opportunity to consider dark issues in an entirely new and potentially efficacious manner.

A Reversal of the Pleasure-Pain Foundation

The last example of the Emoya Luxury Hotel illustrates another facet of dark theming in postmodern times—namely, there is a reversal of the pleasure-pain foundation of tourist and consumer spaces. Most themed and consumer spaces have at their heart the idea that everything within the space—the design, experiences, services, and products—is oriented to the guest's enjoyment and happiness. Service industry workers of such spaces often struggle to deal with this foundation since they are commonly asked to suspend their own happiness for the sake of the guest. But as the Emoya suggests, there may be something darker around the corner when it comes to the fulfillment of the guest's needs. In fact, many spaces and design experiments are slowly altering this assumption that seems so embedded in consumer space.

One of the most prescient spaces that has suggested this new orientation of space in terms of the denial of the guest's pleasure is the contemporary memorial museum or monument. During a series of research visits to Berlin in 2015, I had the opportunity to see, first hand, the ways in which Germans are addressing *Vergangenheitsbewältigung*, roughly, "struggling with or dealing with the past." Berlin has an especially dark history in terms of its National Socialist and Holocaust past and thus it is fitting that its many museums and monuments reflect this sense of struggle. Peter Eisenman's Memorial to the Murdered Jews of Europe was the first of my Berlin research trips that focused on the design responses to dark history. The memorial consists of over 2,700 concrete slabs of different heights that are arranged in rows utilizing changes in elevation, the result of which creates a certain unease in the individual who visits the space. The second space, Daniel Liebeskind's Jewish Museum Berlin, offers similar approaches to design as that of Eisenman's. The visitor notes the many examples of absence within the space—including "voids" that Liebeskind created to express "that which can never be exhibited when it comes to Jewish Berlin history: Humanity reduced to ashes" and the striking Holocaust Tower, which features a very small slit at the top through which sunlight enters—and is asked, as in the case of Eisenman's memorial, to comprehend the incomprehensible in terms of the Holocaust and Berlin's dark past.[24] Most powerful in the Jewish Museum Berlin is the Garden of Exile, which features forty-nine concrete pillars arranged on a 12-degree gradient that is designed, in Liebeskind's words, "to completely disorient the visitor. It represents a shipwreck of history."[25] Both of these examples of Berlin's memorialization and musealization of the past illustrate the requirement of the guest within each space to undergo discomfort as he or she moves through it. This is nothing new for museums and memorials that focus on the Holocaust and genocide, but what is unique is the role that architecture and design plays in this forcing of the guest to experience discomfort and existential anxiety.[26] But what can be said of the creation of such discomfort and pain in the guest in spaces beyond those of museums and memorials?

There is one striking example of the reversal of the pleasure-pain foundation in the world of theme parks—Disney's America in the 1990s. The park would have included historical reconstructions of a Civil War-era village, President's Square (representing the genesis of American democracy), a Native American-themed area, a Civil War-era themeland (complete with a Coney Island-like Monitor and Merrimack battle reconstruction), the landmark of Ellis Island and its representative ethnics, a factory town that denoted the American Industrial Revolution, and a Victory Field that referenced

Image 23.1. Memorial to the Murdered Jews of Europe by Peter Eisenman (Photo by Scott A. Lukas)

the American proclivity for warfare. Most notable in Disney's efforts to re-create the past in this failed theme park was the explicit focus on the Civil War and slavery. Early in the debates over Disney's America, satirical cartoons began to appear that ultimately mocked the idea of Disney dealing with a "serious" topic. Likely, it wasn't much of a help to Disney's cause when Disney officials offered, "We will show the Civil War with all its racial conflict. We want to make you feel what it was like to be a slave or what it was like to escape through the Underground Railroad."[27] In response to such statements, historian William Styron questioned that Disney's approach could "do anything but mock a theme as momentous as slavery…[no] combination of branding irons, slave ships or slave cabins, shackles, chained black people…or treks through the Underground Railroad could begin to define such a stupendous experience."[28] The criticisms of Disney's America and its proposed focus on dark history seem to have in common the notion of the sobriety of history or the idea that only certain spaces, such as museums, should have the right to consider disturbing periods of the past. Had the park been built, we may have witnessed a radical shift in the theme park industry such that a new purpose—and focus—of the guest would have been realized. If the expectation of the guest was to have a splendid time, this would have been likely met with the opposite force—an existential one that would have required the guest to, ironically, have a "bad" (or at least dark and uncomfortable) time at the park.[29]

Dark Theming and Existential and Nihilistic Tendencies

The idea of a space privileging the pain and discomfort of the guest, and not the reverse, reminds of another facet of dark theming—the arena of existentialism and nihilism. Interestingly, we may look to the past to see widespread evidence of existential and nihilistic trends in amusements. In the early part of the twentieth century, the amusement parks of Coney Island—including Sea Lion Park, Steeplechase Park, Luna Park, and Dreamland—offered forms of entertainment, rides, and attractions that covered topics ranging from the Boer War, the Galveston Flood, the Fall of Pompeii, the gates of hell, and offered oddities like "midget" worlds (Lilliputia), fire-fighting demonstrations, the Blowhole Theater, premature baby incubators, even the electrocution of an elephant named Topsy.[30] Many of these attractions also opened in world's fair midways and were ones that generated much of the popularity of late nineteenth- and early twentieth-century outdoor amusement spaces. The nature of these attractions, whose concerns ranged from disaster, warfare, death, religion, and "unnatural" humans, aligns with inherently existentialist and nihilistic tendencies. Existentialism suggests the concern with looking inward—at asking the questions about reality and existence that are not typically addressed in contexts of everyday life—while nihilism considers the absurdity of life, the moments of doubt and uncertainty, and life's capricious and unexplained nature.

Within the world of popular culture, there are numerous examples of such existentialist and nihilistic expressions. The worlds of film and popular television include greater emphasis on disturbing topics, anti-heroes, and narratives that move beyond the typical "good overcoming evil" and overtly happy and cheerful storylines.[31] Audiences are, more and more, desirous of narratives of popular culture that are complex, unfinished, depressing, and ultimately existential in that they require the audience member to deeply contemplate much more than the media form or story at hand. These tendencies have influenced the world of themed and immersive spaces, particularly as we are now witnessing spaces that are reminiscent of dark and disturbing examples that were a part of the Coney Island amusement park tradition.

One of the most curious and controversial of contemporary themed spaces is the Heart Attack Grill in Las Vegas. Not unlike the many other spaces considered in this work, this themed restaurant has received notable negative attention in the

Image 23.2. The Galveston Flood, Coney Island (From the collection of Scott A. Lukas)

Image 23.3. Heart Attack Grill, Las Vegas (Photo by Scott A. Lukas)

national press. In no small part this is due to the unique approach to theming at the restaurant. In 2015, while conducting research at the venue, I was surprised to read these signs on the front of the restaurant:

I am probably the only restaurateur in the entire world who is unapologetically telling you that my food is bad for you, that it will kill you, and that you should stay away from it...We're passed [sic] the point of no return at the Heart Attack Grill, we have blood on our hands at this point...These people have the right to weigh what they want to weigh, to eat what they want to eat, and I have the right to serve them that food!...I make good money selling unhealthy food, but at least I'm honest.

These and many other quotes by Jon Basso, the restaurant's founder, adorned the front of the space during my visit. The quotes suggest the complexity of the construction of dark theming, especially in the contradictory messages they contain—on the one hand, Basso takes responsibility for serving unhealthy food, and on the other, he argues for the right of any person to eat what he or she wants to eat. The restaurant also features a hospital theme, scantily clad waitresses dressed as nurses, a scale for guests to weigh themselves (with the offer of "Over 350 Lbs Eats Free"), a "Last Supper" painting featuring all the various recognizable fast food cartoon characters, and menu items that reflect the theming—Single Bypass Burger, Flatliner Fries, and other variations. As a themed space, the restaurant is like many other spaces in that it focuses on a consistent theme that is noticeable and evocative, but what is so obviously different about the Heart Attack Grill is the fact that it has meditated on its theme at such a conceptual and political level.[32] Lost in the media's moralism about the restaurant is the venue's uniqueness in terms of how it has earnestly and reflexively focused on its complicity in nutritional issues. The Heart Attack Grill's founder Jon Basso has called his guests the "avant-garde of nutritional risk takers," and while this use of the avant-garde may seem tongue in cheek, the nature of such an existentially focused restaurant suggests some interesting affinities with the world of conceptual aesthetics.[33]

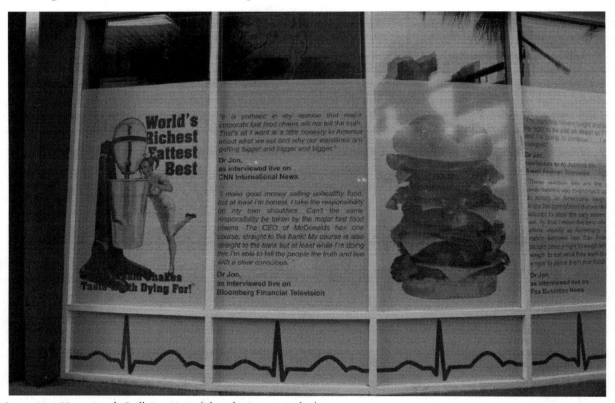

Image 23.4. Heart Attack Grill, Las Vegas (Photo by Scott A. Lukas)

A Conceptual Side of Dark Theming

Conceptual spaces are ones that challenge the traditional understandings, uses, and constructions of theming and immersion. Such venues are "type breakers" as they suggest new ways of understanding traditional spaces and, indeed, they point us in new directions because as conceptual spaces they get us to think about theming and immersion (and their referents) in the deepest senses possible. The Museum of Jurassic Technology in Culver City, California is one example of a conceptual space. One could call it a museum, but this misses the point of the space, which is to challenge our perceptions of what a museum is. An exhibit like the one in which a bat is suspended mid-flight in a piece of solid concrete—and which, it is said, was to have gotten stuck in the middle of the object while using its unique technique of traveling through solid objects—asks the guest to reflect on the idea of a museum itself, including the issue of what is true and untrue in it. A second space that is worth mentioning is Dennis Severs' House in London. Like the Museum of Jurassic Technology, Dennis Severs' House challenges the visitor's perceptions of a museum or interpretive center. Many of the exhibits are offered in fanciful ways that seem to "wink" at the guest, as if playing a joke on him or her. As well, an evocative use of sensory design—ranging from aural, olfactory, and other senses—suggests a much different approach to the staid museum that lacks full sensory and evocative potentials. Conceptual spaces are type breakers particularly because they force the guest to reconsider everything that he or she had known before about the type of space, issue, or experience at hand. Neither the Museum of Jurassic Technology nor Dennis Severs' House are, per se, spaces of explicit dark theming, but their nature as conceptual spaces—as places that challenge guests in so many unique ways—suggests an allegiance to the other spaces described in this research and a reminder of the need to revise old and limited definitions of dark tourism.

Dark theming indicates a growing conceptual trend in popular amusements—a trend that asks critical questions of designers, operators, and guests of themed spaces, as well as their cultural critics. Spaces that rely on a conceptual focus suggest that the guests who visit them use them to contemplate existential, social, political, and other issues. Because of this focus, we might say that such spaces exhibit the idea of what Umberto Eco called the "open work"—a "text" that allows the "reader" to make conclusions and interpretations because of the room, or opportunity, that the "author" has given him or her.[34] The desire to create more open and contemplative spaces will, no doubt, necessitate new innovations in the worlds of themed and immersive space design, but one curious issue about contemporary spaces—especially those that explicitly deal with dark or controversial topics—is whether some designers will create innovative conceptual spaces that nonetheless lack important foci of guest input, reflexivity, and the like. As an example, we note the growth of toilet- and Nazi-themed restaurants and cafes around the world. Both types of themed spaces are dark spaces in that they deal with controversial or difficult topics. We may consider such spaces ones that exhibit what Georges Bataille denoted as the "low" or that which is underground, subversive, and Rabelaisian.[35] While toilet- and Nazi-themed restaurants express Bataille's "low," they, quite problematically, fail at political levels. In the case of toilet-themed venues, the "low" begins and ends with the toilet bowl. Never is the guest asked to contemplate issues that could be associated with toilets—excrement, filth, waste, sacrifice, and so forth—instead the guest is left to be simply amused with the ubiquitous toilets within the space. In the case of the Nazi-themed restaurant, unfortunately the guest is not asked to reflect on the ills of National Socialism, the Holocaust, or associated issues; instead, it would appear that as in most of the cases of such dark themed venues, the guest is asked to simply eat and take in the décor—a pure pandering to the lowest common denominator of shocking design and materiality.[36]

Conceptual spaces of the sort that I have described in this writing should do more than merely shock us. As well, they may do more than simply get us to think about the world in more avant-garde senses. They may suggest an awakening within the world of themed space design in which designers will tackle more complex projects that push the limits of the past. In other work, I have suggested that conceptual space will likely involve nine areas of innovation of the future—ranging from the increased use of irony, to mysticism, reflexivity, and flux.[37] One area of new emphasis involves the use of dark theming for reflexive purposes.

Reflexivity and Pedagogy in Themed and Immersive Spaces

While conducting research at the 2015 World Exposition in Milan, Italy, I came across the interesting space of the Swiss Pavilion. Like much of the expo, the Swiss Pavilion emphasizes the expo's overall theme of food through the lens of scarcity and environmentalism. What is more is that the designers of the pavilion emphasized that scarcity must be connected to issues of personal responsibility and the need for praxis or action in social settings. As they state:

> The journey through the towers is guided by this leitmotif, thus prompting visitors to reflect—on the basis of their own personal experience—on the global availability of food and sustainable development throughout the food value chain. Visitors will be free to take away or consume any amount of the products. How much will be

left for later visitors—and for how long—will be determined by the consumer behaviour and level of awareness of each visitor.[38]

The pavilion is constructed with four towers—each of which has a finite amount of four key food items (coffee, apple, water, salt), each chosen for their relevance as Swiss foodway symbols as well as their connection to key issues of global sustainability and scarcity. Within the space, the guest is challenged in two senses—each of which emphasizes two important facets of dark theming. These include reflexivity or the tendency of such theming to force the guest to reflect on his or her own condition, often resulting in realizations of complicity in systems of oppression, and pedagogy, or the use of theming to instruct, didactically, in such a way that the guest may be changed after visiting the space. As Paul Williams notes, many memorial museums are accustomed to using both reflexivity and pedagogy as means of creating empathy between guests and victims of the past, present, or future during the course of the visit.[39] Yet, there is a difference in terms of the constructions of darkness that we note in a space like the Swiss Pavilion at the 2015 World Exposition in Milan and the memorial museums described by Williams. In the case of some museums of genocide, the emphasis on victimization and troubling acts of the past may not always inspire the guest to take action in the present. In the case of other spaces, including the Museum of Tolerance in Los Angeles and the Swiss Pavilion at the exposition, the guest is asked to both reflect and to take a position. In the Museum of Tolerance case, the visitor is asked to focus on his or her own prejudice, hopefully for the purpose of change; in the case of the Swiss Pavilion, the individual is forced to reflect on the consumption "problem" (as in a brain teaser or scenario) at hand—the scarcity of the four food items—and then is asked to analogize that scarcity with the overall shortage of food in the world as well as related environmental and social issues.

Image 23.5. Swiss Pavilion, World Expo 2015, Milan (Photo by Scott A. Lukas)

As pedagogical venues in which guests are asked to consider disturbing topics in reflexive senses, such spaces also suggest a last facet of dark theming—that of the political and of social justice. Within the world of popular culture and consumerism, more and more, we see examples of politics, ethics, and social justice being a primary concern of the company or brand at hand, the act of consumption on the part of the consumer, and the overall meaning that is attributed to the entirety of the brand or product as it is a part of the world. Patagonia's Footprint Chronicles, which focus on the company's responsibility to the environment and its workers, is one example of a new corporate agenda that considers social justice as part and parcel of its operation and brand identity.⁴⁰ A quasi-themed space, Whole Foods, also expresses similar commitments to the environment, social justice, and its workers. In 2014, Whole Foods in Reno, Nevada themed a small area of its store to resemble a Ghanaian indigenous dwelling and with it included information about "Investing in a Future without Poverty." Some critics have expressed, somewhat cynically, that such examples of consumer and brand activism are ineffective, at best, or a ploy to increase sales, at worst.⁴¹ Theme parks, including Disney's Animal Kingdom, have also invited guests to ponder environmental, political, and social justice issues all the while partaking in experiences that are deemed to be entertaining.

The challenge in these and many other cases is to avoid the harsh dichotomies and simplifications that are often suggested by critics and instead partake in the interesting and innovative spaces—both material and discursive—that invite the most critical of debates. Not only will we see more innovative and exciting theming and immersion of the sort exhibited at the 2015 World Expo in Milan, we will likely come to realize that much more is at stake in the world of popular themed amusements than we had realized. With new theming and immersive designs, we may only hope that the moral, political, social, and existential narratives that they entail, as well as their criticism, will be as innovative.

Notes

1. Maurice Blanchot, *The Writing of the Disaster* (Lincoln: University of Nebraska Press, 1986), 4. Note: a video of this chapter is available at <https://youtu.be/sHLSPuGJdoA>.

2. Alissa Walker, "A Fake Slum for Luxury Tourists Who Don't Want to See Real Poverty," *Gizmodo*, November 25, 2013.

3. In addition to the Shanty Town, the Emoya has a second hotel that features a Basotho Village. See <http://www.emoya.co.za/p17/accommodation/emoya-estate-for-luxury-accommodation-in-bloemfontein.html>.

4. I originally suggested the concept of dark theming in 2007 and hope to use this writing as a reevaluation of that initial work. See Scott A. Lukas, "A Politics of Reverence and Irreverence: Social Discourse on Theming Controversies," in *The Themed Space: Locating Culture, Nation, and Self*, ed. Scott A. Lukas (Lanham, MD: Lexington, 2007), 271–293.

5. Philip Stone, "A Dark Tourism Spectrum: Towards a Typology of Death and Macabre Related Tourist Sites," *TOURISM: An Interdisciplinary International Journal* 54, no. 2 (2006): 146.

6. Online Etymology Dictionary, <http://www.etymonline.com/index.php?term=dark>.

7. For more on thanatourism see, A.V. Seaton, "Guided by the Dark: From *Thanatopsis* to Thanatourism," *International Journal of Heritage Studies* 2, no. 4 (1996): 234–244.

8. P.E. Tarlow, "Dark Tourism: The Appealing 'Dark Side' of Tourism and More," in *Niche Tourism–Contemporary Issues, Trends and Cases*, ed. Marina Novelli (Amsterdam: Elsevier, 2005), 47–58. Chris Rojek, "Fatal Attractions," in *Ways of Escape: Transformations in Leisure and Travel* (London: Macmillian, 1993), 136–172.

9. One exception is Paul Williams, *Memorial Museums: The Global Rush to Commemorate Atrocities* (Oxford: Berg, 2007).

10. Williams, *Memorial Museums*, 77.

11. Another example of this involved many of the park's staff working feverishly to scrape bubblegum off of the ground prior to the visit of Six Flags' CEO at the time, Bob Pittman. For more, see Scott A. Lukas, "How the Theme Park Gets Its Power: Lived Theming, Social Control, and the Themed Worker Self," in *The Themed Space: Locating Culture, Nation, and Self*, ed. Scott A. Lukas (Lanham, MD: Lexington, 2007), 183–206.

12. Stephen M. Fjellman, *Vinyl Leaves: Walt Disney World and America* (Boulder, CO: Westview, 1992), 106.

13. This section is influenced by the literature on the doppelgänger brand image or the "family of disparaging images and meanings about a

brand that circulate throughout popular culture." Craig J. Thompson, Aric Rindfleisch, and Zeynep Arsel, "Emotional Branding and the Strategic Value of the Doppelgänger Brand Image," *Journal of Marketing* 70 (January 2006): 50.

14. Anne Ellegood, "The Isle of Porcine Romance," *MOUSSE*–Archive–Issue #24–Paul McCarthy, <http://moussemagazine.it/articolo.mm?id=562>.

15. Mitch Albom, *The Five People You Meet in Heaven* (New York: Hyperion, 2003). Robert Stuart Nathan, *Amusement Park* (New York: Dial Press, 1977). Lincoln Child, *Utopia* (New York: Doubleday, 2002). Julian Barnes, *England, England* (New York: Vintage, 2000). For more on these contexts of death and themed spaces, see Scott A. Lukas, "The Theme Park and the Figure of Death," *InterCulture* 2 (May 2005, <https://www.academia.edu/273918/The_Theme_Park_and_the_Figure_of_Death>.

16. Anon, "Homeless-Inspired Sheets Bring Street into the Bedroom," *The Huffington Post*, March 18, 2010 <http://www.huffingtonpost.com/2009/10/22/homeless-inspired-sheets_n_330908.html>.

17. See <http://www.dutchbydesign.com/home-duvet-cover-double>.

18. John Lennon and Malcolm Foley, *Dark Tourism* (London: Continuum, 2000), 11.

19. For more on the DDR Museum and other dark themed spaces, see my video page on YouTube <https://www.youtube.com/playlist?list=PLTetG9GSbApBYkZGa2dlcKflJVmNGQy6a>.

20. Susan Stone, "DDR Living: Museum Offers 'Ostalgic' Look at East Germany," *Spiegel*, July 20, 2006, <http://www.spiegel.de/international/ddr-living-museum-offers-ostalgic-look-at-east-germany-a-427579.html>.

21. As Neil Harris has astutely said, "Today's museums…are no longer accepted simply as custodians of truth." Neil Harris, "Museums and Controversy: Some Introductory Reflections," *The Journal of American History*, December 1995: 1104.

22. Malte Steinbrink, "'We Did the Slum!'–Urban Poverty Tourism in Historical Perspective," *Tourism Geographies* 12, no. 2 (2012): 213.

23. Rachael Antony and Joël Henry, *The Lonely Planet Guide to Experimental Travel* (Melbourne: Lonely Planet, 2005).

24. See, <http://www.jmberlin.de/main/EN/04-About-The-Museum/01-Architecture/01-libeskind-Building.php>.

25. See, <http://www.jmberlin.de/main/EN/04-About-The-Museum/01-Architecture/01-libeskind-Building.php>.

26. Another excellent example of such a memorial is the Monument against Fascism in Hamburg-Harburg, Germany.

27. Mike Wallace, *Mickey Mouse History and Other Essays on American Memory* (Philadelphia: Temple University Press, 1996), 164.

28. Wallace, *Mickey Mouse History*, 165.

29. For more on the Disney's America controversies, see Scott A. Lukas, "History Magic: From Coney Island to the Theme Park," <https://www.academia.edu/3744931/History_Magic>. Interestingly, in 2015 the artist Bansky opened a theme park that was a parody of Disneyland. It was known as Dismaland. For more see, Christopher Beanland, "Theme Parks Continue to Draw in Thrill-Seekers Despite The Risks–So Why Are We so Addicted?" *The Independent*, September 16, 2015, <http://www.independent.co.uk/travel/news-and-advice/theme-parks-continue-to-draw-in-thrillseekers-despite-the-risks--so-why-are-we-so-addicted-10483525.html>.

30. Rem Koolhaas, Delirious New York (New York: Montacelli Press, 1994). See "Coney Island: The Technology of the Fantastic," 29–79.

31. For more on the general influences of nihilism on popular culture, see Thomas Hibbs, *Shows About Nothing: Nihilism in Popular Culture* (Waco, TX: Baylor University Press, 2012); on nihilism and film, see Scott A. Lukas and John Marmysz, "Introduction: Fear, Cultural Anxiety, Transformation and the Film Remake," in *Fear, Cultural Anxiety and Transformation: Horror, Science Fiction and Fantasy Films Remade*, eds. Scott A. Lukas and John Marmysz (Lanham, MD: Lexington Books, 2008); and for more on the antihero trend in popular culture, Scott A. Lukas, *The Immersive Worlds Handbook: Designing Theme Parks and Consumer Spaces* (New York: Focal, 2012), 51 and Scott A. Lukas, "Controversial Topics: Pushing the Limits in Themed and Immersive Spaces," *Attractions Management* 4 (2015): 50–54.

32. Another example of a space that has suggested a political and existential agenda served with its food is the Conflict Kitchen in Pittsburgh, Pennsylvania. The restaurant serves cuisine from nations that are in conflict with the United States. See, <http://conflictkitchen.org>. A second space worthy of mention is Parque EcoAlberto's (Mexico) Caminata Nocturna. The night hike is intended to replicate an illegal and dangerous border crossing. See, <http://ecoalberto.com.mx>.

33. See, <http://www.heartattackgrill.com/heart-attack-grill-s-media-contact-information.html>.

34. Umberto Eco, *The Open Work* (Cambridge: Harvard University Press, 1989).

35. See Denis Hollier, *Against Architecture: The Writings of Georges Bataille* (Cambridge: MIT Press, 1992), 102.

36. For more on the Nazi-themed restaurant trend, see Scott A. Lukas, *Theme Park* (London: Reaktion, 2008), 212–214.

37. See Scott A. Lukas, "Research in Consumer Spaces: Emergent Issues," <https://www.academia.edu/3746281/Research_in_Consumer_Spaces>.

38. Swiss Pavilion, <http://www.padiglionesvizzero.ch/en/swiss-pavillon-2/the-towers-3/>.

39. Williams, *Memorial Museums*, 33.

40. See <http://www.patagonia.com/us/footprint>.

41. See Josée Johnston, "The Citizen-Consumer Hybrid: Ideological Tensions and the Case of Whole Foods Market," *Theory and Society* 37, no. 3 (June 2008): 229–270.

PART IX

The View of the Critic

Municipal Baths and Beach, Coney Island, N. Y.

24

Complicated Agency

By Brian Lonsway

I want to start with the obvious, or at least what is obvious to me: themed environments are authentic. They are in every way genuine, original, real, primary. They are of their own, and fashion themselves after other environments not to imitate them, but rather to reconstruct or re-contextualize them in new (authentic) ways. Yet somehow—unfathomably to me—this is not an accepted truism, especially in certain scholarly circles. There, it appears essential to position themed environments in an invented hierarchy of authenticity, below environments defined *prima facie* as "real," or "original," or (perhaps most frightening to me) "natural." The goal of this positioning is ultimately to empower human agency with a comfort of truth that gives us a reason to exist, authentically. The "fake," by denying us contact with the real, must somehow make our humanity, our *raison d'être*, less valuable. But are we not simply playing a semantic game when we decry a real experience as fake? Whether or not a themed environment may appear to simulate another (apparently not themed) environment, in the way Las Vegas' Venetian Hotel and Casino is fashioned from references to Venetian architecture, my experience of the Venetian is every bit as real as my experience of Venice. The Venetian itself: every bit as real as Venice itself. My experience in a themed environment, constructed and narratively framed as it may be, is real, sensorial, and personally meaningful; as a result of such an experience, have I not in fact become more empowered with the complexities of my reality?

What underlies the discrimination of authentic from inauthentic environments—and the naïve and unfortunate association of theming with the latter—is the belief that the creators of themed environments wish somehow to be duplicitous, to trick us into believing that we are where we are not or who we are not (thus the corporeal fear of becoming "fake," etymologically to be of obscure origin, to be "in the fold.") But the history of themed environment design, from ancient cultures to the brandscape, reveals this not to be the case. The theme is meant, quite explicitly, to complement our identities; to enrich our play; to provide a more curious, and often more provocative, reality rather than to detract from it. Distraction, maybe; detraction, no.

Only by acknowledging the authenticity of the themed environment can we begin with a foundation for critical inquiry that considers them alongside every other environment of our construction (material or cultural): parks, cities, houses, cemeteries, hospitals, and so forth. (It's worth noting that these, too, have been themed either implicitly or explicitly, to varying degrees depending on their own collective histories and cultural contexts.) The value of this point of departure is that we are able to better understand the agencies of and behind themed environments, as well as what the impacts of these agencies have on their inhabitation, than if themed environments are taken to be something other than or apart from our "more authentic" environments. We are, in other words, able to level the playing field and open our inquiry into the themed environment armed with valuable tools of spatial/environmental critique that have been evolved for the analysis of other spatial forms. And vice versa. Critiquing Disneyland, in other words, should fundamentally be no different than critiquing the Victoria and Albert, or my house.

None of this is to say, however, that there isn't something complicated about the themed environment, especially as the lines blur between what is and what isn't explicitly themed. In 2009's *Making Leisure Work: Architecture and the Experience Economy*, I pulled apart many of the narrative constructions of the themed environment, seeking to better understand what makes it tick and how its spatialized narratives have impacted lived experience.[1] Whether exploring the visual design techniques of a mid-century American theme park, the cultural veracity of cheese-making in a Japanese themed residential village in the Netherlands, or the psychological impacts of themed environment design for Alzheimer's care, I have to testify to the often complicated roles that people are anticipated, expected, or required to play to make the themed experience a success. Whether an owner, designer, visitor, resident, employee, or critic, the very real—very authentic—impact of the themed environment is to complicate your agency at the service of the thematic backstory.

This, in fact, is the art and science of the themed environment: the careful material construction and managerial maintenance of the "sticky" (to borrow Malcolm Gladwell's term for a brand narrative that sticks with you) backstory—the (literally) composed narratives that guide all design and construction. Understanding these acts as intending to complement rather than deceive allows the critic to see their power on the terms of the creators: a power to expand the narrative potentials of the built environment. As I and others have written, this is the core inspiration of the so-called "Experience Economy."[2] In a saturated glocalized service economy where offerings can easily lack distinction, the tenants of the Experience Economy propose that human experience itself is an essential medium of differentiation in the contemporary marketplace. B. Joseph Pine and James Gilmore, the prime movers of the Experience Economy framework, offer that the customer (transformed by a brand experience) is the real product of the Experience Economy. Pine and Gilmore's writings and consultancy build upon the already well-established efforts of Hollywood, the Walt Disney Company, and their successors to merge the storytelling capacity of spatial and cultural experience with the storytelling needs of successful public relations/branding campaigns. Not all theming is so explicitly tied to branding initiatives of course; at its core, theming is ultimately about impacting human experience through immersion in a narrative. But when tied to a company's bottom-line through advertising or customer experience budgets, the very expensive propositions of the Experience Economy are meticulously planned and managed, translating to an obsessive management of the narratively-framed customer experience. In the Disney theme parks for example, where no expense is spared to assure a fluid and consistent experience for the visitor, attractions are repaired and visually touched-up nightly and every detail from hardware (screws, hinges, and so forth) to hairnets are consistent with an area's backstory documents.[3]

The realization of these details, whether as obsessive as Disney's or more akin to those informing our experiences at Barnes and Noble, Starbucks, Trader Joe's, or Chipotle, is a significant design undertaking that requires intense collaboration between designers and brand managers. Companies rely on designers' abilities to create immersive experiences across media (including space, like the space of a retail outlet, for example) that directly engage customers. But what are they engaging? Sensory capacity? Physical movement? Psychological aptitude? Mental acuity? All of these, yes, but also quite importantly: human agency. If the transformation of the customer through a transformational experience *is* the product of the Experience Economy, then it is precisely the impact on human agency that is the holy grail of brand marketing.

The entirety of the theme-based experience economy is to affect agency in this way: ideally, to fold in layers of positive experience that leave one feeling "in good hands," "taken care of," "enriched," "fulfilled," or "transformed" by the company or organization in question. If I want a consistently known coffee experience around the world, Starbucks will dependably fulfill this desire. If I want to feel like I'm bargain shopping while embracing euro-contemporary design, Ikea will take care of me. These stores—these experiences—do not destroy or defeat my human agency (in limited scope of this example, to remove my ability to shop elsewhere). Rather, they fold in additional layers of brand affiliation that are meant to complement (and complicate) my spatial experience.

The more spatially immersive a theme (at the service of a commercial brand or not), the greater the effect on agency there can be. The fantastical narratives underpinning a theme park (and the design realizations that spatialize them) are intended to immerse the visitor completely within the story, actively shifting the visitor's agency toward that of a role-player within the narrative itself. Of course, the shift can never be complete. Disney doesn't expect to trick a visitor to Tomorrowland to believe that they're visiting the future. Rather, they seek to convince them that they are believably visiting a segment of a theme park that is based on stories about the future. They are concerned, in other words, with providing an authentic experience of a real place (called Tomorrowland) in the real world. Similarly, while much has been written about the ersatz of Main Street, U.S.A., the nineteenth-century-Americana-themed entrance promenade at Disneyland and its progeny, the specific design goal of Main Street, U.S.A. is to embed visitors in a controlled experience of the very twentieth-century Main Street, U.S.A.—not of a simulacrum of an idealized nineteenth-century American main street. Walt may have modeled the company's first design on a mash-up of waning American main streets, but it was to Disneyland he was drawing them, not to those waning urban centers.

"Fake," as I mentioned earlier, has at its etymological roots a notion of folding: specifically, a loop one makes when coiling a rope.[4] From there, through senses of concealed origins, contrivances, and ultimately counterfeits, fake has come to its present definition. A fake, we take for granted, is something to be dismissed, something not authentic. "Complicated," too, finds its roots in the fold: here, a folding together.[5] But the complication is not a fake; both may be folds, but they are folds of a very different nature. Complications reveal entanglements *within* our (authentic) experiences; fakes conceal their loops outside of them. It is for this reason that I find it essential for a study of themed environments that we see their folds of narrative as complications rather than fakes. It is the very authenticity of the themed environment that complicates our lived experiences; it isn't a reductively polarizing matter of authentic experience versus fake experience. Rather, it is a complicated matter of complicated experiences that the layers of narrative impose on us. And it also complicates my job as a critic. But that's the fun part.

My choice of "complicated" over "complex" is intentional. I rest my understanding on their difference with the following quite simple explanation by Paul Cilliers.

> If a system—despite the fact that it may consist of a huge number of components—can be given a complete description in terms of its individual constituents, such a system is merely *complicated*. Things like jumbo jets or computers are complicated. In a *complex* system, on the other hand, the interaction among constituents of the system, and the interaction between the system and its environment, are of such a nature that the system as a whole cannot be fully understood simply by analysing its components. Moreover, these relationships are not fixed, but shift and change, often as a result of self-organisation.[6]

I foist the term "complicated" on the question of agency to argue that even the strange layers of experience that affect our activities and our choices in the themed environment are "merely" complicated, and not complex. Of course there are complex aspects to everything, and the themed environment is no exception; I write this well aware of the limits of the claim. Just try to wrangle with the history and politics of the formation of Walt Disney's Retlaw Enterprises and Reedy Creek Development District, both created to surreptitiously acquire Florida land and form a new form of geo-political entity to manage it.[7] I am not intending to suggest that agency itself is not a complex concept, but rather to argue that, within the complexities of our agency, the impacts of the themed environment are but complications.

The framework of agency that I am using here is one loosely affiliated with actor network theory, built upon in recent years by a handful of architectural theorists seeking to better understand the politics of our relationship to the built environment.[8] These politics involve multiple agencies that include the activities of real estate developers, building owners, municipalities and their representatives, designers, engineers, employees, residents, visitors, passers-by, and others. And, as offered to us by at least certain interpretations of actor network theory, we can include the agency of the objects and artifacts produced by these individuals and their activities. As humans, we employ this agency to act in particular ways in particular situations, with and against the myriad other agencies in our contexts. In architectural theory, the understanding of an agency constituted by the capabilities, capacities, and powers of the actor-network—the interchanges between components in a system—has opened up a rich exploration of the complexities of our power relationships to the built environment. I have argued that the theming narratives themselves—including the bodies that invent and manage them—are essential actors in this network, shifting (complicating) the kind of agency we have when our physical spatial environments are constructed to maintain adherence to a sticky backstory. We are required to engage these stories, even if our engagement is to reject or avoid them, and construct our agency in direct relationship to them. Is there a story? What is it? Am I part of it? How? What do I feel about the story? Is it changing my behavior? What do I think of this? How can or should I act?

My experience with diverse rhetorics surrounding the themed environment, from personal testimonials and corporate ephemera to scholarly writing, fandom websites, and "critical" guidebooks, has revealed a tendency to oversimplify the impacts of these constructions. On one hand, there is the enthusiastic fan who sees Disney as simply a fun place to visit without acknowledging its vast commercial efforts to wrap its visitors ever more inside its brand. On the other hand, there is the critic who dismisses the themed environment outright, as either a corporate blight on the landscape or simply a subject not worthy of study. None of these simplifications help us advance a productive and proactive critical theory of—or critical engagement with—the themed environment. A more richly nuanced understanding is required, one that reveals the shifted agencies of the themed environment, but which does not mark them impenetrably complex.

What I hope to offer with the provocation of complicated agency is not only a more direct embrace of the nuances of recent re-engagements with questions of agency in the context of the built environment, but a way to enfold layers of once-perceived contradictions, dualist dialectics, and over-simplified power dynamics into a more relevant and empowering critical framework that helps us better understand the effects of the themed environment.

KidZania

I would like to take as my case study a recently formed and rapidly expanding themed environment that manifests these complications in a profound way: KidZania. KidZania is itself a complicated concept. Founded in 1996 under the vision of Xavier López Ancon and Luis Javier Laresgoiti as a hybrid day care center/entertainment destination, KidZania (originally *La Ciudad de los Niños*, or The Children's City/The City of Children) currently manages 20 "edutainment" destinations across the globe (with others announced for the next few years) for four to fourteen year olds. Each location features a diverse set of experiences based on adult jobs, from airline pilots to firefighters and car mechanics to fast food burger flippers. These are set within a themed interior designed around the principles of a western-style streetscape, with each venue encapsulated in its own thematic enclosure inside the various buildings (see image 24.1). The streetscapes are generally two-story, although everything is scaled down to kids' size, making it a bit uncanny for a 6'-2" voyeur like myself to even enter the interior's interiors. (In fact, parents are strongly discouraged from entering the "active" areas so kids can be entirely only their own with the center's own adult leaders.) Radio broadcasts created by kids in the on-air studio are carried on radios throughout the center, newborn babies are taken care of, back accounts are opened, surgeries are performed, pizzas are made, and degrees are sought. KidZania is kind of "Job Experience Theme Park" or Grownup-land.

The jobs in KidZania operate in each center's own narratively constructed civic sphere according to the principles of (or at least the narrative of the principals of) the free market. Given 50 KidZos (the local currency) upon entry, children can earn additional KidZos "working" at various venues, with a sliding scale of incomes roughly modeled after adult job salaries. KidZos can be spent as well, sometimes to buy things like groceries (plastic props which have to be returned to the store), sometimes to buy trinkets or memorabilia (that are then owned by the purchaser), and sometimes to pay for designated work experiences. Should KidZanians open a bank account, they can deposit their KidZos and manage them through a debit card. Should they pay for and sit in on a college course, their earnings go up. If they're unsure of which job to start with, children can go the job placement center, fill out a skill-evaluation test, and receive a recommended career path. Each venue has around 60 jobs that can be performed, each located in its own iconographically styled interior that is arrayed along the streetscape of KidZania.

It is truly a remarkable experience. I have a young child, and while I visited Dubai's KidZania solo, I couldn't help but see it through his eyes. It is a playground that materializes all the props, clothing, and environmental and sensorial cues that form the ecology of a child's fantasy role-play. Their carefully crafted spatial relationships maintain the grander theme of KidZania, immersing the child not only within each activity, but across them, in a narrative of KidZanian urban life and political identity. It is a highly immersive experience, for the adult as well as the kid, and as such, really mucks with our sense of agency.

KidZania's complications begin even within its own identity. KidZania is both the name of the company and the name of the geo-political identity that each venue portrays. KidZania is described as a kind of nation-state—formed through political foment among children—with each venue ambiguously serving both as a replication of *the* KidZanian urban center and/or *one of* the many independent KidZanian cities. Within the company's corporate hierarchy, directors of each venue are considered (and semi-officially titled) mayors, with governors above them, and with Lopez himself as president (although he jokes he should be considered dictator because he wasn't elected).[9]

Image 24.1. Part of the streetscape in KidZania Dubai (Photo by Brian Lonsway)

The backstory of KidZania's political identity is an origin story, filled with frustration, liberation, and independence as its core themes.

The Time Had Come

The kids of the world became utterly fed up. Looking at the way the adults were running the world had become an exercise in exasperation. Governments operated inefficiently, societies were becoming inequitable, valuable resources were routinely squandered and values were seemingly more and more negotiable.

With principles wavering and violence increasing, it became apparent that kids would be inheriting a less than ideal world. Something had to be done and they were the ones prepared to do it.

The kids decided to create their own nation

This was a world full of opportunities where kids could assert themselves and be responsible. This was a world full of possibilities for sharing ideas and gaining knowledge. And this was a world where kids could think and act independently from adults. What the kids envisioned, was a real world made perfect which ultimately made it "the place" where kids wanted to be.

A declaration is made

Following the spirit of many independent thinkers in history, kids decided to mark this moment and write an official Declaration of Independence. This proclaimed their sovereignty as a group united in purpose and announced their new world's existence.[10]

Ultimately, the backstory continues, a *League of RightZ* is established, with a group of mascots defined as RightZkeepers appointed "to guarantee that KidZania's belief system would always be represented and also to ensure the RightZ would be remembered forever."[11] This is followed by an anthem, a flag, a language (English that selectively uses "K" or "Z" for effect, like "Kai" for hi, or "Z-U" for see-you) the currency (KidZos), and the governance system that moves from president, locally elected kid's Congrezzes, and on-site adult "Zupervisors."[12]

Within this political structure, work (on the part of the kids-as-visitors) occurs within a public-private continuum (which jobs are modeled on the public sector and which are modeled on the private sector varies from country to country—"country" here referring to the officially recognized geopolitical entity within which a KidZania sits). Some jobs, such as fighting fires and policing streets are more or less identified with the culturally recognized costumes and symbols of the host country. Others result from close partnerships established with national or international brands.

> *A child, whose responsible caregivers choose to wait in the second floor Parent's Lounge (where children are not allowed), decides to visit the Coca-Cola bottling plant to "learn the process of manufacturing their own bottle of Coca-Cola, from the bottle hygiene and cleansing process, to filling and packaging."*[13] *After paying with her KidZania credit card (filled with KidZos from her entrance fee and other earned jobs) the girl dons a Coke-red trademark-emblazoned apron, retrieves an empty plastic bottle, washes it, places it in a disinfecting light-box, fills it with syrup, adds carbonated water, seals it, disinfects it again, and labels it. The process takes all of 90 seconds, and involves the moving of a bottle and the pressing of buttons. It is overseen by a trained Zupervisor who has the particular challenge of assuring that this girl, like all the children, avoids spilling her very full bottle of Coke when removing it from the carbonation machine and capping it. During this process, she has been watched by other caregivers—by those with children four years and under from inside the main bottling room, and by other parents of older children who have nonetheless chosen to escort their children through the streets of KidZania.*
>
> *In the midst of bottling, a fire alarm sounds—the hotel across the street from the bottling plant is "on fire." In short order, the sound of a fire truck appears in the distance (see image 24.2). Of course, to the Zupervisor (and anyone who has been to this KidZania before), this is a regular occurrence, with the Flamingo (get it—"Flaming-o") hotel bursting into audio-visual flames multiple times a day. But to the bottling plant employees, this is an intense distraction. The young girl's gaze averts from the bottling process, and others' necks are craned to see across the street, only to be frustrated by the crowds gathered on the street between the plant and the hotel. Soon, a fire truck arrives on scene, and children wearing fire-fighter outfits step out and up to a set of hoses to spray water (actual water) onto the building. Sensors are activated by water pressure to turn off the fire effects so that the kids are ultimately able to put the fire out on their own. Crisis averted, the fire subsides, and the children are trucked back to the fire station to collect their wages and move on to their next experience.*
>
> *The girl departs the bottling plant with her own DIY bottle of Coke, returns her apron, and moves on.*

There is no doubt that even this brief exposure has some educational value as a hands-on experience, especially to the older child if reinforced and discussed afterwards by caregivers. This belief is at the core of KidZania's "CSR," or Corporate Social Responsibility mission—to be an educational destination that is at the same time entertaining. But as themed environments of this immersive caliber are expensive to create and maintain, KidZania's mission (the corporate mission, that is, not the narrative mission of KidZania the "country") calls for a strong brand-affiliation strategy to ensure global appeal, return visitorship, and a willingness to spend heavily on admission prices. The pure genius of KidZania is that it enfolds immersive environment design, a unique take on environmental branding, and fantasy child's play into a seamless spatial experience that is immensely profitable. KidZania leverages environmental immersion as an "interactive publicity" opportunity for companies who partner with KidZania, constructing KidZania's own brand through brand affiliations with others.[14] In addition to direct funds, partners provide professional expertise, props, and other complementary materials so that a visitor's

Image 24.2. A fire truck negotiating the streets of KidZania Dubai (Photo by Brian Lonsway)

experience with their brand feels "authentic," and is well aligned with jobs and skills appropriate to the partner's brand. KidZania represents environmental branding at its apotheosis—a highly controlled narrative brand experience.

Kids flip burgers at a McDonald's, work at a Coca-Cola bottling production line, tune up a car at an A C Delco service Station, buy groceries at a Waitrose, or clean teeth at a Colgate dental clinic. Not only do children wear branded outfits and become exposed to the brand through expected product placements and environmental graphics, but most powerfully, their play-work involves the performance of actions that reinforce their connection to the brand.

> We have a very strong principal that what we do is to copy real life so when you're walking down the street you don't have say "supermarket" or "gas station," you have Walmart or HSBC.[15]

Lopez's claim is warranted by a certain measure; the environment might appear less true-to-life if it avoided brands entirely. He claims that these brands "authenticate the content."[16] Children are likely exposed to them in their everyday lives, and have already processed their messages well before coming to KidZania. But, while optional or incidental in a child's fantasy grown-up play, here brands are unavoidable. The most common indictment of KidZania leveled by critics, these brands in fact form a core part of KidZania's business model.

In the case of the bottling plant, the company has just engaged a young consumer directly in the very act of *producing* a key component of the brand. Their play has resulted in them "being a grown-up at a Coca-Cola plant," and they have their very own bottle of Coke—produced by their very own hands—to prove it. It's a novel take on what Pine and Gilmore have called "Paying Labor" where one pays to have a work experience that both edifies the consumer and provides products or services to the host.[17] (Perhaps the most well known retail example of this is the Build-a-Bear workshop stores, where you pay to build—select a skin for, stuff, and clothe and decorate—your own stuffed bear.) What is unique about the paying labor model of KidZania is that, while a child may walk away with a trinket that they produced, this "job" itself is at the service of the larger job they are performing, complementing the real-life work of the brand manager.

It's a "win-win"…win…operation, according to Xavier López Ancon:

> The KidZania business model is two-fold: on one side we are a family edutainment center where kids role-play

and can get a sense of life as an adult. On the other hand, KidZania is a new marketing media for brands. I think it is a win-win-situation: marketing partners win because they can get their brand, products or services closer to kids and their families; children win because they have a fun and educational place to play, learn and have a good time and parents win because they see their kids having fun and also learning important life lessons.[18]

The "real-life" aspect of each work experience is reinforced (in the real-life that occurs within KidZania) by being immersively situated within the bustle of a city "outside. "KidZania's major events, like the hotel fire, parades, or the singing of the KidZania welcome song, occur on the streets of the city, bringing life to what otherwise amounts to an idiosyncratically sculpted corridor. The economy of KidZos, the volatile currency that undergirds both formally structured (for example, the bottling plant) and loosely structured (for example, purchasing an item at the in-KidZania shopping mall) experiences coheres the narrative and calibrates them to the free market. And, while mostly invisible to the children visiting a KidZania location, the political narrative that underpins the civic backstory and the civic nomenclature of the corporate hierarchy wraps the entire organization—company, franchises, employees, and visitors—directly into one consistent backstory. This highly unique construction operates like a controlled petri dish for immersive branding experiences.

The Critic and the Designer (or "Criticism and Design")

The social critic typically frames such a controlling environment as exemplifying all that is wrong with corporate empowerment over the consumer. The architectural critic typically frames it as ersatz, cheese, novelty of the worst kind, detracting from the true power of architecture to positively transform experience. The experience designer conceives and realizes it as a contemporary evolution of centuries of speculation and design production, exploring the heights of affective multi-channel, multi-sensory environment design. The partner sees it as a one-of-a-kind opportunity for "interactive publicity" or brand immersion. The enthusiastic child engages it as a stimulating and safe play-scape where activities and their outcomes are wholly in their control. Through the very same artifacts, environmental cues, and activities, each of these perspectives contributes to the complicated folds of agency experienced in KidZania. It is empowering *and* disempowering, supportive *and* challenging of free will, educational *and* consumerist. In fact, such polarities are already absorbed into both the backstory and the company's business model itself, as we have seen. They only appear as contradictions when we attempt to apply many of the conventional analytical tools of the critic.

And this is the claim that I am ultimately seeking to make, that the many layers of backstory that undergird the intensely themed environment complicate our capacity to make easy claims about these categorizations—but that they *only* complicate them, laying them open to empowering critical analysis if (and only if) this critical analysis embraces alternative frameworks.

Even when critical theory moves beyond reductive qualitative assessments and into more productive ground, the very concept of the themed environment continues to be vexing. Barthes's "mythography" or Baudrillard's "simulacra" still stand as first-generation western theoretical frameworks in this area, but each still polarizes: an imbalanced power dynamic of the "writers" and "readers" of cultural myths (a prescient analogue to the themed backstory) in the case of Barthes, and a theoretical separation of the real from the signs of the real in the case of Baudrillard.[19] As we get closer to the subject of themed environments with works such as Daniel Boorstin's *The Image* or Dean MacCannell's *The Tourist*, we get even farther from a nuanced understanding as qualitative assessments like the former's "pseudo-events" and the latter's work/leisure polarities kick in.[20] Even Foucault's otherwise prescient theorization of the heterotopia begat our more contemporary "third space" frameworks, acknowledging yet still extracting the themed environments from the cultures of everyday life.[21] The majority of critical work on themed experience design continues, even in the ensuing decades, to insist that we understand themed environments apart from lived experience, setting up a *prima facie* argument for why they must be treated (critically) differently. In a similar vein, negative critiques of themed environments often stem from an argument that these environments (and their owners and designers) "make passive" their inhabitants through strategies of control. Such passive individuals are argued to have their agency substantially curtailed or delimited by these strategies, and critical frameworks present what is "wrong" with the structures within which these passive actors are operating—or frequently what is wrong with the structures (economies, cultural beliefs, and so forth) behind these structures. Either the "extractive" or "passive-actor" reading is offered as a precondition for change: a change that, still persistent from Marx, is often perceived as necessarily revolutionary.

Actor network theory gets us closer to a productive alternative, affording an understanding of an owner-designer-environment-inhabitant-etc. network that produces conditions for the formation of agency. Here, agency is a result of interactions among components of the network, and must of necessity establish itself dynamically, contextually, *in situ*. This framework operates at two levels in my critique: both at a level that sees the themed environment as a component of everyday lived experience, and at a level that sees the individual person as a component of the themed experience. This negates the "extractive" theoretical frameworks that require that the themed environment be established as something "other" than normative lived experience. And it negates the "passive-actor" theoretical frameworks that require that individual's agency be seen as curtailed or delimited by controlling environmental strategies. What it leaves us with, however, is a more complicated understanding of agency, one that requires us to pull apart the many network relations in play to better understand its potentials

I can trace the concept of complicated agencies to an earlier exploration I conducted in themed environments in *Making Leisure Work*. Here, focused primarily on the various forms of "textual" encounter one might have with the backstories of themed environments, I uncovered a category of practices that shared the function of providing "extra-thematic readings" of otherwise extremely narrative spaces. Whether they were websites that provided detailed reviews and access strategies for the bathrooms of Disneyland or guidebooks for avoiding overly long queues at theme parks, these efforts represent a productive agency that both enjoys and finds onerous the dominant narrative frameworks of the themed environment.[22] They are neither explicitly critical of, nor overwhelmingly exuberant about their subjects. They treat them as matter-of-fact subjects: entertainment destinations that simply complicate quotidian events, like finding a bathroom when you need it.

These, among many other practices, represent the potentials of a form of criticism that acknowledges the complications of agency in places like KidZania. They explicitly lay out the layers of narratives that are present, the subjective needs of the individual actors, and both the enjoyment and displeasure that comprise the themed environment. Their analysis is typically deeper than that of the cultural critic. This is often because their authors' pleasure in their subject brings them into frequent contact with it, but is also, in many cases like that of the Unofficial Guides book series and website, because the rigor of their data collection operations is directly tied to income and profit.[23] Their limit, however, is that they fail to provide an interpretive framework that is larger than their subject. They choose instead to exploit the rigorous analysis of complicated agencies in practical terms, to aid the wearied or anxious visitor who wants both a commodified entertainment experience and as much subjective autonomy as the destination can afford.

Nevertheless, I believe formal criticism has a lot to learn from this. It must move beyond the polarizing tendencies of critical discourse that deny a more rigorous analysis of the agencies at play in the themed environment. If it can do this, the complications of these agencies become evident. The strange paying-labor self-branding play-work of KidZania can be unfolded and seen as something more rich, conflicted, and multi-layered than critical writing has assumed that it is. Ultimately, this is a trajectory for critical work that itself has greater agency than criticism's traditionally narrow audience allows; accessibly presented, its findings and interpretations could truly engage the design, production, and inhabitation of intensely themed environments, empowering those who play and/or work on, with, or in them with a greater capacity to express their agency in ways that are not passive with regard to the overarching narratives. This essay is intended as a start.

Notes

1. Brian Lonsway, *Making Leisure Work: Architecture and the Experience Economy* (Oxford: Routledge, 2009).

2. Lonsway, *Making Leisure Work*; Anna Klingmann, *Brandscapes, Architecture in the Experience Economy* (Cambridge: MIT Press, 2007); B. Joseph Pine and James H. Gilmore, *The Experience Economy: Work is Theater and Every Business a Stage* (Cambridge: Harvard Business School Press, 1999).

3. The design specifications for the Main Street, U.S.A. attraction at Disney theme parks call for the exclusive use of flat-head screws for signs that can be seen by the public. Use of the Phillips screw, while substantially time-saving for regular maintenance, would be anachronistic in a nineteenth-century themed attraction as the invention was not made until the twentieth century. At the Karamelle-Kuche shop in the Germany pavilion at Epcot's World Showcase, hosts wear hairnets as fashion rather than hygiene. Servers in the food stations at other nations' pavilions do not wear hairnets, an accommodation allowed by the state of Florida's adoption of The US Department of Health and Human Services' Food Code, available at <http://www.myfloridalicense.com/dbpr/hr/statutes/documents/2009FoodCode_As_Adopted.pdf>. Traditional German bakeries, however, as a matter of both custom and regulation, include hairnets or hair covering of some kind as an identifiable component of the uniform. See Centre de Promotion et de Recherche der Handwerkskammer in Zusammenarbeit mit dem Verband der Patrons Boulangers-Pâtissiers. Leitlinien-zur-Guten-Hygiene-Praxis für Bäcker, available at <http://hygiene-for-cleaners.eu/media/HACCP_Leitlinien/Leitlinie_Baeckerei.pdf?wb_session_id=56a5fab1c044bcecf7bda63f3cbd2ca4>. Hairnets in this case serve as one of a number of attempts to authenticate the ethnicity of Karamelle-Kuche employees.

4. OED Online, Oxford University Press, <http://www.oed.com>.

5. OED Online.

6. Paul Cilliers, *Complexity and Postmodernism: Understanding Complex Systems* (London: Routledge, 1998).

7. Stephen Fjellman, *Vinyl Leaves: Walt Disney World and America* (Boulder, CO: Westview, 1992).

8. Keller Easterling, *Organization Space: Landscapes, Highways, and Houses in America* (Cambridge: MIT Press, 1999). Easterling, *Extrastatecraft: The Power of Infrastructure* Space (New York: Verso, 2014). Nishat Awan et. al., *Spatial Agency: Other Ways of Doing Architecture* (London: Routledge, 2011). Lisa Findley, *Building Change: Architecture, Politics, and Cultural Agency* (London: Routledge, 2005). Kim Dovey, *Framing Places: Mediating Power in Built Form* (London: Routledge, 1997). Florian Kossak et. al. *Agency: Working With Uncertain Architectures* (London: Routledge, 2009).

9. Rebecca Mead, "When I Grow Up: The Theme-Park Chain where Children Pretend to Be Adults," *The New Yorker*, January 19, 2015, <http://www.newyorker.com/magazine/2015/01/19/grow>.

10. KidZania Dubai, "What is KidZania?" <http://www.kidzania.ae/en/WhatisKidZania/OurStory.aspx>.

11. KidZania London, "Our Story," <http://london.kidzania.com/en-uk/about_kidzania/story>.

12. KidZania Kuala Lumpur, "The Glossary of Terms of KidZania," <http://www.kidzania.com.my/about-kidzania/glossary-of-terms>.

13. KidZania Dubai, "City Tour—Industry: Coca-Cola Bottling Plant," <http://www.kidzania.ae/en/CityTour/Industry/BottlingPlant.aspx>.

14. "Performance With a Purpose—KidZania's Win, Win, Win Plan," April 9, 2011, <http://www.blooloop.com/features/performance-with-a-purpose-kidzania-s-win-win/362#.VhpB7rTHpTO>.

15. "Performance With a Purpose."

16. Jude Webber, "Lunch with the FT: Xavier López Ancona," *Financial Times*, <http://www.ft.com/intl/cms/s/2/1bc2e7f6-17e1-11e4-b842-00144feabdc0.html#axzz3i7syfn1o>.

17. B Joseph Pine and James H. Gilmore, "Take This Job and Sell It: Charging Customers to Help Stage Events," <http://strategichorizons.com/TakeThisJobandSellIt.pdf>.

18. "Performance With a Purpose."

19. Jean Baudrillard, *Simulacres et simulation* (Paris: Editions Galilée, 1981). Roland Barthes, *Mythologies* (Paris: Éditions du seuil, 1957).

20. Dean McCannell, *The Tourist: A New Theory of the Leisure Class* (New York: Schocken Books, 1975). Daniel J Boorstin, *The Image; Or, What Happened to the American Dream?* (New York: Antheneum, 1961).

21. Michel Foucault, *The Order of Things: An Archaeology of the Human Sciences* (New York: Pantheon Books, 1971). Homi Bhabha, *The Location of Culture* (London: Routledge, 1994). Edward Soja, *Thirdspace: Journeys to Los Angeles and Other Real-and-Imagined Places* (Hoboken, NJ: Blackwell Publishers, 1996).

22. Lonsway, *Making Leisure Work*, 213.

23. "Historic Disneyworld Crowds," touringplans.com, <http://unofficialguide.com/walt-disney-world/historical-crowds>.

25

North Dakota Wins the Internet

Sincerity and Irony in an Olive Garden Review

By Michael Mario Albrecht

On March 7, 2012, Marilyn Hagerty, a food critic for the *Grand Forks Herald* penned a review of the Olive Garden, which had recently opened in Grand Forks, North Dakota. In an era in which snark and irony dominate the terrain of foodie culture, the eighty-five-year-old Hagerty's review stands out for its earnest treatment of the omnipresent restaurant upon its arrival in Grand Forks. Hagerty reviewed the restaurant through the eyes of a person who had never been to the enormously popular chain restaurant. She writes: "the place is impressive. It's fashioned in Tuscan farmhouse style with a welcoming entryway." She continues, noting that "the chicken Alfredo ($10.95) was warm and comforting on a cold day. The portion was generous. My server was ready with Parmesan cheese."[1] Towards the end of the review, she observes that "all in all, it is the largest and most beautiful restaurant now operating in Grand Forks. It attracts visitors from out of town as well as people who live here."[2] Hagerty's earnest prose along with her effusively positive review of the restaurant proved to be popular not only among her loyal Grand Forks readers, but also to a national audience as her local review of the restaurant "went viral" and was picked up by websites and blogs across the country. A *Huffington Post* article outlining the phenomenon notes that by March 9, two days after Hagerty's post, the review had garnered an impressive 270,000 hits.[3] Even I was caught up in the excitement surrounding the article; having previously published a scholarly article about the Olive Garden, I was interviewed about the enormous success of Hagerty's review for *The USA Today*.[4]

The varying responses to the Olive Garden review demonstrate multiple positions that the restaurant occupies in contemporary culture. These responses suggest that the restaurant serves as a cultural signifier, and that the experience associated with patronizing the restaurant and of dining experiences in general carry a surfeit of meanings. This overdetermination allows for discourses of reverent adoration to circulate in the same cultural milieu as ironic condemnation of the establishment and the meanings that it evokes. The possibility of both earnest and ironic readings reflect not just a relationship to the Olive Garden in particular, but also to the larger category of themed spaces as they come to occupy an increasing presence in the everyday life of contemporary consumer culture. In this chapter, I look at the different modes of engagement vis-à-vis themed spaces between irony and sincerity. Towards these ends, I examine the ways in which scholars have taken up the notions of irony and sincerity since the 1990s. Critics of themed commercialized spaces have suggested irony as a means of counteracting the potential alienation of an environment that increasingly takes on the logic of a theme park. However, critics of irony have lamented the loss of "real" engagement in one's environments and have suggested that irony leads towards cynicism and nihilism. The viral sensation of Marilyn Hagerty and the competing responses to the review's popularity bring the differences between ironic and sincere sensibilities into stark relief. Further, this difference sets up a political distinction between a "blue-state" sensibility that thrives on snark and inhabits the coasts, and a "red-state" sensibility that proliferates in "flyover country" and embraces the simplicity of sincerity. Ultimately, I argue that the question of whether irony or sincerity is a better mode of being-in-the-world is unimportant; instead, this distinction works to mark its proponents as particular types of differentiated subjects in a culture increasingly dominated by themed spaces.

Themed Spaces

The proliferation of restaurants like the Olive Garden is part of a larger phenomenon in which the logic of themed spaces is increasingly prevalent in contemporary consumer culture. In *The Theming of America*, sociologist Mark Gottdiener developed the notion of themed environments, and describes them as "large material forms that are socially constructed which serve as containers for human interaction. These milieus are social spaces within which the public can mingle."[5] He goes on to note that "themed material forms are also products of a cultural production process that seeks to use constructed spaces as symbols."[6] For Gottdiener, these themed environments are products of a contemporary culture dominated by consumerism in late capitalism. While themed amusement parks are the most obvious example of themed spaces, scholars have suggested that themed spaces are increasingly prolific in contemporary consumer society. In "How the Theme Park Gets Its Power," Scott A. Lukas specifically ties the themed space of the theme park to Starbucks, the omnipresent corporate coffee chain. Lukas specifically addresses the performative aspects of themed spaces, noting that "even outside of theme parks, people are more accustomed with staged or superficial modes of conversation and performance that take place in venues like Starbucks."[7] These staged or superficial modes of engagement—which characterize Starbucks as well as restaurants like the Olive Garden—extend not only to the employees of the themed spaces, but also to its patrons as well of those who offer critique of those spaces in reviews and related commentary.

Literary scholar Melissa Jane Hardie specifically addresses the notion of ironic engagement as it operates through themed spaces. In "Torque," she interrogates the phenomenon of roadside attractions that proliferate outside of Dollywood, the theme park in the Great Smoky Mountains overseen by country singer Dolly Parton and based on an idealized version of her early life in rural Tennessee. Dollywood is an homage to Americana in the mountainous regions of Tennessee and abuts Smokey Mountain National Park. For Hardie, the roadside attractions that populate the road between the national park and the theme park stand in contrast to the natural authenticity of the national park and the constructed authenticity of the theme park. She posits the roadside attractions as a "third zone—the citations and catalogs of the roadside connoisseur of vernacular culture."[8] She goes on to assert that the characteristic mode of engagement for these roadside attractions "is ironic, and its ambition is to place the affective effects of vernacular culture within the framework of a self-consciously parodic nostalgia."[9] Hardie underscores the role that ironic engagement plays in themed spaces, and offers a way of thinking about themed restaurants such as the Olive Garden as sites of self-conscious parody. I would expand upon Hardie's argument and claim that the vernacular culture allows for both the possibility of an ironic engagement as well as an earnest engagement, and that the divide between these sensibilities often falls along political and cultural divides.

The Olive Garden as a themed space shares certain qualities with the roadside attractions that Hardie analyzes; chain restaurants such as the Olive Garden proliferate in the contemporary roadside spaces—strips near the exits of freeways. For certain cultural critics, an ironic relationship is the only one appropriate for these ostensibly inauthentic spaces. Critiques of themed spaces such as the Olive Garden rely upon their artificiality and ostensible inauthenticity to delegitimize the spaces. Lukas explains that "many people have been unable to accept theming as a legitimate form of culture because of the assumption that it produces stereotypical, inauthentic, and simulated reflections on people, things, cultures, places, and moments of history."[10] The assumption that theming produces inauthentic spaces marks those who frequent those spaces without ironic distance as similarly inauthentic; the spaces implicitly interpolate their consumers as stereotypical, inauthentic, and simulated. The critiques of themed spaces that Lukas outlines differentiate those who patronize the restaurants from those who avoid such spaces. The responses to Hagerty's review work to constitute the Olive Garden as a particular kind of themed space and to differentiate those who enjoy the restaurant sincerely, and those who can only enjoy it ironically to mask the disdain for those types of themed spaces.

Responses to Hagerty's Article

Marilyn Hagerty's review of the Olive Garden evoked a plethora of responses across the contemporary media landscape. Many of the pieces that engaged Hagerty's review featured a snarky attitude towards Hagerty and the seemingly naïve sincerity that she exudes in her piece. The day after Hagerty's initial posting, Emily Weiss from the Minneapolis-based weekly *City Pages* titled her article "Olive Garden Review: The Greatest Restaurant Review Ever Written."[11] She begins her article: "After a great run writing reviews for *City Pages*, I will probably need to tender a letter of resignation because Marilyn Hagerty, Eatbeat columnist for *Grand Forks Herald*, just won restaurant reviewing. Forever." In this response, Weiss is employing not only a traditional version of irony in which one says the opposite of what one means, but is also employing an ironic sensibility in which nothing is to be taken seriously in the postmodern landscape of contemporary media culture. Positioning postmodernism as lacking seriousness is a consistent claim by its opponents, but literary critic Linda Hutcheon warns against this line of critique. In *A Poetics of Postmodernism*, she writes that "many of the foes of postmodernism see irony as fundamentally antiserious, but this is to mistake and misconstrue the power of doublevoicing."[12] She goes on to argue that irony "is intricately involved in seriousness of person and theme. In fact irony may be the only way we *can* be serious today."[13] Through her use of irony, Weiss highlights Hagerty's earnestness, which is an unacceptable mode of engagement for a certain segment of the population in the contemporary media environment—especially as it pertains to a themed space like the Olive Garden—because it disavows the power of doublevoicing that Hutcheon outlines.

Weiss was not alone in her ironic engagement with Hagerty's review; snarky comments abound in the myriad reactions to Hagerty's piece, and much of the sarcasm seems to stem from the fact that Hagerty's review was an earnest assessment of the restaurant while reading like an article from *The Onion*, a newspaper and website known for its deadpan irony. *The Onion*, as well as television shows such as *The Simpsons* and *The Daily Show*, and websites such as Gawker, which broke the Hagerty piece on a national level, proliferate in contemporary popular culture and use irony as their *lingua franca*. The Hagerty review inverts the logic of *The Onion*, which features "fake" news pieces that are often mistaken as real; instead, Hagerty's review is a "real" news piece that is so earnest and sincere as to be mistaken as satire.

The Gawker summary and comments are notable for their insistence on discourses of irony and snark that juxtapose with the earnest sincerity of Hagerty. Emma Carmichael penned the Gawker summary, and her deadpan assessment of the original review is itself dripping with irony. Using direct quotes from Hagerty, Carmichael luxuriates in the absurdity of the review. She writes, "the recently-opened Olive Garden in Grand Forks, N.D., is off to a great start, according to Marilyn Hagerty, longtime food critic for the Grand Forks Herald. The restaurant 'is the largest and most beautiful' in town and has been patronized by visitors 'from out of town as well as people who live here,' Hagerty reports in yesterday's positive review."[14] Carmichael's review derives its irony by reporting about the Hagerty article in a straightforward way, though Carmichael's audience ostensibly recognizes the absurdity of both the original piece and the "straight" retelling of the review by Carmichael. However, the comments on the Gawker website span a broad range from subtle acknowledgements of Carmichael's sly irony to indignation over the treatment of Hagerty as a foil for an insider joke. MaurZedong writes in defense of Hagerty. He/she asserts that "I live in Grand Forks, and Marilyn Hagerty is a beloved figure of the community here…To be fair, she's reviewing the restaurants so that Grand Forks citizens know what to expect when they go to that specific location…Sometimes I think New Yorkers are the ones living in a bubble."[15] Some commenters seemed perplexed about why Gawker would want to highlight this particular review. Milk Shakin' Daft Bollocks etc. asks: "Some[one] explain to me. Why is this a story? I don't get the references or the joke. Unless it is laughing at funny little provincial people going about their little lives and their adorable little newspaper."[16] In reaction to commenters who ostensibly do not get the joke, Bs Baldwin is happy to explain: "Are people missing the fact that she reviewed the Olive Garden? It's the ultimate chain restaurant, there is nothing unique to it that stands out that deserves to be reviewed."[17] Many of the responses to Hagerty's review were indeed mocking her quaint provincialism. The differences in responses by Milk Shakin' Daft Bollocks and Bs Baldwin mirror the larger divide between the sincere and the ironic—a divide that runs through many of the comments.

Commenter A. Nonie Meus is able to articulate both extremes of this divide by couching his/her apparent distain for Carmichael in irony. The commenter writes: "this is the kind of snide asshole-ish post that makes people outside of New York hate people who live in New York. Congratulations, Emma Carmichael, you are much, much better as a person than people who live in North Dakota. Enjoy your take-out Ethiopian food at lunch! God, can you IMAGINE living somewhere without an Ethiopian restaurant?"[18] A. Nonie Meus espouses the standard critique of irony in which those who adopt an ironic sensibility are doing so at the expense of those who embrace a more sincere way of being-in-the-world. Further, he/she highlights a set of geographical and cultural assumptions in which those who live in urban centers on the coasts, such as New York City, embrace irony as a way of mocking those who live in less cosmopolitan areas. Finally, after posing in opposition to the cultural elite that embrace irony, A Nonie Meus inverts his/her own logic and identifies him/

herself as a member of that cultural elite. In the last sentence when he/she rhetorically ponders what it might be like to live in a place without an Ethiopian restaurant, such a restaurant—and ethnic dining in general—stands in for a practice enjoyed by a cosmopolitan elite rather than a provincial Midwesterner who earnestly enjoys the Olive Garden.

While many of the snarky responses to Hagerty's piece use literary irony (saying the opposite of what one means) in their reviews and critiques, the predominant way in which irony circulates is through a larger mode of engagement with contemporary society. This ironic mode of being-in-the-world stems in part from a suspicion that the logic of themed spaces has come to proliferate contemporary consumer culture and that the only acceptable way of engaging such superficial simulations is by abandoning sincerity and not taking anything too seriously. Though he does not use the language of themed spaces, French theorist Jean Baudrillard in *Simulacra and Simulations* famously suggests that the "real" world increasingly reflects the logic of the theme park. He maintains that "Disneyland exists in order to hide that it is the 'real' country, all of 'real' America that is Disneyland."[19] For those who despair the world Baudrillard describes in which everything is a themed space, a detached ironic relationship to those spaces becomes the only outlet of resistance against an increasingly themed world.

Critiques of Irony

Writing at the turn of the twenty-first century, many scholars characterized the 1990s as an age of irony, and one of depthlessness and callous indifference. Among those who feared the proliferation of this new ironic sensibility was law professor Jedediah Purdy. In his best-selling jeremiad *For Common Things*, Purdy laments that "the point of irony is a quiet refusal to believe in the depth of relationships, the sincerity of motivation, or the truth of speech—especially earnest speech."[20] Foreshadowing the reaction to Hagerty's review by more than a decade, Purdy goes on to argue that "an endless joke runs through the culture of irony, not exactly at anyone's expense, but rather at the expense of the idea that anyone might take the whole affair seriously."[21] Purdy also locates the propensity for ironic sensibility in the hubs of New York and Los Angeles. He maintains that "irony does not reign everywhere; it cannot be properly said to reign at all. It is most pronounced among media-savvy young people...New York and Hollywood, well populated with Ivy League-educated scriptwriters, produce a popular culture drenched in irony."[22] Hagerty's review serves as the perfect foil to attract the type of ironic responses that Purdy despises. Her sincerity coupled with her location in the "flyover country" of North Dakota allow her to stand in for a cultural wasteland in need of ironic displacement.

Purdy's schema reinforces a divide between hip urbanites who embrace irony and uncool Midwestern salt-of-the-earth folk who embrace sincerity and piety. Hagerty's review went viral because it was decidedly uncool and unaware. As blogger Cassandra Willyard explains, "Hagerty's review is unintentionally funny in its earnestness. She reviews the restaurant with dogged thoroughness."[23] To emphasize her lack of hipness, *The Grand Forks Harold* sent the octogenarian reviewer to New York City where she brought her humble critical style to bear on New York City cuisine, from fine dining to street-vendor hot dogs. Andy Newman, A blogger from the *New York Times* interviewed Hagerty as she tried a street-vendor hot dog, and Haggerty opined that she thought "the hot dogs could be a little hotter," but that she liked "this combination of mustard and onions."[24] Newman also notes that Hagerty was unfamiliar with the term "Halal food," which characterized the particular hot dog stand that she patronized, and when it was explained to her, she remarked that "I'm Lutheran, so that wouldn't apply to me."[25] Though he is simply reporting on his interaction with the food critic, Newman positions Hagerty's earnest midwestern sensibilities as incompatible with the hip cosmopolitan streets of New York City. Hagerty's adventures in the metropolis replicate the situational irony that characterizes the fish-out-of-water comedy. However, embedded in this journey is an assumption of a peculiar mode of engagement with New York culture that is foreign to the North Dakotan food critic. The Midwesterner Hagerty reviews the cosmopolitan cuisine of the city with the utmost sincerity, and in so doing offers a critique of the sensibilities that ostensibly characterize New York City. According to Newman's blog, after having a hot dog for lunch, Hagerty was looking forward to trying the Olive Garden in Times Square. She notes that "it will be...interesting to see if it's any different. It's pleasant to dine at the Olive Garden."[26] The blog interview highlights the steadfast refusal of the critic to engage the cuisine of New York City on any terms but the ones that solidified her as an established food critic in Grand Forks.

Irony and Politics

Divergent narratives about the Olive Garden restaurant and differing modes of engagement with themed spaces align with an increasingly politically segregated U.S. population. Sociologist Bill Bishop outlines a phenomenon wherein conservatives and liberals have moved away from each other spatially and are now less likely to live in proximity to each other in the United States. In *The Big Sort*, he maintains that this spatial segregation has moved the country further apart culturally.[27] Liberals tend to live in "blue" states, but more specifically live in urban enclaves that tend to be nearer to the coasts. Conservatives tend to live in "red" states, and cluster in suburban areas and dominate the vast rural "heartland" of America that exists between the coasts. He goes further and argues that "people were reordering their lives around their values, there tastes, and their beliefs. They were clustering in communities of like-mindedness."[28] Sociologists Pamela Kock and Lala Steelman outline the perceived difference between those in red states and those in blue states in terms of stereotypes. They outline these stereotypes, arguing that "red state residents are presumably humble, spirited fans for their teams, churchgoers…and stalwart supporters of Vintage American values. In contrast, blue state residents are portrayed as showy, drive Volvos, drink lattes."[29] Chain restaurants and themed spaces dominate suburbia, and affinity for one is characteristic of a red-state mentality. One could add irony to the list of stereotypes that characterize "blue" American, and sincerity as a perceived quality of "red" America. Regardless of the validity of the cultural stereotypes, the popularity of Hagerty's article resonates with widely held cultural assumptions about the "kind of people" who live in places like Grand Forks, North Dakota and frequent restaurants like the Olive Garden. For one to enjoy the snarky responses to the Hagerty article, one must maintain an ironic sensibility, which often correlates to a set of values that mark one as a "blue-state" liberal. Similarly, for one to take offense at the mockery of Hagerty, one would more likely align with those "red-state" values of sincerity and earnestness.

Irony and sincerity are not merely two modes of address or being-in-the-world that tend to differ in red states and blue states. Inherent in irony is a doubly binding political position. In *Irony*, cultural theorist Claire Colebrook outlines this seeming dilemma. For the postmodernist, irony offers a way out of the stultifying structures of contemporary consumer culture. She asserts that "this form of postmodern irony is argued to be politically liberating; because no common ground is assumed, a life marked by irony remains open and undetermined."[30] Thus, the commentators making snarky comments about Hagerty's review are operating in a framework that this mode of address might open up the closed themed space that the Olive Garden represents. However, in so doing they are necessarily working through an elitist set of relations wherein the ironist—intentionally or not—positions him/herself as more knowledgeable, savvy, or clever than one who adheres to sincere sensibilities. Colebrook maintains that "at the very least, irony is elitist: to say one thing and mean another, or to say something contrary to what is understood, relies on the possibility that those who are not enlightened or privy to the context will be excluded."[31] This elitism and exclusion informs the comments of those defending Hagerty and her review; commenters felt that the snarky reviews were overly harsh and reflected an implied or explicit elitism on the part of the ironist.

Sincerity vs. Irony

The snarky replies to Hagerty's review exemplify an ironic sensibility that works to characterize the ironist as urban, educated, elite, and hailing from a "blue state." For many, the dismissive tone of ironic detachment is problematic, and some pine for a resurgence of sincerity. Since Purdy's critique of the culture of irony, pundits have portended the death of ironic culture on several occasions, the most famous of which was in the era immediately following the events of September 11, 2001. In the days after the attacks, *Vanity Fair* editor Graydon Carter predicted that "there's going to be a seismic change. I think it's the end of the age of irony."[32] Similarly, David Rosenblatt opined later in the month in *Time* magazine that "one good thing could come from this horror. It could spell the end of irony."[33] He goes on to argue (in a piece that is retrospectively ironic) that "the good folks in charge of America's intellectual life have insisted that nothing was to be believed or taken seriously…with a giggle and a smirk, our chattering classes—our columnists and pop culture makers—declared that detachment and personal whimsy were the tools for an oh-so-cool life."[34] For Carter, Rosenblatt, and others, the very real seriousness that characterized the 9/11 attacks left no room for the shallowness of irony. The proclamations of irony's death reflect a desire for a return to an imagined time when meaning was more stable; inherent in discourses of the death of irony is a conservative longing for an idyllic moment when things ostensibly had more meaning.

Irony has not in fact died in the years since 9/11; rather, the era has flourished with concomitant strains of irony and sincerity that reflect larger political and social divisions. In response to pundits such as Carter and Rosenblatt, *Salon* columnist David Beers locates the coterminous popularity of the seemingly incompatible sensibilities in the days immediately following the 9/11 attacks. He suggests that critics were incorrect when asserting that irony represented "the nihilistic shrug of an irritatingly shallow smartass."[35] Instead, he holds that in the decade preceding 9/11, "ironic farce has been largely consumed as a side dish to sentimental earnestness."[36] He ultimately hoped that a "real" irony (one devoid of nihilism) would emerge after 9/11. While Beers defended the political potential of irony, sociologist Jeffrey Guhin questions whether irony is "good for America." Guhin looks at both proponents and skeptics of the usefulness of irony and asserts that both groups "fundamentally agreed on the threat of nihilism" and that irony might potentially lead to nihilism.[37] The underlying assumption in assertions of the death of irony as well as attempts to justify it is that irony maintains the potential for nihilism; all draw on a desire for things to matter. Some critics and scholars have suggested a shift away from irony altogether, while others have made distinctions between "good" irony, which leads towards some kind of meaningfulness, and "bad" irony, which leads only to nihilism.

Thus, the different understandings of Marilyn Hagerty's article are not just about the Olive Garden; they are indeed arguments about what mode of being-in-the-world is good for America. The restaurant stands in synecdochically for a contemporary consumer culture dominated by themed spaces and an anxiety about the implications of an increasingly themed existence. To dismiss Hagerty's article is to reject a large number of people in the U.S. who both enjoy eating at the Olive Garden and enjoy the familiarity and sincerity of reviews like Hagerty's.

The sincerity of Hagerty's article circulates against an ironic sensibility that allowed the review to achieve national attention. American Studies scholar R. Jay Magill, Jr. wrote two books that address the notions of irony and sincerity respectively. In *Chic Ironic Bitterness*, he holds that "there is an unspoken understanding within this ironic sensibility that mainstream American culture fundamentally perpetuates an illusion of suburban tranquility, beneath the surface of which lies turmoil, misery, and despair."[38] He goes on to specifically isolate chain restaurants such as the Olive Garden as sites that construct this illusory suburbia that the ironist despises. In his schema, the ironist condemns "restaurants that attempt historical or ethnic authenticity through mass-produced faux elements, such as 'rustic' walls, waxed decorative breads, old wine bottles…these restaurants would include the chains Olive Garden, TGI Friday's, Houlihan's, Chili's, Ruby Tuesday, or Cracker Barrel."[39] Beyond this condemnation, these restaurants become the source material for the ironist's derision. The ironist finds humor in Hagerty's review of the Olive Garden because of the juxtaposition of his/her sincerity with the assumed vapidity of chain restaurants. Magill avers that sincerity involves a level of depth that the ironist disavows while the Olive Garden has no such depth. He argues that being sincere "means confronting one's innermost thoughts or emotions and relaying them to others straightforwardly, no matter how relevant to the topic, injurious to one's reputation, or embarrassing."[40] Implicit in Magill's argument is a critique of the people who enjoy the highly successful restaurant, and its suburban setting which is becoming increasingly homogenized and themed. For him, a return to sincerity is important, but themed spaces that do not possess the depth for which Magill longs are not conducive to producing the sincere experience that depth would provide. I maintain that while Magill's ostensible goal is to find depth in experience, he implicitly constructs a cultural and political divide between those like Hagerty who enjoy the restaurant sincerely, and those who with smug assuredness maintain that a more authentic experience lies outside of the homogeneous boundaries of themed space.

Themed Spaces and Their Engagement

Themed spaces have emerged as a dominant part of contemporary culture. Drawing from Gottdiener, Scott A. Lukas suggests that perhaps the first themed spaces were the caves of Lascaux, and that such spaces have been a part of human environments since then. For him, the fact that those caves have meaning many thousands of years later is important to understanding the caves and the themed spaces that have existed since then. He writes that "if the 'real' happens to be themed, as becoming more the case in all venues of everyday life, then we can only hope that the relations that emerge in themed spaces can be as meaningful as those of the symbolic caves of Lascaux."[41] The question of meaning emerges in debates about the respective benefits of irony and sincerity; whereas the ironist uses his/her cool detachment to create meaning and distinction in increasingly undifferentiated spaces of contemporary society, critics of irony lament the loss of stable meaning in a world of increasing detachment. Marilyn Hagerty's review was a short-lived viral sensation, the likes of which abound in contemporary media culture. However, the strong, diverse reactions to her piece offer a window into a set of social and political anxieties that proliferate in contemporary consumer culture. These anxieties reflect a set of assumptions about themed spaces, the question of meaningful existence, and political affinities in the twenty-first century. If themed spaces do indeed bring meaning into everyday life, the meanings they produce are multiple, complicated, and contested, and modes of engagement in these spaces reflect those multiplicities, complications, and contestations.

Notes

1. Marilyn Hagerty, "The Eatbeat: Long-awaited Olive Garden Receives Warm Welcome," *Grand Forks Herald*, March 7, 2012,<http://www.grandforksherald.com/accent/food/2350615-eatbeat-long-awaited-olive-garden-receives-warm-welcome>.

2. Hagerty, "The Eatbeat."

3. "Marilyn Hagerty's Olive Garden Review for *Grand Forks Herald* Goes Viral," *Huffington Post*, March 9, 2012, <http://www.huffingtonpost.com/2012/03/08/marilyn-hagerty-olive-garden_n_1332753.html>.

4. Dan Vergano, "Ask an Expert: Olive Garden Review Brouhaha," *The USA Today*, March 15, 2012, <http://content.usatoday.com/communities/sciencefair/post/2012/03/marilyn-hagerty-ask-an-expert-olive-garden-review-brouhaha/1#.VaAUEPlViko>.

5. Mark Gottdiener, *The Theming of America: Drams, Visions, and Commercial Spaces* (Boulder, CO: Westview Press, 1997), 4–5.

6. Gottdiener, *The Theming of America*.

7. Scott A. Lukas, "How the Theme Park Gets its Power: Lived Theming, Social Control, and the Themed Worker Self," in *The Themed Space: Locating Culture, Nation, and Self*, ed. Scott A. Lukas (Lanham, MD: Lexington Books, 2007), 192.

8. Melissa Jane Hardie, "Torque: Dollywood, Pigeon Forge, and Authentic Feeling in the Smokey Mountains," in *The Themed Space: Locating Culture, Nation, and Self*, ed. Scott A. Lukas (Lanham, MD: Lexington Books, 2007), 31.

9. Hardie, "Torque."

10. Lukas, "How the Theme Park Gets its Power," 183.

11. Emily Weiss, "Olive Garden Review: The Greatest Restaurant Review Ever Written," *City Pages*, March 8, 2012, <http://www.citypages.com/restaurants/olive-garden-review-the-greatest-restaurant-review-ever-written-6603934>.

12. Linda Hutcheon, *A Poetics of Postmodernism: Theory, History, Fiction* (New York: Routledge, 1988), 39.

13. Hutcheon, *A Poetics of Postmodernism*.

14. Emma Carmichael, "Grand Forks Olive Garden Receives Positive Review," Gawker, March 8, 2012, <http://gawker.com/5891587/grand-forks-olive-garden-receives-positive-review>

15. MaurZedong, March 8, 2012 (11:07 PM), comment on Emma Carmichael, "Grand Forks Olive Garden Receives Positive Review," Gawker, March 8, 2012, <http://gawker.com/5891587/grand-forks-olive-garden-receives-positive-review>.

16. Milk Shakin' Daft Bollocks etc, March 8, 2012 (12:35 PM), comment on Emma Carmichael, "Grand Forks Olive Garden Receives Positive Review," Gawker, March 8, 2012, <http://gawker.com/5891587/grand-forks-olive-garden-receives-positive-review>.

17. Bs Baldwin, March 8, 2012 (3:55 PM), comment on Emma Carmichael, "Grand Forks Olive Garden Receives Positive Review," Gawker, March 8, 2012, <http://gawker.com/5891587/grand-forks-olive-garden-receives-positive-review>.

18. A. Nonie Meus, March 8 2012 (12:20 PM), comment on Emma Carmichael, "Grand Forks Olive Garden Receives Positive Review," Gawker, March 8, 2012, <http://gawker.com/5891587/grand-forks-olive-garden-receives-positive-review>.

19. Jean Baudrillard, *Simulacra and Simulation* (Ann Arbor: University of Michigan Press, 2000), 12.

20. Jedidiah Purdy, *For Common Things: Irony, Trust, and Commitment in America Today* (New York: Vintage Books, 2000), 10.

21. Purdy, *For Common Things*.

22. Purdy, *For Common Things*.

23. Cassandra Willyard, "Marilyn Hagerty's Fleeting Fame," The Last Word on Nothing, March 15, 2012, <http://www.lastwordonnothing.com/2012/03/15/marilyn-hagertys-fleeting-fame/>.

24. Andy Newman, "For a Professional Midwest Palate, a First Taste of a Dirty-Water Dog," *New York Times*, March 13, 2012, <http://cityroom.blogs.nytimes.com/2012/03/13/for-a-professional-midwest-palate-a-first-taste-of-a-dirty-water-dog/?_r=0>.

25. Newman, "For a Professional Midwest Palate, a First Taste of a Dirty-Water Dog."

26. Newman, "For a Professional Midwest Palate, a First Taste of a Dirty-Water Dog."

27. Bill Bishop, *The Big Sort: Why the Clustering of Like-Minded America is Tearing Us Apart* (Boston: Mariner Books, 2009).

28. Bishop, *The Big Sort*, 12.

29. Pamela Ray Koch and Lala Carr Steelman, "'From Molehills Mountains Made': An Examination of Red and Blue State Cultural Stereotypes," *Cultural Sociology* 3, no. 1 (2009): 166.

30. Claire Colebrook, *Irony* (New York: Routledge, 2004), 18.

31. Colebrook, *Irony*, 18–19.

32. David Beers, "Irony is Dead! Long Live Irony!," *Salon*, September 25, 2001, <http://www.salon.com/2001/09/25/irony_lives/>.

33. Roger Rosenblatt, "The Age of Irony Comes to an End," *Time*, September 24, 2001, <http://content.time.com/time/magazine/article/0,9171,1000893,00.html>.

34. Rosenblatt, "The Age of Irony Comes to an End."

35. Beers, "Irony is Dead! Long Live Irony!"

36. Jeffery Guhin, "Is Irony Good For America: The Threat of Nihilism, the Importance of Romance, and the Power of Cultural Forms," *Cultural Sociology* 7, no. 1 (2013): 24.

37. Jeffery Guhin, "Is Irony Good For America: The Threat of Nihilism, the Importance of Romance, and the Power of Cultural Forms," *Cultural Sociology* 7, no. 1 (2013): 24.

38. R. Jay Magill, Jr., *Chic Ironic Bitterness* (Ann Arbor: University of Michigan Press, 2007), 30.

39. Magill, Jr., *Chic Ironic Bitterness*.

40. R. Jay Magill, Jr., *Sincerity* (New York: W. W. Norton and Company, 2012), 13.

41. Lukas, "How the Theme Park Gets its Power," 201.

26

Judgments Passed

The Place of the Themed Space in the Contemporary World of Remaking

By Scott A. Lukas

The replacement of reality with selective fantasy is a phenomenon of that most successful and staggeringly profitable American phenomenon, the reinvention of the environment as themed entertainment. — Ada Louise Huxtable[1]

The one thing I can say is that simplistic attempts to imitate the traditional architecture of places rarely work, and end up looking and feeling more like theme parks. — Paul Goldberger[2]

In 2015, the curious Caverne du Pont d'Arc opened near Vallon-Pont-d'Arc in the south of France. What makes this site so remarkable is the considerable effort that went into fashioning this cave art site in the image of Chauvet Cave, one of the most celebrated sites of Paleolithic cave art. Like an earlier replica of another famous cave art site—Lascaux II, which opened in 1983—Caverne du Pont d'Arc offers visitors the opportunity to immerse themselves in a symbolic world of mystery, creativity, and spirituality. At a cost of over $60 million USD and utilizing some of the most cutting-edge scanning and reproduction technologies, the replica cave project, which has been called a "true prototype" by its creators, has enthralled some and enraged many more. Upon the opening of the tourist venue, journalists exclaimed the site was a "perfect fake"—a version that was "better than nothing" or the "next best thing" as compared to the "original" cave art site.[3] In spite of the efforts to preserve France's many cave art sites from algal slime—which impacted dramatically the site of Lascaux and which resulted in an international symposium organized by the French Ministry of Culture in 2009 to consider solutions to this issue of heritage conservation—many critics struggled with the idea of a "replica" version of an "original" site of cave art and, with their views, suggested a revival of age-old criticisms of art and imitation—from Plato to Walter Benjamin.[4] Indeed, one critic expressed that Caverne du Pont d'Arc was a space in which "the execution is flawless, [but] the issue is whether you can suspend your disbelief."[5] While some popular travel review sites heralded Caverne du Pont d'Arc and Lascaux II as "formidable feat[s]" and, simply, "awesome," many popular, fan-based sites, like TripAdvisor, offered much less enthusiastic reviews. As one individual commented in a review that was titled "Fake fake faux fake fake fake fake," "I couldn't get past the fact that it was a reproduction. Go Walter Benjamin!"[6] Indeed, Walter Benjamin, whose work on the effect of mechanical reproduction on the fate of art is prescient to this day, would be proud of both these replica cave art sites and the contrasting social commentary that has emerged in their wake.[7]

I use these initial spaces of reproduced cave art sites as introductions to a complex set of judgments that I wish to analyze. The focus of this chapter is on the space of critique that has emerged in reference to the many instances of themed, immersive, and consumer space that have appeared after their earlier versions in spaces like Chauvet, Lascaux, and numerous other sites of cave art. In other writing, I have expressed that the original themed spaces were, indeed, spaces like those of prehistoric cave art.[8] Like the themed spaces of the consumer present, sites of Paleolithic cave art suggest the significance of symbolism in space in concert with specific human behaviors, actions, and states of mind. Of course, the themed and immersive spaces of the contemporary world are drastically different in terms of their imbrication in systems of consumption, domination, hegemony, and the like. In terms of this comparison, it is curious, if not humorous, to consider that save the examples in Gary Larson's *The Far Side*, indigenous criticism of the spaces of cave art did not

Image 26.1. Cave Art (© Nathanphoto | Dreamstime.com)

occur.[9] From what we may infer, very little criticism took place during the Upper Paleolithic, the period in which cave art played a prominent role in early human life—aesthetics without criticism…indeed, a very unique period of human history! Interestingly, archaeologists are in disagreement in terms of the functions of cave art in this period of early human history, and thus it is quite curious to imagine the near religious fervor that unites many contemporary critics in the sensibility that original sites of cave art like Chauvet and Lascaux possess a certain spirit of authenticity—a sense of mana—as compared to their re-creations in Caverne du Pont d'Arc and Lascaux II, which are deemed faux and inauthentic.[10] In the contemporary world, the status of such re-created spaces of cave art bears little difference in comparison with that of themed and immersive spaces—whether themed casinos in Las Vegas, theme parks in Orlando, or many other spaces that have as part of their foundation an emphasis on re-creation or remaking. Ultimately, they share a status of the profane.

The Profane Nature of the Remake

Much of my research has focused on the significance of forms of cultural remaking—on the various ways in which the world is remade and retold in material, ideological, technological, and personal senses. Whether a film remake in which a classic and previous version is retold in a new time period (perhaps with an updating of characterization, setting, or other contextual elements of the original), or a personal makeover in which an individual (often on a reality television show) is given new clothes, bodily adornment, or physicality in terms of plastic surgery, or, appropriate to this study, a themed space in which a place, time period, or culture is refashioned for a new place, time, and culture in architectural and other senses, the variety and contexts of forms of remaking are immense and multifaceted. In terms of themed and immersive spaces, one of the clear concerns expressed by social critics is the illicit nature of such remaking—the ways in which presumed originals are eroded, tarnished, and deprived of their auras as they are refashioned in new architectural, material culture, and performative forms. Ada Louise Huxtable and Paul Goldberger, both of whom I have quoted in the epigraphs, have been two of the most outspoken and public critics of what is often called vernacular, consumer, or even theme park architecture. In their minds, theme parks, themed spaces, consumer branded cityspaces (Universal CityWalk), and even sites of historical reenactment (Colonial Williamsburg) share in common simplistic, imitative, and inauthentic approaches that exemplify the "replacement of reality with selective fantasy."[11] Much of Huxtable's *The Unreal America* is dedicated to analyses of the many ways in which themed spaces—including Disney theme parks, the casinos of the Las Vegas Strip, and the reenactments of Colonial Williamsburg—represent a degradation of architecture, sociality, identity, even society itself. Likewise, the many essays, articles, and public lectures of Paul Goldberger—who like Huxtable received a Pulitzer Prize for Criticism and created a powerful public voice for American architecture—parallel Huxtable's view of themed spaces. Notably, Goldberger has used the image of the "theme park" as both a stand-in and a straw man for his otherwise prescient critiques of contemporary architecture, spatial planning, and aesthetics and design.[12] I will address these critiques of Huxtable and Goldberger later in this chapter, however, it is important to note that their concerns about such spaces and their myriad implications—ranging from the Jane Jacobs' criticism of the loss of cityspace organicism, to issues of inauthenticity, and many others—are not minority viewpoints.[13] More and more, contemporary academic *and* popular criticism of popular, consumer, and themed architecture represents a citation—direct or indirect—of Huxtable's and Goldberger's critiques. Even counterculture figure Henry Rollins recently wrote a controversial series of essays about the Las Vegas Strip in which he opined about the "knockoff Eiffel Tower" and Vegas' being "amateur hour for chumps."[14]

Image 26.2. The Las Vegas Strip (Photo by Scott A. Lukas)

No doubt, Goldberger and Rollins would agree that themed spaces like those on the Las Vegas Strip are too phony, inauthentic, campy, consumerist, to be taken seriously.[15] Such concerns resonate more generally with global- and macro-level critiques of consumer society and, specifically, its penchant for remaking things—be they films or famous places. In the case of the latter, perhaps it is the scale of the theming that is inappropriate (such as in the case of Paris Las Vegas with a 1:2 Eiffel Tower reproduction), or it could be that the elements chosen for the themed space are too predictable, even stereotypical (such as in the use of gondoliers at the Venetian in Las Vegas), or it could be that the values, behaviors, and contexts selected for the space are considered inappropriate for various reasons (such as the spaces of the New York–New York in Las Vegas that are focused primarily on consumerist endeavors). There are many other concerns, but what each of these shares is the sensibility that theming is a profane practice. It is fitting that "profane" has a spatial etymology in offering (in Latin *profanus*) something "out in front [or outside] of the temple."[16] As Mircea Eliade once wrote, a sacred space such as a church points to

> the threshold that separates the two spaces [and] also indicates the distance between two modes of being, the profane and the religious. The threshold is the limit, the boundary, the frontier that distinguishes and opposes two worlds—and at the same time the paradoxical place where those worlds communicate, where passage from the profane to the sacred world becomes possible.[17]

In Eliade's general focus on the church (sacred) and the non-church (profane), and in the more specific example of the non-themed and themed space, we see the very curious circumstance in which the two spaces impinge on one another. Interestingly, one of the most curious decisions made at the version of Chauvet Cave at Caverne du Pont d'Arc was to fashion the space inside a rather abstract and nonrepresentational exterior architecture. One of the project's creators offered that this decision was quite deliberate: "We didn't want an ambiguity between the real [cave] and the false one. That's why the false cave is included in a building and we do not go down into the underground. We don't want to lie to people; we say that they're entering a false cave."[18] It would seem that the creators of this remade version of Chauvet Cave were quite cognizant of the concerns that would be raised about this version of the iconic space of prehistory, yet, this was not necessarily enough to contain the entirety of the criticism and we thus note a curious tendency of critics emphasizing the profane nature of spatial forms of remaking, regardless of the specifics or contexts of the spaces at hand.

The anxiety about remaking and its associated forms—notably mimesis or imitation—has a particularly long history. Beginning with Plato and his observations in *The Republic*, the mimetic potential of art was seen as a threat to the cosmic order. "Imitation is far removed from the truth, for it touches only a small part of each thing and a part that it itself is only an image," Plato offers, and it could certainly result in a viewer/user of images, things, or contexts that bear the mark of remaking being unable to "distinguish between knowledge, ignorance, and imitation."[19] As Susan Sontag writes, "Plato's view [is] that all art is an elaborate *trompe-l'oeil*, and therefore a lie."[20] Plato's concerns about mimesis are quite problematic as they fail to recognize that the truth, as Nietzsche reminds us, is context dependent; as well, even if an imitative form "touches only a small part of each thing," that touch can be quite provocative in terms of how the new, remade form impacts the world and those around it. While critics have argued that the remake's state (and appeal) is profane, when we review the nature of remaking in all cultures, including indigenous ones, we discover a much different sensibility. In many cultures, there is a sense of respect afforded to the remake, particularly because it is able to unify disparate time, space, material, and existential states of the world.[21] The etymology of remaking invites us to celebrate the "force," "movement away," "undoing" and, simultaneously, "back to the original place," "again," and "repetition." Thus, remaking is both a destroyer and a creator, a bringer of new ideas as well as a conservative maintainer of the past.[22] In the conclusion of this chapter, I will argue that it is this illicit nature of remaking's potentiality—especially its ability to unite disparate and contradictory times, cultures, people, and contexts—that makes it such an appealing force in the contemporary world. Strangely, this power of remaking has been lost on the many critics of themed and immersive spaces.

The Space of Criticism

In his 1907 essay on Coney Island titled "Boredom," socialist writer Maxim Gorky expressed a scathing critique of one of the United States' most famous amusement venues.[23] While Gorky wrote of Coney's "depravity…organized as a paying business" and spoke of the need to "free the people from the slavery of a varied boredom," there is another side of his diatribe that expresses a curiosity, if not admiration, of Coney Island's electrical amusement spectacle.[24] Reading Gorky's words, we are perhaps reminded of the curious nature of critique—especially that applied to spaces of consumption. As Rita Felski writes,

> Critique is drawn to an either/or schema: if we are not suspicious, we must be subservient; if we are not critical, we are doomed to be uncritical.[25]

Gorky's perspective on Coney Island, though more rhetorically fanciful, parallels the interpretations of many observers and researchers of today's amusement spaces. As we note in Felski's views, very commonly, there is a strict dichotomy established by the critic between those in the know (and critical) and those unable to know (and thus uncritical), and, as such, we are reminded of a curious and somewhat ironic point about the criticism that is applied to consumer spaces. The etymology of "critic" implies a spatial act of separation (from *krinein*, "to separate, decide"), and reviewing the term "distance," we note the meanings of "quarrel, discord" and "remoteness, space between things or places."[26] Thus, I would suggest that while criticism of the sort of Gorky's (or any of the contemporary critics of themed spaces) appears to be something, discursively, that is above, not a part of, or separate from the space of concern, we need to "spatialize" criticism (to locate it) in order to more fully grasp its nature and to, presumably, transform its core.

In the literature on themed, immersive, and consumer spaces, there is a notable contrast (and distance) between the interpretations, experiences, and attitudes of the guest who visits these spaces (as well as the designers and operators connected to them) and the academic researcher or cultural critic who encounters these same environments. The guest visits such spaces for pleasure, release, enjoyment, and other reasons while the researcher/critic visits the same spaces for analytical, critical, and academic reasons. Though each of the parties is a part of the same space—and in some cases the critic may not actually visit the physical space—we note that, in the end, each is separated by a significant distance. As an anthropologist who has worked both in the theme park industry and has studied the numerous discourses that, in part, constitute the industry, I am often beguiled by the separation that I have noted between these worlds. Academic and high culture criticism (such as that emanating from the *New York Times* or other high-brow publications) of theme parks and related venues exist in a world (and habitus) much removed from the spaces themselves. Some analysts of these venues have spent little time conducting ethnographic research on site, and while this is not a prerequisite for understanding the nature of such spaces, it does suggest a certain abstraction through disconnection that is often displayed in the resultant discourse. The critiques that have been offered of themed and immersive spaces are varied, though for the purposes of argument, we may simplify them and consider that the foundation they all share is the notion that themed and immersive spaces are inauthentic, fabricated, faux, and simulated and that (in terms of their effects on workers, guests, and society at large) such spaces result in the negative cultural, political, and economic effects of hegemony, consumerism, hedonism, and conformity.[27]

These critiques of themed and immersive spaces have certainly played powerful roles in our understandings of the contemporary consumer world and its many spaces, yet it is worth taking a step back and focusing more generally on what critique has meant for its various political, aesthetic, and literary worlds. As Rita Felski suggests in her important study of criticism, *The Limits of Critique*, a literary, art, social, or other critic has as his or her focus a sense of suspicion in regards to the world or, more specifically, the exact object of criticism—whether it be a poem, work of visual art, or a themed space.[28] And, as Paul Ricoeur reminded, certain "lies and illusions of consciousness" are embedded in the world and our everyday experiences of it and thus it is incumbent on the critic to use suspicion as a means of motivating others—members of taste cultures, citizens, and everyday people—to resist these effects of the world.[29] A critic's sense of suspicion could be rooted in any number of concerns and could imply a range of possible effects. Felski, in her reading of Ricoeur, suggests that a common orientation of criticism and the "hermeneutics of suspicion" is a focus on:

> expos[ing] hidden truths and draw[ing] out unflattering and counterintuitive meanings that others fail to see…[and] revers[ing] the falsifications of everyday thought, to "unconceal" what has been concealed, to bring into daylight what has languished in deep shadow.[30]

A general disenchantment with the world and its products, modes, or experiences is what typically orients a critic, as does a sense of what Susan Sontag notes as a "discrepancy" between worlds—further reminding us of the curious spatial (and divisive) nature of the act of criticism.³¹ We also note in the distance that separates the critic from the space an assumed role in which the individual acts in passing judgment about the space, its contexts, people, and experiences.³² As an individual connected to the space, the critic thus acts upon it—by passing judgment—and figuratively lacks a middle voice. We refer to the middle voice as that, between the active and passive voices, which is unaccusative, in the midst of, and generally able to be a part of a context—as both actor and acted upon—and not above or distant from it. What the voice of criticism reminds us of, as I will discuss later, is the need to address the nature of critique in terms of the "results" or after effects of the criticism that has been applied to the spaces considered. In addition to the distance that is noted in terms of the critic's relationship with the space, the outcome of the critic's discourse is also, spatially, removed from the spaces of design, operation, and use. Often, because of its level of abstraction and disconnection from the direct spaces of criticism, the discourse of criticism does not flow, necessarily, into the worlds of these spaces. The flow of some forms of critical discourse, notably that of social media, popular journalism, and Internet review and feedback discussion fora (such as Yelp, TripAdvisor, Cruise Critic, and other sites) does result in some direct impacts on the spaces in question. In a sense, such discourse represents a virtualization of the guest relations comment sheets of the past and while they do carry with them a sense of efficacy in terms of the guest's ability to reflect upon and, perhaps, change the space in question, academic and cultural critics would likely be dismayed with both the lack of (cultural) critical context in such discourse and the fact that the channeling of such criticism is towards the economic and capitalistic ends of the company that controls the space. Of course, even when the criticism is more directly tied to the space of concern, there is no guarantee that its role will be "productive" in the senses that I am suggesting. In the example of larger public charrettes, such as in the major ones that occurred as part of the World Trade Center redevelopment in New York City following September 11, disagreement, bureaucracies, and forces external and often invisible to the processes within the charrette spaces resulted in notable challenges in terms of the after effects of the criticism, collaboration, and dialogue that were a part of the processes.³³ In the case of the debates related to the World Trade Center redevelopment, we are reminded that agon often occurs when the stakes of the debate are high and its rhetoric serious and sober. Typically, we note that the debates connected to themed and immersive spaces have a much more whimsical, if not kitsch quality.

The Plastic Palm Tree: Critique as Kitsch

In 2009, prior to an academic conference on theme parks, I conducted a research visit to Europa-Park, located in Rust, Germany. My contact at the park was an architect who graciously spent the better part of a day with me—reviewing his architectural drawings and theming design processes in his office and also taking me through the park's Iceland themeland of which his design played a major role. Following our visit, I was introduced to a member of park management. I was quite surprised by the manager's opening words: "Yes, I hear that you are really nice. This is good to hear. The last time anthropologists called us up on the phone for information about our park, well, they were very mean to us. They said that all we were involved with here is fakery." It was interesting to hear this commentary on academic research. Indeed, in my many years working in the theme park industry, studying themed spaces as an academic, and acting as a consultant to the theming industry, I have noted extreme contradictions in terms of the views of those involved in these differing fields. At the time, it occurred to me that the differences experienced by Europa-Park management in terms of these two contrasting visits of academics to their park was a matter of differing methodologies or ethnographic stylistic differences of the researchers. Some years later, I now have a much broader sensibility about these differences. They reflect the contrast of viewing a themed space like that of a theme park as an object of kitsch (an unserious, fake thing) or as an object of study and criticism (as a serious, sober entity). Viewing a themed space through the lens of kitsch could result, theoretically, in opportunities to see such a space through new eyes in ways that are commonly missed by typical guests. However, the focus of such criticism seems to have greater basis in rhetorical and affective play. We are reminded of this with this passage from the work of Ada Louise Huxtable: "There are rain forests in Las Vegas that casino guests find infinitely more impressive than the South American variety."³⁴

Though Huxtable's observation has little ethnographic foundation, we might acknowledge the mood of her description given the fact that there are guests who are very enamored with the theming of Las Vegas casinos. Yet, on closer inspection we begin to note a hyperbolic quality to her rhetoric that not only parallels that of Gorky at Coney Island but reminds us of the unfortunate divisive nature of such criticism. Let us imagine, for the moment, that there are such guests who actually find faux, remade, and themed rainforests to be "more impressive than the South African [and presumably 'real']

Image 26.3. Iceland, Europa-Park (Photo by Scott A. Lukas)

variety." We may reflect on circumstances in which a given person might indeed find any number of so-called re-created forms as preferable to a presumed original that may also be assumed to have influenced the remade form. Consider, as an example, an art enthusiast who has great desire for certain artworks—perhaps oil paintings—that depict another place in the world. Would this same criticism of Huxtable's be applied to this person? And, if so, would we be able to see that this criticism and, likely, many others in which an anxiety about presumed originals and copies is expressed are based on judgments about taste and what thoughts, actions, perceptions, and feelings are deemed to be appropriate in life? If so, sociologist Herbert Gans would remind us that such judgments are illusory and are reflective more of the specific biases and uncritical assumptions of the particular critic—as he suggests, there exists no distinction between high and low culture, other than that which emerges in the consciousness of the critic.[35] As well, we should be reminded that the simplicity that is inherent in Huxtable's assertion about fake and real rain forests is rooted in a notion of the original as a source of mana or aura and the remake as a derivative, unoriginal copy.[36] As Thibaut Clément offered, "by depicting the [theme] park as 'fake,' scholarly interpretations suggest the existence of an objective reality against which the [theme] park may be judged and interpreted."[37] Extending Clément's concern, we might ask: why has an emphasis on the "fake" been so deliberately present in theme park critiques?

We have been conditioned to be suspicious of the themed, consumer spaces in the world (and their plastic palm trees), when, in fact, we should be equally concerned about the many discourses that have been generated in their wake. Earlier, I spoke of the possibility that a guest in a themed casino in Las Vegas could, indeed, find the faux rain forests in one to be impressive, even more desirable than the ones found in South America and I suggested that this argument is disingenuous for its reliance on cut-and-dry dichotomies of originals and copies and for its inherently judgmental nature. Let me add to these concerns and offer that it is unlikely that so many guests would, at least in the number that Huxtable implies in her quote and through the overall argument within her text, prefer remade rain forests over real versions. Yet, even if this

Image 26.4. Indoor Palm Trees, Hyatt Regency Orange County (Photo by Scott A. Lukas)

were the case, the fact that Huxtable's simplistic dichotomy has even framed this debate—and has influenced the work of numerous critics of themed and consumer spaces—says something quite profound about the nature of criticism. Particularly as this type of criticism resonates so strongly with matters of taste, we may say that it, ironically enough, approaches a form of kitsch, in spite of the fake forms that it so loathes and their kitsch qualities that it identifies in connection with consumer society.

In their study of sociological deviance, Joel Best and Kathleen S. Lowney focus on the case of the reputation of Walt Disney Corporation.[38] They point to the interesting fact that the many criticisms of the Walt Disney Corporation—ranging from religious, political, social, and academic versions—originate from both right- and left-wing political spectrums. Criticisms of Disney's theme parks, as Greil Marcus illustrates, are reductionistic and shallow, ultimately acting (as discursive constructs) as "empty vessels" of language and politics.[39] What, then, might be imagined as alternatives to such forms?

The Futures of Critique

Earlier, I wrote of the profane status that has been afforded to the themed space as it represents a specific instance of more general forms of consumer, popular culture, and media remaking. The many concerns that have been expressed of themed and immersive spaces—whether those authored by academic researchers or public critics like Huxtable and Goldberger—are misguided not because of the errors of their authors committed at their onset but because of problems connected to the deployment, outcome, and process of critique. We might imagine critique of the future as not any less "critical," so to speak, as compared to work of the past, but more in tune with eros (as opposed to agon), trust (as contrasted with suspicion), and the prefix "re" (as compared to the prefix "de").[40] Along these lines, then, let us imagine four possible directions of the futures of critique.

First, is the need to reorient popular and academic understandings of remaking such that we move beyond the typical critiques that are founded in simplistic, reductionistic, and romantic notions of originality. In my own work on forms of remaking—ranging from film remakes to the remade spaces of theme parks—I have noted much more nuance, alterity, and variation in the ways in which previous versions are reconstituted in new versions, and the fact of the very active involvement of their forms' actors in their new constitution. No doubt, as Harold Bloom reminds us of the agon and the "anxiety of influence" in the world of poetry and art that occurs when any predecessor and successor "meet," we are likely to discover new forms of turmoil and debate, as well as compromise and growth, in such understandings to come.[41]

Second, is the need to consider remaking as a sacred and generative form, particularly as it brings forth new, radical, and dialogic forces, processes, and forms in the world. As I have written, the potentials of remaking include the opportunity to unsettle the appeal to the Truth, to imagine new and inorganic selves, to create new visions of the world that offer opportunities for radical political and community forms, and to fashion new worldview and cosmology that is founded on the reaffirmative and recombinatory dynamics of remaking.[42] As Lawrence Lessig has reminded us in many ways, remaking—more specifically as remixing—is a generative process that involves the creation of meaning only through reference, citation, use, and even misuse, of a previous or original form.[43]

Image 26.5. Haw Par Villa, Singapore (Photo by Scott A. Lukas)

Third, is the desirability of reforming criticism—both academic and popular—in such a way that it creates new opportunities for dialogue, community, and multi-level forms of participation. As Bruno Latour argues:

The critic is not the one who debunks, but the one who assembles. The critic is not the one who lifts the rugs from under the feet of the naive believers, but the one who offers the participants arenas in which to gather.[44]

We should reimagine critique as an opportunity for opening up, not closing down, dialogue, debate, and consideration of the many themed and immersive spaces in the world around all of us.

Finally, we should acknowledge the value of resituating criticism—of themed spaces and of all forms of consumer, media, and popular culture—within new venues of possibility. Mary Flanagan, in her text *Critical Play*, expresses the opportunities that are present in the world of critical and radical game design such that new, insurgent, hybrid, and avant-garde spatialities are created.[45] Flanagan references these new spatialities through Edward Soja's concept of the "thirdspace," in which:

> everything comes together…subjectivity and objectivity, the abstract and the concrete, the real and the imagined, the knowable and the unimaginable, the repetitive and the differential, structure and agency, mind and body, consciousness and the unconscious, the disciplined and the transdisciplinary, everyday life and unending history.[46]

In this final sense of spatializing critique, we might look to Soja's notions to suggest that the future critique practices that are applied to themed and immersive spaces be governed by more of a reflexive, connected, and dialogic sensibility that affirms not its own rhetorical, political, and virtuosic impulses, as it so often has, but that it situates its urges within a more communal, and mutable, space.

Notes

1. Ada Louise Huxtable, *The Unreal America: Architecture and Illusion* (New York: New Press, 1999), 14. Note: a video of this chapter is available at <https://youtu.be/IR6xqNG8L1k>.

2. Anne W. Semmes, "Paul Goldberger Speaks to His Book and to Architecture," *Greenwich Time*, November 6, 2009, <http://www.greenwichtime.com/news/article/Paul-Goldberger-speaks-to-his-book-and-to-206782.php>.

3. As quoted in promotional materials by Sarah Griffiths, "They Look Like Sketches from Walt Disney's Studio But These Amazing Prehistoric Paintings Were Actually Drawn 36,000 Years Ago," *Dailymail.com*, April 8, 2015, <http://www.dailymail.co.uk/sciencetech/article-3030493/Step-inside-world-s-largest-replica-CAVE-French-cavern-contains-1-000-prehistoric-paintings-recreated-using-3D-scanning.html>. James Stewart, "Prehistoric Ardèche Cave Art Brought to Life in €55m Replica," *The Guardian*, April 18, 2015, <http://www.theguardian.com/travel/2015/apr/18/france-ardeche-cave-pont-darc>. James Adams, "Faux Real?: France Spent $75-Million Rebuilding Its Prehistoric Past," *Globe and Mail*, May 22, 2015, <http://www.theglobeandmail.com/life/travel/a-journey-through-the-prehistoric-past-or-merely-a-passable-replica/article24548547/>.

4. See, <http://www.editions-msh.fr/livre/?GCOI=27351100548910>.

5. Stewart, "Prehistoric Ardèche Cave Art Brought to Life in €55m Replica."

6. Anon. "Grotte De Lascaux (Lascaux Caves), Fodor's Review," <http://www.fodors.com/world/europe/france/the-dordogne/things-to-do/sights/reviews/grotte-de-lascaux-475215>. Therese I, ""Fake fake faux fake fake fake fake," Review on TripAdvisor, Lascaux II, August 7, 2013, <http://www.tripadvisor.com/ShowUserReviews-g2044790-d246632-r171579063-Lascaux_II-Montignac_Dordogne_Aquitaine.html>.

7. Walter Benjamin, "The Work of Art in the Age of Mechanical Reproduction," in *Illuminations* (New York: Schocken Books, 1969), 217–251.

8. Scott A. Lukas, *Theme Park* (London: Reaktion, 2008), 10–11. Scott A. Lukas, *The Immersive Worlds Handbook: Designing Theme Parks and Consumer Spaces* (New York: Focal, 2012), 7.

9. In one specific example of *The Far Side*, Larson shows a couple dining at a table in a cave with walls adorned with forms of cave art. In a sense, Larson's cartoon suggests a humorous version of a prehistoric themed restaurant.

10. For a brief overview of theories of cave art, see, Margaret W. Conkey, "A Century of Paleolithic Cave Art," *Archaeology* 34, no. 4 (July/August 1981): 20–28.

11. Huxtable, *The Unreal America*, 14.

12. In fact, Goldberger uses the word "theme park" to refer to spaces that are not proper theme parks and are, in fact, themed spaces. This, however, seems to confirm the fact that his rhetorical deployment of "theme park" represents a stand-in for any form of popular, consumerist architectural inauthenticity. Many of his essays and lectures are available on his website, <http://www.paulgoldberger.com>.

13. Jane Jacobs, *The Death and Life of Great American Cities* (New York: Vintage, 1992).

14. Henry Rollins, "Las Vegas Is Out of Ideas," *LA Weekly*, August 7, 2014, <http://www.laweekly.com/music/henry-rollins-las-vegas-is-out-of-ideas-4989162.> It should be noted that Rollins' column received notable negative reaction from Vegas locals. As one example of such a response see, PJ Perez, "10 Things Henry Rollins Doesn't Know About Las Vegas," *Los Angeles Magazine*, October 24, 2014, <http://www.lamag.com/las-vegas/10-things-henry-rollins-doesnt-know-las-vegas/>.

15. I should note that I generally enjoy both the work of Goldberger and Rollins—having heard Goldberger and Rollins speak (separately, of course) in Reno, Nevada on four different occasions. I did not get the opportunity to ask Rollins about his views of themed architecture, but on the occasion of meeting Goldberger following one of his talks, I found that he was generally unimpressed with themed architecture, as well as its study.

16. Online Etymology Dictionary, <http://www.etymonline.com/index.php?term=profane>.

17. Mircea Eliade, *The Sacred and the Profane: The Nature of Religion* (New York: Harvest, 1957), 25.

18. Adams, "Faux Real?"

19. Plato, *Republic,* in Readings in Classical Political Thought, ed. Peter J. Steinberger (Indianapolis, IN: Hackett, 2000), 305.

20. Susan Sontag, "Against Interpretation," in *Against Interpretation and Other Essays* (New York: Delta, 1966), 4.

21. Allen F. Roberts, "The Ironies of System D," in *Recycled Re-Seen: Folk Art from the Global Scrap Heap*, eds. Charlene Cerny and Suzanne Seriff (New York: Henry N. Abrams, 1996), 82–101. See also, Gwyneira Isaac, "Mediating Knowledges: Zuni Negotiations for a Culturally Relevant Museum," *Museum Anthropology* 28, no. 1 (2005): 3–18.

22. See Scott A. Lukas and John Marmysz, "Horror, Science Fiction, and Fantasy Films Remade," in *Fear, Cultural Anxiety, and Transformation: Horror, Science Fiction, and Fantasy Films Remade*, eds. Scott A. Lukas and John Marmysz (Lanham, MD: Lexington, 2010), Scott A. Lukas, "Remaking as Potential: A Summary of Issues," <https://www.academia.edu/4182920/Remaking_as_Potential_A_Summary_of_Issues>, and Scott A. Lukas, A Case for Remakes, the State of 'Re,'" <https://www.academia.edu/4062209/A_Case_for_Remakes_the_State_of_Re_> for more on these many contexts of the remake.

23. Maxim Gorky, "Boredom," *The Independent*, August 8, 1907, 309–317.

24. Gorky, "Boredom," 311, 314.

25. Rita Felski, *The Limits of Critique* (Chicago: University of Chicago Press, 2015), 51.

26. Online Etymology Dictionary, <http://www.etymonline.com/>.

27. One of the most comprehensive reviews of the critiques of (Disney) theme parks is offered by Thibaut Clément, "'Locus of Control': A Selective Review of Disney Theme Parks," *InMedic* 2 (2012), <http://inmedia.revues.org/463>.

28. Felski, *The Limits of Critique*.

29. Paul Ricoeur, *Freud and Philosophy: An Essay on Interpretation* (London: Yale University Press, 1970), 356.

30. Felski, *The Limits of Critique*, 1, 31.

31. Sontag, "Against Interpretation," 5, 6. Note that Sontag's "worlds" refer to those of art and aesthetics.

32. Etymologically, "critic," also refers to anyone who is able to pass judgment. Online Etymology Dictionary, <http://www.etymonline.com/>.

33. Some of these dynamics are expressed in Richard Hankin's documentary about the redevelopment of the World Trade Center site, *16 Acres* (2012).

34. Huxtable, *The Unreal America*, 81.

35. Herbert Gans, *Popular Culture and High Culture: An Analysis and Evaluation of Taste* (New York: Basic Books, second edition, 1999).

36. While Walter Benjamin's work on reproduction and the work of art is highly significant in terms of understanding the contemporary worlds of remaking, copying, and remixing, we should also be aware of criticisms of this work that suggest the overall productive value of remaking. For one such criticism, see, Bruno Latour and Adam Lowe, "The Migration of the Aura or How to Explore the Original Through Its Fac Similes," in *Switching Codes: Thinking Through Digital Technology in the Humanities and the Arts*, ed. Thomas Bartscherer (Chicago: University of Chicago Press, 2011), 275–297.

37. Clément, "'Locus of Control.'"

38. Joel Best and Kathleen S. Lowney, "The Disadvantage of a Good Reputation: Disney as a Target for Social Problems Claims," *The Sociological Quarterly* 50, no. 3 (Summer 2009): 431–449.

39. Greil Marcus, "Forty Years of Overstatement: Criticism and the Disney Theme Parks," in *Designing Disney's Theme Parks: The Architecture of Reassurance*, ed. Karal Ann Marling (Paris: Flammarion, 1997), 201–207. On the empty vessel, see, Slavoj Žižek, *Enjoy Your Symptom!: Jacques Lacan in Hollywood and Out* (New York: Routledge, 2007), 154. Note that in the film *The Pervert's Guide to Ideology* (2012), Žižek, more generally, extends the "empty vessel" simile to ideology itself.

40. Felski, *The Limits of Critique*, 17.

41. Harold Bloom, *Agon: Towards a Theory of Revisionism* (New York: Oxford University Press, 1983), and *The Anxiety of Influence: A Theory of Poetry* (New York: Oxford University Press, 1997).

42. See, Scott A. Lukas, "Remaking as Potential."

43. Lawrence Lessig, *Remix: Making Art and Commerce Thrive in the Hybrid Economy* (New York: Penguin, 2008), 74. See, also, the documentary film *RiP!: A Remix Manifesto* (2008, directed by Brett Gaylor) for more on the potentialities of remixing.

44. Bruno Latour, "Why Has Critique Run Out of Steam?: From Matters of Fact to Matters of Concern," *Critical Inquiry* 30, no. 2 (Winter 2004), 246.

45. Mary Flanagan, *Critical Play: Radical Game Design* (Cambridge: MIT Press, 2013), 253.

46. Edward W. Soja, *Thirdspace* (Malden, MA: Blackwell, 1996), 57.

PART X

The Place of the Future

27

Disney's Immersive Futurism

By Davin Heckman

In order to understand Disney's futurism and its realization in immersive environments, one must consider its three expressions of the future: Tomorrowland, Walt Disney's plan for EPCOT, and the EPCOT Center theme park. This essay will draw a line from the 1939–40 World's Fair in New York (for which Disney developed several attractions), the creation of Disneyland in California, Walt Disney's dream of a planned community called EPCOT, and the final expression of this dream as a theme park. Key to the formation of these material speculations is a tension between utopian thought and consumer society, which convert radical thought about the future into a series of sponsored "attractions." This chapter will explore the idea of the future as experienced from the vantage point of postwar America.

Disney's Immersive Environments

This essay discusses the dialectical development of Disney's futurism, beginning with the company's first installations for the 1939–40 World's Fair, many of which were incorporated into the Disneyland theme park. From this initial success, Walt Disney developed his ideas for a planned community, EPCOT. The ideas for EPCOT, while truly utopian in their ambition, were partially implemented after Walt Disney's death as the Epcot Center theme park at the Walt Disney World Resort in Florida. Today, the immersive futurism of the Disney experience is expanded to include Magic+ wristbands and has been incorporated into a larger discourse about the seamless access to themed environments. What readers will see, I hope, is the comprehensive scale of transmedia storytelling by way of the development of cultural institutions with access to many media channels.

Walt Disney's vision of an Experimental Prototype Community of Tomorrow, or EPCOT, was initially imagined as both a planned community and a laboratory for innovation. In Disney's words,

> EPCOT will take its cue from the new ideas and new technologies that are now emerging from the creative centers of American industry. It will be a community of tomorrow that will never be completed, but will always be introducing and testing and demonstrating new materials and new systems. And EPCOT will always be a showcase to the world of ingenuity and imagination of American free enterprise.[1]

Conceptually, EPCOT owes a great deal to the tradition of American technical utopianism, with nods to Colonial beliefs about the "City on a Hill," Frontier mythologies of "virgin land," Industrial Age stories of the "self-made man," progressive faith in finding "the one best way," and post-war consumer ideologies. In fact, one could draw a line through American history and see all these themes as variations on an American identity built around self-actualization and change. Contemporary readers might identify this common theme as resonant with neoliberal or postdigital ways of being. In any case, the notion that freedom is a kind of personal optimization aided by new technology and that utopia is best pursued through a civic collaboration with industry is a key aspect of Disney's vision for EPCOT. Understanding this mode of utopianism can help contemporary citizens understand a key aspect of American culture.

Sensing this continuity, Sharon Zukin, in *Landscapes of Power*, draws the connection between Disneyland and EPCOT and the 1893 World's Columbian Exposition in Chicago. Zukin points to the Columbian Exposition's attractions: "amusement parks and rides, stage-set representations of vernacular architecture, state-of-the-art technology, and a special construction of an ideal urban community."[2] It is also worth noting, that Frederick Jackson Turner's "Frontier Thesis" (which was a meditation on the implications of coast-to-coast settlement of the North American continent) also made its debut at this very same fair. As I discuss in *A Small World: Smart Houses and the Dream of the Perfect Day*, the end of territorial expansion into the West pushed American capitalism inward, turning the process of expansion towards optimization and management of existing resources, markets, and risks.[3] Consider, for instance, the arc from Frederick Winslow Taylor's early-twentieth-century "Scientific Management" studies, the emergence of consumer psychology in the mid-twentieth century, the massive push towards privatization in the latter twentieth century, and the twenty-first-century culture of sousveillance and analytics, and we can see the transition towards ever more granular theories of governmentality that informs this trajectory into the future.[4] It's no wonder that the twenty-first-century Epcot is realized purely as an entertainment destination, enfolded into a multimodal crossmedia experience that includes "smart bands" that can monitor (and improve!) one's progress through the park.

But lest we dwell too deeply on the conceptual implications of Epcot, it is important to map out the aesthetic expressions of the park, its origins, and the ultimate failure of this aesthetic as a prediction. In addition to the 1893 Columbian Expo, the 1939–40 "World of Tomorrow" World's Fair in New York deserves credit for laying the foundations of Disney's futurism. Perhaps the most commonly referenced antecedent to the aesthetic of 1960s American suburbia is General Motors' Highways and Horizons Exhibit, specifically Norman Bel Geddes' Futurama, an attraction that took attendees over a scale model of a futuristic American city.[5] Riders were treated to the following narrative description of a model superhighway:

> Looming ahead is a 1960 Motorway intersection. By means of ramped loops, cars may make right and left turns at rates of speed up to 50 miles per hour. The turning-off lanes are elevated and depressed. There is no interference from the straight ahead traffic in the higher speed lanes.[6]

As Helen Burgess notes in her ambitious study of the exhibit:

> In a montage of stock images, the film announced the coming of the world of tomorrow by tapping into narratives of progress and manifest destiny. The film then went on to showcase the Futurama model exhibit, showing close-ups of the Futurama diorama in action, and ended with shots of the popular exhibition building itself, replacing the familiar "the end" with "Without End" to signifying that the future was something to strive for indefinitely.[7]

Beyond simply envisioning future spaces as static objects, the Bel Geddes exhibit links this vision of the future with the dynamism of physical automobility and with a narrative of open-ended possibility.

At the opening of the Disneyland theme park in 1955, Tomorrowland was a key piece of the narrative theme world Disney aimed to create. In his 1955 dedication speech, Walt Disney described Tomorrowland as follows:

> Tomorrowland, a vista into a world of wondrous ideas, signifying Man's achievements, a step into the future with predictions of constructive things to come. Tomorrow offers new frontiers in science, adventure, and ideals, the Atomic Age, the challenge of outer space and the hope for a peaceful and unified world.[8]

Early attractions included Space Station X-1 (a simulated view of America from space), Hall of Aluminum Fame (an exhibit about aluminum building materials sponsored by Kaiser Aluminum), Circarama (a 360-degree cinematic experience), and The World Beneath Us (an exhibit on energy exploration sponsored by Richfield). These inaugural attractions were followed by Astro-Jets and the Bathroom of Tomorrow (in 1956), the Monsanto House of the Future (in 1957), the General Electric Carousel of Progress and Flight to the Moon (both in 1967).[9] Disney also contributed to the 1964 World's Fair in New York. WED developed attractions for Ford Motors ("Magic Skyway"), Pepsi-Cola ("It's a Small World," see image 27.1), General Electric ("Progressland," see image 27.2), and the State of Illinois ("Great Moments with Mr. Lincoln").[10] A key theme in Disney's development of Tomorrowland (and one which overlaps significantly with his contributions from the 1964 World's Fair) is the strong reliance on corporate partnerships. A number of these attractions, apart from being fun, is the obvious narrative of a better tomorrow through technology.

Image 27.1. Pepsi-Cola "It's A Small World" Advertisement from the 1964/1965 New York World's Fair Official Guide

For instance, Monsanto's House of the Future was intended to highlight the possibilities of plastic. As guests would walk through the house, they were greeted by the following narration:

> The architects who designed this house sought to develop a plan which would be logical from the standpoint of everyday family living. Yet, at the same time, they were determined to create a home free from the preconceived notions of a house made from conventional building materials. Constructed of a few large parts instead of many small ones, the design takes advantage of the almost unlimited flexibility of plastics in building.[11]

Like Buckminster Fuller's Dymaxion House, the Monsanto house resembled a flying saucer. Built entirely from plastic, the house emphasized the utility and strength of its novel materials. But a key narrative approach to this attraction, following the overwhelming display of novelty, was to suture this exceptional model back to the everyday: "Those of you who have visited us previously know that many of the exciting uses of plastics you saw here before, now have become commonplace in houses from New England to California."[12]

Prior to the 1950s, the focus of American engineering and design was heavily pragmatic. In keeping, perhaps, with the interests of a rapidly developing nation (which saw the fast adoption of electricity, the telephone, radio, and, eventually, television), the overwhelming aesthetic prior to this period seems remarkably reserved. In *Taylored Lives*, Martha Banta explains that much of the energy of innovation as manifested in the lives of the consumer was fairly instrumental in its focus. Banta identifies in this era, a shift in daily life that is primarily focused on increased efficiency: "the touch of the invisible hands, hands that guided what we may call the corporate relations between management practice and theory, and the practice and theory of the narrative act."[13] Resonant with Thoreauean values like thrift and self-reliance, scientific management as a pre-war paradigm of popular "futurism" was fairly straightforward in the improvement it promised. Still, the internalization of this kind of self-governance of the subject would cultivate an important component that would aid the development of what would follow.

With the widespread incorporation of television into the space of the home following World War II (as well as shifts towards suburban development, automobile transportation, and the "open plan" design), the stage was set for an accelerated consumerism. In fact, the stability and growth of the economy required an accelerated consumerism. Though the shift from rational, pragmatic marketing to expressive, stylized appeals had been brewing for years, it was during this period that the latent industrial capacity, technical developments, and cultural trajectory saw the emergence of a new kind of futurism.[14] The narrative of progress became a stylized design aesthetic, Populuxe, which celebrated the notion of a massively attainable "good life," characterized by the consumption of mass produced goods, often with a space age feel. This design paradigm persisted through the 1960s, and Disney's 1966 vision of EPCOT is a clear expression of this spirit. Vestiges of this futurism survived well into the 1980s, but a variety of forces—desktop computing, the exhaustion produced by the decades-old Cold War, the neoliberal disenchantment with central planning—all contributed to nostalgic, ironic, and/or eclectic aesthetics that revised the power and meaning of the "space age" style that it displaced.

What survived and actually emerged more fully formed as the definitive design feature of the late twentieth century was mediality itself. It was not this or that particular design aesthetic that persisted as the chief characteristic of postmodern design, but the plasticity of the interface and its ability to integrate itself into experience (a phenomenon that McLuhan describes in his famous catchphrase, "the medium is the message"). First the TV and then the explosion of a variety of recordable, playable, customizable media (Betamax, VHS, Walkman, Cable, Console, Computer, Discman, DVD, TiVo, Internet, iPod, Mobile, Tablet, among others) emerged to establish narrativity, modularity, and playability as the design feature of the early twenty-first century.

The rise of content was anticipated by Disney's desire to connect the immersive environment to his original overwhelming preoccupation—media:

> Driven by the desire to take his passion for storytelling far beyond the confines of two-dimensions, he landed on the idea that visitors who stepped into this park should feel as though they stepped into a movie. Every inch of the place should be a part of a story, as in a movie or television show.[15]

The challenge, but also the genius, from a transmedia perspective is to build bridges that connect the exceptional experience on display to the lifeworld of the user. In *Technics and Civilization*, Mumford uncovers a key affinity between the exceptional and mundane by way of consumer technologies: "the machine came into our civilization, not to save man from the servitude of ignoble forms of work, but to make more widely possible the servitude to ignoble standards of consumption."[16] More appropriate to this discussion, Mumford maps this tendency onto the suburban home:

> This private world, as lived in Suburbia or in the more palatial country houses, is not to be differentiated by any objective standard from the world in which the lunatic attempts to live out the drama in which he appears to himself to be Lorenzo the Magnificent or Louis XIV. In each case the difficulty of maintaining an equilibrium in relation to a difficult or hostile external world is solved by withdrawal, permanent or temporary, into a private retreat, untainted by most of the conditions that public life and effort lay down.[17]

Concurrent with the built environment that Disney wished to create, the home itself had become an immersive media landscape in this era. Anticipating the twenty-first-century preoccupation with prosumer activity and cultures of fandom in the culture industries, the merging of the lifeworld of the user with the romance of the storyworld requires a careful mapping of the exceptional onto the everyday and back again. While the ultimate fate of the Monsanto House speaks to the success (or lack thereof) of the storytelling strategy in this instance, the enduring nature of the Disney parks (and the obsessive unofficial documentation of even defunct attractions by fan communities) speaks to the general power of Imagineering.

Against the development of the Disneyland theme park, Disney himself also dreamed of something more significant: The Experimental Prototype Community of Tomorrow. Far from transient spectators enjoying the ephemeral pleasures of themed attractions, the people who enjoyed EPCOT would live there, work there, raise their families, and pioneer a new way of life. In October 1966, Walt Disney shared this utopian dream with the world: "when EPCOT has become a reality and we find the need for technology that don't [sic] even exist today, it's our hope that EPCOT will stimulate American industry to develop new solutions that will meet the needs of people expressed right here in this experimental community."[18] Disney continued, "It will never cease to be a living blueprint of the future where people actually live a life they can't find anyplace else in the world." On another occasion, he explained, "It's like the city of tomorrow ought to be, a city that caters to people as a service function."[19] Of course, to make this model work, EPCOT would be owned entirely by the corporation, with no voting, no home ownership, and no independent employment. All would work for EPCOT and all would prosper under the constant revolution of technological progress.[20]

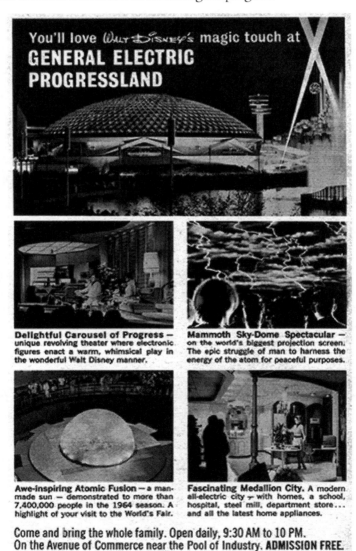

Image 27.2. General Electric "Progressland" Advertisement from the 1964/1965 New York World's Fair Official Guide.

The utopia offered by EPCOT was one of constant, rational change. Anticipating current trends in digital rights management, the subjects of EPCOT would be served by constant updates, improvements, and upgrades. Beyond the fun thematic flourishes on display in Tomorrowland, the real insight of EPCOT is in its anticipation of futuristic processes. The replacement of democracy with corporate control, the valorization of the upgrade, the moderation of risk through social planning, the rationalization of chaotic social practices—the future procedural organization of EPCOT, though never actually built in the way that Disney imagined, has proven to be prophetic in its own way.

Walt Disney died two months after sharing his plan for EPCOT with the world. His more "sensible" brother, Roy, took charge of WED, and Walt's wild-eyed notion of a utopian social experiment on the company's dime was set aside. In the early 1980s, EPCOT returned, in the form of the EPCOT Center, as a companion theme park to the Magic Kingdom in Florida. In contrast to planned community, a 1982 article on the park published in *OMNI* magazine reported: "The EPCOT that will open this fall will have no permanent residents. The company has adopted the line that the tens of thousands of daily visitors to the Florida Disney complex will be its residents."[21]

And though we can lament pragmatism that shifted EPCOT from a social experiment into, yet, another theme park, there is something appropriate about this development if viewed from a historical perspective. The EPCOT Center marks a late stage of development in the arc of progress that stretches from the frontier model of capitalist expansion towards the colonization of the self in the early twenty-first century.[22]

The latest phase of Disney's immersive futurism, is neither EPCOT nor Tomorrowland, or perhaps it is both and much more: MyMagic+.[23] Updating the design logic of themed environments and perhaps fulfilling in an ironic way, Disney's original hope for EPCOT, the introduction of the MagicBand seeks to integrate the user's complete experience through constant monitoring. As Ian Bogost notes:

> I learn that in addition to the expected RFID allowing short-range communication at touch-points—room entry, park admission, and points of purchase—the MagicBand also includes a long-range radio transceiver, which communicates with receivers located throughout the Disney properties. The FAQ clarifies, in the vaguest possible way, that these long-range readers are used "to deliver personalized experiences…as well as provide information that helps us improve the overall experience in our parks."[24]

Guests can use a variety of services on the web-based MyMagic+ to reserve spots in the "FastPass" system (which is like an appointment-only express line for attractions), plan their itinerary, and access information about their vacations. This information is mapped onto the data gathered through the MagicBand, which can be used to unlock hotel rooms, access FastPass reservations, make purchases, and optimize service. From Disney's end, the MagicBand allows the corporation to analyze consumer behaviors and manage traffic.

As its name suggest, the MagicBand employs a rhetoric that is more Fantasyland than Tomorrowland, which is perhaps appropriate in this world of proprietary technologies and the top-down algorithmic mysteries that animate the contemporary fictions of digital populism. It is here that the dream of a controlled, corporate utopia of interminable technical upgrades and constant data surveillance reaches a pinnacle. From another vantage point, this is a futurism that doesn't send you to Mars and provide a spaceship within which to do it, it is a future which provides endless storytelling choices and nowhere to go—*utopia*, in the strictest sense of the word.

The lesson, if there is one to be learned from the long arc of immersive storytelling as pioneered by the incorporated genius of Disney (the corporation) is that immersive environments thrive insofar as they have a strong, distributed narrative backbone. Centralized design is important on the front end, but the key to user experience is the degree to which the supplied experience is personally held. This transmedia approach, which permits many navigable and personalized paths through content, is not dependent on the constraints and affordances of media channels. Rather it is dependent on one's strategic use of those channels to achieve storytelling aims. Where affordances are strong, heavily designed experiences are possible and encouraged. Where constraints are strong, the user has an opportunity to experience the negative capability of the work through a form of participation or imaginative play. This, of course, says nothing of the political, social, and subjective implications of themed spaces in general or in their particular iterations—these should be understood with the same critical scrutiny that previous generations have applied via semiotics, literary criticism, rhetorical analysis, art history, and political economy. What it does tell us is that critical approaches must take a step back and situate individual experiences, specific attractions, the historical development of spaces, the progress of media industries and technologies, and the ideal of the consumer experience within a grammar that allows us to discern their impact on daily life in the twenty-first century.

Notes

1. "E.P.C.O.T Film (1966)," *The Original E.P.C.O.T.*, <https://sites.google.com/site/theoriginalEpcot/>.

2. Sharon Zukin, *Landscapes of Power: From Detroit to Disney World* (Berkeley: University of California Press, 1991), 225.

3. To read in greater detail about the idea of the Smart House and the development of the house of the future in the United States (and Disney's role in this narrative), please see: Davin Heckman, *A Small World: Smart Houses and the Dream of the Perfect Day* (Durham, NC: Duke University Press, 2008). The "riskless risk" is a critical term used by Russel Nye, and employed by John Hannigan to describe the function of entertainment in the postmodern city. As Hannigan argues, the object of Urban Entertainment Destinations, the quintessential consumer environment, is to provide intense experiences safe from the threat of harm—a riskless risk. For a more detailed discussion of this concept, see, John Hannigan, *Fantasy City: Pleasure and Profit in the Postmodern Metropolis* (New York: Routledge, 1999), 71–74.

4. For more information on scientific management, read: Frederick Winslow Taylor, *The Principles of Scientific Management* (New York: Dover, 1998). For more information on governmentality and surveillance, see Michel Foucault, "Technologies of the Self," in *Technologies of the Self: A Seminar with Michel Foucault*, eds. Luther H. Martin, et al. (Amherst: University of Massachusetts Press, 1988), 16–49.

5. Larry Zim, et al., *The World of Tomorrow: The 1939 New York World's Fair.* (New York: Harper and Row, 1988), 207–208.

6. Zim et al., *The World of Tomorrow*, 109.

7. Helen Burgess, "Futurama, Autogeddon: Imagining the Superhighway from Bel Geddes to Ballard," *Rhizomes* 8 (Spring 2004): par. 10, <http://www.rhizomes.net/issue8/burgess.htm>.

8. "Tomorrowland Dedication," <https://www.youtube.com/watch?v=fMV_fTDvhJc>.

9. Werner Weiss, "Other Tomorrowland Attractions," *Yesterland*, <http://www.yesterland.com/spaceman.html>.

10. Bob Thomas, *Walt Disney: An American Original* (New York: Simon and Schuster, 1976), 313.

11. A virtual tour and complete audio recording of the attraction's original 1957 narration is available at "Monsanto House of the Future," Visions Fantastic, <http://visionsfantastic.com/visions/dlr/disneyland/tom/history/monsanto.html>.

12. "Monsanto House of the Future," *Visions Fantastic*.

13. Martha Banta, *Taylored Lives: Narrative Productions in the Age of Taylor, Veblen, and Ford* (Chicago: University of Chicago Press, 1993), 14.

14. Interestingly, Edward Bernays had produced the Democracity display for the 1939 World of Tomorrow Fair. For more discussion of Bernays, see Adam Curtis, *The Century of the Self*, BBC Four, 2002.

15. Imagineers, *Walt Disney Imagineering: A Behind the Dreams Look at Making the Magic Real* (New York: Hyperion, 1998), 11.

16. Lewis Mumford, *Technics and Civilization*, (New York: Harcourt, Brace and World, 1962), 105–106.

17. Mumford, *Technics and Civilization*, 313.

18. "E.P.C.O.T Film (1966)," *The Original E.P.C.O.T.*

19. Thomas, *Walt Disney*, 349.

20. Thomas, *Walt Disney*, 349.

21. Tim Osonko, "Tomorrow Lands," *OMNI* (Sept 1982), 68–72, 106–107. 70.

22. Further cementing the relationship between these tendencies are Walt Disney's own invocation of the frontier in his 1966 announcement: "We think the need is to start from scratch on virgin land and building [*sic*] a special kind of new community." "E.P.C.O.T Film (1966)," *The Original E.P.C.O.T.*

23. "My Magic+," *Walt Disney World*, <https://disneyworld.disney.go.com/plan/my-disney-experience/my-magic-plus/>.

24. Ian Bogost, "Welcome to Dataland," *Medium*, July 29, 2014, <https://medium.com/re-form/welcome-to-dataland-d8c06a5f3bc6>.

28

Resetting the Clock

Theme Parks, New Urbanism, and Smart Cities

By Markus Reisenleitner

On October 10, 2013, Los Angeles Mayor Eric Garcetti, a former visiting professor at the University of Southern California with degrees in Urban Planning and Political Science and at the time just 100 days in office, announced his "Great Streets Initiative":

> The program focuses on improving street life as the "backbone" for urban planning. In his announcement, Mayor Garcetti reminded us of the walk-friendly history of this great city we all love—a city that was built by the Red Car [tramway system], designed to encourage walking to transit, and support people of all backgrounds who lived in our communities—until we shifted our priorities to value our cars, how fast we could travel and how conveniently we could park. He plans to return to our roots and transform the main streets of up to 40 neighborhoods into vibrant, pedestrian-friendly destinations.[1]

Mayor Garcetti's initiative was a clear shift away from the 1980s and 1990s "city of quartz" imaginary of LA—a city besieged by Asian capital and hovering on the brink of riots and gang warfare, a rapidly de-industrializing site of disempowerment for the racialized male body where flows of people, capital, and cultural memes were hierarchically demarcated along ethnic, racial, and class lines in films such as *Die Hard* (1988), *Rising Sun* (1993), and *Falling Down* (1993), and rejuvenated in the *Fast and Furious* (2001) franchise.[2] It is also a shift away from Rayner Banham's 1973 magisterial rehabilitation, if not celebration, of Los Angeles' freeways, vernacular architecture, and suburban sprawl.[3] Rather, this new vision for Los Angeles champions a utopian future Los Angeles that is walkable, pedestrian-friendly, and ecologically healthy, with adequate public transportation and accessible public space around a rejuvenated downtown. The city's pseudo-Hispanic past, already turned into a tourist-friendly theme park pueblo around Olvera Street during the 1930s, has once again been recuperated for Los Angeles's urban imaginary and folded into a utopian vision that resonates with core values such as community, walkability, vibrant street life, and neighborliness, imagined as common to all Angelinos and to be implemented through planning decisions that make it possible to overcome racial tension and social inequality and provide communities with the good life.[4]

This program, somewhat incongruous and surprising for a city like Los Angeles, is built upon what is arguably now a commonsensical affective structure that informs politicians' and urban planners' strategies to deal with whatever ails the global city of the twenty-first century: pollution, suburban sprawl, alienation, gated communities, racial tensions, and fear of crime. The imaginary of a prelapsarian urban environment that is not dependent on cars, provides public space for communities and families, and, as a side effect, increases property values and business opportunities, is of course nothing new, but in a city that has such close connections to Walt Disney and the film industry, it raises the question in how far the re-invention of Los Angeles around its downtown core is merely a rhetorical appeal to the nostalgic visions of small-town America that Disneyland literally shrunk into the global commodity of Main Street, U.S.A.

What might be surprising is that the affective investment in a nostalgic vision of the urban in Los Angeles' current re-invention is complemented by another, very different urban imaginary that has emerged, or rather, re-emerged, in contemporary desires for a different urbanism: the utopia of a city mobilizing contemporary digital technologies of massive data collection and algorithmic analysis as a basis for decision-making that can alleviate the city's contemporary so-called problems, that is, the "smart cities" initiatives.

> In December 2013, Los Angeles Mayor Eric Garcetti issued an executive order instructing each city department to gather all the data it collects and share it on a publicly accessible website by early the following year. In February 2014, he appointed Los Angeles' first Chief Innovation Technology Officer, and a few months later he launched DataLA, the city's online data portal. The launch, aimed at a generation who had grown up with smart phones, the internet, and GIS mapping, was promoted with a hackathon hosted at City Hall.[5]

In what follows, I discuss the connections and intersections between the aesthetic and social utopias promoted by New Urbanism's immersive spaces (the alleged theming or Disneyfication of the postmodern and, arguably, post-postmodern city) and the algorithmically-driven fantasies of control and social engineering mobilized for planning "smart cities." Theming and immersive spaces emerge as the foundation of imaginaries of urban dwelling that profoundly influence the planning and development of twenty-first-century urban spaces.

The theming of contemporary cities is often seen as "Americanizing" processes of urban change that disregard historically grown material structures or rework them into unrecognizable utopias of sociability. In this context, it is crucial to acknowledge that the United States is not a primarily urban society. Rather, its entry into modernity, and consequently its national imaginary, have been profoundly dominated by the small town, which "has been, since the mid-nineteenth century, a part of the fictional imagination," a utopia traced meticulously by Miles Orvell and described as a "story of the effort, and the failure, to define community."[6] Main Street, the heart of the small town, is a trope invented in the nineteenth century that found its apotheosis in Disneyland, which brought together, through the mechanism of a theme park, the often contradictory and ambiguous notions of community, family values, and commerce that informed the trope and its conceit of building community through a particular spatial formation. While actual small towns were often pretty dismal and socially oppressive places that young people could not wait to escape from, the image of Main Street, by conflating social imaginaries and a particular building aesthetic, provided, according to Orvell, both a nostalgic imaginary of an American golden age, a powerful homegrown antithesis to the international style that permeated the modern city, metonymically represented by New York's and Chicago's skyscrapers, and a vision of how a built environment could be mobilized to (re-)create community—precisely what Disneyland's downscaled entryway tries to recuperate as a form of prosthetic childhood memory.

The American Main Street imaginary also provided a fulcrum for the attacks on modernism that resulted from its failure to socially engineer and aesthetically plan more equitable, livable, and functional cities on a global scale. While the attacks on modernism that resulted in the postmodern rallying cry to "learn from Las Vegas" targeted the housing projects and rational layouts of the inner cities that had become all but uninhabitable in the United States and had produced the racialized blight of an urban underclass, the neo-traditional approach that took its cues from Disney (and the nostalgia Disney builds on) targeted modern city planning's failure to accommodate the middle-class by militating against suburban sprawl, bedroom communities, and car culture, and their consequences on family and street life. Branded as "New Urbanism," the neo-traditional approach to tackling urban issues literally codifies the nostalgia that inspired Disneyland into a few simple principles that profess to stem directly from an appreciation of historical models indicative of universal (or universalizable) human values and "a new image of the good community."[7]

One of the first and probably best-known developments of New Urbanism is the resort town of Seaside, Florida, a planned town on Florida's Gulf Coast (a.k.a. "the Redneck Riviera") in 1981. Masterminded by architects Andrés Duany and Elizabeth Plater-Zyberk and their firm DPZ, Seaside, population 2,000—supposedly the size of a typical town of the 1920s and 1930s—takes its stylistic cues from the Old South and sets out to build a community through a "rediscovery of planning and architectural traditions that have shaped some of the most livable, memorable communities in America—urban precincts like Boston's Back Bay and downtown Charleston, South Carolina; neighborhoods like Seattle's Capitol Hill and Philadelphia's Germantown; and traditional small towns where life centers around a courthouse square, common, plaza, train station or main street."[8] With strict building codes inspired by historical models, Seaside was the first example of

Image 28.1. Celebration, Florida (Photo by Markus Reisenleitner)

the "Traditional Neighborhood Approach" that DPZ would develop into the codified tenets of New Urbanism with the foundation of the Congress of New Urbanism (CNU, 1993) and their book *Suburban Nation*, an urban planning bestseller that has been seen as the twenty-first century response to (and continuation of) Jane Jacobs' 1961 manifesto that similarly rallies against suburbs and motorization:

> "[C]odes dictate the proportion of building heights to street width, ensuring that each type of street has a distinct spatial character…basic building block of DPZ's community plans is the neighborhood, which is sized (from 40 to 200 acres) and configured (a radius of no more than one-quarter mile) so that most of its homes are within a three-minute walk of neighborhood parks and a five-minute walk of a central square or common."[9]

The result is a town that mobilizes eclectic stylistic references to architectural history to implement a particular vision of community, imagined as a form of sociability that needs to be resurrected from the past: "Seaside, Florida, is a town designed as an 'ideal' community, where houses have front porches and verandas, picket fences and sleeping porches; here, streets are carved and paved with brick, and sidewalks are made of pebbles and seashells. It is the kind of place where you might imagine your grandparents grew up."[10]

Of course, chances are high that even middle-class Americans' grandparents would have grown up in an entirely different, less Rockwellian, more Orwellian place. It would be easy to debunk a resort town with faux historical styles as yet another example of postmodern architecture's eclectic and apolitical appropriation of past models—a "fantasy theme park village" built to provide a refuge for well-heeled, white-bread Midwesterners from the hardships of winter that lets them experience the utopia of small-town communities during spring break.[11] But Seaside, and the New Urbanism movement in general,

Image 28.2. Seaside, Florida (Photo by Markus Reisenleitner)

Image 28.3. Celebration, Florida (Photo by Markus Reisenleitner)

struck a chord with city planners and communities because they promised to address at a very fundamental level the problematic of urban modernity while also speaking to the desire that planning decisions and aesthetic choices can address and improve this problematic. The language of "improvement," accompanied by buzzwords such as "smart growth," played well in an economic environment in which property value was on everybody's minds.[12] New Urbanism promised solutions inspired by (imagined) histories—learning from small-town pasts—that had the potential to re-build communities and neighborhoods. The CNU provided an organizational framework for New Urbanists. The relatively small scale of New Urbanism planning—that is, its being centered around the concept of the "neighborhood"—made it relatively easy to put theory into practice, while the populist and eclectic rhetoric, modeled after what had worked for theme parks, helped communicate the message to officials and stakeholders, often mobilizing innovative forms of communication, such as DPZ's "charrettes"—seven-day meetings with community stakeholders who were asked to contribute their own ideas that were translated, on-site, into planning and hand-drawn visualizations. The CNU has met regularly since 1993, and has established chapters, produced publications, television programs, and a YouTube channel, and thus successfully established itself as a "movement" with a streamlined, uncomplicated, apolitical, and capital-friendly message that is strongly rooted in an optimistic belief in spatial determinism and social engineering through architecture and planning at the local, community level.[13] "Neighborhood," the basic building block of "community," is imagined as something that supposedly existed unproblematically in a simpler (pre-automobile) past and now only in need of re-engineering through deliberate pseudo-historical references in the manner of staging that theme parks had pioneered.

Image 28.4. 2009. Epcot. Photo by Markus Reisenleitner

The Walt Disney Company demonstrated this intimate connection between theme parks and utopian desires for a different kind of urbanity when it developed the town of Celebration in the 1990s on Disney property close to Orlando, and it is arguably in the history of Celebration that we can discern the common lineage of new urbanist utopias and smart cities most clearly. Celebration can be considered the realization of Walt Disney's initial concept for EPCOT, the "Experimental Prototype Community of Tomorrow," that he had planned as a utopian city of commerce and technology, inspired by the world fairs of 1893 (the "Chicago Columbian") and 1939 (the "[New York City] World of Tomorrow"), but with a healthy dosage of social control, "as influenced by urban planner Victor Gruen," the inventor of the shopping mall.[14] Disney's approach to town planning foreshadows some of New Urbanism's tenets with its emphasis on "mixed-use development to revitalize dying city centers" and reduced traffic.[15] While "ur-EPCOT was the last gasp of the paternalist company town," Celebration maintains Walt's utopian spirit but marries it to the Main Street U.S.A. nostalgia that had already been successfully translated into community utopianism by the neo-traditionalists in their attempt to revive and re-interpret a supposedly lost sense of place and community not reliant on cars.[16] Again, the architecturally re-imagined past obliquely references the Old South, but Disney's Imagineers originally intended to go far beyond design, style manuals, and floor plans:

> [A] key part of the Imagineering process is developing what is called a "backstory" for the product, the mythological history that provides a focus as the development proceeds. Concocting a backstory for a town did not seem too different from concocting one for a new ride. But some of the ideas were ripe. At one point, the Imagineers suggested the tale of a city rising from the ashes of General Sherman's march across the South, though that fact that he never set foot in Florida did not seem to matter. In the end, the more pragmatic development people recognized that the town would not be a ride or a movie, but a real place.[17]

Image 28.5. Celebration, Florida (Photo by Markus Reisenleitner)

Despite abandoning the idea of a fictitious history for Celebration, master planners Robert A.M. Stern and Jacquelin Robertson designed Celebration to look as though it had "grown up organically over time," even if the results are somewhat contrived, as Andrew Ross, who spent his sabbatical there in 1997, observes in his aptly titled book *The Celebration Chronicles: Life, Liberty and the Pursuit of Property Values in Disney's New Town*: "In Celebration…everything, even if it is 'slightly aged'…looks freshly minted. The preference for porches and gingerbread detail made of polymerized materials instead of wood (highly rottable in this climate) means that the real aging process will have a struggle on its hands."[18] While architectural critics were largely dismissive of Celebration's "inauthenticity" and themed origins, Ross troubles the false dichotomy that underwrites the town's aesthetic dismissal:

> For some time now, it has been considered a feat of publicly minded heroism to save and restore old buildings. By contrast, constructing old buildings from scratch is considered a morally corrupt act of forgery. One enterprise is true and noble, the other is false and vulgar. According to this double standard, gentrifying urbanites are serving an admirable cause by restoring Federal townhouses, while well-heeled suburbanites who move into brand-new neo-traditionalist communities are fodder for the heritage machine that merchandizes a counterfeit past. This is no small irony in a country whose most cherished public buildings are often ardent copies of ancient European originals.[19]

Ross reminds us here of earlier movements that have informed at least part of New Urbanism's agenda not completely unrelated to theming urban spaces, especially Jane Jacobs' spearheading a preservationist movement that "convinced an entire generation of the environmental sanity of preserving the high-density urban neighborhoods that planners were itching to condemn as urban slums."[20] Well intended, they were also fodder for the gentrification onslaught of the 1980s that freely mixed downtown revitalization with Disney-like theming in places such as Boston's Quincy Market, New York's Times Square, and a number of waterfront revitalization projects that, hoping to be "saved by the mouse," have re-imagined their pasts architecturally in ways not dissimilar from the New Urbanists.[21]

Image 28.6. Rosemary Beach, Florida (Photo by Markus Reisenleitner)

Other recent developments, such as Rosemary Beach, down the road from Seaside, also designed by Andrés Duany and Elizabeth Plater-Zyberk (in 1995) and characterized by its "incorporation of the European Colonial architecture of the West Indies, New Orleans, and St Augustine as the prototypical house design," substantiate what Celebration had intimated: that at least in the American utopian imaginary, there is a close connection between the desire for sustainable, walkable, equitable, and mixed-use urban environments and the kind of social and aesthetic control that theme parks' Imagineers impose on anyone who enters their spaces.[22] New Urbanism's principles have, in turn, had an effect on the restoration, commodification, and gentrification of historical town centers, and the intricate layering of imaginaries. This became manifest when DPZ, whose projects had been so strongly influenced by the architecture of New Orleans, were retained in the rebuilding process of that city after Hurricane Katrina.[23]

Paradoxically, it is in this turn to the past, conjured up as an immersive themed environment, that we can locate the structures of desire that connect new urbanism and smart cities. Visions of smart cities are built on the powerful imaginary of (and desire for) algorithms that can make sense of data distilled from the complexities of urban life. In this discourse, the social whole is imagined as a marketplace modeled on data-driven derivative trading. Practices of acting on the urban environment are framed as formalized "models" that rely on scalability and predictability patterns derived from a data-driven analysis of the past while informing "value" in monetary terms (that is, the value of property), supported by the ancillary, less clearly defined value system of family, community, safety, and livability, distilled into corporate public relations messages that appeal to commonsensical imaginaries of what would be desirable in contemporary cities. The past is no longer "the multiplicity of histories that is the spatial...with all its happenstance juxtapositions and unintended emergent effects" but rather a resource for providing models that serve as guarantors against the randomness and unpredictability of the urban, simplified through what are fundamentally engineering practices imposed on data as well as spaces, and serving as the foundation of imposed and imposable social reform through a particular (and equally limited) notion of community.[24]

It should thus come as no surprise that the rhetorical invocations of smart cities, in conjunction with the new urbanist principles of walkability, neighborliness, and Main Street theming, provide a seductive template for city politicians, urban planners, and middle-class families. By merit of its limited reach and "do-ability," this palatable and hegemonic consensus agenda does not need to address the underlying issues that result from global capital hitting the ground in a world city and creating or reinforcing economic, ethnic, and legal status divides. Rather, this rhetoric speaks to the mediated libidinal economies tied to turning the clock back to a time before the freeways and automobile started to characterize notions of living in (or near) a metropolis. Historically and/or ethnically distinct and demarcated neighborhoods, transformed into stylishly themed environments—what Sharon Zukin calls "domesticated by cappuccino," "a scenario in which urban space is 'Imagineered' as an entertainment event for the consumption of those who can afford it"—regulated algorithmically through the supposedly benevolent and "bottom-up," transparent, and hackable affordances of "smart" technologies, promise a version of urban life that is promoted as the benign outcome of shared and predictable histories.[25]

But disregarding the multiplicity of historical forces that converge in a city invariably has unintended and occasionally dire consequences: smart technologies invariably fail, and neighborliness can become quite oppressive and contentious. The challenge for urban planners, something that has haunted modernism's version of social Imagineering since its beginnings, remains the same for cities of the twenty-first century: How to plan for the unplannable and take seriously a concept of history "as a source of a liberating certainty that anything could happen," especially in the global city.[26]

Notes

1. Los Angeles Walks, "Mayor Garcetti Announces the Great Streets Initiative, Los Angeles Walks," <http://www.losangeleswalks.org/mayor-garcetti-announces-the-great-streets-initiative/>.
2. Mike Davis, *City of Quartz: Excavating the Future in Los Angeles* (New York: Verso, 1990).
3. Reyner Banham, *Los Angeles: The Architecture of Four Ecologies* (New York: Penguin Books, 1973).
4. See William Estrada, *Los Angeles's Olvera Street* (Charleston, SC: Arcadia, 2006).

5. Mark Vallianatos, "How LA Used Big Data to Build a Smart City in the 1970s," *Gizmodo*, June 22, 2015, <http://gizmodo.com/uncovering-the-early-history-of-big-data-in-1974-los-an-1712551686>.

6. Miles Orvell, *The Death and Life of Main Street: Small Towns in American Memory, Space and Community* (Chapel Hill: University of North Carolina Press, 2012).

7. Jill Grant, *Planning the Good Community: New Urbanism in Theory and Practice* (New York: Routledge, 2006), 3.

8. Todd W. Bressi, "Planning the American Dream," in *The New Urbanism: Toward an Architecture of Community*, eds. Peter Katz, Vincent Joseph Scully, and Todd W. Bressi (New York: McGraw-Hill, 1994), Kindle version.

9. Andres Duany, Elizabeth Plater-Zyberk, and Jeff Speck, *Suburban Nation: The Rise of Sprawl and the Decline of the American Dream* (New York: North Point Press, 2000). Orvell, *The Death and Life of Main Street*. Bressi, "Planning the American Dream," Kindle version.

10. Andres Duany and Seaside Institute, eds., *Views of Seaside: Commentaries and Observations on a City of Ideas* (New York: Rizzoli, 2008), text cited is from the cover.

11. Rosalyn Fraad Baxandall and Elizabeth Ewen, *Picture Windows: How the Suburbs Happened* (New York: Basic Books, 2000), 252.

12. Bressi, "Planning the American Dream."

13. Grant, *Planning the Good Community*.

14. Cher Krause Knight, *Power and Paradise in Walt Disney's World* (University Press of Florida, 2014), 112.

15. Krause Knight, *Power and Paradise in Walt Disney's World*.

16. Andrew Ross, *The Celebration Chronicles: Life, Liberty and the Pursuit of Property Values in Disney's New Town* (New York: Ballantine Books, 1999), 55. Douglas Frantz and Catherine Collins, *Celebration, U.S.A.: Living in Disney's Brave New Town* (New York: Henry Holt and Co, 1999), 43.

17. Frantz and Collins, *Celebration, U.S.A.*, 52.

18. Ross, *The Celebration Chronicles*, 10.

19. Ross, *The Celebration Chronicles*, 65.

20. Ross, *The Celebration Chronicles*, 67.

21. John Hannigan, *Fantasy City: Pleasure and Profit in the Postmodern Metropolis* (New York: Routledge, 1998), 192.

22. Richard Sexton, *Rosemary Beach* (Gretna: Pelican Pub. Company, 2007), text cited is from the cover.

23. Doug MacCash, "Urban Planner Andres Duany Shows off His Bywater House Prototypes," *NOLA.com*, <http://blog.nola.com/dougmaccash/2009/01/post_14.html>; Andres Duany, "Restoring the Real New Orleans," Newgeography.com," March 18, 2009, <http://www.newgeography.com/content/00673-restoring-real-new-orleans>; Douglas A. Blackmon and Thaddeus Herrick, "New Urbanist Tries to Rebuild New Orleans Neighborhoods," *Chicago Tribune*, May 14, 2006, <http://articles.chicagotribune.com/2006-05-14/business/0605140416_1_andres-duany-new-orleans-city-council-new-urbanism>; Fred A. Bernstein, "Seaside at 25: Troubles in Paradise," *The New York Times*, December 9, 2005, <http://www.nytimes.com/2005/12/09/travel/escapes/seaside-at-25-troubles-in-paradise.html>.

24. Massey, "Travelling Thoughts," in *Without Guarantees: In Honour of Stuart Hall*, eds. Lawrence Grossberg, Angela McRobbie, and Paul Gilroy (London: Verso, 2000), 231.

25. Sharon Zukin, *Naked City the Death and Life of Authentic Urban Places* (New York: Oxford University Press, 2010), 4.

26. Meaghan Morris, *Too Soon Too Late: History in Popular Culture* (Bloomington: Indiana University Press, 1998), 26.

29

Theming and Immersion in the Space of the Future

By Scott A. Lukas

We are all interested in the future, for that is where you and I are going to spend the rest of our lives... and remember my friend, future events such as these will affect you in the future. — The Amazing Criswell, from the opening of *Plan 9 from Outer Space* (1959), directed by Edward D. Wood, Jr.

In 2015, a few days prior to a presentation on immersion that I was offering at IAAPA's (International Association of Amusement Parks and Attractions) Attractions Expo, I had the opportunity to visit Celebration, Florida—the famous planned community that was initially created by the Walt Disney Company. I was particularly excited to visit Celebration as my last research trip was in 2008 and I hoped to get a better feel on how this community, which was originally described by Disney as "a place that takes you back to that time of innocence," had persisted over the many years since my last visit. Celebration has always been a notable blip on my theme park radar. Academic critics, including Andrew Ross, have often cited this community as illustrative of Disney's encroachment on cities (and everyday life) and journalists have pointed to the numerous contradictions between Disney's original vision of its New Urbanist town and contemporary realities (suicide, murder, police standoffs, foreclosures, shoddy workmanship, wife swapping, shuttered businesses) that suggest something other than a "place...of innocence."[1] My visit began with a survey of the town's most famous architectural sites—those of Michael Graves, Philip Johnson, Robert A.M. Stern, Robert Venturi and Denise Scott Brown, Graham Gund, Charles Moore, and Cesar Pelli—and I discovered that many of them had changed hands or purposes since their initial incarnations, but most unsettling to me was the work by the last architect, Cesar Pelli. Pelli created the iconic Art Deco theater that was occupied by AMC until 2010 when it closed. The theater is located in a prominent place just across from many of Celebration's bucolic water features and as I was attempting to capture video to document its place among the other iconic architectural structures in the town, I paused for a moment to reflect on what the building's status meant for Celebration. The windows were covered, the building completely deserted, yet, curiously enough, on the outside of the structure a prominent sign proclaimed, "Celebration, Florida—One of America's Ten Most Beautiful Neighborhoods, *Forbes*, 2011" (see image 29.1).[2]

I couldn't help but reflect on the irony, and tragedy, inherent in that proclamation. One of Celebration's most iconic buildings was now just a memory of the town's unsettling journey into time. In fact, it is time that orients my feelings experienced at Celebration and my overall focus in this chapter. More and more, my research on themed and immersive spaces has begun to emphasize the issues of time and temporality.[3] In this work, I am particularly interested in the place of the future as it connects with theming and immersion in a number of significant respects. As the epigraph by the Amazing Criswell offers in its amusing redundancy and tautology, the future is a curious place as it is both a projection of time-forward offered in the present and a reflection prior of time-backwards as it is realized in the next present that takes place after the first. My visit to Celebration prompted me to reflect on the uncanny nature of the future as it is realized in architectural visions. The late futurist Terence McKenna, in his suggestions for "psychedelic society," offered that the achievement of a new society was imaginable by "living as far into the future as possible."[4] On first glance, McKenna's notion of such a form of living seems oxymoronic, but upon review, it suggests a coming to terms with the limitations of the present—a utopian sensibility that is reflected in the meaning of the Latin *futurus* or "going to be, yet to be."[5] There is a yearning, a sense of discovery, and a hopeful optimism reflected in both McKenna's futurism and the etymology of "future," and, I would add, a similar meaning to be discovered in spaces like those found in Celebration, Florida.

Image 29.1. Celebration, Florida (Photo by Scott A. Lukas)

Upon returning from Celebration in 2015, I reviewed my Flickr images from my previous trip in 2008 and began to ruminate on the beguiling temporal issues that were wrapped up in these two sets of images separated by seven years. In the midst of this review, I was also preparing my IAAPA talk on the subject of immersion. Interestingly, one of my foci was the issue of what immersion and theming would look like in the future. I could only reflect back on the trip to Celebration and began to think about the unfulfilled nature of this town's theming, architecture, design, and associated community values. In 1994, when the community opened, the visions of Celebration as a "place…of innocence" likely seemed perfectly reasonable—after all, Disney has been one of the most successful theme park companies, and thus it was a good bet that Celebration would be a "success." Tom Vanderbilt once wrote that "Disney hints at the fact of our anxiety about being unable to build the future," and it seems that in the case of Celebration, Disney's typical ability to suggest a future of American towns was limited.[6]

Alexander Wilson has written of the many ways in which Disney's theme park projects, notably Epcot, rely on utopian thought.[7] Of course, as Wilson and many others have illustrated, this utopian vision did not begin with Disney theme parks. Many years before them, the world exposition or world's fair tradition ushered in a concern with the future that many would say is equally obsessive, idealistic, and unrealistic. It is this focus on the futuristic projections found in the world exposition tradition that I wish to consider in this writing. My specific concern is the visions that I noted in ethnographic work conducted at Expo 2015 in Milan, Italy. I selected this most current incarnation of the world exposition as it best reflects my sensibility of the future of theming and immersion as a "space"—both material and conceptual.

Visions from the World Exposition

The world exposition, dating from the 1851 version of the Crystal Palace to the 2015 iteration in Milan, has always acted as a predictive space—one that points to the future in both optimistic and pessimistic senses. Through its technological, branded, commercial, cultural, and material cultural presentations, it suggests a future that could be possible. Today, as we look back on visions like those of Norman Bel Geddes' Futurama (the 1939–1940 New York World's Fair), we might chuckle and indeed wonder how such a vision of a fully automated highway system (among other offerings), that seems so

Image 29.2. Celebration Town Cinema by Cesar Pelli (Photo by Scott A. Lukas)

patently ridiculous to us today, could have been imagined.[8] But herein lies the problem with such assertions of the world exposition's failure as a utopian form—the expo may, in fact, somewhat portend how the world will appear. For all of the criticisms of the futurism of the world exposition, we see that the form *has* impacted the world in some practical senses. We may consider that many of the visions that began at expos did, in fact, take shape in society in a variety of senses. Architectural futurism of the time, like the Eiffel Tower in Paris (Exposition Universelle of 1889) and the Space Needle in Seattle (Century 21 Exposition of 1962), persisted and came to impact the future of urbanism in these cities.[9] Technological innovations (ranging from the electrical outlet to the video teleconferencing device) and branded or consumer forms (such as the ice-cream cone and Cracker Jack) saw their first, imaginative moments as forms at the world's fair.[10] At Expo 2015, the World Expo Museum, not surprisingly, focused on the many innovations of these sorts as part of its display of the value of the exposition form.[11] Thus, I would argue that the world exposition has always occupied a conceptual space of the future. Of course, one of the challenges faced by any exposition is the fact that these many architectural, technological, and consumer-branded forms may be more futuristic than futurist—more utopian dreaming than predictive realism.[12]

In the course of my research at the Milan expo, I came across fewer of the future-that-might-be models that are illustrated by Futurama and other such world exposition attractions. One notable example was a miniature model of future farming, new approaches to power, and other technologies at the pavilion of Kuwait.[13] Kuwait's expo offering was the closest to a representation of the future that was a common facet of expos of the past. Many other pavilions, such as those of Germany and Italy, offered visions of the future but only in a muted and micro sense. Individual technologies and innovative food systems—as opposed to entire cities—were the emphases. A number of the nations at the exposition seemed to avoid all contact with the future and instead focused on a positive and progressive present—the idea being that the nation in question is already doing its job in terms of protecting the environment, focusing on sustainability, and the like. As I will suggest later, the impetus behind this movement away from the predictive role of the expo may relate to overall pessimism and nihilism that has impacted more and more cultures in the contemporary world. Embedded in the etymology of the term "utopia" is the meaning of "nowhere," which relates to the fact that some pavilion designers have taken to heart the idea that the expo's project of predicting and dictating the future is, perhaps, an imaginary and thus unnecessary one.[14] Beyond the future-focus of the form, the world exposition offers an additional space of the future—this the more literal one in which it projects new, future-looking, and sometimes predictive versions of themed and immersive spaces. Like any consumer space in the world, the themed, immersive, and often avant-garde architectural spaces of the world exposition offer, for any expo guest, a notion of how future, non-expo spaces may look someday.

Spatial Futures

The world exposition of 2015 was, like the expositions of 1851 and 1893, a complex, curious, and contradictory form. During my exploration of the vast grounds of the Milan version, I struggled to make sense of the expo's overall theme of "Feeding the Planet, Energy for Life" in terms of its varied representation in the many corporate, nation, and civil organization pavilions. In all, 145 nations, 17 organizations, and 21 corporations participated in the exposition. Many of the pavilions were designed by some of the world's most celebrated architects, and just as these architects' styles differed greatly so did the architectural, design, interactive, and conceptual approaches of the exposition's pavilions. One of my research concerns was to analyze the predictive nature of these pavilions. Their designs have had an impact on the themed and immersive spaces that we find in today's theme parks, themed restaurants, branded and lifestyle stores, but, unlike these spaces, the architecture and design approaches of exposition pavilions often take a deliberately iconic, eclectic, if not outlandish focus.[15] Highly symbolic architecture, such as that of supersized versions of specific products and brands (for example, Uniroyal's Giant Tire at the 1964–1965 New York World's Fair), has always been a part of the world's fair and world exposition tradition, and certainly we see some indirect influences of these architectural forms on the spaces common to the Las Vegas Strip; theme park zones like those of Wisconsin Dells (Wisconsin), Pigeon Forge (Tennessee), Orlando (Florida); and certain contemporary branded and iconic stores—notably the Fry's Electronics chain.[16] But, what about additional influences that we may begin to attribute to this and still-to-come expositions?

Image 29.3. Austria Pavilion, World Expo 2015, Milan (Photo by Scott A. Lukas)

One expression of this future is a divide between representational and abstract or postmodern space. The pavilion of Austria, for example, represented a typical Austrian forest in an attempt to convey the overall theme of the space which focused on air, breathing, and life (see image 29.3). In contrast, that of Vanke (the corporate real estate group of Asia) was a postmondern, abstract form designed by architect Daniel Libeskind who is known for his work on aspects of the rebuilding of the World Trade Center in New York as well as postmondern, angular spaces like the Jewish Museum Berlin and Crystals shopping mall at CityCenter in Las Vegas. These two versions of World Exposition 2015 could not be greater contrasts in terms of architecture, expression of theme, and conception. Their difference is also illustrative of the evolution we note in terms of more permanent zones of consumer architecture. The Las Vegas Strip underwent a themed revolution in the late 1980s/early 1990s as a number of themed casinos opened—Treasure Island, Luxor, Excalibur, Aladdin, Paris, Mirage, New York–New York, and the Venetian. In the late 2000s, however, a movement away from theming took shape. New casino and hotel projects, including the Wynn and CityCenter, eschewed place-, culture-, or context-based representational architecture and design in lieu of high-class, affective, and abstract forms of design. Many themed casinos, including Treasure Island, Luxor, and Excalibur, initiated detheming or retheming efforts. In 2007, amidst these radical changes at the Luxor, Luxor President Felix Rappaport offered that:

> We're not a British museum with ancient artifacts, we're a casino-resort…This was a brilliantly conceived building from the outside. The pyramid always created a sense of wow and wonder, but the inside never delivered on that promise…The brilliance of the Egyptian theme is in the pyramid. Inside, however, it seemed a restaurant or bar was given a trite Egyptian name and the job was done. Las Vegas has moved beyond that overall theming in the last five to 10 years.[17]

Interestingly, the next large casino to be built on the Las Vegas Strip, Resorts World Las Vegas, will have what is described as an "Authentic Chinese Theme."[18] Indeed, we may likely see a movement back to theming, at least in terms of the casino and related hotel industries, for the fact that it so greatly contrasts with what some have identified as the anemic and bland forms of architecture that took hold in the late 1990s.[19] Aside from stating how this future may appear, we may consider that consumer and branded architectural spaces to come will represent a wrestling with this divide between the representational and the abstract forms of design.[20]

The Milan expo's architectural and design contrasts were many. In addition to those of pavilion design that have been mentioned, there were notable differences in terms of the conceptual and contextual issues that were connected to the spatial design of the pavilions. For the first time at a world exposition, the smaller country pavilions were clustered not by geographical proximity nor location of the nations but by food products or climatic zones shared among the clustered nations. Nine clusters—that included Rice; Cacao and Chocolate; Coffee; Spices; among others—suggested the possibility of using architecture and site planning at an exposition space in a new and more conceptual sense. Moving beyond geographic and cultural essentialism, the different approach to organizing smaller nations at the exposition offered important insights about new forms of political, economic, technological, and (inter)cultural connectivity in the world. In addition, other experimental approaches to design and concept—such as Slovenia's abstract and metonymic approach to food, environment, and industry, as well as experiments of various sorts in the pavilions of Slovakia and Estonia—offered ideas about how the future of themed and immersive space does not, necessarily, need to rely on cultural and national essences.[21]

In fact, a number of these pavilions suggested experiments of the spatial-conceptual sort that are reflected in innovative spaces like Dennis Severs' House in London and the Museum of Jurassic Technology in Culver City, California. An exciting potential suggested by both the exposition and the museum spaces mentioned is conceptual design that may approach more experimental expressions in spaces on the horizon, including those of a typically consumer and branded nature. As I have suggested in other work, there is a clear possibility that such conceptual and contextual experimentation may result in more complex engagement of guests in spaces of the future.[22]

In addition, as we note with the futuristic efforts of Disney's Epcot, every exposition has portended a fascinating, and often too fantastical, technological future. At the 2015 version of the exposition, Germany had one of the most curious approaches to both technology as future and the future as technology. Unlike many other pavilions that simply celebrated technology as the redeemer of the future and that also expressed an overreliance on *techne* (to reference Heidegger), Germany instead utilized what it termed a "seed book"—a mysterious piece of cardboard with a white surface that each guest received upon entry to the pavilion.[23] The seed book was an integral component of the pavilion space—it both reflected the common use of technology in the expo space as a supreme, deified form and, more importantly, connected to the thematic and contextual issues of the pavilion. Most notably, the seed book was the device by which pavilion guests interacted with a series of characters—individuals who represented Germany's diverse cultural, foodway, and ethnic traditions—and political and environmental contexts that were connected to the actions of these characters as well as the guests.

There are many technological influences that will impact the design of themed and immersive spaces to come. Most notable is the development of augmented and virtual reality forms within space, the use of mobile media in new senses, and the overall shift of focus from passive to active users and creators of technology (in terms of guests). In this last area, we may look to the important work of Henry Jenkins in terms of convergence culture and transmedia storytelling.[24] Additionally, as more and more consumer spaces utilize new forms of technology and spatial interaction, we will see an expansion of the themed and immersive space beyond the time-space of the attraction itself. In the sense of a "lifespace," we will begin to see that experience with the space will occur not only during the physical visit of the guest to that space but in the "spaces" that are entailed in the before and after of the guest's visit, thus suggesting new experiments with time and temporality in these spaces on the horizon.[25]

As I will reflect later, a major component of the annual IAAPA conference in Orlando, Florida is an elaborate trade show that features many of the suggested technological futures of themed and immersive spaces—notably forms that include rides, attractions, video games, and related media. It is worth noting that many of the firms that design attractions for world expositions (such as BRC Imagination Arts) also design attractions for theme parks, museums, and branded spaces.[26] Thus, there is a clear degree of continuity—professional, technical, conceptual, and material—that may be located in the interfacing of exposition spaces and those of theming and immersion outside of expos.

Beyond the micro arena of the consumer space, we note that numerous researchers have pointed to the ways in which forms of theming and immersive technology have impacted the world outside of theme parks and consumer spaces. Notable in terms of this influence is the effect of theming and associated theme park architectural, design, and management technologies on cities and forms of urban development.[27] In the future, cities will, no doubt, reflect what some consider to be the encroachment of theming and consumer spatial forms on urban spaces. More specifically, we will continue to see the impact of theming and immersive techniques on spaces that traditionally have been less common sites for such approaches. Museums, interpretive centers, and even libraries (such as the Cerritos Millennium Library), have relied on theming, experiential design, and other forms of spatial immersion to retell the contexts of their spaces for guests.[28] It is also worth noting that not all of the spatial futures of theming and immersion will take place in public consumer venues. In fact, more and more, we are witnessing the expansion of theming and immersive contexts to the home and lifeworld of the everyday individual. Popular shows on television, particularly those that emphasize a "before and after" focus, suggest that the home, itself, is an apt site for the deployment of performative, affective, and thematic narratives.[29] Specific versions of such deployment, such as tiki, exemplify what some might argue is the democratization of forms that were, in the past, under the control of corporate and branded entities.[30]

Returning to the case of the Milan expo, one of the most significant pavilions that suggested a unique and provocative vision of the future of themed and immersive space was that of Brazil. Brazil's pavilion featured a rope net that served as the top of the structure which guests navigated.[31] Guests were encouraged to walk across the net in a challenging operation that often involved their losing balance (see image 29.4). The effect of the pavilion, conceptually, was to suggest to the guest the challenge of negotiating the future of uncertain political, environmental, and social realities. It was quite easy, one noted, to be thrown off one's course by a guest who had lost his or her balance; yet, interestingly, it was also easy to interpret that by relying on the assistance of those in your group (as they held on to you and you to them), one could more easily make one's way to the end of the net structure. Thus, Brazil's pavilion used architecture in a very conceptual and potentially political sense; and this leads to a final possible version of the themed and immersive space—that of the political future.

The Space of Collective Futures

The example of Brazil's dramatic pavilion reminds of the cases of utopian visions that I addressed earlier—Terence

Image 29.4. Brazil Pavilion, World Expo 2015, Milan (Photo by Scott A. Lukas)

McKenna's "psychedelic society" and the planned township of Celebration, Florida. In both of these cases, we note a powerful suggestion about the alteration of society—in the first, through psychedelic drugs (and other forms of "living as far into the future as possible"), and in the second, through new approaches to urbanism, architecture, and community life—yet both, for different reasons, fail to achieve the utopian intentions of its founders. As models, though, they do provide powerful suggestions of how the future may appear.

Returning to Expo 2015, we note a number of pavilions that stressed specific values that seemed to align both contexts of the future considered in this writing—the material and the conceptual—with notions of *bonum commune communitatis* (the greater good of the community). The pavilion of South Korea focused on traditional forms of food storage and combined these with a powerful reflexive focus—"You Are What You Eat," as one of the pavilion signs reminded visitors. Likewise, the Swiss pavilion, which represented the height of politics and conceptual design, utilized four key food items—coffee, water, salt, and apple—and asked the guest to consider her or his behavior as it related to consumption, sustainability, among other issues.[32] Yet, it was Pavilion Zero—a pavilion organized by the host country (as well as the United Nations)—which promised to reflect on the thematics that connected to the overarching concerns of the exposition and which made the most dramatic statements about the future.

This pavilion, composed of twelve rooms inside one of the largest structures on the expo site, focused on the various human impacts on the environment in a variety of experimental, conceptual, and political installations. A dramatic topographic map (over 100 feet in length) illustrated an evolutionary progression represented by spatial models of various forms of human life—beginning with foraging, moving to agriculture, and culminating in a global city (Chicago). Another room included expansive artistic representations of trash and food rubbish, while a massive video screen that resembled a stock market ticker board and included video loops of television shows, media events, and branded phenomena provided an important reflection on the dramatic world in which most guests live (see image 29.5).[33] Interspersed throughout the rooms of Pavilion Zero were signs that included texts like, "Man felt the necessity to intervene on [*sic*] the environment, modifying it," and spoke of "our power over the strength of nature" and the need to address the "paradox of waste." The end of the pavilion, most optimistically as compared to the other exhibits, suggested some nations' "best practices" that had been successful in attempting to curb the powerful and damaging effect of humans on ecosystems and their species.[34] Yet, even in this last exhibit, one might argue that the overall mood of Pavilion Zero was depressing and nihilistic. As I have written of elsewhere, it is this spirit of the dark, depressing, and nihilistic sort that may be most appropriate to the design, context, intent, and existential focus of themed and immersive spaces to come.[35]

Image 29.5. Pavilion Zero, World Expo 2015, Milan (Photo by Scott A. Lukas)

Such nihilistic designs and content may also have the ability to stress that each and every guest approach the spaces at hand (and the many other spaces and realities through which each guest travels) with much more awareness, connection, reflexivity, and, ultimately, consider his or her complicity in the most pressing issues that are impacting the world. High time it may be to move so-called serious, political, and activist topics from the confines of certain museums and interpretive centers and into the consumer spaces of the future. Of course, as we saw with Disney's America—a failed attempt to theme serious and depressing history in a theme park that was to have been located in Manassas, Virginia—communities of various origins and concerns will likely have a say in such forward-looking and controversial spaces. Interestingly, it is community and its political appeals that has provided an important direction for the future of themed and immersive spaces.

Indeed, though not influenced directly by the exposition tradition, contemporary communal, experimental, and participatory communities like Burning Man (which takes place annually in the Black Rock Desert near Reno, Nevada) and Christiania (a former military base in Copenhagen which was taken over by squatters and artists in the 1970s and which has declared itself an independent and sovereign nation) illustrate that many political potentials of future themed and immersive space may be located at the intersections of architecture and community, design and activism, theming and political participation.

A third and most curious example of themed communal spaces of the future is the experimental art installation Dismaland that was organized by the elusive artist Banksy. Banksy's approach was to mimic or mock Disneyland and the overall theme park form by inviting 58 artists to create artistic installations that focused on key contemporary social topics that included the media and paparazzi, the European refugee crisis, among other topics. Banksy's vision was deeply ironic and satirical, though this was lost on the many journalists and critics who called Dismaland "bad and boring," "uninteresting," even "kitsch."[36] Ironically, in a world whose critics proclaim that we would be better off without Disney and other themed spaces, it is the space of Disney's erasure and remaking—in Dismaland—that attracted similar equally visceral criticisms.[37] Strangely enough, even a space like Banksy's, which could—one never knows—end up influencing the design and content of the world's next immersive spaces, is not deemed to be an appropriate vision of spatial or critical futures. Indeed, as Tom Vanderbilt has written, one of the greatest values of the Disney theme park has been its ability to imagine a future—something which others have been unable to do.[38] So, one might ask in the simplest terms possible: if not Disneyland and if not its erasure and satirical critique in Dismaland, then what?

Epilogue: The IAAPA Attractions Expo

During my time at the IAAPA conference in 2015, at which I gave my address on the future of theming and immersion, I had the opportunity to visit the Trade Show—a massive display of the architectural, material cultural, technological, and service futures of the amusement park industry. The Trade Show offered a variety of the latest rides, coin-op games, management systems, photo and social media technologies, and many other offerings, all within an indoor and outdoor space that featured a staggering 1,000 exhibitors covering nine miles of exposition space. My first moments inside the Trade Show were akin to experiencing the awe and excitement that I have often felt when first visiting a new theme park. Initially, I struggled to comprehend the show in a holistic sense—how exactly may we make sense of these disparate technologies, services, rides, and attractions? What do they suggest about the future of amusement and theme park attractions? How can we be sure that these, indeed, are the reflections of the future? What factors might result in their "sticking" in terms of having a profound or meaningful impact on the spaces that I study?

Image 29.6. Exodrome by the company Exo, IAAPA 2015 (Photo by Scott A. Lukas)

As I always do, I took copious fieldnotes and jotted down many reflections that I had on these and other questions. I previewed a number of rides, including one called the Exodrome by the company Exo. It was, as many rides are these days, a hybrid entity—a combination of video game simulator and theme park ride. The literature that accompanied the ride, in fact, stated that "Exo was created as a blend of the best from video games and amusement rides."[39] During the demo, I was given a lengthy list of instructions in terms of securing myself in the ride, which spun dramatically upside down, and was instructed as to how to operate the virtual guns in the many software options that ranged from *Crazy Toys*, to *Warflyer*, and *Bounty Roller Coaster 2*. I chose the last option and, after strapping myself in, went about the challenge of trying to shoot the many virtual targets all the while spinning upside down and rocking back and forth in my ride vehicle. Near the end of my ride, my avatar rode near some water features on the screen and, much to my surprise, mild jets of water began to spray my face. After exiting the ride, I asked the attentive corporate representative if I indeed had experienced water on my face. "Yep, that's the future that you felt!"

Notes

1. The "place…of innocence" is described in Abby Goodnough, "Disney Is Selling a Town It Built to Reflect the Past," *New York Times*, January 16, 2004. In addition to Andrew Ross, *The Celebration Chronicles: Life, Liberty and the Pursuit of Property Values in Disney's New Town* (New York: Ballantine Books, 1999), see Douglas Frantz and Catherine Collins, *Celebration, U.S.A.: Living in Disney's Brave New Town* (New York: Henry Holt and Co, 1999). For more on the contradictory contemporary histories of the community, see Ed Pilkington, "How the Disney Dream Died in Celebration," *The Guardian*, December 13, 2010, "The Dark Heart of Disney's Dream Town: Celebration Has Wife-Swapping, Suicide, Vandals…and Now Even a Brutal Murder," *DailyMail.com*, December 9, 2010, and Kelsey Campbell-Dollaghan, "Celebration, Florida: The Utopian Town That America Just Couldn't Trust," *Gizmodo*, April 20, 2014. Note: a video of this chapter is available at <https://youtu.be/rr7BKKObAqE>.

2. See, John Giuffo, "America's Prettiest Neighborhoods," *Forbes*, September 22, 2011.

3. My work in this area has been influenced by my participation in the many time and temporality events and publications initiated by Filippo Carlà (University of Exeter) and Florian Freitag (Johannes Gutenberg University Mainz). See, also, Scott A. Lukas, "Time and Temporality in the Worlds of Theme Parks," in *Here You Leave Today: Time and Temporality in Theme Parks*, eds. Filippo Carlà, Florian Freitag, Sabrina Mittermeier, and Ariane Schwarz (Hanover, Germany: Wehrhahn, 2016).

4. Terence McKenna, Psychedelic Society (1984), <https://www.youtube.com/watch?v=c9RxtZlkQGs>.

5. Online Etymology Dictionary, <http://www.etymonline.com/index.php?term=future>.

6. Tom Vanderbilt, "It's a Mall World After All: Disney, Design, and the American Dream," *Harvard Design Magazine* 9 (Fall 1999): 89–93.

7. Alexander Wilson, "Technological Utopias," *South Atlantic Quarterly* 92, no. 1 (1993): 157–173. See, also, Davin Heckman, "Disney's Immersive Futurism" in this collection.

8. A video overview of Futurama is available at <https://archive.org/details/ToNewHor1940>.

9. See, Javier Monclús, *International Exhibitions and Urbanism: The Zaragoza Expo 2008 Project* (Surrey, England: Ashgate, 2009) and Julie Sze, "Imagining Ecological Urbanism at the World Expo," Chapter 5 of *Fantasy Islands: Chinese Dreams and Ecological Fears in an Age of Climate Crisis* (Berkeley: University of California Press, 2015) for more on the world exposition tradition and urbanism.

10. Curiously, a number of websites have focused on spot-checking the "accuracy" of expo and theme park "predictions" of the future. As an example, see, Seth Porges, "Fact-Checking 5 Epcot Rides That Predicted the Future," *Popular Mechanics*, December 17, 2009, <http://www.popularmechanics.com/adventure/a4552/4325511/>.

11. See my YouTube site for a video overview of the museum, <https://www.youtube.com/watch?v=BallgoTPJ4E>.

12. While the meanings of these two terms may be, arguably, similar, I would suggest that the connotation of "futuristic" relates to technological or other projections of what is to come while "futurist" suggests a more global vision of the society of the future, particularly in dictating trends and future states of culture or being.

13. See my YouTube site for a video overview of the pavilion, <https://www.youtube.com/watch?v=cIOZxGgGgSc>.

14. Online Etymology Dictionary, <http://www.etymonline.com/index.php?term=utopia>.

15. The world exposition tradition has impacted significantly the traditions of theme parks. See, Scott A. Lukas, "How the Theme Park Got Its Power: The World's Fair as Cultural Form," in *Meet Me at the Fair: A World's Fair Reader*, eds. Laura Hollengreen, Celia Pearce, Rebecca Rouse, and Bobby Schweizer (Pittsburgh: ETC Press, 2013), 383–394.

16. Uniroyal highlights the significance of this branded, iconic architecture in terms of its corporate history. See, <http://www.uniroyaltires.com/assets/pdf/AboutUniroyalGiantTire.pdf>.

17. Anon. "Farewell to Egypt," *Las Vegas Review-Journal*, July 12, 2007, <http://www.reviewjournal.com/business/farewell-egypt>. See also, Sonya Padgett, "Curtains Drop on Themed Hotel-Casinos," *Las Vegas Review-Journal*, September 28, 2008, <http://www.reviewjournal.com/life/curtains-drop-themed-hotel-casinos>. Perhaps the most telling metaphor of the detheming effect in Las Vegas is found with the closure of the pirate-themed Sirens show at the Treasure Island and the show's replacement with a rather mundane (and unthemed) CVS drug store. See, Norm Clarke, "Treasure Island Closes Strip-side 'Sirens of TI' Show," *Las Vegas Review-Journal*, November 22, 2013, <http://www.reviewjournal.com/columns-blogs/norm-clarke/treasure-island-closes-strip-side-sirens-ti-show>.

18. See, <http://www.rwlasvegas.com/>.

19. See Joel Bergman, "Themed Space Design Retrospective," in *The Immersive Worlds Handbook: Designing Theme Parks and Consumer Spaces* (New York: Focal, 2013), 250–253.

20. For example, Joe Rhode, Imagineer behind Disney's Animal Kingdom, discussed the idea that abstraction has less of a role than representational forms of architecture and theming. This discussion occurred at a lunch discussion and tour at Disney's Animal Kingdom at the 2015 IAAPA Attractions Expo in Orlando, Florida.

21. For more on culture and essence at the Milan Expo, see See, Scott A. Lukas, "Cultural Thresholds at World Expo 2015 (Milan)," *OAA Perspectives: The Journal of the Ontario Association of Architects* 23, no. 4 (Winter 2015/2016).

22. See Scott A. Lukas, "Theme Parks: From Cultural Remaking to Social Justice, or Towards a Theme Park of Discomfort and the Uncanny," <https://www.academia.edu/3798322/Theme_Parks_From_Cultural_Remaking_to_Social_Justice_or_Towards_a_Theme_Park_of_Discomfort_and_the_Uncanny>.

23. Martin Heidegger, *The Question Concerning Technology, and Other Essays* (New York: Harper, 1977). For a video of the seed book, see my expo video, <https://www.youtube.com/watch?v=Va0maCxAKXA>.

24. See, Henry Jenkins, *Convergence Culture: Where Old and New Media Collide* (New York: New York University Press, 2008), and Henry Jenkins, "Convergence," in *The Immersive Worlds Handbook: Designing Theme Parks and Consumer Spaces* (New York: Focal, 2013), 245–247.

25. Scott A. Lukas, "From Themed Space to Lifespace," in *Staging the Past: Themed Environments in Transcultural Perspectives*, eds. Judith Schlehe, Michiko Uike-Bormann, Carolyn Oesterle, and Wolfgang Hochbruck (Bielefeld, Germany: Transcript, 2010), 135–153.

26. See <http://brcweb.com/>, Bob Rogers and Carmel Lewis, "Technology as Storytelling," in *The Immersive Worlds Handbook: Designing Theme Parks and Consumer Spaces* (New York: Focal, 2013), 215–219. See, also, Lukas, "How the Theme Park Got Its Power," 404–405.

27. See, Eric Avila, *Popular Culture in the Age of White Flight: Fear and Fantasy in Suburban Los Angeles* (Berkeley: University of California Press, 2006) and John Hannigan, *Fantasy City: Pleasure and Profit in the Postmodern Metropolis* (London: Routledge, 1998).

28. See my video, "Theming in the Experience Economy–Cerritos Millennium Library," <https://youtu.be/2Sbld_lchtA>.

29. One example of such a show is the defunct *Monster House* (2003–2006) on Discovery Channel in which houses were remodeled, often with an extreme theme. The world of bars has also experienced similar emphases on the use of theming to give new life to a struggling establishment. One such show is Spike TV's *Bar Rescue* with Jon Taffer.

30. See Scott A. Lukas, "The Cultures of Tiki," in this collection.

31. See my video of the pavilion experience, <https://youtu.be/Jyc3hFF0BGQ>.

32. See Scott A. Lukas, "Dark Theming Reconsidered," in this volume, for more on the contexts of the Swiss pavilion.

33. See <http://www.expo2015.org/en/pavillion-zero> for more on the design context of the pavilion.

34. See my walkthrough videos on Pavilion Zero, <https://www.youtube.com/watch?v=s6HrnnpbN9Q> and <https://www.youtube.com/watch?v=HZUyI9U1xYY>.

35. See Scott A. Lukas, "Dark Theming Reconsidered," in this volume; Scott A. Lukas, "Controversial Topics: Pushing the Limits in Themed and Immersive Spaces" (Masterclass), *Attractions Management* 20 (Quarter 4, 2015): 50–54; and Scott A. Lukas, "A Politics of Reverence and Irreverence: Social Discourse on Theming Controversies," in *The Themed Space: Locating Culture, Nation, and Self*, ed. Scott A. Lukas (Lanham, MD: Lexington, 2007), 271–293.

36. Mike Nudelman, "Banksy's 'Dismaland' Is Art About Nothing–and We're Over It," *Business Insider*, August 24, 2015, <http://www.businessinsider.com/banksys-dismaland-is-bad-and-boring-2015-8>, Shailee Koranne, "Dismaland Is Not Interesting and Neither Is Banksy," *Huffington Post Canada*, August 23, 2015, <http://www.huffingtonpost.ca/shailee-koranne/banksy-and-dismaland_b_8049062.html>, Dan Brooks, "Banksy and the Problem with Sarcastic Art," *New York Times Magazine*, September 10, 2015, <http://www.nytimes.com/2015/09/10/magazine/banksy-and-the-problem-with-sarcastic-art.html?_r=0>. See, also my discussion of Dismaland in Christopher Beanland, "Theme Parks Continue to Draw in Thrill-Seekers Despite the Risks–So Why Are We So Addicted?" *The Independent*, September 2, 2015, <http://www.independent.co.uk/travel/news-and-advice/theme-parks-continue-to-draw-in-thrill-seekers-despite-the-risks-so-why-are-we-so-addicted-10483525.html>.

37. For more on Dismaland see Florian Freitag, "Autotheming: Themed and Immersive Spaces in Self-Dialogue," and See Scott A. Lukas, "Judgments Passed: The Place of the Themed Space in the Contemporary World of Remaking," both in this collection.

38. See Vanderbilt, "It's a Mall World After All."

39. Exo, "Better Than Reality!," marketing brochure, 3.

30

Research Dialogue

The Place of the Future

By Filippo Carlà, Florian Freitag, Gordon Grice, Scott A. Lukas

This chapter is the second of two research dialogues that focus on the insights that may be gained from research collaborations within the worlds of themed and immersive spaces. The dialogue focuses on the idea of creating cross-pollination between the academic and design arenas of themed and immersive spaces. The research group that forms this conversation has begun a series of field, design, and academic critical experiments that focus on fuller understandings of these spaces. This second dialogue will focus on the contexts of the Place of the Future and will suggest some senses of how themed and immersive spaces, and their criticism, might exist in the future.

Lukas: Perhaps we could begin with a focus on themed and immersive spaces of the future. What might we expect these spaces to be, in terms of their design, their uses, and the criticism that will be applied to them?

Grice: This is a big question and maybe it's one that I don't feel all that competent to answer. I could say that virtual experience will soon supplant actual experience and that our everyday environment will become so immersive that the few remaining non-immersive environments will be eagerly sought. At the very least, the words "virtual" and "immersive" will need to be periodically redefined or superseded. We're already seeing retronyms such as "physical environment" and "actual experience" (to distinguish them from virtual environments and experiences), as well as brick-and-mortar businesses, (as opposed to e-commerce). How will the brave new digital/virtual world affect our entertainment choices? Will we need to leave our homes for anything ever again?

—What's on tonight?

—London in the tenth century.

—Will I need a sweater?

Carlà: This is a question I cannot really answer. I think we will see shifting interests in the themes to be represented, since they change according to identity structures, political interests, and also fashions. A successful movie can have, for example, a big impact. What I do see is in any case that the interest for the past is not going to decrease, while the "crisis of the future" is always more visible, so I expect an always stronger concentration on historical themes (real or fantastic) and on nostalgia as a central cultural factor.

Freitag: Successful theming depends, amongst other things, on recognizability and relatability. Therefore, I think, themed spaces will always be somewhat "conservative," using images, symbols, and the like that have been well established through other media and that have proven successful with a sizable audience. That does not necessarily mean that new and original themes are impossible, but they require a bigger effort from both the designer and from the visitor, and I would suggest that not too many themed spaces, at least not commercial ones, are going to run that risk.

Lukas: These are all excellent points, and I agree that we will likely see some combination of nostalgia, recognizability, and varied experiments with time. I would also add to these predictions and suggest that we might see that more spaces will begin to focus even more exclusively on the inward experiences of the guest—creating with them the sense that the theming and immersion of those spaces are entirely focused on the unique interests, lifestyle, and personalities of the guest. To go back to the issue of time and temporality, could any of you perhaps comment on how the constructions of time and temporality in themed and immersive spaces will be different in the future?[1]

Carlà: Again, this is very hard to foresee. There is a huge amount of literature on how the perception of time and temporality has changed in the second half of the twentieth century, substantially switching from the "modern" *regime de temps*, characterized by the idea of the "timeline" and a clear separation of past, present, and future (Koselleck), to a "postmodern" one, in which the three time levels collapse onto each other creating a "broader present" (Gumbrecht) —with the consequence of a stronger need for "presentification" which is the very foundation of the immersive environments.[2] This implies a "death of the future" (Assmann, Hölscher), so our inability to think of the future as a completely different world, ruled by completely different political and social structures—we rather conceive of it as a hypertechnological present.[3] As all ways of perceiving temporality, this is a cultural construct and will change, but when and how...it is impossible to know.

Freitag: I would suggest that time in themed and immersive spaces will become even more multi-layered and complex. A few examples such as FastPass and ExpressPass have radically changed the way visitors use themed spaces in general and theme parks in particular, and I expect to see more of this in the future, even though such a rationalization of leisure time may seem somewhat paradoxical. Rather than being cut off from events and developments outside the themed space, visitors can keep in touch with them via their smart phones. New ride systems allow vehicles to speed up, slow down, and even come to a complete stop during a ride instead of just moving through the circuit at one fixed speed. Finally, seasonal events have become more and more important, taking over rides and entire sections at theme parks.

Lukas: I wanted to mention a brief encounter that the three of us had in the hours following our research trip to Universal Studios Hollywood. You will recall that we chose to eat at the themed restaurant Bubba Gump Shrimp Company and one of the more interesting moments came when we began to interact with our server who seemed to be overly performative in the playing-out of his role as a server at the restaurant. During our conversation, I mentioned a famous anecdote of Sartre's about a server in a French restaurant and the idea that the server was displaying inauthenticity in terms of his own approach to service.[4] I recall that both of you found the server's approach to playing out the restaurant's theme to be too over the top. In the interest of commenting on what authenticity might look like for the future of themed and immersive spaces, perhaps both of you could comment on this exchange and some of the implications of it.

Carlà: In immersive spaces, authenticity is surely not an absolute quality of the objects, but it is a subjective quality, determined by the feelings of the visitors.[5] So the point is what most visitors perceive as authentic—in that occasion, the performance was, in our perception, inauthentic because it pushed too far. If you reconstruct, I don't know, a medieval castle, and make it completely shining and white, people won't like it, because they expect medieval castles to be dark, dusty, and a bit dirty. This applies also to discussions on "excessive renovations" of real historical monuments, which have been "too polished." So, authenticity is about expectation and fulfillment of expectations. Too little and too much are wrong in the same way.

Freitag: Exactly. The problem with the server was that I wasn't *expecting* him to act the way he did, which is why I thought his performance was inauthentic. But then, I was ill prepared for the experience in the first place: I have never watched *Forrest Gump*, I did not get any of the references, in fact, I had not even realized the place was themed (except for a vague seaside theme, perhaps). Again, this is about recognizability and relatability. To me, Bubba Gump Shrimp Company failed in both respects. The key to successful theming is not (only) to know your theme, but to know your audience.

Lukas: I find myself coming back to Wayne Curtis' quote that authenticity is "something that looks as you imagine it might."[6] As both of you indicate, there is so much variability in terms of what one of us will recognize in a given theme—its material cues and their antecedents, among other aspects—versus what another will recognize. If we believe what many postmodernist theorists have suggested about contemporary consumer society, it may be more and more difficult to match up all of these differing expectations and interpretations of guests in themed spaces of the future particularly because of the mélange of meanings, symbols, and memes that would appear to exist in the contemporary world. To shift this discussion just a bit, I wondered if you, Gordon, could comment on any senses that you have of future research and design work in these arenas that we have considered?

Grice: Psychologists Marily Oppezzo and Daniel Schwartz recently conducted studies demonstrating that walking doesn't simply stimulate thought, it facilitates the formation of creative thoughts: "Walking opens up the free flow of ideas." They conclude, "While research indicates that being outdoors has many cognitive benefits, walking has a very specific benefit—the improvement of creativity."[7] The objective of our visits to the theme parks was to stimulate our own creative thoughts by walking and observing inquisitively—to notice, and then to notice what we've noticed, as writer Verlyn Klinkenborg might put it—to collect data in the form of unhindered observations, to form ideas, and to discuss these among ourselves to spark further study and examination.[8] Here, it's worth mentioning another of Oppezzo and Schwartz's observations: "Walking increased the tendency to talk, and people were especially loquacious when walking outside." If this sounds like a fancy way of describing something that any group of friends might do at a theme park, there's some truth to that. The difference is that our discussions were aimed at finding sources of creative intuition—sources that might yield further creative ideas. Our observations were made, secure in the knowledge that any observation that one of us made would trigger a response from the others that would lead to insights and deeper discussion—the very basis of Creative Research. It wasn't surprising that our reflections were disparate and our discussions were wide-ranging. What was perhaps surprising—and especially useful—was that many of our observations lay outside of what each of us might have claimed as our own area of expertise. For example, one of my (the architect's) interests is the way that a ride does or doesn't engage the visitor by following a credible story arc. For example, I thought the roller coaster staged its events poorly. This is possibly something that an anthropologist might have been expected to remark on. But Scott, the anthropologist, was busy observing and commenting on view lines and vistas—a topic that interests me immensely, but which I didn't really notice until he mentioned it. Filippo the historian noticed various behavioral patterns, such as visitors' frequent "un-immersion" in the immersive environment by resorting to their cellphones—a cultural phenomenon, surely. And, throughout our visit, Florian, the cultural studies professor, was a constant source of information about the history of the parks. Another surprising discovery was that we all agreed on which attractions we liked the most. The attraction that got top marks from all four of us committed one or two subtle but disturbing architectural faux pas that it took the anthropologist to point out. Much more research is needed and is, we hope, imminent.

Carlà/Freitag: From a scholar's perspective, presenting at conferences and publishing happen after the most important part of one's work—researching, thinking, and writing—has already been done. Transdisciplinary and trans-academic encounters, however, must not be afterthoughts, but instead must happen at a point when they can genuinely impact our thinking about theme parks. We therefore propose collaborative field research or, as Gordon Grice has called it, Creative Research, as a way to bring together scholars and professionals on site—where theme parks and studies on theme parks happen. Creative Research cannot and is not intended to replace "traditional" field research in theme parks. If a scholar intends to do work on a particular park or a particular area in a park, they will still need to go to the park at some point, equipped with a camera and a notepad, in order to systematically examine it. Creative Research, by contrast, can take place at any park and does not have to proceed in a carefully planned, systematic way. It is not an individual exercise, but involves at least two and up to four people (scholars from various disciplines and professionals). It may focus on details such as the design of a specific theme park element or on broader issues like the trend to create autotheming or meta-theme parks (theme parks themed to theme parks).[9] It requires everyone involved to self-consciously reflect on their own perspective and to be ready to translate their thoughts into the language(s) of the other(s). And perhaps most importantly, it requires everyone involved to be open to different ways of thinking, while at the same time maintaining their specific field of expertise and making it immediately and directly comprehensible to the other members of the group. Creative Research will not necessarily directly translate into publishable material. Yet it may radically change the ways scholars, from whatever discipline, think about theme parks. It may draw a scholar's attention to issues that, due to their expert training, they may not even notice anymore. Or it may encourage scholars to write for a broader, transdisciplinary (or even trans-academic) audience, not just for their disciplinary peers. And due to the involvement of professionals, it may ultimately change the way theme parks look and work.

Lukas: Gordon, I wondered if you could comment on the sense that I have that in most cases academics who study theme parks are viewed with some suspicion or resentment by practitioners in the field of themed and immersive space design? What is the source of this and how might we imagine more collaboration and creative research of the sort that you have discussed?

Grice: The distressing part of all this is that, in my experience, practitioners don't appear to pay attention to the research at all. I haven't found prejudices against academics—being a non-academic myself, maybe I'm not sufficiently attuned to it—but there seems to be a lack of awareness or interest in anything theoretical. Is it possible that the world is actually divided into two groups: theorists and practitioners? There is hope. Florian was in Toronto (in 2015) and came to our office to give a brief, excellent talk on the Time and Temporality Project. A surprisingly large group assembled to listen to him and asked penetrating questions at the end. About two-dozen people emailed me afterwards, asking for transcripts of Florian's writing on the subject. Many of those in attendance said that they had no idea how much room for thought there was in the subject of theme parks. I remember being similarly and pleasantly astounded the first time I opened one of your (Lukas') books. There is an eager audience for this. I think it's up to us to get the word out.

Notes

1. Scott A. Lukas' chapter in this collection, "Theming and Immersion in the Space of the Future," also addresses a number of the issues that form the basis of this research dialogue.

2. Reinhart Koselleck, *Vergangene Zukunft: Zur Semantik geschichtlicher Zeiten* (Frankfurt am Main, Germany: Suhrkamp, 2003). Hans Ulrich Gumbrecht, *Unsere breite Gegenwart* (Frankfurt am Main, Germany: Suhrkamp, 2010).

3. Aleida Assmann, *Ist die Zeit aus den Fugen?: Aufstieg und Fall des Zeitregimes der Moderne* (Munich, Germany: Hanser, 2013). Lucian Hölscher, *Die Entdeckung der Zukunft* (Frankfurt am Main, Germany: Fischer Taschenbuch Verlag, 1999).

4. Jean-Paul Sartre, *Being and Nothingness: An Essay on Phenomenological Ontology* (London: Methuen, 1958), 59.

5. Cornelius J. Holtorf, "On Pastness: A Reconsideration of Materiality in Archaeological Object Authenticity," *Anthropological Quarterly* 86 (2013): 427–444.

6. Wayne Curtis, "Belle Epoxy: Has the New Las Vegas, with Its Mishmash Collection of the World's Greatest Cultural Icons, Raised the American Love Affair with the Fake to the Level of High Art?," Preservation (May/June 2000).

7. Marily Oppezzo and Daniel L. Schwartz, "Give Your Ideas Some Legs: The Positive Effect of Walking on Creative Thinking," *Journal of Experimental Psychology: Learning, Memory and Cognition* 40, no. 4 (2014): 1148.

8. Verlyn Klinkenborg, *Several Short Sentences About Writing* (New York: Vintage, 2011), 41.

9. See Florian Freitag's contribution in this collection, "Autotheming: Themed and Immersive Spaces in Self-Dialogue," for more on this phenomenon.

Selected Bibliography

Aagaard, Sine. "Globe 1: A Place of Integration or an Ethnic Oasis?" Pp. 199–212 in *Re-Investing Authenticity: Tourism, Place and Emotions*, edited by Britta Timm Knudsen and Anne Marit Waade. Bristol, UK: Channel View Publications, 2010.

Aalbers, Manuel B. and Magdalena Sabat, "Re-making a Landscape of Prostitution: The Amsterdam Red Light District." *CITY* 16, nos. 1–2 (February–April 2012): 112–128.

Abarbanel, Brett. "Mapping the Online Gambling e-Servicescape: A Conceptual Model." *UNLV Gaming Research & Review Journal* 17, no. 2, (2013): 27–44.

Adams, Judith A. *The American Amusement Park Industry*. Boston: Twayne, 1991.

Adey, Peter. "Above Us Only Sky: Themes, Simulations, and Liverpool John Lennon Airport." Pp. 153–166 in *The Themed Space: Locating Culture, Nation, and Self*, edited by Scott A. Lukas. Lanham, MD: Lexington, 2007.

Adler, Jerry and Maggie Malone. "Theme Cities." *Newsweek*, September 11, 1995.

Agnew, Vanessa. " History's Pure Serene: On Reenacting Cook's First Voyage, September 2001." Pp. 205–218 in *Staging the Past: Themed Environments in Transcultural Perspectives*, edited by Judith Schlehe, Michiko Uike-Bormann, Carolyn Oesterle, and Wolfgang Hochbruck. Bielefeld, Germany: Transcript, 2010.

———. "History's Affective Turn: Historical Reenactment and Its Work in the Present." *Rethinking History* 11, no. 3 (September 2007): 299–312.

Ah-Keng, Kau. "Evaluating the Attractiveness of a New Theme Park: A Cross-Cultural Comparison." Pp. 259–272 in *Tourism Management: Towards the New Millennium*, edited by Chris Ryan and Stephen Page. New York: Routledge, 2000.

Al, Stefan, "Welcome to Theoretical Las Vegas." *Berkeley Planning Journal* 22, no. 1 (2009): 141–146.

Allen, David. Seeing Double: Disney's Wilderness Lodge." *European Journal of American Culture* 31, no. 2 (2012): 123–144.

Amusement Business. "Theming Plays Major Role in Popularity of Coasters." *Amusement Business* 106, no. 20 (1994): 22–25.

Anderson, Dana. "Sign, Space, and Story: Roller Coasters and the Evolution of a Thrill." *The Journal of Popular Culture* 33, no. 2 (Fall 1999): 1–22.

Anderson, Grace. "Entertainment Architecture." *Architectural Record*, September 1989.

Anderton, Frances. "The World According to Disney." *Architectural Record*, September 1988.

Andorka Jr., Frank H. "Theme Dreams." *Hotel & Motel Management* 213, no. 17 (1998): 42–44.

Angelo, Bonnie and Stacy Perman. "Hungry for Theme Dining." *Time* 148, no. 5.

Anthes, Bill. "Learning from Foxwoods: Visualizing the Mashantucket Pequot Tribal Nation." *American Indian Quarterly* 32, no. 2 (2008): 204–218.

Antonucci, Rocco. "In the Clouds of Joseph Farcus: The Phenomenology of Going to Sea in the Era of Supermodernity." *Design Issues* 25, no. 4 (Autumn 2009): 36–50.

Apfel, Ira. "Magic-Theme Restaurants Conjure Up Spellbinding Sales." *Restaurants USA*, February 1998.

Archer, Kevin. "The Limits to the Imagineered City: Sociospatial Polarization in Orlando." *Economic Geography* 73, no. 3 (July 1997): 322–336.

Arkell, Harriet. "Indonesian Café Owner Sparks Outrage after Opening Nazi-Themed Restaurant Complete with Waiters Dressed as SS Officers." Daily Mail.com, July 19, 2013.

Arndorfer, Jim. "McSploitation." Pp. 173–181 in *Boob Jubilee: The Cultural Politics of the New Economy*, edited by Thomas Frank and David Mulcahey. New York: W. W. Norton, 2003.

Aronstein, Susan L. "Pilgrimage and Medieval Narrative Structures in Disney's Parks." Pp. 57–76 in *The Disney Middle Ages: A Fairy-Tale and Fantasy Past*, edited by Tison Pugh and Susan Aronstein. New York: Palgrave Macmillan, 2012.

Aronstein, Susan L. and Laurie A. Finke. "Discipline and Pleasure: The Pedagogical Work of Disneyland." *Educational Philosophy and Theory* 45, no. 6 (2013): 610–624.

Atkinson, Connie Zeanah. "Whose New Orleans?: Music's Place in the Packaging of New Orleans for Tourism." Pp. 171–182 in *Tourists and Tourism: A Reader*, edited by Sharon Bohn Gmelch. Long Grove, IL: Waveland, 2004.

Augé, Marc. *Non-Places: An Introduction to Supermodernity*. London: Verso, 2009.

Auslander, Mark. "Touching the Past: Materializing Time in Traumatic 'Living History' Reenactments." *Signs and Society* 1, no. 1 (Spring 2013): 161–183.

Baber, Katherine and James Spickard. "Crafting Culture: 'Tradition,' Art, and Music in Disney's 'It's A Small World.'" *The Journal of Popular Culture* 48, no. 2 (April 2015): 225–239.

Bagaeen, Samer. "Brand Dubai: The Instant City; or the Instantly Recognizable City." *International Planning Studies* 12, no. 2 (May 2007): 173–197.

Bagli, Charles V. "Novelty Gone, Theme Restaurants Are Tumbling." *New York Times*, December 27, 1998.

Baldwin, Deborah. "Main Street as Memory Lane." *New York Times*, January 10, 2002.

Balides, Constance. "Jurassic Post-Fordism: Tall Tales of Economics in the Theme Park." *Screen* 41, no. 2 (2000): 139–160.

Ball, Edward. "To Theme or Not to Theme: Disneyfication without Guilt." Pp. 31–37 in *The Once and Future Park*, edited by Deborah Karasov and Steve Waryan. New York: Princeton Architectural Press, 1993.

Baptista, João Afonso. "Tourism Moral Imaginaries and the Making of Community." Pp. 125–146 in *Tourism Imaginaries: Anthropological Approaches*, edited by Noel B. Salazar and Nelson H. H. Graburn. New York: Berghan, 2014.

Barbas, Samantha. "I'll Take Chop Suey: Restaurants as Agents of Culinary and Cultural Change." *The Journal of Popular Culture* 36, 4 (2003): 669–686.

Barber, Stephen. *Projected Cities: Cinema and Urban Space*. London: Reaktion, 2012.

Barreneche, Gabriel Ignacio. "The Dystopic Theme Park: The Role of Lorelei in Marcelo Cohen's *El oído absoluto*." *Romance Quarterly* 55, no. 2 (2008): 128–139.

Barron, Kelly. "Theme Players." *Forbes* 163, no. 6 (March 22, 1999).

Bartkowiak, Mathew J. "Behind the Behind the Scenes of Disney World: Meeting the Need for Insider Knowledge." *The Journal of Popular Culture* 45, no. 5 (2012): 943–959.

Bartling, Hugh. "The Magic Kingdom Syndrome: Trials and Tribulations of Life in Disney's Celebration." *Contemporary Justice Review* 7, no. 4 (2004): 375–393.

Bayless, Martha. "Disney's Castles and the Work of the Medieval in the Magic Kingdom." Pp. 39–75 in *The Disney Middle Ages: A Fairy-Tale and Fantasy Past*, edited by Tison Pugh and Susan Aronstein. New York: Palgrave Macmillan, 2012.

Beanland, Christopher. "Theme Parks Continue to Draw in Thrill-Seekers Despite The Risks—So Why Are We so Addicted?" *The Independent*, September 16, 2015.

Beard, Richard R. *Walt Disney's Epcot Center: Creating the New World of Tomorrow*. New York: Harry N. Abrams, 1982.

Beardsworth, Alan and Alan Bryman. "The Wild Animal in Late Modernity: The Case of the Disneyization of Zoos." *Tourist Studies* 1, no. 1 (2001): 83–104.

———. "Late Modernity and the Dynamics of Quasification: The Case of the Themed Restaurant." *The Sociological Review* 47, no. 2 (May 1999): 228–257.

Bedford, Leslie. *The Art of Museum Exhibitions: How Story and Imagination Create Aesthetic Experiences*. Walnut Creek, CA: Left Coast Press, 2014.

Beeton, Sue. *Travel, Tourism and the Moving Image*. Clevedon, UK: Channel View Publications, 2015.

———. *Film-induced Tourism*. Clevedon, UK: Channel View, 2005.

Bégout, Bruce. *Zeropolis: The Experience of Las Vegas*. London: Reaktion, 2003.

Bell, Claudia and John Lyall. *The Accelerated Sublime: Landscape, Tourism, and Identity*. Westport, CT: Praeger, 2002.

Bell, Jonathan, ed. *Carchitecture*. London: Birkhäuser, 2001.

Bell, Rick, Herbert L. Meiselman, Barry J. Pierson, and William G. Reeve. "Effects of Adding an Italian Theme to a Restaurant on the Perceived Ethnicity, Acceptability, and Selection of Foods." *Appetite*, 22 (1994): 11–24.

Benbow, S. Mary. "Zoos: Public Places to View Private Lives." *The Journal of Popular Culture* 33, no. 4 (Spring 2000): 13–23.

Benston, Liz. "Six Questions: Joel Bergman, Architect of Themed Megaresorts." *Las Vegas Sun*, October 8, 2008.

Bergren, Ann. "Jon Jerde and the Architecture of Pleasure." *Assemblage*, no. 37 (December 1998): 8–35.

Best, Joel and Kathleen S. Lowney. "The Disadvantage of a Good Reputation: Disney as a Target for Social Problems Claims." *The Sociological Quarterly* 30, no. 3 (Summer 2009): 431–449.

Betsky, Aaron. "Theme Wars Rage in Vegas." *Architectural Record* 180, no. 8 (1992).

Bettany, Shona and Russell W. Belk. "Disney Discourses of Self and Other: Animality, Primitivity, Modernity, and Postmodernity." *Consumption Markets & Culture* 14, no. 2 (2011): 163–176.

Bezdecny, Kris. "Imagineering Uneven Geographical Development in Central Florida." *Geographical Review* 105, no. 3 (July 2015): 325–343.

Bhatt, Ritu, "Aethetic or Anaesthetic: A Nelson Goodman Reading of the Las Vegas Strip." Pp. 19–30 in *Relearning from Las Vegas*, edited by Aron Vinegar and Michaek J. Golec. Minneapolis: University of Minnesota Press, 2009.

Bieger, Laura. *Ästhetik der Immersion: Raum-Erleben zwischen Welt und Bild: Las Vegas, Washington und die White City*. Bielefeld, Germany: Transcript, 2007.

Bjerregaard, Peter. "De-connecting Relations: Exhibitions and Objects as Resistance." Pp. 45–63 in *Objects and Imagination: Perspectives on Materialization and Meaning*, edited by Øivind Fuglerud and Leon Wainwright. Oxford: Berghahn, 2015.

Blair, Carole and Neil Michel. "Commemorating in the Theme Park Zone: Reading the Astronauts Memorial." Pp. 29–83 in *At the Intersection: Cultural Studies and Rhetorical Studies*, edited by Thomas Rosteck. New York: Guilford, 1999.

Blake, Peter. "The Lessons of the Parks." Pp. 425–439 in *The Art of Walt Disney: From Mickey Mouse to the Magic Kingdoms and Beyond*, edited by Christopher Finch and John Lasseter. New York: Harry N. Abrams, 2011.

Bohl, Charles C. *Place Making: Developing Town Centers, Main Streets, and Urban Villages*. Washington, D.C.: Urban Land Institute, 2002.

Borchard, Gregory A. and Anthony J. Ferri. "When in Las Vegas, Do as the Ancient Romans Did: Bread and Circuses Then and Now." *The Journal of Popular Culture* 44, no. 4 (August 2011): 717–731.

Borges, Sofia, Sven Ehmann, and Robert Klanten. *WorkScape: New Spaces for New Work*. Berlin: Gestalten, 2013.

Borghini, Stefania *et. al.* "Why Are Themed Brandstores So Powerful? Retail Brand Ideology at American Girl Place." *Journal of Retailing* 85, no. 3 (September 2009): 363–375.

Borrie, William T. "Disneyland and Disney World: Designing and Prescribing the Recreational Experience." *Loisir et Société/Society and Leisure* 22, no. 1 (1999): 71–82.

Bosker, Bianca. *Original Copies: Architectural Mimicry in Contemporary China*. Honolulu: University of Hawaii Press, 2013.

Botticello, Julie. "Lagos in London: Finding the Space of Home." *Home Cultures* 4, no. 1 (2007): 7–23.

Boyle, David. *Authenticity: Brands, Fakes, Spin and Lust for Real Life*. New York: Harper Perennial, 2006.

Braithwaite, David. *Fairground Architecture: The World of Amusement Parks, Carnivals, and Fairs*. New York: Frederick A. Praeger, 1968.

Branham, Joan. "The Temple that Won't Quit: Constructing Sacred Space in Orlando's Holy Land Theme Park." *Harvard Divinity Bulletin* 36, no. 3 (Autumn 2008): 18–31.

Brannen, Mary Yoko. "Bwana Mickey: Constructing Cultural Consumption at Tokyo Disneyland." Pp. 216–234 in *Remade in Japan*, edited by Joseph Tobin. New Haven, CT: Yale University Press, 1992.

Bransford, Walt. "The Past Was No Illusion." Pp. 197–205 in *Meet Me at the Fair: A World's Fair Reader*, edited by Laura Hollengreen, Celia Pearce, Rebecca Rouse, and Bobby Schweizer. Pittsburgh: ETC Press, 2013.

Briefel, Aviva. "Mickey Horror Escape from Tomorrow and the Gothic Attack on Disney." *Film Quarterly* 68, no. 4 (Summer 2015): 36–43.

Briggs, Nigel "Reaching a Broader Audience." *The Public Historian* 22, no. 3 (Summer, 2000): 95–105.

Brigham, Ann. "Behind-the-Scenes Spaces: Promoting Production in a Landscape of Consumption." Pp. 207–223 in *The Themed Space: Locating Culture, Nation, and Self*, edited by Scott A. Lukas. Lanham, MD: Lexington, 2007.

———. "Consuming Pleasures of Re/Production: Going Behind the Scenes in Spielberg's *Jurassic Park* and at Universal Studios Theme Park." *Genders* 36 (2002).

Brode, Douglas. "Of Theme Parks and Television: Walt Disney, Rod Serling, and the Politics of Nostalgia." Pp. 183–194 in *Disneyland and Culture: Essays on the Parks and Their Influence*, edited by Kathy Merlock Jackson and Mark I. West. Jefferson, NC: McFarland, 2010.

Brown, Janelle. "The Consumer Incarnation of Microsoftiness." *Salon*, June 29, 1999.

Brown, Roni. "Designing Differently: the Self-Build Home." *Arts and Humanities Journal of Design History* 21, no. 4 (2008): 359–370.

———. "Identity and Narrativity in Homes Made by Amateurs." *Home Cultures* 4, no. 3 (2007): 213–238.

Brown, Stephen and Anthony Patterson. "Knick-Knack, Paddy-Whack, Give a Pub a Theme." *Journal of Marketing Management* 16 (2000): 647–662.

Brumback, Nancy. "Museum Piece?" *Restaurant Business* 99, no. 24.

———. "Theme Song." *Restaurant Business* 103, no. 13: 42–43.

Bruner, Edward M. *Culture on Tour: Ethnographies of Travel*. Chicago: University of Chicago Press, 2004.

Bryant, Raymond L. "Consuming Burmese Teak: Anatomy of a Violent Luxury." Pp. 239–256 in *Consuming Space: Placing Consumption in Perspective*, edited by Michael K. Goodman, David Goodman, and Michael Redclift. Burlington, VT: Ashgate, 2010.

Bryman, Alan. *The Disneyization of Society*. London: Sage, 2004.

———. "The Disneyization of Society." *The Sociological Review* 1999: 25–47.

———. "McDonald's as a Disneyized Institution: Global Implications." *American Behavioral Scientist* 47, no. 2 (2003): 154–167.

Buchanan, Chris. "The Long Road to Riches." *Mail & Guardian Friday*, June 30–July 6, 2000.

Buda, Dorina Maria. *Affective Tourism: Dark Routes in Conflict*. London: Routledge, 2015.

Bukatman, Scott. "There's Always Tomorrowland: Disney and the Hypercinematic Experience." *October* 57 (Summer 1991): 55–78.

Bull, Michael. *Sound Moves: iPod Culture and Urban Experience*. London: Routledge, 2008.

Bunten, Alexis Celeste. "Deriding Demand: Indigenous Imaginaries in Tourism." Pp. 80–102 in *Tourism Imaginaries: Anthropological Approaches*, edited by Noel B. Salazar and Nelson H. H. Graburn. New York: Berghan, 2014.

Burka, Madeleine. "Evolution, Not Revolution: Theme Restaurants Come of Age." *Restaurants USA*, December 1999.

Burnside, Mary Wade. "Halloween Theming Growing Trend in Europe, Asia." *Amusement Business* 114, no. 9.

Business Pundit. "15 Amazingly Creative Themed Office Spaces." *Business Pundit*, May 3, 2013.

Business Wire. "Airline to Middle-earth Scores a Flying Hat-Trick with New Lord of the Rings 747: The Return of Aragorn and Legolas." *Los Angeles Times*, November 17, 2003.

Carlà, Filippo and Florian Freitag. "Strategien der Geschichtstransformationen in Themenparks." Pp. 131–149 in *Geschichtstransformationen: Medien, Verfahren und Funktionalisierungen historischer Rezeption*, edited by Sonja Georgi, Julia Ilgner, Isabell Lammel, Cathleen Sarti, and Christine Waldschmidt. Bielefeld, Germany: Transcript, 2015.

———. "Ancient Greek Culture and Myth in the Terra Mítica Theme Park." *Classical Receptions Journal* 7, no. 2 (2015): 244–246.

Carnegie, Elizabeth. "'It Wasn't All Bad': Representations of Working Class Cultures within Social History Museums and Their Impacts on Audiences." *Museum and Society* 4, no. 2 (July 2006): 69–83.

Carnegie, Elizabeth and Scott McCabe. "Re-enactment Events and Tourism: Meaning, Authenticity and Identity." *Current Issues in Tourism* 11, no. 4 (2008): 349–368.

Carr, Adrian. "Understanding the 'Imago' Las Vegas: Taking our Lead from Homer's Parable of the Oarsmen." *M@n@gement* 4, no. 3 (2007): 122–140.

Carr, Austin. "The Messy Business Of Reinventing Happiness: Inside Disney's Radical Plan to Modernize Its Cherished Theme Parks." *Fast Company*, May 2015: 100–116.

Carson, Charles. "Whole New Worlds: Music and the Disney Theme Park Experience." *Ethnomusicology Forum* 13, no. 2 (2004): 228–235.

Carver, Francisco Asensio. *Theme and Amusement Parks*. New York: Arco, 1997.

Cashill, Robert. "Architecture/Themed Entertainment: The Jekyll and Hyde Club." *Entertainment Technology Communications* 30, no. 2: 44–7.

———. "Theming the History of Hong Kong." *TCI: Theatre Crafts International* 31, no. 1 (January 1997): 7–8.

———. "Theming beyond The Great Wall." *TCI: Theatre Crafts International* 30, no. 7 (August/September 1996): 8–9.

Cass, Jeffrey. "Egypt on Steroids: Luxor Las Vegas and Postmodern Orientalism." Pp. 241–64 in *Architecture and Tourism: Perception, Performance, and Place*, edited by D. Medina Lasansky. Oxford: Berg, 2004.

Cass, Jeffrey and Dion Dennis. "Ground Zero: Las Vegas' Luxor." *CTHEORY* 19, no. 3, Event-scene 32, November 6, 1996.

Chambers, Erve. *Native Tours: The Anthropology of Travel and Tourism*. Long Grove, IL: Waveland, 2009.

Chamish, Barry. "Bible-Themed Park Fares Well in Land of Political Instability." *Amusement Business* 106, no. 43: 45.

Chang, Lan-Yun. "Sensation Seeking and Customer Perceptions of Thematic Entertainment: Evidence From Theme Motels in Taiwan." *Social Behavior and Personality* 37, no. 6 (2009): 753–766.

Chang, T. C. "Theming Cities, Taming Places: Insights from Singapore." *Geografiska Analer: Series B, Human Geography* 82, no. 1 (2000): 35–54.

Chaplin, Sarah. *Japanese Love Hotels: A Cultural History*. London: Routledge, 2007.

———. "Heterotopia Deserta: Las Vegas and Other Spaces." Pp. 340–361 in *Designing Cities: Critical Readings in Urban Design*, edited by Alexander R. Cuthbert. Oxford: Blackwell, 2003.

———. "Authenticity and Otherness: The New Japanese Theme Park." Pp. 77–79 in *Architectural Design: Consuming Architecture*, edited by Maggie Toy. West Sussex, UK: John Wiley and Sons, 1998.

Chappell, Edward A. "The Museum and the Joy Ride: Williamsburg Landscapes and the Spectre of Theme Parks." Pp. 119–156 in *Theme Park Landscapes: Antecedents and Variations*, edited by Terence Young and Robert Riley. Washington, D.C.: Dumbarton Oaks Research Library and Collection, 2002.

Chase, John. "The Garret, the Boardroom, and the Amusement Park." *Journal of Architectural Education* 47, no. 2 (1993): 75–87.

Chena, Hung-Bin, Shih-Shuo Yehb, and Tzung-Cheng Huanc. "Nostalgic Emotion, Experiential Value, Brand Image, and Consumption Intentions of Customers of Nostalgic-Themed Restaurants." *Journal of Business Research* 67, no. 3 (March 2014): 354–360.

Chhabra, Deepak, Woojin Leea, and Shengnan Zhaoa. "Epitomizing the 'Other' in Ethnic Eatertainment Experiences." *Leisure/Loisir* 37, no. 4 (2013): 361–378.

Chiang, Connie Y. "Monterey-by-the-Smell: Odors and Social Conflict on the California Coastline." *Pacific Historical Review* 73, no. 2 (2004): 183–214.

Chicone, Sarah J. and Richard A. Kissel. *Dinosaurs and Dioramas: Creating Natural History Exhibitions*. Walnut Creek, CA: Left Coast Press, 2013.

Christersdotter, Maria. "Mobile Dreams." Pp. 92–111 in *Experiencescapes: Tourism, Culture, and Economy*, edited by Tom O'Dell and Peter Billing. Frederiksberg: Copenhagen Business School Press, 2005.

Chung, Chuihua Judy, Jeffrey Inaba, Rem Koolhaas, Sze Tsung Leong, Tae-wook Cha, et al. *Harvard Design School Guide to Shopping*. New York: Taschen, 2001.

Chytry, Josef. "Walt Disney and the Creation of Emotional Environments: Interpreting Walt Disney's Oeuvre from the Disney Studios to Disneyland, Calarts, and the Experimental Prototype Community of Tomorrow (EPCOT)." *Journal of Vacation Marketing* 7, no. 4 (2012): 316–332.

Cicora, Elaine T. "Your Place or Mayan?" *New Times*, Cleveland Scene, October 25, 2006.

Clandfield, Peter. "Passing Time at West Edmonton Mall." Pp. 153–166 in *The Globetrotting Shopaholic: Consumer Spaces, Products, and their Cultural Places*, edited by Tanfer Emin Tunc and Annessa Ann Babic. Newcastle Upon Tyne, UK: Cambridge Scholars Publishing, 2008.

Clanton, Brett. "Hollywood's Out, Carnival's In: Restaurant Gets New Theme." *New Orleans City Business* 21, no. 32: 7.

Clark, Gregory. "Rhetorical Experience and the National Jazz Museum in Harlem." Pp. 113–135 in *Places of Public Memory: The Rhetoric of Museums and Memorials*, edited by Greg Dickinson, Brian L. Ott, and Carole Blair. Tuscaloosa: University of Alabama, 2010.

Clave, S. Anton. *The Global Theme Park Industry*. Oxfordshire, England: CABI, 2007.

Clément, Thibaut. "'Locus of Control': A Selective Review of Disney Theme Parks." *InMedia* 2 (2012).

Coates, Nigel. *Guide to Ecstacity*. London: Laurence King, 2003.

Coffer, David. "Operators' Creativity Flourishes with Theme Restaurants." *Nation's Restaurant News,* December 30, 2014.

Cohen, Erik. "Authenticity and Commoditization in Tourism." *Annals of Tourism Research* 15, no. 3 (1988): 371–386.

———. "A Phenomenology of Tourist Experiences." *Sociology* 13, no. 2 (May 1979): 179–201.

Collins, Larry K. and Lorna Collins. *31 Months in Japan: The Building of a Theme Park*. Lincoln, NE: iUniverse, 2005.

Conlin, Jonathan. *The Pleasure Garden, from Vauxhall to Coney Island*. Philadelphia: University of Pennsylvania Press, 2012.

Cooper, Marc. "Searching for Sin City and Finding Disney in the Desert." Pp. 325–350 in *Literary Las Vegas*, edited by Mike Tronnes. New York: Henry Holt, 1995.

Corn, Joseph J. and Brian Horrigan. *Yesterday's Tomorrows: Past Visions of the American Future*. Baltimore, MD: Johns Hopkins University Press, 1996.

Cornelis, Pieter. "Time and Temporality in Theme Parks: An Economic Perspective." In *"Here You Leave Today": Time and Temporality in Theme Parks,* edited by Filippo Carlà, Florian Freitag, Sabrina Mittermeier, and Ariane Schwarz. Hanover, Germany: Wehrhahn, 2016.

Crabtree, James. "Laws of Attractions: Inside India's Largest Theme Park." *Caravan,* July 1, 2013.

Crang, Mike. "Living History: Magic Kingdoms or a Quixotic Quest for Authenticity?" *Annals of Tourism Research* 23, no. 2 (1996): 415–431.

Croce, Paul Jerome. "A Clean and Separate Space: Walt Disney in Person and Production." *The Journal of Popular Culture* 25, no. 3 (Winter 1991): 91–103.

Crockett, David and Lenita Davis. "Commercial Mythmaking at the Holy Land Experience." *Consumption Markets and Culture* (2015): 1–22.

Cronin, Anne M. *Advertising, Commercial Spaces and the Urban*. London: Palgrave Macmillan, 2010.

Culverwell, Wendy. "Cool Spaces: Comic-themed Meeting Rooms at New Relic Inc." *Portland Business Journal*, March 5, 2013.

Curtis, Wayne. "From Tiki to Tacky–and Back." *Atlantic Monthly* 308, no. 4 (2011): 28.

———. "Tiki: How Sex, Rum, World War II, and the Brand-New State of Hawaii Ignited a Fad That Has Never Quite Ended." *American Heritage* 57, no. 4 (August/September 2006): 38–46.

———. "The Tiki Wars." *Atlantic Monthly* 287, no. 2. (2001).

———. "Belle Epoxy." *Preservation* May/June 2000.

D'Arcens, Louise. "Laughing in the Face of the Past: Satire and Nostalgia in Medieval Heritage Tourism." *Postmedieval: A Journal of Medieval Cultural Studies* 2, no. 2 (2011): 155–170.

Dale, Crispin and Neil Robinson. "The Theming of Tourism Education: A Three-domain Approach." *International Journal of Contemporary Hospitality Management* 13, no. 1 (2001): 30–35.

Davies, Alice and Kathryn Tollervey. *The Style of Coworking: Contemporary Shared Workspaces*. Munich, Germany: Prestel, 2013.

Davies, Paul. "The Algiers Motel." Pp. 97–108 in *Stripping Las Vegas: A Contextual Review of Casino Resort Architecture*, edited by Karin Jaschke and Silke Ötsch. Weimar, Germany: University of Weimar Press, 2003.

———. "Sites of Vicarious Consumption: Hollywood's Living (Room) History." Pp. 72–75 in *Architectural Design: Consuming Architecture*, edited by Maggie Toy. West Sussex, UK: John Wiley and Sons, 1998.

———. "New York, New York: Las Vegas' Latest Hotel Takes Theming to New Heights." *Blueprint* no. 134 (December 1996): 20–22.

Davis, Susan G. "Landscapes of Imagination: Tourism in Southern California." *Pacific Historical Review* 68, no. 2 (May 1999): 173–191.

———. *Spectacular Nature: Corporate Culture and the Sea World Experience*. Berkeley: University of California Press, 1997.

———. "The Theme Park: Global Industry and Cultural Form." *Media Culture and Society* 18 (July 1996): 399–422.

Davis, Tracy C. "Theatrical Antecedents of the Mall that Ate Downtown." *The Journal of Popular Culture* 24, no. 4 (Spring 1991): 1–15.

DeAngelis, Michael. "Orchestrated (Dis)orientation: Roller Coasters, Theme Parks, and Postmodernism." *Cultural Critique* no. 37 (Autumn 1997): 107–129.

De Groote, Patrick. "Globalisation of Commercial Theme Parks, Case: the Walt Disney Company." *Applied Studies in Agribusiness and Commerce* 38 (2009): 22–28.

De la Mare, Nick. "Why Schools and Hospitals Should Be More Like Theme Parks." *Fast Company*, January 20, 2016.

DeLyser, Dydia. "Authenticity on the Ground: Engaging the Past in a California Ghost Town." *Annals of the Association of American Geographers* 89, no. 4 (December 1999): 602–632.

De Vries, Tity. "Ambiguity in an Alaskan History Theme Park: Presenting 'History as Commodity' and 'History as Heritage.'" *The Public Historian* 29, no. 2 (Spring 2007): 55–79.

Delany, Samuel R. *Times Square Red, Times Square Blue*. New York: New York University Press, 1999.

Dennett, Andrea Stulman. "A Postmodern Look at EPCOT's American Adventure." *Journal of American Culture* 12, no. 1 (Spring 1989): 47–53.

Denson, Charles. *Coney Island: Lost and Found*. Berkeley: Ten Speed Press, 2004.

Desmond, Jane C. *Staging Tourism: Bodies on Display from Waikiki to Sea World*. Chicago: University Of Chicago Press, 2001.

Detweiler, Eric. "Hyperurbanity: Idealism, New Urbanism, and the Politics of Hyperreality in the Town of Celebration, Florida." Pp. 150–171 in *Disneyland and Culture: Essays on the Parks and Their Influence*, edited by Kathy Merlock Jackson and Mark I. West. Jefferson, NC: McFarland, 2010.

Dickinson, Greg. "Joe's Rhetoric: Finding Authenticity at Starbucks." *Rhetoric Society Quarterly* 32, no. 4 (Fall 2002): 5–27.

———. "Memories for Sale: Nostalgia and the Construction of Identity in Old Pasadena." *The Quarterly Journal of Speech* 83, no. 1 (February 1997): 1–27.

Dickinson, Greg, Brian L. Ott, and Eric Aoki. "Spaces of Remembering and Forgetting: The Reverent Eye/I at the Plains Indian Museum." *Communication and Critical/Cultural Studies* 3, no. 1 (2006): 27–47.

Dickerson, Marla. "Self-Styled Keepers of the Magic Kingdom." *Los Angeles Times*, September 12, 1996.

Disney Book Group. *Marc Davis: Walt Disney's Renaissance Man*. New York: Disney Editions, 2014.

Dixon, Kevin. "Football Fandom and Disneyisation in Late-modern Life." *Leisure Studies* 33, no. 1 (January 2014): 1–21.

Dodsworth, Clark. "Theme Parks in the Digital Age." *Animation World Magazine* 3.9 (December 1998).

Dombek, Kristin. "Murder in the Theme Park: Evangelical Animals and the End of the World." *The Drama Review* 51, no. 1 (Spring 2007): 138–153.

Doorley, Scott and Scott Witthoft. *Make Space: How to Set the Stage for Creative Collaboration*. Hoboken, NJ: Wiley, 2012.

Doss, Erika. *Memorial Mania: Public Feeling in America*. Chicago: University of Chicago Press, 2010.

———. "Making Imagination Safe in the 1950s: Disneyland's Fantasy Art and Architecture." Pp. 179–190 in *Designing Disney's Theme Parks: The Architecture of Reassurance*, edited by Karal Ann Marling. Paris: Flammarion, 1997.

Draper, Susana. *Afterlives of Confinement: Spatial Transitions in Postdictatorship Latin America*. Pittsburgh: University of Pittsburgh Press, 2012.

Dreschke, Anja. "Playing Ethnology." Pp. 253–267 in *Staging the Past: Themed Environments in Transcultural Perspectives*, edited by Judith Schlehe, Michiko Uike-Bormann, Carolyn Oesterle, and Wolfgang Hochbruck. Bielefeld, Germany: Transcript, 2010.

Drummond, Kent. "Shame, Consumption, Redemption: Reflections on a Tour of Graceland." *Consumption Markets & Culture* 14, no. 2 (2011): 203–213.

Dunlop, Beth. *Building a Dream: The Art of Disney Architecture*. New York: Harry N. Abrams, 1996.

Dunne, Carey. "8 Of Google's Craziest Offices." *Fast Company*, April 10, 2014.

During, Simon. "Mimic Toil: Eighteenth-Century Preconditions for the Modern Historical Reenactment." *Rethinking History* 11, no. 3 (September 2007): 313–333.

Dutton, Barbara. "Pirates, Primates and Pyramids: To Compete with Area Attractions, Regional Waterparks Look into Theming to Set Them Apart." *Parks and Recreation* 39, no. 11 (November 2004): 84–88.

Ebenkamp, Becky. "Tiki's Transcendency." *Brandweek* 38, no. 9 (1997).

Ebster, Claus. "The Role of Authenticity in Ethnic Theme Restaurants." *Journal of Foodservice Business Research* 7, no. 2 (2005): 41–52.

Eco, Umberto. *Travels in Hyperreality*. San Diego: Harcourt Brace Jovanovich, 1986.

Edensor, Tim and Uma Kothan. "Sweetening Colonialism: A Mauritian Themed Resort." Pp. 189–206 in *Architecture and Tourism: Perception, Performance, and Place*, edited by D. Medina Lasansky. Oxford: Berg, 2004.

Edwards, John S. A. and Inga-Britt Gustafsson. "The Room and Atmosphere as Aspects of the Meal: A Review." *Journal of Foodservice* 19, no. 1 (February 2008): 22–34.

Ehmann, Sven, Sofia Borges, and Robert Klanten. *Brand Spaces: Branded Architecture and the Future of Retail Design*. Berlin: Gestalten, 2013.

Eisen, David. "The De-Theming of Luxor." *Travel Agent* 330, no. 9 (2007): 24.

Ek, Richard. "Regional Experiencescapes as Geo-economic Ammunition." Pp. 69–91 in *Experiencescapes: Tourism, Culture, and Economy*, edited by Tom O'Dell and Peter Billing. Frederiksberg: Copenhagen Business School Press, 2005.

Elliott, Anthony and John Urry. *Mobile Lives*. New York: Routledge, 2010.

Emerson, Chad Denver. *Project Future: The Inside Story Behind the Creation of Disney*. Lexington, KY: Ayefour Publishing, 2010.

Emmons, Natasha. "New Library's Design Taps Park Theming Talent." *Amusement Business* 114, no. 7.

Enders, Deborah G. "Are Thrills Giving Way to Shared Emotional Experiences? High Tech or High Touch." *Amusement Business* 105, no. 37: 32.

Engelhardt, Tom and Edward T. Linenthal (eds.) *History Wars: The Enola Gay and Other Battles for the American Past*. New York: Holt, 1996.

Engler, Mira. "Theme Towns: The Pitfalls and Alternatives of Image Making." *Small Town* 24, no. 4 (January-February 1994): 14–23.

Eroglu, Sevgin and Karen Machleit. "Atmospheric Factors in the Retail Environment: Sights, Sounds and Smells." *Advances in Consumer Research* 20, no. 1 (1993): 34.

Falk, John H. *Identity and the Museum Visitor Experience*. Walnut Creek, CA: Left Coast Press, 2009.

Falk, John H. and Lynn D. Dierking. *Museum Experience Revisited*. Walnut Creek, CA: Left Coast Press, 2012.

Fan, Stephen (ed.). *Suburbanisms: Casino Urbanization, Chinatowns, and the Contested American Landscape*. New London, CT: Lyman Allyn Art Museum, 2014.

Fehlmann, Marc. "As Greek As It Gets: British Attempts to Recreate the Parthenon." *Rethinking History* 11, no. 3 (September 2007): 353–377.

Feige, Michael. "Mini Israel and the Subversive Present." In *"Here You Leave Today": Time and Temporality in Theme Parks*, edited by Filippo Carlà, Florian Freitag, Sabrina Mittermeier, and Ariane Schwarz. Hanover: Wehrhahn, 2016.

———. "Mini Israel: The Israeli Place between the Global and the Miniature." Pp. 328–342 in *Jewish Topographies: Visions of Space, Traditions of Place*, edited by Julia Brauch, Anna Lipphardt, and Alexandra Nocke. Burlington, VT: Ashgate, 2008.

Feinberg, Sandra and James Robert Keller. *Designing Space for Children and Teens in Libraries and Public Places*. Chicago: American Library Association, 2010.

Ferchland, William. "Themes Used Widely to Boost Business." *Tahoe Daily Tribune*, April 27, 2006.

Findlay, John M. *Magic Lands: Western Cityscapes and American Culture after 1940*. Berkeley: University of California Press, 1993.

Fırat, A. Fuat. "The Meanings and Messages of Las Vegas: The Present of our Future." *M@n@gement* 4, no. 3 (2007): 101–120.

Fırat, A. Fuat, Simone Pettigrew, and Russell W. Belk. "Themed Experiences and Spaces." *Consumption Markets & Culture* 14, no. 2 (2011): 123–124.

Fırat, A. Fuat, and Ebru Ulusoy. "Living a Theme." *Consumption Markets & Culture* 14, no. 2 (2011): 193–202.

Fjellman, Stephen M. *Vinyl Leaves: Walt Disney World and America*. Boulder, CO: Westview, 1992.

Fodness, Dale D. and Laura M. Milner. "A Perceptual Mapping Approach to Theme Park Visitor Segmentation." Pp. 246–258 in *Tourism Management: Towards the New Millennium*, edited by Chris Ryan and Stephen Page. New York: Routledge, 2000.

Forgetta, John. "Architect Brings Art to the Table." *Daily Variety* 270, no. 5.

Fortune, Ron. "Desert Passage Soon Passé: Aladdin Mall Undertakes 'De-theming.'" *Gaming Today*, April 4, 2006.

Foster, Derek. "Wii're Here for a Good Time": The Sneaky Rhetoric of Wii-Themed Parties. *The Journal of American Culture* 33, no. 1 (2010): 30–39.

———. "Love Hotels: Sex and the Rhetoric of Themed Spaces." Pp. 167–181 in *The Themed Space: Locating Culture, Nation, and Self*, edited by Scott A. Lukas. Lanham, MD: Lexington, 2007.

Foster, Jamye and Melinda A. McLelland. "Retail Atmospherics: The Impact of a Brand Dictated Theme." *Journal of Retailing & Consumer Services* 22 (January 2015): 195–205

Fox, William L. *In the Desert of Desire: Las Vegas and the Culture of Spectacle*. Reno: University of Nevada Press, 2005.

———. *Driving by Memory*. Albuquerque: University of New Mexico Press, 1999.

Francaviglia, Damien. "Branson, Missouri: Regional Identity and the Emergence of a Popular Culture Community." *Journal of American Culture* 18, no. 2 (Summer 1995): 57–73.

Francaviglia, Richard V. "Frontierland as an Allegorical Map of the American West." The Western Historical Quarterly 30, no. 2 (Summer 1999): 155–182.

———. *Main Street Revisited: Time, Space, and Image Building in Smalltown America*. Iowa City: University of Iowa Press, 1996.

———. "History after Disney: The Significance of Imagineered Historical Places." *The Public Historian* 17, no. 4 (Autumn, 1995): 69–74.

———. "Main Street U.S.A.: A Comparison/Contrast of Streetscapes in Disneyland and Walt Disney World." *The Journal of Popular Culture* 15, no. 1 (Summer 1981): 141–156.

Franci, Giovanna. *Dreaming of Italy: Las Vegas and the Virtual Grand Tour*. Reno: University of Nevada Press, 2005.

Frantz, Douglas and Catherine Collins. *Celebration U.S.A.: Living in Disney's Brave New Town*. New York: Owl Books, 2000.

Freitag, Florian. "'Like Walking into a Movie': Intermedial Relations between Disney Theme Parks and Movies." *The Journal of Popular Culture* (forthcoming).

———. "Amerikanisierung, Glokalisierung, Branding. EuroDisney, 1992." Pp. 165–198 in *Transkulturelle Dynamiken: Aktanten – Prozesse – Theorien*, edited by Jutta Ernst and Florian Freitag. Bielefeld, Germany: Transcript, 2015.

Freitag, Florian and Ariane Schwarz, "Thresholds of Fun and Fear: Borders and Liminal Experiences in Theme Parks." *OAA Perspectives: The Journal of the Ontario Association of Architects* 23, no. 4 (Winter 2015/2016): 22–23.

Frenkel, Stephen, Judy Walton, and Dirk Andersen. "Bavarian Leavenworth and the Symbolic Economy of a Theme Town." *Geographical Review* 90, no. 4 (October 2000): 559–184.

Friedberg, Anne. *The Virtual Window: From Alberti to Microsoft*. Cambridge, MA: MIT Press, 2006.

———. *Window Shopping: Cinema and the Postmodern*. Berkeley: University of California Press, 1994.

Friedman, Bill. "Casino Design and Its Impact on Player Behavior." Pp. 69–86 in *Stripping Las Vegas: A Contextual Review of Casino Resort Architecture*, edited by Karin Jaschke and Silke Ötsch. Weimar, Germany: University of Weimar Press, 2003.

———. *Designing Casinos to Dominate the Competition*. Reno, NV: Institute for the Study of Gambling and Commercial Gaming, 2000.

Friess, Steve. "CityCenter: Vegas 4.0: How Frank Gehry, Nancy Rubins, Cesar Pelli, Maya Lin and Others are Reinventing California's Favorite Playground." *LA Weekly*, December 2, 2009.

Gapps, Stephen. "Mobile Monuments: A View of Historical Reenactment and Authenticity from Inside the Costume Cupboard of History." *Rethinking History* 13, no. 3 (September 2009): 395–409.

Gardner, Andrew. "The Past as Playground: The Ancient World in Video Game Representation." Pp. 255–272 in *Archaeology and the Media*, edited by Timothy Clack and Marcus Brittain. Walnut Creek, CA: Left Coast Press, 2007.

Gatterer, Harry and Hanni Rützler. *Hotel der Zukunft: Die Wichtigsten Trendfelder für die Hotellerie*. Stuttgart, Germany: Matthaes Verlag, 2012.

Gegax, T. Trent. "Booming Amusement Parks: The Theme Is Extreme." *Newsweek*, March 30, 1998, 12.

Gibson, David. *The Wayfinding Handbook: Information Design for Public Places*. New York: Princeton Architectural Press, 2009.

Gill, Patrick. "Themed Restaurant Chains are Catching On." *The Moscow Times*, October 15, 2002.

Giroux, Henry A. and Grace Pollock. *The Mouse that Roared: Disney and the End of Innocence*. Lanham, MD: Rowman and Littlefield, 2010.

Goldberg, Alan. "Identity and Experience in Haitian Voodoo Shows." *Annals of Tourism Research* 10, no. 4 (1983): 479–495.

Goldberger, Paul. "What Happens in Vegas: Can You Bring Architectural Virtue to Sin City?" *The New Yorker*, October 4, 2010.

———. "Architecture View: A Curious Mix of Versailles and Mickey Mouse." *New York Times*, June 14, 1992.

———. "From English Pub to Chinese Pagoda: EPCOT's Eerie but Endearing Sameness." *New York Times*, February 3, 1985.

———. "Mickey Mouse Teaches the Architects." *New York Times Magazine*, October 22, 1971.

Golec, Michael J. "Format and Layout in *Learning from Las Vegas*." Pp. 31–47 in *Relearning from Las Vegas*, edited by Aron Vinegar and Michaek J. Golec. Minneapolis: University of Minnesota Press, 2009.

Goodman, Michael K., David Goodman, and Michael Redclift. "Introduction: Situating Consumption, Space and Place." Pp. 3–40 in *Consuming Space: Placing Consumption in Perspective*, edited by Michael K. Goodman, David Goodman, and Michael Redclift. Burlington, VT: Ashgate, 2010.

Gordon, Tammy S. "Heritage, Commerce, and Museal Display: Toward a New Typology of Historical Exhibition in the United States." *The Public Historian* 30, no. 3 (Summer 2008): 27–50.

Goss, Jon. "The Magic of the Mall: Form and Function in the Retail Built Environment." *Annals of the Association of American Geographers* 83, no. 1 (1993): 18–47.

Gottdiener, Mark. *The Theming of America: American Dreams, Media Fantasies, and Themed Environments*. 2nd ed. Boulder, CO: Westview, 2001.

———. *Life in the Air: Surviving the New Culture of Air Travel*. Lanham, MD: Rowman and Littlefield, 2000.

———. "Consumption of Space and Spaces of Consumption." Pp. 12–15 in *Architectural Design: Consuming Architecture*, edited by Maggie Toy. West Sussex, UK: John Wiley and Sons, 1998.

———. "Themed Environments of Everyday Life: Restaurants and Malls." Pp. 74–87 in *The Postmodern Presence*, edited by Arthur Asa Berger. Walnut Creek, CA: AltaMira, 1998.

Graham, Otis L. Jr. "Editor's Corner: Learning Together: Disney and the Historians." *The Public Historian* 16, no. 4 (1994): 5–8.

———. "Editor's Corner: Who Owns American History?" *The Public Historian* 17, no. 2 (1995): 8–11.

Gran, Anne-Britt. "Staging Places as Brands–Visiting Illusions, Images and Imaginations." Pp. 22–37 in *Re-Investing Authenticity: Tourism, Place and Emotions*, edited by Britta Timm Knudsen and Anne Marit Waade. Bristol, UK: Channel View Publications, 2010.

Gray, Fred. *Designing the Seaside: Architecture, Society and Nature*. London: Reaktion, 2006.

Grech, Daniel. "An Eatery that Links Its Ware with Software." *Business News New Jersey*, May 5, 1997.

Greco, JoAnn. "Mall Makeovers." *Planning* 75, no. 7 (July 2009): 10–14.

Grice, Gordon S. "Temporality as Storyline, in the Design of Themed Environments." In *"Here You Leave Today": Time and Temporality in Theme Parks* edited by Filippo Carlà, Florian Freitag, Sabrina Mittermeier, and Ariane Schwarz. Hanover, Germany: Wehrhahn, 2016.

———. "Thresholds: Introduction." *OAA Perspectives: The Journal of the Ontario Association of Architects* 23, no. 4 (Winter 2015/2016): 14–17.

———. "When Is an Entrance Not an Entrance?" *OAA Perspectives: The Journal of the Ontario Association of Architects* 23, no. 4 (Winter 2015/2016): 24–25.

Grier, Sonya A., Anne M. Brumbaugh, and Corliss G. Thornton. "Crossover Dreams: Consumer Responses to Ethnic-Oriented Products." *Journal of Marketing* 70, no. 2 (April 2006): 35–51.

Griffin, Sean P. *Tinker Belles and Evil Queens: The Walt Disney Company from the Inside Out*. New York: New York University Press, 2000.

Griffiths, Alison. *Shivers Down Your Spine: Cinema, Museums, and the Immersive View*. New York: Columbia University Press, 2013.

Groves, Derham. "Hong Kong Disneyland: Feng Shui Inside the Magic Kingdom." Pp. 138–149 in *Disneyland and Culture: Essays on the Parks and Their Influence*, edited by Kathy Merlock Jackson and Mark I. West. Jefferson, NC: McFarland, 2010.

Groves, Kursty and Will Knight. *I Wish I Worked There!: A Look Inside the Most Creative Spaces in Business*. Hoboken, NJ: Wiley, 2010.

Guier, Cindy Stooksbury. "Themed Experience Right in Style." *Amusement Business* 111, no. 37 (13 September 1999): 9–10.

———. "Theming Usage Varies, but Can Be Critical to Success." *Amusement Business* 111, no. 37 (13 September 1999): 10–12.

Guzman, Rafer. "Hotel Offers Kids a Room with a Logo." *Wall Street Journal*, October 6, 1999.

Gwynne, Robert N. "Creating Palate Geographies: Chilean Wine and UK Consumption Spaces." Pp. 215–238 in *Consuming Space: Placing Consumption in Perspective*, edited by Michael K. Goodman, David Goodman, and Michael Redclift. Burlington, VT: Ashgate, 2010.

Gyimóthy, Szilvia. "Thrillscapes: Wilderness Mediated as Playground." Pp. 254–265 in *Re-Investing Authenticity: Tourism, Place and Emotions*, edited by Britta Timm Knudsen and Anne Marit Waade. Bristol, UK: Channel View Publications, 2010.

———. "Nostalgiascapes: The Renaissance of Danish Countryside Inns." Pp. 112–127 in *Experiencescapes: Tourism, Culture, and Economy*, edited by Tom O'Dell and Peter Billing. Frederiksberg: Copenhagen Business School Press, 2005.

Hagen, Joshua. "The Most German of Towns: Creating an Ideal Nazi Community in Rothenburg ob der Tauber." *Annals of the Association of American Geographers* 94, no. 1 (March 2004): 207–227.

Hall, Dennis. "Civil War Reenactors and the Postmodern Sense of History." *Journal of American Culture* 17, no. 3 (September 1994): 7–11.

Hall, Martin. "The Reappearance of the Authentic." Pp. 70–101 in *Museum Frictions: Public Cultures/Global Transformations*, edited by Ivan Karp, Corinne A. Kratz, Lynn Szwaja, and Tomás Ybarra-Frausto. Durham, NC: Duke University Press, 2006.

Hall, Martin and Pia Bombardella. "Las Vegas in Africa." *Journal of Social Archaeology* 5, no. 1 (February 2005): 5–24.

Hamilton, Carolyn. *Terrific Majesty: The Powers of Shaka Zulu and the Limits of Historical Invention*. Cambridge: Harvard University Press, 1998.

Handler, Richard and Eric Gable. *The New History in an Old Museum: Creating the Past in Colonial Williamsburg*. Durham, NC: Duke University Press, 1997.

Handler, Richard and William Saxton. "Dyssimulation: Reflexivity, Narrative, and the Quest for Authenticity in Living History." *Cultural Anthropology* 3, no. 3 (1988): 242–260.

Hannam, Kevin and Chris Halewood. "European Viking Themed Festivals: An Expression of Identity." *Journal of Heritage Tourism* 1, no. 1 (2006): 17–31.

Hannigan, John. "Themed Environments." Pp. 806–810 in *Encyclopedia of Urban Studies*, edited by E. Ray Hutchison. London: SAGE, 2009.

———. "Casino Cities." *Geography Compass* 1, no. 4 (July 2007): 959–975.

———. *Fantasy City: Pleasure and Profit in the Postmodern Metropolis*. London: Routledge, 1998.

Hansen, Zia. "Interview with Zia Hansen from Avery Brooks and Associates, Interior Architects." Pp. 87–90 in *Stripping Las Vegas: A Contextual Review of Casino Resort Architecture*, edited by Karin Jaschke and Silke Ötsch. Weimar, Germany: University of Weimar Press, 2003.

Hardie, Melissa Jane. "Torque: Dollywood, Pigeon Forge, and Authentic Feeling in the Smoky Mountains." Pp. 23–37 in *The Themed Space: Locating Culture, Nation, and Self*, edited by Scott A. Lukas. Lanham, MD: Lexington, 2007.

Harries, Karsten. "Theory as Ornament." Pp. 79–95 in *Relearning from Las Vegas*, edited by Aron Vinegar and Michaek J. Golec. Minneapolis: University of Minnesota Press, 2009.

Harris, Neil. "Expository Expositions: Preparing for the Theme Parks." Pp. 19–28 in *Designing Disney's Theme Parks: The Architecture of Reassurance*, edited by Karal Ann Marling. Paris: Flammarion, 1997.

Harris, Steven and Deborah Berke, eds. *Architecture of the Everyday*. Princeton: Princeton Architectural Press, 1997.

Hart, Hugh. "Las Vegas Grows Up: Architecture Review." *LA Weekly*, December 2, 2009.

Hart, Lain. "Authentic Recreation: Living History and Leisure." *Museum and Society* 5, no. 2 (July 2007): 103–124.

Harvey, Penelope. *Hybrids of Modernity: Anthropology, the Nation State and the Universal Exhibition*. London: Routledge, 1996.

Haussman, Glenn. "Hotels Shed Hyper-Themes." *Travel Agent* 331, Issue 1 (2007): 16.

Hede, Anne-Marie and Maree Thyne. "A Journey to the Authentic: Museum Visitors and Their Negotiation of the Inauthentic." *Journal of Marketing Management* 26, nos. 7–8 (2010): 686–705.

Hell, Julia and George Steinmetz. "Ruinopolis: Post-Imperial Theory and Learning from Las Vegas." *International Journal of Urban and Regional Research* 38, no. 3 (May 2014): 1047–1068.

Heller, Alfred. *World's Fairs and the End of Progress*. Corte Madera, CA: World's Fair Inc, 1999.

Hellier-Tinoco, Ruth. "Embodying Touristic Mexico: Virtual and Erased Indigenous Bodies." Pp. 71–78 in *Meet Me at the Fair: A World's Fair Reader*, edited by Laura Hollengreen, Celia Pearce, Rebecca Rouse, and Bobby Schweizer. Pittsburgh: ETC Press, 2013.

Hench, John. *Designing Disney: Imagineering and the Art of the Show*. New York: Disney Editions, 2003.

Henderson, Justin. *Casino Design: Resorts, Hotels, and Themed Entertainment Spaces*. Gloucester, MA: Rockport, 1999.

Hendry, Joy. "The Past, Foreign Countries and Fantasy…They All Make for a Good Outing: Staging the Past in Japan and Some Other Locations." Pp. 41–56 in *Staging the Past: Themed Environments in Transcultural Perspectives*, edited by Judith Schlehe, Michiko Uike-Bormann, Carolyn Oesterle, and Wolfgang Hochbruck. Bielefeld, Germany: Transcript, 2010.

———. "Japan's Global Village: A View from the World of Leisure." Pp. 231–244 in *A Companion to the Anthropology of Japan*, edited by Jennifer Robertson. New York: Wiley-Blackwell, 2008

Hermanson, Scott. "Truer than Life: Disney's Animal Kingdom." Pp. 199–230 in *Rethinking Disney: Private Control, Public Dimensions*, edited by Mike Budd and Max H. Kirsch. Middletown, CT: Wesleyan University Press, 2005.

Herwig, Oliver and Florian Holzherr. *Dream Worlds: Architecture and Entertainment*. Munich, Germany: Prestel, 2006.

Herzog, Lawrence A. *From Aztec to High Tech: Architecture and Landscape across the Mexico-United States Border*. Baltimore: Johns Hopkins University Press, 2001.

Hess, Alan. *Googie Redux: Ultramodern Roadside Architecture*. San Francisco: Chronicle Books, 2004.

———. "Beautiful Chaos: The Latest Collision of New and Old on the Strip Is Not Always Pretty, but Effective." *Las Vegas Life*, November 1999, 42–44.

———. *Viva Las Vegas: After-hours Architecture*. San Francisco: Chronicle Books, 1993.

———. *Googie: Fifties Coffee Shop Architecture*. San Francisco: Chronicle Books, 1986.

Hiaasen, Carl. *Team Rodent: How Disney Devours the World*. New York: Ballantine Publishing Group, 1998.

Hibbard, Don. *Designing Paradise: The Allure of the Hawaiian Resort*. Princeton: Princeton Architectural Press, 2006.

Hickey, Dave. "Real Fakery." Pp. 66–67 in *Spectacle*, edited by David Rockwell. New York: Phaidon, 2006.

Higgs, Eric and Jennifer Cypher, "Colonizing the Imagination: Disney's Wilderness Lodge." Pp. 403–423 in *From Virgin Land to Disney World: Nature and Its Discontents in the USA of Yesterday and Today*, edited by Bernd Herzogenrath. Amsterdam: Rodopi, 2001.

———. "Manufacturing Natural Heritage: Disney's Wilderness Lodge." *Tourism Development: The Theming of Vernacular Settings* 104

(1998): 1–12, Center for Environmental Design Research, International Association for the Study of Traditional Environments, Traditional Dwellings and Settlements, Working Paper Series. Berkeley: University of California.

Hildebrandt, John. "Cedar Point: A Park in Progress." *The Journal of Popular Culture* 15, no. 1 (Summer 1981): 87–107.

Hjemdahl, Kirsti Mathiesen. "History as Cultural Playground." *Ethnologia Europaea* 32, no. 2 (2002): 105–124.

Hochbruck, Wolfgang and Judith Schlehe. "Introduction: Staging the Past." Pp. 7–20 in *Staging the Past: Themed Environments in Transcultural Perspectives,* edited by Judith Schlehe, Michiko Uike-Bormann, Carolyn Oesterle, and Wolfgang Hochbruck. Bielefeld, Germany: Transcript, 2010.

Hoelscher, Steven D. *Picturing Indians: Photographic Encounters and Tourist Fantasies in H. H. Bennett's Wisconsin Dells.* Madison: University of Wisconsin Press, 2008.

———. *Heritage on Stage: The Invention of Ethnic Place in America's Little Switzerland.* Madison: University of Wisconsin Press, 1998.

Hoffstaedter, Gerhard. "Representing Culture in Malaysian Cultural Theme Parks: Tensions and Contradictions." *Anthropological Forum* 18, no. 2 (July 2008): 139–160.

Holbrook, Morris B. and Robert M. Schindler. "Market Segmentation Based on Age and Attitude Toward the Past: Concepts, Methods, and Findings Concerning Nostalgic Influences on Customer Tastes." *Journal of Business Research* 37, no. 1 (September 1996): 27–39.

Hollands, Robert and Paul Chatterton. "Producing Nightlife in the New Urban Entertainment Economy: Corporatization, Branding and Market Segmentation." *International Journal of Urban and Regional Research* 27, no. 2 (June 2003): 361–385.

Holliday, Ruth and Tracey Potts. *Kitsch!: Cultural Politics and Taste.* Manchester: Manchester University Press, 2012.

Hollinshead, Keith. "Theme Parks and the Representation of Culture and Nature: The Consumer Aesthetics of Presentation and Performance." Pp. 269–289 in *The SAGE Handbook of Tourism Studies,* edited by Tazim Jamal and Mike Robinson. Los Angeles: Sage, 2009.

Holtorf, Cornelius J. "Changing Concepts of Temporality: From Age to Pastness in Heritage and Theme Parks." In *"Here You Leave Today": Time and Temporality in Theme Parks,* edited by Filippo Carlà, Florian Freitag, Sabrina Mittermeier, and Ariane Schwarz. Hanover, Germany: Wehrhahn, 2016.

———. "On Pastness: A Reconsideration of Materiality in Archaeological Object Authenticity." *Anthropological Quarterly* 86 (2013): 427–444.

———. "The Zoo as a Realm of Memory." *Anthropological Journal of European Cultures* 22 (2013): 98–114.

———. "The Presence of Pastness: Themed Environments and Beyond." Pp. 23–40 in *Staging the Past: Themed Environments in Transcultural Perspectives,* edited by Judith Schlehe, Michiko Uike-Bormann, Carolyn Oesterle, and Wolfgang Hochbruck. Bielefeld, Germany: Transcript, 2010.

———. "Imagine This: Archaeology in the Experience Society." Pp. 47–64 in *Contemporary Archaeologies: Excavating Now,* edited by Cornelius Holtorf and Angela Piccini. Berne: Peter Lang, 2009.

———. "On the Possibility of Time Travel." *Lund Archaeological Review* 15 (2009): 31–41.

———. "Time Travel: A New Perspective on the Distant Past." Pp. 127–132 in *On the Road: Studies in Honour of Lars Larsson,* edited by Birgitta Hardh, Kristina Jennbert, and Deborah Olausson. Stockholm: Almquiest & Wiksell, 2007.

———. *From Stonehenge to Las Vegas: Archaeology as Popular Culture.* Walnut Creek, CA: Altamira, 2005.

Hong, Michael. "Interview with Michael Hong from The Jerde Partnership." Pp. 91–96 in *Stripping Las Vegas: A Contextual Review of Casino Resort Architecture,* edited by Karin Jaschke and Silke Ötsch. Weimar, Germany: University of Weimar Press, 2003.

Hornskov, Søren Buhl. "On the Management of Authenticity: Culture in the Place Branding of Øresund." Pp. 80–92 in *Re-Investing*

Authenticity: Tourism, Place and Emotions, edited by Britta Timm Knudsen and Anne Marit Waade. Bristol, UK: Channel View Publications, 2010.

Hornstein, Katie. "The Price of Things: Art, Industry and Commodity Culture at the Exposition Universelle of 1855 in Paris." Pp. 169–174 in *Meet Me at the Fair: A World's Fair Reader*, edited by Laura Hollengreen, Celia Pearce, Rebecca Rouse, and Bobby Schweizer. Pittsburgh: ETC Press, 2013.

Horton, James and Oliver Lois E. Horton, eds. *Slavery and Public History: The Tough Stuff of American Memory*. Chapel Hill, NC: The University of North Carolina Press, 2008.

Houston, H. Rika and Laurie A. Meamber. "Consuming the 'World': Reflexivity, Aesthetics, and Authenticity at Disney World's EPCOT Center." *Consumption Markets & Culture* 14, no. 2 (2011): 177–191.

Howe, Katherine. "Vacation in Historyland." Pp. 195–206 in *Disneyland and Culture: Essays on the Parks and Their Influence*, edited by Kathy Merlock Jackson and Mark I. West. Jefferson, NC: McFarland, 2010.

Howland, Dan. *The Journal of Ride Theory Omnibus*. Portland, OR: Ride Theory Press.

Hsieh, Tsuifang and Yungkun Chan. "Interactive Quality Control of Service Encounters in Theme Restaurants." *Journal of Global Business Issues* 3, no. 2 (Summer/Fall 2009): 85–94.

Huddleston, Gene. "McDonald's Interior Décor." *Journal of American Culture* 1, no. 2 (Summer 1978): 363–369.

Hughes, Deborah L. "Debating the African Village." Pp. 61–69 in *Meet Me at the Fair: A World's Fair Reader*, edited by Laura Hollengreen, Celia Pearce, Rebecca Rouse, and Bobby Schweizer. Pittsburgh: ETC Press, 2013.

Huhtamo, Erkki. *Illusions in Motion: Media Archaeology of the Moving Panorama and Related Spectacles*. Cambridge: The MIT Press, 2013.

Huijbens, Edward H. "Developing Wellness in Iceland: Theming Wellness Destinations the Nordic Way." *Scandinavian Journal of Hospitality and Tourism* 11, no. 1 (2011): 20–41.

Hume, Ivor Noël. "Resurrection and Deification at Colonial Williamsburg, USA." Pp. 90–103 in *The Constructed Past: Experimental Archaeology, Education and the Public*, edited by Philippe Planel and Peter G. Stone. London: Routledge, 1999.

Hutcheon, Linda. *A Theory of Adaptation*. New York: Routledge, 2012.

Huxtable, Ada Louise. *The Unreal America: Architecture and Illusion*. New York: New Press, 1999.

Ijzereef, Gerard F. "The Reconstruction of Sites in the Archaeological Themepark ARCHEON in the Netherlands." Pp. 171–180 in *The Constructed Past: Experimental Archaeology, Education and the Public*, edited by Philippe Planel and Peter G. Stone. London: Routledge, 1999.

Imada, Adria L. "Hawaiians on Tour: Hula Circuits through the American Empire." *American Quarterly* 56, no. 1 (March 2004): 111–149.

Imagineers, The. *The Imagineering Field Guide to Disney California Adventure at Disneyland Resort*. New York: Disney Editions, 2014.

———. *Walt Disney Imagineering: A Behind the Dreams Look at Making More Magic Real*. New York: Disney Editions, 2010.

———. *The Imagineering Field Guide to Disney's Hollywood Studios*. New York: Disney Editions, 2010.

———. *The Imagineering Field Guide to Disneyland*. New York: Disney Editions, 2008.

———. *The Imagineering Field Guide to Disney's Animal Kingdom at Walt Disney World*. New York: Disney Editions, 2007.

———. *The Imagineering Field Guide to Epcot at Walt Disney World*. New York: Disney Editions, 2006.

———. *The Imagineering Workout*. New York: Disney Editions, 2005.

———. *The Imagineering Field Guide to Magic Kingdom at Walt Disney World*. New York: Disney Editions, 2005.

———. *The Imagineering Way: Ideas to Ignite Your Creativity.* New York: Disney Editions, 2003.

———. *Walt Disney Imagineering: A Behind the Dreams Look At Making the Magic Real.* New York: Disney Editions, 1998.

Immerso, Michael. *Coney Island: The People's Playground.* Piscataway, NJ: Rutgers University Press, 2002.

Ingram, Susan. "Themeparks, Nostalgia, Retro." In *"Here You Leave Today": Time and Temporality in Theme Parks,* edited by Filippo Carlà, Florian Freitag, Sabrina Mittermeier, and Ariane Schwarz. Hanover, Germany: Wehrhahn, 2016.

Ingram, Susan and Markus Reisenleitner. "Faking Translation in Hallstatt: A Visit to *Hallstatt Revisited I.*" *TranscUlturAl* 6.1 (2014): 43–52.

Irazábal, Clara. "Kitsch Is Dead, Long Live Kitsch: The Production of Hyperkitsch in Las Vegas." *Journal of Architectural and Planning Research* 24, no. 3 (Autumn 2007): 199–223.

Isaac, Gwyneira. "Responsibility Towards Knowledge: The Zuni Museum as a Mediator between Anglo-American and Zuni Knowledge Systems." Pp. 303–321 in *Contesting Knowledge: Museums and Indigenous Perspectives,* edited by Susan Sleeper-Smith. Lincoln: University of Nebraska Press, 2009.

Isenstadt, Sandy. "Recurring Surfaces: Architecture in the Experience Economy." *Perspecta* 32 (2001): 108–119.

Isozaki, Arata. "Theme Park." *The South Atlantic Quarterly* 92, no. 1 (1993): 175–182.

Ives, David. "Welcome to World World." *New York Times Magazine,* December 17, 1995.

Jackson, Kathy Merlock. "Synergystic Disney: New Directions for Mickey and Media in 1954–1955." Pp. 19–28 in *Disneyland and Culture: Essays on the Parks and Their Influence,* edited by Kathy Merlock Jackson and Mark I. West. Jefferson, NC: McFarland, 2010.

———. "Autographs for Tots: The Marketing of Stars to Children." Pp. 207–214 in *Disneyland and Culture: Essays on the Parks and Their Influence,* edited by Kathy Merlock Jackson and Mark I. West. Jefferson, NC: McFarland, 2010.

Jakle, John A. and Keith A. Sculle. "Concept Restaurants." Pp. 277-195 in *Fast Food: Roadside Restaurants in the Automobile Age.* Baltimore, MD: Johns Hopkins University Press, 1999.

Jang, SooCheong (Shawn), Yinghua Liu, and Young Namkung. "Effects of Authentic Atmospherics in Ethnic Restaurants: Investigating Chinese Restaurants." *International Journal of Contemporary Hospitality Management* 23, no. 5 (2011): 662–680.

Jansen, Robert S. "Jurassic Technology? Sustaining Presumptions of Intersubjectivity in a Disruptive Environment." *Theory and Society* 37 (2008): 127–159.

Jansson, Andre. "The City In-Between: Communication Geographies, Tourism and the Urban Unconscious." Pp. 38–51 in *Re-Investing Authenticity: Tourism, Place and Emotions,* edited by Britta Timm Knudsen and Anne Marit Waade. Bristol, UK: Channel View Publications, 2010.

Jaschke, Karin. "Casinos Inside Out." Pp. 109–32 in *Stripping Las Vegas: A Contextual Review of Casino Resort Architecture,* edited by Karin Jaschke and Silke Ötsch. Weimar, Germany: University of Weimar Press, 2003.

Jaspistos. "Competition: Themed Eating." *Spectator,* November 13, 2004.

Jeffers, Carol S. "In a Cultural Vortex: Theme Parks, Experience, and Opportunities for Art Education." *Studies in Art Education* 45, no. 3 (Spring, 2004): 221–233.

Jencks, Charles. "Ersatz in LA." *Architectural Design* 43, no. 9 (September 1973): 596–601.

———. *The Language of Post-modern Architecture.* 4th ed. New York: Rizzoli, 1984.

Jenkins, Henry. *Convergence Culture: Where Old and New Media Collide.* New York: New York University Press, 2008.

Jensen, Jakob Linaa. "Online Tourism – 'Just Like Being There?'" Pp. 213–225 in *Re-Investing Authenticity: Tourism, Place and Emotions,* edited by Britta Timm Knudsen and Anne Marit Waade. Bristol, UK: Channel View Publications, 2010.

Jerde, Jon. "Capturing the Leisure Zeitgeist: Creating Places to Be." Pp. 69–71 in *Architectural Design: Consuming Architecture*, edited by Maggie Toy. West Sussex, UK: John Wiley and Sons, 1998.

Jewell, Nicholas. *Shopping Malls and Public Space in Modern China*. Surrey, England: Ashgate, 2015.

Johnson, David M. "Disney World as Structure and Symbol: Re-creation of the American Experience. *The Journal of Popular Culture* 15, no. 1 (Summer 1981): 157–165.

Johnson, Lesley, Karl J. Mayer, and Elena Champaner. "Casino Atmospherics from a Customer's Perspective: A Re-Examination." *UNLV Gaming Research & Review Journal* 8, no. 2 (2004): 1–10.

Jones, Gordon L. "Little Families: The Social Fabric of Civil War Reenacting." Pp. 219–234 in *Staging the Past: Themed Environments in Transcultural Perspectives,* edited by Judith Schlehe, Michiko Uike-Bormann, Carolyn Oesterle, and Wolfgang Hochbruck. Bielefeld, Germany: Transcript, 2010.

Jones, Karen. "'The Old West in Modern Splendor': Frontier Folklore and the Selling of Las Vegas." *European Journal of American Culture* 29, no. 2 (2010): 93–110.

Judd, Dennis R. and Susan S. Feinstein, eds. *The Tourist City*. New Haven, CT: Yale University Press, 1999.

Kalshoven, Petra Tjitsk. "Things in the Making: Playing with Imitation." *Etnofoor* 22, no. 1 (2010): 59–74.

Kane, Josephine. *The Architecture of Pleasure: British Amusement Parks 1900–1939*. Burlington, VT: Ashgate, 2013.

Kaplan, Caren. "A World without Boundaries: The Body Shop's Trans/National Geographics." *Social Text* 43 (Autumn 1995): 45–66.

Kaplan, Mike. *Theme Restaurants*. Glen Cove, NY: Pbc Intl, 1998.

Kärrholm, Mattias. *Retailising Space: Architecture, Retail and the Territorialisation of Public Space*. Burlington, VT: Ashgate, 2012.

Kasson, John F. *Amusing the Million: Coney Island at the Turn of the Century.* New York: Hill and Wang, 1978.

Kaufman, Leslie. "Our New Theme Song." *Newsweek*, June 22, 1998.

Kazakina, Katya. "Eastern Bloc Party." *New York Times*, June 25, 2000.

Keasler, Misty. *Love Hotels: The Hidden Fantasy Rooms of Japan*. San Francisco: Chronicle Books, 2006.

Keating, Sheila. "One-track Mind." *The Times* (London), May 4, 2002.

Kersel, Morag and Yorke Rowan. "Beautiful, Good, Important and Special: Cultural Heritage, Archaeology, Tourism and the Miniature in the Holy Land." *Heritage and Society* 5, no. 2 (102): 199–220.

King, Margaret J. "The Disney Effect: Fifty Years After Theme Park Design." Pp 223–226 in *Disneyland and Culture: Essays on the Parks and Their Influence*, edited by Kathy Merlock Jackson and Mark I. West. Jefferson, NC: McFarland, 2010.

———. "'Disneyfication'? Some Pros and Cons of Theme Parks. 'Never Land' or Tomorrowland?" *Museum* 43, no. 1 (1991): 6.

———. "The Theme Park Experience: What Museums Can Learn from Mickey Mouse." *The Futurist* 25, no. 6 (November-December 1991): 24–31.

———. "Disneyland and Walt Disney World: Traditional Values in Futuristic Form." *The Journal of Popular Culture* 15 (1981): 116–140.

———. "The New American Muse: Notes on the Amusement/Theme Park." *The Journal of Popular Culture* 15, no. 1 (Summer 1981): 56–62.

King, Margaret J. and J. G. O'Boyle. "The Theme Park: The Art of Time and Space." Pp. 5–18 in *Disneyland and Culture: Essays on the Parks and Their Influence*, edited by Kathy Merlock Jackson and Mark I. West. Jefferson, NC: McFarland, 2010.

Kirshenblatt-Gimblett, Barbara. *Destination Culture: Tourism, Museums, and Heritage*. Berkeley: University of California Press, 1998.

Kirsner, Scott. "Are You Experienced?: From Anheuser-Busch's Exclusive Tropical Paradise to VW's 3-D Marketing Brandland, the Personalized Theme Park Is Here." *Wired* 8.07 (July 2000).

———. "Experience Required." *Fast Company* 39 (September 2000).

Kirsten, Sven. *Tiki Pop: America Imagines Its Own Polynesian Paradise*. Köln, Germany: Taschen, 2014.

———. *The Book of Tiki*. Köln, Germany: Taschen, 2003.

Klanten, Robert, K. Bolhöfer, and Sven Ehmann. *Out of the Box! Style & Architecture Brand Experiences Between Pop-Up and Flagship*. Berlin: Gestalten, 2011.

Klanten, Robert, Sven Ehmann, and Sofia Borges. *Let's Go Out!: Interiors and Architecture for Restaurants and Bars*. Berlin: Gestalten, 2012.

Klanten, Robert, Anna Sinofzik, and Floyd Schulze. *Introducing Culture Identities: Design for Museums, Theaters and Cultural Institutions*. Berlin: Gestalten, 2013

Klara, Robert. "Familiar Themes." *Restaurant Business* 100, no. 10.

Klein, Norman. *The Vatican to Vegas: A History of Special Effects*. New York: New Press, 2004.

———. "Scripting Las Vegas: Noir Naïfs, Junking Up, and the New Strip." Pp. 17–29 in *The Grit beneath the Glitter: Tales from the Real Las Vegas*, edited by Hal K. Rothman and Mike Davis. Berkeley: University of California Press, 2002.

———. "Scripted Spaces: Navigating the Consumer Built City." Pp. 80–83 in *Architectural Design: Consuming Architecture*, edited by Maggie Toy. West Sussex, UK: John Wiley and Sons, 1998.

Klingmann, Anna. *Brandscapes: Architecture in the Experience Economy*. Cambridge, MA: MIT Press, 2007.

Klitgaard Povlsen, Karen. "Cool Kullaberg–The History of a Mediated Tourist Site." Pp. 121–137 in *Re-Investing Authenticity: Tourism, Place and Emotions,* edited by Britta Timm Knudsen and Anne Marit Waade. Bristol, UK: Channel View Publications, 2010.

Knight, Cher Krause. *Power and Paradise in Walt Disney's World*. Gainesville: University Press of Florida, 2014.

———. "What Time Is It? Subverting and Suppressing, Conflating and Compressing Time in Commodified Space and Architecture." *Analecta Husserliana* 78 (2003): 325–336.

———. "Beyond the Neon Billboard: Sidewalk Spectacle and Public Art in Las Vegas." *Journal of American and Comparative Cultures* 25, no. 1/2 (Spring 2002): 9–13.

Knudsen, Timm and Anne Marit Waade. "Authenticity in Tourism and Spatial Experience–Rethinking the Relation between Travel, Place and Emotion in the Context Of Cultural Economy and Emotional Geography." Pp. 1–21 in *Re-Investing Authenticity: Tourism, Place and Emotions*, edited by Britta Timm Knudsen and Anne Marit Waade. Bristol, UK: Channel View Publications, 2010.

Koolhaas, Rem. *Delirious New York*. New York: Montacelli Press, 1994.

Koolhaas, Rem and Hans Ulrich Obrist. "Re-learning from Las Vegas." Interview with Denise Scott Brown and Robert Venturi. Pp. 150–157 in *Content*, edited by Rem Koolhaas. Köln, Germany: Taschen, 2004.

Kornfeld, Alana B. Elias and Valerie Reiss. "WWBD?" *Newsweek*, August 14, 2006.

Kotler, Philip, Donald Haider, and Irving Rein. *Marketing Places*. New York: Free Press, 2002.

Kozinets, Robert V. *et al*. "Ludic Agency and Retail Spectacle." *Journal of Consumer Research* 31, no. 3 (December 2004): 658–672.

———. "Themed Flagship Brand Stores in the New Millennium: Theory, Practice, Prospects." *Journal of Retailing* 78, no. 1 (Spring 2002): 17–29.

Krasniewicz, Louise. "Taking a Chance on Chance." *Expedition* 50, no. 2 (Summer 2008): 6–13.

Kratz, Corinne A. and Ivan Karp. "Wonder and Worth: Disney Museums in World Showcase." *Museum Anthropology* 17, no. 3 (October 1993): 32–42.

Krausz, Tibor. "Bangkok's 'Hitler Chic' Trend Riles Tourists." CNN.com, February 27, 2012.

Kroker, Arthur and Marilouise Kroker. "Treasure Island at the Mirage," "Las Vegas Theme Park," "Luminous Luxor Las Vegas." Pp. 94–97, 103, in *Hacking the Future*. New York: St. Martin's, 1996.

Kuenz, Jane. "It's a Small World after All: Disney and the Pleasures of Identification." *South Atlantic Quarterly* 92, no. 1 (1993): 63–88.

Kurtti, Jeff. *Walt Disney's Imagineering Legends and the Genesis of the Disney Theme Park*. New York: Disney Editions, 2007.

LaFantasie, Glenn W. "The Foolishness of Civil War Reenactors." *Salon*, May 8, 2011.

La Gallienne, Richard. "Human Need of Coney Island." *Cosmopolitan* 39 (July): 239–246.

Laing, Angus, Terry Newholm, and Gill Hogg. "Space for Change or Changing Spaces: Exploiting Virtual Spaces of Consumption." Pp. 257–276 in *Consuming Space: Placing Consumption in Perspective*, edited by Michael K. Goodman, David Goodman, and Michael Redclift. Burlington, VT: Ashgate, 2010.

Lainsbury, Andrew. *Once Upon an American Dream: The Story of Euro Disneyland*. Lawrence: University Press of Kansas, 2000.

Lankauskas, Gediminas. "Sensuous (Re)Collections: The Sight and Taste of Socialism at Grūtas Statue Park, Lithuania." *Senses and Society* 1, no. 1 (2006): 27–52.

Larsen, Hanne Pico. "A Ferris Wheel on a Parking Lot: Heritage, Tourism, and the Authenticity of Place in Solvang, California." Pp. 93–106 in *Re-Investing Authenticity: Tourism, Place and Emotions*, edited by Britta Timm Knudsen and Anne Marit Waade. Bristol, UK: Channel View Publications, 2010.

Lasansky, D. Medina. "Tourist Geographies: Remapping Old Havana." Pp. 165–188 in *Architecture and Tourism: Perception, Performance, and Place*, edited by D. Medina Lasansky. Oxford: Berg, 2004.

Lavin, Sylvia. *Kissing Architecture*. Princeton: Princeton University Press, 2011.

Lebensztejn, Jean-Claude. "Photorealism, Kitsch, and Venturi." Pp. 49–78 in *Relearning from Las Vegas*, edited by Aron Vinegar and Michaek J. Golec. Minneapolis: University of Minnesota Press, 2009.

Lee, Chih-Jen, Deng-Chuan Cai and Tung-Jung Sung, "The Study of Non-Linear Relationships in Theme Restaurant Servicescape Attributes," *Bulletin of Japanese Society for the Science of Design* 62, no. 1 (2015): 29–38.

Lego Muñoz, Caroline and Natalie T. Wood. "A Recipe for Success: Understanding Regional Perceptions of Authenticity in Themed Restaurants." *International Journal of Culture Tourism and Hospitality Research* 3, no. 3 (2009): 269–280.

Lego Muñoz, Caroline, Natalie T. Wood, and Michael R. Solomon. "Real or Blarney?: A Cross-Cultural Study of Perceived Authenticity in Irish Pubs." *Journal of Consumer Behaviour* 5, no. 6 (2006): 222–234.

Lego Muñoz, Caroline K., Natalie T. Wood, Michael R Solomon, and Stephanie McFee. "A Thirst for the Real Thing in Themed Retail Environments: Consumer Authenticity in Irish Pubs." *The Journal of Foodservice Business Research* 5, no. 2 (2010): 61–74.

Lennon, John and Malcolm Foley. *Dark Tourism*. London: Continuum, 2000.

Leyda, Jay. *Eisenstein on Disney*. Calcutta: Seagull Books, 1986.

Lindgren, Anne-Li, Anna Sparrman, Tobias Samuelsson, and David Cardell. "Enacting (Real) Fiction: Materializing Childhoods in a Theme Park." *Childhood* 22, no. 2 (May 2015): 171–186.

Little, Kenneth. "Belize Ephemera, Affect, and Emergent Imaginaries." Pp. 220–241 in *Tourism Imaginaries: Anthropological Approaches*, edited by Noel B. Salazar and Nelson H. H. Graburn. New York: Berghan, 2014.

Liu, Melinda. "Mao Will Serve You Now." *Newsweek* 158, nos. 15/16 (2011): 74–75.

Loftus, Regina, Paul Roellke, and Victoria Tafferner. "Ventures into History." Pp. 235–252 in *Staging the Past: Themed Environments in Transcultural Perspectives*, edited by Judith Schlehe, Michiko Uike-Bormann, Carolyn Oesterle, and Wolfgang Hochbruck. Bielefeld, Germany: Transcript, 2010.

Lonsway, Brian. "The Dubai Mall." *Journal of Architectural Education* 67, no. 1 (2013): 152–153.

———. *Making Leisure Work: Architecture and the Experience Economy*. New York: Routledge, 2009.

———. "The Experience of a Lifestyle." Pp. 225–246 in *The Themed Space: Locating Culture, Nation, and Self*, edited by Scott A. Lukas. Lanham, MD: Lexington, 2007.

Lounsbury, Carl R. "Beaux-Arts Ideals and Colonial Reality: The Reconstruction of Williamsburg's Capitol, 1928–1934." *Journal of the Society of Architectural Historians* 49, no. 4 (December 1990): 373–389.

Lovelock, Brent and Kirsten Lovelock. *The Ethics of Tourism: Critical and Applied Perspectives*. London: Routledge, 2013.

Lowenthal, David. *The Past is a Foreign Country – Revisited*. 2nd edition. Cambridge: Cambridge University Press, 2014.

———. "The Past as a Theme Park." Pp. 11–23 in *Theme Park Landscapes: Antecedents and Variations*, edited by Terence Young and Robert Riley. Washington, D.C.: Dumbarton Oaks Research Library and Collection, 2002.

———. *The Past is a Foreign Country*. Cambridge: Cambridge University Press, 1999.

Lugosi, Peter. "Mobilising Identity and Culture in Experience Co-creation and Venue Operation." *Tourism Management* 40 (2014): 165–179.

Lukas, Scott A. "Time and Temporality in the Worlds of Theme Parks." In *"Here You Leave Today": Time and Temporality in Theme Parks*, edited by Filippo Carlà, Florian Freitag, Sabrina Mittermeier, and Ariane Schwarz. Hanover, Germany: Wehrhahn, 2016.

———. "Cultural Thresholds at World Expo 2015 (Milan)." *OAA Perspectives: The Journal of the Ontario Association of Architects* 23, no. 4 (Winter 2015/2016): 26–27.

———. "Thresholds and Themed and Immersive Spaces." *OAA Perspectives: The Journal of the Ontario Association of Architects* 23, no. 4 (Winter 2015/2016): 28–29.

———. "Controversial Topics: Pushing the Limits in Themed and Immersive Spaces" (Masterclass), *Attractions Management* 20 (Quarter 4, 2015): 50–54.

———. "How the Theme Park Got Its Power: The World's Fair as Cultural Form." Pp. 383–394 in *Meet Me at the Fair: A World's Fair Reader*, edited by Laura Hollengreen, Celia Pearce, Rebecca Rouse, and Bobby Schweizer. Pittsburgh: ETC Press, 2013.

———. "Culture Sampling." Unpublished paper. <https://www.academia.edu/2249945/Culture_Sampling>.

———. *The Immersive Worlds Handbook: Designing Theme Parks and Consumer Spaces*. New York: Focal, 2013.

———. "From Themed Space to Lifespace." Pp. 135–153 in *Staging the Past: Themed Environments in Transcultural Perspectives*, edited by Judith Schlehe, Michiko Uike-Bormann, Carolyn Oesterle, and Wolfgang Hochbruck. Bielefeld, Germany: Transcript, 2010.

———. *Theme Park*. London: Reaktion, 2008.

———. "The Themed Space: Locating Culture, Nation, and Self." Pp. 1–22 in *The Themed Space: Locating Culture, Nation, and Self*, edited by Scott A. Lukas. Lanham, MD: Lexington, 2007.

———. "Theming as a Sensory Phenomenon: Discovering the Senses on the Las Vegas Strip." Pp. 75–95 in *The Themed Space: Locating Culture, Nation, and Self*, edited by Scott A. Lukas. Lanham, MD: Lexington, 2007.

———. "How the Theme Park Gets Its Power: Lived Theming, Social Control, and the Themed Worker Self." Pp. 183–206 in *The Themed Space: Locating Culture, Nation, and Self*, edited by Scott A. Lukas. Lanham, MD: Lexington, 2007.

---. "A Politics of Reverence and Irreverence: Social Discourse on Theming Controversies. Pp. 271–293 in *The Themed Space: Locating Culture, Nation, and Self*, edited by Scott A. Lukas. Lanham, MD: Lexington, 2007.

---. "The Theming of Everyday Life: Mapping the Self, Life Politics, and Cultural Hegemony on the Las Vegas Strip." *Community College Humanities Review* 27 (2006-2007): 167–192.

---. "The Theme Park and the Figure of Death." *InterCulture* 2 (May 2005).

---. "An American Theme Park: Working and Riding Out Fear in the Late Twentieth Century." Pp. 405–428 in *Late Editions 6, Paranoia within Reason: A Casebook on Conspiracy as Explanation*, edited by George E. Marcus. Chicago: University of Chicago Press, 1999.

Luna, Ian. *Retail: Architecture and Shopping*. New York: Rizzoli, 2005.

Luscombe, Belinda. "Creating Spaces." *Time*, September 16, 2002.

Lyon, David. *Jesus in Disneyland: Religion in Postmodern Times*. Cambridge: Polity, 2000.

MacCannell, Dean. *The Tourist: A New Theory of the Leisure Class*. Berkeley: University of California Press, 2013.

---. *The Ethics of Sightseeing*. Berkeley: University of California Press, 2011.

---. "The Ego Factor in Tourism." *Journal of Consumer Research* 29, no. 1 (June 2002): 146–151.

---. "A Semiotic of Attraction." Pp. 109–133 in *The Tourist: A New Theory of the Leisure Class*. New York: Shocken Books, 1989.

---. "Staged Authenticity." Pp. 91–107 in *The Tourist: A New Theory of the Leisure Class*. New York: Shocken Books, 1989.

MacDonald, George F. and Stephen Alsford. "Museums and Theme Parks: Worlds in Collision?" *Museum Management and Curatorship* 12, no. 2 (1995): 129–147.

MacLaurin, Donald J. and Tanya L. MacLaurin. "Customer Perceptions of Singapore's Theme Restaurants." *Cornell Hotel and Restaurant Administration Quarterly* 41, no. 3 (2000): 75–86.

---. "Future Trends For the Theme-restaurant Business." *Cornell Hotel and Restaurant Administration Quarterly* 41, no. 3 (2000): 84.

Macleod, David. "Scottish Theme Towns: Have New Identities Enhanced Development?" *Journal of Tourism and Cultural Change* 7, no. 2 (2009): 133–145.

Magnet, Shoshana. "Playing at Colonization: Interpreting Imaginary Landscapes in the Video Game *Tropico*." *Journal of Communication Inquiry* 30, no. 2 (April 2006): 142–162.

Mair, Heather. "Searching for a New Enterprise: Themed Tourism and the Re-making of One Small Canadian Community." *Tourism Geographies* 11, no. 4 (2009): 462–483.

Malamud, Margaret. *Ancient Rome and Modern America*. New York: Wiley-Blackwell, 2008.

---. "Roman Entertainments for the Masses in Turn-of-the-Century New York." *The Classical World* 95, no. 1 (2001): 49–57.

---. "Pyramids in Las Vegas and in Outer Space: Ancient Egypt in Twentieth–Century American Architecture and Film." *The Journal of Popular Culture* 34, no. 1 (2000): 31–47.

---. "As the Romans Did? Theming Ancient Rome in Contemporary Las Vegas." *Arion* 6, no. 2 (1998): 11–39.

Månsson, Maria. "Negotiating Authenticity at Rosslyn Chapel." Pp. 169–180 in *Re-Investing Authenticity: Tourism, Place and Emotions*, edited by Britta Timm Knudsen and Anne Marit Waade. Bristol, UK: Channel View Publications, 2010.

Marcus, Greil. "Forty Years of Overstatement: Criticism and the Disney Theme Parks" Pp. 201–207 in *Designing Disney's Theme Parks: The Architecture of Reassurance,* edited by Karal Ann Marling. Paris: Flammarion, 1997.

Marin, Louis. "Utopic Degeneration: Disneyland." Pp. 239–258 in *Utopics: The Semiological Play of Textual Spaces*. Amherst, NY: Humanity Books.

Marling, Karal Ann. "Imagineering the Disney Theme Parks." Pp. 29–177 in *Designing Disney's Theme Parks: The Architecture of Reassurance*, edited by Karal Ann Marling. Paris: Flammarion, 1997.

———. "Elvis Presley's Graceland, or the Aesthetic of Rock n' Roll Heaven." *American Art* 7, no. 4 (Autumn 1993): 72–105.

Maroon, Bahíyyih. "Leisure Space: Thematic Style and Cultural Exclusion in Casablanca." Pp. 137–151 in *The Themed Space: Locating Culture, Nation, and Self*, edited by Scott A. Lukas. Lanham, MD: Lexington, 2007.

Mathieu, Paula. "Economic Citizenship and the Rhetoric of Gourmet Coffee." *Rhetoric Review* 18, no. 1 (Autumn 1999): 112–127.

Mayer, Florian. *The Disney Theme Parks: Home to the Mouse, Hyperreality and Consumerism*. Munich, Germany: Verlag, 2007.

Mayer, Karl J. and Lesley Johnson. "A Customer-based Assessment of Casino Atmospherics." *UNLV Gaming Research & Review Journal* 7, no. 1 (2003): 21–31.

Mbembe, Achille. "Aesthetics of Superfluity." *Public Culture* 16, no. 3 (Fall 2004): 373–405.

McCarthy, Anna. *Ambient Television: Visual Culture and Public Space*. Durham, NC: Duke University Press, 2001.

———. "Brand Identity at NikeTown." Pp. 410–414 in *Signs of Life in the USA: Readings on Popular Culture for Writer*, edited by Sonia Maasik and Jack Solomon. 4th ed. Boston: Bedfords/St. Martin's, 2003.

McClung, Gordon W. "Theme Park Selection: Factors Influencing Attendance." Pp. 233–245 in *Tourism Management: Towards the New Millennium*, edited by Chris Ryan and Stephen Page. New York: Routledge, 2000.

McCombie, Mel. "Art Appreciation at Caesars Palace." Pp. 53–64 in *Popular Culture: Production and Consumption*, edited by Denise D. Bielby and C. Lee Harrington. London: Blackwell, 2000.

McCullough, Edo. *Good Old Coney Island*. New York: Fordham University Press, 1999.

McDowell, Bill. "Bread and Circuses: The Theme Restaurant Revolution." *Restaurants and Institutions* 105, no. 11: 50–72.

McMorrough, John. "On Billboards and Other Signs around (*Learning from*) Las Vegas." Pp. 129–146 in *Relearning from Las Vegas*, edited by Aron Vinegar and Michaek J. Golec. Minneapolis: University of Minnesota Press, 2009.

McNeill, Donald. "The Airport Hotel as Business Space." *Geografiska Annaler: Series B, Human Geography* 91, no. 3 (2009): 219–228.

———. "The Hotel and the City." *Progress in Human Geography* 32, no. 3 (2008): 383–398.

McNeill, Donald and Kim McNamara. "The Cultural Economy of the Boutique Hotel: The Case of the Schrager and W Hotels in New York." Pp. 147–162 in *Consuming Space: Placing Consumption in Perspective*, edited by Michael K. Goodman, David Goodman, and Michael Redclift. Burlington, VT: Ashgate, 2010.

———. "Hotels as Civic Landmarks, Hotels as Assets: the Case of Sydney's Hilton." *Australian Geographer* 40, no. 3 (2009): 369–386.

Meamber, Laurie A. "Disney and the Presentation of Colonial America." *Consumption Markets & Culture* 14, no. 2 (2011): 125–144.

Mechling, Elizabeth Walker and Jay Mechling. "The Sale of Two Cities: A Semiotic Comparison of Disneyland with Marriott's Great America." *The Journal of Popular Culture* 15, no. 1 (Summer 1981): 166–179.

Meiselman, Bell R. et. al. "Effects of Adding an Italian Theme to a Restaurant on the Perceived Ethnicity, Acceptability, and Selection of Foods." *Appetite* 22, no. 1 (1994): 11–24.

Melotti, Marxiano. "Gladiator for a Day: Tourism, Archaeology, and Theme Parks." In *"Here You Leave Today": Time and Temporality in Theme Parks*, edited by Filippo Carlà, Florian Freitag, Sabrina Mittermeier, and Ariane Schwarz. Hanover, Germany: Wehrhahn, 2016.

———. "The Last Gladiators: History, Power and Re-enactment," *Les usages publics du passé* (2015).

———. "In Search of Atlantis: Underwater Tourism Between Myth and Reality." *AP: Online Journal in Public Archaeology* 4 (2014): 95–116.

Mendelsohn, Adam E. "Be Here Now." *Art Monthly* 300 (October 2006): 13–16.

Mennel, Barbara. *Cities and Cinema*. New York: Routledge, 2008.

Mennel, Timothy. "Victor Gruen and the World's Fair that Wasn't." Pp. 323–330 in *Meet Me at the Fair: A World's Fair Reader*, edited by Laura Hollengreen, Celia Pearce, Rebecca Rouse, and Bobby Schweizer. Pittsburgh: ETC Press, 2013.

Mermigas, Diane. "Imagineering: Disney's Secret Weapon." *Electronic Media* 19, no. 40 (2000): 22–23.

Message, Kylie. *New Museums and the Making of Culture*. New York: Berg, 2006.

Michaelides, Stephen. "What Goes Around, Comes Around." *Restaurant Hospitality* 94, no. 78: 152.

Mikunda, Christian. *Brand Lands, Hot Spots and Cool Spaces: Welcome to the Third Place and the Total Marketing Experience*. London: Kogan Page, 2004.

Miles, Steven. *Retail and the Artifice of Social Change*. London: Routledge, 2015.

———. *Spaces for Consumption*. London: Sage, 2010.

Miller, Carolyn Handler. *Digital Storytelling: A Creator's Guide to Interactive Entertainment*. Third edition. New York: Focal, 2014.

Miller, Julie. "San Francisco Follows Theme Trend on Vegas Strip." *Hotel and Motel Management* 212, no. 14 (1997): 7.

Miller, Richard K. "Unique and Theme Restaurants." Pp. 244–251 in *Restaurant and Foodservice Market Research Handbook*. Loganville, GA: Richard K Miller & Associates, 2007.

Miller, Ross. "Euro Disneyland and the Image of America." *Progressive Architecture* 10 (October 1990): 92–95.

Milman, Ady. "Evaluating the Guest Experience at Theme Parks: An Empirical Investigation of Key Attributes." *International Journal of Tourism Research* 11, no. 4 (July/August 2009): 373–387.

———. "The Future of the Theme Park and Attraction Industry: A Management Perspective." *Journal of Travel Research* 40, no. 2 (2001): 139–147.

Mintz, Lawrence. "In a Sense Abroad: Theme Parks and Simulated Tourism." Pp. 183–192 in *Tourists and Tourism: A Reader*, edited by Sharon Bohn Gmelch. Long Grove, IL: Waveland, 2004.

———. "Simulated Tourism at Busch Gardens: The Old Country and Disney's World Showcase, Epcot Center." *The Journal of Popular Culture* 32, no. 3 (Winter 1998): 47–58.

Mitchell, Patricia B. "Theme and Decor: How Important to Restaurants?" *Register and Bee* (Danville, Virginia), April 7, 1991.

Mitrasinovic, Miodrag. *Total Landscape, Theme Parks, Public Space*. Burlington, VT: Ashgate, 2006.

Mittermeier, Sabrina. "Utopia, Nostalgia, and Our Struggle with the Present: Time Travelling through Discovery Bay." In *"Here You Leave Today": Time and Temporality in Theme Parks*, edited by Filippo Carlà, Florian Freitag, Sabrina Mittermeier, and Ariane Schwarz. Hanover, Germany: Wehrhahn, 2016.

Moggridge, Bill. *Designing Interactions*. Cambridge: The MIT Press, 2007.

Moore, Alexander. "Walt Disney World: Bounded Ritual Space and the Playful Pilgrimage Center." *Anthropological Quarterly* 53, no. 4 (1980): 207–218.

Moore, J. Duncan, "A Mickey Mouse Operation: Louisiana Hospital Learns Customer Service Lessons from Disney." *Modern Healthcare*, April 14, 1997.

Morris, Brian. "Architectures of Entertainment." Pp. 205–219 in *Virtual Globalization: Virtual Spaces/Tourist Spaces*, edited by David Holmes. London: Routledge, 2001.

Moscardo, Gianna M. and Philip L. Pearce. "Historic Theme Parks: An Australian Experience in Authenticity." *Annals of Tourism Research* 13, no. 3 (1986): 467–479.

Moss, Mark. *Shopping as an Entertainment Experience*. Lanham, MD: Lexington, 2007.

Munarriz, Rick Aristotle. "Theme Restaurants Battle Extinction." *The Motley Fool*, February 28, 2006.

Muschamp, Herbert. "Disney: Genuinely Artificial, Really Surreal." *New York Times*, October 4, 1998.

Muto, Shoichi. *Las Vegas: 16 Hotel and Casinos, 5 Theme Restaurants*. Tokyo: Shotenkenchiku-sha, 1997.

Mylchreest, Ian. "Stores with Ethnic Themes Set to Be the Next Stage." *Las Vegas Business Press* 21, no. 27 (2004): 19.

Nadis, Fred. "Nature at Aichi World's Expo 2005." *Technology and Culture* 48, no. 3 (July 2007): 575–581.

Ndalianis, Angela. "Dark Rides, Hybrid Machines and the Horror Experience." Pp. 11–26 in *Horror Zone: the Cultural Experience of Contemporary Horror Cinema*, edited by Ian Conrich. London: I.B. Tauris, 2010.

Nelson, Andrew. "Cinema from Attractions: Story and Synergy in Disney's Theme Park Movies." *CINEPHILE* 4, no. 1 (Summer 2008): 36–40.

Nelson, Steve. "Reel Life Performance: The Disney-MGM Studios." *The Drama Review* 34, no. 4 (1990): 60–78.

———. "Walt Disney's EPCOT and the World's Fair Performance Tradition." *The Drama Review* 30, no. 4 (1986): 106–46.

Neuman, Robert. "Disneyland's Main Street, U.S.A., and Its Sources in Hollywood, U.S.A." Pp 37–58 in *Disneyland and Culture: Essays on the Parks and Their Influence*, edited by Kathy Merlock Jackson and Mark I. West. Jefferson, NC: McFarland, 2010.

Newman, Morris. "The Strip Meets the Flaming Volcano." *Progressive Architecture,* February 1995: 82–86.

Nichols, Chris. *The Leisure Architecture of Wayne McAllister*. Salt Lake City, UT: Gibbs Smith, 2007.

Nielsen, Niels Kayser. "'The Summer We All Went to Keuruu' – Intensity and Topographication of Identity." Pp. 52–64 in *Re-Investing Authenticity: Tourism, Place and Emotions*, edited by Britta Timm Knudsen and Anne Marit Waade. Bristol, UK: Channel View Publications, 2010.

Nooshin, Laudan. "Circumnavigation with a Difference? Music, Representation and the Disney Experience: 'It's a Small, Small World.'" *Ethnomusicology Forum* 13, no. 2 (November 2004): 236–251.

Norman, Don. *The Design of Everyday Things*. Revised and expanded edition. New York: Basic Books, 2013.

———. *Emotional Design: Why We Love (or Hate) Everyday Things*. New York: Basic Books, 2005.

Nye, Russel B. "Eight Ways of Looking at an Amusement Park." *The Journal of Popular Culture* 15, no. 1 (Summer 1981): 3–75.

O'Brien, James. "Las Vegas Today: Rome in a Day: Corporate Development Practices and the Role of Professional Designers." *Journal of Architectural Education* 54, no. 2 (2000): 68–79.

Ockman, Joan and Saloman Frausto, eds. *Architourism*. Munich, Germany: Prestel, 2005.

O'Connora, Kaori. "Kitsch, Tourist Art, and the Little Grass Shack in Hawaii." *Home Cultures* 3, no. 3 (2006): 251–271.

O'Dell, Tom. *Spas: The Cultural Economy of Hospitality, Magic and the Senses*. Lund, Sweden: Nordic Academic Press, 2010.

———. "Experiencescapes: Blurring Borders and Testing Connections." Pp. 1–35 in *Experiencescapes: Tourism, Culture, and Economy*, edited by Tom O'Dell and Peter Billing. Frederiksberg: Copenhagen Business School Press, 2005.

———. *Culture Unbound: Americanization and Everyday Life in Sweden*. Lund, Sweden: Nordic Academic Press, 1997.

Oesterle, Carolyn. "Themed Environments–Performative Spaces: Performing Visitors in North American Living History Museums." Pp. 157–175 in *Staging the Past: Themed Environments in Transcultural Perspectives*, edited by Judith Schlehe, Michiko Uike-Bormann, Carolyn Oesterle, and Wolfgang Hochbruck. Bielefeld, Germany: Transcript, 2010.

Oettermann, Stephan. *The Panorama: History of a Mass Medium*. New York: Zone, 1997.

Olesen, Bodil Birkebæk. "Ethnic Objects in Domestic Interiors: Space, Atmosphere and the Making of Home." *Home Cultures* 7, no. 1 (2010): 25–41.

Olson, Scott Robert. "The Extensions of Synergy: Product Placement Through Theming and Environmental Simulacra." *Journal of Promotion Management* 10, nos. 1/2 (2004): 65–87.

Onosko, Tim. *Fun Land U.S.A.* New York: Arno.

Ooi, Can-Seng. "A Theory of Tourism Experiences: The Management of Attention." Pp. 53–68 in *Experiencescapes: Tourism, Culture, and Economy*, edited by Tom O'Dell and Peter Billing. Frederiksberg: Copenhagen Business School Press, 2005.

Ooi, Can-Seng and Birgit Stöber. "Authenticity and Place Branding: The Arts and Culture in Branding Berlin and Singapore." Pp. 66–79 in *Re-Investing Authenticity: Tourism, Place and Emotions*, edited by Britta Timm Knudsen and Anne Marit Waade. Bristol, UK: Channel View Publications, 2010.

Opel, Andy and Jason Smith. "Zootycoon: Capitalism, Nature, and the Pursuit of Happiness." *Ethics and the Environment* 9, no. 2 (Fall–Winter 2004): 103–120.

Østergaard, Jesper and Dorthe Refslund Christensen. "Walking towards Oneself–Authentification of Place and Self." Pp. 241–253 in *Re-Investing Authenticity: Tourism, Place and Emotions*, edited by Britta Timm Knudsen and Anne Marit Waade. Bristol, UK: Channel View Publications, 2010.

Ostwald, Michael J. "Identity Tourism, Virtuality and the Theme Park." Pp. 192–204 in *Virtual Globalization: Virtual Spaces/Tourist Spaces*, edited by David Holmes. London: Routledge, 2001.

Ötsch, Silke. "Earning from Las Vegas." Pp. 133–152 in *Stripping Las Vegas: A Contextual Review of Casino Resort Architecture*, edited by Karin Jaschke and Silke Ötsch. Weimar, Germany: University of Weimar Press, 2003.

Ott, Brian L., Eric Aoki, and Greg Dickinson. "Ways of (Not) Seeing Guns: Presence and Absence at the Cody Firearms Museum." *Communication and Critical/Cultural Studies* 8, no. 3 (2011): 215–239.

Page, Stephen. "Theme Parks, Introduction." Pp. 227–232 in *Tourism Management: Towards the New Millennium*, edited by Chris Ryan and Stephen Page. New York: Routledge, 2000.

Paradis, Thomas. "From Downtown to Theme Town: Reinventing America's Smaller Historic Retail Districts." Pp. 57–74 in *The Themed Space: Locating Culture, Nation, and Self*, edited by Scott A. Lukas. Lanham, MD: Lexington, 2007.

———. "Theming, Tourism, and Fantasy City." Pp. 195–209 in *A Companion to Tourism*, edited by Alan A. Lew, Allan M. Williams, and Colin Michael Hall. London: Blackwell, 2004.

———. *Theme Town: A Geography of Landscape and Community in Flagstaff, Arizona*. Lincoln, Neb.: iUniverse, 2003.

———. "The Political Economy of Theme Development in Small Urban Places: The Case of Roswell, New Mexico." *Tourism Geographies* 4, no. 1 (2002): 24–43.

Parascandola, Louis J. and John Parascandola, eds. *A Coney Island Reader: Through Dizzy Gates of Illusion*. New York: Columbia University Press, 2014.

Paterson, Mark W. D. *Consumption and Everyday Life*. London: Routledge, 2006.

Pearce, Philip L. and Gianna Moscardo. "Tourist Theme Parks: Research Practices and Possibilities." *Australian Psychologist* 20, no. 3 (November 1985): 303–312.

Pearson, Sarina. "Persistent Primitivisms: Popular and Academic Discourses about Pacific and Māori Cinema and Television." *Journal of the Polynesian Society* 122, no. 1 (2013): 21–44.

———. "The Influence of Fiction and Cinematic Excess on the Factual." *Journal of Pacific History* 45, no. 1 (2010): 105–116

Pegler, Martin M. *Entertainment Destinations: Cinemas/Center/Casinos/Clubs/Cruise*. New York: Visual Reference Publications, 2000.

———. *Theme Restaurant Design: Entertainment and Fun Dining*. New York: Retail Reporting Corp, 1997.

Penner, Barbara. "Doing It Right: Postwar Honeymoon Resorts in the Pocono Mountains." Pp. 207–226 in *Architecture and Tourism: Perception, Performance, and Place*, edited by D. Medina Lasansky. Oxford: Berg, 2004.

Pettigrew, Simone. "Hearts and Minds: Children's Experiences of Disney World." *Consumption Markets & Culture* 14, no. 2 (2011): 145–161.

Philips, Deborah. "Narrativised Spaces: The Functions of Story in the Theme Park." Pp. 91–108 in *Leisure/Tourism Geographies: Practices and Geographical Knowledge*, edited by David Crouch. London: Routledge, 1999.

Pike, David. "The Walt Disney World Underground." *Space and Culture* 8, no. 1 (February 2005): 47–65.

Pine, Joseph B. II and James H. Gilmore. *Authenticity: What Consumers Really Want*. Boston: Harvard Business School Press, 2007.

———. *The Experience Economy: Work Is Theatre and Every Business a Stage*. Boston: Harvard Business School Press, 1999.

Pinoniemi, Lynn. "Theming Parks: Creating Memorable Playgrounds by Building on a Theme." *Parks and Recreation*, November 2003.

Postrel, Virginia. *The Substance of Style*. New York: Harper Collins, 2003.

Potteiger, Matthew and Jamie Purington. *Landscape Narratives: Design Practices for Telling Stories*. New York: John Wiley and Sons, 1998.

Prentice, Claire. *The Lost Tribe of Coney Island: Headhunters, Luna Park, and the Man Who Pulled Off the Spectacle of the Century*. New York: New Harvest, 2014.

Project on Disney, The. *Inside the Mouse: Work and Play at Disney World*. Durham, NC: Duke University Press, 1995.

Project on Vegas, The. *Strip Cultures: Finding America in Las Vegas*. Durham, NC: Duke University Press, 2015.

Quainton, David. "Prepare for Impact (Advice Bureau Theming)." *Event Magazine* (UK), August 2009: 43–44.

Quirk, Vanessa. "China Replicates Austrian Village." *Arch Daily*, June 12, 2012.

Quitzau, Maj-Britt and Inge Røpke. "Bathroom Transformation: From Hygiene to Well-Being?" *Home Cultures* 6, no. 3 (2009): 219–242.

Rabinovitz, Lauren. *Electric Dreamland: Amusement Parks, Movies, and American Modernity*. New York: Columbia University Press, 2012.

Rahn, Suzanne. "The Dark Ride of Snow White: Narrative Strategies at Disneyland." Pp 87–100 in *Disneyland and Culture: Essays on the Parks and Their Influence*, edited by Kathy Merlock Jackson and Mark I. West. Jefferson, NC: McFarland, 2010.

Raz, Aviad E. "Domesticating Disney: Onstage Strategies of Adaptation in Tokyo Disneyland." *The Journal of Popular Culture* 33, no. 4 (Spring 2000): 77–99.

———. *Riding the Black Ship: Japan and Tokyo Disneyland*. Cambridge: Harvard University Asia Center, 1999.

Real, Michael R. "The Disney Universe: Morality Play." Pp. 46–89 in *Mass-Mediated Culture*. Englewood Cliffs, NJ: Prentice-Hall, 1977.

Redclift, Michael. "Frontier Spaces of Production and Consumption: Surfaces, Appearances and Representations on the Mayan Riviera." Pp. 81–96 in *Consuming Space: Placing Consumption in Perspective*, edited by Michael K. Goodman, David Goodman, and Michael Redclift. Burlington, VT: Ashgate, 2010.

Reed, Nancy B. "The Classical Heritage in Neon Lights: Las Vegas, Nevada." *Journal of American & Comparative Cultures* 24, nos. 1-2 (Spring/Summer 2001): 147–152.

Reijnders, Stijn. *Places of the Imagination: Media, Tourism, Culture*. Surrey, England: Ashgate, 2013.

Ren, Hai. *The Middle Class in Neoliberal China: Governing Risk, Life-Building, and Themed Spaces*. New York: Routledge, 2012.

———. "The Landscape of Power: Imagineering Consumer Behavior at China's Theme Parks." Pp. 97–112 in *The Themed Space: Locating Culture, Nation, and Self*, edited by Scott A. Lukas. Lanham, MD: Lexington, 2007.

Renaut, Christian. "Disneyland Paris: A Clash of Cultures." Pp 125–137 in *Disneyland and Culture: Essays on the Parks and Their Influence*, edited by Kathy Merlock Jackson and Mark I. West. Jefferson, NC: McFarland, 2010.

Rentschler, Ruth and Anne-Marie Hede, eds. *Museum Marketing: Competing in the Global Marketplace*. Oxon, UK: Routledge, 2007.

Rieger, Bernhard. "Floating Palaces." *History Today* 55, no. 2 (2005): 37–43.

Riewoldt, Otto. *Brandscaping: Worlds of Experience in Retail Design*. Basel, Switzerland: Birkhäuser, 2002.

Rinella, Heidi Knapp. "Heavy Roman Theming Makes Way for Truly Upscale Restaurants." *Las Vegas Review Journal*, August 6, 2006.

Ringaard, Dan. "Travel and Testimony, Rhetoric of Authenticity." Pp. 108–120 in *Re-Investing Authenticity: Tourism, Place and Emotions*, edited by Britta Timm Knudsen and Anne Marit Waade. Bristol, UK: Channel View Publications, 2010.

Ritzer, George. *Enchanting a Disenchanted World: Revolutionizing the Means of Consumption*. Thousand Oaks, CA: Pine Forge, 2005.

Ritzer, George, and Todd Stillman. "The Modern Las Vegas Casino-Hotel: The Paradigmatic New Means of Consumption." *M@n@gement* 4, no. 3 (2007): 83–99.

Robinson, Shirleene. "Inventing Australia for Americans: The Rise of the Outback Steakhouse Restaurant Chain in the USA." *The Journal of Popular Culture* 44, no. 3 (2011): 545–562.

Robles, Fanny. "*Blanche et Noir*, by Louise Faure-Favier: When France Falls in Love with Senegal at the Paris Exposition Universelle of 1900." Pp. 53–60 in *Meet Me at the Fair: A World's Fair Reader*, edited by Laura Hollengreen, Celia Pearce, Rebecca Rouse, and Bobby Schweizer. Pittsburgh: ETC Press, 2013.

Rockwell, David and Chee Pearlman. *What If...?: The Architecture and Design of David Rockwell*. New York: Metropolis Books, 2014.

Rollins, Henry. "Las Vegas Is Out of Ideas." *LA Weekly* (Blog) August 7, 2014.

Ron, Amos. "Holy Land Protestant Themed Environments and the Spiritual Experience." Pp. 111–133 in *Staging the Past: Themed Environments in Transcultural Perspectives*, edited by Judith Schlehe, Michiko Uike-Bormann, Carolyn Oesterle, and Wolfgang Hochbruck. Bielefeld, Germany: Transcript, 2010.

Roost, Frank. "Synergy City: How Times Square and Celebration Are Integrated into Disney's Marketing Cycle." Pp. 261–298 in *Rethinking Disney: Private Control, Public Dimensions*, edited by Mike Budd and Max H. Kirsch. Middletown, CT: Wesleyan University Press, 2005.

———. "Recreating the City as Entertainment Center: The Media Industry's Role in Transforming Potsdamer Platz and Times Square." *Journal of Urban Technology* 5, no. 3 (1998): 1–21.

Rose, Frank. *The Art of Immersion: How the Digital Generation Is Remaking Hollywood, Madison Avenue, and the Way We Tell Stories*. New York: W. W. Norton and Company, 2012.

Rose, Mariah S. "Granddaddy of All Theme Restaurants." *ColoradoBiz* 26, no. 8 (August 1999): 16.

Ross, Andrew. *The Celebration Chronicles: Life, Liberty, and the Pursuit of Property Values in Disney's New Town.* New York: Ballantine Books, 1999.

Rowe, Megan. "Edgy Hotel Restaurants." *Restaurant Hospitality* 95, no. 3 (2011): 28–32.

———. "The Theme's The Thing." *Restaurant Hospitality* 91, no. 7 (2007): 36–44.

Roy, Kisholoy. "Theme Restaurants and Bars in India: The Factors Behind Their Growth." *ICFAI Journal of Services Marketing.* 6, no. 1 (2008): 70–76.

Rubin, Barbara. "Aesthetic Ideology and Urban Design." *Annals of the Association of American Geographers* 69, no. 3 (1979): 339–361.

Rubin, Michael S., Robert J. Gorman, and Michael H. Lawry. "Entertainment Returns to Gotham." *Urban Land* 53, no. 8 (1994): 64.

Rubinstein, Ed. "Mars 2112 to Beam Restaurantgoers into the 22nd Century." *Nation's Restaurant News,* 32, no. 29: 158–159.

Rugare, Steven. "The Advent of America at EPCOT Center." Pp. 103–112 in *Cartographies: Poststructuralism and the Mapping of Bodies and Spaces,* edited by Rosalyn Diprose and Robyn Ferrell. Australia: Allen and Unwin, 1991

Rugoff, Ralph. "Honey, I Shrunk the City." Pp. 25–29 in *Circus Americanus.* London: Verso.

Russell, Deborah. "New Restaurant Brings Bit of Nashville to L.A." *Billboard,* September 3, 1994.

Russell, James S. "Theming vs. Design." *Architectural Record* 185, no. 3: 90–93.

Rutes, Walter A., Richard H. Penner, and Lawrence Adams. *Hotel Design, Planning, and Development.* New York: W. W. Norton and Company, 2001.

Rutheiser, Charles. *Imagineering Atlanta: The Politics of Place in the City of Dreams.* London: Verso, 1996.

Ruzich, Constance M. "For the Love of Joe: The Language of Starbucks." *The Journal of Popular Culture* 41, no. 3 (2008): 428–441.

Rykwert, Joseph. "Is Euro Disney a Substitute for Paris?" *Times Literary Supplement,* September 9, 1992.

Salamone, Virginia A. and Frank A. Salamone. "Images of Main Street: Disney World and the American Adventure." *Journal of American Culture* 22, no. 1 (Spring 1999): 85–92.

Salazar, Noel B. *Envisioning Eden: Mobilizing Imaginaries in Tourism and Beyond.* New York: Berghan, 2013.

———. "Imagineering Tailor-Made Pasts for Nation-Building and Tourism: A Comparative Perspective." Pp. 93–109 in *Staging the Past: Themed Environments in Transcultural Perspectives,* edited by Judith Schlehe, Michiko Uike-Bormann, Carolyn Oesterle, and Wolfgang Hochbruck. Bielefeld, Germany: Transcript, 2010.

Sallaz, Jeffrey J. "The Disneyfication of the World: A Grobalisation Perspective." *American Sociological Review* 77, no. 1 (February 2012): 99–119.

Sally, Lynn. "Luna Park's Fantasy World and Dreamland's White City: Fire Spectacles at Coney Island as Elemental Performativity." Pp. 39–55 in *The Themed Space: Locating Culture, Nation, and Self,* edited by Scott A. Lukas. Lanham, MD: Lexington, 2007.

———. "Fantasy Lands and Kinesthetic Thrills: Sensorial Consumption, the Shock of Modernity, and Spectacle as Total-Body Experience at Coney Island." *Senses and Society* 1, no. 3 (November, 2006): 293–309.

———. *Fighting the Flames: The Spectacular Performance of Fire at Coney Island.* New York: Routledge, 2006.

Salvail, Andre. "Fashion Cafe Goes Out of Style in N.O." *New Orleans City Business* 19, no. 4: 1–3.

Samuelson, Dale and Wendy Yegoiants. *The American Amusement Park.* St. Paul, MN: MBI, 2001.

Sandbye, Mette. "Making Pictures Talk–The Re-opening of 'a Dead City' through Vernacular Photography as a Catalyst for the

Performance of Memories." Pp. 182–198 in *Re-Investing Authenticity: Tourism, Place and Emotions*, edited by Britta Timm Knudsen and Anne Marit Waade. Bristol, UK: Channel View Publications, 2010.

Sandlin, Jennifer and Julie Maudlin. "Disney's Pedagogies of Pleasure and the Eternal Recurrence of Whiteness." *Journal of Consumer Culture* (September 2, 2015).

Sandvik, Kjetil. "Crime Scene as Augmented Reality-Models for Enhancing Places Emotionally by Means of Narratives, Fictions and Virtual Reality." Pp. 138–153 in *Re-Investing Authenticity: Tourism, Place and Emotions*, edited by Britta Timm Knudsen and Anne Marit Waade. Bristol, UK: Channel View Publications, 2010.

Santesso, Aaron. "Living Authenticity: The World's Fair and the Zoo." Pp. 41–51 in *Meet Me at the Fair: A World's Fair Reader*, edited by Laura Hollengreen, Celia Pearce, Rebecca Rouse, and Bobby Schweizer. Pittsburgh: ETC Press, 2013.

Santos, Paula Mota. "Calling Upon the Lost Empire: The Evocative Power of Miniatures in a Portuguese Nationalist Theme Park." Pp. 52–73 in *Tourism and the Power of Otherness: Seductions of Difference*, edited by David Picard and Michael A. Di Giovine. Bristol, UK: Channel View Publications, 2014.

Savage, Kirk. *Monument Wars: Washington, D.C., the National Mall, and the Transformation of the Memorial Landscape*. Berkeley: University of California Press, 2011.

Von Schaewen, Deidi and John Maizels. *Fantasy Worlds*. New York: Taschen, 1999.

Schadla-Hall, Tim. "Shakespeare's Globe: 'As Faithful a Copy as Scholarship … Could Get'; 'a Bit of a Bastard.'" Pp. 104–123 in *The Constructed Past: Experimental Archaeology, Education and the Public*, edited by Philippe Planel and Peter G. Stone. London: Routledge, 1999.

Schatzker, Mark. "Historical Fiction: How Do Medieval-Themed Restaurants Get It Wrong?" *Slate*, October 6, 2004.

Schenker, Heath. "Pleasure Gardens, Theme Parks, and the Picturesque." Pp. 69–89 in *Theme Park Landscapes: Antecedents and Variations*, edited by Terence Young and Robert Riley. Washington, D.C.: Dumbarton Oaks Research Library and Collection, 2002.

Schickel, Richard. *The Disney Version: The Life, Times, Art and Commerce of Walt Disney*. Third edition. Chicago: Ivan R. Dee, 1997.

Schlehe, Judith. "Cultural Politics of Representation in Contemporary Indonesia." *European Journal of East Asian Studies* 10 (2011): 149–167.

Schlehe, Judith and Michiko Uike-Bormann. "Staging the Past in Cultural Theme Parks: Representations of Self and Other in Asia and Europe." Pp. 57–91 in *Staging the Past: Themed Environments in Transcultural Perspectives*, edited by Judith Schlehe, Michiko Uike-Bormann, Carolyn Oesterle, and Wolfgang Hochbruck. Bielefeld, Germany: Transcript, 2010.

Schmid, Heiko. *Economy of Fascination: Dubai and Las Vegas as Themed Urban Landscapes*. Urbanization of the Earth, Vol. 11. Stuttgart, Germany: Borntraeger, 2009

Schmitt, Bernd H. and Alex Simonson. *Marketing Aesthetics: The Strategic Marketing of Brands, Identity and Image*. New York: Free Press, 1997.

Schneekloth, Lynda H. and Robert G. Shibley. *Placemaking: The Art and Practice of Building Communities*. New York: Wiley, 1995.

Schneiderman, Deborah. *Inside Prefab: The Ready-made Interior*. New York: Princeton Architectural Press, 2012.

———. "The Prefabricated Kitchen: Substance and Surface." *Home Cultures* 7, no. 3 (2010): 243–262.

Schnell, Steven M. "Creating Narratives of Place and Identity in Little Sweden, U.S.A." *Geographical Review* 93, no. 1 (January 2003): 1–29.

Schüll, Natasha Dow. "Oasis/Mirage: Fantasies of Nature in Las Vegas." Pp. 377–402 in *From Virgin Land to Disney World: Nature and Its Discontents in the USA of Yesterday and Today*, edited by Bernd Herzogenrath. Amsterdam: Rodopi, 2001.

Schwartz, David G. "The Conjuring of The Mirage." *Vegas Seven*, April 30, 2014.

———. *Suburban Xanadu: The Casino Resort on the Las Vegas Strip and Beyond.* New York: Routledge, 2003.

Schwartz, Hillel. *The Culture of the Copy: Striking Likenesses, Unreasonable Facsimiles.* New York: Zone, 1996.

Schwartz, Nelson D. "How Investors Got 86ed by Theme Restaurants." *Fortune* 137, no. 4 (1998).

Schwarz, Angela. "Past, Present and Future in one Place: Nineteenth-Century World's Fairs and the Emergence of Theme Parks." In *"Here You Leave Today": Time and Temporality in Theme Parks,* edited by Filippo Carlà, Florian Freitag, Sabrina Mittermeier, and Ariane Schwarz. Hanover, Germany: Wehrhahn, 2016.

Schwarz, Ariane. "Staging the Gaze: The Water Coaster Poseidon as an Example of Staging Strategies in Theme Parks." In *"Here You Leave Today": Time and Temporality in Theme Parks,* edited by Filippo Carlà, Florian Freitag, Sabrina Mittermeier, and Ariane Schwarz. Hanover, Germany: Wehrhahn, 2016.

Scibelli, Cathy. "Forget the Prozac, Give Me a Dose of Disney." Pp. 215–222 in *Disneyland and Culture: Essays on the Parks and Their Influence,* edited by Kathy Merlock Jackson and Mark I. West. Jefferson, NC: McFarland, 2010.

Seelye, Katharine. "The Sun Sets on a Symbol Of Western-Themed Dining." *New York Times*, October 20, 2013.

Selberg, Torunn. "Journeys, Religion and Authenticity Revisited." Pp. 228–240 in *Re-Investing Authenticity: Tourism, Place and Emotions,* edited by Britta Timm Knudsen and Anne Marit Waade. Bristol, UK: Channel View Publications, 2010.

Shanken, Andy. "Confederates on the Fairway: A Civil War Themed Subdivision in Rural Ohio." *Landscape Journal* 26, no. 2 (2007): 287–301.

Shaw, Gareth and Allan M. Williams. *Tourism and Tourism Spaces.* London: Sage, 2004.

———. "Theming the Landscape." Pp. 207–210 in *Critical Issues in Tourism: A Geographical Perspective.* London: Blackwell, 2002.

Sherry, John F. "The Work of Play at American Girl Place." *Social Psychology Quarterly* 72, no. 3 (September 2009): 199–202.

———. *Servicescapes: The Concept of Place in Contemporary Markets.* Chicago: NTC Business Books, 1998.

Sherry, John F. et al. "Being in the Zone: Staging Retail Theater at ESPN Zone Chicago." *Journal of Contemporary Ethnography* 30, no. 4 (2001): 465–510.

———. Gendered Behavior in a Male Preserve: Role Playing at ESPN Zone Chicago." *Journal of Consumer Psychology* 14, nos. 1/2 (2004): 151–158.

Shields, Rob. "The Tourist Affect: Escape and Syncresis on the Las Vegas Strip." Pp. 105–126 in *Ecologies of Affect: Placing Nostalgia, Desire, and Hope,* edited by Tonya K. Davidson, Ondine Park, and Rob Shields. Waterloo, Canada: Wilfrid Laurier Unkversity Press, 2011.

———. "Architecture as a Good" P. 95 in *Architectural Design: Consuming Architecture,* edited by Maggie Toy. West Sussex, UK: John Wiley and Sons, 1998.

———. *Lifestyle Shopping: The Subject of Consumption.* London: Routledge, 1992.

Siano, Joseph. "A '*Star Trek*' Voyage Lands in Las Vegas." *New York Times*, January 25, 1998.

Siegel, Greg. "Disneyfication, the Stadium, and the Politics of Ambiance." Pp. 299–324 in *Rethinking Disney: Private Control, Public Dimensions,* edited by Mike Budd and Max H. Kirsch. Middletown, CT: Wesleyan University Press, 2005.

Simon, Bryant. *Boardwalk of Dreams: Atlantic City and the Fate of Urban America.* New York: Oxford University Press, 2006.

Simon, Nina. *The Participatory Museum.* Museum 2.0 (Self Published), 2010.

Simpson, David. "Tourism and Titanomania." *Critical Inquiry* 25, no. 4 (Summer, 1999): 680–695.

Simpson, Tim. "Macau Metropolis and Mental Life: Interior Urbanism and the Chinese Imaginary." *International Journal of Urban and Regional Research* 38, no. 3 (2014): 824–832.

———. "Chinese Tourists, Themed Casinos, and Consumer Pedagogy in Macau." Pp. 157–174 in *The Communicative City and Urban Communication in the 21st Century: Urban Communication Reader 3*, edited by Matthew D. Matsaganis, Victoria J. Gallagher, and Susan J. Drucker. New York: Peter Lang, 2013.

———. "Tourist Utopias: Las Vegas, Dubai, Macau." Asia Research Institute Working Paper Series, Issue 177. National University of Singapore, 2012.

———. "Materialist Pedagogy: The Function of Themed Environments in Post-Socialist Consumption in Macau." *Tourist Studies* 9, no. 1 (2009): 60–80.

———. "Macau's Mediterranean Motifs." *World Architecture* 12 (2009): 104–111.

———. "Themed Environments, Suburbs, and the Middle Class in Bangkok." *Etnofoor* 14, no. 1 (2001): 7–30.

———. "Streets, Sidewalks, Stores, and Stories: Narrative and the Uses of Urban Space." *Journal of Contemporary Ethnography* 29, no. 6 (2000): 682–716.

Sindi, Rena Kirdar. *Be My Guest: Theme Party Savoir-Faire*. New York: Assouline, 2002.

Sion, Brigitte, ed. *Death Tourism: Disaster Sites as Recreational Landscape*. Calcutta: Seagull Books, 2014.

Sjöholm, Carina. "Murder Walks in Ystad." Pp. 154–168 in *Re-Investing Authenticity: Tourism, Place and Emotions*, edited by Britta Timm Knudsen and Anne Marit Waade. Bristol, UK: Channel View Publications, 2010.

Sklar, Martin. *Dream It! Do It!: My Half-Century Creating Disney's Magic Kingdoms*. New York: Disney Editions, 2013.

Slagle, Jefferson D. "The Heirs of Buffalo Bill: Performing Authenticity in the Dime Western." *Canadian Review of American Studies/Revue canadienne–américaine d'études* 39, no. 2 (2009): 119–138.

Smith, Adam I.P. "It's Magnificent But Is It History?" *History Today* 51, no. 5 (2001): 36–37.

Smith, Cynthia Duquette and Teresa Bergman. "You Were on Indian Land: Alcatraz Island as Recalcitrant Memory Space." Pp. 160–188 in *Places of Public Memory: The Rhetoric of Museums and Memorials*, edited by Greg Dickinson, Brian L. Ott, and Carole Blair. Tuscaloosa: University of Alabama Press, 2010.

Smith, Katherine. "Mobilizing Visions: Representing the American Landscape." Pp. 97–128 in *Relearning from Las Vegas*, edited by Aron Vinegar and Michaek J. Golec. Minneapolis: University of Minnesota Press, 2009.

Snow, Richard F. "Disney: Coast to Coast." *American Heritage* 38, no. 2 (February–March 1987).

Snyder, Eldon E. "The Chautauqua Movement in Popular Culture: A Sociological Analysis." *Journal of American Culture* 8, no. 3 (Fall 1985): 79–90.

Solnit, Rebecca. "Las Vegas, or the Longest Distance between Two Points." Pp. 277–291 in *Wanderlust: A History of Walking*. New York: Penguin, 2001.

Solomon, Michael R. *Conquering Consumerspace: Marketing Strategies for a Branded World*. New York: AMACOM, 2003.

Sorkin, Michael. "See You in Disneyland." Pp. 205–232 in *Variations on a Theme Park*, edited by Michael Sorkin. New York: Noonday, 1992.

Souther, J. Mark. "The Disneyfication of New Orleans: The French Quarter as Facade in a Divided City." *The Journal of American History* 94, no. 3 (December 2007): 804–811.

Southworth, Michael. "Reinventing Main Street: From Mall to Townscape Mall." *Journal of Urban Design* 10, no. 2 (2005): 151–170.

Specialty Retail. "Why Theme Restaurants Fail (and How They Succeed)." *Specialty Retail*, March 1999.

Spence, Charles and Betina Piqueras-Fiszman. *The Perfect Meal: The Multisensory Science of Food and Dining.* New York: Wiley-Blackwell, 2014.

Sperb, Jason. *Disney's Most Notorious Film: Race, Convergence, and the Hidden Histories of Song of the South.* Austin: University of Texas Press, 2013.

———. "Take a Frown, Turn It Upside Down: Splash Mountain, Walt Disney World, and the Cultural De-rac[e]-ination of Disney's Song of the South (1946)." *The Journal of Popular Culture* 38, no. 5 (August 2005): 924–938.

Spotte, Stephen H. *Zoos in Postmodernism: Signs and Simulation.* Madison, NJ: Fairleigh Dickinson University Press, 2006.

Squires, Nick. "Anger in Italy Over a Chain of Mafia-themed Restaurants in Spain." *The Telegraph*, February 19, 2014.

Statesman. "Durga in Themeland." *The Statesman* (India), October 2, 2006.

Stausberg, Michael. *Religion and Tourism: Crossroads, Destinations and Encounters.* New York: Routledge, 2011.

Stegmeier, Diane. *Innovations in Office Design: The Critical Influence Approach to Effective Work Environments.* Hoboken, NJ: Wiley, 2008.

Stein, Andi. *Attracting Attention: Promotion and Marketing for Tourism Attractions.* New York: Peter Lang, 2015.

———. *Why We Love Disney: The Power of the Disney Brand.* New York: Peter Lang, 2011.

Stein, Andi and Beth Bingham Evans. *An Introduction to the Entertainment Industry.* New York: Peter Lang, 2009.

Stein, Harvey. *Coney Island.* New York: W. W. Norton & Company, 1998.

Steinbrink, Malte. "'We did the Slum!' – Urban Poverty Tourism in Historical Perspective." *Tourism Geographies* 14, no. 2 (2012): 213–234.

Steiner, Michael. "Frontierland as Tomorrowland: Walt Disney and the Architectural Packaging of the Mythic West." *Montana: The Magazine of Western History* 48, no. 1 (Spring, 1998): 2–17.

Steinglass, Matt. "Why a Casino that Looks Like a Tuscan Village Is One of South Africa's Most Democratic Public Spaces." *Metropolis*, October 2002.

Steinkrüger, Jan-Erik. "Other Times and Other Spaces: The Construction of Difference in Themed Spaces." In *"Here You Leave Today": Time and Temporality in Theme Parks,* edited by Filippo Carlà, Florian Freitag, Sabrina Mittermeier, and Ariane Schwarz. Hanover, Germany: Wehrhahn, 2016.

———. *Thematisierte Welten: Über Darstellungspraxen in Zoologischen Gärten und Vergnügungsparks.* Bonn, Germany: Transcript, 2013.

Stern, Jane and Michael Stern. "When the Theme's the Thing." *Gourmet* 56, no. 11 (1996): 152–155.

Stern, Robert A. M. "The Pop and the Popular at Disney." *Architectural Design* 67, nos. 7/8 (1992): 20–23.

Stevenson, Jill. "Embodying Sacred History: Performing Creationism for Believers." *The Drama Review* 56, no. 1 (Spring 2012): 93–113.

Strömberg, Per. "Theming." *The Wiley Blackwell Encyclopedia of Consumption and Consumer Studies.* 1–5 (Online).

Sturken, Marita. *Tourists of History: Memory, Kitsch, and Consumerism from Oklahoma City to Ground Zero.* Durham, NC: Duke University Press, 2007.

Suitner, Johannes. *Imagineering Cultural Vienna: On the Semiotic Regulation of Vienna's Culture-led Urban Transformation.* Bielefeld, Germany: Transcript, 2015.

Sundbo, Jon and Flemming Sørensen, eds. *Handbook on the Experience Economy.* Cheltenham, UK: Edward Elgar, 2013.

Surrell, Jason. *The Haunted Mansion: Imagineering a Disney Classic.* New York: Disney Editions, 2015.

———. *The Haunted Mansion: From the Magic Kingdom to the Movies*. New York: Disney Editions, 2009.

———. *The Disney Mountains: Imagineering At Its Peak*. New York: Disney Editions, 2007.

———. *Pirates of the Caribbean: From the Magic Kingdom to the Movies*. New York: Disney Editions, 2006.

Svonkin, Craig. "A Southern California Boyhood in the Simu-Southland Shadows of Walt Disney's Enchanted Tiki Room." Pp. 107–124 in *Disneyland and Culture: Essays on the Parks and Their Influence*, edited by Kathy Merlock Jackson and Mark I. West. Jefferson, NC: McFarland, 2010.

Swain, Margaret Byrne. "Myth Management in Tourism's Imaginariums: Tales from Southwest China and Beyond." Pp. 103–124 in *Tourism Imaginaries: Anthropological Approaches*, edited by Noel B. Salazar and Nelson H. H. Graburn. New York: Berghan, 2014.

Synnott, Marcia G. "Disney's America: Whose Patrimony, Whose Profits, Whose Past?" *The Public Historian* 17, no. 4 (Autumn, 1995): 43–59.

Tao, I. M., Yasuhiko Taguchi, and Takeshi Saito. *American Theme Restaurants*. Tokyo: Shotenkenchiku Sha, 1999.

Telotte, J. P. "Disney and 'This World's Fair Thing.'" Pp. 409–422 in *Meet Me at the Fair: A World's Fair Reader*, edited by Laura Hollengreen, Celia Pearce, Rebecca Rouse, and Bobby Schweizer. Pittsburgh: ETC Press, 2013.

———. "Theme Parks and Films–Play and Players." Pp. 171–182 in *Disneyland and Culture: Essays on the Parks and Their Influence*, edited by Kathy Merlock Jackson and Mark I. West. Jefferson, NC: McFarland, 2010.

Teunissen, Martine. "Staging the Past in the Revolutionary City: Colonial Williamsburg." Pp. 177–198 in *Staging the Past: Themed Environments in Transcultural Perspectives*, edited by Judith Schlehe, Michiko Uike-Bormann, Carolyn Oesterle, and Wolfgang Hochbruck. Bielefeld, Germany: Transcript, 2010.

Theodossopoulos, Dimitrios. "Scorn or Idealization? Tourism Imaginaries, Exoticization and Ambivalence in Emberá Indigenous Tourism." Pp. 57–79 in *Tourism Imaginaries: Anthropological Approaches*, edited by Noel B. Salazar and Nelson H. H. Graburn. New York: Berghan, 2014.

Thompson, Craig J. and Zeynep Arsel. "The Starbucks Brandscape and Consumers' (Anticorporate) Experiences of Glocalization." *Journal of Consumer Research* 31, no. 3 (December 2004): 631–642.

Thompson, Frederic. "Amusing the Million." *Everybody's Magazine* 19 (July to December, 1908): 378–387.

———. "Amusement Architecture." *The Architectural Review* 16, no. 7 (July 1909): 85–89.

Thompson, Jenny. *Wargames: Inside the World of 20th Century Reenactors*. Washington, D.C.: Smithsonian Books, 2004.

Thorns, David C. "Theme Parks and Theme Parks–History and Development." Pp. 138–140 in *The Transformation of Cities: Urban Theory and Urban Cities*. New York: Palgrave Macmillan, 2002.

Tonnaer, Anke. "Envisioning the Dutch Serengeti: An Exploration of Touristic Imaginings of the Wild in the Netherlands." Pp. 242–259 in *Tourism Imaginaries: Anthropological Approaches*, edited by Noel B. Salazar and Nelson H. H. Graburn. New York: Berghan, 2014.

Trentmann, Frank. "Multiple Spaces of Consumption: Some Historical Perspectives." Pp. 41–56 in *Consuming Space: Placing Consumption in Perspective*, edited by Michael K. Goodman, David Goodman, and Michael Redclift. Burlington, VT: Ashgate, 2010.

Trouillot, Michel-Rolph. *Silencing the Past: Power and the Production of History*. Boston: Beacon Press, 1997.

Tsai, Chen Tsang and Lu Pei-Hsun. "Authentic Dining Experiences in Ethnic Theme Restaurants." *International Journal of Hospitality Management* 31, no. 1 (2012): 304–306.

Tuan, Yi-Fu. *Topophilia: A Study of Environmental Perception, Attitudes, and Values*. New York: Columbia University Press, 1990.

Tuan, Yi-Fu and Steven D. Hoelscher. "Disneyland: Its Place in World Culture." Pp. 191–200 in *Designing Disney's Theme Parks: The Architecture of Reassurance*, edited by Karal Ann Marling. Paris: Flammarion, 1997.

Turan, Zeynep. "Material Objects as Facilitating Environments: The Palestinian Diaspora." *Home Cultures* 7, no. 1 (2010): 43–56.

Turley, L.W. and Jean-Charles Chebat. "Linking Retail Strategy, Atmospheric Design and Shopping Behaviour." *Journal of Marketing Management* 18, nos. 1/2 (February 2002): 125–144.

Turner, Rory. "Bloodless Battles: The Civil War Reenacted." *The Drama Review* 34, no. 4 (Winter, 1990): 123–136.

Twohig, David. *Living in Wonderland: Urban Development and Placemaking*. Hampshire, UK: Harriman House, 2014.

Tyson, James L. "Eat Fast, before the Crocodile Snaps Its Jaw." *Christian Science Monitor*, May 13, 1996.

Upton, Dell. "Signs Taken for Wonders." Pp. 147–162 in *Relearning from Las Vegas*, edited by Aron Vinegar and Michaek J. Golec. Minneapolis: University of Minnesota Press, 2009.

Ureta, Sebastian. "Domesticating Homes: Material Transformation and Decoration Among Low-income Families in Santiago, Chile." *Home Cultures* 4, no. 3 (2007): 311–336.

Urry, John and Jonas Larsen. *The Tourist Gaze 3.0*. London: SAGE, 2011.

Vanderbilt, Tom. "It's a Mall World After All: Disney, Design, and the American Dream." *Harvard Design Magazine* 9 (Fall 1999).

Van Eeden, Jeanne. "Theming Mythical Africa at the Lost City." Pp. 113–122 in *The Themed Space: Locating Culture, Nation, and Self*, edited by Scott A. Lukas. Lanham, MD: Lexington, 2007.

———. "The Colonial Gaze: Imperialism, Myths, and South African Popular Culture." *Design Issues* 20, no. 2 (Spring, 2004): 18–33.

Van Maanen, John. "Displacing Disney: Some Notes on the Flow of Culture." *Qualitative Sociology* 15, no. 1 (1992): 5–35.

Van Maanen, John and Gideon Kunda. "Life with Tinkerbell," (part of "Real Feelings: Emotional Expression and Organizational Culture"). In *Research in Organizational Behavior* 11, edited by L. L. Cummings and Barry M. Staw. Greenwich, CT: JAI Press 1989.

Van Melik, Irina Van Aalst, and Jan Van Weesep. "Fear and Fantasy in the Public Domain: The Development of Secured and Themed Urban Space." *Journal of Urban Design* 12, no. 1 (February 2007): 25–42.

Van Wert, William F. "Disney World and Posthistory." *Cultural Critique* no. 32 (Winter 1995–1996): 187–214.

Vellinga, Marcel. "The Inventiveness of Tradition: Vernacular Architecture and the Future." *Perspectives in Vernacular Architecture* 13, no. 2 (2006/2007): 115–128.

Venturi, Robert and Denise Scott Brown, "Constructing Decoration." Pp. 64–65 in *Spectacle*, edited by David Rockwell. New York: Phaidon, 2006.

Venturi, Robert, Denise Scott Brown, and Steven Izenour. *Learning From Las Vegas: The Forgotten Symbolism of Architectural Form*. Cambridge: MIT Press, 1993.

Vinegar, Aron. "The Melodrama of Expression and Inexpression in the Duck and Decorated Shed." Pp. 163–193 in *Relearning from Las Vegas*, edited by Aron Vinegar and Michaek J. Golec. Minneapolis: University of Minnesota Press, 2009.

———. *I Am a Monument: On Learning from Las Vegas*. Cambridge: MIT Press, 2008.

Waddell, Ray. "Themed Restaurants Seek Country Club Atmosphere." *Amusement Business* 107, no. 22.

———. "From Simple to Elaborate, Theming Discussed During WWA Symposium." *Amusement Business* 110, no. 42: 2–4.

Waldrep, Shelton. *The Dissolution of Place: Architecture, Identity, and the Body*. Burlington, VT: Ashgate, 2013.

———. "Postmodern Casinos." Pp. 137–166 in *Productive Postmodernism: Consuming Histories and Cultural Studies*, edited by John Duvall. Albany: State University of New York Press, 2002.

Walker, Derek. "Architecture and Themeing." *Architectural Design* 52, nos. 9/10: 28–31.

Wallace, Michael. *Mickey Mouse History and Other Essays on American Memory*. Philadelphia: Temple University Press, 1996.

———. "Serious Fun." *The Public Historian* 17, no. 4 (Autumn, 1995): 83–89.

———. "Visiting the Past: History Museums in the United States." *Radical History Review* 1981, no. 25: 63–96.

Wallis, Mark. "The New You: Best Practice in Historical Live Interpretation." Pp. 199–204 in *Staging the Past: Themed Environments in Transcultural Perspectives*, edited by Judith Schlehe, Michiko Uike-Bormann, Carolyn Oesterle, and Wolfgang Hochbruck. Bielefeld, Germany: Transcript, 2010.

Walonen, Michael K. "The Spatial/Political-Economic Dynamics of Theme Parks in Contemporary Transatlantic Fiction." Pp. 151–164 in *Contemporary World Narrative Fiction and the Spaces of Neoliberalism*. London: Palgrave, 2016.

Walsh, Kevin. *The Representation of the Past: Museums and Heritage in the Post-modern World*. New York: Routledge, 1992.

Wanhill, Stephen. "Creating Themed Entertainment Attractions: A Nordic Perspective." *Scandinavian Journal of Hospitality and Tourism* 2, no. 2 (2002): 123–144.

Wardle, Kelly. "Dream A Little Theme." *Special Events Magazine*, August, 2005.

Warren, Stacy. "EPCOT: Disney's (sort of) World's Fair." Pp. 447–455 in *Meet Me at the Fair: A World's Fair Reader*, edited by Laura Hollengreen, Celia Pearce, Rebecca Rouse, and Bobby Schweizer. Pittsburgh: ETC Press, 2013.

———. "Saying No to Disney: Disney's Demise in Four American Cities." Pp. 231–260 in *Rethinking Disney: Private Control, Public Dimensions*, edited by Mike Budd and Max H. Kirsch. Middletown, CT: Wesleyan University Press, 2005.

———. "Cultural Contestation at Disneyland Paris." Pp. 109–125 in *Leisure/Tourism Geographies: Practices and Geographical Knowledge*, edited by David Crouch. London: Routledge, 1999.

Wasko, Janet. *Understanding Disney: The Manufacture of Fantasy*. Cambridge: Polity, 2001.

Wasserman, Louis. *Merchandising Architecture: Architectural Implications and Applications of Amusement Themeparks*. Sheboygan, WI: privately printed, 1978.

Wassler, Philipp, Xiang (Robert) Li, and Kam Hung. "Hotel Theming in China: A Qualitative Study of Practitioners' Views." *Journal of Travel and Tourism Marketing* (May 14, 2015).

Webb, Sam. "Monaco Wherever You Go: Super Yacht Designed to Mimic Billionaires' Playground City." *Daily Mail*, January 8, 2014.

Weinstein, Raymond M. "Disneyland and Coney Island: Reflections on the Evolution of the Modern Amusement Park." *The Journal of Popular Culture* 26, no. 1 (Summer 1992): 131–164.

Weiss, Rachel, Andrew Hale Feinstein, and Michael Dalbor. "Customer Satisfaction of Theme Restaurant Attributes and Their Influence on Return Intent." *Journal of Foodservice Business Research* 7, no. 1 (2004): 23–41.

Weissmann, Arnie. "De-theming Resorts and Upending Reputations." *Travel Weekly*, October 8, 2007.

Welch, Michael. *Escape to Prison: Penal Tourism and the Pull of Punishment*. Berkeley: University of California Press, 2015.

Weschler, Lawrence. *Mr. Wilson's Cabinet Of Wonder: Pronged Ants, Horned Humans, Mice on Toast, and Other Marvels of Jurassic Technology*. New York: Vintage, 1996.

West, Brad. "Consuming National Themed Environments Abroad: Australian Working Holidaymakers and Symbolic National Identity in 'Aussie' Theme Pubs." *Tourist Studies* 6 (2006): 139–155.

West, Mark I. "Animator as Architect: Disney's Role in the Creation of Children's Architecture." Pp. 29–36 in *Disneyland and Culture: Essays on the Parks and Their Influence*, edited by Kathy Merlock Jackson and Mark I. West. Jefferson, NC: McFarland, 2010.

———. "Tom Sawyer Island: Mark Twain, Walt Disney, and the Literary Playground." Pp. 101–106 in *Disneyland and Culture: Essays on the Parks and Their Influence*, edited by Kathy Merlock Jackson and Mark I. West. Jefferson, NC: McFarland, 2010.

West, W. Richard. *The Changing Presentation of the American Indian*. Seattle: University of Washington Press, 2004.

Wharton, Annabel Jane. *Selling Jerusalem: Relics, Replicas, Theme Parks*. Chicago: University of Chicago Press, 2006.

Wheeler, Alina. *Designing Brand Identity: An Essential Guide for the Whole Branding Team*. New York: Wiley, 2012.

White, Leanne and Elspeth Frew. *Dark Tourism and Place Identity: Managing and Interpreting Dark Places*. London: Routledge, 2013.

Whitely, Nigel. "Learning from Las Vegas…and Los Angeles and Reyner Banham." Pp. 195–210 in *Relearning from Las Vegas*, edited by Aron Vinegar and Michaek J. Golec. Minneapolis: University of Minnesota Press, 2009.

Whitfield, Stephen J. "Frontiers of the World's Columbian Exposition." Pp. 83–95 in *Meet Me at the Fair: A World's Fair Reader*, edited by Laura Hollengreen, Celia Pearce, Rebecca Rouse, and Bobby Schweizer. Pittsburgh: ETC Press, 2013.

Wickstrom, Maurya. *Performing Consumers: Global Capital and Its Theatrical Seductions*. New York: Routledge, 2006.

Williams, Kevin and Michael Mascioni. *The Out-of-Home Immersive Entertainment Frontier: Expanding Interactive Boundaries in Leisure Facilities*. Surrey, UK: Gower, 2014.

Williams, Michael. "Disney's California Adventure Theme Park: Rhetorical Shape of a California Dream." *Lore* 3, no. 1 (2003): 61–70.

Williams, Michael Ann and Larry Morrisey. "Constructions of Tradition: Vernacular Architecture, Country Music, and Auto-Ethnography." Pp. 161–175 in *People, Power, Places: Perspectives in Vernacular Architecture* 8. Knoxville: University of Tennessee Press, 2000.

Williams, Paul. *Memorial Museums: The Global Rush to Commemorate Atrocities*. Oxford: Berg, 2007.

Willim, Robert. "Looking With New Eyes at the Old Factory: On the Rise of Industrial Cool." Pp. 36–52 in *Experiencescapes: Tourism, Culture, and Economy*, edited by Tom O'Dell and Peter Billing. Frederiksberg: Copenhagen Business School Press, 2005.

Willis, G. E. "Army Hits Hole in One with New Restaurant Concept." *Army Times* 57, no. 48: 24–25.

Willis, Susan. "Disney's Bestiary." Pp. 53–74 in *Rethinking Disney: Private Control, Public Dimensions*, edited by Mike Budd and Max H. Kirsch. Middletown, CT: Wesleyan University Press, 2005.

Wilson, Alexander. "The Betrayal of the Future: Walt Disney's EPCOT Center." Pp. 118–128 in *Disney Discourse: Producing the Magic Kingdom*, edited by Eric Smoodin. New York: Routledge, 1994.

———. *The Culture of Nature*. Cambridge: Blackwell, 1992.

Witcomb, Andrea. *Re-Imagining the Museum: Beyond the Mausoleum*. New York: Routledge, 2003.

Witz, Leslie, Ciraj Rassool, and Gary Minkley. "Repackaging the Past for South African Tourism." *Daedalus* 130, no. 1 (Winter, 2001): 277–296.

Wolcott, Victoria W. *Race, Riots, and Roller Coasters: The Struggle over Segregated Recreation in America*. Philadelphia: University of Pennsylvania Press, 2014.

Wong, Kevin K. F. "Strategic Theming in Theme Park Marketing." *Journal of Vacation Marketing* 5, no. 4 (1999): 319–332.

Wood, Natalie T. and Caroline Munoz. "No Rules, Just Right or Is It? The Role of Themed Restaurants as Cultural Ambassadors." *Tourism and Hospitality Research* 7, no. 3–4 (2007): 242–255.

Wright, Chris. "Natural and Social Order at Walt Disney World; the Functions and Contradictions of Civilising Nature." *The Sociological Review* 54, no. 2 (May 2006): 303–317.

Wright, Talmadge. "Themed Environments and Virtual Spaces: Video Games, Violent Play, and Digital Enemies." Pp. 247–270 in *The Themed Space: Locating Culture, Nation, and Self*, edited by Scott A. Lukas. Lanham, MD: Lexington, 2007.

Wynn, Steve. "Reinventing Vegas." Pp. 62–63 in *Spectacle*, edited by David Rockwell. New York: Phaidon, 2006.

Xiao, Qu, Hanqin Qiu Zhang, and Hui Huang. "The Effects of Hotel Theme Strategy: An Examination on the Perceptions of Hotel Guests on Theme Elements." *Journal of China Tourism Research* 9, no. 1 (January 2013): 133–150.

Yandell, Stephen. "Mapping the Happiest Place on Earth: Disney's Medieval Cartography." Pp. 21–38 in *The Disney Middle Ages: A Fairy-Tale and Fantasy Past*, edited by Tison Pugh and Susan Aronstein. New York: Palgrave Macmillan, 2012.

Yano, Christine R. *Pink Globalization: Hello Kitty's Trek Across the Pacific*. Durham, NC: Duke University Press, 2013.

Yeoh, Brenda S. A. and Peggy Teo. "From Tiger Balm Gardens to Dragon World: Philanthropy and Profit in the Making of Singapore's First Cultural Theme Park." *Geografiska Annaler*. Series B, Human Geography 78, no. 1 (1996): 7–42.

Young, Renee. "Merchant of Vegas: New $1.2 Billion Las Vegas Hotel Gambles on the Beauty, Romance and Visionary Spirit of Venice." *Building Design and Construction* 40, no. 9 (September 1999): 32–36.

Young, Terence. "Grounding the Myth-Theme Park Landscapes in an Era of Commerce and Nationalism." Pp. 1–10 in *Theme Park Landscapes: Antecedents and Variations*, edited by Terence Young and Robert Riley. Washington, D.C.: Dumbarton Oaks Research Library and Collection, 2002.

Zeisel, John. *Inquiry by Design: Environment/Behavior/Neuroscience in Architecture, Interiors, Landscape, and Planning*. New York: W. W. Norton, 2006.

———. "Environmental Design Effects on Alzheimer Symptoms in Long-Term Care Residences." *World Hospitals and Health Services* 36, no. 3 (2000): 27–31.

Zukin, Sharon. "Disney World: The Power of Facade/The Facade of Power." Pp. 217–250 in *Landscapes of Power: From Detroit to Disney World*. Berkeley: University of California Press, 1991.

Contributors

Stefan Al is a Dutch architect, urban designer, and Associate Professor of Urban Design at the University of Pennsylvania. His research focuses on contemporary urbanization, with books published including *Factory Towns of South China*, *Villages in the City*, and *Mall City*. He is currently working on books about Las Vegas, Macau, and high-density urban form. In an international career to date, Al has worked as a practicing architect on renowned architectural projects such as the 2,000-feet high Canton Tower in Guangzhou, the preservation of world heritage in Latin America at the World Heritage Center of UNESCO, and a new eco-friendly city in India.

Michael Mario Albrecht is an Assistant Professor of Media Communication at Eckerd College in St. Petersburg, Florida. His work is situated broadly within critical cultural studies. His particularly scholarly interests include: media studies, popular culture studies, television studies, political theory, popular music studies, tourist studies, and gender and sexuality studies. He has previously written about the Olive Garden in "'When You're Here, You're Family': Culinary Tourism and the Olive Garden Restaurant" in a 2011 article for *Tourist Studies*. The piece in this collection is in many ways a follow-up to that article. His first book, *Masculinity in Contemporary Quality Television*, was published by Ashgate Press in 2015.

Stephen Brown is the P.T. Barnum Professor of Branding at Ulster University, Northern Ireland. He has published numerous books including *Fail Better*, *Free Gift Inside*, and *Wizard: Harry Potter's Brand Magic*. In addition, he has written four novels, none of which bothered the bestseller lists.

Filippo Carlà is a Lecturer in Classics and Ancient History at the University of Exeter (United Kingdom). After studying Ancient History at the Universities of Turin and Udine (Italy), he taught and researched at the Universities of Heidelberg and Mainz (Germany). His main research interests are the socio-economic and cultural history of the Roman world and the reception of Classical Antiquity in modern and postmodern culture. Together with Irene Berti, he edited the volume *Ancient Magic and the Supernatural in the Modern Visual and Performing Arts* (Bloomsbury, 2015). He is a member of the international research network "Imagines: The Reception of Antiquity in the Visual and Performing Arts" and he leads, together with Florian Freitag, the research project "'Here You Leave Today': Time and Temporality in Theme Parks," in which he particularly analyzes the representations of Ancient Greece in theme parks across the world.

Kent Drummond is a faculty member in Management and Marketing at the University of Wyoming. His current research analyzes re-productions and re-consumptions of contemporary cultural icons, including the Beatles, the Royal Opera House, and *Wicked*.

Derek Foster (Ph.D., Carleton University, 2004) is an Associate Professor of Communication Studies in the Department of Communication, Popular Culture, and Film at Brock University in Ontario, Canada. He is the Graduate Program Director of Brock University's MA in Popular Culture and the President of the Popular Culture Association – Canada. His research focuses on visual rhetoric and popular media in the public sphere. He has numerous publications studying discourses of reality television and the rhetoric of other forms of visual and material culture and is currently investigating the visual and material rhetoric of film and television-based memorials and commemorative exercises.

Florian Freitag studied English and French at the University of Konstanz, at Yale University, and at the University of British Columbia. He received his Ph.D. in American Studies from the University of Konstanz in 2011. Since then he has been lecturer (*wissenschaftlicher Mitarbeiter*) in American Studies at Johannes Gutenberg University Mainz. Freitag's main research interests include Comparative North American studies, literary regionalism, Periodical studies, Performance studies, and Theme Park studies. Freitag is the author of *The Farm Novel in North America* (2013) and the co-editor of a collection on transcultural dynamics as well as a special issue of the *European Journal of American Studies* on North American regionalism. His other work has appeared in *Amerikastudien/American Studies*, *Studies in American Naturalism*, *Canadian Literature*, *The Journal of Popular Culture*, *Classical Receptions Journal*, and the *Palgrave Handbook of Comparative*

North American Literature. Freitag's current publication projects include an edited collection about time and temporality in theme parks, a study of the depiction of the future in Disney theme parks, and a monograph on the representation of New Orleans in popular culture. Together with Filippo Carlà, he leads an interdisciplinary research group on theme parks, funded by the German Research Foundation (DFG). During the academic year 2015–2016, Freitag was a Volkswagen Foundation Fellow at CUNY.

Gordon Grice is an architect, editor, writer, illustrator, and creative director. During his 40 years as a freelance consultant, Gordon has worked with a variety of clients and audiences around the world. Currently, as Creative Director at Forrec, Gordon's responsibilities include creative and art direction, creative writing, thematic development, and professional outreach. For the past twenty years, Gordon has been active as a writer and editor, having published more than two-dozen books dealing with design and architectural illustration. Since 1997, he has served as editor of the Ontario Association of Architects' (OAA) quarterly journal *OAA Perspectives* and recently released *100 + 25 Years: OAA Perspectives on a Quarter-Century*, an OAA 125th-anniversary retrospective, co-edited with Ian Ellingham. Gordon is a Past President and Senior Advisor to the American Society of Architectural Illustrators (ASAI) and serves as jury consultant and editor for the society's annual international illustration competition and publication *Architecture in Perspective*. He is a member of the Toronto Society of Architects, the OAA Honours and Awards Committee, the Royal Architectural Institute of Canada (RAIC), the Massey College Quadrangle Society, and the RAIC College of Fellows. In 2014, Gordon was honored with the OAA's medal of the Order of Da Vinci, for distinguished service to the profession. Gordon's recent professional presentations include illustration roundtables at the ASAI/UIA Conference in Tokyo, 2011 and the ASAI Conference in San Francisco, 2013, "Drawing in the Digital Age" (DDA) at the 2013 OAA Toronto Conference, the 2013 IIDEX Conference, the 2014 RAIC Winnipeg Conference, and the 2014 ASAI Dallas Conference. In 2014, Gordon presented a paper at the Time and Temporality Conference in Mainz Germany and participated in a roundtable at the American Studies Association annual conference in Los Angeles. At the same time, he and his colleagues, Filippo Carlá, Florian Freitag, and Scott A. Lukas, initiated an ongoing "ambulatory creative research" project.

Davin Heckman is an Associate Professor of Mass Communication at Winona State University. He serves on the board of the Electronic Literature Organization and is Managing Editor of Electronic Book Review. He is the author of *A Small World: Smart Houses and the Dream of the Perfect Day* (Duke University Press), a text which explores automation, lifestyle narratives, and the "house of tomorrow." His articles on electronic literature and digital culture appear in places like Culture Machine, Dichtung Digital, and Leonardo Electronic Almanac. During the 2011–2012 academic year, Davin was a Fulbright Scholar in Digital Culture at the University of Bergen. His current research addresses poetics and estrangement in digital literature. He lives in Winona, Minnesota with his wife and a disorganized gang of clever, occasionally unruly, little adventurers.

Cornelius Holtorf is a Professor of Archaeology and Director of the Graduate School in Contract Archaeology GRASCA at University in Kalmar, Sweden. In recent years he has worked mainly in the fields of public archaeology and heritage theory. His current research interests include applied archaeology and heritage, heritage futures, heritage values, migrant heritage, and the current meanings of archaeological sites and artifacts (contemporary archaeology). Holtorf is Associate Editor of the academic journals *Heritage & Society* and *Journal of Contemporary Archaeology*. He has published numerous academic papers and was a Senior Editor of *The Oxford Companion to Archaeology* (Oxford University Press, 2012). At the moment he is increasingly interested in knowledge transfer between academia and society. He recently concluded two projects: one entitled "One Hundred Thousand Years Back and Forth: Archaeology Meets Radioactive Waste," co-financed by Linnaeus University and Swedish Nuclear Fuel and Waste Management Co. (SKB), and another one on "Heritage Values, Communities and Authenticity" developing a policy document "Nara+20" relevant to global cultural heritage. He is currently participating in a major international research project "Assembling Alternative Futures for Heritage," funded by the Arts and Humanities Research Council, UK, 2015–2019 with numerous partners including the One Earth: New Horizons Message initiative developing a space message.

Susan Ingram is Associate Professor in the Department of Humanities at York University, Toronto, where she is affiliated with the Canadian Centre for German and European Studies and the Research Group on Language and Culture Contact.

She is the general editor of Intellect Book's Urban Chic series, the co-author of the volumes on Berlin and Vienna, and the editor of the World Film Locations volume on Berlin. A past president of the Canadian Comparative Literature Association, her research interests revolve around the institutions of European cultural modernity and their legacies.

Lei Jia is a doctoral student in Marketing at the College of Business, University of Wyoming. His research focuses on experiential consumption, sensory marketing, and contextual influences on consumer behavior.

Christina Kerz is a lecturer and Ph.D. student at the Institute of Geography at the University of Mainz, Germany, and managing editor of the book series *Media Geography at Mainz*. Her main research interests address topics in social and urban geography with a focus on questions relating to aesthetics, emotions, heritage, tourism, and identities. She is building her studies on qualitative research methods and empirical fieldwork, adopting mostly phenomenological and constructivist perspectives. In her dissertation project she explores the relationship between atmosphere and authenticity as constructed and perceived in Colonial Williamsburg in Virginia, United States.

Brian Lonsway is an architectural designer, theorist, and educator who writes on the interrelationships between the built environment and the technologies and practices which produce it. His first book, *Making Leisure Work: Architecture and the Experience Economy*, surveys the evolution and convergence of various histories and theories of late-twentieth-century design practice, and explores their sometimes unwitting agency in the development of consumer-centric landscapes. He has written on virtual environments, shopping malls, computer-aided design, and Alzheimer's clinics as important agents or artifacts that represent the powerful agency of design in contemporary life. His current research is centered on exploring the inherent transdisciplinary of design, and the intersection of disciplinary and professional identities with alternative models of design practice. With Kathleen Brandt, he is a partner in KBL Studios. Their work includes the co-development and co-direction of Thinklab, an experimental resource for transdisciplinary thinking on complex problems; and the conceptualization and design of The Einhorn Next Generation Design Studio, both forward-looking spatial environments that seek to critically engage the future of design practice, research, and pedagogy. As well, with Kathleen, Brian is a co-founder, designer, and design editor of *Public: a Journal of Imagining America*, an innovative multimedia, interdisciplinary peer-reviewed journal of public scholarship in the arts, humanities, and design.

Scott A. Lukas received his Ph.D. in Cultural Anthropology at Rice University and has taught Anthropology and Sociology at Lake Tahoe Community College and Valparaiso University, and, in 2013, was Visiting Professor of American Studies at the Johannes Gutenberg University of Mainz, Germany. He is the author/editor of *The Immersive Worlds Handbook* (Focal, 2012), *Theme Park* (2008, Arabic translation, 2010), *The Themed Space: Locating Culture, Nation, and Self* (2007), *Fear, Cultural Anxiety, and Transformation: Horror, Science Fiction, and Fantasy Films Remade*, (co-edited with John Marmysz, 2009), *Recent Developments in Criminological Theory* (co-edited with Stuart Henry, 2009), and *Strategies in Teaching Anthropology* (co-editor, 2010). He has been recognized with the McGraw-Hill Award for Excellence in Undergraduate Teaching of Anthropology by the American Anthropological Association (2005), a Sierra Arts Foundation Artist Grant Program Award in Literary-Professional (2009), the Lake Tahoe Community College Distinguished Faculty Member Award (2012), and the California Hayward Award for Excellence in Education (2003). He appeared in the documentary *The Nature of Existence* and has provided interviews for and had his work discussed in To the Best of Our Knowledge, Atlas Obscura, The Huffington Post UK, *The Daily Beast*, *Slate*, *The Independent*, *The Chicago Tribune*, *The Washington Post*, *The Financial Times of London*, *USA Today*, and *Caravan* (India). He is a former theme park trainer, has worked as a consultant for major media and theme park corporations, and has provided keynote addresses and talks at major theme park industry conferences, including those of the Themed Entertainment Association and the International Association of Amusement Parks. He maintains a YouTube channel that features video documentation of themed and immersive spaces from around the world (https://www.youtube.com/channel/UCfWefMpOPy7ENr27waGDSTQ).

Steven Miles is Professor in Sociology at Manchester Metropolitan University (United Kingdom) and author of *Retail and the Artifice of Social Change* (Routledge, 2015). His particular interest is in the role of consumption in impacting on questions of identity—both at the individual level and that of the city. His Ph.D. looked at how young people use consumption in the construction of their identities in an apparently fragmented world. Since that time he has broadened his interest into consumption spaces and how it is that consumption defines consumers' relationship with the city by defining consumption as an ideological orthodoxy. His key publications include *Consumerism as a Way of Life* (Sage, 1998) and *Youth Lifestyles in a Changing World* (Oxford University Press, 2000) and *Spaces for Consumption: Pleasure and Placelessness in the Post-Industrial City* (Sage, 2010). He is co-author of *Consuming Cities* (Palgrave Macmillan, 2004) with Malcolm Miles. He has also published in *Sociology, Urban Studies, Cultural Trends,* and *The International Journal of Cultural Policy*. Miles is critical of the role culture plays in constructing narratives around the city and he designed the methodology for the research programme *Impacts08*—the biggest research programme of its kind which looks at the social, cultural, and economic impact of the European Capital of Culture in Liverpool. He is currently editor of the *Journal of Consumer Culture*.

Celia Pearce is a game designer and curator, She is the co-editor of *Meet Me at the Fair: A World's Fair Reader* (ETC Press, 2014) and the author of *Communities of Play* (MIT Press, 2009), as well as numerous other books, papers, and book chapters. She is currently an Associate Professor of game design in the College of Arts Media and Design at Northeastern University. Previously, she was at the Georgia Institute of Technology, where she directed the Experimental Game Lab and the Emergent Game Group. Prior to entering academia, she worked in the theme park and museum industries where she designed award-winning attractions, including concept design for a world's fair pavilion in Japan.

Markus Reisenleitner received his Ph.D. from the University of Vienna and is Professor of Humanities at York University in Toronto, Canada. He was the Director of York University's Graduate Program in Humanities from 2010–2015. He is also affiliated with the Graduate Program in Communication and Culture, the Graduate Program in History, and the Canadian Centre for German and European Studies at York. Before joining York's Division of Humanities in 2006, he taught at the University of Vienna (1991–2000), the Vienna campus of the University of Oregon's International Program (1991–1998), the University of Alberta (1998–2001), and Lingnan University in Hong Kong (2001–2006), where he was Head of the Department of Cultural Studies from 2004–2006. Markus Reisenleitner is past President of the Canadian Comparative Literature Association. His research is situated at the intersections of Cultural History and Cultural Studies. His current work focuses on the imaginaries of mobility, community, fashion and style in the global digital city. He has also worked and published on urban imaginaries of modernity, digital humanities, e-learning, and memory and nostalgia in popular and digital culture. Publications include *Wiener Chic: A Locational History of Vienna Fashion* (Intellect, 2013, co-authored with Susan Ingram), *Historical Textures of Translation: Traditions, Traumas, Transgressions* (Mille Tre, 2012, co-edited with Susan Ingram), and *Urban Imaginaries in the Asia-Pacific* (Interasia Cultural Studies Special Issue, Routledge, 2008, co-edited with Meaghan Morris and Caroline Turner).

Bobby Schweizer is a professional lecturer in the College of Computing and Digital Media at DePaul University. In addition to teaching in the School of Design, his research areas include videogame space, expressive environments, and cities. He co-authored *Newsgames: Journalism at Play* (MIT Press, 2010) and co-edited *Meet Me at the Fair: A World's Fair Reader* (ETC Press, 2014).

Tim Simpson is Associate Dean of the Faculty of Social Sciences, and Associate Professor in the Department of Communication, University of Macau, where he has worked since 2001. He is the co-author (with UK-based photographer Roger Palmer) of the volume *Macao Macau* (Black Dog Publishing, 2015), and editor of the forthcoming book *Tourist Utopias: Offshore Islands, Enclave Spaces and Mobile Imaginaries* (Amsterdam University Press). His recent work has been published in journals in the areas of geography, sociology, urban studies, critical theory, and tourism studies. He is currently under contract with University of Minnesota Press to publish a monograph entitled *Macau: Casino Capitalism and the Biopolitical Metropolis*.

Jan-Erik Steinkrüger works as a scientific assistant at the Geographical Department of the University of Bonn. After studying philosophy, politics, and geography at the University of Bonn, he wrote his doctoral thesis in historical geography on the representation of Africa in zoological gardens and theme parks past and present. In it he showed how the negotiation of cultural difference—between cultures and between culture and nature—and its representation has been used in public discourse to negotiate social distinctions within society. His main interest in the research of themed spaces is the role of landscape as a semiotic system representing other landscapes. His research and teaching foci are historical and cultural geographies, animal geographies, geographies of belief systems, and geographies of tourism and leisure. Currently, Steinkrüger is working on the topic of the perception of stray animals and animal shelters.

Per Strömberg is an architectural historian from Uppsala University and defended his thesis *Upplevelseindustrins turistmiljöer* (*Tourist Environments in the Era of the Experience Economy*) in 2007 about themed environments and conceptualization of tourist attractions and hotels in today's tourism industry. The Royal Academy of Letters, History, and Antiquities in Sweden awarded his thesis as "deserved scholarly work" in 2008. His contribution to this anthology partly derives from his doctoral thesis. In 2009–2012, he held the postdoctoral position at BI Norwegian Business School in Norway at the Centre of Experience Economy. This postdoctoral project focused on the reuse of buildings as a cultural innovation strategy in tourism, event, and retailing. One example of the outcome of this project is the article "Funky Bunkers. The Post-Military Landscape as a Readymade Space and a Cultural Playground" in the anthology *Ordnance: War +Architecture & Space* (Ashgate). Since 2012, Strömberg has worked at University College of Southeast Norway as an Associate Professor in Tourism Management. A recent publication is an entry on "theming" in *The Wiley Blackwell Encyclopedia of Consumption and Consumer Studies* (2015).

Jeanne van Eeden has spent most of her academic career in the Department of Visual Arts at the University of Pretoria, where she started teaching Art History in 1985. From 1995 onwards, she spearheaded the development of visual culture as a subject in the Department. She was Head of the Department between March 2007 and February 2015 and was also Chair of the Arts Cluster in the Faculty of Humanities between 2012 and 2014. She has been rated by the South African National Research Foundation as an established researcher. Jeanne has published almost thirty articles in peer-reviewed journals and twelve chapters in national and international scholarly books, including most recently a contribution on Southern African design to the *Bloomsbury Encyclopedia of Design* (2015). In addition, she was the co-editor of the book *South Africa Visual Culture* (Van Schaik, 2005) that established the relevance of the study of visual culture in South Africa. Her interest in themed and commodified spaces started with her doctoral study on The Lost City theme park in South Africa. Her current research focuses mainly on South African postcards as a neglected channel of ideological discourse. Jeanne serves on the editorial committee of the academic journal, *De Arte*, and has been the editor of the academic journal *Image & Text* since 2011. She is an ad hoc referee for the following national and international journals: *Acta Academica, Africa Today, Annals of Tourism Research, Body and Society, Communicatio, Critical Arts, De Arte, Historia, Journal of Design History, Literator, Journal of African Languages,* and *South African Journal for Cultural History*. She has delivered more than twenty papers at national and international conferences and is an ad hoc external examiner for six South African universities. She has successfully supervised almost thirty Masters and Doctoral students and has been an active member of the South African Visual Art Historians since the 1980s.

About the ETC Press

ETC Press is a publishing imprint with a twist. We publish books, but we're also interested in the participatory future of content creation across multiple media. We are an academic, open source, multimedia, publishing imprint affiliated with the Entertainment Technology Center (ETC) at Carnegie Mellon University (CMU) and in partnership with Lulu.com. ETC Press has an affiliation with the Institute for the Future of the Book and MediaCommons, sharing in the exploration of the evolution of discourse. ETC Press also has an agreement with the Association for Computing Machinery (ACM) to place ETC Press publications in the ACM Digital Library, and another with Feedbooks to place ETC Press texts in their e-reading platform. Also, ETC Press publications will be in Booktrope and in the ThoughtMesh.

ETC Press publications will focus on issues revolving around entertainment technologies as they are applied across a variety of fields. We are looking to develop a range of texts and media that are innovative and insightful. We are interested in creating projects with Sophie and with In Media Res, and we will accept submissions and publish work in a variety of media (textual, electronic, digital, etc.), and we work with The Game Crafter to produce tabletop games.

Authors publishing with ETC Press retain ownership of their intellectual property. ETC Press publishes a version of the text with author permission and ETC Press publications will be released under one of two Creative Commons licenses:

- **Attribution-NoDerivativeWorks-NonCommercial:** This license allows for published works to remain intact, but versions can be created.
- **Attribution-NonCommercial-ShareAlike:** This license allows for authors to retain editorial control of their creations while also encouraging readers to collaboratively rewrite content.

Every text is available for free download, and we price our titles as inexpensively as possible, because we want people to have access to them. We're most interested in the sharing and spreading of ideas.

This is definitely an experiment in the notion of publishing, and we invite people to participate. We are exploring what it means to "publish" across multiple media and multiple versions. We believe this is the future of publication, bridging virtual and physical media with fluid versions of publications as well as enabling the creative blurring of what constitutes reading and writing.

http://www.etc.cmu.edu/etcpress/wellplayed
Twitter: @etcwellplayed

Made in the USA
Middletown, DE
16 February 2018